AF900092

Manual of Forensic Science

Manual of Forensic Science: An International Survey

Edited by
Anna Barbaro

CRC Press
Taylor & Francis Group
Boca Raton London New York

CRC Press is an imprint of the
Taylor & Francis Group, an **informa** business

CRC Press
Taylor & Francis Group
6000 Broken Sound Parkway NW, Suite 300
Boca Raton, FL 33487-2742

First issued in paperback 2020

ISBN-13: 978-1-4987-6630-2 (hbk)
ISBN-13: 978-0-367-77826-2 (pbk)

Library of Congress Cataloging-in-Publication Data

Names: Barbaro, Anna, editor.
Title: Manual of forensic science : an international survey / edited by Anna Barbaro.
Description: 1 Edition. | Boca Raton : CRC Press, [2018] | Includes bibliographical references and index.
Identifiers: LCCN 2017015348| ISBN 9781498766302 (hardback : alk. paper) |
ISBN 9781315181424 (ebook)
Subjects: LCSH: Forensic sciences—Handbooks, manuals, etc. | Criminal investigation—Handbooks, manuals, etc.
Classification: LCC HV8073 .M25545 2017 | DDC 363.25—dc23
LC record available at https://lccn.loc.gov/2017015348

Visit the Taylor & Francis Web site at
http://www.taylorandfrancis.com

and the CRC Press Web site at
http://www.crcpress.com

Contents

Editor

Anna Barbaro earned a PhD in forensic genetics from the University of Santiago de Compostela, Spain, a post-degree diploma from the School of Specialization in Applied Genetics (University La Sapienza in Rome) and a master diploma in Psychological and Behavioral Techniques of the Criminal Investigation (Msc) from the University La Sapienza in Rome (Italy). She also has a diploma of Expert in Criminal Investigation and a diploma of Superior Expert in Criminal Profiling. She is the Chief of the Forensic Genetics Department at Studio Indagini Mediche E Forensi (SIMEF) in Reggio Calabria, Italy. She teaches forensic genetics at the second master level in forensic sciences at the University of Rome La Sapienza, Italy along with several other courses. She is an expert consultant for the Italian Court of Justice and is the author of more than 100 papers on forensic DNA analysis. She serves as the founder and president of the Wordwide Association of Women Forensic Experts (WAWFE), she is the Honor Dean of the Superior School of Criminalistics and Criminology (Spain), and Honor Member of several international scientific associations. She is also a member of the editorial board for various international scientific journals and serves as an expert reviewer for some forensic journals; and is a speaker at national and international conferences.

Contributors

Samar Ahmed is an associate professor in the Department of Forensic Medicine and Toxicology, Ain Shams University, Cairo, Egypt. She is education oriented and is a leading educationist by training. She is also responsible for program development and evaluation as well as international projects. She graduated from Ain Shams University and after earning her doctorate degree attained a master's degree in health professions education from Maastricht University and a fellowship in health professions education from the FAIMER Institute in Philadelphia.

She has experience in forensic curricula development and has taken many initiatives in the development of the learning of forensic science at various stages of education. She is a reviewer for many journals in the area of medical education and is an expert in the area with a large body of international publications in the field. Dr. Ahmed has an interest in forensic psychiatry and has been involved in many initiatives to work with patient offenders funded by the European Union. She is currently creating a Center of Excellence in Forensic Psychiatric Research.

Dalia M. Al-Saif, MD, is a consultant Forensic Medical Examiner and Head of the Education and Training Section, Center of Forensic and Legal Medicine, Eastern Province, Saudi Arabia. She is board certified in forensic medicine and works as an expert witness in medicolegal cases including child abuse. She is a lecturer and provides training on the evaluation of sexual abuse victims. Al-Saif is a member of many local and international associations related to forensic medicine and child abuse, and has published many scientific papers related to this field.

Adrienne Brundage, MD, is a forensic entomologist and lec-turer at Texas A&M University, and an adjunct professor at the University of Florida. She has been consulting on casework for nearly 20 years, and is a member of the American Board of Forensic Entomologists.

Jason H. Byrd, MD, is an associate professor and associate director of the William R. Maples Center for Forensic Medicine at the University of Florida's College of Medicine, Gainesville. He is a board certified forensic entomologist and diplomate of the American Board of Forensic Entomology. He was twice-elected President of the American Board of Forensic Entomology, and is both a past and the current President of the North American Forensic Entomology Association. He served for over a decade as a faculty member of the Virginia Institute of Forensic Science and Medicine and currently serves as an executive manager for the International Veterinary Forensic Sciences Association and as the Director of Education for the ASPCA Veterinary Forensic Sciences Program. Dr. Byrd has combined his formal academic training in entomology and forensic science to serve as a consultant and educator in both criminal and civil–legal investigations throughout the United States and internationally.

Maria Cecilia Pastor Carson graduated with a DDS in Odontology from the Faculty of Odontology, Catholic University Santa Maria, Arequipa, Peru. She specialized in orthodontics (UAP University, Lima, Peru); expertise dentistry from col. number 018 (Col Lima, Peru); and forensic odontology (University Cientifica del Sur, Lima). She serves as the WAWFE coordinator of Peru and is the vice president of the Peruvian Association of Forensic Dentistry (APOFOR). She is a member of the Peruvian Society of Legal and Forensic Dentistry and Criminology, the Argentina Society of Legal Odontology (SADOL), the Iberoamerican Society of Odontoestomatology (SOFIA), the South American Association of Forensic Dentistry (AOFS), the American Association for Orthodontics (United States), the Paulista Society of Orthodontics (Brazil), and the Society of Six Elements (Peru). She is also a speaker at national and international conferences.

Francisco R. Carvallo Chaigneau, DVM, DSc, DACVP, obtained his DVM from the Universidad Austral de Chile, Valdivia (2001), a doctor of science from the Universidad Nacional Autonoma de Mexico, Mexico City (2007), and completed a 3-year veterinary pathology residency at the University of Connecticut, Storrs, and received Diplomate status from the American College of Veterinary Pathologists in 2011. He then moved to the Universidad de Chile, Department of Animal Pathology where he served as an assistant professor. He joined the California Animal Health and Food Safety Laboratory System (CAHFS), at San Bernardino, as an assistant professor of Clinical Diagnostic Veterinary Pathology in 2014. Dr. Carvallo has had numerous presentations in international conferences and publications in peer-reviewed journals.

Stephen Cole works with Acumé Forensics, Ltd.

Michael Dixon is a technical director at Acumé Forensics (West Yorkshire, United Kingdom), with a first class honors degree and is a professional member of the Chartered Society of Forensic Sciences. An expert in digital media and how it can be used in the field of forensics and law enforcement, he works in television, producing reconstructions and technical graphics.

Stephen Driver is a facial imaging expert and forensic artist.

Lori D. Frasier, MD, is a professor of pediatrics and director of the Center for the Protection of Children at Penn State Health Children's Hospital and Penn State Hershey College of Medicine, Hershey, Pennsylvania. She is board certified in pediatrics and child abuse pediatrics. Dr. Frasier has written extensively and lectured internationally on topics in child abuse and child sexual abuse. She has been a part of many committees and expert panels which have developed the guidelines and current medical approaches to sexually abused children and adolescents.

Ghada Hasabo, MD, is a lecturer of Forensic Medicine and Clinical Toxicology, Faculty of Medicine, Cairo University, Egypt. She is also an International Certified Professional Trainer at the Management Development Institute, Missouri State; and an anesthesiology, pain management, and postsurgical ICU specialist. Dr. Hasabo has been published and serves as a reviewer and editor for a number of international publications in the field of forensic and toxicology sciences. She is also a member of many international organizations for women rights and refugee aid.

Mack S. House, Jr., is a crime scene investigator diver technologist (CSIDT), published author, and internationally reputed expert in underwater forensics crime scene investigation. He invented the CSIDT International Weapons and Body Containment Devices and is an active member of the International Crime Scene Investigators Association (www.icsia.org), Forensic Experts Incorporated (www.feinc.net), the International Association of Coroners and Medical Examiners, and the Evidence Partnership Ltd. of Forensic and Policing Service Association and Global Forensic Directory.

Linda Huber graduated from the University of California, Los Angeles and is a forensic scientist at the Orange County Sheriff's Department in Los Angeles, California. She also serves as an adjunct professor at Citrus Community College, Glendora, California.

Shelina Khalid Jilani is a forensic expert specializing in facial mapping at Acumé Forensics. As a forensic and medical science graduate from the University of Bradford, she is currently pursuing a PhD at the Centre of Visual Computing, University of Bradford, West Yorkshire, United Kingdom. She is a professional member of the Chartered Society of Forensic Science and British Association of Human Identification (BAHID). Her research interests include ethnic classification of faces and human verification from photographic images.

Kay Michiels, LLM, teaches law and forensics at Avans University of Applied Sciences, the Netherlands. She is the coordinator of the minor Chain of Evidence and project member of the EFEN network.

Amarnath Mishra, PhD, is an assistant professor at the Amity Institute of Forensic Sciences, Amity University, Noida, India. Dr. Mishra has worked as an associate professor in the Department of Forensic Medicine of Tribhuvan University, National Medical College, Nepal. He received an MSc in forensic science with a specialization in DNA forensic and toxicology from Allahabad Agricultural Institute–Deemed University, Allahabad, India in collaboration with the Central Forensic Science Laboratory, Hyderabad, India; and an MSc in biochemistry from UPRTOU, Allahabad, India. He received an MPhil with a specialization in DNA forensic and toxicology from Vinayaka Missions University, Salem, Tamil Nadu, India. He received a PhD in forensic science with a specialization in forensic and analytical toxicology from Sam Higginbottom Institute of Agriculture, Technology and Sciences, Deemed University, Allahabad in collaboration with Central Forensic Science Laboratory, Chandigarh, India. He has published 2 books and more than 15 research articles in reputed peer-reviewed international and national journals. He has also participated in various oral and poster presentations during international and national conferences and seminars. He serves as editor, guest editor, reviewer, and editorial board member with various international and national journals of concerned specialization and subjects. He is a member of various international and national professional bodies. He is also a visiting/guest faculty at various colleges and universities.

Nino Nardareshvili serves with the Ministry of Internal Affairs of Georgia—Forensic Criminalistics Main Division, Tbilisi, Georgia.

Filomena Paciello has a law degree from the University of Perugia, and a master's in forensic science—criminology, investigation, security, and intelligence—from the University of Rome "La Sapienza," Italy Stage at SIMEF Study Medical and Forensic Investigations Study in Reggio Calabria, School in Ethics and Techniques of Criminal Law at Criminal Chamber of Rome. She is also an Expert Criminologist and Expert in Civil–Military Cooperation.

Andrew R. Reitnauer is a Certified Senior Crime Scene Analyst (CSCSA) through the International Association for Identification. For the past 12 years, he has been an active Latent Print Examiner, Senior Crime Scene Responder, Forensic Photographer, and Section Supervisor. In addition to casework duties, he has also served as a primary trainer for new examiners and outside agencies, and is the owner of Delta Forensics, LLC, where he performs case consultations and offers training classes to members of the professional community. He is a Past-President and current Chairman of the Board of Directors for the New York Division of the IAI and is an active member of three IAI Divisions. He was an initial member of the OSAC Friction Ridge Subcommittee and was the Chairman of the Latent Print Technical Working Group for the State of New York.

Alan Diego Briem Stamm, graduated Odontology DDS from the Faculty of Odontology of the University National of Northeast, Corrientes, Argentina. He is a Diploma school graduate specializing in legal dentistry (University of Rosario, Argentina); a Diploma school graduate specializing in Forensic Medicine (University of Corrientes, Argentina); and a Diploma school postgraduate level 1 and 2 course in Forensic Odontology (University of Córdoba, Argentina). He is currently pursuing a doctorate in dentistry, 3rd cohort at the University of Corrientes. He is a professor of legal dentistry, Faculty of Dentistry, University of Buenos Aires (UBA), Argentina; a subdirector specializing in forensic odontology, Faculty of Dentistry, University of Buenos Aires; a professor forensic odontology, Licenciature in Criminalistic, University Institute of Federal Police (IUPFA); a subdirector of Forensic Science International Management, Worldwide Group Police; a professor of forensic odontology at level 1 and 2 Multidisciplinary Course International Forensic Science and Criminalistic, Fiep Foundation, Worldwide Group Police; a dentist expert in the Forensic Medicine Division of the National Gendarmerie Argentina; the and the coordinator in Argentina for the Worldwide Association of Women Forensic Experts (WAWFE). He is a member of the Peruvian Society of the Forensic Dentistry and Criminalistic (SPOLFOC) and of the South American Association of Forensic Dentistry (AOFS). He is the past treasurer of the Argentinian Society of Legal Dentistry (SADOL); past chairman of the Iberoamerican Society of Forensic Odontoestomatology (SOFIA). In addition, he is the author of articles in scientific journals and a speaker at national and international conferences.

Lerah Sutton is a doctoral candidate in forensic anthropology at the University of Florida (UF), Gainsville, specializing in decomposition, forensic taphonomy, and comparative osteology. She works as a graduate assistant at the William R. Maples Center for Forensic Medicine and a research fellow at the UF-ASPCA Veterinary Forensic Sciences Program. She is also a teaching assistant for the forensic science master's degree program, UF, the nationally recognized Hume Honors College, and the UF-ASPCA veterinary forensic sciences master's degree program. In her positions, she responds to death investigation scenes, speaks at workshops and conferences, consults and offers hands-on field exercises and trainings for law enforcement, conducts original research, and interacts with students seeking higher education in the forensic sciences. Sutton earned a master's degree in forensic science from the University of Florida after earning a bachelor's degree in anthropology with the highest honors, also from the University of Florida. She has been employed by the UF Maples Center throughout her higher education. Sutton previously worked at the Florida District 7 & 24, Office of the Medical Examiner, where she provided administrative support and assisted in the morgue. After completing her PhD in 2017, she plans to obtain a faculty position teaching forensic science and medicine, conducting research, and working as a consultant to law enforcement agencies. She is also currently working on developing a new master's degree program in forensic medicine to be offered at the University of Florida.

Víctor Toledo González obtained his veterinary science degree in 1999 and master's degree in 2009 from the Universidad de Chile. He developed his professional career as an assistant professor in the Anatomy Unit in the Department of Biological Sciences and then in the Animal Pathology Department (last 4 years) in Santiago, Chile. He is currently pursuing a doctorate in forensic sciences at the University of Alcalá de Henares, Henares, Spain. Dr. Toledo is the creator, founder, and president of the Iberoamerican Association of Medicine and Forensic Veterinary Sciences AG. In addition, he is the General Secretary and Director of the Department of Veterinary Forensic Veterinary Medicine in Chilean Criminalists Association AG (COLCRIM). He has participated as a monitor in activities related with crime scene investigation of wildlife animals in technical programs of collaboration between Chile and the United States. He has given numerous presentations at national and international conferences related with forensic veterinary science.

Mark Wood is a graphic designer and photographer, with more than 20 years of experience as a creative professional and educator. He has developed professional training classes and taught both undergraduate and postgraduate courses. In addition, he has delivered train-the-trainer courses for the Apple Authorized Training Program. Wood is the author of the only Apple authorized book on Pages, Numbers, and Keynote, and writes on a broad range of digital imaging topics.

Anita Zannin, MSFS, holds two bachelor of science degrees, one in forensic chemistry and a second in criminal justice, and a master of science degree in forensic science. She taught both graduate and undergraduate courses at Syracuse University, taught as faculty and a lab instructor at more than 10 Bloodstain Evidence Institutes, a 40-hour basic bloodstain pattern interpretation course, and is a visiting professor at Francisco Marroquin Law School in Guatemala where she primarily teaches crime scene and homicide investigation. Prior to entering the forensics field, Zannin worked and studied in the medical field for many years. Zannin is a member of several professional organizations and is an internationally recognized expert in bloodstain pattern analysis and has been accepted as an expert in both federal and state courts. She has worked on criminal and civil cases in the United States, Canada, Australia, and the United Kingdom.

CHAPTER 1

Crime Scene Investigation

Anita Zannin and Linda Huber

CONTENTS

1.1 INTRODUCTION

Crime scene investigation may occur as a result of relatively minor offenses such as property crimes or thefts to very violent crimes such as rape, torture, and murder. The crime scene investigator (CSI) is the "gatekeeper" to the criminal justice system. The evidence that is collected, the procedures that are followed, and a thorough understanding of the potential value of different kinds of evidence can make the difference between a successful prosecution (the right person being prosecuted for the right crime) or the exoneration of an innocent individual, and an unsuccessful prosecution (either that charges cannot be brought, or an innocent person is wrongly prosecuted). The old cliché "garbage in, garbage out" was never as appropriate as in this context! If the CSI fails to recognize evidence, or the potential probative value of a piece of evidence, crimes may remain unsolved or unprosecutable, or the wrong person is charged.

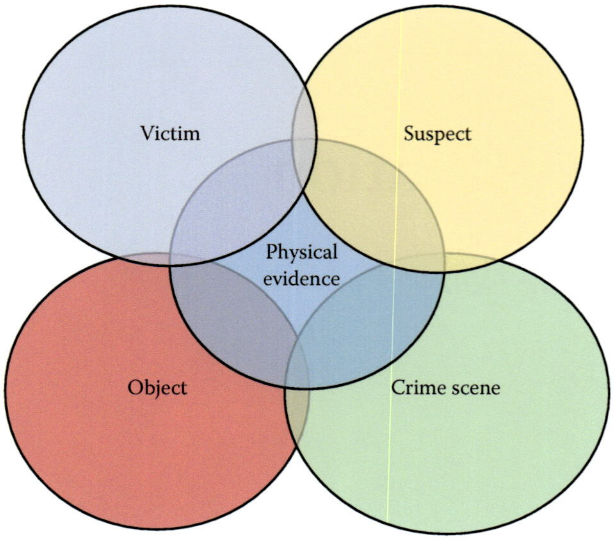

FIGURE 1.1 The interrelationships between people, places, and things within a crime scene.

The goal of a crime scene investigation is to recognize, collect, preserve, and test physical evidence in an effort to reconstruct the events that occurred. Physical evidence can link suspects to victims, individuals to objects, and crime scenes, and vice versa. This concept is represented in Figure 1.1.

The tenet that physical evidence can provide linkage to people, places, or things is based upon Locard's exchange principle, which states:

> *Whenever two objects come into contact, there is always a transfer of material. The methods of detection may not be sensitive enough to detect this, or the decay rate may be so rapid that all evidence of transfer has vanished after a given time. Nevertheless, the transfer has taken place.*
>
> —Edmond Locard (1877–1966)

Crime scene investigation can be defined as a legal, purposeful, planned, and systematic process, conducted by competent investigators who possess the requisite knowledge, skills and abilities to search for, discover, protect, document, collect, package, label, preserve, and transmit physical evidence associated with a suspected criminal event to a forensic science facility for safekeeping and eventual scientific examination and analysis (Rini, n.d.).

1.2 CLASSIFICATION OF THE CRIME SCENE

Crime scenes may be classified in several ways:

Type of crime: Homicide, suicide, sexual assault, robbery, and so on, are examples of defining a scene by the type of alleged crime or incident.

Location: A scene may be described by its physical location, such as indoor, outdoor, vehicle, aquatic, and so forth.

Behavioral: A crime scene may be defined by the apparent behavior associated with the scene, such as organized, disorganized, passive, or active.

Size: Less commonly, a scene may be defined as macroscopic or microscopic. An example of a macroscopic scene might be a stabbing victim, stabbed in a house, who is transported in a car, and the body dumped in a creek. All the associated scenes would be considered to be under the heading of macroscopic. A microscopic scene is more related to the physical and trace evidence associated within the macroscopic scene and body itself. Using the previous example, this could include hairs and fibers in the vehicle used to transport the body or on the knife, tire tracks or footwear impressions located near the body, and bloodstains located on the victim, in the house or in the car utilized for transporting the body.

Site of first alleged criminal activity: More commonly, when there are multiple scenes related to a particular event, they may be referred to as primary, secondary, and tertiary. The primary scene is the site of the first criminal activity. This is not necessarily where the body is located. In the stabbing example from the previous **Size** category, the house where the stabbing occurred would be the primary scene. Some agencies utilize only primary and secondary classifications, where secondary refers to any subsequent scenes as secondary. Therefore, in the above example, both the car and dump site would be secondary scenes. Other agencies utilize secondary and tertiary designations, where secondary scenes include any subsequent scenes, such as dump sites, paths to/from, and so on and tertiary refers to any vehicles utilized in the crime. Referring again to the above example, the primary scene would be the house where the stabbing occurred, the secondary scene would be the body dump site, and the car would be the tertiary scene. Suppose that the body was transferred from a car to a van that then took the body to the dump site; both the car and the van would be tertiary scenes using this classification method.

It is important to note that the designations of primary, secondary, and tertiary in no way signify the importance or priority of scenes, rather, simply a sequence of events. Scenes may also be referred to as dynamic or static. A scene and the evidence contained therein is always undergoing change and/or degradation, even if not visible to the naked eye, including during the investigative process, until the evidence is collected. With this understanding, an unprocessed scene is considered dynamic. After a scene has been processed, it is considered static.

1.3 GENERAL CRIME SCENE PROCEDURES

The first person to arrive at a scene is referred to as the first responder. Depending on how a call comes in, this may be police officers, fire department, or emergency medical personnel. For the purposes of this writing, when referring to the "first responder," this will refer to the first responding police officer.

1.3.1 First Responder

The first responder(s) will be the only individual(s) to observe a scene in its most pristine state, and their observations are critical. There are a number of duties that the first responder must carry out: most importantly, he/she must ensure safety of the scene and the people associated with it, including him/herself and the victim(s).

- If the victim is alive, the first responder should assist the victim until appropriate medical personnel arrive to take over. If the victim is deceased, the first responder should take measures to prevent any changes to the body.
- If the suspect is still on scene, search for and arrest, as appropriate.
- Detain witnesses—If possible, witnesses should be separated both from each other and from the scene in order to preserve their objectivity. For the same reason, witnesses should not be returned to the scene. This is not to say that an individual would deliberately mislead (although some will); however, if they are returned to the scene, the possibility exists that their minds will subconsciously attempt to "fill in the blanks" and/or explain why certain pieces of evidence appear as they do (e.g., "Well, he must have fallen backward to have blood in that location—I thought I saw him fall to the side"). It is well documented that the majority of wrongful convictions are based on erroneous eyewitness testimony. Most people are not expecting to witness a violent crime, and therefore are not prepared to "record" every detail. Knowing that witness statements may vary, conflict, and/or contain inaccuracies, every effort should be taken to avoid additional "contamination."
- Establish scene security—How this is accomplished will depend on the location of a crime scene and can include official vehicles to block off streets, barrier tape, or other means available until additional assistance arrives. A crime scene log should be initiated, documenting the name, date, in/out times, and duty or agency of those individuals with access to the crime scene. This helps prevent unauthorized individuals or officials from entering the scene. No eating, drinking, smoking, restroom use, and so on, should be allowed within the secured area.
- Document and communicate to the investigator all movements, actions, and any alterations within the scene. For instance, if, upon arrival, a victim is found prone in a small space between the sink and bathtub, and the first responder had to pull the victim out and turn him over to check for signs of life, this is critical for the investigators to know, as it is no longer a pristine scene and will have undoubtedly created some artifactual evidence.

1.3.2 Crime Scene Security

Because crime scene investigation procedures are based upon Locard's exchange principle, it is of utmost importance to establish scene security so as to avoid unnecessary contamination by nonessential personnel. This can be accomplished by using multiple layers of security, for example:

- Zone (or Level) 1—Is the immediate crime scene, where the highest level of restriction is in force. Only essential personnel (those processing the scene) should be in this area. For example, if a crime occurred in the gymnasium of a school, only essential personnel should be in the gymnasium.
- Zone (or Level) 2—Is a wider perimeter around Zone 1, where access should be restricted to only individuals performing official duties. This is the zone in which incident command or a command center would be located. Using the above example, Zone 2 could be the entire school building.
- Zone (or Level) 3—Is an even wider perimeter than Zone 2, where members of the media can be located, while excluding the general public. Again using the school example, Zone 3 could be the entire school property.

Figure 1.2 illustrates this concept using the school example above.

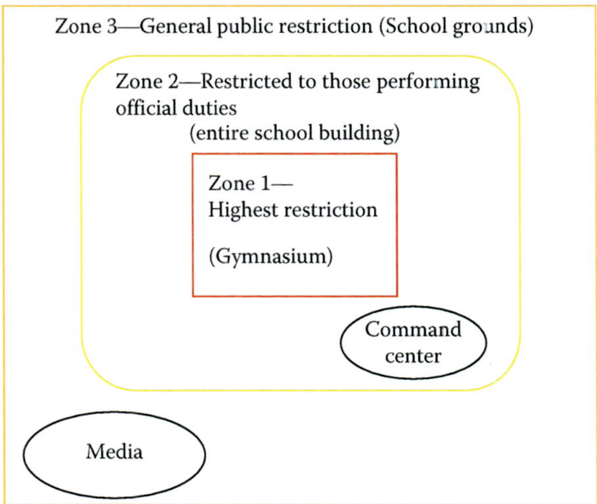

FIGURE 1.2 Example of multilevel scene security.

It is important to note that the perimeter(s) initially established may have to be adjusted once the crime scene personnel arrive and evaluate the scene.

1.3.3 Crime Scene Investigator(s)

Upon arrival to the scene, the CSI(s) should sign in on the previously established crime scene log. If one has not yet been initiated, the CSI should initiate the crime scene attendance log and obtain as much information as possible regarding other undocumented individuals who may have been at the scene. After signing in, the CSI should have a conference with the first responder and/or on-scene detective (if arrived) to understand the circumstances of the scene as known at that time. This does not mean the CSI's "theory" of what occurred and should include only facts known.

CSIs must also ensure that they will be conducting a legal search. In the United States, searches can be conducted in the following circumstances:

- *Consent*—The person who owns or has the legal ability to consent can give permission to conduct a search of an area of interest.
- *Exigent circumstances*—Exigent circumstances are those situations where evidence will be damaged or lost if it is not collected immediately, or if there is an immediate risk of serious injury or death. An example of an exigent circumstance could be that, upon police arrival, a suspect runs to the bathroom to attempt to flush drugs, and the drugs were recovered. This would not give permission to search the rest of the bathroom or house for drugs. With the drugs and suspect secured, a search warrant should be obtained to search the remainder of the residence.
- *Search warrant*—A legal, thorough search warrant is the best way to gain access to the area of interest, as this reduces the likelihood of evidence later being deemed inadmissible for various reasons, such as the individual from whom consent was obtained didn't have the legal authority to do so or the judge disagrees that exigent circumstances existed.

1.3.4 Security and Safety

During the initial conference, potential safety issues, both situational and infectious, should be considered and discussed. For example, if there has been a multiple shooting, the scene must be cleared by police prior to entry of the crime scene team. If there is apparent unrest, suspect(s) still at large, or it is a high-profile case, a plan to protect the CSI(s) while they are processing the scene should be dealt with. Additionally, the description of the scene from the first responder will help the CSI to assess potential hazards and determine what personal protective equipment (PPE) is likely to be needed or if additional assistance from specialty teams like hazmat or bomb squad is required before beginning scene processing. The CSI(s) must evaluate the scene and use their judgment and training to determine the safety of a situation. CSI personnel should not feel pressured to process a scene or perform a procedure if they reasonably believe their personal safety will be compromised.

1.3.5 Initial Walk-Through

The initial walk-through is also referred to as the primary survey. The only individuals who should be included in the walk-through are the first responder, CSI, and case detective (if on scene). This orients the CSI and detective to the scene, and the first responder should describe his/her paths within the scene in addition to any item that was changed, removed, or otherwise altered. This information is critical, especially in scenes where there was a great deal of activity prior to the CSI arrival, when it comes time to reconstruct the scene. It can be helpful to take some initial "establishing" photographs during the walk-through, as this is the most pristine state that the CSI will observe the scene. The CSI should:

- Be aware of current and upcoming weather and environmental conditions that might alter or destroy evidence. Precautions should be taken to protect and collect any evidence that might be affected by adverse weather or environmental conditions. For example, strong winds or rain could potentially alter or destroy evidence. If this situation occurs, the evidence should be photographed, documented with measurements, and collected as soon as possible.
- Make note of transient and/or conditional evidence that will require immediate processing, collection or protection. Transient evidence is temporary evidence, such as odors or hair/fiber evidence that is not adhered to something, such that it might be lost with normal actions performed during scene processing. Conditional evidence is evidence that is the result of an action, such as entries and exits (transferred evidence), lights (did first responder turn on/off?), or moved furniture (occurred during incident or to create access for first responder?). Evidence may be both transient and conditional, for example, a cigarette burning in an ashtray. The burning cigarette is transient because it will stop burning at some point

and conditional because someone had to light the cigarette to cause it to burn (this may also give information as to when the incident occurred).

- Identify points of entry and exit and note contamination caused by first responder(s). Also identify paths of movement within the scene. Ideally, there should be only one point of entry and exit, and a path through the scene for personnel and equipment.
- Brief initial observations should be recorded. This is not the detailed narrative that will be completed at a later time, but rather a "snapshot" that deals with the nuts-and-bolts information of who, what, where, when, and how.
- Determine needs in terms of personnel, equipment, PPE, and specialists (if applicable and available). Notify appropriate parties, as per policy, as to necessary additional personnel, equipment, or specialists that are needed.
- Determine the extent of your search area. As mentioned above, this may result in the expansion of your initial crime scene perimeter.
- If there is a decedent present, coordinate processing with the coroner/medical examiner personnel.
- Determine the need for barriers to reduce observation by the public and press photographers. Situations may also arise that require CSI personnel to process an area of the scene in order to create a pathway to the decedent.
- Conduct the walk-through slowly, being very cognizant of where personnel are stepping and anything that is touched. Take extreme care not to disturb the scene in any way during this initial walk-through.
- Take in the big picture and do not mark or move anything.
- Look for evidence mentioned by the briefing officer and investigator. Does what is seen fit the information provided? Try and think through the actions of the perpetrator. Does the evidence observed fit the hypothesis? Or, does it reveal a different scenario? Note that it may not always be possible to accurately reconstruct the actions of the perpetrator due to lack of sufficient evidence.

Once the walk-through is complete, the lead CSI (team leader) will determine the best approach to the scene that will result in the most efficient, but thorough search for and collection of evidence, and determine the roles of each team member. In the most ideal circumstance, the following roles should be assigned:

- Team leader
- Photographer/videographer
- Note-taker
- Sketcher
- Evidence collector(s)
- Evidence custodian

Many departments are too small to have a different individual assigned to each role, and one person may have to fill two or more roles, so this requires a bit more attention when planning the scene approach, to ensure an efficient work-flow that maintains the integrity and thoroughness of the search and collection of evidence. CSI personnel should not be rushed or allow themselves to be rushed by others, should take control, and be firm if necessary. Ultimately, the CSI personnel are the ones responsible for the integrity of the evidence collected and presented in court.

After the approach is decided and roles are assigned, a search for evidence is conducted, documented, and collected (to be described in greater detail below).

1.3.6 Final Walk-Through

Prior to releasing the scene, a final walk-through is conducted to ensure that no evidence was inadvertently overlooked and all equipment has been retrieved. The possibility of returning to a scene once it has been released is highly unlikely; therefore, this is a good time to review your notes to ensure that all measurements and observations have been documented. Discuss the scene search and evidence recovered with relevant personnel. This is a good time to photograph the scene in its final condition if damage was done during processing (e.g., demolition of walls to recover bullets). All death investigations should be conducted as homicide investigations, until the evidence proves otherwise. There is only one opportunity to collect the evidence, and this mind-set will help prevent overlooking evidence that may be important later as the investigation develops.

1.3.7 Post-Scene Communication with Investigators

After the evidence associated with the crime scene investigation has been submitted to the crime laboratory, the crime scene investigator becomes the case manager or liaison between the crime lab and the investigators.

Once evidence is transported back to the CSI office/lab, follow-up examinations can be performed. This can include things like processing certain pieces of evidence for fingerprints that could not be performed at the scene, photographing pieces of evidence in more detail, or examining clothing for the presences of gunpowder particles that requires the use of illuminated magnifiers and microscopes. Additionally, the detective's ongoing investigation of the case may lead to additional information that may require another search and/or collection of evidence.

1.3.8 Submission of Evidence

It is not practical or financially feasible to submit every piece of evidence to the laboratory for testing. Therefore, based on the particular case circumstances, evidence selected for testing should be those which will, regardless of results, provide the most useful information in determining the essential facts of the case. Similarly, not all pieces can be utilized for all types of testing. One may have to choose which testing will yield the most probative information. For example, consider a pistol with a textured grip. Should it be submitted for fingerprint processing or DNA to attempt to establish possession? In this case, since it is difficult to obtain latent prints from this type of surface, submitting it for low copy number (sometimes called "touch") DNA may be more probative. If the subject was not wearing gloves, it is more likely that skin cell and/or sweat (especially in the context of committing a crime) can be recovered than fingerprints from the grip of the pistol.

FIGURE 1.3 Overall photograph. (From the authors' files.)

1.4 DOCUMENTATION

1.4.1 Photography

Proper scene photography is critical to thoroughly documenting a scene for proper case disposition at a later time. The goal of photo-documenting the scene is to provide a true and accurate representation of the scene when it is reviewed by others at a later time and/or use in court proceedings. The photographs should provide the viewer with a "snapshot" of the scene, as seen by the photographer, and reveal the different stages of the scene investigation. Typically, photography is done after the initial walk-through or after videography. An organized, systematic method should be utilized, with the general flow of:

- *Overall photographs* (Figure 1.3)—These pictures are also known as "establishing" pictures and include interior and exterior photographs. These are typically done prior to any movement of evidence or placement of evidence markers as a way of documenting the scene in its initial state. Exterior views should include outbuildings, surroundings, street signs, address placards and/or mailbox showing address, and paths to/from the scene. Interior views should be overlapping in order to be able to "stitch" the photographs together for a panoramic depiction of the room(s). A convenient way to achieve this is to utilize the corners of the room as your focal point, or utilize the four compass points: north, south, east and west. These should also include doors/doorways into and out of the scene, and windows and routes leading to and away from the scene. Overall photographs provide context and show relationships between pieces of evidence.
- *Mid-range photographs* (Figure 1.4)—As the title suggests, these photographs are taken at a distance between overall and close-up, and the focus is individual pieces of evidence in relationship to one another and other items within the scene. The number of photographs taken in this range will vary based on the specifics of the particular scene, and should progress in a step-wise manner. Different lenses, f-stops, or lighting may need to be utilized to achieve good-quality results.
- *Close-up photographs* (Figure 1.5)—These photographs again feature the individual pieces of evidence, but at a much closer range to show greater detail and should be examination quality. The photograph of a 1 millimeter bloodstain is going to require a different technique than a bloodstained shoe. Generally, the flash will need to be detached from the camera body, or a ring flash utilized. Different lighting techniques may

FIGURE 1.4 Mid-range photograph. (From the authors' files.)

FIGURE 1.5 Close-up photograph. (From the authors' files.)

need to be utilized to capture sufficient detail. These photographs should be both with and without scales. Therefore, there should be a progression of overall, mid-range, close-up without scale, close-up with scale, photograph area underneath, behind, and so on, after the item is collected to show there is or is not additional evidence covered by the object, for example, a cartridge case found on the ground after the gun is collected.

It is good practice, after the overall or mid-range photographs are taken, to place the evidence markers and re-photograph from at least the overall perspective. This is of great assistance to individuals who have to examine the photographs at a later time. Camera settings that provide the best depth of focus should be utilized. It is also good practice to start the photograph series with a placard that contains the name of the case, date, time, photographer name, and a gray scale.

Given the prevalence of digital cameras today, there is debate as to whether photography logs are necessary, since all the camera information and settings are contained within the metadata. Some are of the thought that "the picture should speak for itself." While that is true, realistically, some scenes are more difficult to photograph than others, and optimal views may not be able to be obtained, and the photograph's context is unclear. In these types of situations, a photo log that includes, at the very least, the picture number and description would be invaluable. Therefore, a log should be created as part of standard procedure so the photographer doesn't have to decide whether the scene warrants one or not.

Whenever possible, photographs should be taken 90 degrees from the subject of interest in order to minimize distortion. This is a necessity if the photograph is going to be considered examination quality. The photograph should be free of distortion, correctly exposed, and in sharp focus. This may require stools, stepladders, tripods, and bubble levels to accomplish. Efforts should be made not to capture personnel, hands, feet, or other extraneous objects.

Last, the camera should be set to "continuous" numbering mode so that each photograph has its own unique number and numbering doesn't reset to zero when the camera is turned off or the SIM card is replaced. Once photographing a scene is finished, the pictures should be downloaded to a "master" file that is never altered. Make three CDs—one for the unit, one for the prosecutor, and one for the defense—and seal them in an evidence bag. Once these steps are taken, a copy of the master folder can be made, to which corrections can be made (brightness, contrast, hue, etc.). Some departments have software through which the photos must be imported, and the software assigns its own number to the photograph. Photographs should never be deleted, even if they are of poor quality or captured inadvertently. The SIM card can be forensically wiped and reused, or, some departments use a new card for each scene.

The digital camera has made it much easier to take many photographs and allows an immediate review of quality so additional photographs can be taken if one or more are not of acceptable quality. Therefore, photographers should not go into a scene with a predetermined number of photographs that they will take, or be conservative in their photography—if in doubt, photograph it! And remember the axiom *if it wasn't photographed, it wasn't seen.*

There are several "special" photography scenarios that may need to be utilized, including, but not limited to, low light photography, aerial photography, and photographing the scene post evidence retrieval that documents changes or damage that occurred as a result of evidence collection activities (e.g., wall damage after projectile retrieval). Every potential scenario cannot be described in detail here due to space requirements. However, there are many resources that describe and instruct in great detail how best to deal with a variety of photography situations/challenges.

1.4.2 Videography

Many agencies routinely videotape crime scenes. This gives the viewer a much better sense of spatial orientation that cannot be achieved with still photography. Videography should be completed after the initial walk-through, prior to still photography.

Audio should be turned off, and the video should not be narrated. As with still photography, personnel and equipment should not be seen in the video. Additionally, as with still photography, the approach should be planned and systematic, and the video should begin with a placard with the case name, date, time, location and videographer's name. The video should start from the outside of the structure, surroundings, and route to the scene. Once in the scene, the goal should be to provide a general orientation of the scene. Remembering to cover all four compass points should assist in thorough video documentation. Also very useful is to record video from the victim's viewpoint; get as close as possible to the victim without compromising evidence, and again, cover the four compass points.

Transitions should be smooth, movement slow and even, and not jump from area to area. If the scene is dark or there are a large amount of shadows, extra lighting should be utilized. Review the tape on-scene after completion, and re-shoot if needed. Videos should never be edited or erased and, in most situations, must be in their original condition to be admissible as evidence. This recording is now evidence and should be handled in a manner similar to the still photographs.

1.4.3 Note-Taking

Note-taking is an activity that is completed as an ongoing activity at the time the tasks are performed, so that there is a contemporaneous written record of crime scene activities that is not affected by memory loss at a later time. Notes should be taken in chronological order, detailed and legible. Sloppy notes or vague statements can later be misinterpreted in court. Notes should never be discarded or erased. Errors are corrected according to each agency's policy and procedures.

Fulsome note-taking will be invaluable if and when the case goes to court, as many cases do not go to court for a year or longer, and will assist in giving a complete "picture" to the reader. Cryptic notes tend to cause more questions and skepticism.

The following information should be included in crime scene notes:

- Case Information
  - Date, time and method of notification, and what information was received.
  - Date, time of arrival, transportation method, individuals present upon arrival, and any notifications that may need to be made.
- Description of Scene
  - Location type and condition, weather (and impending weather, if applicable), major structures, and any transient or conditional evidence identified.
  - Victim description (note that in most areas, the body cannot be moved without the permission of the medical examiner or coroner), position, clothing, obvious wounds, lividity, jewelry (also important to document a lack of jewelry), and presence or absence of any identification.
  - CSI team: personnel names and roles, initial and final walk-through times, beginning and ending times of activity and any variations from procedure, unusual circumstances, or, if evidence was moved or somehow altered, why and how that occurred.
- Location of Evidence
  - Where the individual items of evidence were discovered. Measurement from two fixed points allows for accurate reconstruction.
  - Designate pieces of evidence or groupings of evidence with numbered or lettered evidence markers.
- Evidence List
  - Both a general statement of evidence collected (e.g., "45 pieces of evidence were recovered from the kitchen and bedroom") in addition to a detailed evidence log that describes the piece of evidence, any visible manufacturer information (e.g., brand name, serial numbers, headstamps), time collected, and who collected it.

1.4.4 Sketching

Sketching is a very important task to complete, as this is what depicts the scene and the relationships among evidence items with accurate measurements, at a glance.

Sketches are useful in depicting the overall layout of the scene and allow for selectivity by including only details that are important to the case. The two most popular sketching perspectives are the bird's-eye view (overhead, as seen from above, looking straight down) and the elevation (side view). The overhead view depicts items in a scene on a single horizontal plane, while the side view is useful when a vertical plane is necessary (e.g., bloodstains present on a wall). The two basic types of sketches are the rough sketch (an example can be seen at: http://www.tpub.com/maa/12740_files/image608.jpg), which is done at the scene and is not usually to scale, and the finished sketch (an example can be seen here: http://www.creatiline.com/tag/finished-sketch-crime-scene). Keep in mind that the information obtained for the rough sketch will be utilized to create the finished sketch for presentation in court. If you are unsure about whether or not to take a measurement, or include an item, it is better to obtain more information than necessary than to need it and not have it. The finished sketch is completed from the information from the rough sketch, but "cleaned up" (in the sense that it is neater) and done with the presence of relevant measurements, scale, orientation, and legend.

Three-dimensional laser scanning systems are currently being adopted by an increasing number of law enforcement agencies. These scanners can be quickly deployed to measure and map indoor and outdoor scenes. This mobile laser device has the capability of collecting thousands of measurements per second while an embedded high-resolution digital camera takes photographs. Once the information is scanned and photographed, computer software can generate diagrams, perform scene reconstruction, and provide accurate measurements.

There are templates available of commonly encountered items that can be easily used in the field that allow the preparer to create a rough sketch more neatly and easily. An example is shown in Figure 1.6.

FIGURE 1.6 Arrowhead Forensics master crime scene sketching kit (http://www.crimescene.com/store/A-6340 CSK.Shtml). Variously themed templates are available for purchase individually to customize as needed.

What to include in the sketch:

- Case identifier, date, CSI personnel drawing sketch
- A scale or designated "not to scale" note somewhere on the sketch
- Legends that are used to designate important features in the sketch (e.g., color red for blood).
- Directionality (i.e., compass or indication of north direction)
- All significant objects, structures, and items of evidence with measurements

Three methods for obtaining measurements for a crime scene sketch:

- *Triangulation*—Two fixed points (things that are not easily changed, such as corners in a room, door frames, trees) are selected and the distance from each point to the piece of evidence is noted. If, for example, there is a body on the floor, and the legs are spread apart, measurements from each fixed point to the top of the head and to the bottoms of the right foot and left foot should be recorded. These measurements would allow a body to be positioned in the most accurate position possible, rather than if measurements were taken only from the fixed points to the head (this would allow the rest of the body to be placed anywhere in a 360-degree circumference).
- *Polar coordinates*—This method also uses two fixed points, but also uses angles. For example, evidence #1 is located 2′3″ from a wall and 20 degrees southeast. Angles can be measured with a compass or transit.
- *Baseline*—Again, two fixed points are utilized, such that a straight line is drawn between the points. The evidence is measured by its distance down the line and perpendicular to the line.

Computer software is available to assist in finished sketches and/or create professional, scaled renderings.

1.5 SEARCH METHODS

A variety of search methods exist, as there are many different types of scenes. This allows investigators to select the most appropriate method(s) for their specific scene. The choice of method may be dictated by the location, size, or circumstances of the scene. Once the search method has been selected, conduct a cautious search of all the visible areas, focusing on avoiding loss of evidence or evidence contamination. After this search has been conducted and the evidence has been photographed and

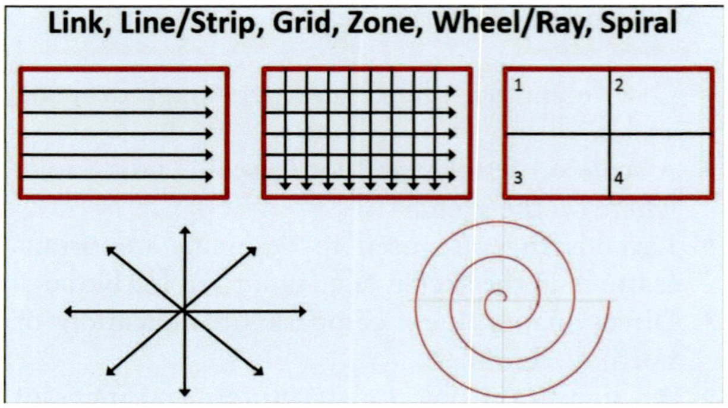

FIGURE 1.7 Search methods.

documented, a more vigorous search can be conducted of those areas that are concealed (e.g., moving furniture to look for cartridge cases). This general-to-specific approach ensures a thorough search of the scene. Figure 1.7 is a graphic summarizing the methods described.

Link—Very common, based upon the linkage theory: once a piece of evidence leads to another (e.g., a fingerprint on a murder weapon is identified to a known individual, individual's house and vehicle searched and reveals bloody clothing, DNA testing of those clothes is consistent with victim), experiential, logical, and systematic. Works with all scenes: small, large, indoor or outdoor.

Line—Often used for large, outdoor scenes. A coordinator is needed and searchers are often volunteer and need instruction.

Grid—Similar to line; essentially two line searches that are 90 degrees from one another. This method can be quite productive, but is more time-consuming.

Zone—Best for defined zones, such as houses or buildings with rooms. Often combined with other methods; good for search warrants. Teams are assigned small zones for searching.

Wheel or Ray—Used in special circumstances, limited applications: small, circular scenes.

Spiral—Best used on scenes without physical barriers (e.g., open water), limited applications, spirals may be inward or outward, must be able to trace a regular pattern with fixed diameters.

1.6 EVIDENCE COLLECTION AND PACKAGING

Evidence collection begins after the scene has been searched, evidence has been located and marked, photography has taken place, and sketches have been drawn. Evidence should be collected in such a manner as to protect it from breakage, contamination, and loss. Packaging will be evidence dependent and CSI personnel should determine what type is appropriate (e.g., paper bags, envelopes, cans, jars, boxes). Each package of evidence should be sealed at the closure in a way that access into the package would be obvious. This can be done by using tamper-evident evidence tape or other nonremovable tape marked with the date and initials of CSI personnel who collected the item.

The outer packaging (there should be at least two layers to protect the integrity of the evidence in the event that the outer packaging is damaged or otherwise compromised) should be marked with the following information: case identifiers, item descriptions, date and time of collection, and who collected the evidence. This initiates the evidence trail or chain of custody. This is the most commonly accepted method for authentication of evidence. It documents the transfer of custody of evidence from one person to another starting with its collection at the crime scene, through various analysts at the crime lab conducting examinations of the evidence, and its possible presentation in court. This ensures that what it presented in court is the same item collected. Each transfer is documented with a signature, date, and time. A record of the chain of custody protects against the possibility of evidence being adulterated or tampered with. Therefore, a break in the chain of custody can result in evidence being inadmissible in court.

As noted previously, proper packaging is key to evidence preservation and is specific to the type of evidence collected. The following are examples of the different types of evidence that may be encountered at a crime scene and how they should be properly packaged.

1.6.1 Fingerprinting

Fingerprints fall in the category of pattern evidence, and because no two people (to date) have been found to have identical fingerprints, including identical twins, it is evidence that can be used to identify (or exclude) individuals. The two main features upon which the discipline of fingerprint analysis are (1) uniqueness—as previously mentioned, each individual's fingerprints are unique; and (2) persistence—fingerprints do not change over an individual's lifetime, provided there is no damage to the dermal layer. This discipline is concerned with identifying friction ridge characteristics, composed of ridges and furrows on the skin, and can be found on the fingers, palms, and soles of the feet.

The three types of fingerprints generally found at crime scenes and/or on pieces of evidence are as follows:

1. *Patent*—A patent print is visible to the naked eye and does not require additional processing in order to identify it as a fingerprint. It may even

be suitable for comparison without additional processing. These fingerprints can be made of several kinds of substances such as dirt, blood, grease, etc.

2. *Latent*—Is not visible to the naked eye and requires additional processing or enhancement in order to visualize and possibly make a comparison. These are typically composed of sweat, lipids, and/or proteins secreted from the pores on the skin. There are many contaminants from the environment that may also be present within the chemical composition of the fingerprint.
3. *Plastic*—More correctly referred to as an "impression" because it is a recognizable fingerprint indentation in a soft substrate, such as putty, tar, wax, soap, etc. These fingerprints are three-dimensional and may not require additional processing in order to visualize.

Occasionally, a latent print can be enhanced sufficiently and photographed simply with oblique lighting or use of an alternate light source. The processing of latent prints will be largely dependent upon the surface on which the print is located. This is accomplished by two general categories, described below.

1.6.1.1 Physical

Physical processing does not involve utilizing chemicals or chemical reactions to increase visibility. Dusting with powder is a common and economical method. When a print is gently dusted, with brushes composed of fine fibers, fine particles of the dust adhere to the residue that created the print, providing enhanced contrast and visibility. There are several powder colors available, with different formulations (e.g., carbon, aluminum) in order to create optimal contrast, since prints may be found on a wide variety of substrates (see Table 1.1).

The MagnaBrush™ was the first magnetic fingerprint "brush" available, and this is a variant on the standard brush-and-powder approach. There is no actual brush in a magnetic device. Rather, there is a magnet within the device that creates a "brush" out of metal-based, magnetic powder. Because there is no actual brush, and the wand can remove excess powder from the substrate, this is a less abrasive method; therefore, it has less chance of inadvertently damaging a print. See Table 1.1 for a summary of methods.

Tape lifting is another physical method of processing fingerprints, where the print (either processed or patent) is physically removed from the surface by means of transparent lifting tape. The tape is then adhered to a backing that provides optimal contrast. There are a variety of products that provide both the lifting tape and the background on which to mount it (e.g., hinge-lifters). Figure 1.8 is an example of scaled hinge lifts available at Arrowhead Forensics.

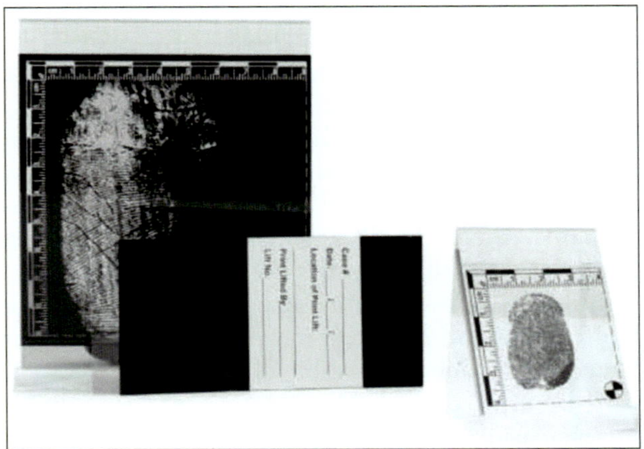

FIGURE 1.8 Arrowhead Forensics scaled hinge lifts (http://www.crimescene.com/store/A-2801KC.shtml).

TABLE 1.1 Fingerprint Processing Method Examples

Method	Composition	Best Surfaces	Application
Powder	Carbon, aluminum, lycopodium based	Nonporous, select porous	Fiberglass, camel hair, or feather brushes*
Magnetic	Iron oxide (may be mixed with black carbon and silicon dioxide, aluminum, titanium dioxide, lycopodium, etc.) for colored and dual contrast formulations	Nonporous, porous	Magnetic wand
Lifting	Transparent adhesive tape and backing cards	Nonporous, select porous	Transparent adhesive tape, manual pressure
Small Particle Reagent	Various compositions and colors ex, molybdenum disulfide, zinc carbonate, crystal violet, etc.	Wet or previously wet surfaces	Fine mist spray

* Due to the increased sensitivity of DNA testing, some agencies use disposable, one-use-only brushes to avoid cross contamination of surfaces and of the powders (re-dipping into a powder jar). Additionally, powder can be dispensed in smaller amounts from its original container to a separate "working" container, for use only on the scene at hand and any remaining powder in the "working" container discarded upon completion of the scene processing in order to avoid contamination of the stock powder.

Small particle reagent (SPR) is also considered a physical method, although it is liquid and sprayed onto the surface. It is essentially a liquid fingerprint powder for use on wet or previously wet items. SPR will adhere to the print residues and the excess SPR is removed with a spray bottle of water.

1.6.1.2 Chemical

There are a number of chemical reagents and processes available for processing latent prints, so that it is not feasible to discuss every available option here. Some of the most commonly used at crime scenes (as opposed to in the laboratory) will be addressed.

Ninhydrin—reacts with the amino acids in the fingerprint residue and turns a purplish color. It may be applied via spraying, dipping, or painting and is very useful on porous substances. The reaction process may be somewhat slow and may be accelerated by heat and humidity. It can be used alone, or as part of a multistep process. There are also derivatives, or analogues that assist with better visualization in conjunction with lasers and/or special illumination methods.

Iodine fuming—Elemental iodine is a substance that sublimes. In other words, it can pass from solid to gas form without turning into a liquid. It is applied via a fuming gun, or in a cabinet that then becomes filled with iodine fumes. This is a good method for items that may be valuable, as without also using a "fixing" component, the iodine enhanced print does not last indefinitely.

Cyanoacrylate—Also known as "super glue fuming." This method is also somewhat slow and requires a cabinet or chamber (portable chambers are available, or can be created easily, but care should be taken to ensure scientific protocols and controls are utilized) in which the fuming can occur. Heating can accelerate the process. The cyanoacrylate is heated to induce fuming, and a moisture source is needed to create optimal relative humidity. Alternatively, a vacuum method is also available. A "test" latent print of the individual performing the enhancement can be added to the chamber in a location that is viewable from the outside of the chamber in order to monitor the progress of development. If a print is not fumed enough, it can be subjected to another fuming session. However, overfuming a print may render it unusable. A cyanoacrylate processed print will be a whitish color. At this point, the print may be enhanced sufficiently to allow comparison, but is often followed by dusting or another processing, like dye staining. This method is useful on a variety of surfaces.

Amido Black—Used to enhance bloody prints. Therefore, these prints are not strictly latent, as there is usually some visualization of at least a partial pattern in order to prompt the use of the amido black. Although not specific for blood, this reagent also reacts with the proteins found in blood and turns a dark blue/black.

These are just a very few of the methods available, and further research is recommended. The processing method(s) chosen are most often based upon the surface to be developed, with the two biggest categories of porous or nonporous. It is not uncommon to find tape, duct or otherwise, that has been used during the commission of a crime. Dry ice, sub-zero freezers, or liquid nitrogen may be used to separate layers of tape without damaging latent prints that may be present on the adhesive side. Dye-type stains have often been used, and there is also a product called "sticky side powder" that is now available, specifically for this situation. Various methods and combination of methods have been utilized to attempt to develop latent prints on human skin, with greater or lesser levels of success. Because human skin conditions (alive, deceased, submerged in water, decomposing, etc.) and the conditions in which they are found will vary significantly, there is no standardized method(s) for developing latent prints on human skin.

The Chesapeake Bay Division of the International Association for Identification (2013) website provides an excellent reference list with clickable links that detail composition of reagent/method, how to utilize the method, the most appropriate materials on which the method should be used, along with the positive and potentially problematic issues associated with each. This reference can be accessed here: http://www.cbdiai.org/Reagents/main.html.

Photography should always be performed prior to any processing or lifting. After an establishing photograph, to show context, a macro lens or setting should be used, the print should fill the frame, and the camera should be perpendicular to the surface being photographed. Locations such as light switches, door handles, and so on, that may need to be used by crime scene personnel should be processed and preserved immediately. Items that can be removed should be packaged so as to prevent any alteration of potential fingerprint evidence and submitted to the crime laboratory for processing.

Documentation should include the name or initials of the individual collecting the evidence, date/time/location of collection, and the case number. If small items, or pieces removed from larger items, are submitted, information regarding the component's orientation should be submitted (up, down, front, back, compass points, etc.).

1.6.2 Trace Evidence Collection

Arson evidence—Generally comes in two different forms: fire debris and liquid samples. Fire debris containing possible ignitable liquids should be sealed in new metal friction lid containers (paint cans) to prevent the loss of vapors to the outside environment. Note that the interior of the can should be Teflon coated (to guard against corrosion). Liquid samples (flammable or otherwise) should be collected in glass jars or vials (never plastic) and sealed with Teflon-coated caps. As an added precaution, the jar or vial should be placed into an appropriately sized paint can containing padding material. This ensures that in the event of breakage or leakage, the liquid remains contained and avoids possible contamination of other evidence.

The evidence submitted for explosives analysis consists of pre-blast or post-blast materials. Pre-blast samples are often small in quantity, and post-blast samples typically consist of the remnants of an exploded device. Often, explosive residue may exist on the post-blast materials. The amount of sample that is available will dictate the method of collection. Glassine bindles and 1 dram vials are ideal for collecting small amounts of powder. Larger samples, usually involving post-blast materials, can be packaged in metal friction lid containers (paint cans).

Glass—There are several different types of glass: soda-lime glass is the type most commonly found in windows and bottles. Pyrex™ is borosilicate glass and is more resistant to shock, and heat changes and resists alteration by nearly every chemical except hydrofluoric acid. Tempered glass is also sometimes referred to as "safety glass." Tempered glass is stronger than typical window glass and, when broken, "dices" into small pieces without sharp edges as opposed to breaking into shards with sharp pieces and edges. This glass is commonly used in vehicle side and rear windows but may also be found in large commercial windows, doors, and even shower doors and some home windows, depending on their location. Laminated glass is what is usually found in vehicle windshields and is usually composed of two layers of tempered glass, with a high-strength sheet of plastic sandwiched in between the layers. This sandwich construction increases the strength of the glass, and the plastic can hold on to broken pieces upon breaking, among other capabilities. What is referred to as "bulletproof glass" is usually composed of multiple layers of laminated glass.

Glass evidence may be found in a variety of incidents such as burglaries, hit and run accidents, and homicides.

Glass evidence may be evaluated for fracture match comparison (fitting pieces together, as in a jigsaw puzzle), to determine the sequence of events (such as gunshots, as a fracture pattern can assist with determining the order of shots) or the direction of force or, by their optical and chemical properties, comparing fragments found at the scene to fragments found on victims or suspects.

Glass evidence should be meticulously documented, both photographically, in notes, and sketches. Orientation documentation (ex. inside/outside surfaces), in addition to documenting whether the fragments were collected from the inside or outside and should be packaged separately, is extremely important if a direction-of-force determination will be required. All glass fragments present should be collected, as even very small pieces may be able to be used in fracture match comparisons (and other testing).

Glass evidence should not be packaged in glass containers. Container selection will be at the investigator's discretion, depending on the nature and size of fragments in addition to the examinations that will be required. Paper bindles, coin envelopes, small plastic vials, and puncture-proof plastic containers are examples that may be used. Fragments should be packaged, sealed, and labeled separately. Textiles and tools (such as clothing, shoes, bats, rocks, etc.) that may contain microscopic glass fragments should be handled minimally (wet or bloodstained items should be allowed to air-dry first) and then wrapped completely in paper, sealed, and labeled. More than one layer of packaging may be prudent. If size prevents collection of all the glass, samples should be collected near the point(s) of impact and from distant corners, then packaged, sealed and labeled separately. The investigator should also be cognizant of other potential evidence that may be present, such as blood, hair, or fibers that may be present on the glass, and prioritize collection and processing of the various types of evidence.

Hair and fibers—Can be valuable in many different types of cases, including, but not limited to, rape, assault, burglary, hit-and-run, and homicide. Hair and fiber evidence can be useful in linking suspects with victims, places, and/or items.

When hairs or fibers are visible and firmly attached to an object:

- They should be left intact and in place.
- Diagram and note the number of hair/fibers and exact location of each fiber on each item, in addition to photography.
- After documentation is complete, label and package separately and securely to prevent the hair/fibers from becoming dislodged during transportation, but such that they will be contained within the packaging in the event that they do become separated from the item.
- Packaging selection should be appropriate for the type of item to which the hair/fibers are adhered.
- Labeling should be referenced in notes.

If hair/fibers are visible but loosely attached, or if firmly attached to an item that cannot be sent to the laboratory (e.g., due to size):

- Diagram and note the number of hair/fibers and exact location of each fiber on each item, in addition to photography.
- Carefully remove hair/fibers with clean tweezers. It would be appropriate to utilize more than one

set of tweezers such that one can be wiped with disinfectant and allowed to dry while other hair/fibers are being collected. The exact procedure will involve judgment based on number and types of fibers being collected, but should always be done in a manner that eliminates or reduces potential cross-contamination as much as possible, and in accordance with departmental procedures.

- Hair/fibers can be packaged in a variety of containers including but not limited to paper bindles, coin envelopes, and plastic or glass vials (that seal tightly). Care should be taken to ensure that the hair/fibers do not come into adhesive during collection or packaging.
- Label (case, description, location/source, item number, date/time, and name of collector) and reference in notes.
- Other circumstances may exist where an alternate method can/should be employed. For instance, if the investigator arrives at a site where a body has been dumped, actions like moving the body or removing clothing to be sent to the lab can cause the loss of hair and fiber evidence. Further, perhaps it is a night scene and with limited lighting available. The best solution is to tape lift the body (or clothing on the body) in situ. If the situation does not permit the immediate tape lifting to occur, then the body is placed in the body bag clothed and the body is tape-lifted back at the coroner's office prior to autopsy and the body bag is collected for trace evidence examination. Tape lifts are labeled according to area (i.e., front of shirt, back of shirt, etc.). Tape lifts may also be appropriate when there is a large number of hairs/fibers, or item is covered in hairs/fibers.

If the victim or suspect clothing may has hair/fiber evidence:

- Each item should be diligently kept separate. Victim and suspect clothing should be examined in different rooms or areas.
- Identification marks should be placed on the garment in an easily accessible place that does not damage or obscure potential evidence on the item. Garment labels are a good location for these marks.
- Examine for and avoid disturbing other types of evidence that may be present on the clothing, such as blood or other biological fluids, soil/dirt, dust or other material adhering to the item. If other types of evidence are present on the item, prioritize what should be enhanced/collected/sampled prior to packaging using established protocols.
- Fold and wrap (dry) articles separately in new paper bags or butcher/craft-type paper wrapping. At least two labeled layers are advisable.

To collect hairs/fibers that may be present in the hair of victims or suspects, hair should be combed with a new, fine-toothed comb over a new piece of clean (preferably white) paper. Using care, fold the paper, together with the comb, into a bindle, to avoid loss of trace evidence. The secure bindle can then be placed into a labeled outer wrapping or bag.

Control samples—Should be submitted, as these are comparative analyses. For example, if fibers are found on the socks or shoes of a victim who alleges being raped in a car, samples of the car's floor mats should be obtained.

Hair control samples—Head, pubic, and animal hair control samples may need to be collected, and should include the roots. This means that the hairs have to be pulled out:

Head: Approximately 50 representative pulled head hairs should be obtained optimally including hairs from both temple areas, crown, and the base of the neck. If there are multiple colors/lengths, samples from each color and length should be obtained, and each area, color, and length should be packaged and labeled separately. Documentation should include the individual's age and overall hair color in addition to any signs of hair treatment.

Pubic: Approximately 30 representative pulled pubic hairs should be obtained from different parts of the pubic area, packaged, and labeled separately to include the individual's name, case number, and area from which the hairs were collected, along with the CSI's name/initials and date/time.

Note: If the individual is not deceased, he/she can be asked to pull both head and pubic hairs themselves in the presence of the investigator.

Animal: Both combed and pulled should be collected, packaged, and labeled separately. Pulled hairs should be collected from the head, back, tail, and belly areas and include both the coarse outer hair and the finer fur hair as well as samples from all major color areas (if multicolored or striped). Each area should be packaged and labeled separately to include CSI name/initials, date/time, case and item numbers, body area from where the sample was obtained, species (cat, dog, rodent, etc.), and other available ID information for the animal that will distinguish it from other animals that may be involved in the case.

Investigators should always exercise extreme diligence and caution when handling suspect and victim items to prevent cross-contamination, as it may not be known until sometime later in the investigation if hairs or fibers are contained within submitted evidence.

Paint—Paint-chip evidence may be present and useful in cases such as hit-and-run incidents, motor vehicle accidents, burglaries, or other incidents involving forced entry or the forcing open of safes, cash registers, and so on.

Automobile: Samples should be obtained from any areas exhibiting fresh damage on pertinent vehicles, collecting all layers down to the metal substrate. Although the outer color of the vehicle may appear to be the same, there may be different types or compositions in different areas on the same vehicle. This is especially true if the vehicle is repainted. Optimally, if full-thickness chips can be recovered by slightly bending the metal and flaking off the sample chips, this is preferable. If not, a clean knife blade can be utilized to scrape off a full thickness sample. The blade should be thoroughly wiped off, or a new blade used between different areas of the vehicle to prevent cross-contamination. Samples from different areas should be packaged and labeled separately.

If cross-transfer is suspected (for example, a hit-and-run involving more than one vehicle), control samples should be taken from areas immediately adjacent to each area of transfer collected. This will assist in distinguishing the paint that was originally on the vehicle from paint that was transferred.

Clothing: Paint transfers on clothing may be very small or even microscopic. If the clothing is wet, it should be dried (air-dried or drying cabinet) before packaging. Avoiding excessive handling, carefully fold or roll in paper or place into a new, clean paper bag. Again, a second outer wrap is advised to prevent loss or contamination if the packaging should get damaged or otherwise compromised. Loose chips may be collected, packaged in paper bindles, and submitted with the clothing in order to prevent damage/breakage of the chip. Prior to collection, documentation (sketch, notes, photography) should be done in order to identify the location of the chip on the clothing.

Loose chips: May be located on clothing (as above) or on the ground near impact points and should be collected and packaged in paper bindles. Documentation should include the location from where the chips were collected.

Forced entry/burglary: Tools used to gain entry may contain paint evidence, in addition to other materials like drywall, plaster, safe insulation, etc. The ends of the tools suspected to have been utilized should be wrapped in a paper bag, sealed with tape to prevent loss. Consideration should be given to other types of evidence that may be present (e.g., fingerprints, DNA) and processing prioritized accordingly. Samples from all areas that the tool is suspected to have been in contact with should be obtained and should again be full thickness. The tool may also have transferred material onto the areas it was utilized; therefore, tool marks should be carefully examined for this type of evidence. *Never* attempt to "fit" the tool into marks or impressions at the scene, as this can result in additional transfer of materials, rendering subsequent analysis useless in terms of significance of presence/absence of a particular substance.

If the entire item can be submitted to the lab, this will ensure that all layers are present, and is especially useful if the specimen is small or difficult to remove.

Paper bindles, small glass or plastic vials with secure lids are good choices for packaging this type of evidence. Envelopes (bindles may be placed in envelopes) are not optimal unless the specimen is of a larger size; however, personnel must ensure that all edges are sealed. Likewise, plastic bags are not the best choice for this type of evidence, as it can be difficult to remove small chips.

Labeling should include CSI name/initials, date/time, case numbers, and source information.

Insects—Entomological evidence can be useful for several aspects of an investigation, such as postmortem interval (PMI), especially in deaths that occurred long enough prior where rigor mortis, algor mortis, and livor mortis are not very useful in assisting with PMI, if a body has been moved/disturbed after death, presence and/or position of wound sites, drugs/poisons (entomotoxicology), length of neglect or abuse in living victims and in wildlife crimes.

Of the major insect groups associated with cadavers, blowflies, flesh flies, and house flies are among the insects that arrive in the early stages of decomposition. Carrion beetles are early to mid-range arrivals, and cheese skippers and dermestids arrive later in the process. The life cycle of the fly is the most reliable to assist in determining an approximate time of death.

Collect both live and fixed specimens—Several of the largest larvae should be collected in various areas of the body, in addition to the "wandering" larvae that are moving away from the body (can be a radius of several feet) to locate an appropriate place to generate pupal casings. Use anatomical drawings in your notes to document where specimens were collected.

Approximately half the larvae should be kept alive by placing them into a cardboard container with air holes and a small amount of wet cat food or other raw meat. Live larvae can be raised/hatched to determine the length of the life cycle and speciation determined.

The other half should be fixed by first immersing in water brought to boiling and then heat turned off for 1 to 5 minutes immediately after collection (hours should not elapse from collection to fixing). Then the larvae are removed from the hot water and preserved in 70%—80% alcohol (ethanol is preferential, but can be difficult to obtain, 50% isopropyl alcohol can also be utilized). This provides a "snapshot" in the larval growth cycle at the time of collection.

Adult flies can also be collected; however, without proper equipment (nylon nets), this may be difficult for a typical crime scene unit. Adult blowflies can be kept alive in a vial with the lid screwed on—no air is required. Consultation with an entomologist may be the best course of action for this, and advice regarding collection and fixation of other insects that may be present, as the types of insects found will be unique to the geographical area. Likewise, if a qualified entomologist can attend the scene, he/she will be able to rapidly discern the most useful specimens.

1.6.3 DNA and Blood Evidence Collection

DNA can be found in all cells of the body that contain a nucleus. This includes the cells in blood, saliva (from buccal cells and white blood cells carried within saliva, as saliva is 99.5% water), hair, semen, vaginal secretions, skin, and sweat. The majority of DNA evidence is collected using sterile cotton-tipped swabs, often with "ultra-pure" water (distilled/sterile), if the evidence has dried on the collection surface. The swabs are then air-dried and stored frozen prior to analysis.

Fingernail and knuckle swabs are generally collected when the decedent appears to have been involved in a struggle or altercation. Sexual assault swabs are collected from six locations for women and four locations for men. Peri-anal, anal, oral, and exterior penile swabs are collected from men. Peri-anal, anal, peri-vaginal, vaginal, oral, and breast swabs are collected from women. Buccal swabs are generally collected from suspects to analyze as a DNA standard.

Current DNA technology has become much more sophisticated than the methods originally established in this field. Sensitivity levels in the detection of DNA have increased to the point the "touch DNA" is being collected and analyzed as evidence. These are situations where DNA has been successfully recovered from objects or victims that have had skin contact with the suspect. Other situations where DNA has been identified from individuals that have simply spoken while positioned over the evidence has led to increased precautions involving contamination. Individuals in close proximity to objects or victims with potential touch DNA are advised to wear masks.

With the potential for touch (low copy number) DNA to be present on a body for collection, it is important for CSI personnel to understand where touch DNA might be present for various situations. Collecting knuckle, hand, and facial swabs from a decedent who may have been in a physical altercation with the suspect prior to his death can yield touch DNA. Other potential avenues can include swabbing the neck of a victim who has been manually strangled or swabbing the clothing of a victim who has been moved or dragged. Each case and situation is unique. Understanding touch DNA and how it may relate to certain situations is a valuable tool when determining where evidence can be found.

1.6.4 Firearms and Related Collection

Firearms should be unloaded and packaged in an appropriate-sized cardboard box (special crime scene collection boxes designed to package various-sized firearms are available for purchase, and examples of Arrowhead Forensics tie-down boxes are shown in Figure 1.9) and secured in a way to ensure safety and prevent the loss of fingerprints, trace evidence, and DNA evidence. Cable ties can be used to secure the firearm to the interior of the box. In the event that a firearm cannot be unloaded (due to damage), precautions must be taken to ensure the safety of all personnel involved in the collection, transport and examination of this piece of evidence. Magazines

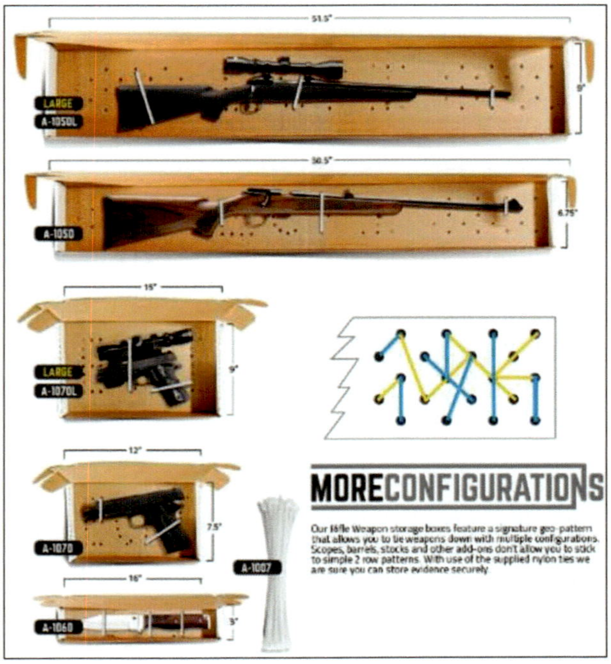

FIGURE 1.9 Arrowhead Forensics tie-down weapon storage boxes (http://www.crime-scene.com/store/a-1070-weapons-storge-box.shtml).

associated with the firearm should be securely packaged with the firearm.

Cartridge cases, cartridges, shot shells, bullets, and other firearms-related evidence should be packaged separately into individual coin envelopes to ensure that potential evidence such as fingerprints, trace, DNA, and markings are not lost or obliterated. These coin envelopes can then be consolidated and placed into a master envelope for submission.

Gunpowder particles may be difficult to observe due to their size. The use of oblique lighting can help in detecting their presence. Once located they can be taped or hand-picked (with gloves on) and transferred into paper bindles.

It is becoming increasingly common that agencies do not collect gunshot residue (GSR) from the hands of possible "shooters." This is because the probative value is not what it once was believed to be, as merely being present in the vicinity during the discharge of a firearm may result in the deposition of GSR on the clothing or bodies of individuals nearby.

TASER devices should also be rendered safe prior to collection and packaging by ensuring that the safety switch in engaged. Package the TASER with the battery in place and secured with cable ties inside an appropriately sized cardboard box. Removal of the battery could result in the loss or contamination of data recorded during its use. Treat the probes as biological sharps evidence and packaged in a puncture-proof container. TASER doors and AFID (anti-felon identification) tags can be packaged in a coin envelope. TASER components can be submitted in a master envelope separate from the TASER device.

A tool, as defined by the Association of Firearms and Tool Mark Examiners (AFTE) (n.d.) is, "An object used to gain mechanical advantage. Also thought of as the harder of two objects which when brought into contact with each other, results in the softer one being marked".

Toolmark items are generally separated into two broad categories, impressed marks and striated marks, along with several subcategories. While the discipline of firearm examination is a part of the toolmarks umbrella, firearms will be discussed separately, and this section will concentrate more on toolmarks such as those created by screwdrivers, pry bars, chisels, and so on.

According to the Indianapolis–Marion County Forensic Services Agency (2008), Evidence Submission Guideline #11:

> *Impressed or compression marks are produced when a tool is placed against an object and enough pressure is applied to the tool that it leaves an impression in the object. The class characteristics (shape) can suggest the type of tool used to produce the mark. The individual characteristics, if present, can be used to identify the tool with the mark.*
>
> *Striated toolmarks are produced when a tool is placed against an object softer than itself and with pressure applied, the tool is moved across the object producing a scrape. The parallel surface irregularities produced by this scraping action are known as a striated toolmark. These are also referred to as friction marks, abrasion marks and scratch marks.*
>
> *Some toolmarks are a combination of both features. Laboratory examinations and comparisons of toolmarks recovered from a crime scene, with tools from a suspect, can often provide conclusive evidence to link a specific tool to a specific crime scene. This evidence combined with the investigators information can sometimes produce invaluable links to suspects in a crime.*

At a crime scene, toolmark evidence may be found in various areas, most commonly entries/exits, windows, safes, and so on, where a tool was used to pry something open. Additionally, if a tool was used in an assault, there may be marks on surrounding objects if the assailant missed his/her target.

The CSI should not move doors, windows, and so on, where there are toolmarks in a manner that could compromise latent fingerprint evidence. The area should be documented fully in notes, sketches (to include distance from a fixed point and distance above the floor) and photographs, overall, to show its placement within the scene, and close up, with and without scale.

Comparisons cannot be made solely from photographs, but they may assist an examiner when submitted with the evidence.

If the pattern is on a small item, the entire item should be submitted to the laboratory, packaged carefully to avoid alteration and/or loss of trace evidence that may be adhered to the tool.

If the pattern is on an item that cannot readily be transported, it may be possible to cut out the section of interest. A large enough section above and below the pattern should be included to minimize risk of unintentionally altering the pattern.

If the surface containing the mark(s) is painted, paint scrapings should be recovered and submitted to the laboratory, as there may be particles that are visible only microscopically on the working surface of the tool.

If neither of the above options are viable, a MIKROSIL cast may be made (after thorough documentation) and submitted to the laboratory. If there is loosely adherent material within the pattern, this should be carefully recovered and the pattern processed for latent prints before the casting takes place. If more than one cast is made, they should be packaged separately, with different item numbers.

A suspected tool should *never* attempt to be "fit" into the pattern, as this can alter both the pattern and tool surface and could result in the loss of trace evidence. Likewise, evidence tape should never be applied to a tool's working surface.

Toolmark evidence packaging information should include, at a minimum, the orientation of the item (top, bottom, front, back etc.), the name or initials of the individual who recovered the evidence, date/time of collection and case number.

1.6.5 Miscellaneous Evidence Collection

When the scene is that of a death, it is important to remember that the scene itself is under the purview/control of the police department, and the body is under the purview/control of the medical examiner's (ME's) or coroner's office. As a result, evidence collection from the body or clothing of the decedent will have to be coordinated between the agencies. The body should not be moved or otherwise altered until the ME or coroner office permits such movement.

All packaging of evidence should be completed at the time of collection during the crime scene investigation. However, exceptions are made when dealing with clothing or bedding that has been saturated with blood, water, or other biological fluids. To avoid possible contamination due to mold and microbial growth, these items of evidence should be thoroughly dried before being stored frozen. The best method for drying is by hanging individual pieces that have been covered on both sides by a continuous piece of butcher paper and secured at the ends and sides with staples, as shown in Figure 1.10. This enables proper airflow while protecting the evidence against contamination. Any loose trace evidence material will be retained at the bottom paper fold. Plastic trays can be placed beneath to collect any excess drippings that may occur during the drying process.

Clothing or bedding that is not saturated should be packaged individually. An ideal method is to individually package each article of clothing for one individual (victim or suspect) and then combine these individual packages into a master bag for that individual. Victim and suspect clothing is *always* packaged separately. If the article of clothing has significant bloodstain patterns that will be documented to a larger extent at the laboratory, the article of clothing can be laid flat on a piece of butcher paper and sandwiched by another piece of butcher paper. The article of clothing can then be carefully folded and packaged for transport. The presence of butcher paper ensures that the article does not fold onto itself, thus eliminating the possibility of the pattern being obliterated.

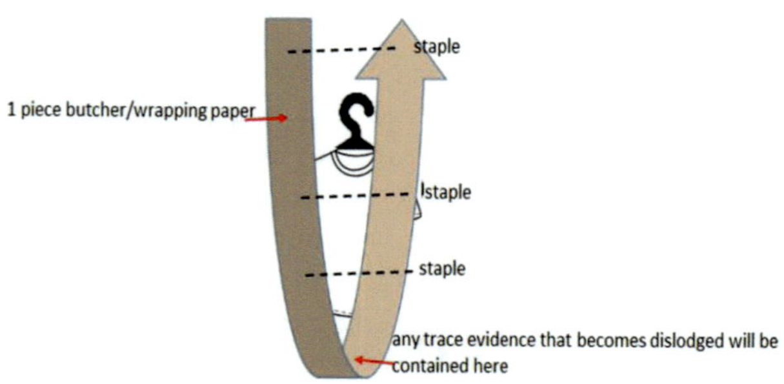

FIGURE 1.10 Example of drying technique for wet items of evidence.

Footwear and tire-tread evidence can be important in many different types of crimes to establish an individual's presence (more accurately, his or her footwear's presence, as it may not be possible to prove that the footwear wasn't used by someone other than its owner) or their vehicle's presence at a scene. Somewhat similar to fingerprint evidence, these can exist in two- or three-dimensional configurations. Two-dimensional patterns are those found on solid-type surfaces, such as tile, wood, linoleum, paper carpet, clothing, and so on. For example, dirt or blood on the bottom of a shoe can be transferred to the floor when the individual subsequently walks across it, leaving a print of the shoe tread. Three-dimensional patterns are those made on softer types of surfaces that deform the surface, such as snow, mud, sand, and so on.

A great deal of information may be able to be ascertained from footwear evidence. Some examples include identification or elimination of footwear, number of participants, confirm or refute statements.

1.6.6 Comparison Samples

Comparison or "known" samples should always be collected and packaged separately from questioned samples.

1.6.7 Presumptive Field Tests

The most common presumptive testing performed in the field is for bloodstains; please refer to the Bloodstain Pattern Analysis (BSPA) chapter for a review of some of the presumptive methods. The appropriate dictionary definition (as noted in the BSPA chapter) that applies to presumptive field tests is "*giving grounds for reasonable belief or opinion*" (http://www.merriam-webster.com/dictionary/presumptive). This is important to keep in mind when conducting presumptive tests and determining their significance. A presumptive test does not confirm the presence of blood, for example. A positive presumptive test gives the investigator reasonable belief that the questioned substance is, in fact, blood, in order to determine the appropriate next step in evidence processing and/or collection.

Presumptive tests are available in a variety of sensitivities and specificities. A very sensitive test means that it can detect a very small amount of the questioned substance. Continuing with blood as an example, a test with high specificity increases the likelihood that the questioned substance is, in fact, blood. In other words, a specific test does not give a positive reaction with many substances other than the one for which it is designed (false positives). Tests may be sensitive, but not specific, meaning that they can detect a small amount of blood, but can cause a positive reaction with substances other than blood. Alternatively, again continuing with the blood example, tests may be very specific, but not very sensitive, meaning that a positive reaction indicates that the substance is more likely blood, but it cannot detect very small amounts of blood. The best situation is to have a test that is both very sensitive and specific. The tests utilized will be determined by department policy and/or the nature of the investigation.

Presumptive tests for fluids such as semen, saliva, urine, and so on, are usually performed in the laboratory. However, the CSI may search for and collect samples of suspected biological stains in the field using an alternate light source (ALS). The following link provides a convenient resource for the wavelength, eye protection and camera filters suggested for various items for which the CSI may search: http://www.horiba.com/fileadmin/uploads/Scientific/Documents/Forensics/fls.pdf.

Additionally, there are some tests for lead or other trace metals, hairs/fibers, and drugs that are utilized in the field by some agencies. Please refer to the appropriate sections.

1.7 CHAIN OF CUSTODY

A properly documented chain of custody, from the moment an item of evidence is collected until its presence in the courtroom, is critical for successful case resolution. One break in the chain of custody can result in critical evidence being excluded for use in court at a later time.

A chain of custody form, an example of which can be seen at http://www.apd.army.mil/jw2/xmldemo/r195_5/r195-5f2-2b.png, is utilized whenever an item of evidence is transferred, or retrieved for tests/examination/analysis. Documented information should include:

- Name of individual handling/transferring the item
- Date and time item was retrieved, transferred or otherwise handled
- Reason(s) for handling of item
- Any changes made to the evidence

For items removed for additional photography, for example, the package should be opened in an area away from the original evidence seal, thereby leaving it intact. The item being photographed should be laid out on clean wrapping paper for the duration of the examination. Then, both the wrapping paper and the original packaging should be included when the item is repackaged. This minimizes the potential for loss of trace evidence and keeps the original packaging available for inspection, if necessary.

1.8 RECONSTRUCTION

If the ultimate goal of crime scene investigation, to be able to reconstruct the events that gave rise to the physical evidence, is kept in mind, it is clear why meticulous documentation and attention to detail is critical.

Also important to remember is that not all scenes can be reconstructed to the point that an exact sequence of events can be determined, as often there may be more than one action that could give rise to a given piece or set of evidence. The same is true for sequencing events—while it is sometimes possible to determine certain parts of the overall sequence (e.g., the glass was broken first, then the footwear pattern occurred on the broken glass), the investigator must be cognizant of the limitations of the various disciplines and render only defensible opinions.

1.9 CONCLUSION

The material contained in this chapter is meant to be a brief overview for guidance rather than a comprehensive manual. Each section could be a chapter in and of itself! Investigators should always adhere to their agency's specific standard operating procedures (SOPs). If deviation from established procedures is necessary, the rationale for the deviation and approval sought should be well documented. Some material is repeated, as it contains critical points that bear repeating.

It is always better to take the time to consult with a subject matter expert when needed, or contact the laboratory with unusual or complex situations instead of improperly or incompletely recovering or documenting necessary evidence.

The role of the crime scene investigator is to locate, collect, and preserve physical evidence, not to "prove" a case. The CSI should remain open-minded and objective in order to assure that scenes are processed objectively and not lean toward proving the theory that was presented upon arrival.

Figure 1.11 shows the "Dynamic Evidence Funnel" (Rini, 2005), which very concisely shows the overall flow of physical evidence from scene to court and the personnel involved at each stage of the process.

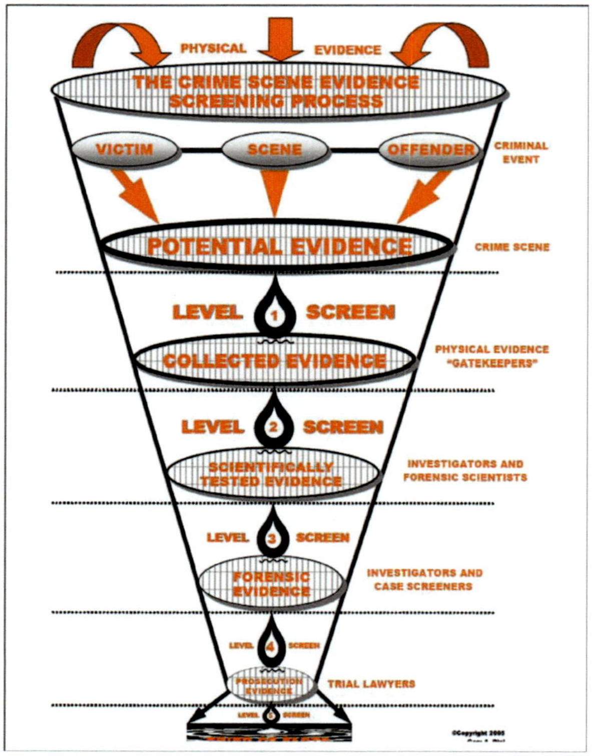

FIGURE 1.11 Dynamic Evidence Funnel. (Courtesy of Gary A. Rini, MFS, Gary Rini & Associates.)

A successful crime scene investigation will discover sufficient physical evidence to establish the fact that a crime has occurred, and that the suspected criminal event occurred at a specific place and with certain limitations, within a specific time frame. In addition, the physical evidence should serve as a means to include or exclude individuals who have been implicated or associated with the criminal event (Rini, n.d.).

BIBLIOGRAPHY

Association of Firearms and Tool Mark Examiners. (n.d.) Accessed 3/15/15. http://afte.org/.

Chesapeake Bay Division of the International Association of Identification. 2013. *Latent Fingerprint Processing Techniques—Selection & Sequencing Guide*. Accessed 2/13/15. http://www.cbdiai.org/Reagents/main.html.

Fisher, Barry A. J. 1993. *Techniques in Crime Scene Investigation*. Fifth Edition. Boca Raton, FL: CRC Press.

Indianapolis–Marion County Forensic Services Agency. 2008. *Evidence Submission Guideline #11*. Accessed 2/15/15. http://www.indy.gov/egov/county/fsa/documents/toolmark.pdf.

James, S. and Nordby, J. 2009. *Forensic Science an Introduction to Scientific and Investigative Techniques*. Third Edition. Boca Raton, FL: CRC Press.

Quality Documents Program. 2006. Accessed 4/15/15. http://www.nfstc.org/download/65.

Rini, Gary A. n.d. Crime Scene Investigation Definition. *Handout*.

Rini, Gary A. 2005. Dynamic Evidence Funnel. *Handout*.

U.S. Department of Justice, Federal Bureau of Investigation, Laboratory Division. 2001. *Processing Guide for Developing Latent Prints*. Accessed 2/01/15. http://www.fbi.gov/about-us/lab/forensic-science-communications/fsc/jan2001/lpu.pdf.

CHAPTER 2

Crime Scene Investigation in the Underwater Environment

Underwater Forensics

Mack S. House, Jr.

CONTENTS

A crime scene is first a medical concern and then a legal one.

> *The recovery of human remains or submerged victim is no different than any other crime scene investigation. You still have a crime scene, a victim and a suspect.*
>
> —Hayden Baldwin, Retired Illinois State Police (www.icsia.org)

2.1 CRIME SCENES PROCESSES

When an individual submits an application for the position of crime scene technician, there are usually variations in the so-called minimum requirements. Depending on the geographical location, which plays an important role in the talents needed, requirements vary. The applicant may be required to have an associate's degree in criminal justice or a similar subject; however, the applicant may have enough experience in the field to bypass this requirement, provided he or she demonstrates a competency level equivalent to the degree applicant.

The typical duty description will include the ability to process a crime scene in a competent manner. This includes the ability to search and recover latent palm and fingerprints. Crime scenes will also include trace evidence such as DNA.

Many of the postings for crime scene technicians, also known as crime scene investigators (CSIs), found on various search engines are vague in their job descriptions.

Again, it comes down to geographical locations and size of the department posting the position, for example, coastal locations, mountain locations or resort locations.

When one considers discussions involving forensics, as it relates to crime scene investigations, one must also understand the underlying principles that provide the foundation of each element.

When discussing the roles of those involved in crime scene investigations, first understand the importance of formal education and the subjects required. There must be a broad base knowledge that includes both theoretical and practical problems that must be solved. It is in no way teaching the student what to think, or what to expect, but rather teaching the student how to think and realize that the only constant found in crime scene investigations is predictable unpredictability.

Protocols and recovery are, in many ways, one and the same. However, one must understand several principles directly involved with the recovery of the submerged victim. Contamination and cross contamination must be understood at all levels. When one considers the "contaminants" found in most rivers, lakes, and streams, one must also include variations in human disease processes.

What effect does a chemically contaminated underwater environment have on a particular victim? If the victim is taking a prescribed antibiotic, such as metronidazole, a synthetic antiprotozoal antibacterial agent, then the "normal" biodegradation or stages of decomposition will change.

The recovery and preservation of an underwater crime scene occur simultaneously.

The victim must be handled in such a manner that precision and methodology must be thoroughly and completely understood. It is true that once an object is moved, it can never be placed exactly as it was originally found. The same goes for the moving of the victim, and postmortem wounding must remain a concern.

Documentation, photographic, video, sketches, GPS, the "Take Slate," and other means of completing the process must be done thoroughly, methodically, and completely. There are no reasons suitable that could justify the failure or incomplete documentation of the scene completely.

The crime scene diagram, or sketching, is a methodical process, which should follow the same sequence in every crime scene investigation. Typically, the rough sketch begins with the outer perimeter of the scene, usually from an above viewpoint, as if the roof of the building were absent. Once the outer perimeter is drawn, it can then be subdivided into rooms, hallways, and so on. Then windows, wall openings and partitions can be added. Large furniture and bodies can be added to the diagram once each room has been reviewed. A separate diagram of each room may be necessary to document smaller items.

Measurements should be consistent in each crime scene. If an outer wall is used as a beginning point, then the outer walls should be the starting point throughout the documentation process. In the process of measuring distances, it is best to use a retractable tape measure. I would discourage using any measuring device that is nonporous, such as wood, most plastics, and rubber-encased measuring tapes. It is important that the measuring device used be thoroughly decontaminated as soon as practical. The decontaminant should contain SD alcohol as its primary ingredient and be applied a minimum of two times. The measuring device should not be retracted until the exposed area is thoroughly decontaminated.

If approved by your particular department, generic "blueprints" of typical residences, including mobile homes and apartments, are always a good source of sketching. Rooms, hallways, closets, windows, entryways, and related areas need only have their dimensions added. There is an advantage in having the various layout styles of blueprints on hand for reference.

Scale is sometimes referred to as measurements; however, a scale is a reference to the size of an object compared to a known object, for example, a dollar bill compared to a handgun. In using a scale, it is best to use the same scale or something as close to it as possible in every case. If you opt to use a common 25 cent coin (quarter) as a scale, then it is easier for you to relate to size when questioned on the witness stand. Remember to decontaminate the scale you use prior to placing it back where you keep it.

2.1.1 Plumb and Level

The plumb and level are additional methods used to show elevation and angle of a substance or object. This information is needed in situations where gravitational pooling is in question or the splatter patterns of a particular substance need clarification. This information is used in court as well as the lab to establish the facts of the case or methods used to determine or clarify a specific fact or question that may be presented. For example, there may be a question regarding the position of a victim leaning out of the driver side of a vehicle, if it is unclear to the court that the driver side of the vehicle is actually leaning 27 degrees lower than the passenger side. Clarification must be made that further explains that the vehicle is in this position because of the vehicle being on an embankment. Photographs may not clarify this position by themselves regardless of the amount of photos taken. A photograph or sequence of photographs, showing a plumb and level in the foreground, which shows a view of the vehicle from behind or from the front, will clarify the circumstances in which the vehicle was found. This in turn gives an explanation as to the position of the victim. The plumb and level is a valuable tool since very few crime scenes occur on flat land or surfaces.

Every department that I have researched requires the ability to sketch a crime scene thoroughly and completely. As you may have guessed, documentation is required as well. This does not mean that you have a laptop computer with spell check to accomplish your tasks. Your ability to take good notes will be an invaluable asset. You will always find that the hiring agency requires the ability of the applicant to prepare detailed reports using proper grammar and punctuation. Of course, you should have the ability to communicate verbally and be as articulate in written form as well.

2.1.2 The Creation of the Human Model

The human model is a measurement of the victim and suspect regarding pant, shirt, shoe sizes, height, weight, and so on. This is in addition to full-body photographs, verified measurements received from the medical examiner. Weight and stature often play an important role in the evaluation process of what took place at the crime scene. All the information, including photographs, provides clarification to the court and jurors regarding the actual events that took place. It is the sequence in which the events actually took place (when, where, how) and precipitating events that bring clarity.

The Human Model procedure may or may not be acceptable to your department or lab procedure and protocol.

2.1.3 Prepares Evidence

In the process of preparing evidence, the first consideration is to ensure that the crime scene has been thoroughly documented, including photographs. Documentation should always indicate the location of each piece of evidence, and then the collection and preparation process can begin. To be methodical in both collection and preparation, the collection of the most fragile or smallest evidence will usually be the starting point. As long as there is an established method, the collection and preparation process should go smoothly and completely. Always be prepared to photograph evidence that is located under the initial evidence. Sometimes this is referred to as stacked or layered evidence photography. As long as the disassembly or removal is well documented in written and photographic form, the technician or technologist is doing his or her job.

Always keep in mind that there are no suitable circumstances in which evidence that may contain moisture be packaged in paper or plastic for a period lasting more than two hours. Moisture, absence of light and warm environment contribute to bacterial growth, which can alter and destroy the existing evidence. Packaging evidence that may cross-contaminate each other must be placed in separate containers or packages. The preparation of evidence is dependent on the type of evidence, its location, its condition, and the existing circumstances at the time of its discovery. Again, it is important to keep in mind the potential for contamination of equipment and personnel.

2.1.4 Maintains Fingerprint Records

The responsibility of maintaining fingerprint records differs from one department to another. Each department has their own protocols for record keeping, thereby suiting their individual needs.

It is understood by crime scene investigators (CSIs) that fingerprint records include fingerprints, palm prints and bare footprints. In some cases, ear prints are included in this list, and they should be. After all, the outer rim (helix) of the human ear is unique from one individual to another. Do not forget that each of these prints contain oil from the skin which may contain additional evidence.

2.1.5 Conducts Latent Fingerprint Examinations

Fingerprint examination has become so automated that it is almost an exception rather than a rule for a technician to examine latent prints. With so many advancements in the field of forensic science, it seems as though technicians' involvement is not necessary; however, it is beneficial for the technician to understand and be able to apply the principles of fingerprint identification and examination.

2.1.6 Attends Training

In many instances, technicians limit their training to the requirements of the department. Most consider these training sessions to be the minimum standards for maintaining the required continuing education points; however, this mind-set does not benefit the technician and his or her ability to excel. In selection and attendance of various training topics available, one cannot restrict oneself to the minimum requirements of the department and expect to be a proficient professional in one's field. In support of this opinion, I offer the obvious differences as well as the similarities of the submerged victim and the land-based (including shallow-grave) victim. These are two completely different environments and circumstances, yet there are many commonalities that both exhibit.

2.1.7 Conducts Training

For the technician who is selected or required to conduct training, he or she must carefully outline the subjects to be covered and thoroughly cover the subjects within the outline. The subject matter may or may not include topics that the attendee is familiar with, and even if the subject is known, the training should go well beyond the attendee's current knowledge. The technician that is selected to conduct a training session will, or at least should, research the subject matter in order to expand the current knowledge base. When I was attending Anesthesia Technology School, we were required to conduct training sessions on a weekly basis, and the attendees included anesthesiologists, anesthetists, and related professionals.

Now that is what you might call a bit of peer pressure, but it most certainly prompted us to become proficient in our knowledge base, training, and speaking ability. In the field of anesthesiology, you either know and understand what you are doing or you are not in the field of anesthesia; it's just that simple.

2.1.8 Knowledge and Abilities

For the CSI, knowledge and abilities are two separate issues. Understanding the abilities of the experts in the lab and established protocols regarding evidence does not imply that the CSI has the same abilities as the laboratory expert. It is important that the CSI understand the lab professionals' needs and the best methods to achieve those needs. It is equally important for the CSI to have the ability to investigate the crime scene with the needs of the lab in mind. So, the knowledge of what is needed and why promotes the abilities and insight of the CSI. For example, the CSI knows that the evidence (a handgun) should, per lab protocol, not be exposed to sunlight and should be kept chilled equal to, or lower than, the temperature in which the evidence was found. Because the CSI is knowledgeable regarding lab protocols, he or she performs CSI duties in a more conscientious, deliberate and methodical fashion.

2.1.9 Special Requirements

In most instances, the special requirements include required successful completion of a thorough background check, physical examination (which may vary from department to department), psychological evaluation and of course the dreaded polygraph. This (the polygraph) brings to mind what Marcus Aurelius must have been thinking when he wrote that the "Character is determined more by the lack of certain experiences than by those one has had."

2.1.10 Nature and Scope of Working Conditions

When discussing the working conditions the CSI is required to cope with, the list can, from a realistic standpoint, be endless. To say that the CSI oversees a variety of complex crime scenes is indeed an understatement. The working conditions that the CSI must cope with would devastate and sicken most people in today's society. Think of the incomprehensible variables the CSI faces in the "typical" homicide investigation. Now, let's add just a bit more to the "list" of working conditions: sexual assaults, home invasions, armed robberies, domestic violence, infant-child and pregnant female homicides, death by vehicle investigations, dismemberment and burnings, dumping bodies in a river or lake, and so on. The variations in each of these examples are almost as endless as the examples themselves. In a typical 8-hour shift, 5.5 hours is spent processing crime scenes. In a typical week of 40 hours, 28 hours will be dedicated to crime scene investigations. The remaining 12 hours of this 40-hour week are spent maintaining equipment, preparing reports, testifying in court, continuing education, and reviewing laboratory protocol updates.

CSIs are required to perform their task regardless of the circumstances. Crime scene searches often require extensive stooping, climbing, reaching, and kneeling regardless of the existing weather conditions. The CSI is also required to carry, pick up, and handle a variety of objects, which will vary in weight, shape, and size. In the performance of the CSI duties, the required physical and mental challenges that he or she will be exposed to are unpredictable and often difficult to manage. Physical endurance is important in order to be able to manage these requirements; however, one cannot dismiss the importance of one's mental strength and stability. In discussing the mental strength of the CSI, one must consider the advantage and importance of critical incident stress management or debriefing.

2.1.11 Summary

It is obvious that there is a lack of universal standardization, other than the basics, regarding requirements for the crime scene technician. Geographical location, department size, and crime rate have an impact on the criteria necessary to become a non-degree CSI. This does not imply that the professional ethics associated with the CSI have been compromised; it simply means that a CSI in a Midwestern state (population of 650) is not under the same pressure as a CSI in New York City. I think it would be rather difficult for the New York City CSI to transfer to a Midwestern city that has a population of 650 and perhaps even more so for the Midwestern CSI to transfer to New York City. The difference in requirements is obvious; never mind the differences in stress levels.

From the beginning of processing a crime scene, one must not forget the advances in crime scene investigative techniques and the technology supporting these advances and the crime scene investigative results.

Technology comes twofold for the CSI. The foundation, considered by many, is advancements in medical research. Next is the support and availability of advanced technology in design, capabilities, and selection of tools that are available to the CSI. Keeping pace with these advancements will not be an easy task for the CSI because suitability is an integral part of the tool selection process.

2.2 PROCESSES CRIME SCENES

The primary difference in the job description between the land-based CSI and the CSIDT (crime scene investigator diver technologist) is the environment in which the crime scene exists. There are considerable differences between the "liquid" environment and "gas" environment. The preparation requirements are as different as the environments, and the time elements are not the same. For the CSIDT, processing the crime scene begins at the conclusion, usually at the water's edge, of the land-based CSI processing protocols. In other words, once CSIs have completed their evaluation and processing protocol, the CSIDT begins their processing protocol. For example, CSIs stop processing at the water's edge, and CSIDTs begin their processing at the water's edge. Communication between the two teams is imperative in order to ensure that the crime scene is thoroughly processed.

The search, location, and verification of evidence and victim are considerably more complicated, hazardous and time-consuming for the CSIDT than for the CSI. For the CSIDT, processing the crime scene is not simply recovering the evidence and/or victim, which is nothing more than a salvage job. Processing the crime scene is a methodical process, just as it is for the CSI.

The location and documentation of all evidence, including photographic documentation, is not much different from CSI protocol. The CSIDT does not have to contend with the weather to the degree that the CSI does; however, the variables that exist in the underwater environment can be far more challenging.

The photographic documentation process includes, to a degree, the same process that the CSI follows. The main differences between the two are that the CSIDT may not be able to photograph the overhead view in the same fashion as the CSI. The CSIDT photographs the victim, making the head of the victim magnetic north for diagram reference. He or she will then photograph the victim by referencing the eight points of the compass for each photograph taken, all of which is done on the horizontal plane. The CSIDT will then photograph the victim from above using a protractor-style format, which provides 0-, 30-, 60-, 90-, 120-, 150-, and 180-degree views of the victim. This procedure is repeated, from different long axis points, as needed, while maintaining approximately the same distance from the victim. Evidence, such as a handgun, is photographed in like fashion. Unlike the CSI, the CSIDT is required to document the depth, water temperature, and current where the victim is located. In addition to this documentation, water and soil samples are taken proximate to the location of the victim. These samples are classified as evidence and are processed in the same manner as any other evidence. The only exception to this protocol is that these samples are chilled (packaged on ice) to the same or lower temperature in which they were located. They may not be exposed to sunlight or any heat source while in the possession of the CSIDT. The chain of custody, for the CSIDT, is strictly adhered to, and release forms, an intricate part of his or her CSIDT logbook—a court-ready document—must be completed.

2.2.1 Maintains Issued Equipment

There are considerable differences in the equipment issued to the CSIDT. The CSIDT does not require items like fingerprint powder, swabs, luminal, and so on. Conversely, the CSI does not require a diving cylinder, EXO-26, "halo" light source, and so on. Other than the CSIDT diving equipment, there may be considerable likeness in equipment used or needed by the CSIDT and CSI. Depending on geographical location and department requirements, the equipment may be identical, especially if the CSIDT serves both land-based and the water environment investigations. The decontamination procedures are also quite different because of the environmental exposure. When one takes into consideration the condition of the victim and the unknown medical condition in which the victim may be, there is little difficulty in understanding the biological concerns. For example, if the victim is in the advanced stages of decomposition, the CSIDT must process the crime scene per protocol, regardless. Since the CSIDT is required to photograph, measure, and so on, in great detail, which requires close proximity to the victim and being in the same column of water, is that not virtually the same as being in the same bathtub as the victim? The decontamination process is rather extensive and methodical.

In maintaining equipment, the CSIDT follows the guidelines as set forth by the manufacturer of each piece. This includes but is not limited to life-support systems, communication and umbilical lines, environmental protection, camera, video and closed-circuit TV systems, halo lighting systems, and so on. Additional maintenance includes DOT (Department of Transportation) hydrostatic testing of diving cylinders as set forth by DOT and team protocols.

2.2.2 Prepares Evidence

In the process of preparing evidence, the CSIDT must use discretion in many areas. It is not a simple task to prepare evidence in a liquid environment. The CSIDT must contend with water currents and limited visibility but with the slow and deliberate movements necessary to prepare the evidence in a responsible manner. Aside from the documentation process, the CSIDT must make sure that measurements are accurate and that all evidence has been photographed. Movement cannot disturb the "crime scene," and since the CSIDT does not use fins, as associated with the recreational diver, hand and foot movement must be done carefully. The preparation of the victim may require bagging the hands (preservation of unseen evidence) of the victim and photographing each step of the process. The victim is always placed in the face-up position prior to taking the victim to the surface. It is the discretion of the CSIDT as to whether or not the victim is to be placed in containment prior to being brought to the surface. Handguns, knives, and like kinds of evidence are always contained prior to transporting to the surface. All firearms are put into a "SAFE" status prior to closing the containment device. Either a CSI supervisor or police department supervisor confirms this via observation on closed-circuit TV.

2.2.3 Maintains Fingerprint Records

Since the CSIDT is not involved in fingerprinting the victim underwater, he or she will supplement this art by assisting the land-based CSI as permitted by department policy. In maintaining records, the CSIDT will assist the CSI in his or her protocol and procedures as established by department policy.

2.2.4 Conducts Latent Fingerprint Examinations

The participation of the CSIDT in latent fingerprint examination can be either on his or her own or under the supervision of a qualified CSI. This largely depends on the department protocol and the active position of the CSIDT as being employed as both a CSI and a CSIDT.

2.2.5 Attends Training

The CSIDT is responsible for maintaining a minimum number of continued education points in both land-based and water-based categories. He or she must attend training classes and or seminars required by their certification as a CSIDT as well as the required points as a CSI. As a CSIDT, the training requirements include land-based training as well as the practical application of training in the water environment, for example, mock homicide and boating incidents, respectively. In addition to this training, the CSIDT is required to attend classes on boating safety as well as safe diving standards and safe diving operations as they apply to the surface support vessel-diving platform.

Training records are an important part of the CSIDT logbook.

2.3 PSYCHOLOGICAL CONSIDERATIONS

Although there may be some degree of controversy as to the "most practical approach" in dealing with the psychological issues that an individual may encounter in this field of study, in my opinion, the following information should assist CSI and CSIDT teams in their understanding of just what the heck PTSD (posttraumatic stress disorder) and the "Critical Incident Stress Debriefing" is all about.

The psychological issues that are associated with the CSI's job description are not a concern that has just recently become known. CSI psychological issues are often related to those of war veterans, which have been studied for many years. When one considers the differences between the CSI's circumstances and his or her degree of exposure and the CSIDT's circumstances and degree of exposure, one realizes that there are considerable differences between the two. For example, when the CSI approaches the crime scene, the crime scene is, more often than not, in plain view. When the CSIDT approaches the crime scene, he or she is subjected to an environment that has little to no visibility at all. The CSI sees the victim from a distance and can view the body either continuously or intermittently, whereas the CSIDT may not see the victim until he or she is within a few inches of the victim and with considerable variations in available light or lighting. There is considerable difference in viewing a victim who is floating on the surface and seeing the victim for the first time a few inches away in a deep dark and often cold lake or river.

For those who are not aware of the personality changes that take place in this line of work, I would ask this question: Have you ever noticed how "naive" the "newbie" is when he or she first comes on board as the new CSI? If he or she is on your team, then you will observe, firsthand, the changes this person goes through, whether they be gradual or accelerated and depending on caseload and circumstance. How often, in your observation of a colleague's newness, have you gone back in time, remembering how you were when you first started as a CSI or CSIDT? Everything was so new and different, and you could not understand how the "veterans" could be so cold or indifferent during the investigation process. Remember the first time you thought you would never stop throwing up? Do you remember your first "burned victim"? I am quite sure that you remember your first infant or child investigation. Do you recall the unbelievable odor that your uniform had when you picked it up to put it in the laundry right after taking a rather lengthy shower? I bet you made sure it smelled nice when it was all done, not that you would have taken a "sniff" before you placed it in the dryer and again when you took it out to hang up. But after all that washing, drying and sniffing, didn't it have just a little bit of odor remaining?

Better wash it a second time just to make sure. After all, you would not want to go to work and have someone say that you smelled like a morgue or some sort of body fluid. Did you find it easy to freak out the newbie by sending him or her on a wild goose chase or having him or her do things you figured you had done too many times already? Perhaps a victim who was in the advanced stages of "decomp" was too much to let pass by for the newbie.

The newbie seems so innocent and so trusting with good intentions, yet there is something about him or her that makes you wonder about yourself. You try to hide these thoughts by making jokes, poking fun at someone, complaining about your next assignment, and being on guard with every question the newbie asks.

You may even find yourself doing something wrong that the newbie points out, but, by gosh, that doesn't make any difference at that point, because you are the senior CSI or CSIDT and it's done your way. Then you begin to sort things out, desperately trying to figure out a way to correct the mistake by weaving it into some new protocol or procedure that you decided to use on this particular investigation.

Each of us can "remember when," but how much, within our own personality, has changed since the "when?" Sometimes in looking back, it is difficult to imagine how you did some of the things you did, and how many times you could have been hurt or even killed. Between the changes in protocol and the advances that have been made in the past 5 years technologically, it is a bit scary to think about all the diseases you have been exposed to, not counting the ones you are not aware of. Have you ever wondered why you have become such a critic when watching one of the CSI movies or TV shows? You catch things that no one else would have a clue about, and then they wonder how you saw it and they didn't. Of course you are too critical when watching the show or movie, and soon you find that people would rather watch it without you being there or hearing your "big word" comments.

Depending on how seasoned you are, at some point in time, you have probably had days that you wish never started. There are as many variables and differences in experiences as there are people who read this book or any other. Everyone has their own experiences and ways of dealing with them. Sometimes it is a bit unnerving to think back on some of these experiences for many reasons. One of the first lessons we learn in this line of work is what I call predictable unpredictability. If one keeps this thought in their mind when going to a crime scene, there will be very few, if any, surprises to be found. Some of them are good experiences, but some of them are very uncomfortable to recall or remember. For many of us, there are some we would rather forget entirely but, for some reason, they will resurface every now and then. You finally learn how to shrug these thoughts off, or so you think, only to realize that every time they reoccur they are different. The longer you are in this field of work, the more memories you accumulate. Even though some are good and others are "bad," the accumulation of these memories can and often does have a negative effect on your personality and attitude. I suppose that you could refer to this as sort of a "CSI psychological effect."

In the process of developing a basic understanding of the long-term effects, psychologically, of what the CSI and CSIDT have to deal with, also understand the primary difference between the CSI and the CSIDT. The CSI, or "land-based" crime scene investigator, is in the company of several people and often has many distractions to deal with, which may offer a break in their train of thought or documentation process: the kidding around, shaking hands every now and then, and idle chit-chat, as it were, are all distractions of a sort. The CSIDT, on the other hand, is in an environment which offers few if any distractions, and he or she must document, in fine detail, the victim.

You cannot turn around and chat with one of the police officers or medics on the scene or walk up and give someone a big hug. The only communication the CSIDT has is with their communications person and their fellow diver or divers. The only other sounds they hear are their breathing and exhaust bubbles. Visibility is often very limited, and their environment is often very cold and indifferent. Under these conditions, they must search for, locate, evaluate, photograph, and begin their documentation process. They must avoid drifting into the victim, which happens all too often, and at the same time try to avoid the body fluids that surround the victim. The CSIDT does not have the opportunity to observe the victim from a distance prior to the victim's documentation process. More often than not, the victim may not come into view until the CSIDT is within 5 feet of the victim, and that is on a good day. CSIs are never "blindfolded" until they are within a few feet of the victim and most certainly are not subjected to some animal or other creature exiting the body because of their presence. The CSIDT is in a completely different world with many different situations to deal with and the understanding that the only predictable circumstance they will encounter is unpredictability. The TV shows and movies that portray the CSI are a total departure from reality. The CSI and CSIDT are not in search of or interested in ratings, or how "hot" they look; crime scene investigations, forensics, is a science that has no time or interest in such self-centered ideology. For the CSI or CSIDT, there is one constant, whatever it is, it is. The circumstances are as they are and the job they are there to do, they do regardless of the circumstances. We don't have people lined up for an autograph or some ridiculous photo shoot at the end of our day or shift, but when we have finished our day, there is a quiet and humble sense of accomplishment that "ratings" cannot buy. Autographs and photo shoots would actually be more of an insult than a compliment. The job of the CSI and CSIDT, can be very lonely and often you feel alone; however, each of us chose this field of study, and by gosh we should be proud of our individual accomplishments.

So, what is the best way to approach or discuss the obvious psychological effects of being a CSI or CSIDT? There are as many opinions as there are books on this subject. To say or advocate one set of solutions over another would be unfair to the reader. Psychology is not an exact science and from the research I have done regarding this subject, there is no single or simple answer.

So, for the sake of discussion, just what exactly is this so-called Critical Incident Stress Debriefing?

First, a "critical incident" could be a common occurrence such as an officer having to shoot a suspect in self-defense. Although such an incident sounds rather "simplistic," it is not. One must consider the psychological effect such an incident has on the officer. Almost any type of event that causes a distressing or profound change in one's physical or psychological well-being will alter, to some degree, their emotional state. Sometimes strong emotions are attached to an event that will either inhibit their ability to function in a "normal" capacity at the time of the event, or be delayed till a later time, depending on the individual.

From a clinical point of view, certain traumatic events and the impact that they may have on an individual are reasonably predictable. Exposure to a critical incident, long term or short term, often has a considerable impact on that person's ability to function in a "normal" capacity. The first documented cases of traumatic stress go back to military personnel who had been involved in combat. At that time, the term used to describe the psychological effects was "transient situational disturbances."

The term "short-term crisis reactions" has been used to identify individuals or groups who had been exposed to events such as domestic violence, child abuse, rape (male and female), violence in the workplace, floods and industrial fires.

As it turns out, the term "debriefing" referrers to a specific technique designed to help individuals in dealing with psychological as well as physical symptoms that are associated with one's exposure to a critical situation or event. Debriefing also assists the individual in recognizing the proper way in which he or she vents frustrations, thoughts and emotions: in other words, to assist the individual in the way in which they process the event and proper reflection on the impact that the incident has or is having on them. The short-term crisis reaction may also be referred to as a catastrophe of emotion, which includes denial, rage, confusion, humiliation, grief, and suicidal/homicidal thoughts.

Individuals and their personalities, experiences and predispositions they may have, psychology, is as varied as a group of fingerprints. Place 100,000 fingerprints on a billboard, and they all look the same, yet there are distinct differences in each one of them. If there is a "support group" for PTSD, critical incident stress or similar "disorder" that you have given thought to attending, I will offer this advice:

- Understand the goals of the program. This could include something similar to a twelve-step program.
- Get into an employee assistance program or find a counselor who specializes in this "disorder" and one who fits your personality and needs.
- Stick with the program and follow the advice of your counselor.
- *Do not get involved in what is referred to as thirteen-stepping.* "Thirteen-stepping" is a term used in other organizations that implies that a person is there for the purposes of, to be

> politically correct and very subtle, "pro-creative dating." The "thirteen stepper" has no intent of following the program. This is quite prevalent in many programs, and these people will do nothing more than complicate and/or destroy your life.

Marcus Aurelius said it best when he wrote, "Through not observing what is in the mind of another, a man has seldom been seen to be unhappy; but those who do not observe the movements of their own minds must of necessity be unhappy."

From this point, we will review some of the latest research regarding the subject of posttraumatic stress disorder (PTSD) and critical incident stress debriefing.

PTSD as well as Critical Incident Stress are disorders that can be associated with any overwhelming life experience, especially since many of the "events" we encounter are those which are unpredictable and beyond our control. This includes the witnesses of the event who are not directly involved, such as bystanders and yes, family members as well. In every journal and study I have reviewed, the groups who are always included in the "statistical information" are law enforcement and EMS (emergency medical services), which includes CSI and support personnel.

When one considers all things, that is, the appearance and condition of most victims, the evidence and documentation requirements, and the time spent photographing and the detail in which all of the documentation must be done, they all add up! All too often, the result is the investigator has a bad attitude that she/he has become complacent or coldhearted in her or his job. Is this a realistic observation by peers or supervisors? No. More often than not, it is a sign of being, as they say, "burned out." Why not refer to this condition as *stressed out*? "Stressed out" is ambiguous term and does not identify the real issue, which is often hidden. In other words, it is more of a slang term used when the real issue is unknown. Having a "bad day" is also a term generally used in the place of stressed out, depending on the circumstances.

On average, a relatively short "recoup" time is necessary to alleviate this problem. The issues that brought about the stress are transient and have very little impact on any individual.

Being *burned out* is considered by most psychologists to be totally different. The fact that people use both terms to describe an individual's "day" does not clarify the differences between the two. This term is used more metaphorically than descriptively. The best way to define burnout is to consider the accumulation of emotional distress that is imposed on anyone involved in this field. Psychologists will often refer to the accumulation of this type of stress as posttraumatic stress disorder, or PTSD. Further, when afflicted with this disorder, one loses one's perspective to the point of becoming negative and withdrawn. Think of it this way: the scenes that you will be exposed to, rather intimately, would physically sicken the "normal" person. Exposure, at this level, to some of the most heinous crimes within the grasp of anyone's imagination, is, in and of itself, psychologically damaging. The facts and details involved in a given case often leave the news media in some protected fairytale world. The grotesque scenes that you will be dealing with are "normal" working conditions. There is no such thing as prepping the victim prior to your observation. You will be observing, documenting, photographing, touching and moving these victim(s) and/or their body parts several times before the next assignment! If that sounds too "matter-of-factly," then include, within the documentation process, the sight, sounds that will obviously occur, the smell or odors that you will encounter, the taste and the touch that you will have to endure, repeatedly.

Is there any wonder, then, that the families of the CSI and CSIDT are perhaps the most affected because of the nature of the job? All too often, the family winds up being last on the priority list instead of being first. The accumulation of crime scenes becomes overwhelming and the effort to *block out* or *forget* what they are being subjected to takes quite a toll. Because there are so many issues to deal with—for example, victims' families, the separation between her/his family and the victim's family—everything becomes so minute that the issues often "merge."

Any individual who is being "pessimistic," as they say, can, and often does, become the victim of an "insidious infection." The hopeless feelings and frustration that are all too often associated with this sort of depressive state of mind are almost predictable. Although it is true that different individuals deal with circumstances differently, the psychological pattern in this line of work has its own, unbiased, unique form.

Another perspective—the individual who has to go off to war will see, firsthand, a degree of devastation and blatant disregard for human life that is beyond comprehension.

More often than not, the individual had no idea that such horror existed in this world other than what he or she had seen on edited television or at the movies. For those involved in the field of forensics, which is reality and not some choreographed television show or movie, the same types, different causes, of devastation will occur, but over a longer period of time and in much smaller portions. Every single day that you are on the job brings different circumstances, different events, different cultures to deal with, different environments, different attitudes, and so on. All these issues change to some degree with every season and of course, the "full moon" nights seem to bring about weird events regardless.

Nonetheless, there remain psychological circumstances, some of which are beyond one's control. The important issue or question here is, what are the best treatment options available for those of us who are involved in this field of work and are required to do the things that our jobs require?

Studies that have been conducted over the past ten to fifteen years have shown that psychological debriefing has become popular and has been adopted by many settings or groups; however, the evidence regarding its use, according to these studies, and the benefits derived from debriefing is indeed lacking. It is important to understand that the primary difference between those of us who go on to develop PTSD and those of us who do not is based more on how we individually "cope" with trauma.

It is important that the CSI and CSIDT understand that traumatic experiences will produce some degree of aftereffects. Since this line of work exposes an individual to repeated experiences with varying degrees of psychological trauma, being diagnosed with PTSD is not uncommon. The team's primary physician should address preventative measures and established protocol guidelines regarding "counseling" and alternative therapy options that have proven to be effective.

I would again suggest that the team consider a hospice organization for input and suggestions. Hospice is the best source I have found which may provide a realistic solution and most certainly positive feedback regarding this issue.

There are three main types or classifications of PTSD, and the list given here does not imply that these classifications appear or occur in any particular order.

Also, keep in mind that these are examples and do not include individual responses to PTSD, because to say that any particular response is "typical" or "common" is not true.

2.3.1 Avoidance

- Feeling emotionally "detached" or complacent with others
- Avoiding circumstances and feelings or activities that may remind you of certain circumstances or events
- Inability to forget or set aside particular events that have occurred
- Seclusion and the loss of interest in activities you once enjoyed and to a degree, life in general as it "used" to be
- An overwhelming sense of loss regarding your future
- Your inability to keep your job or perform in a "normal" capacity

2.3.2 Re-Experiencing

- Memories of a certain event, whether they are vague or specific.
- Scary physical responses, because they are unfamiliar and come without warning, to even subtle reminders of an event (e.g., suffocating feeling, pounding heart, lightheadedness, nausea or diarrhea, muscle tension and sometimes a burning sensation in your legs or arms, feeling cold or sweating for no apparent reason)
- Nightmares (waking up to a particular "sound" or "feeling" something next to you)
- Feelings of intense distress because of uncertain feelings

2.3.3 Anxiety

- Fight-or-flight mind-set, or, as some call it, always on "red alert"
- Inability to slow down your thoughts, which leads to difficulty falling asleep
- Difficulty in your ability to focus or concentrate
- Agitation and irritability which may lead to outbursts of anger or hostility
- Always on edge or uncontrollable, having mixed feelings and being easily startled

Some of the more common symptoms or complaints found in the posttraumatic stress disorder patient include the following:

- Headaches, stomach problems that may lead to GERD (gastroesophageal reflux disorder), nonspecific chest pain
- Hypochondria or feelings that something is physically wrong without a well-founded reason
- Dramatizing certain situations to an unrealistic level
- Overstating events or adding to an event
- Panic attacks
- Almost always short-tempered and irritable
- Shame, or blaming ones self for the outcome of certain events or circumstances
- Alcohol and/or drug abuse
- Different levels or degrees of depression and unrelenting feelings of hopelessness
- Suicidal thoughts and/or feelings which may or may not instill fear instead of consideration or intent to follow through with these thoughts or feelings
- Feelings of being alone or that no one cares
- Feelings of being betrayed and mistrusting others

Under "normal conditions" a traumatic event or series of events that lead a person into the posttraumatic stress disorder are those who have a single encounter, such as in the 9/11 incidents or witnessing a homicide. Both can be considered overwhelming and, depending on the individual, frightening. The only difference between people who immerse themselves in the event by continually "replaying" the event and those who do not immerse themselves in the event, is dependent on how well they "cope" with the trauma. All too often, people will dwell on a given event to the point of either obsessing on it or allowing it to control their life. In any event, it is best to psychologically arm yourself with as much knowledge and understanding as possible in order to prevent or at least understand and be aware when something is getting the best of you.

Being aware of what may happen if certain things go unchecked is a positive step in the right direction, and one you will never regret.

It would be incorrect to say or imply that there is a specific "combination" or recipe that will prevent PTSD or like kinds of disturbances. As in almost any kind of therapy, your choice should be a therapist that fits you and your personality: someone who specializes in PTSD and understands you and your specific, unique needs, that is, investigating multiple homicide victims.

It is important that you, as an individual, understand that if you try to suppress your memories, they will eventually get the better of you. Just when you think you have everything under control (an illusion), the panic attack, depression or any of the symptoms will reemerge with vengeance.

The part of PTSD that will not be apparent right away is the harm it is causing your friends and family and your ability to function in your job.

Whatever you do, do not be the "suck it up" or "macho" kind of person who has all the control and does not need help. If you should ever become or feel that way, then it is already apparent that you need help sooner rather than later. When someone tells you that PTSD, anxiety, depression, and so on, is not a sign of some sort of weakness, they are telling you the truth because it most certainly is not. There is a method in conducting a crime scene investigation both on land and underwater. There is a sequence of events that must take place in order to establish a reasonable outcome. When it comes to issues regarding PTSD, the same circumstances apply. There is a method, a step-by-step process, that one should follow in order to alleviate the overwhelming feelings associated with PTSD. You had a FTO (field training officer) when you first began crime scene investigations, and it was he or she who guided you through the "hoops," as it were. Well, when it comes to PTSD, the same process should be followed. Your therapist or physician is your FTO to guide you through the hoops. You have the guidance, support and respect of a colleague, and a light at the end of the tunnel.

Consider three good, sound reasons for seeking the help and advice of a physician and/or therapist.

- **Health-Related Problems**—Who hasn't heard on every radio and TV about the impact that stress has on your heart and body as a whole? Exercise, good diet, and a better lifestyle will decrease your risk of heart disease. There have been studies that have shown a direct relationship between PTSD and heart trouble. Anyone experiencing these symptoms should certainly understand why there is a link between the two. Do a little research on depression as it relates to the immune system, and you will begin to understand that PTSD is not a simple side effect of your job description. In fact, there is nothing simple at all about PTSD.
- **Early Treatment**—The sooner you recognize that you may have a problem with PTSD, the sooner you should seek help. As a matter of fact, if a co-worker thinks you are getting stressed out, then be smart enough to at least consult your physician or therapist. The one thing that can be worse than being stressed out today is to be stressed out again tomorrow. Everyone's treatment is different, and each treatment requires the careful and methodical treatment of these unique needs by a well-qualified person, someone who truly understands and someone who shows compassion. There are some great therapists who are very well qualified to help those who are in this line of work.
- **Family Life**—There should be no question regarding the impact that PTSD has on family as well as friends. Have you ever been around someone who is depressed or cynical more often than not? And how much fun was that? Did you stay around that person for very long periods of time? How about having a friend or acquaintance that was a wreck because of a divorce?

Always negative and complaining, never mind being condescending toward just about every one they see or meet. Having to deal with these sorts of issues, when it is a loved one, is entirely different and yes, it does have quite an impact on the family as a whole. To think that you can hide your PTSD issues is an illusion that you share with no one other than yourself.

Self-delusion is part of PTSD, and you can change that if you seek the right help and stick with the right program. Your therapist is your teacher as well as your sounding board, and once you establish a working relationship with him or her, things will change without your realizing it. It works; I assure you it does because no one can work in this field for any length of time and not be affected.

> *Constant exposure to dangers will breed contempt for them.*
>
> —Seneca

2.4 PROCESSING THE CRIME SCENE

As most job position postings would have it, there are many questions involving the position requirements and duties. There are few, if any, postings at this point in time that list positions for the "Crime Scene Diver Technologist." When departments or organizations begin posting these positions, I hope they are a bit more specific. There is just too much ambiguity in job position postings at this time.

I would like to take a bit of time to "review" one of the typical postings that anyone may come across.

> *Process crime scenes to include the search and recovery of trace, DNA and other physical evidence. Take photographs and prepares sketches and reports for presentation in court and provide court testimony.*

Five people can read the same requirement, and it is more than likely you will have different interpretations from each individual.

This is not a bad thing, mind you, but how many people would pick up on the key words, "presentation" and "testimony," when referring to court proceedings? Please understand that "presentation" does not mean that you simply show up, take a seat on the witness stand, and show them what you have. Testimony is not simply stating the facts that you know because you are also going to be cross-examined and questioned regarding your findings and every reference imaginable regarding your evidence and chain of custody, to name a few. Unless you have had to testify in a court proceeding, I suspect that you are not aware of the true meaning of *accountability* and *listening*.

Always remember that a CSIDT has considerable accountability, especially in the presentation and explanation of evidence she or he presents to the court. Part of that accountability is, in fact, to know and understand *every* possible aspect of each and every item of evidence you are accountable for *before* it is presented.

The process of "sketching" is different in that the use of a "compass rose" and topographical maps are common criteria. They afford a more descriptive format, which includes information not commonly used by surface investigations. An example of this information is the topography of a given body of water, which includes depth indicators and shoreline parameters. Reference points are often included within this classification of map as well as scale and legend. Maritime ("marine") "plotting maps" include various information sources which are helpful in the documentation process. A copy of the map may be included with other documentation material. This will aid in the "reconstruction" (triangulation) of a case if needed in the future, that is, a case that is "reopened." These elements are an intricate part of the evidence log.

2.4.1 Classification of Evidence

There are 10 primary classifications of evidence the CSIDT should relate to during the crime scene process. Understanding each one, as each applies to each individual crime scene, is an invaluable asset.

- **Admissible** evidence is any evidence a judge finds, or accepts as being useful in determining the facts presented.
- **Circumstantial** evidence is any evidence that is presented in a trial setting that does not originate from an "eyewitness."
- **Corroborating** evidence is any form of evidence which confirms or strengthens existing evidence.
- **Demonstrative** evidence refers to an actual object, such as a photograph, sketch, or other media, which is an accurate representation of the facts as presented.
- **Documentary** evidence is any paper or document presented into evidence, provided it meets the requirements as set forth in the rules of evidence.
- **Preponderance** of the evidence, associated with civil trials, refers to the greater weight of the evidence as required in a civil court case.
- **Evidence Suppression** is any evidence the presiding disallows.
- **Tainted** evidence, associated with criminal court, is any evidence or information that has been obtained illegally, for example, through an illegal search. Tainted evidence is also referred to as "fruit of the poisonous tree."
- **Evidence weight** verifies value and believability in the evidence that has been presented.
- **Incontrovertible evidence** is that which is so conclusive that there can be *no other truth to the matter*.

2.4.2 Training

The terms "diver" and "diving team" refer to the crime scene investigator diver technologist (CSIDT) and the CSIDT support personnel.

When most agencies address "training" issues, they are somewhat vague in their requirements. It is common to see the phrase "attends training on a variety of forensic topics annually," which is open to too much interpretation by the employee. When it comes time to address this statement, "attends training on a variety of forensic topics annually," I will always reply by saying, "This does not mean that you are required to attend training once or twice a year. This means that for your benefit and knowledge base as a CSIDT, you need to attend as many training classes as you can on a wide variety of subjects that relate to your job, *in what you do.*"

Diversity is a good thing but you must be, out of necessity, a bit more job-specific. Yes, it is imperative to attend training classes on forensic topics, as that is part of your job description as a CSIDT, but equally important is to achieve safe diving operation protocol and standards. There are actually two jobs involved with the CSIDT:

- First, crime scene investigations
- Second, training as a commercial scientific diver specializing in crime scene investigations

Training includes but is in no way limited to the following:

- Diving on simulated crime scenes, multicasualty boating accidents, multivictim motor vehicle accidents, i.e., school bus that has run off a bridge or into any water environment.
- Circumstances and situations, including potential contamination, the diver may face in any given crime scene situation.
- Job hazard analysis or evaluation.
- Specialized diving equipment.
- Specialized crime scene equipment, specifically designed or modified for underwater use.
- Review of diving time table protocols, e.g., U.S. Navy no-decompression timetables. This includes RN (residual nitrogen) time tables as well.

It is to the benefit of all concerned to consider working with the Coast Guard Auxiliary, Wildlife Officers, Police Boating Enforcement, ALE and other agencies to advance the team concept while increasing the team member's knowledge base.

For example, have you ever considered attending one of the classes offered by hospice organizations? Well, if not, I suggest you reconsider. The information and insight regarding the death and dying patient is invaluable because it affects you as a human being with feelings, admittedly or not. After all, is it not to your advantage to be well versed in this part of life? It is not uncommon to be approached by family members, usually when you are not suspecting that the people near you are part of the deceased's family. Attending such classes will also help you to deal with the issues you face in the life/death process. Hospices are wonderful organizations with a variety of services, and they are so accommodating to those with questions and or concerns. Your department or organization should consider attending hospice training a prerequisite or at least include this course in CE requirements.

2.4.3 General Course of Study

The minimum requirements, as a general course of study, based on OSHA (Occupational Safety and Health Administration), U.S. Coast Guard and Environmental Protective Agency guidelines. These guidelines are very specific and implemented as part of the on-site team safety manual. Any modification to these *minimum* guidelines is on the verifiable side of safety.

2.4.3.1 Section I

Minimum Requirements:

- Each team member must maintain a current certification, by an accredited agency (e.g., American Red Cross), in emergency first aid, which shall include basic life support.
- Each team member who is subject to hyperbaric conditions shall be required to take and satisfactorily complete courses in human anatomy and physiology.
- The team "standby diver" is required to be a designated CSIDT. However, in such a circumstance, the standby diver may not be involved in *any* crime-scene-related procedures but still be required to pass the CSIDT diver training.
- The surface support communications officer is not required to be "diver certified." However, the communications officer is required to maintain and test all communication systems—e.g., radios, cell phones, licenses if applicable, diver communication systems, all vessel lighting systems, and day shapes and night lighting (OSHA)—and be well versed in safe diving operations.
- The team safety officer must have and maintain current certification, as a minimum, as an Emergency Medical Technician–Intermediate and have on board a copy of the emergency medical manual and applicable medical equipment.
- The team's designated person in charge must be current in their training as a CSIDT, which includes having a current and up-to-date *CSIDT Diver Log Book* and being well versed in all

aspects of assigned diving operations, safety protocols, vessel safety as mandated by the U.S. Coast Guard and established emergency procedures.

- The Team Surface Support Pilot must be current in approval for piloting as well as maintaining safety inspection of such vessel by the U.S. Coast Guard Auxiliary or other certifying agency. A current copy of Chapman's *Piloting and Team Safety Manual* shall be on board the vessel at all times. The surface support vessel pilot is in charge of all vessel operations and movement, and responsible for maintaining a log of all maintenance, repairs and motor hours.

2.4.4 CSIDT Diver Logbook

The CSIDT diver logbook is considered a court-ready document that pertains to a particular case. The CSIDT diver logbook also provides a documented history of previous investigations as well as training. The CSIDT diver logbook contains the diver photograph, positive identification, medical history, inoculations, medication history, latest physical exam, and examining physician. As a court-ready document, the CSIDT logbook contains the incident referral number or case/complaint number, which identifies a particular case or investigation. There is an attachment to the CSI who was involved in the case by including the CSI's name and identification number. The CSIDT logbook should be kept in a safe location, and if the team-training officer or medical examiner wants to make a copy of a particular page of the book for reference to a particular case, the copy must comply with the rules of evidence. All pages must be bound and all pages must be numbered. Three-ring binders, for example, are not permitted.

In conclusion, the Crime Scene Investigator Diver Technologist is one of the most professional and well-trained divers in the industry. Well versed in matters of legal proceedings, rules of evidence, chain of custody, documentation, safe diving protocols, safe diving practices, OSHA and U.S. Coast Guard regulations, surface support vessel piloting, blood-borne pathogens, contamination, decontamination, pre-contamination, job hazard analysis, human anatomy and physiology, pharmacology, photography, and confidentiality.

The CSI television shows that people watch are nothing like the reality of crime scene investigation. Starched clean lab coats, nice dresses and suits, clean neat laboratories, and so on, are all for ratings and theatrics. It would be nice if things were so neat and relaxed, but they aren't. Becoming a true CSI requires a lot of education, patience, and determination.

CHAPTER 3

Bloodstain Pattern Analysis

Anita Zannin

CONTENTS

3.1 INTRODUCTION

Is bloodstain pattern analysis (BSPA) a science, or an art? That question is asked in courtrooms all across the country, especially after the 2006 National Academy of Sciences (NAS) report. The answers to this question have been as varied as the types of BSPA practitioners. Some say science, some say art, some say a little of both. My typical answer to this question is that it is a "discipline based on scientific principles." While BSPA is not a "hard" science, it is based on the principles of the hard sciences of physics, mathematics, biology and chemistry. There is an element of subjectivity, and the analysis rendered is ultimately an opinion—as is the case with several other forensic science disciplines. Reproducibility is an important concept in the sciences. When a fluid is acted upon by a force, it will behave in a predictable manner. This predictability and reproducibility is what allows BSPA to be taught over and over again. Bloodstain pattern analysis is not serology, or DNA; it is the analysis and interpretation of the size, shape, distribution, and location of bloodstains in order to determine the events which gave rise to their origin. It is the study of the static aftermath of a dynamic, bloodshedding event. BSPA is used, in conjunction with other forensic disciplines, such as forensic pathology and DNA, to assist in reconstructing a scene to determine the most likely scenario(s).

3.2 HISTORY

Often, it is thought that bloodstain pattern analysis (BSPA) is a relatively new discipline in forensic science. However, the reality is that BSPA has a long history, dating back to the 1500s, in Europe.

1895—Dr. Eduard Piotrowski produced a book, complete with color plates, entitled *Uber Entstehung, Form, Richtung und Ausbretung der Blutspuren nach Hiebwunden des Kopfes* (Concerning Origin, Shape, Direction and Distribution of the Bloodstains Following Head Wounds Caused by Blows). This appears to be the first truly scientific study of BSPA, including the understanding and application of the scientific method.

1939—French scientist Dr. Victor Balthazard et al. presented their paper, *Des Gouttes De Sang Projete* (Research on Blood Spatter) at the 22nd Congress of Forensic Medicine. The first page of this paper states, "This research paper was to pinpoint characteristic elements of a bloodstain which might give decisive hints as to its origin." This original research included study of trajectories, the trigonometric relationship (the ratio between width and length of a bloodstain), an awareness of target surface considerations and the understanding that the dynamics of a bloodshedding event could not always be copied under laboratory conditions.

The first significant documentation of BSPA in the United States came from Dr. Paul Kirk, a professor at the University of California at Berkley. In 1953, Kirk published a book entitled *Crime Investigation—Physical Evidence and the Police Laboratory* with a section called "Blood: Physical Investigation," which included examination of angular and velocity effects on bloodstains. In 1955, Dr. Kirk authored a lengthy affidavit in the case of *Ohio v. Sheppard* (the case upon which the movie *The Fugitive* is based). In this affidavit, Kirk reviewed the investigation, drying times, and adopted a "whole scene" approach and established the relative positions of the victim and attacker at the time of the beating. This was a significant milestone for bloodstain evidence in the legal system. Dr. Kirk encouraged Herbert L. MacDonell to continue with bloodstain pattern research and to apply for a grant from the Law Enforcement Assistance Administration (LEAA). MacDonell did apply for and receive that grant, resulting in the 1971 publication of *Flight Characteristics and Stain Patterns of Human Blood* (MacDonell and Bialousz, 1973).

The parallels between Balthazard and MacDonell's work truly speak to the reproducibility of this discipline. One should remember that, in the late '60s and early '70s, the Internet, as we know it today, did not exist, so previous research on the subject was not as easy as it is today. This means that the work of Balthazard and MacDonell were completed independently of one another.

In March of 1973, the first BSPA course (Institute on the Geometric Significance of Human Bloodstain Evidence) was taught by MacDonell. This was the beginning of the development of BSPA as a recognized field in the legal system in the United States. Since then, many 40-hour basic BSPA courses were taught, and many of those students, too numerous to name here, have gone on, conducted additional research and now teach the discipline themselves. MacDonell revised his initial research publication as more literature was located (by hand—MacDonell obtained the last known copy of Piotrowski's work in Krakow, Poland), research conducted, cases evaluated and court decisions rendered, with his last publication, *Bloodstain Patterns—Second Revised Edition* in 2005 (MacDonell, 2005). In 2004, MacDonell was awarded an honorary ScD for his many contributions to the field of forensic science. The professional organization for bloodstain pattern analysts, the International Association of Bloodstain Pattern Analysts (IABPA) was founded in 1983 and today has over 900 members worldwide. Each year, there is a U.S. and European IABPA conference held. This is by no means a complete history of BSPA, but meant to give a brief evolution of the discipline.

Probably the earliest recorded association of blood with crime is in the Bible:

> *God asked Cain, "Where [is] Abel thy brother?" Cain replied, "I know not: [Am] I my brother's keeper?"*
>
> *And he said, "What hast thou done? The voice of thy brother's blood crieth unto me from the ground. And now [art] thou cursed from the earth, which hath opened her mouth to receive thy brother's blood from thy hand; when thou tillest the ground, it shall not henceforth yield unto thee her strength; a fugitive and a vagabond shalt thou be in the earth."*
>
> —Genesis 4:10–12, n.d.

There are many popular art examples, Shakespeare's *MacBeth*, Akseli Gallen-Kallela's 1897 oil painting *Fratricide*, and *Charlie Chan at the Racetrack* all the way to current-day television programs such as *CSI* (*Miami, New York, Las Vegas*) and *Dexter*, a bloodstain pattern analyst with a police department who is also a serial killer.

3.3 BSPA ROLE

Some things BPA can reveal are as follows:

- What type of event occurred? (e.g., a stabbing or beating vs. a shooting)
- How many blows were struck? (a minimum number of blows)
- Did the victim move after injury?
- Position of participants
- How long did the attack continue? (can be a factor in charging the accused or at sentencing)
- Was the attacker injured?
- Which stains should be analyzed?
- Support or refute statements
- Sequencing events

It is important to understand that all of the above are not necessarily able to be ascertained from all scenes. In *some* cases, all of the above might be able to be determined. In other cases, perhaps only a few of these items can be ascertained. Still other cases may reveal *none* of the above. Sometimes there may be very complex, overlapping patterns, limited available information or extensive alteration of the scene. In these types of scenarios, it may be that the most responsible opinion to have is to *not have an opinion*. It is critical for an analyst to understand the limitations of the discipline and not render an opinion that cannot be scientifically supported.

3.4 BIOLOGY/PHYSIOLOGY/ANATOMY

Blood in an incompressible fluid. This means that blood doesn't reduce in volume with an increase in pressure. The two main functions of human blood are transportation and defense. Transportation includes supplying the necessary nutrients, hormones, and so on, as well as waste product removal. The defense function includes fighting infection and clotting.

Human blood is composed of both liquid and solid (cellular) portions (see Figure 3.1). The liquid portion of the blood is called plasma and constitutes 55% of the total blood volume. Ninety percent of plasma is water. Also within the plasma is found salts, hormones, proteins, lipids, ABO antibodies, glucose, fibrinogen and clotting factors. Once clotting has occurred, the liquid portion is referred to as serum. White blood cells (WBCs) and platelets are found in a layer called the buffy coat. This constitutes less than 1% of the total blood volume; therefore, it is included in the total cellular percentage, at 45%.

The bulk of the cellular component of blood is comprised of the red blood cells (RBCs), where hemoglobin and ABO antigens are located. Mature RBCs have the shape of a biconcave disc and do not have a nucleus. Because there is no nucleus, it is not the RBCs that are used for nuclear DNA analysis, as is sometimes misunderstood. Each RBC contains approximately 280 million hemoglobin molecules (Sears, 2002), and each hemoglobin molecule can carry up to four oxygen molecules. Therefore, hemoglobin's primary function is the transportation of oxygen from the lungs to the tissues and of carbon dioxide to the lungs for gas exchange.

WBCs are the cells in the blood which are utilized for nuclear DNA analysis, as these cells are nucleated cells. There are several types of WBCs; however, generally speaking, their main function is fighting infection. WBCs are significantly larger and less plentiful than RBCs. RBCs are small and flexible enough to be able to pass through capillaries (approximately 3 to 10 microns in diameter) single file (Secomb, 1991).

Our bodies contain three categories of blood vessels: veins, arteries, and capillaries. In general, arteries carry blood away from the heart, while veins carry blood to

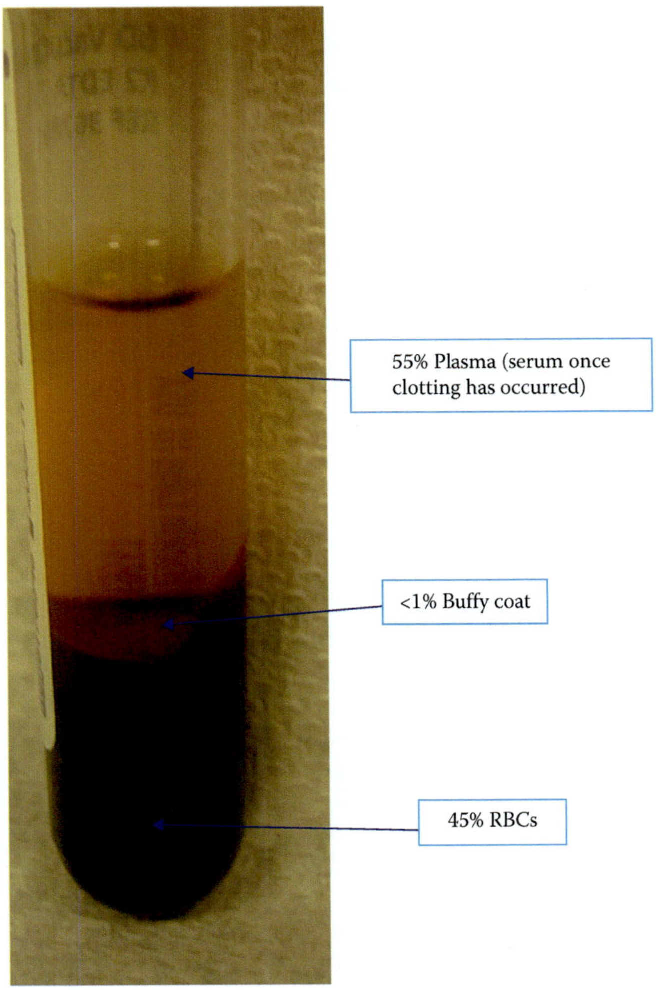

FIGURE 3.1 Components of blood in a blood tube after centrifugation.

the heart. Arteries are thick-walled vessels that contain smooth muscle. These vessels pulse in the same cadence as an individual's heartbeat. The smooth muscle contractions are what propel the blood through arteries and create significant pressure in these vessels. Veins are comparatively thin-walled vessels that have valves within to prevent backflow; think of saloon doors that open in only one direction. Skeletal muscle movement is what propels the blood through veins, and they have significantly less internal pressure than arteries. If the valves become dysfunctional, varicosed veins may result. Capillaries are very small vessels that act as a sort of "bridge" between veins and arteries. It is in these vessels that gas and nutrient exchange takes place.

The amount of blood in a human body is related to body weight. Blood volume is approximately 7% of an individual's body weight. For example, a 150lb individual's blood volume is calculated in the following manner:

$$\begin{aligned} 150 \text{ lbs} &= \sim 68 \text{ kg} \\ (68\,\text{kg})(.07) &= 4.76 \text{ kg} \\ 1 \text{ kg of blood} &= 1 \text{ liter of blood, therefore} \\ 4.76 \text{ kg} &= 4.76 \text{ liters of blood} \end{aligned}$$

There are a number of medical conditions that can cause bleeding, both internally and externally. This is important to remember when evaluating a scene—not all scenes are criminal in nature. Bloodstained scenes may be the result of homicidal or assaultive behaviors, but they may also be suicides, accident, or natural in nature, and it is imperative that the analyst approach the scene with an open mind.

3.5 SCENE AND EVIDENCE PRECAUTIONS

A bloodstained scene can be a dangerous environment for many reasons; items such as hypodermic needles, loaded firearms, broken glass, knives, and so on, may be present. This section however, will discuss dangers presented by the blood itself.

Blood can carry many infectious diseases, such as HIV, Hepatitis B, and Hepatitis C, to mention a few. The HIV virus is relatively fragile outside the body, but Hepatitis C can remain in dried blood for several days. Because of this, it is important to approach each scene as though it is infectious and utilize the proper personal protective equipment (PPE). Gloves should always be used when dealing with blood evidence. Tyvek suits, or protective disposable lab coats, should be used to protect the analyst's clothes from becoming contaminated with blood. Masks, eyewear, and hair coverings should be utilized when there is a chance of splashing or aerosolized blood and to protect from inadvertent contamination of the scene with the analyst's own DNA. Shoe covers should always be utilized, both to protect footwear and to protect the scene from contamination by items that may be transferred from the tread of the analyst's footwear.

3.6 CATEGORIES OF BLOODSTAINS

Depending on whose terminology one uses, the overall categories may differ. For the purposes of this writing, the categories used will be those outlined by James, Kish, and Sutton, 2005. Those categories are passive, spatter, and altered, under which are several subcategories (see Table 3.1). Also, the Scientific Working Group on Bloodstain Pattern Analysis (SWGSTAIN) compiled a list of recommended terminology that the IABPA has adopted.

Generally, bloodstains included in the passive category are those that are under the influence of only gravity, or transfer stains, where a blood-bearing object transfers liquid blood onto another surface. Examples include blood dripping from a finger; a victim who is lying on the ground whose blood is "seeping" out of wounds, creating an area of pooling (non-absorbent surface) or saturation (absorbent surface); and a bloody hand touching a wall. Spatter includes impact—such as occurs in a beating or shooting; "secondary," also known as satellite spatter; and projected patterns. Projected patterns are those which are acted on by a force greater than that of gravity and occur from something other than impact, such as arterial gushing and expirated bloodstain patterns. Altered bloodstain patterns are those that have undergone some sort of physiological, physical/mechanical, or chemical change, such as diluted bloodstains, or patterns created by insects. While the word "altered" may seem to imply a negative or deliberate change in order to deceive connotation, that is not what is meant by its use in bloodstain categorization. While patterns in this category can include deliberate changes to the bloodstains, in this context, it simply means that there has been some change. These categories will be examined in more detail below.

TABLE 3.1 Bloodstain Categories

Passive	Spatter	Altered
Contact	Impact mechanism	Clotted
Drop(s)	Secondary mechanism	Diluted
Flow	Projection mechanism	Dried
Saturation/Pooling	–	Diffused
Free-Falling Volume	–	Insects
–	–	Sequenced
–	–	Voids

The volume of an "average" drop of passively falling blood has been reported to be .05 mL with a diameter in the air of 4.56 mm. There are several factors that influence the volume and diameter of a blood drop, including the nature of the surface from which the blood falls (e.g., dripping from the end of a baseball bat vs. the tip of a knife), the rate of bleeding, the distance fallen (to a point), and the effect of a force (such as impact) acting on the blood. There are several resources available that document many of these factors based on experimentation.

Blood exhibits cohesive forces in order to achieve the most stable configuration by reducing the exposed surface area. This creates surface tension that is resistant to penetration—like "skin." A common experience that most people have had is watching water bugs walk across the surface of the water. This is possible because of the water's surface tension. The surface molecules have unequal molecular attractive forces acting on them—air on one side and other water molecules on all other sides.

A drop of blood will fall when the gravitational attraction, or some other force, overcomes its surface tension.

There are a number of potential reasons that a stain may exhibit certain characteristics—for example, you could have a small drop of blood that, size-wise, is consistent with impact spatter, but may have simply dripped off of something with a small surface area, or dripped close to the surface. Blood does not spontaneously "break up"; something has to happen to it (e.g., an impact) for this to happen.

The nature of the target surface is of tremendous importance. Generally, when blood strikes a smooth, hard, nonporous surface, the drop will be smooth and round, as can be seen in Figure 3.2. If a drop of blood strikes something soft and porous, spines, satellite spatter, and/or scalloping may be observed (see Figure 3.3). This occurs because the fibers or other microscopic projections penetrate the surface tension and rupture the drop. Blood (or any other liquid) does not fall in the shape of a teardrop, as is often seen in drawings, paintings, advertisements, and even weather maps. Once a drop of blood breaks free, it organizes into the most efficient possible configuration, which is that of a sphere. Some oscillation from spherical to "egg-shaped" may be observed.

Spines are fine projections that are still attached to the parent drop (as seen in Figure 3.3). Satellite spatter is disconnected from the parent drop (seen radiating circumferentially around the parent drop in Figure 3.3). Scalloped edges (not pictured) have a "wavy" sort of appearance.

When blood strikes a surface at 90 degrees, the resulting stain is round in appearance. As the angle of impact becomes more acute, the stain becomes more elongated, as shown in Figure 3.4.

The angle of impact is the internal angle between the flight path of the blood drop and the surface it strikes. There is a trigonometric relationship between the length and width of a bloodstain. To calculate the angle of impact, the width (at the center, widest part of the bloodstain) and length ("rounding" distortion at the terminal edge where necessary) are measured. The width is divided by the length, providing a ratio of 1 or less. This ratio is the sine of the internal angle. In order to find the angle, a scientific calculator is utilized to find the $\sin^{-1}$ (inverse sine). Each calculator is a little different, but buttons labeled "inv," "2nd," "function," and so on, and the sin key will result in the angle of impact. A passive 90-degree drop will have a ratio of 1 because its length and width are equal. A drop whose width is

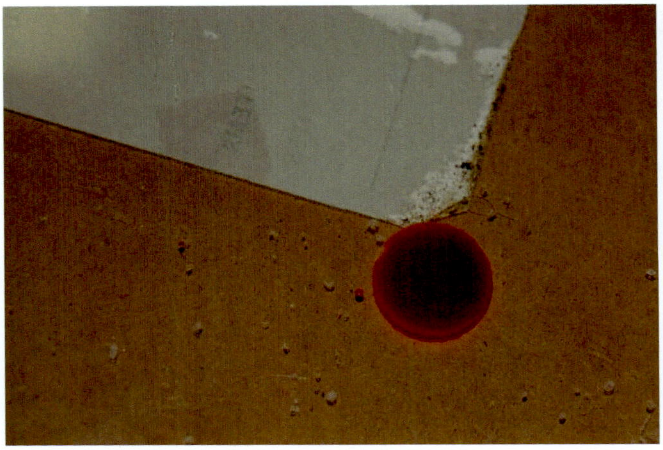

FIGURE 3.2 Glass—smooth edges, accompanying a drop seen to the left.

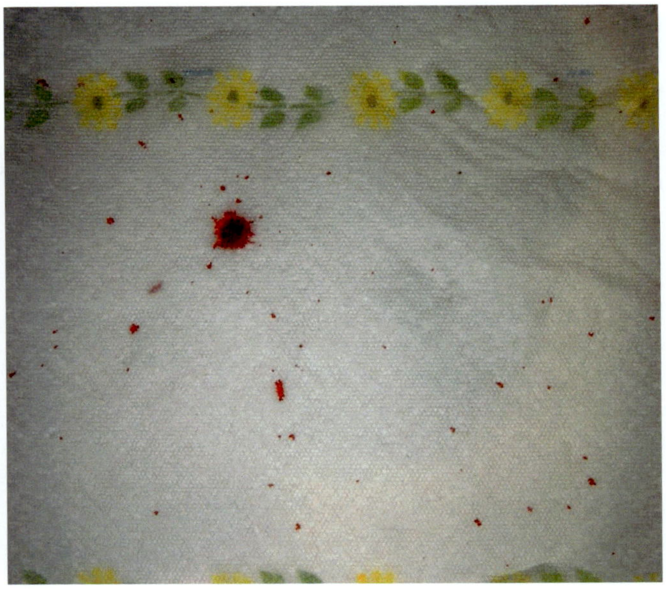

FIGURE 3.3 One drop on a paper towel, note the spines and satellite spatter.

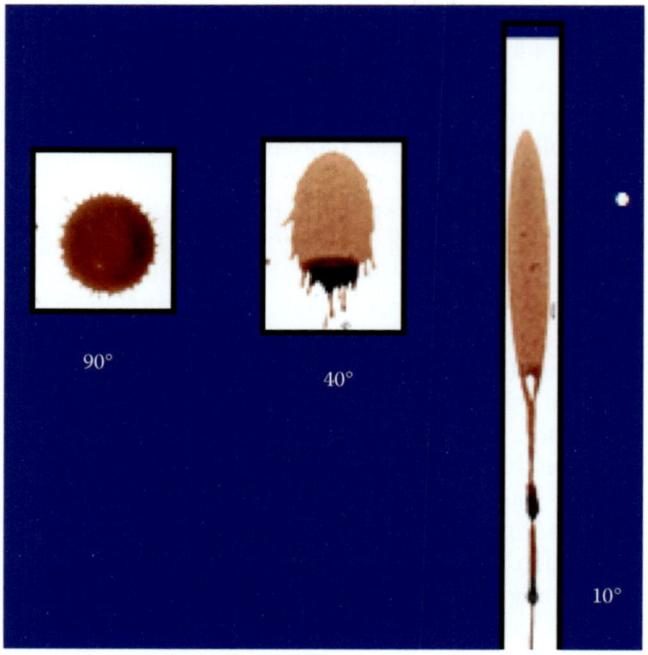

FIGURE 3.4 Decreasing angle of impact.

half its length will result in a ratio of .5, and a 30-degree angle of impact. For example:

$$W = 5\,\text{mm Angle of impact} = (\text{Width} / \text{Length})^{\sin-1}$$

$$L = 10\,\text{mm Ratio: } (5\,\text{mm} / 10\,\text{mm}) = .5$$

$$\text{Angle of impact} = (.5)^{\sin-1} = 30°$$

It is impaortant to note that the units of measurement must be the same for the width and length (e.g., both in millimeters, or both in inches) so that they cancel out to reveal a unitless ratio.

The area of convergence is the place, in two dimensions, where the bloodshedding occurred. In other words, the location on the surface (wall, floor, etc.). This is determined by drawing a line, or using string on-scene, from the leading edge (this is where the blood drop impacts the surface) of the bloodstain, projecting it backward following the line of its long axis. This is done for several stains from within the pattern, to achieve a representative sampling. Where the lines or strings cross, is the area of convergence. The area of origin is the three-dimensional location where the bloodshed occurred. After finding the area of convergence and calculating the angle of impact as described above, each line or string is raised, with the use of a zero baseline protractor, to its calculated angle. An alternate way to determine how far off the surface an event occurred is the tangent method. The formula is as follows: Tan(angle of impact) = Z/measured distance, where the measured distance is the measurement from the leading edge of the stain to the area of convergence. Rearranging the formula to solve for "Z" results in the following: Z = Tan(angle of impact)(measured distance), so, the tangent of the calculated angle of impact multiplied by the measured distance. For example:

Calculated angle of impact = 20°
Distance from leading edge to convergence
= 28 inches
Tan(angle of impact) = Z/measured distance
Tan(20) = Z/28
Tan(20) = .36397...
Tan(20)(28) = Z
(.36397)(28) = 10.2 inches

It is important to note that the area of origin will be the height/distance past which the event could not have occurred, because the "stringing" method does not take into account the effects of gravity and air resistance. BSPA is not a precise discipline—these methods will not reveal *exactly* where the blood source was located, but it can give an idea of whether the victim was lying down, sitting, or standing, which is then compared against the statements of suspects, witnesses, and victims (if living). For example, a wife claims that she was "just looking at her husband's gun" when it "went off all of a sudden as he was walking in the room." After analysis, the bloodstains on the floor are determined to fall between a 10- and 20-degree angle of impact. This would indicate that her statement is not consistent with the physical evidence—the blood source was on the ground, not "walking into the room." Computer software has been developed in order to produce "virtual" stringing known as directional analysis of bloodstain patterns. Programs such as BackTrack™ and Hemospat™ are examples of programs that allow the user to utilize photographs and measurements of bloodstains from actual crime scenes to determine the areas of origin. Buck et. al published the journal article "3D Bloodstain Pattern Analysis: Ballistic Reconstruction of the Trajectories of Blood Drops and Determination of the Centres of Origin of the Bloodstains." This approach utilized computer-aided design (CAD), photogrammetry, tachymetry, ballistics software, and laser scanning and rendered a true-to-scale 3D rendering of the scene and the relevant bloodstain pattern information.

3.6.1 Contact Patterns

Contact patterns are generally referred to as transfer patterns, of which there are many types. A transfer pattern requires contact between two items, at least one of which is wet with blood. Sometimes, a transfer pattern may have recognizable features that may provide information about the object that created it, such as a potential weapon shape, hair, footwear, and fabric. It is not uncommon to see a mirror image of the object that created the pattern, when blood is transferred from one part of the body to another, or with the folding over of fabrics. Fingerprints, palm prints, foot and/or footwear transfer patterns may be transferred with sufficient detail that an identification is possible, depending on the target surface.

Hair compression transfer patterns and hair swipes are often easily recognized by the fine, wispy nature of the pattern. Sometimes, hair may be present within the pattern.

Swipe patterns are included in the category of passive patterns. Swipe patterns result from the contact of a bloody surface with a non-bloody surface exhibiting relative motion between the two. As a general rule, the feathered end of a swipe pattern reveals the direction of travel as in Figure 3.5.

James et al. (2005) include wipe patterns in the passive category, but acknowledge that wipe patterns may also be included in the altered category. The SWGSTAIN definition of a wipe pattern is "an altered bloodstain pattern resulting from an object moving through a preexisting wet bloodstain." Wipe patterns are common in cleanup efforts and are also seen in sequenced patterns.

Figure 3.5 reveals both swipe and wipe patterns on a wall. When a bloodstained object first makes contact with a surface, it is generally where there will be the most pressure applied, and the surface may exhibit a non-specific stain. As the bloody object travels along and eventually departs from the surface, the amount of pressure lessens, producing the feathered edge characteristics. Therefore, the directionality in Figure 3.5 would be from right to left. The wipe stains are those which have passed through the existing spatter on the wall, removing the centers and altering the edge characteristics.

FIGURE 3.5 Wall exhibiting both swipe and wipe patterns. Directionality is from right to left.

3.6.2 Flow Patterns

Flow patterns occur when there is a great enough volume of blood that it is unable to adhere to the target surface. Gravity and object topography/contour dictate the direction of flow patterns. These patterns are useful in determining if a victim (or bloodstained item) moved or was moved after bleeding started. When a flow pattern is still wet, a flow line's direction will change with the position of the body/object. For instance, if flow patterns are identified on an individual's leg with directionality from the knee to the foot, but the individual is found lying down on the ground, it can be determined that the victim was in a seated or standing position for a period of time, to allow the blood to dry sufficiently that no change in directionality is exhibited, before moving or being moved to the ground. Within the yellow box of Figure 3.6 are shown flow patterns on the victim's thigh, knee, and calf that are inconsistent with the position in which she is photographed.

3.6.3 Drop(s) and Free-Falling Volumes

Passive drops are usually fairly easily identifiable, as seen earlier in Figure 3.2, on glass. Passive drops on carpet appear to have much smaller diameters due to their absorption into the carpet. Often seen are drip trails when the blood source moves between two or more places, such as an individual walking away with a dripping weapon, or a bleeding victim walking around the scene. Directionality is not always evident, however, with sufficient velocity; sometimes edge characteristics and wave cast-off can help determine the direction of travel. Wave cast-off is

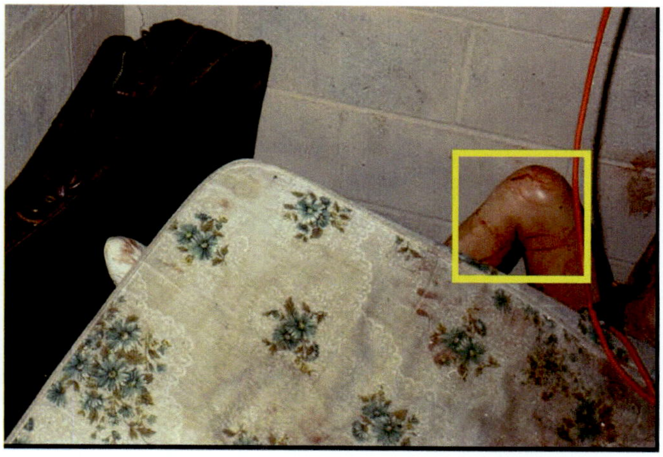

FIGURE 3.6 Flow patterns inconsistent with position.

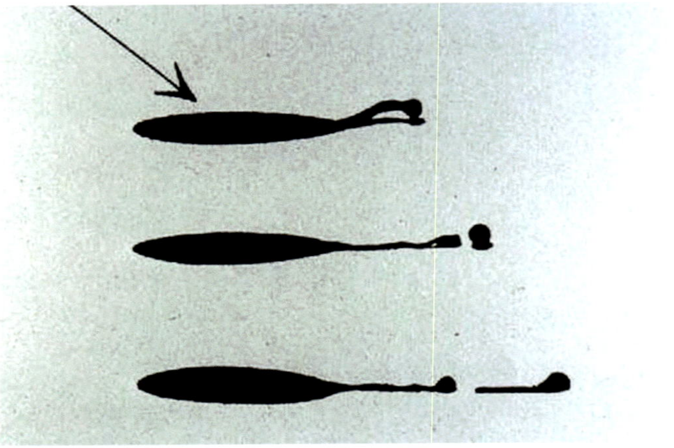

FIGURE 3.7 Mechanism of wave cast-off formation by high-speed photography. (Courtesy of Herbert L. MacDonell, hereafter HLM.)

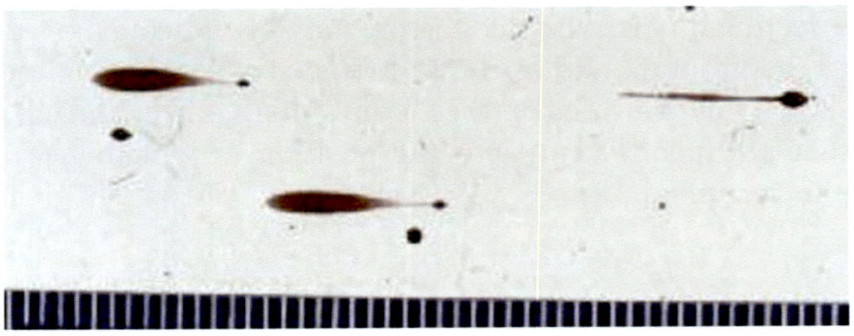

FIGURE 3.8 Example of a wave cast-off. (Courtesy of HLM.)

a smaller blood drop thrown from the parent drop upon impact. Figure 3.7 shows the mechanism of wave cast-off formation. Figure 3.8 is an example of wave cast-off. There is significant distance between the top parent stain and its wave cast-off. When there are overlapping stains, it may be difficult to match the parent stains with their wave cast-off. However, if a line is drawn through the long axis of the wave cast-off, similar to what is done for area of convergence, and projected back, it is often possible to assign the wave cast-off to the appropriate parent stain. The terminal end of the bloodstain at the bottom of Figure 3.8 shows a similar geometry to the wave cast-off pictured above it—however, it has not broken free. A word of caution—if a wave cast-off is viewed without its parent stain, one might determine its directionality to be opposite its actual direction of travel due to the amount of blood at its "head" and thin tail. However, wave cast-off is discernable from a parent stain in its geometry. The parent stain has an elliptical shape with a tapered end, whereas wave cast-off has a more rounded end and a straight "neck" (as opposed to tapering to a point).

When a passively dripping blood source does not move, and blood drips into itself, it creates a discernable drip pattern, as seen in Figure 3.9, that creates small

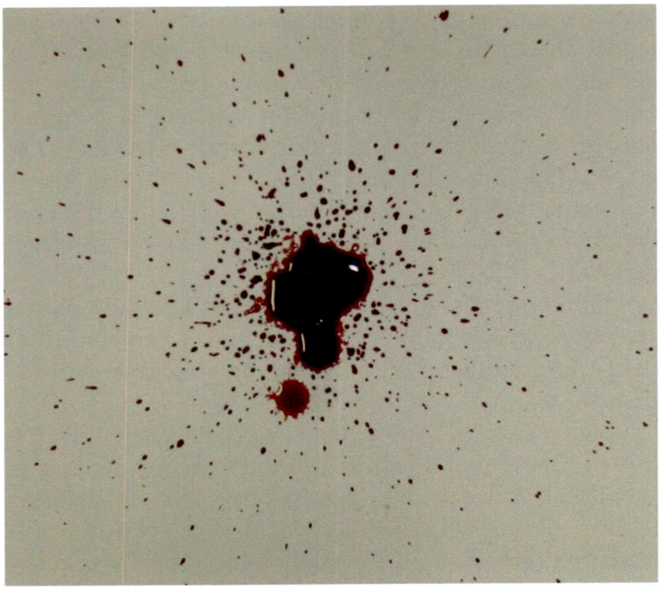

FIGURE 3.9 Drip pattern.

(usually around 1 mm in size), round to oval satellite spatter in a radiating pattern around the parent stain. Typically, there is not a great deal of obvious directionality as compared to projected patterns discussed later. The satellite spatter (or secondary spatter) is formed when drops continue to strike each other; the small stains are formed and are spattered into the air, out and away from the forming pool.

Large, free-falling volumes are those of ~1 mL or more falling all at once as opposed to drop by drop; this is also referred to as splashed blood.

3.6.4 Saturation/Pooling

As mentioned, the SWGSTAIN definitions of saturation and pooling are as follows:

Saturation Stain: A bloodstain resulting from the accumulation of liquid blood in an absorbent material.

Pool: A bloodstain resulting from an accumulation of liquid blood on a surface.

Figure 3.10 illustrates pooling on a non-absorbent surface resulting from the passive flowing of blood out of multiple gunshot wounds (GSWs). Figure 13.11 reveals saturation staining of absorbent bedding.

3.6.5 Impact Spatter

The old classification of bloodstains was based on the velocity at which the blood source was impacted and the size of the bloodstains that resulted. However, there

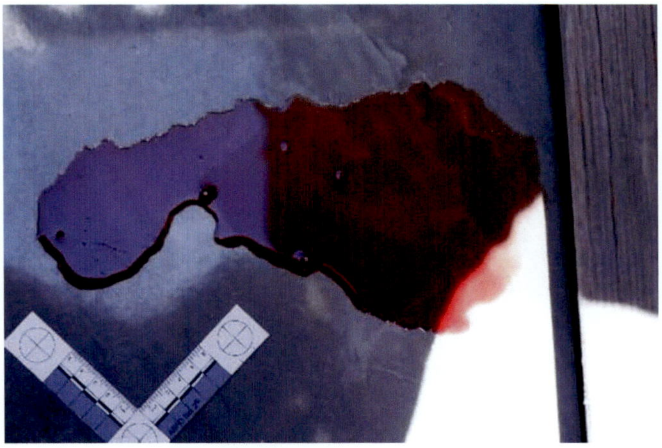

FIGURE 3.10 Pooling on a non-absorbent surface.

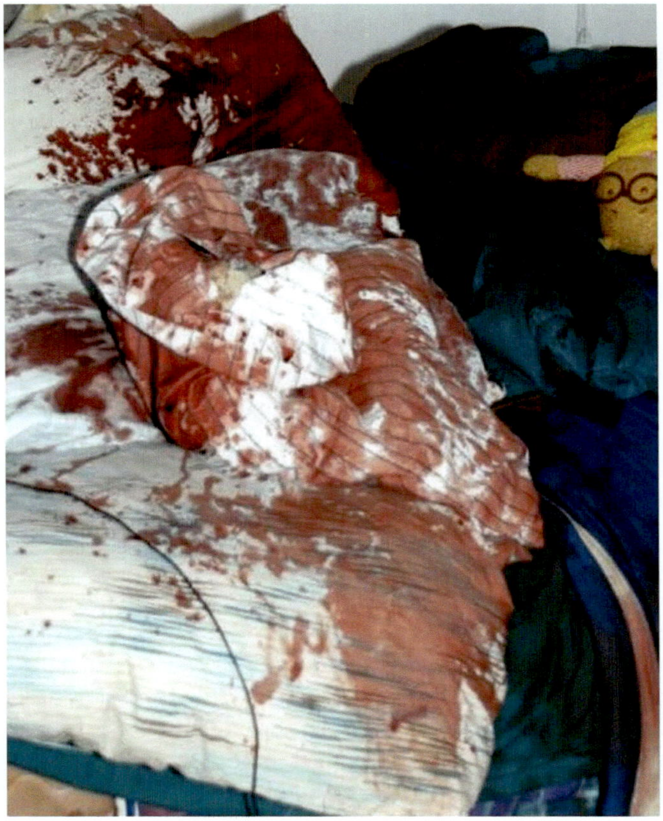

FIGURE 3.11 Saturation staining on an absorbent surface.

is enough overlap between the categories as they relate to bloodstain size, that new classification and terminology has been proffered. The old terminology referring to impact spatter was low-velocity impact spatter (LVIS), medium-velocity impact spatter (MVIS), and high-velocity impact spatter (HVIS). The new method of referring to these categories still relies on the sizes of the stains; however, it focuses more on the overall size, shape, distribution and location in the context of specific case information, instead of a strict classification based on size alone. For instance, if a person had a bloody nose that gushed onto the floor and another person was standing next to him/her, we might find stains around 1 mm in size on the pant leg of the innocent bystander. The resulting pattern may be incorrectly classified as impact spatter without case-specific information, instead of satellite spatter from a free-falling large volume of blood.

Impact spatter that is consistent with a beating or stabbing tends to have the preponderance of bloodstains with a diameter of approximately 1–3 mm. However, there can be a wide variation from 1 to 3 mm based on type of weapon, amount of exposed blood, and several other factors. The velocity of the force that impacts the blood source is generally between 5 and 25 feet/second. There must be blood exposed before it can be spattered. This means that in the absence of something like a crushing head blow, it would not be surprising not to see any blood spatter resulting from a single blow to the head. Individuals who administer a beating or stabbing may or may not become spattered with blood themselves.

There are many factors that determine whether or not an assailant becomes spattered with blood, some of which include the length, weight, and shape of the weapon; the direction of force; the number of blows; the relative positions and movements of the victim and attacker, to name a few. An absence of blood spatter on an assailant does not prove nonparticipation for several reasons: the factors mentioned above regarding the spattering of blood, that an assailant may have changed clothes prior to apprehension or wore an outer protective layer that was discarded, or administered the beating without clothes on and showered. There are, however, areas that assailants often overlook when cleaning up. Items like socks, shoe laces, and jewelry are good places to look for bloodstains that may have been overlooked, or not easily cleaned. Conclusions about bloodstains on clothing should be rendered cautiously, as the weave of the fabric may distort the shape of the original bloodstain; where, for example, a 90-degree impact angle may appear more ovoid in shape, or vice versa. This phenomena may also be observed on unfinished wood as the grain may distort the stain.

The distribution of bloodstains in a beating often appears in a radiating pattern around the origin, not unlike a sunburst, on either vertical or horizontal surfaces, as seen in Figure 3.12.

In many cases, calculating the angle of impact and stringing is not critical, as the victim's location at the time of bloodshed can be ascertained by observation. For example, in the scene depicted in Figure 3.12, impact spatter is also seen on the side of the bathtub (right side of photograph). Additional photos show impact spatter on the bottom of the sink and on the right side (as viewed upon entering the bathroom) of the toilet. This means that it had to occur below the bottom of the sink and in

FIGURE 3.12 Radiating pattern and relative void where the victim's head was located at the time of a beating.

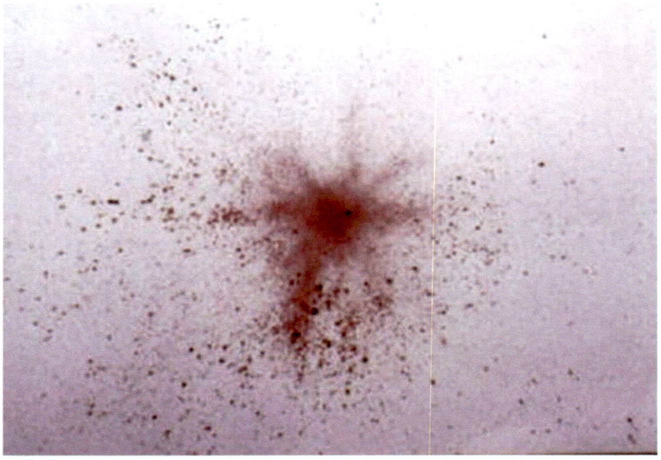

FIGURE 3.13 Impact spatter associated with a gunshot. Note the misting around the bullet hole.

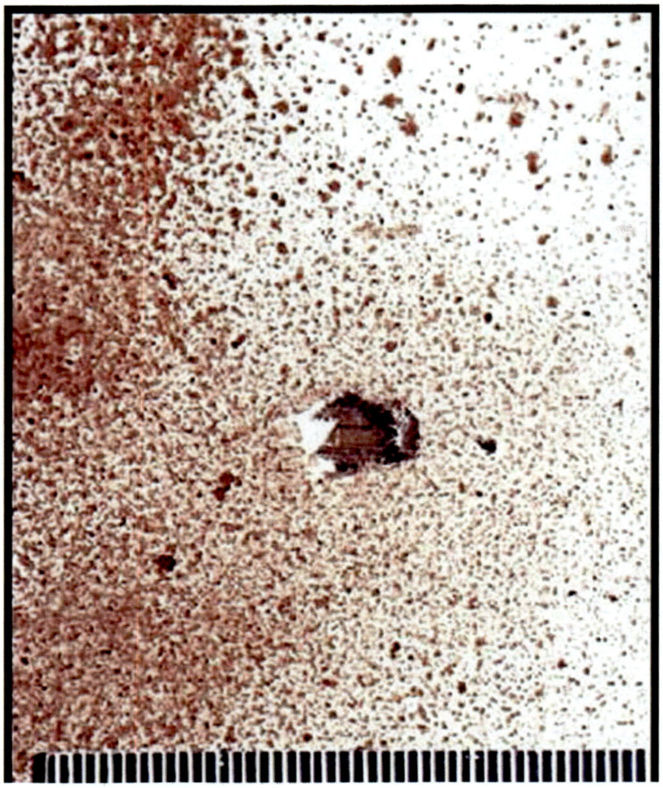

FIGURE 3.14 Close-up of misting. (Courtesy of HLM.)

between the toilet and bathtub. So, simply with observation, the area of assault can often be easily identified. Clearly, this may not be the case with multiple victims and complex, overlapping patterns.

Impact spatter consistent with gunshot wounds (GSWs) is generated by a force impacting the blood source at greater than 100 feet per second. In these patterns, there is also a range of spatter sizes that may be seen, from .01 mm to 3 mm or greater, as seen in Figure 3.13. The defining feature of this type of spatter is that the preponderance of stains are less than 1 mm and have been described as mist-like or aerosolized in appearance, as can be seen in Figure 3.14. Two types of spatter may result from a gunshot wound; forward spatter and back spatter. Forward spatter is what comes out of the exit wound with the projectile in a perforating GSW. Back spatter is what comes out of the entrance wound back toward the muzzle of the firearm and shooter. If the GSW is a penetrating wound, there is no exit wound, therefore no possibility of forward spatter. Generally, forward spatter is greater in volume and travels significantly farther than back spatter, as a result of the energy transfer from the projectile.

Research by Dr. Martin Fackler suggests that the collapse of the temporary wound cavity in contact or close-range GSWs is responsible, at least in part, for spatter production. Gases, heat and a projectile exit the muzzle of a firearm when fired. These gases, therefore pressure, are transmitted to the body tissues when fired at contact or close range. The permanent cavity is that produced by the projectile. The temporary cavity is a significantly larger cavity as a result of the transferred gases and energy, that is much like a balloon, surrounding the permanent cavity. The tissue of the temporary cavity collapses after the passage of the projectile. It is this collapsing that is proposed to force blood out of the entrance and/or exit wounds, creating spatter.

In actual casework, due to the dynamic nature of violent assaults and the proximity, color, and texture of surface on which the blood lands, the mist-like stains may never be identified. Additionally, these very small stains typically travel approximately only 1 to 4 feet (with some exceptions) due to air resistance and dry almost immediately. If there is an object close enough to the blood source to receive the mist-type spatter, the stains may be easily disturbed or destroyed with normal actions of investigators, depending on the nature of the surface. To assist with understanding why the small stains do not travel very far, an analogy would be the difference in trying to throw a handful of flour versus a handful of rocks—the bigger, heavier rocks will go significantly farther. The blocking effects of hair and clothing must also be taken into account, as they can easily block the very small stains from depositing on surrounding objects. With a single shot to the chest of a clothed victim, one would not expect to see spatter on surrounding objects. The amount of spatter depends on several factors, including but not limited to wound location, type of ammunition, caliber of firearm, muzzle to target distance, number of shots fired, and the presence or absence of clothing, hair, or other intermediate objects.

If there is nothing nearby on which the mist can deposit or is blocked, the only observed pattern might be more similar to that seen with a beating or stabbing. Case-specific information is always important to help narrow down the possible mechanisms that caused the pattern. The barrels of firearms should always be examined for the presence of blood. This can be especially important in suicide vs. homicide investigations, where range of fire and firearm orientation may be factors necessary to discern. There is a "drawback" effect produced by the rapid contraction of gases within the barrel of a firearm that creates a partial vacuum. In contact and near-contact wounds, blood can be drawn into the barrel, up to several inches, depending on factors like type of firearm, ammunition and distance from the wound as documented in a 1977 study by MacDonell and Brooks. It is important to note that the lack of blood in a barrel of a firearm does not exclude its involvement in the shooting.

3.6.6 Cast-Off—Projected

There are two types of cast-off, not to be confused with wave cast-off. The first type is cessation cast-off. Cessation cast-off occurs when a bloody object comes to a sudden stop and blood is projected off the end of an object. Frequently, cessation cast-off is obscured by impact spatter and may be difficult, or impossible, to differentiate.

The second type of cast-off is usually simply referred to as "cast-off." This type of cast-off refers to blood that is released from an object due to its motion. This is usually seen in beatings and stabbings on walls and ceilings when the bloody object is swung vertically. If the object is swung in a horizontal manner, as in a baseball swing, cast-off may be present on the walls in a horizontal configuration. Cast-off is identifiable by its linear nature and changing directionality through the arc of the swing, as seen in Figure 3.15. Stains will be round at any area where the object swung is at a 90-degree angle from the

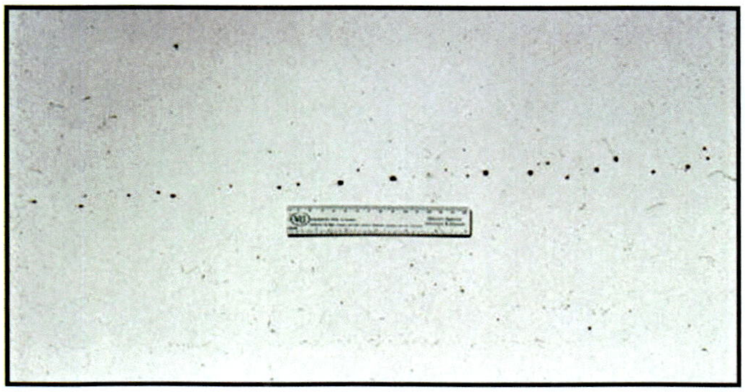

FIGURE 3.15 Cast-off—note the linear configuration, round stains in middle, and the right to left directionality on the left side of the photo. (Courtesy of HLM.)

target surface. For example, when a person is swinging a bloodied weapon in a vertical, overhead swing, you may see round stains (indicating a 90-degree angle of impact), on the ceiling directly overhead, when the weapon is perpendicular to the ceiling.

There are many factors that determine the configuration of cast-off patterns. Some of these include the number of blows struck, the material of which the weapon is made, shape and length of weapon, the amount of blood available, and the force of the swings. The overall size can be consistent with that of impact spatter, but may also be larger. While the stain sizes often remain similar throughout a cast-off pattern; the "downswings" may produce somewhat smaller stains, as the force of the downswing can be greater than the upswing.

Cast-off patterns may be found on ceilings, walls (side swing), or even floors, depending on the relative positions of the assailant and victim. Cast-off patterns may also be seen on clothing. Sometimes, cast-off stains are found on the shoulder, back and/or back of the leg of the assailant. Cast-off patterns on the front of clothing should be carefully considered, as this may indicate proximity to the event, even without participation.

3.6.7 Expirated—Projected

Expirated bloodstains are those which are created as a result of air pressure. This may be due to blood in the nose, mouth, or airways; air mixed with blood in the chest or abdominal wounds; or positioning of victim, such as with his/her head in and breathing breathing into a pool of blood. The size of such bloodstains varies greatly, as it will depend on how forcefully the blood was expelled. As seen in impact spatter, the greater the force, the smaller the bloodstains. As a result, expirated patterns may be confused with impact spatter—either that which is seen with a beating/stabbing, or what is seen with gunshot wounds. One must be very cautious

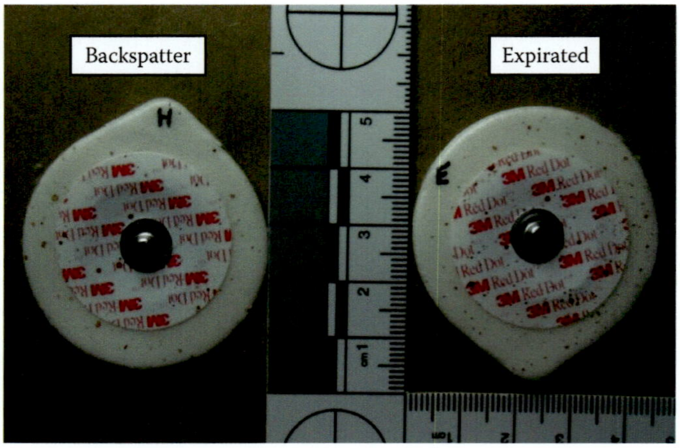

FIGURE 3.16 Heart monitor electrodes. Left: Exposed to backspatter. Right: Exposed to expirated blood.

and consider all possibilities when examining cases where both impact spatter and expirated may be present. Figure 3.16 depicts electrodes with laboratory-created patterns that compare backspatter from a gunshot with expirated bloodstain patterns to show how similar the two types of patterns can be in terms of their overall size, shape, and distribution.

There may be some characteristics that allow differentiation of the patterns. For instance, air bubbles may be present. The presence of air bubbles is essentially conclusive that there is some sort of airway injury. However, the absence of air bubbles does not mean that the pattern cannot be expirated. There are several variables, such as the origin of the expirated blood (from mouth, nose, wound), the nature of the injury causing the bleeding, the nature of the target surface, and the force with which blood is expirated that may affect whether air bubbles may be present and/or seen. In some cases, when blood with air bubbles dries, there are bubble rings that remain. A bubble ring is the outline within a bloodstain that remains where the bubble had been before it ruptured and/or dried. While the description may sound similar to that of a perimeter stain (discussed in the section on altered bloodstains), they are visually different from one another. The outline of a bubble ring may be thicker, thereby creating what looks like little vacuoles or craters, where the perimeter stain is generally flat and is the outline of a stain that has been wiped through before it was dry.

Bilateral patterns may be identified if blood is projected from both nares, by, for example, sneezing with blood in the nasal cavity. Additionally, sometimes mucous strands are identified with blood projected from the nose or mouth. Expirated blood may appear lighter in color due to dilution from saliva when blood is expirated from the mouth. It is important to keep in mind that a lack of dilution and/or air bubbles does not eliminate a pattern from being expirated. Field tests for salivary amylase (an enzyme found in saliva) are available that may assist investigators with determining origin. Analysts must remain objective and open-minded when evaluating bloodstain patterns in a case. There will be times when it is impossible to determine whether a pattern is impact spatter or expirated. If, for example, there is a victim who has a perforating GSW to the head, so both forward and backspatter are possibilities, and the victim has blood coming out of his/her nose and mouth. Bloodstains that are approximately 1 mm in size are found on the wall near the victim, and salivary amylase testing is negative. The best conclusion that the analyst could come to is that the pattern could be either impact spatter or expirated blood, because there are no other factors to make one or the other more likely. If there are factors that allow the analyst to form an opinion that one mechanism is more likely than another, they must be a scientifically defensible.

It is easy to get engrossed in the minutiae of individual bloodstains and "not see the forest for the trees," so the analyst must always remember to take into consideration the overall size, shape, and distribution of the bloodstains when forming opinions. Bloodshedding events are commonly very dynamic, chaotic events, and it may not be possible to explain every single bloodstain with the available information, so a responsible analyst should report all possible mechanisms.

3.6.8 Arterial Bleeding—Projected

As previously mentioned, arteries have a large smooth muscle layer, which contracts in the same cadence as an individual's heart rate; this is how healthcare workers are able to count their patients pulses in their wrist, neck, inside of the elbow, foot, groin, and so on—anywhere there is a palpable pulse. This also makes arteries more resistant to collapsing than veins, as they have tension in them, somewhat like a taut rubber band. If an artery is completely severed, as in the top illustration of Figure 3.17, it is common for the ends to retract under the skin, subcutaneous fat, and muscle (imagine cutting a taut rubber band and the ends "snap back"). This causes a "spraying" type of pattern, somewhat like what happens if you place your thumb over a garden hose. This spraying type of arterial bleeding is seen in Figure 3.18. A crushed artery may also produce this type of pattern. It is not uncommon to also see the overall "peaks and valleys" in the pattern, corresponding to the contraction and relaxation of the heart—much like an electrocardiogram strip that is also seen in Figure 3.18 for comparison purposes. As the individual's blood pressure drops, the relative height of the "peaks" will become smaller.

If an artery is partially severed or is superficial, where the cut ends are exposed to the external environment, as

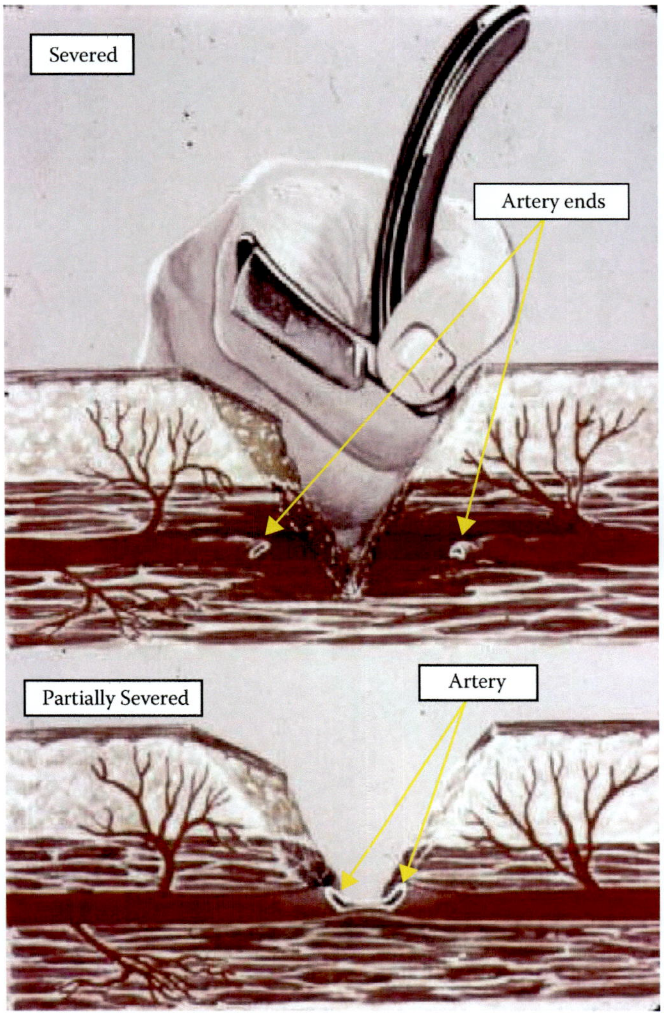

FIGURE 3.17 Top: Artery completely severed, ends retracted under tissue. Bottom: Partially severed, cut ends of artery exposed. (Courtesy of HLM.)

seen in the bottom illustration of Figure 3.17, the resulting bloodstain patterns appear as distinct "pulses," where individual heartbeats can be counted. This individual pulsing type of arterial bleeding can be seen in Figure 3.19. In some cases, it is possible to see features of a combination of the two types of arterial bleeding outlined here, where distinct pulses can be seen in addition to the overall "peaks and valleys"; however, they may appear more rounded "hills" as opposed to sharp "peaks."

3.6.9 Altered Bloodstains

An altered bloodstain, according to SWGSTAIN, is one with characteristics that indicate a physical change has occurred. These changes can be the result of usual physiological phenomena, actions, insects, chemicals, and so on.

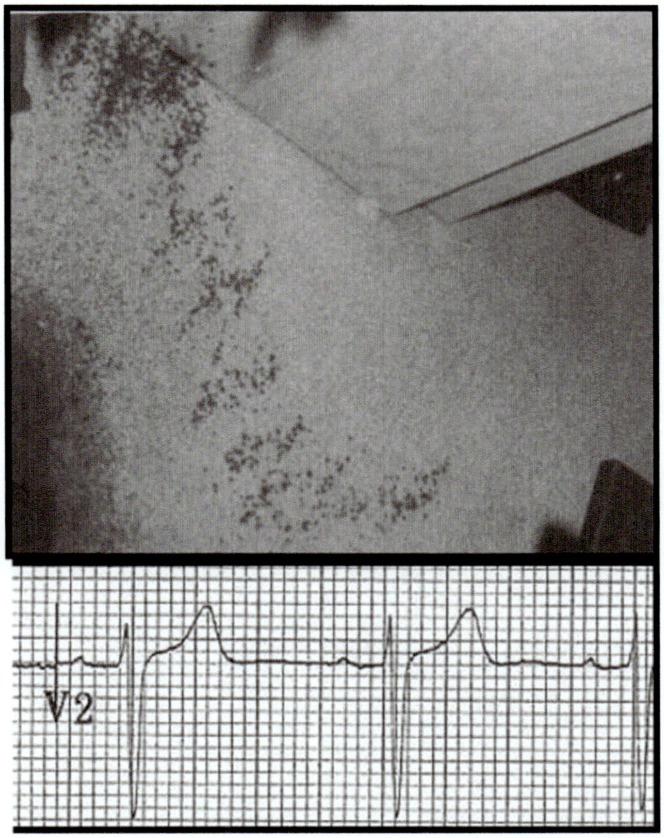

FIGURE 3.18 Arterial "spraying" with comparison to an EKG strip, illustrating the contraction/relaxation cycles of the heart. (Courtesy of HLM and author's files.)

3.6.10 Clotted Blood

When an individual suffers a bloodletting injury, there is a complex clotting cascade that takes place in order to stop the bleeding and form a scab. However, blood will clot when it is outside the body as well. This can be observed rather quickly (within minutes) in a blood tube that does not have an anticoagulant in it when one has blood drawn for medical testing. When clotting occurs in a pool of blood, serum separation will be seen, as seen in Figure 3.20. Also seen in Figure 3.20 is capillary diffusion—blood/serum is drawn from a higher concentration to a lower concentration in defiance of gravity, on the shirt sleeve.

The length of time required for clotting and serum separation is affected by many variables. These include the initial volume of blood, temperature, humidity, substrate on which blood is located, and source of blood. The source of blood is important because wounds that involve the head or otherwise breach the spinal canal may result in the mixing of cerebrospinal fluid (CSF) with the blood, which is known to significantly accelerate the clotting process. Figure 3.21 shows serum separation

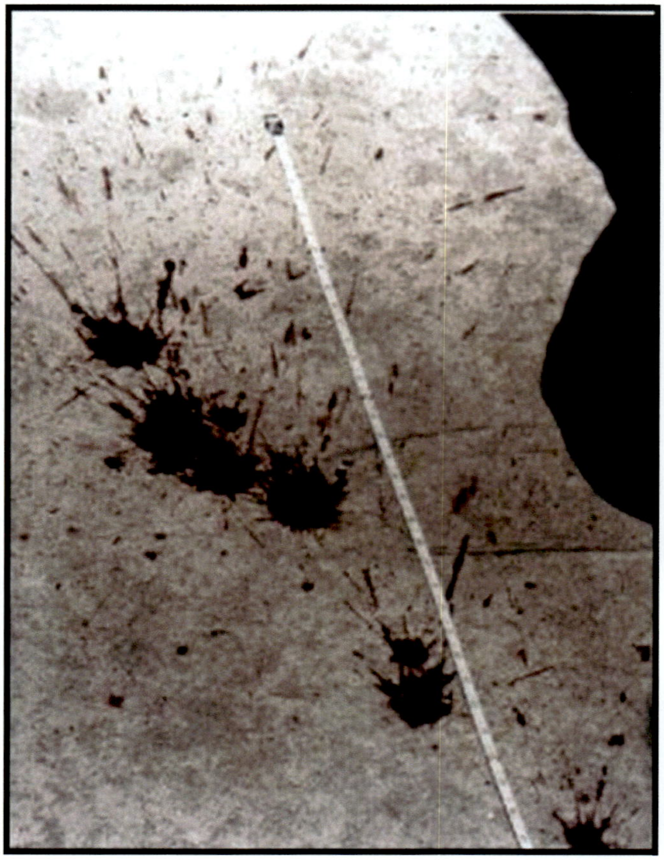

FIGURE 3.19 Distinct "pulses" of a victim with cut carotid artery crawling. (Courtesy of HLM.)

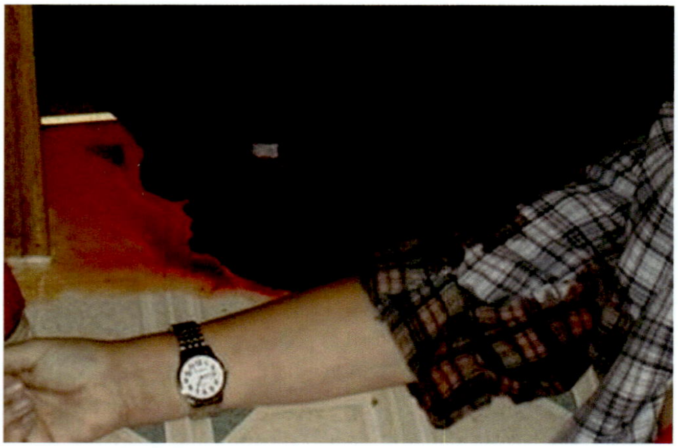

FIGURE 3.20 Clotting, serum separation, and capillary diffusion.

on an absorbent surface, in this case, a carpet. Note the darker, "thicker" appearance of the clotted area toward the bottom of the photo, and the lighter periphery of the serum. This is often how serum separation appears on porous surfaces.

When clotting or clotted blood continues to be impacted, small clots that have been spattered may be

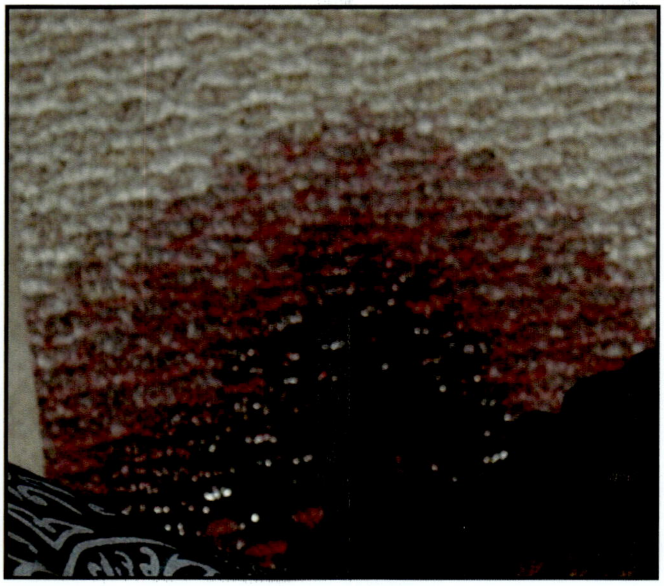

FIGURE 3.21 Clotting and serum separation on a carpet.

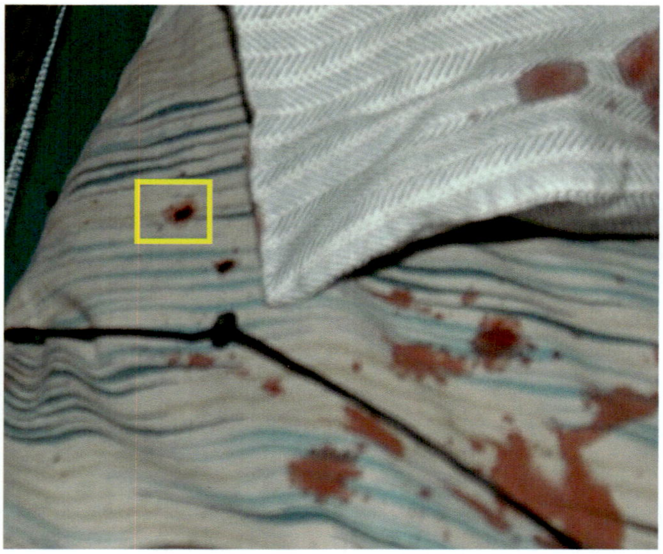

FIGURE 3.22 Yellow box—clotted spatter associated with a stabbing.

seen as depicted within the yellow box in Figure 3.22. Generally, when fresh blood is spattered, it will dry before a clot can form. Therefore, if clotted spatter is seen, this may give an indication of how long an attack continued, which, in some areas, may be a factor in what charges are sought against a defendant. The length of an attack can also be a significant factor in sentencing, particularly in areas that have the death penalty, when the prosecution is attempting to show the particularly heinous, atrocious and cruel nature of the attack.

If a time-lapse estimate is requested by investigating agencies or counsel associated with a case, this should be done very conservatively due to the large number of variables involved. Sometimes the best an analyst can report is a sequence of events, without assigning specific time frames.

Drying time estimates should also be addressed very conservatively, as many of the same variables (temperature, humidity, substrate, amount, etc.) affect drying time as well. Additionally, it is not uncommon for an attorney to ask something like "How long would it have taken for the victim's hair (shirt, pants, etc.) to become saturated with blood?" This too should be approached very cautiously and conservatively if the analyst wasn't at the scene when the injuries and subsequent bleeding occurred, which is usually the case. For example, a GSW to the head may cause blood to gush out of the nose like a faucet, whereas a similar GSW to the head in someone else may cause only a few drops of blood to drip out of the nose. Although both examples have a GSW to the head, the first victim's clothing would become saturated in a matter of seconds, where the second victim's clothing may not become saturated at all, or would take many minutes. Once again, it cannot be overstressed that the only proffered opinions should be those that are defensible.

3.6.11 Diluted Bloodstains

Diluted bloodstains are those that have been altered by addition of a liquid. This may be environmental, such as snow or rain; physiological, such as tears, perspiration, or saliva; or deliberate, such as seen in cleanup efforts. Diluted blood is generally darker around the periphery. Figure 3.23 shows a sink with both whole blood and diluted stains. Especially around the drain, note that these stains exhibit the typical darker periphery characteristic. It is important to note that bathrooms should always be examined, as assailants may go there to clean up and victims often go to the bathroom to determine the severity of their injuries. Figure 3.23 is from a woman who was attacked by a dog and went to the bathroom to check the severity of injuries to her face.

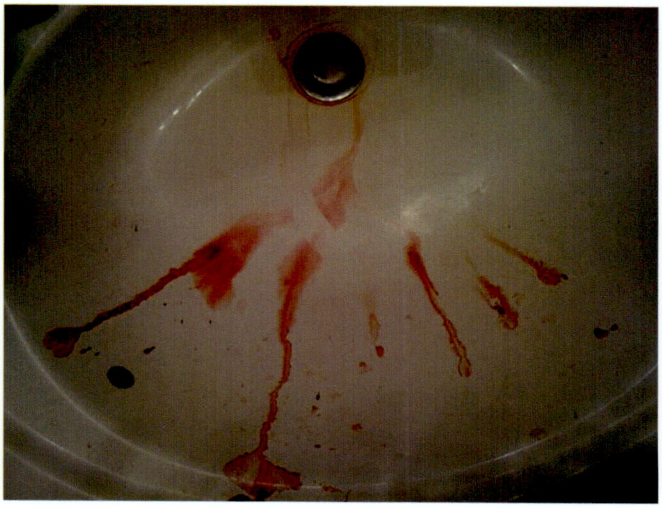

FIGURE 3.23 Diluted bloodstains around a drain, right side and just left of center of photo. Note darker periphery.

Figure 3.24 shows spatter and transfer bloodstains altered by a cleanup attempt. Figure 3.25 depicts a bloodstain altered by saliva. Note the glossy appearance (air bubbles are also present).

During an altercation, or life and death struggle, it is not uncommon for participants to perspire profusely. Figure 3.26 shows bloodstains diluted with perspiration on the shirt of a perpetrator in a stabbing attack.

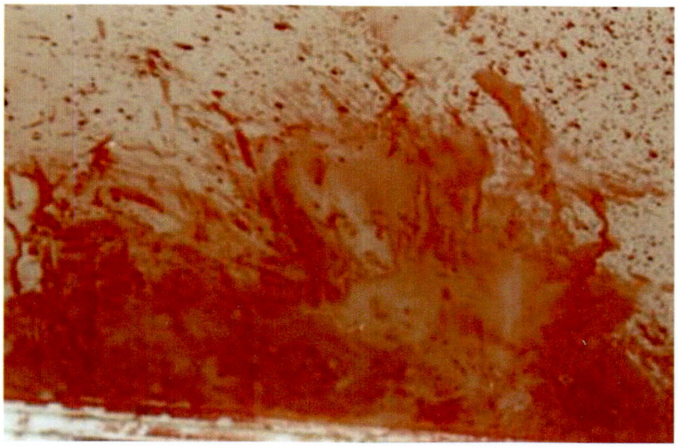

FIGURE 3.24 Bloodstains altered by a cleanup attempt.

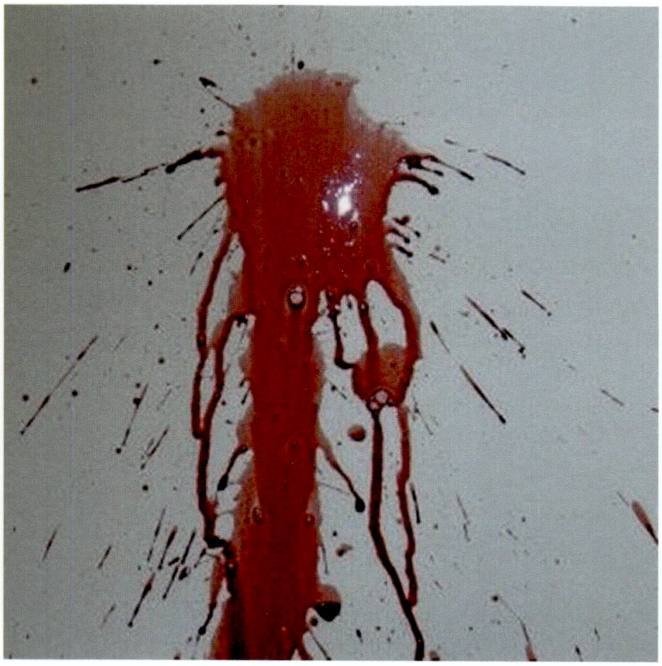

FIGURE 3.25 Bloodstains altered by saliva.

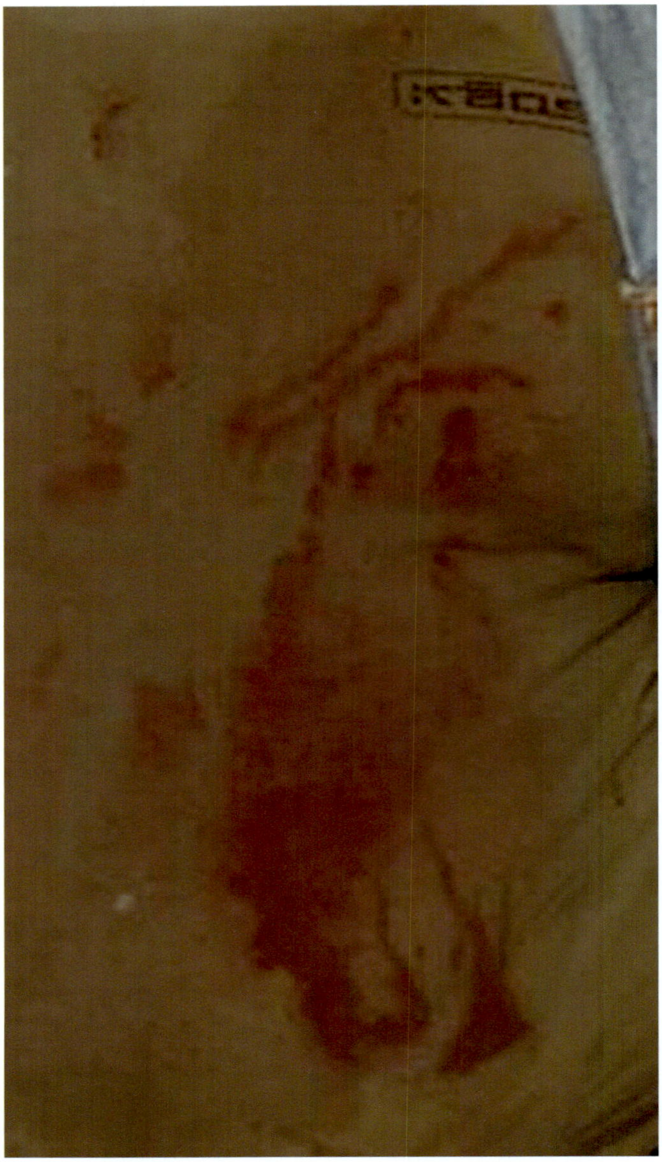

FIGURE 3.26 Bloodstains diluted by perspiration.

Bloodstains that are found in places where the stains may be further altered by a change in temperature/humidity, such as a walk-in freezer, should be dealt with first and thoroughly photographed (be sure photographs are acceptable), and presumptive testing completed, if necessary, prior to permitting a significant change in the environment (such as leaving the freezer door open for prolonged periods of time).

3.6.12 Dried Bloodstains

As has been discussed previously, environmental factors, target surface and amount of blood are important when considering the drying times of blood. Under "room temperature" conditions, small spatter stains, thin/light

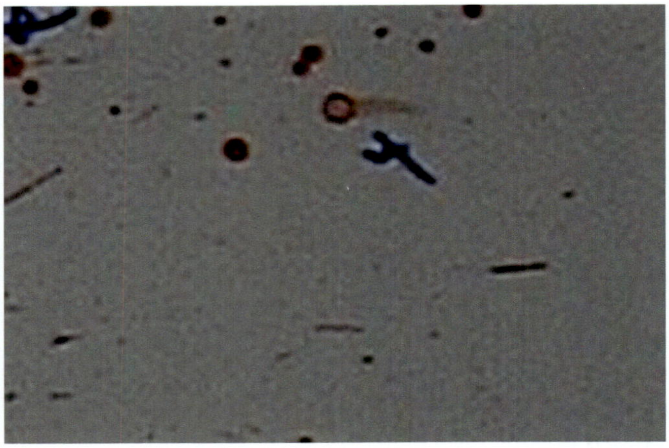

FIGURE 3.27 Bloodstain wiped through after 4 minutes, leaving the peripheral rim intact.

transfer stains and flow patterns with a small volume of blood can dry within a few minutes on non-porous surfaces. Larger volumes of blood will take longer to dry, and surfaces that can be saturated (e.g., carpet, bedding) usually take longer than the same volume of blood on a nonporous surface.

Generally, drying time is decreased with elevated temperature and lower humidity. Conversely, drying time is increased with lower temperature and increased humidity. Increased airflow, such as produced by fans, wind, and breezes from open windows, will affect drying times. Casework will often present features of both of the aforementioned generalities. For example, in areas closer to the equator, one may find a situation with increased temperature and increased humidity. Experiments may need to be performed in cases where drying times are a significant issue. In these cases, the size of the bloodstains, temperature, humidity, target surface, and airflow should be replicated as closely as possible.

Bloodstains dry from the periphery toward the center. Figure 3.27 illustrates this principle. Next to the number 4, a stain that has been wiped through, 4 minutes after it was deposited, is seen. The peripheral rim is intact, but the center of the stain has been removed. This is referred to as a skeletonized stain, or a perimeter stain. This drying principle holds true with all types of stains, pools, saturation, flow patterns, and so on. In some instances, the center of the stain may dry and begin to flake away, as seen in Figure 3.28. This is often seen on smooth and varnished type surfaces or on surfaces with a greasy film.

Dried bloodstains on different types of skin may appear very different from one another. Blood in a uniform layer that has dried relatively quickly and without disturbance, may have a "crazed" or cracked appearance, as seen in Figure 3.29. This phenomenon can be seen on several other types of target surfaces as well. Blood

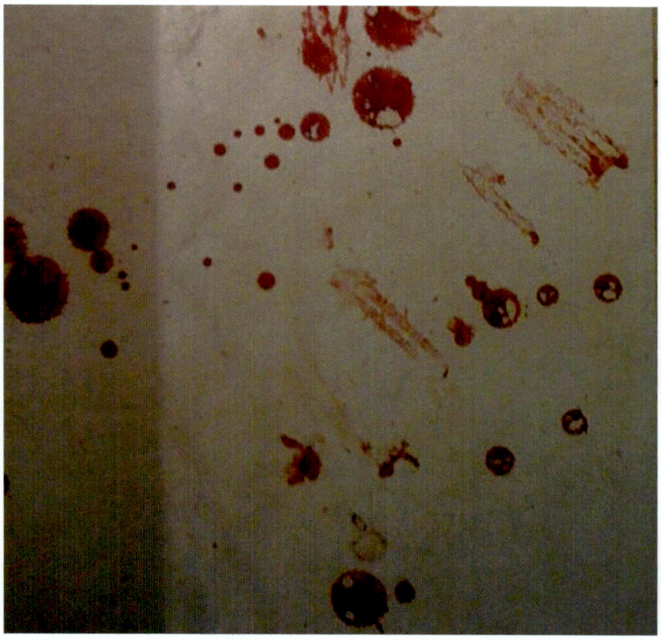

FIGURE 3.28 Bloodstain on a tile floor that has begun to flake off, leaving the periphery intact.

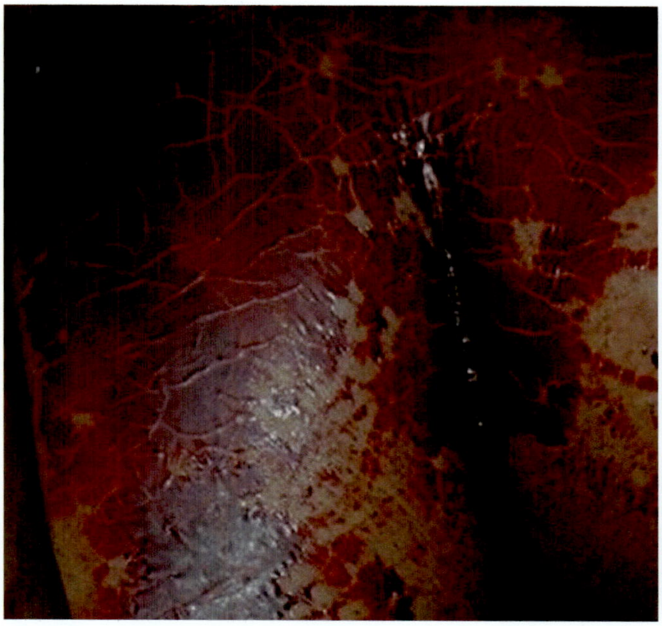

FIGURE 3.29 Dried blood on skin exhibiting "crazing."

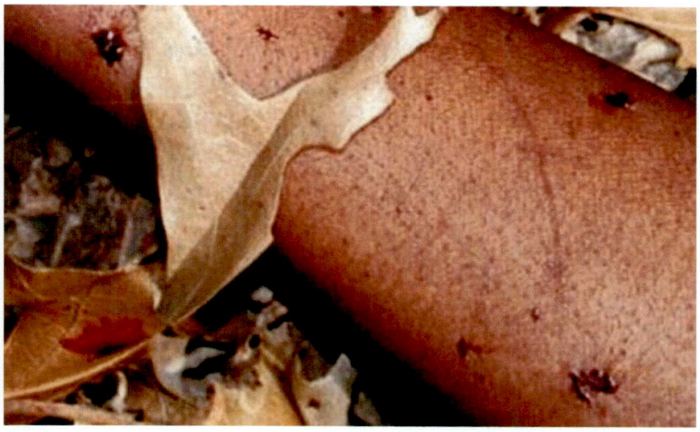

FIGURE 3.30 Dried blood on skin with a "puckered" appearance.

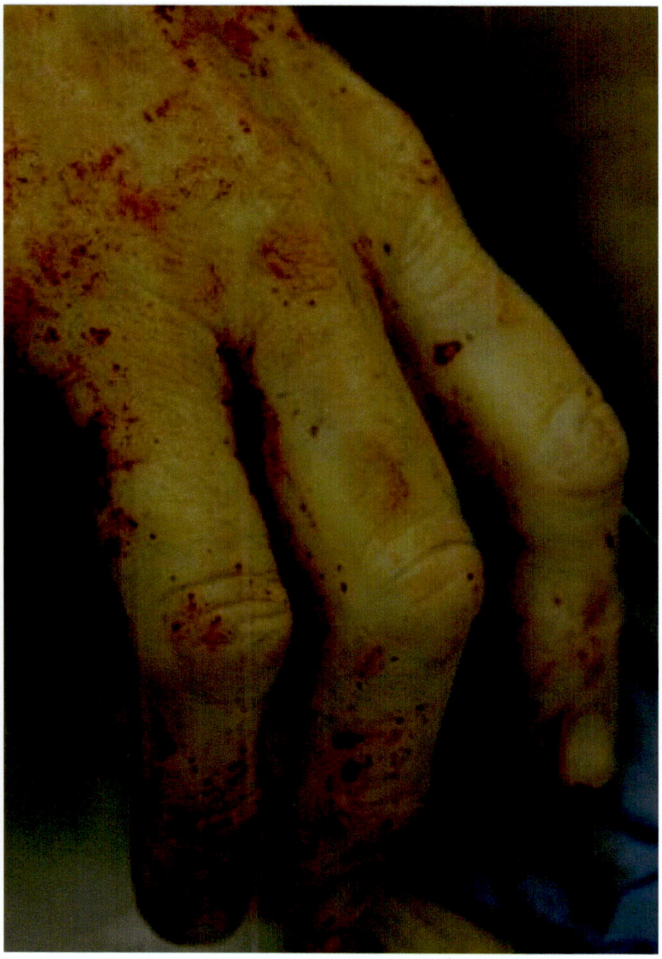

FIGURE 3.31 Dried blood on skin with a "crusty" appearance.

that is deposited in thicker, smaller drops or spatter can appear "puckered," as seen in Figure 3.30. Still others may appear more, as most people without experience in the discipline might expect—somewhat of a "crusty" appearance, as shown in Figure 3.31.

It is important to note that the type of skin (ethnicity, age, medical conditions, etc.) in addition to the use of products on the skin, along with the usual environmental factors, can affect the appearance of the bloodstains. Spatter patterns and expirated patterns exhibiting directionality may remain intact on hands, arms, or other body areas that may assist with positioning in reconstruction, if needed.

The aging of bloodstains (meaning, when was the blood deposited?) has been an elusive task. There has recently been work published using hyperspectral imaging in the aging of bloodstains that may have more promise than previous aging attempts. It is commonly thought that bloodstains darken, from red to a rusty type color to black, as they age. While bloodstains do tend to darken as they age, attempting to estimate age of a bloodstain by its color, without experimenting with replicate conditions particular to that case, is not scientifically defensible. Bloodstains deposited on a piece of glass and a piece of wood at the same time and subsequently examined a week later may show surprising results. The one on the wood may appear much darker, while the one on glass may still appear red due to the light that is transmitted through the glass. Consider bloodstains on two identical lightbulbs in lamps with blood deposited at the same time. One lamp was never turned on, while the other remained on for an hour before being shut off. Once law enforcement arrives, in both instances, the bulb will be cold, but the stains on the two lightbulbs may look very different. Depending on when law enforcement arrives, the amount of blood deposited, temperature, and so on, the bloodstains on the bulb that was never turned on may still be "tacky" or even wet, while the bloodstains on the bulb that had been on may be dry, darker and perhaps even starting to flake off. Absent case specific experiments (whose estimates should still be conservative, as not every variable can be replicated), it is best to be conservative—if the blood was still wet upon arrival, then it can be concluded that it was recently deposited. If the blood is dry upon arrival, then it can be concluded that some time has passed since it was deposited. Epstein and Laber, in 1983, published data in *Experiments and Practical Exercises in Bloodstain Pattern Analysis*, taking into account several environmental factors, surfaces characteristics, and volumes of blood up to 10 mL that can be used as a general guide/reference.

3.6.13 Diffused/Capillary Action

Diffusion is defined as the net movement of a substance from an area of high concentration to an area of low concentration. Capillary action refers to the ability of a liquid to flow in small/narrow spaces in defiance of gravity and without the assistance of external forces. This occurs when the adhesive forces, which are the forces between two dissimilar substances, between the liquid and the container, are greater than the cohesive forces within the liquid. Cohesive forces are forces between like substances. Therefore, conversely, if the cohesive forces are greater than the adhesive forces between the liquid and container, a reverse flow will occur. It is capillary action that is the principle at work when using paper towels or sponges when cleaning up a liquid. Figure 3.32 shows diffusion and capillary action: diffusion, because the movement is from an area of high concentration (the blood pool on the floor), to low concentration; and capillary action, because the liquid portion of the blood is being drawn up the shirt—from the floor/back of the body to the front of the body, in defiance of gravity. Some individuals may be familiar with the term "wicking," which is often used to describe capillary action. The rate at which this phenomenon may occur is highly dependent on the surface, weave, or "grain" involved, in addition to the adhesive forces.

Capillary action is the principle at work in thin layer chromatography, where there is a solid and a mobile phase. In bloodstain cases, the mobile phase is the liquid portion of the blood and the solid phase is the porous material on which it travels. Caution should be exercised when evaluating bloodstains/spatter patterns related to directionality determinations, as the weave of the fabric can distort the shape of the stain—what was dropped at a 90-degree angle and should appear round, may appear somewhat elliptical, and vice versa, an elliptical stain may appear more rounded. Additionally, with some fabrics, it can be extremely difficult to determine on which side of the fabric the blood was deposited. Figure 3.33 shows bloodstains on a microfiber type of material. The green dividing line separates the stains that were deposited on one side from stains deposited on the opposite side. As seen in Figure 3.33, a simple visual examination may not be sufficient to make the determination. This author has seen this issue in several types of material. Experimentation may be required on unusual or unfamiliar materials.

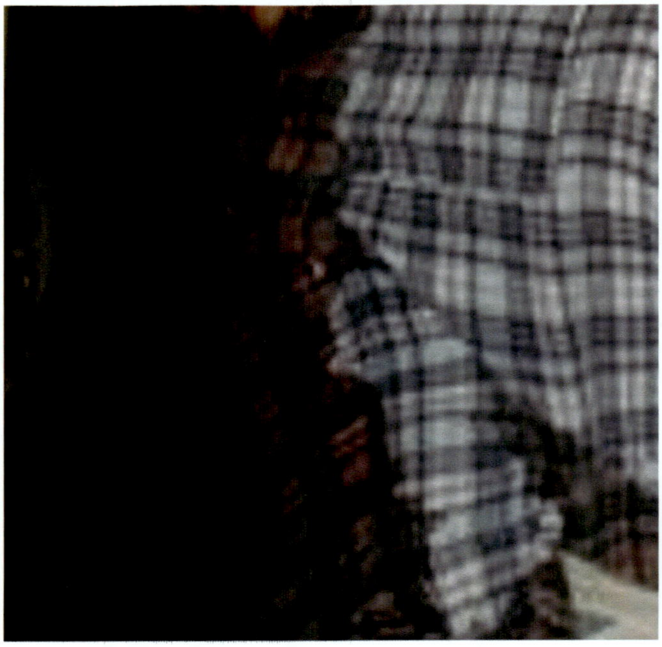

FIGURE 3.32 Diffusion and capillary action.

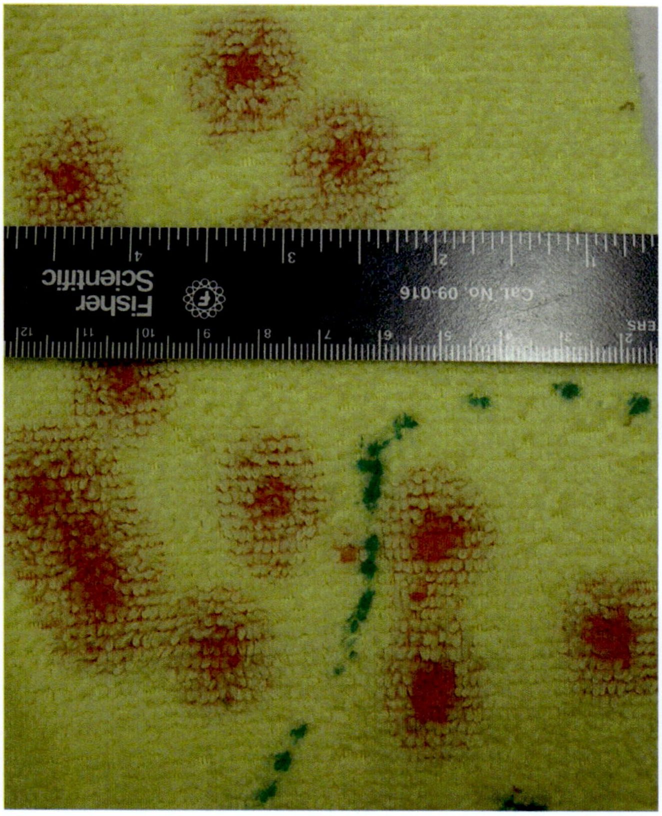

FIGURE 3.33 Microfiber material, green line separating stains deposited on opposite sides.

3.6.14 Insects (and Other Animals)

Not uncommonly, a victim or victims, whether by homicide, suicide, accidental, or natural deaths, are not discovered until they are significantly into the decomposition process. Indeed, sometimes the first indication of a dead body may be extensive fly activity around the trunk of a car, for example, or vultures circling in an outdoor area. Maggots can ingest up to approximately 95% of a body's mass, who will then turn into flies. Flies can create very small stains that may be confusing to the analyst at a scene where other small stains may be present, such as a beating or shooting. The appearance of these artifacts may differ from dome-shaped, as a result of the sucking action of their proboscis (sometimes characterized as "lappers and suckers" as opposed to "biters" like a horsefly), to a swiped appearance as a result of defecation, or transferred from walking through liquid blood.

These stains are often seen concentrated around light sources, windows, and ceilings and may also be found on a variety of surfaces, including on the deceased's body and clothing. One of the defining features of these "patterns" is that there is no pattern—there is no defined area of convergence. Figure 3.34 shows an overall view of bloodstains created by flies around the base of a lamp.

FIGURE 3.34 Fly artifacts around a lamp base. (Courtesy of HLM.)

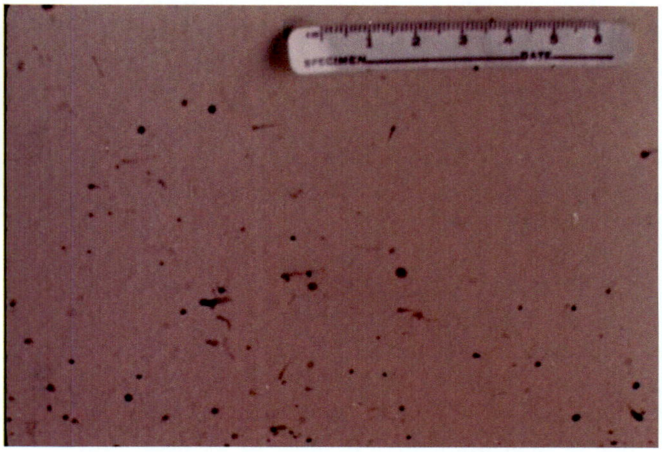

FIGURE 3.35 Close-up of fly artifacts on a ceiling. (Courtesy of HLM.)

Note the void between the ring of stains and the base of the lamp. Likewise, it is common to see bloodstains all around an exposed bulb, but not on the bulb itself, if on. Figure 3.35 shows a close-up image of some of the stains from the same scene, on the ceiling. Note the variable appearance of the stains in addition to the random apparent "directionality." Some additional items to consider when evaluating if the stains are related to the mechanism that caused death are as follows:

- Is there a lack of edge characteristics that would be expected on a given surface?
- Is there evidence of fly activity (alive or dead flies present)?
- Are there stains in other rooms that do not appear to be connected to the incident? Compare stains in other rooms to those near the body.
- Do they look like known fly artifacts?

3.6.15 Sequenced Bloodstains

It is not uncommon to find multiple and/or overlapping bloodstain patterns at the scene of a death or assault. This may occur for a variety of reasons, from an injured party simply moving around, to a prolonged struggle or assault to staging efforts. Sometimes, the sequence of pattern deposition can be ascertained and, therefore, can be utilized to help to corroborate or refute statements.

For example, at the scene of a beating as seen in Figure 3.36, the victim's husband said that he found his wife beaten when he arrived home. However, looking closely at the blood stains, shows that the sequence of events was s follows:

- Impact spatter deposited on the wall
- Palm print, confirmed to be the husband's, in blood, transferred to wall, and created the perimeter stains seen as his palm wiped out the center of the impact spatter on the wall
- Additional impact spatter deposited on top of the palm print

Can the husband's statement be true? It can be concluded that the person who deposited the bloody handprint (the husband) was present after the beating began and before it ended. Therefore, his statement that he came home and found his wife at some point later is not consistent with the physical evidence.

Figure 3.37 was created in a laboratory setting by students in a basic bloodstain pattern analysis course. By examining the edge characteristics of the swipes, the order of deposition may be able to be determined; see the numbering on photo for order of deposition. The "newest" swipe will disrupt the edges of the previously deposited swipe if it is still at least partially wet.

Another example to consider is a scene where a clean-up was attempted and the body present at the scene. If the body does not disrupt the wiping pattern, it can be deduced that the body was placed there after the wiping occurred. Further, with a significant amount of blood, if no disrupted clots are present, this would indicate that the wiping occurred while the blood was still quite fresh, which may help confirm or refute suspect or witness statements with regard to a timeline of events.

There are several more types of sequencing stains that may be observed that can answer many different types of questions; the preceding figures are a few examples. When determining sequence from photographs, the analyst should be conservative, because in certain circumstances, the determination may not be as straightforward as the figures shown here.

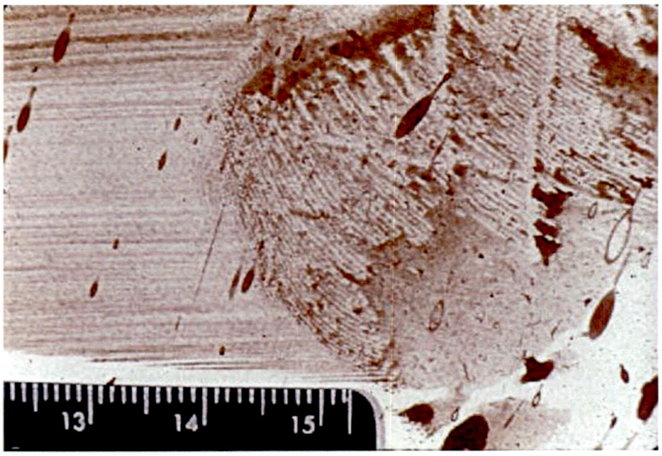

FIGURE 3.36 Sequenced impact spatter, palm transfer creating perimeter stains, then additional impact spatter. (Courtesy of HLM.)

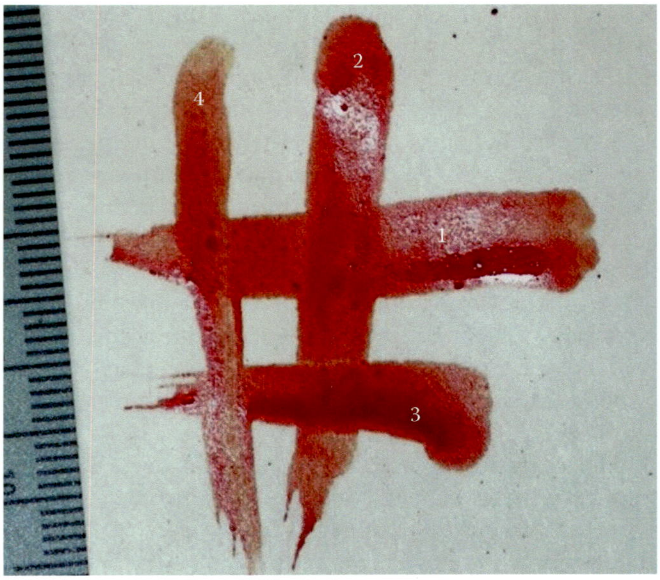

FIGURE 3.37 Sequenced swipe patterns.

3.6.16 Voids Patterns

The currently accepted definition of a void pattern is "an absence of blood in an otherwise continuous bloodstain or bloodstain pattern." Voids can help to place object and/or individuals within a scene.

Recall Figure 3.12 from the impact spatter section. There is a relative void where the victim's head was positioned during the administration of the beating.

Figure 3.38 depicts a laboratory-created void pattern. The target paper was placed behind the right side of the sneaker and a blood-soaked sponge was placed on the left side and was subsequently shot into with a .22 caliber

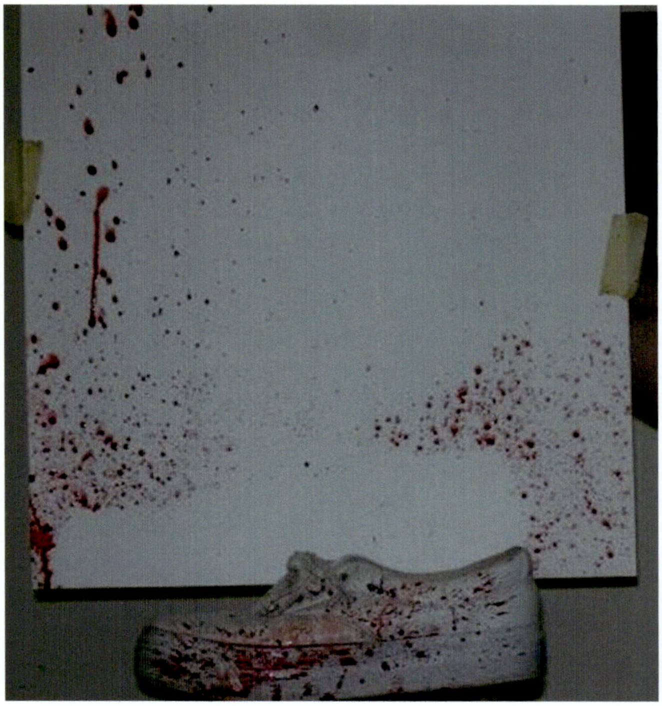

FIGURE 3.38 Laboratory-created void of a sneaker.

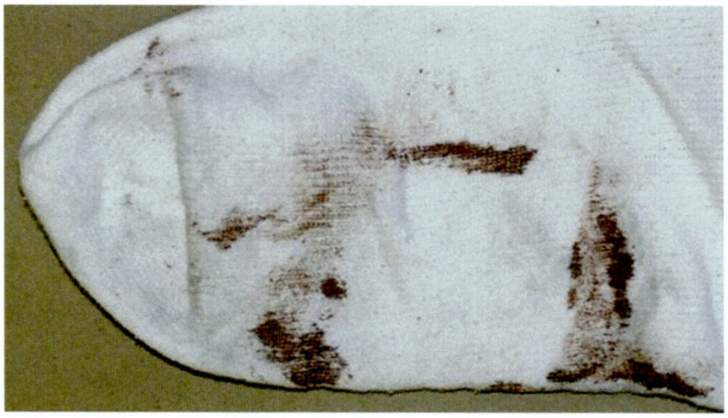

FIGURE 3.39 Void within a transfer pattern on a sock.

revolver. The void created by the sneaker, whose left side intercepted a portion of the bloodstains, can easily be seen on the target paper. Figure 3.39 reveals a square-shaped void within a transfer pattern on a sock recovered at the scene of a stabbing.

A void may reveal a recognizable pattern, or it may only show that something blocked the deposition of blood in that particular area. Voids are commonly seen in between transfer patterns on the extremities of a victim, which may assist with victim positioning. Likewise, voids on the clothing of suspects or victims may indicate how it was worn (e.g., buttoned or unbuttoned), folded, or creased at the time of blood deposition.

FIGURE 3.40 Door and wall with a stick-on ruler grid.

3.7 DOCUMENTATION

It is not uncommon for a bloodstain pattern analysis to be performed "remotely" from photographs and other case documentation. Sometimes, the conclusions that they analyst can reach regarding the significance of particular bloodstains is compromised as a result of incomplete or not appropriately gathered documentation.

Photography is critically important. Photographs should be taken with the standard overall, mid-range, and close-up (preferably macro, where very small stains are involved) protocol. After initial "as found" scene photography is complete, markers may be placed to assist in showing the orientation of the pattern in a particular photograph. This may be accomplished in many ways, depending on the nature and size of the area being photographed. Photographs should be taken in a manner such that the close-up photographs can be easily related to the overall scene. Some methods utilized are gridding off a large area, such as a wall, with either painter's tape, stick-on scales as seen in Figure 3.40, or markers. Individual stains may be circled, as in Figure 3.41,

FIGURE 3.41 Bloodstains on a wall circled by a marker.

to show the overall distribution from a distance. Scales should be utilized when photographing bloodstains, and they should be photographed at 90 degrees from the surface whenever possible to minimize any distortion.

Bloodstains on clothing may be highlighted in different ways as well. Some methods include ring reinforcers (with the paper backing still on), stick-on arrows, triangles created from masking tape, and so on. Clothing should be photographed prior to the placement of any marking devices. Consideration must also be given if there is going to be, or is likely to be, DNA testing.

Videography is also useful in documenting the spatial relationships among objects and stain patterns that may be difficult to discern from two-dimensional photographs.

Written documentation should accurately describe the overall pattern as well as the size, shape, distribution, and location of individual stains. The condition of the blood should also be described; for example, wet, dry, partially dry, crazed, and so on. Areas of bloodstaining can also be indicated on the scaled scene diagram using measurements from triangulation.

Collection of items with bloodstain patterns of interest, or that may be difficult or questionable should be collected in their entirety when possible. When considering bloodstaining on flooring, both a bloodstained sample and a control sample (without visible bloodstaining) should be collected. If carpeting, the carpet and padding should be collected and notation made as to the underlying surface (e.g., hardwood, cement). Additionally, these samples should be labeled so as to indicate what their positions were within the carpet/flooring. Compass directions and measurements via triangulation may be useful in achieving this. The control sample(s) should be sufficient so that both prosecution and defense analysts have adequate material on which experiments can be conducted if necessary. Each person maintains their floors/carpets differently, so the best way to carry out case-specific experiments as closely as possible to the actual conditions is to use flooring from that particular scene. If flooring cannot be collected for logistical or storage reasons, it should be described as thoroughly as possible (e.g., marble tile with apparently sealed grout, linoleum with a hazy appearance). This will allow experts to reconstruct as closely as possible if the case requires a reconstruction. Swabs of wet or dry stains (collected with a swab wet with sterile water) should be collected from a representative sample of each discrete area of bloodstain patterns and from those stains which appear "out of place" (e.g., a passive stain on the back of a single victim found facedown) for presumptive and DNA testing to assist in placing participants in their relative positions in reconstruction efforts, if necessary.

Multiple documentation methods should be utilized to thoroughly document a scene. There may appear to be some overlap in documentation, but it is better to have redundancy instead of a gap that may turn out to be critical. When documenting a scene, the investigator should ask him- or herself, "Could someone unfamiliar with this scene review my documentation and reconstruct this scene?" If the answer is "no," then there must be a gap in documentation that should be revisited.

3.8 PRESUMPTIVE TESTING AND CHEMICAL ENHANCEMENT

The definition of "presumptive" according to merriam-webster.com (Presumptive, n.d.), is "giving grounds for reasonable opinion or belief." Therefore, when conducting presumptive testing either on scene or in the laboratory, a positive result does *not* mean that the suspected stain/sample is, in fact, blood. A positive presumptive test gives the analyst grounds for reasonable belief that the substance is blood and that he or she can continue with the investigation as if it were blood, pending confirmatory or DNA testing.

Historically, the chain of testing was as follows: presumptive → confirmatory → species determination → DNA. Today however, it is very common that the intermediate steps are not performed, and a sample is sent for DNA testing after a positive presumptive test is obtained.

There are a number of presumptive tests available: catalytic color tests, such as phenolphthalein (PTH) (also known as Kastle-Meyer or KM), leucocrystal violet (LCV), Hemastix, leucomalachite green, tetramethylbenzidine (TMB) as well as chemiluminescent and fluorescent preparations. Hexagon OBTI is currently the only presumptive test available that can make the analyst more confident that a suspected sample is, in fact, human blood. While false positives have occurred with some primate blood samples, it did not react with blood from common domestic and farm animals.

It is good practice to collect two swabs of a stain and utilize one for presumptive testing and one to submit for DNA testing, as many of the color tests can render the sample useless for DNA testing. Catalytic color tests are tests that function by utilizing a chromogen solution (color) that is oxidized, usually by a 3% hydrogen peroxide, which is catalyzed by the presence of hemoglobin, and results in a visible color change. These tests should be read within a few seconds of the completion of the application of solutions to the swabs, or the results are not reliable.

Examples of tests that produce light instead of color are chemicals such as Luminol, BlueStar Forensic, and Fluorescein, that are luminescent (Luminol, BlueStar) and fluorescent (Fluorescein), respectively. These chemicals are typically used to identify areas of bloodshed after a cleanup or to enhance bloodstains that may be on a substrate where visualization of bloodstains is difficult. When photographing chemiluminescent or fluorescent reactions, it is preferable to use a technique that reveals both the reaction and the surrounding location. This can be achieved by either "painting with light" or rear-curtain sync techniques. Some agencies will take a photograph of the area in normal light conditions, followed by the chemical enhancement of the same area (that typically looks like areas of light on a black background) and then layer the two photographs in a photo-editing program. While this technique is not impermissible, there are a few steps that should be taken to ensure admissibility. First, once the image of the "normal" lighting conditions is obtained, a tripod must be used. Second, a scale should be placed for the normal light conditions, photographed and left in place for the chemical reaction photographs. The scale will serve as proof that the camera was not moved from its original position and provide an "anchor" to utilize when the photos are layered in the photo-editing program. Unscaled photos, or one scaled photograph with one unscaled photograph, should not be used for layering purposes. Additionally, each step in the photo-editing process should be documented, whether within the software program, in writing, or both, so that the composite image can be deconstructed and reconstructed following the documented steps, by a third party.

All presumptive tests are subject to some false positive results—which is a positive reaction from a substance other than blood, such as vegetable peroxidases and chemical oxidants. There are several studies available that examine the specificity (how likely the test is to react to materials other than blood) and sensitivity (how low of a concentration of blood will the test detect). For color tests, if there is an apparent color reaction before the addition of the oxidizing agent, this is also considered a false positive.

Apparent partial prints in blood may be enhanced to further reveal either ridge or tread detail for potential comparison. Some commonly used chemicals for this purpose include amido black, Hungarian red, aqueous leucocrystal violet, and Coomassie Brilliant Blue. There are advantages and disadvantages to each, and the method should be chosen based on the substrate and the potential probative value.

Positive and negative controls should be performed immediately prior to use in case work to assure that the chemicals are functioning properly. It should be noted that this is a very brief overview of presumptive testing to acquaint the reader with some of the commonly used chemicals. A great deal of literature exists that covers additional testing and enhancement methods.

3.9 EVALUATING A BLOODSTAIN CASE

A bloodstain pattern analyst may be asked to conduct an analysis at various points in the criminal justice process—from responding to a fresh crime scene to evaluating a cold case. This section will also be an overview of some of the most important issues to consider when evaluating a bloodstain case, regardless of where it is within the process, rather than a comprehensive reference manual.

When examining a crime scene, or physical evidence, proper personal protective equipment (PPE) should be utilized. All biological material should be considered infectious and handled accordingly. Additionally, the scene and evidence must be protected from contamination by the analyst. At a fresh scene, a preliminary walk-through should be conducted, initial observations noted, and assessment of what PPE, equipment and personnel will be necessary.

The reconstruction of a bloodstained scene requires the input from other disciplines and information sources, such as the autopsy report, hospital records, witness statements, DNA and other laboratory testing.

Initially, patterns should be identified and described based solely on their size, shape, distribution, and location, without attempting to attribute a specific event that created the pattern—this will be done later. For example, a pattern consisting of small, round stains, between 1 and 3 millimeters in diameter, is located on a wall approximately 12 inches above the floor. The "differential diagnoses" based on this information could be impact spatter, satellite spatter or expirated bloodstains. If there is no pooling of blood nearby, nor evidence that one was cleaned up, or that an object onto which dripping may have occurred had been removed, satellite spatter may be ruled out. After review of EMS, hospital, autopsy reports, scene and autopsy photographs, there is no documentation of blood in the nose, mouth, airway, airway injury, or positioning of the victim such that an expirated pattern is possible (such as breathing into a pool of blood), then expirated bloodstains may be ruled out. This would leave impact spatter and the most likely pattern and would then be correlated with the injuries.

Once DNA testing results are obtained, it may be possible to place individuals in their respective positions. This is especially important when multiple victims are involved.

Each case will have different information available for review. It is important to note that the analyst may find him- or herself in the position of not having sufficient information on which to base an opinion, or many overlapping, complex and/or altered patterns that make rendering an opinion difficult or impossible. It is critical that the analyst recognizes this and reports only conclusions that can be supported by the available evidence.

Several examples of worksheets are available to ensure that examinations are systematic and thorough, whether it is of a scene, clothing, vehicle, or other items of evidence. It is not uncommon for a defense of an accused to be something like, "Look at all the blood at this scene. No blood was found on Mr. Jones' person, clothes or vehicle. Mr. Jones could not have been involved in this crime and not gotten any blood on himself!" Research by MacDonell and Kish has coined the axiom in bloodstain pattern analysis that "absence of evidence is not evidence of absence." This means that simply because a suspect has little or no blood on his or her person or clothing does not mean that he/she was not involved in the incident. There are a number of factors that determine whether or not an assailant becomes spattered with blood, as mentioned earlier, including but not limited to the following:

- The nature of the weapon (length, mass, arc of swing) utilized
- Direction of the blows or sharp force trauma
- The number of wounds and if covered by clothing or hair
- Duration of assault
- The assailant discarded clothing worn during assault and cleaned him- or herself up
- Assailant committed the assault while naked, subsequently cleaned up
- Assailant utilized outer protective clothing

3.10 CONCLUSION

Bloodstain pattern analysis can be a valuable investigative tool. If crime scene investigators and homicide detectives participate in a basic bloodstain pattern analysis course, while it will not make them instant "experts," it will assist them in identifying, understanding and preserving valuable bloodstain evidence for evaluation by an expert that might otherwise be overlooked and lost. Proper documentation is critical for a useful bloodstain pattern analysis.

It should be remembered that bloodstain pattern analysis should be utilized as another "tool" in the investigative toolbox. Because several stain patterns can appear similar to one another, although caused by different mechanisms, one should be critical of an analyst or expert who concludes that a given pattern could have occurred only by one particular mechanism. For instance, in the aforementioned example of the 1–3 millimeter-sized pattern on the wall 12 inches from the floor—if blood was found in the nose and/or mouth of the victim, then the best opinion that can be rendered is that the pattern is *either* impact spatter *or* expirated. For this reason, bloodstain pattern analysis is frequently better utilized in identifying what *could not* have happened.

It is better to be conservative in one's opinion rather than reporting or testifying to opinions that cannot be supported by the physical evidence. The analyst may want to keep in mind, "Would I want to be convicted based on this evidence?" when forming conclusions. If an analyst is unable to be objective, the case should be referred to another analyst. Case-specific experimentation may need to be performed, and if evidence and control samples are properly collected, this will allow the analyst to render the best opinions.

Finally, this chapter on bloodstain pattern analysis is not all inclusive, but meant to assist with understanding some of the basic tenants, procedures and challenges that exist in this discipline.

BIBLIOGRAPHY

Genesis 4:10–12 (King James Version). (n.d.) In *Bible Tools*. Retrieved from https://www.bibletools.org/index.cfm/fuseaction/Bible.show/sVerseID/90/eVerseID/90. Accessed July 5, 2015.

James, S., Kish, P. and Sutton, T.P. 2005. *Principles of Bloodstain Pattern Analysis, Theory and Practice*. Boca Raton, FL: CRC Press/ Taylor & Francis.

MacDonell, H.L. 2005. *Bloodstain Patterns*, Second Revised Edition. Elmira, NY: Golos Printing.

Presumptive. (n.d.). In *Merriam Webster online*. Retrieved from http://www.merriam-webster.com/dictionary/presumptive (Accessed July 5, 2015).

Sears, D.W. 2002. Overview of hemoglobin's structure/function relationships. *Biochemistry and Molecular Biology Education*, 30(3):208.

Secomb, T.W. 1991. Red blood cell mechanics and rheology. *Cell Biophysics*, 18(3):231–251.

CHAPTER 4

Latent Print Examination

Andrew R. Reitnauer

CONTENTS

4.1 INTRODUCTION

The use of fingerprints as a means of personal identification has been used for centuries. Through centuries-old findings, scientists have found that a person's fingerprints were used on stone carving, to leave a personal mark on pottery, and to sign legal documents. Throughout the centuries, the use of fingerprints evolved into a means of personal identification, through the application of a systematic classifications system. The continued advancement of these records is still in use today and is the primary source of individual identification in forensic science.

The 20th century has seen the development of fingerprint processing and collection techniques, allowing examiners and technicians to develop and preserve fingerprint impressions at a crime scene for comparison to known exemplar records. In addition, the advent of digital photography and imaging enhancement has revolutionized the capture of impression evidence beyond the limits of the traditional film darkroom. The International Association for Identification, one of the world's oldest forensic science organizations, has recognized the value of digital imaging as the progression of photography in forensic science. Through the fundamental principles, founded in the traditional sciences of biology, physiology, and physics, the development of fingerprint identification has become a widely accepted means of personal identification.

4.2 HISTORY

Homo sapiens are a subset of the phylum Mammalia. As a part of the early zoological research done by Klaatsch, Reh, Hepburn, Whipple, and Wilder, the formation of volar pads in mammals, and specifically the formation of friction ridge skin in primates, was examined. Their research founded many of the original theories of the development of the hands and feet, and through the additional research of Grew and Bidloo, the anatomical structure of friction ridge skin began to form. In 1685, Marcello Malphighi published his research on the structure and formation of the layers of the skin. Following his research, Mayer and Purkinje continued to develop the theories concerning friction ridge skin, and began to formulate the principles of individuality in reference to a person's fingerprints.

Beginning in the 19th century, researchers and police professionals began to apply the knowledge of their scientific predecessors to the needs of the criminal justice system and government. Sir William Herschel began to use the individuality of friction ridge impressions to validate records and contracts in India. He continued this practice, and expanded the collection of fingerprint records as the Magistrate and Collector at Hooghly, applying them in their criminal court and record system. He is also credited with some of the first research proving the persistency of fingerprints throughout one's lifetime. Dr. Henry Faulds, who conducted medicolegal research, wrote a letter to Charles Darwin in 1880, citing the uniqueness of one's fingerprints, publishing some of his findings in a letter in *Nature*, entitled "On the Skin-Furrows of the Hand" (Faulds, 1880). Faulds published his findings prior to Herschel; however, both men are credited with pioneering efforts in proving fingerprints as a viable means of personal identification. The use of a fingerprint as a means of personal identification in the United States can be linked to a receipt from Gilbert Thompson to acknowledge a financial transaction in 1882, as reported by Ashbaugh.

Perhaps the most well-known scientist in the early stages of fingerprint identification was Sir Francis Galton. He had received correspondence from Dr. Faulds regarding his research, and as an anthropologist, Galton began to explore the unique characteristics of fingerprints and their potential in personal identification. His research led him to compare the aspects of previous systems of identification against the principles of fingerprints. His well-known publication in 1892 described many of the features found in the ridges and furrows of fingerprints (Galton, 1892). This publication went on to describe the features found and their degree of uniqueness when applied to the population, in essence applying the science of fingerprint identification to some population statistics, proving their ultimate value.

While a member of the Central Police Department at La Plata, Argentina, Juan Vucetich began to collect the fingerprints of convicted criminals. By 1891, he had devised a fingerprint classification system (Ashbaugh, 2000). On June 19, 1892, two murdered children were found by their illegitimate mother, Francisca Rojas. Upon examining the scene of the crime, the inspector located a bloodstain, containing a fingerprint, on the bedroom door. The piece of the door was removed and compared to the fingerprint card taken from Francisca Rojas. The impression was identified as her right thumb, leading to an admission that she had killed the children. During the same time, Sir Edward Henry, the Inspector General of Police in the Bengal Province of India, was exploring the systems of personal identification; currently the primary system was anthropometry or Bertillionage, which used the physical measurements of the body, as designed by Alphonse Bertillion. Anthropometry was widely used and accepted until the case of Will West. In 1903, two inmates at Leavenworth Penitentiary named Will West and William West were incarcerated. Both men had a similar record using Bertillionage. William West was already incarcerated for a crime during the time Will West committed his offense. Their fingerprints allowed the two men to be distinguished with separate records (Will West). Henry's exploration lead him to devise a classification system for fingerprints, known as the Henry System, which is still in use today. Following the presentation by Detective John Ferrier of Scotland Yard at the 1904 World's Fair regarding the evolution of fingerprints as reported by these scientists, the current value of fingerprints in the criminal justice system and forensic science became clear.

During the 20th century, a number of advancements were made regarding the use of fingerprints to identify individuals. The use of fingerprint evidence in criminal proceedings became a hallmark in the investigatory process. Detectives and crime scene responders became adept at the development and recovery of latent fingerprint evidence, with the evolution of the physical and chemical processing methods. The application of the ACE-V methodology, as termed by David Ashbaug, became the standard methodology used in the scientific examination of latent print evidence. The methodology has evolved further in today's scientific laboratories, with the application of human factors and quality assurance measures that have helped safeguard the proper application of the scientific basis for conclusion during the examination process.

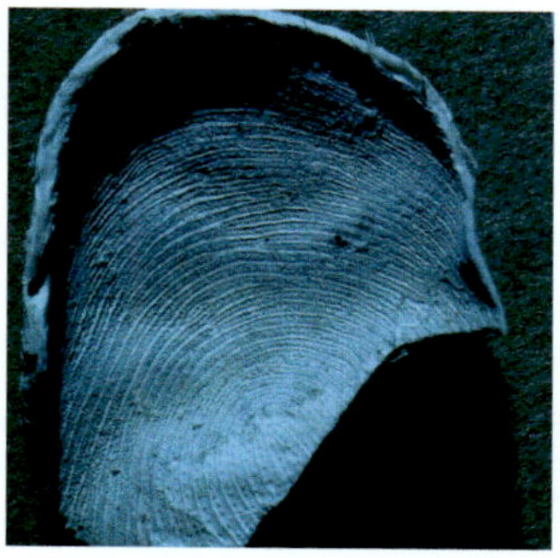

FIGURE 4.1 The base of the epidermis. (Courtesy of Ioan Truta.)

FIGURE 4.2 Example of a permanent injury to the skin. (Courtesy of Ioan Truta.)

4.3 PHYSIOLOGY

The two fundamental principles regarding fingerprints as a means of personal identification, permanence and uniqueness, are founded on the physiological basis of skin formation. The skin is composed of two overall layers, the dermis and the epidermis. The dermis is the innermost layer, and the epidermis is the outer layer, which is where the friction ridges used in forensic examinations are found. As cells are developed by the body, they begin in the basal layers of the dermis, where they continue to develop and migrate outward into the epidermis, where the body continually sheds cells in favor of new ones. Due to the specific structure of these two layers, they maintain a specific formation due to the desmosomes present in the membrane found between the papillary region of the dermis and the basal layer of the epidermis.

The epidermis is composed of five layers, which aid in the development of skin cells migrating to the outer layer. The epidermis is composed of the stratum corneum, stratum lucidum, stratum granulosum, stratum spinosum, and stratum basale. As evident in the figures that follow, there is a specific structure between the epidermis and the dermis. These peaks and valleys continue throughout the entire structure, resulting in the formation of the friction ridges and furrows. This anatomical structure is what leads to the principle of permanence. Throughout a person's lifetime, his or her fingerprints will remain the same, until death and decomposition. Figure 4.1 is a photograph of the base of the epidermis. Visible are the friction ridges, furrows and sweat glands. During the course of one's lifetime, temporary damage can occur to the layers of the skin. If the damage is limited to the epidermal layers, the natural healing process of the skin will replace the damaged cells, and the features of the friction ridge skin will remain the same. If the dermal layer of the skin is damaged, the resulting effect on the epidermal friction ridge detail will be visible in the formation of a scar or similar feature. Figure 4.2 is an example of the resulting effect of a permanent injury of the dermal layer of the skin.

The principle of uniqueness is formed during fetal development. While the overall pattern types may have some genetic influence, the specific individual characteristics are formed during pressure and movement in utero. The location of the volar pads during gestational growth has been shown to have a direct influence on the ultimate pattern type. Volar pads that develop in the center of the distal phalange will become a whorl. If the volar pad develops in a more proximal location on the distal phalange, the resulting fingerprint pattern type will become an arch. Volar pads that develop off center of the distal phalange will become a loop.

The specific ridge pathways that subsequently develop are dependent on the influences born by the fetus during gestation. These specific ridge pathways are what allow fingerprints to be unique to an individual. While identical twins share DNA, they will not have the same fingerprints, which has been proven through research.

4.4 LATENT PRINT DEVELOPMENT

There are three types of fingerprints when considering their deposition on a surface area: latent, patent, and plastic. A latent print is a chance impression left by the contact of the palmar surface of the hands or the plantar surface of the feet onto a secondary surface. These types of impressions are generally invisible to the naked eye, and require an application of a physical or chemical technique to make them visible. Examples of both a patent print (Figure 4.3a) and a plastic print (Figure 4.3b) are provided. A patent print is a type of impression that is readily visible to the naked eye, and has been deposited in ink, mud, blood, or other matrix. Plastic prints are a three-dimensional impression that have been casted into the surface that was contacted. Surfaces such as clay or putty may create a topographic impression of the print. These types of impressions may be recovered through photographic or casting means.

Physical evidence can be divided into two basic categories when considering the application of latent print development techniques: porous and nonporous. Porous evidence is a type of surface that is readily permeable to water such as paper or cardboard. Nonporous evidence is a type of surface that does not absorb water. These types of surfaces may be glass, metal, or plastic, among others. The recognition of the type of evidence received will determine the sequence of development techniques used.

In discussing the various development methods, one must consider the potential permanent, or destructive, nature of the technique to the item. The most common form of a nondestructive development technique is light. Whether applied through ambient lighting, or through the use of an alternate light source (ALS) or forensic laser, the matrix of the impression may have a reaction with the light energy, allowing the friction ridge detail to become visible. The light does not have a destructive property to the physical evidence, with a caveat being any subsequent biological testing in the presence of shortwave UV light, as it may have a denaturing effect. Another example of a nondestructive technique is the use of fingerprint powders. In general, these particulates will adhere to the matrix of the impression, but may be wiped off of the surface area. Many of the chemical reagents that are used, and will be discussed further, are destructive, meaning they have a permanent reaction to the surface area.

When examining evidence, the examiner should always begin with a visual examination of the item—not only to observe any patent or plastic impressions, but to also examine the item for other forms of trace evidence (e.g., hairs and fibers) for collection. At any point of the examination process, if any friction ridge detail is observed that may be suitable for examination purposes, it should be either lifted or photographed following proper collection methods. In addition to the initial visual examination, the examiner may also wish to employ an ALS examination, in order to determine if any impressions are present that may have a natural reaction to the light wavelength; in addition, certain biological materials may fluoresce under an ALS.

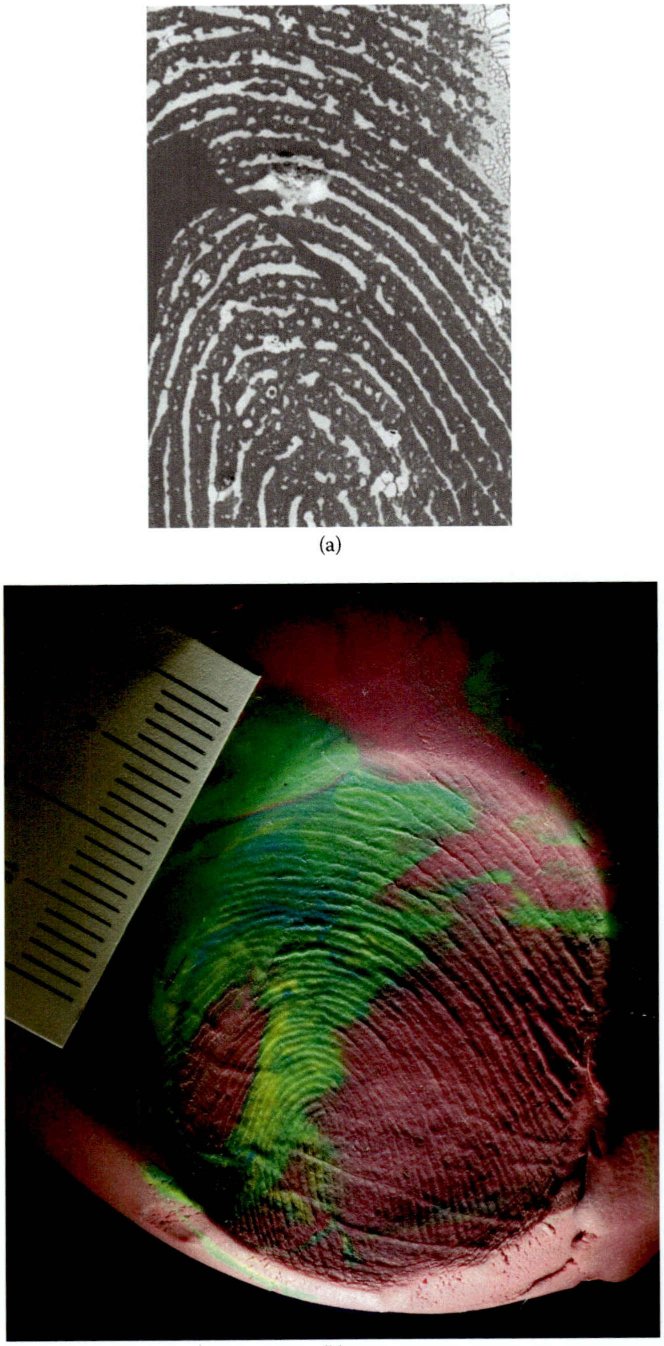

(a)

(b)

FIGURE 4.3 Examples of (a) a patent print and (b) a plastic print. (Courtesy of Andrew Reitnauer.)

4.4.1 Iodine Fuming

Iodine fuming is a technique that is used on porous items to develop latent impressions. The iodine is applied via a wand within an iodine chamber to sublimate the crystals into vapor. When exposed to the iodine vapors, the sebaceous components of the latent print matrix will react to form a light brown reaction. The development is a temporary reaction, thus the results must be photographed immediately. Iodine fuming should be performed under conditions of adequate ventilation. This technique should also not be performed on a live human, due to a possible allergic reaction to the skin.

4.4.2 Hydrochloric Acid Fuming

Hydrochloric acid, or muriatic acid, may be used to develop latent impressions on porous items, especially thermal paper. This technique must be performed in a safe and ventilated area. The item being processed should be held over the container holding the acid. The acidic fumes emitted from the liquid acid will develop with the matrix of the latent impression, resulting in a light green development.

4.4.3 1,8-Diazafluoren-9-One (DFO)

DFO is a fluorescent development technique used on porous items. This reagent is quite sensitive to the amino acids present in the latent print matrix. The reagent is sprayed onto the surface of the item and allowed to air-dry. The item must then be placed into an oven at 100°C for 20 minutes. The resulting development may be viewed under an ALS or forensic laser at a range of 495 nm to 550 nm, using an orange- or red-colored filter. The resulting development must be photographed, as DFO cannot be physically lifted from the item. This technique may be employed as a part of a sequential method; however, it must be used prior to the application of ninhydrin (Figure 4.4).

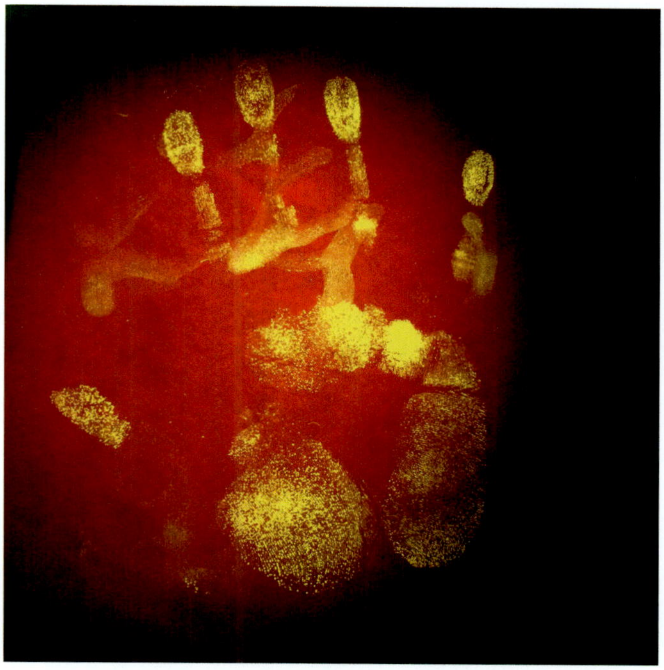

FIGURE 4.4 A result of the DFO technique. (Courtesy of Andrew Reitnauer.)

4.4.4 1,2-Indanedione

1,2-Indanedione is a reagent with a similar application and visualization as DFO. The exception being that 1,2-Indanedione does not require the application of a heat source to develop. This reagent is also an optimal processing technique for use on thermal paper, as the chemical carriers in DFO and ninhydrin may be detrimental to the examination process through a negative reaction with the item. 1,2-Indanedione must be given 72 hours to completely react with latent impressions on thermal paper. The evidence should be visually examined every 24 hours and impressions must be photographed upon visualization. 1,2-Indanedione can also be used in a similar manner as DFO for the development of latent impressions on nonthermal paper. It should be used in a similar method, or in accordance with manufacturer instructions.

4.4.5 Ninhydrin

Ninhydrin or triketohydrindene hydrate is a reagent used on porous items where the development of the latent impressions is a reaction resulting in Ruhemann's purple. The reagent is applied under adequate ventilation conditions, and the application of heat and humidity will accelerate the reaction. Like DFO and 1,2-Indanedione, Ninhydrin is sensitive to the amino acids present in the latent print matrix. While a notable part of the sequential process for porous items, this technique must be applied following the application to DFO, as it will inhibit any subsequent reactions by DFO. Ninhydrin does have a limitation when processing thermal paper, as some of the carriers may adversely react with the item (Figure 4.5).

Ninhydrin may also be used to develop blood impressions on porous surfaces due to its sensitivity to the amino acids in blood. Another application for ninhydrin is its application to raw wood surfaces (Table of Reagents Program). It is recommended to allow the reaction a full 24 hours to complete, and all developed impressions must be photographed.

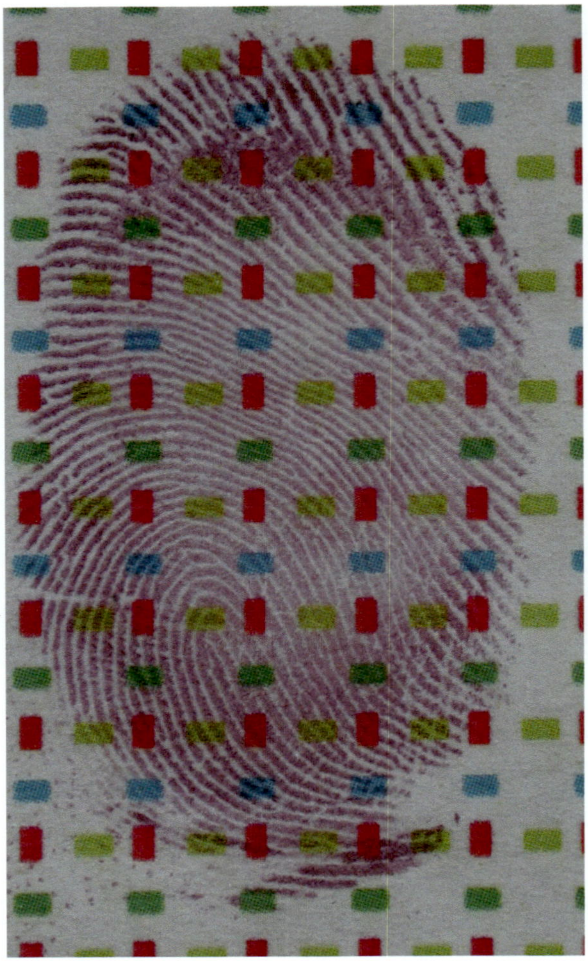

FIGURE 4.5 Example of the ninhydrin technique. (Courtesy of Danielle O'Neill.)

FIGURE 4.6 Example of the zinc chloride technique. (Courtesy of Danielle O'Neill.)

4.4.6 Zinc Chloride

Zinc chloride is a fluorescent technique that is traditionally applied following the development of latent impressions after ninhydrin. The reagent is applied, allowed to air-dry and placed into an oven at 80°–100°C for 40 minutes. This reagent is also sensitive to the components of 1,2-Indanedione and may be used in conjunction when processing evidence to enhance the reactions of these two techniques individually. The visualization for zinc chloride is approximately 500 nm and an orange barrier filter must be used. Any developed impressions must be photographed (Figure 4.6).

4.4.7 Silver Nitrate/Physical Developer

Silver nitrate and physical developer can be discussed together, as silver nitrate is the active reagent in the physical developer solution. A single-step silver nitrate spray reagent is available through some manufacturers; however, physical developer is a multistep development technique. The initial step is a maleic acid prewash for 10 minutes. This prewash step regulates the pH levels of the item, allowing the working solution to properly react with the sebaceous components of the latent print matrix. Examiners must be aware that the application of any outside source of metal will impact the development process. Physical developer is also a preferred reagent for use on items that may have been wet, raw wood or on paper currency. Special disposal may be required due to the presence of silver.

4.4.8 Cyanoacrylate

Cyanoacrylate fuming, or commonly referred to as superglue fuming, is a commonly used technique to develop latent prints on nonporous evidence. In the late 1970s, Japanese scientists discovered the application of cyanoacrylate fuming to the development of latent prints during biological examinations on glass slides (Fingerprint Sourcebook). During this time, the primary means of fingerprint development had been traditional powders;

FIGURE 4.7 Example of the cyanoacrylate technique. (Courtesy of Danielle O'Neill.)

however, this discovery changed the scope of latent print examination. The active chemical, cyanoacrylate, binds to the aqueous components of the latent print matrix. The resulting reaction is a polymerization of the latent print matrix, resulting in a white residue that secures the latent print to the surface area. The application of heat and humidity will enhance the development process as well. Cyanoacrylate is an initial step in examining nonporous evidence that has a great deal of sensitivity in its development potential. The application must be performed either in a chamber or in an area with adequate ventilation, as cyanoacrylate fumes are extremely harmful (Figure 4.7).

4.4.9 Ardrox/Basic Yellow/Rhodamine 6G/MBD/RAY/RAM

This group of processing reagents are all post-cyanoacrylate fluorescent dye stains. They may be composed of different carriers; however, in all of them the active chemical dye is absorbed by the residue left during the cyanoacrylate development process. All of them require a forensic light source, such as an ALS or laser, in order to visualize them properly. Depending on the dye stain used

TABLE 4.1 Reagent Wavelength

Reagent	Wavelength	Barrier Filter
Ardrox	350 nm–435 nm	Yellow
Basic Yellow	415 nm–485 nm	Yellow/Orange
MBD	415 nm–505 nm	Yellow/Orange
Rhodamine 6G (Basic Red 1)	495 nm–540 nm	Orange
RAM (R6G/Ardrox/MBD)	Follow the wavelength and barrier for desired reagent reaction.	
RAY (R6G/Ardrox/Basic Yellow)		

during the examination process, the wavelength used for excitation and the color of the barrier filter will change. Table 4.1 shows the various light wavelengths and barrier colors required for these techniques. The examiner can use different dye stains depending on the circumstances of the examination, and to achieve the desired resulting contrast between the latent impression and the background of the substrate.

4.4.10 Small Particle Reagent

Small particle reagent or SPR is a solution that may be sprayed onto a surface area. It is a suspension of powder in a carrier reagent, and is available in white or black. Small particle reagent must be applied to a surface that is or has been wet. The solution is sprayed onto the surface and allowed to run across the surface, adhering to the latent print matrix.

4.4.11 Gentian Violet

Gentian violet, or crystal violet, is a reagent that is used to develop latent impressions on the sticky side of tape. The active reagent is a biological stain sensitive to the sebaceous components of cells. This dye may also be used to process items that may have been contaminated by fats or oils. The reagent is applied by spraying or dipping, followed by a rinse of distilled water, and may be repeated until the desired reaction is obtained. Once allowed to air-dry, developed latent impressions must be photographed. One must be mindful when photographing transparent tape that the photograph be taken of the side with the developed impression, or the resulting image will be laterally reversed.

4.4.12 Sticky Side Powder

Sticky side powder is a reagent for the development of latent prints on the sticky side on adhesive tape. The powder is suspended in a solution containing a detergent. Upon mixture to the specified proportions, the mixture is applied to the tape and rinsed using distilled water. The powder adheres to the latent print residue, resulting in a gray-colored development. The resulting impressions must be photographed, following the caveat described above.

4.4.13 Sudan Black

Sudan black is a dye stain that is sensitive to oily and fatty compounds. This technique is applied to a surface by spraying or dipping and rinsed with distilled water. The development is a blue-black color. This technique is specifically applicable for the development of latent impressions on items that have been contaminated with grease or food. These results must be photographed for further examination

4.4.14 Powders

One of the oldest recognized methods of the development of latent impressions is through the use of fingerprint powders. The use of fingerprint powders had been well documented as the primary technique used both in the laboratory and at crime scenes for decades. The use of fingerprint powders has the advantage of not requiring the safety precautions of many of the chemical reagents, while one must be cognizant of any respiratory hazards. One of the main advantages to using fingerprint powders is the immediate result obtained once the powder has been applied. Any resulting impression may be photographed and/or lifted for further examination. As the primary objective in developing any latent impression is to maximize the contrast between the friction ridge detail and the substrate for further comparative purposes, there are a large number of fingerprint powders available.

There are four basic types of fingerprint powders, with some variations within. The first is traditional black powder. Typically composed of a carbon-based particulate, the powder is applied with a fiberglass brush by spinning the brush bristles over the area being examined. Any latent print detail will adhere to the particulates. Carbon black, silk black, and the dark components of bichromatic powders will develop a "black" impression on the lighter background. The second type of powder is a traditional white powder. The primary component in current products is titanium dioxide. This type of powder is applied in the same manner as traditional black powder. White, silk white, gray and bichromatic powders will all develop a "white" impression on a darker background. The third type of powder is magnetic. This type of fingerprint powder is applied through the use of a magnetic "wand" style brush. The ferrous particles in the powder mixture adhere to the magnet of the brush and may be lightly applied to the surface of the item. These powders may be dark or light in color, depending on the color of the surface being examined.

FIGURE 4.8 Fingerprint powders. (Courtesy of Danielle O'Neill.)

The final type of fingerprint powders are fluorescent powders. These powders are available in a variety of colors and are visualized through the use of an ALS or forensic laser. These powders are often used on multi-colored surfaces. If photographed, these impressions may require the use of a barrier filter on order to optimize contrast. All types of latent impressions developed may be lifted; however, to examine the lift of a fluorescent impression, the examiner will also require an ALS or laser (Figure 4.8).

4.5 BLOOD REAGENTS

When examining evidence for the presence of fingerprint or palm print impressions, patent prints in blood may be encountered. These types of impressions will require specialized treatment and equipment due to the presence of potential biohazard conditions. An agency's procedures will determine the collection order, methods and testing of any biological material due to the overall considerations of future testing. All blood impressions should be photographed and documented prior to the application of any development reagent. While research has shown that the traditional application of cyanoacrylate fuming and dye stains has not had a detrimental effect on blood impressions, care must be exercised when treating these types of impressions (Pilla and Reitnauer, 2010). Blood impressions must be fixed to the surface prior to the application of the reagent to ensure proper development. Many commercially prepared reagents include the fixative within the reagent solution.

4.5.1 Amido Black

Amido black or napthalene black is a biological stain sensitive to the heme protein groups found in blood. Amido black has been a relied-upon technique in the laboratory setting; however, it may also be used at a crime scene. This reagent may be produced with a methanolic or aqueous carrier. The reagent is typically sprayed onto the surface area and rinsed with the appropriate rinsing agent. When developed, impressions that react with amido black are visualized with a blue-black reaction. Any impressions developed with amido black must be photographed (Figure 4.9).

4.5.2 Leucocrystal Violet

Leucocrystal violet is another type of biological stain sensitive to the proteins commonly found in blood. The reaction of leucocrystal violet (LCV) with blood impressions results in a purple development. However, LCV also has a fluorescent property that will react under the presence of an ALS. Any developed impressions must be photographed, and when utilizing the fluorescent property, the use of a barrier filter may be required.

FIGURE 4.9 Photograph of an amido black impression. (Courtesy of Danielle O'Neill.)

4.5.3 Hungarian Red/Acid Fuschin

Hungarian red is a fluorescent biological stain that reacts with blood proteins. The resulting reaction yields a pink-colored result. In addition to this visual property, Hungarian red is a fluorescent reagent. Under the influence of an ALS, the resulting impression will fluoresce at 515–560 nm. Hungarian red can also be lifted by allowing the reagent to absorb into a white gelatin lifter. These results must be photographed for further examination, and if lifted, the image must be laterally reversed.

4.5.4 Phloxine B

Phloxine B is a derivative of fluorescein, a biological stain for epithelial cells. The reaction with blood impressions results in a pink-colored reaction. This reagent has a secondary property to aid in visualization, where, under direct lighting applied at an appropriate angle, the resulting impression will appear silver due to a reflective property of the reaction. Phloxine B has been shown to have positive results on nontextured surfaces and on surfaces that would benefit from its reflective property (Agarwal et al., 2010). This technique must also be photographed, and may be effectively used at a crime scene.

4.5.5 Acid Yellow 7

Acid Yellow 7 is a fluorescent technique used to develop blood impressions, primarily on dark-colored surfaces. This is a multistep process that must be performed under proper ventilation in laboratory conditions. The first step is a blood fixative, followed by the actual dye stain, and a glacial acid rinse. Acid Yellow 7 fluoresces under 495 nm with a yellow barrier filter. Unlike the other blood reagents discussed, Acid Yellow 7 may be lifted using a black gelatin lifter. After placing the lift on the impression, the dye will transfer to the gelatin lifter and may be viewed under an ALS. This impression must be laterally reversed due to the lifting mechanism. This technique has been shown to be effective on textured surfaces (Agarwal et al., 2010). Unlike the other blood reagents discussed, Acid Yellow 7 may not be used at a crime scene due to the nature of the chemical development process.

4.6 PHOTOGRAPHY

4.6.1 Fundamental Principles

The two basic purposes for an analyst to photograph a subject is to (1) document a scene or object for overall purposes, and (2) capture an impression for critical comparisons. There are legal precedents to both of these categories, and the photographer should be aware of these prior to conducting forensic photography within the scope of examinations.

The legal precedent of an overall photograph was first set forth in 1859, in the case of *Luco et al. v. United States*, 23 Howard 515 (1859). This was a primary example of using flash photography to record a subject. It was determined that an overall photograph had to be "a fair and accurate representation of what was present," in this instance describing a reproduction of a document.

> *We have ourselves been able to compare these signatures by means of photographic copies and fully concur, from evidence oculis subjecta fidelibus, that the seal and the signatures of Pico [The governor of California who was alleged to have signed the grant. Author] are forgeries.*
>
> —*Luco et al. v. United States*, 23 Howard 515 (1859).

The precedent set forth is that the photographer must duplicate the conditions that were present at the time the photograph was taken, regardless of the file type. The lighting, objects, and color tones must be duplicated in the photograph. There has been photographic evidence excluded at trial due to a misuse of white balance, which can alter the colors within the image, or an image being out of focus. These types of errors can be prevented by a complete knowledge of the equipment being used, and the factors that can affect the image.

Impressions that are photographically captured for the purpose of critical comparisons follow different guidelines than overall images. These types of photographs must be over a threshold of resolution and clarity in order for a comparison between a known and unknown sample to be performed.

4.6.2 Types of Lighting

When photographing a subject, there are several types of lighting available for use. Some types of lighting are designed for overall photography, and some for macro photography. Overall lighting types are generally more powerful, requiring a dispersal of light in order to illuminate the subject or area. Macro lighting types are more concerned with angles and directionality. In all areas of photography, the proper use of light will directly determine the quality, and perhaps admissibility, of the image.

The most basic type of lighting is the use of ambient light. If photographing a subject out in the natural world, the sunlight present may be sufficient to illuminate the image. If photographing indoors, the designated lighting of the room may also be sufficient. Note that when using ambient lighting, adjusting the white balance becomes a paramount concern. Since the light is not from a controlled source, the photographer should be mindful of where the lighting source is, and what color temperature is present.

If macro photography is being performed for critical comparisons, all images must be captured when the camera is mounted on a tripod or copy stand (Figure 4.10). Ambient lighting can also be utilized in this type of photography; however, most images will require the use of additional lighting sources.

4.6.3 Macro Photography Lighting

When performing macro photography in a controlled lighting environment, there are a few different techniques that can be used to achieve an optimal result. These techniques focus on the intensity and angle of lighting, which can be used to eliminate glare, highlight contours, and increase contrast. The lighting styles of direct lighting, oblique lighting, bounce lighting, tented lighting, direct reflective lighting, and transmitted lighting can all be used independently or in a system to capture a proper image. As a general rule of thumb, when conducting macro photography, the camera should replace your eye. This means that if you are able to visualize an impression, the camera lens should replace the photographer's eye, while maintaining the lighting system used.

Direct lighting is performed by the use of lighting positioned at approximately 45° from the subject item. The type of lighting source (incandescent, tungsten, fluorescent) can vary depending on the needs of the photographer. However, the white balance of the camera should reflect the color temperature of the lighting used. Figure 4.10 is an example of direct lighting, as performed on a copy stand.

Oblique lighting is similar to direct lighting except for the angle of the light source. While direct lighting is set at approximately 45°, bounce lighting is set at approximately 10°. This placement allows the light source to pass over the surface at a near-parallel direction, highlighting the contours of the item or impression. In instances of indented writing, plastic impressions, or other similar circumstances, this type of lighting can be very beneficial. Similar to direct lighting, any light source may be used, and proper white balance must be considered. Often, optimal visualization with oblique lighting

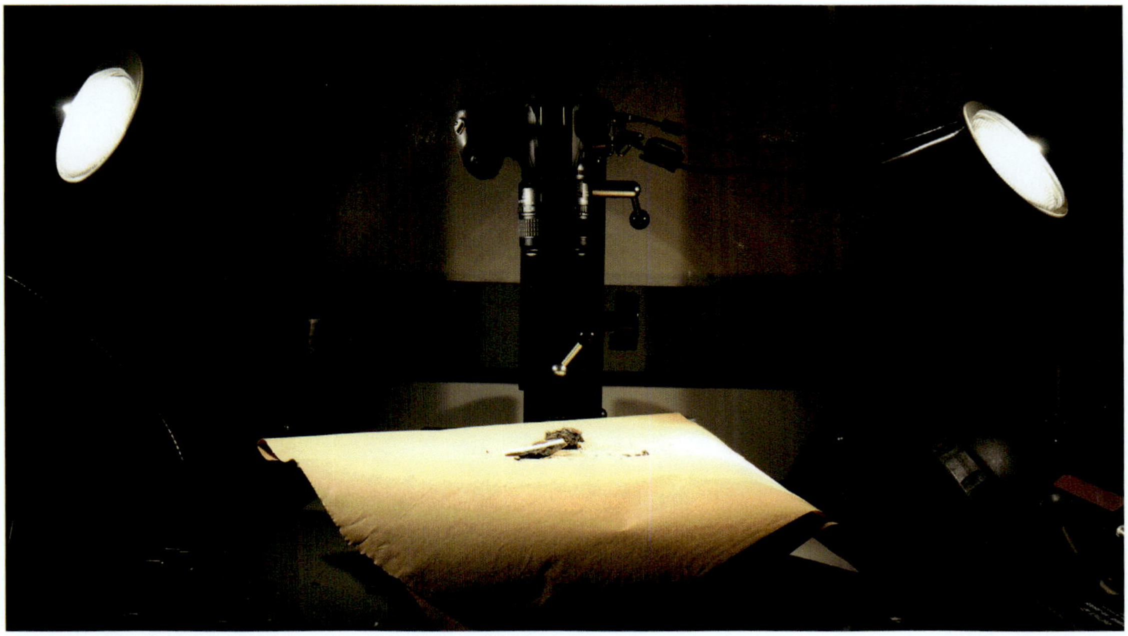

FIGURE 4.10 An example of direct lighting, performed on a copy stand. (Courtesy of Andrew Reitnauer.)

is attained by utilizing the light source from one direction. This directionality can help to visualize the highlights and shadows caused by the lighting of peaks and furrows found in the subject matter.

Oblique lighting can also be beneficial when performing overall photography. The directionality of light can be the most useful tool a photographer can use. As a part of standard documentation in a case involving a vehicle, the photographer should include a photograph of the VIN. Direct lighting will almost always result in a "hot spot" reflection from the windshield. Using the remote cord to operate the flash off of the camera, a useable image can be attained by utilizing an oblique angle with the flash. The light will penetrate the windshield and illuminate the VIN placard.

Bounce lighting involves changing the angle of the light to point away from the subject by creating a "dome" or barrier that can either diffuse the light source, or reflect the light to create an overall illumination of the subject. By creating this type of lighting system, the object or impression will have an even amount of illumination, free from highlights and reflection. Often this type of lighting works positively on dark surfaces where direct light may change the tones present. Also, if the impression being photographed is dark in nature with a low amount of contrast, as compared to the substrate, this type of lighting will enhance the natural contrast present. It can also be useful when photographing a reflective surface. The system can consist of a single piece of paper, or a complex photographic dome. In this example, the lighting system acts to evenly diffuse the light source in order to achieve a proper exposure (Figure 4.11).

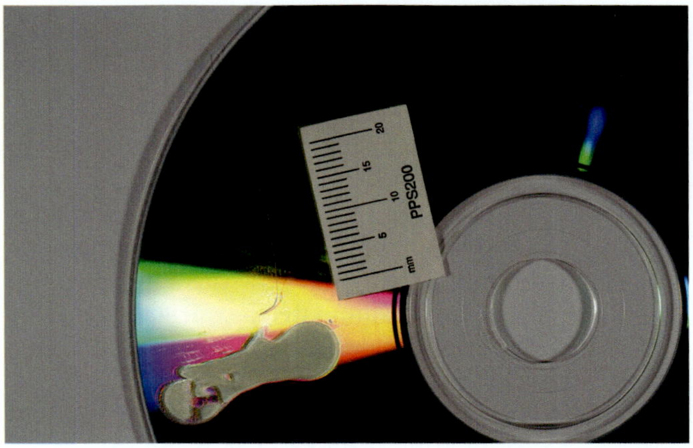

(a)

(b)

FIGURE 4.11 (a) Direct lighting and (b) bounce lighting. (Courtesy of Andrew Reitnauer.)

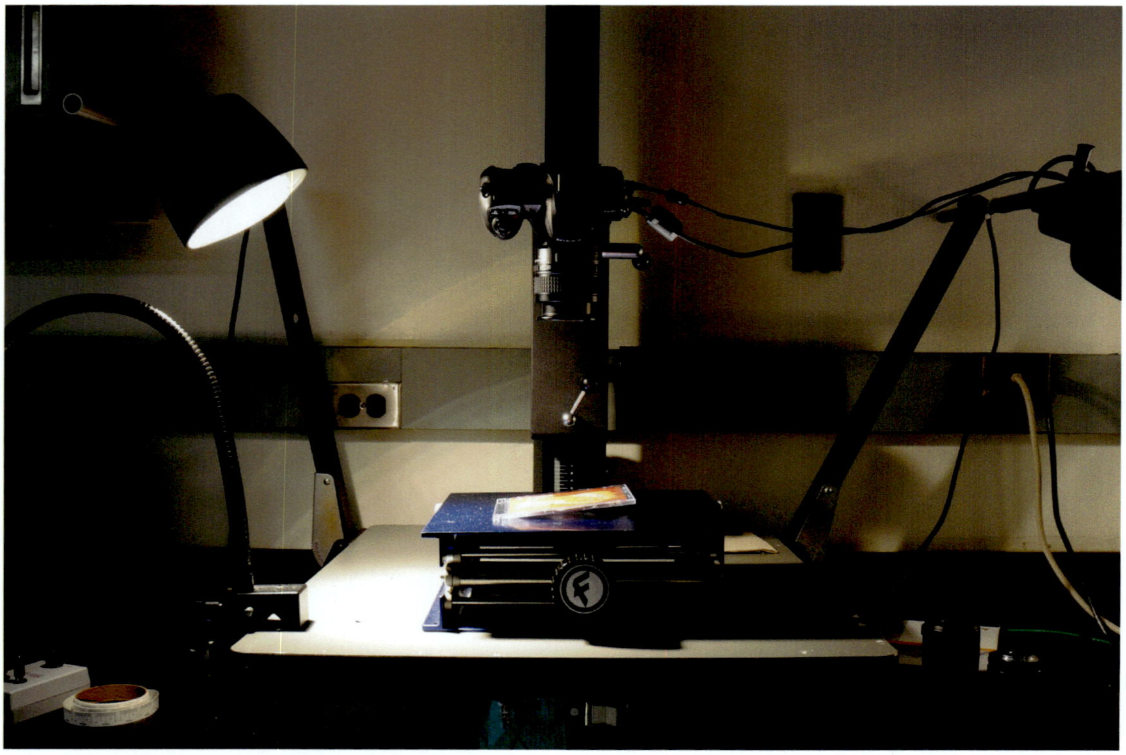

FIGURE 4.12 Direct reflective lighting system. (Courtesy of Andrew Reitnauer.)

Tented lighting is a lighting system similar to bounce lighting. The main difference is that tented lighting is a more ridged structure, while bounce lighting is an adjustable system. The tented lighting system is placed in a manner that will allow the light source to enter from the side to illuminate the surface, or if the tent structure is permeable, the light can be diffused through the tent.

Perhaps one of the most useful lighting systems is direct reflective lighting. The premise behind this type of lighting is using the light source to create a "hot spot" encompassing the impression area. This "hot spot" will eliminate any background noise from the substrate, and turn the impression black on white. A black-on-white image is one where the impression area is black and the background is white. In instances where the background has a lot of color, or patterns that can interfere with the question impression, this type of lighting can help the photographer obtain an optimal exposure. Also, surfaces that are reflective in nature (e.g., mirrors, CDs) can create shadows in the exposure due the way these items are created. The use of direct reflective lighting can eliminate these shadows, allowing the impression to be captured.

When setting up the camera and item to be photographed under direct reflective lighting conditions, the principle of replacing your eye with the camera lens becomes very important. The angles created between the light source, surface of the subject, and the camera must be exact. Capturing the impression is dependent of the creation of a "hot spot" on the surface, which may entail using props to change the angle of the surface area of the subject. Also, different light sources may be used to create this type of lighting system. Ambient light sources, incandescent lights, ALS, and fiber optic illuminators are all examples of lighting sources that can be utilized. Figure 4.12 is an illustration of the direct reflective lighting system, and Figure 4.13 is an example of a palm print photographed using the direct reflective lighting system.

Transmitted lighting is a system where the light source is behind the substrate and the light passes through the surface to optimize the contrast of the subject. If an impression is on a clear surface (e.g., glass, clear plastic), this type of lighting can be beneficial. A benefit is a situation when direct lighting, or other type of lighting system, might cause a distortion between the impression and the area behind the impression. An example of this is shown in Figure 4.14. Also, if there is some sort of contaminant on the surface, such as scratches or dust, transmitted lighting can help to reduce this type of noise. Many different lighting sources can be used to capture an image under this lighting system. Sources used in a laboratory setting such as an ALS, incandescent lighting, and fiber optic illuminators as well as overall flash units can be used.

FIGURE 4.13 An example of a palm print photographed using the direct reflective lighting system.

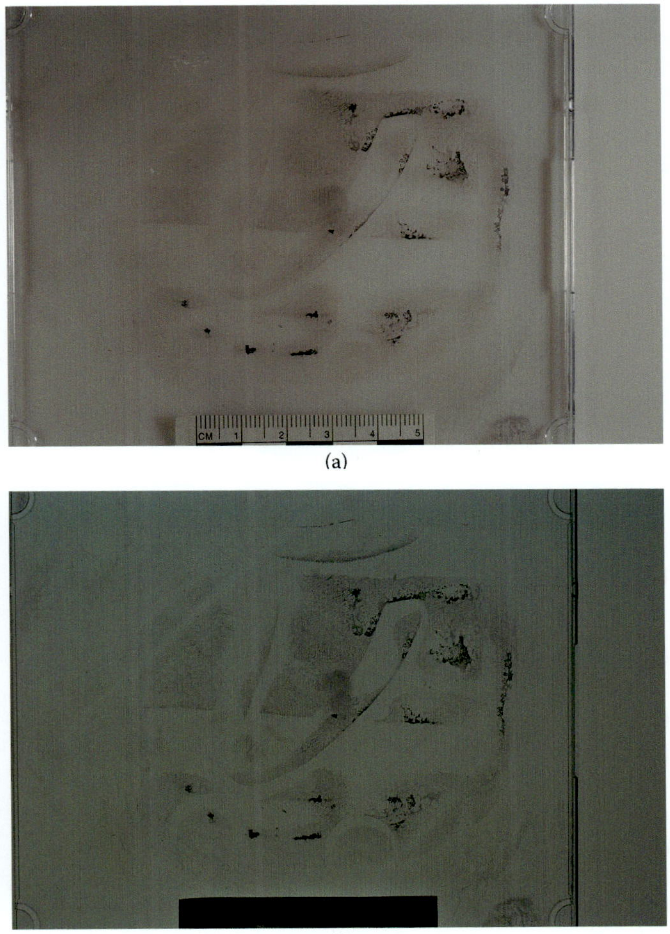

FIGURE 4.14 Transmitted lighting. (a) Footwear impression on a clear CD cover. Using transmitted lighting from the light table behind the CD cover, the impression is clear with individual characteristics present. (b) Footwear impression on a clear CD cover. Using direct lighting the impression seems blurry due to the space between the surface of the CD cover and the background surface. (Courtesy of Andrew Reitnauer.)

4.7 BARRIER FILTERS

The use of barrier filters on a camera can be beneficial to a photographer in two basic functions. The first is to optimize the visualization of fluorescent development. Depending on the technique used and light wavelength present, a specific filter system can allow certain emittance wavelengths to pass through, and block opposing wavelengths. This allows the developed impression to be visualized and background light to be omitted from the image. The following table gives a basic classification of what color filters should be used for corresponding wavelengths.

350 nm–450 nm	Yellow
450 nm–535 nm	Orange
535 nm–585 nm	Red

The examples listed in the table to the left are general guidelines, not steadfast rules. As the ALS wavelengths used increase in length, the darker the barrier filter used will become. This trend is due to the longer emittance of the development reagent's fluorescence, or natural emittance of the subject of the photograph. Typically, these two criteria have a systematic relationship.

All basic photography follow the principles of the basic six-tone color wheel. In order to optimize the image taken using a fluorescent technique, the ALS wavelength's opposing color filter should be utilized. In considering the color wheel depicted in Figure 4.15, an ALS wavelength and filter system should result in an acceptable image based upon the lighting system. Following this principle, a UV lighting source of approximately 350 nm (blue) will require a yellow barrier filter, based upon the opposing positions of these two colors within the wheel.

The second purpose of barrier filter usage is to eliminate varying background colors present in the subject matter. The basic premise is to render the hue of the

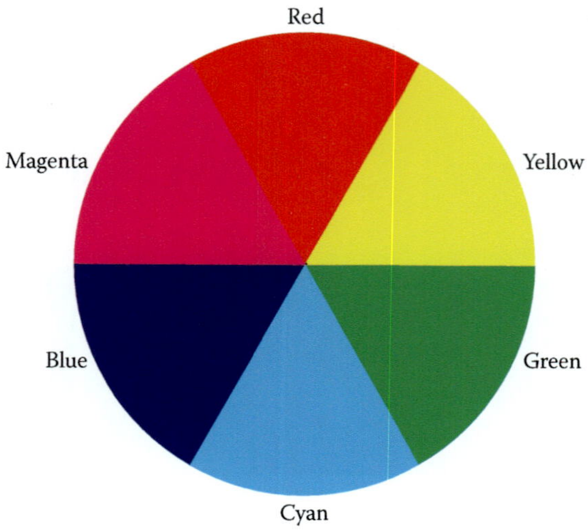

FIGURE 4.15 The basic six-tone color wheel used in basic photography. (Courtesy of Andrew Reitnauer.)

entire image a single color. When the image is opened in a digital imaging program, such as Adobe Photoshop, the entire color saturation can be removed, leaving the photographer with a grayscale image and optimal visualization of the subject matter. The use of a barrier filter, in this type of application, is in conjunction with one of the standard light sources, rather than an ALS. It also requires the photographer to think forward to an enhancement stage. Understanding the capabilities of the software can help a photographer when using barrier filters. The basic principles, regarding opposite colors, of the color wheel can be applied in using enhancement software. However, in this type of use, the filters will absorb the opposing colors. In an example of a latent fingerprint developed with ninhydrin (purple), a green filter will absorb the purple color, rendering it black. Using a cyan filter will absorb blood, also rendering it black.

Another type of filter that can be useful in forensic photography is a polarizing filter. This type of filter is designed to eliminate reflections from objects by blocking light that has wavelengths traveling in a specific direction. By adjusting the filter's position on the camera lens, the directionality of the light being blocked can change. This allows the photographer to adjust the camera in order to eliminate the desired light, resulting in a proper exposure.

4.8 HUMAN FACTORS

Within the current progression of the field of latent print examination, much attention is being given to the areas of human factors and their impact on the results of the examinations, issues such as contextual and conformational bias and the degree to which they may affect the latent print examination. Michele Triplett's Fingerprint Dictionary defines bias as "An influence based on impertinent information rather than objective data, such as irrelevant contextual details surrounding an event" (Triplett, 2010). Research done by Dror has shown that external influences have had an impact on the results reached by examiners (Dror, 2014). In addition, the 2009 report issued by the National Academy of Science discussed the impact that bias may have on the forensic analysis process (National Academy of Science). These external influences must be recognized within the comparison process, as applied by the examiner, and steps should be taken to reduce the risk of bias.

Contextual bias occurs when external information influences the final determination made by the examiner. In the latent print field, this can occur through the influence of department personnel outside of the analyst, the information received as a part of the case documentation, or knowledge of a previous determination by a secondary analyst. In all these examples, the examiner has been exposed to undue influence that may preclude him or her from conducting an unbiased examination of the evidence. In many laboratories, efforts are being made to safeguard the examiners from contextual bias by removing all case documentation that is not pertinent to the examination, shielding the examiners from outside personnel throughout the examination process, and by implementing quality assurance measures. While all forms of contextual bias may not be fully removed from the examination process, the recognition of their influence must be a consideration of the laboratory system.

Confirmational bias occurs when the results of an examination are interpreted to confirm a preexisting theory or proclivity toward a predetermined conclusion. One of the primary methods of avoiding this type of bias is the application of the ACE-V process. Overall, while viewed as a linear approach to latent print examination, determinations are made at intervals based upon the data that is present. The totality of the data, as determined by the examiner, will allow for a proper conclusion to be made. While the linearity of the ACE-V examination process is not finite, the independent interpretations made by the examiner must be a cognitive consideration.

Laboratories may employ quality assurance measures in order to reduce the effects of bias on the analysts and the examination process. In addition to some of the measures mentioned above to reduce the impact of contextual bias, these same measures should be applied to the verification process of the examination. Verifying analysts should be allowed access to not only the exemplar record that was identified, but to all those involved in the case. This task, allows the examiner to have the knowledge that the latent print was identified, but not to which individual. Many laboratories only confirm the conclusions of "identification," rather than verify the sufficiency determinations and resulting conclusions of "exclusion" and "inconclusive." Laboratory policy dictates the technical review methods employed during the examination case review; however, the implementation of these steps also helps safeguard against false negatives and non-consensus sufficiency determinations.

4.8.1 Blind Verification

One method employed by laboratories to ensure the conclusions reached by the independent examinations done by the analysts is through the implementation of blind verification. During a reanalysis, or blind verification, a secondary examiner is reassigned the case to examine, without any prior knowledge of conclusions, or that the evidence had been previously examined. By implementing this type of quality assurance protocol, laboratories may ensure that a sound conclusion has been reached in a case by following the process of separate examiners when observing the same evidence. Human factors that may be present often affect examiners in different ways, and the usage of a blind verification module ensures not only the correct conclusions of identification, exclusion, and inconclusive, but also the application of the method and the sufficiency determinations reached as a result of the analyst.

4.9 LEGAL CONSIDERATIONS AND STANDARDS

In the United States there have been some landmark legal decisions that have determined the admissibility of expert witness testimony. In addition to courtroom testimony, some jurisdictions have additional rules to govern the dissemination of case notes, images, and written documentation to all parties. In addition, there are different standards between the state level courts and the federal level in terms of expert testimony.

In 1923, the United States Supreme Court heard the case of *Frye v. the United States*. In this case, the question to be decided was the admissibility of evidence derived from a systolic blood pressure deception test, a crude precursor of the polygraph machine. The defendant was on trial for murder, and the test had been given to him by investigators. The defense argued that the physiological changes undergone by the defendant during the interrogation and questioning process would also incur similar changes to the defendant.

The question in this case was not the validity of the expert's testimony regarding the implementation of the test, rather to the validity of the test itself. While the appeals court denied the admissibility of the polygraph test itself, it did state that the examination used must be "generally accepted" within the relevant scientific community. When admitting expert testimony in a court proceeding, the basis for the expert opinion now had to be founded in the scientific community as a valid methodology that has been confirmed as an accepted practice of theory. The Frye Standard became the rule of admissibility for the next 70 years in the United States. There are a number of states that currently maintain the Frye standard as the admissibility guideline.

In 1993, the United States Supreme Court heard the case of *Daubert v. Merrell Dow Pharmaceuticals*. This landmark decision changed many of the guidelines regarding the admissibility of expert opinion testimony, as previously outlined in the Frye standard. In this case, the Court noted the applicability of the Federal Rules of Evidence to the Frye standard, and delivered four questions, which experts must satisfy under this new standard (Kiely, 2005).

1. Is there peer-reviewed materials in publication?
2. Is this methodology taught in universities or discussed in professional meetings?
3. Can the methodology be tested for accuracy, and does it have a known error rate?
4. Is the methodology generally accepted in the relevant scientific community?

This new standard focused the admissibility of a scientific method from a general scope of acceptance, to an approach that must meet multiple criteria, including acceptance in the relevant community. These standards were also affirmed in the cases of *General Electric v. Joiner* and *Kumho Tire v. Carmichael*.

The federal rules of evidence are tasked with the guidelines regarding the admissibility of evidence. The rules are broken into several portions, including sections for civil testimony. While the individual rules specify the admissibility of different types of evidence, the sections specific to expert testimony are founded in rules 702 and 703 (Babitsky et al., 2000). In rule 702, if scientific or specialized knowledge will assist the trier of fact in understanding the evidence in question, an expert may form an opinion based upon his or her knowledge, skills, and training. Rule 703 discusses the admissibility of opinion testimony based upon the facts or data upon which the opinion was formed. This rule states that these facts do not need to be submitted into evidence prior to the formation of an opinion.

4.10 LATENT PRINT COMPARISONS

The examination of friction ridge impressions as a means of personal identification has been widely accepted for over a century. The process of latent print comparisons is a subjective discipline, largely based upon the training, knowledge and abilities of the examiner. The process widely used within the field of fingerprint identification, named by David Ashbaugh, is ACE-V (Ashbaugh, 2000). This process is a derivative of the scientific method, and stands for Analysis, Comparisons, Evaluation, and Verification. While developed as a primarily a linear approach to latent print examination, we have seen that this process can be applied in a circular method as well. Each of these steps requires due process and the ability to examine the data present to reach a conclusion. During the course of an examination, an examiner may be required to conduct an analysis of a complex latent impression, interpret factors such as distortion or multiple deposits, determine anatomical aspect, and make a sufficiency determination. Groups such as SWGFAST (Scientific Working Group on Friction Ridge Analysis and Terminology), the new OSAC (Organization of Scientific Area Committees), ENFSI (European Network of Forensic Science Institutes, and INTERPOL have been working to create standards and guidelines concerning the science of fingerprint identification. Through the documentation of best practices, these groups have strived to ensure that the latent print examiners and their laboratories have a reference concerning the relevant issues facing the discipline and the criteria that the examiners may follow.

During the initial analysis phase of a latent print examination, the latent print is analyzed to determine anatomical source, orientation, pattern type, the presence of distortion, and the sufficiency of the impression for further examination. Fingerprints are classified into three basic pattern types: loops, whorls, and arches. The general population is approximately 60% loops, 35% whorls, and 5% arches (Figure 4.16).

In considering palm prints, there are also three areas to consider: the interdigital, thenar, and hypothenar. The interdigital region is located on the upper portion of the palm, beneath the fingers; the thenar is located adjacent to the thumb; and the hypothenar is the side opposite the thumb. Figure 4.17 is an illustration of the areas of the palm.

In addition to the fingertips and the palms, friction ridge skin can also be found on the finger joints. There are some characteristics that are also indicative of the specific location on the hand. These orientation clues present on all areas of friction ridge examination are a key part of the initial analysis process. Certain pattern types may be indicative of a hand, or even a specific finger. The location of a palmar area may lead to a determination of which hand left the impression. Often, impressions from multiple fingers are deposited in a single deposit, creating a simultaneous impression. The orientation of the individual impressions within the group can assist the examiner in determining the fingers present. This type of information can also be useful in determining the criteria of searching an impression in an Automated Fingerprint Identification System (AFIS), in order to narrow the scope of the search against the known exemplar samples.

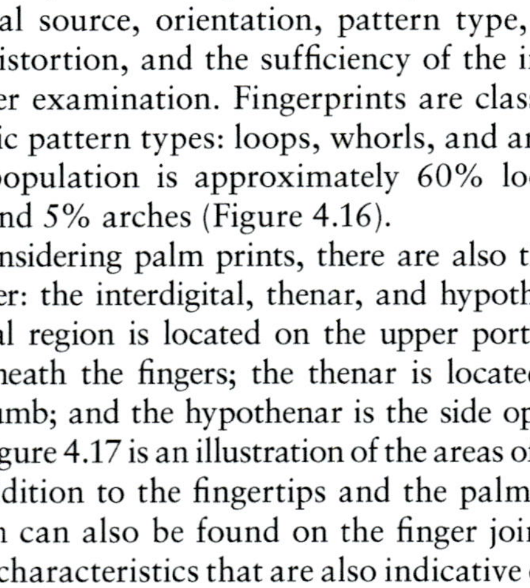

FIGURE 4.16 Fingerprints are classified into three basic pattern types: loops, whorls, and arches. (Courtesy of Ioan Truta.)

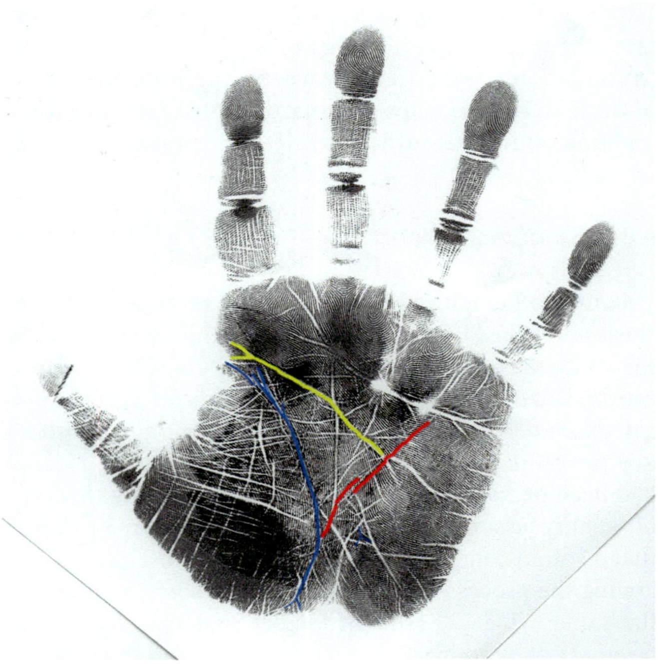

FIGURE 4.17 An illustration of the different areas of the palm. (Courtesy of Andrew Reitnauer.)

In considering the overall pattern type, or level 1 detail of the impression, some overall orientation clues can be used to assist the examiner. Loops may be further classified as ulnar or radial loops, indicating which bone of the forearm the pattern flows toward. This type of classification may be considered only if the hand is known. More commonly, loops are referred to as "left slant" or "right slant" loops, based upon the direction of the ridge flow in the pattern area.

When examining the deposited latent print, left slant loops fill flow down and away to the left side of the impression, and right slant loops will flow down and away to the right side of the impression. Typically, left slant loops are found on the fingers of the left hand and right slant loops tend to be found on the fingers of the right hand. One common crossover is the presence of an opposite loop on the index fingers. In a similar pattern, whorls may have a slant to their axis. Their overall trends follow those of the loop directional patterns. These overall trends can assist an examiner in determining a possible anatomical source for the impression, and assist in narrowing a search in AFIS. For example, if the impression is a left slant loop, a search may be conducted on the left hands and the right index finger.

The palm of the hand has three distinct areas: the interdigital, thenar, and hypothenar. These areas are also separated by the presence of the major creases of the palm. The interdigital region is above, or distal, to the distal transverse crease, or top crease. This area may have up to four deltas, and loop formations may also be found. As described by Ron Smith and reported in Triplett (2010), the delta present beneath the index finger is referred to as the clean delta. Directly beneath the middle and ring fingers are deltas referred to as "snow cone" deltas, due to their overall shape, and beneath the little finger is the "side come" delta. Beginning at the clean delta, an overall flow of friction ridges begins, commonly referred to as the waterfall, that transverses the palm, flowing downward into the hypothenar region (Figure 4.18).

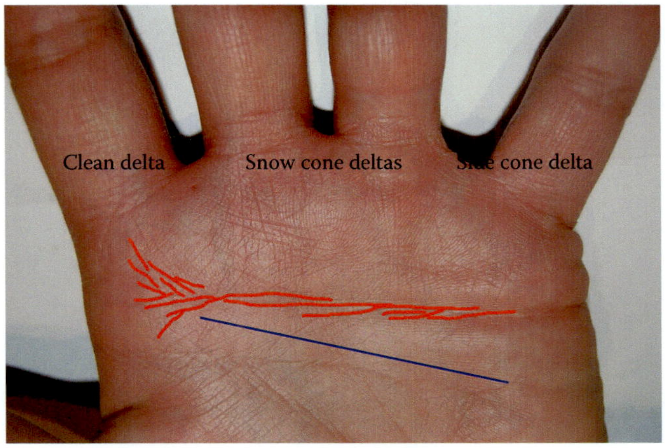

FIGURE 4.18 Example of interdigitals with the presence of deltas, waterfall, and creases. (Courtesy of Andrew Reitnauer.)

The hypothenar region of the palm, located on the opposite side of the palm from the thumb, also has some overall characteristics that can be used during the analysis of a latent impression. Situated below the top crease, the hypothenar has a directionality of ridges that flow down and out, leading toward the bottom edge of the palm. The hypothenar's characteristics include the presence of lateral creases on the outer borders of the palm, toward what is classified as the writer's edge. One of the main features of the hypothenar is the presence of a "funnel" formation within the friction ridges. The ridges tend to diverge at this point, with the lower, or proximal, ridges flowing downward at a sharper degree than the upper, or distal ridges. This overall shape, resembling a funnel, is a feature specific to this region of the palm. The hypothenar may also contain loops, both inward- and outward-facing. Figure 4.19 shows some examples of the features of the hypothenar, with the funnel ridge flow formation in blue.

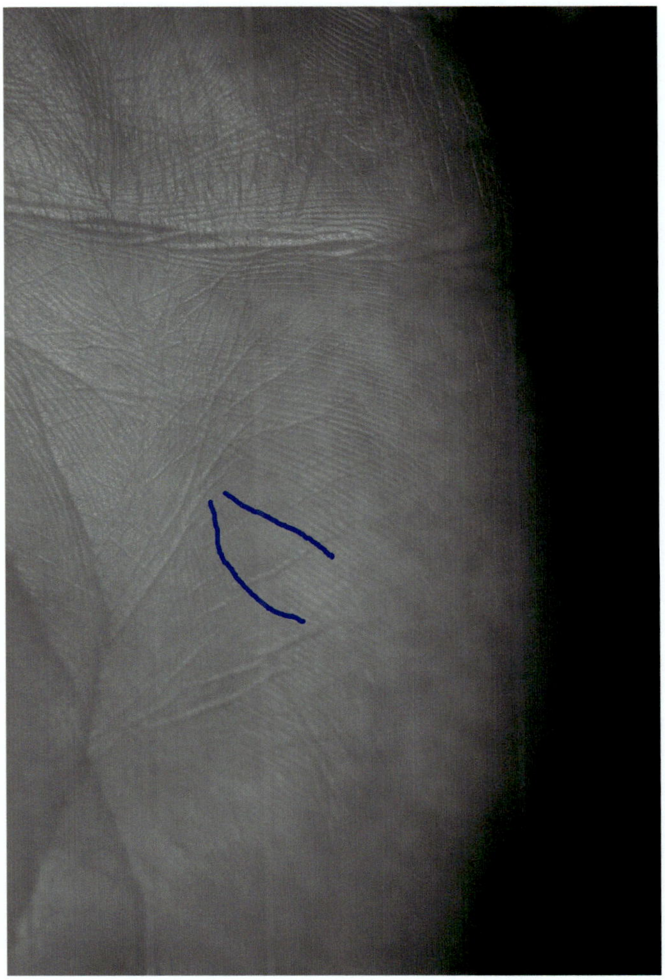

FIGURE 4.19 Examples of the features of the hypothenar, with the funnel ridge flow formation in blue. (Courtesy of Andrew Reitnauer.)

The thenar is the area of the palm near the thumb. It is best characterized by the arcing flow of the ridges. The overall flow of the thenar friction ridges begin at the wrist, flow inward toward the central portion of the palm, turn and flow out of the palm above the thumb joint. The thenar may contain a series of cross-hatching creases, commonly referred to as "cat scratches" (RON). One feature that may be present in the thenar is a vestige. Vestiges appear in approximately 10% of the population and are visualized as a squared-off formation of the friction ridges (see Figure 4.20). Also present is a crease feature caused by the webbing of skin at the base of the thumb, as a result of humans having an opposable thumb. This feature is commonly referred to as a starburst.

There are a number of notable creases within the palm of the hand. The three main creases are the distal transverse crease, proximal transverse crease, and the radial longitudinal crease. At the base of the thumb is a crease referred to as the thumb bracelet, and at the proximal end of the palm is the wrist bracelet.

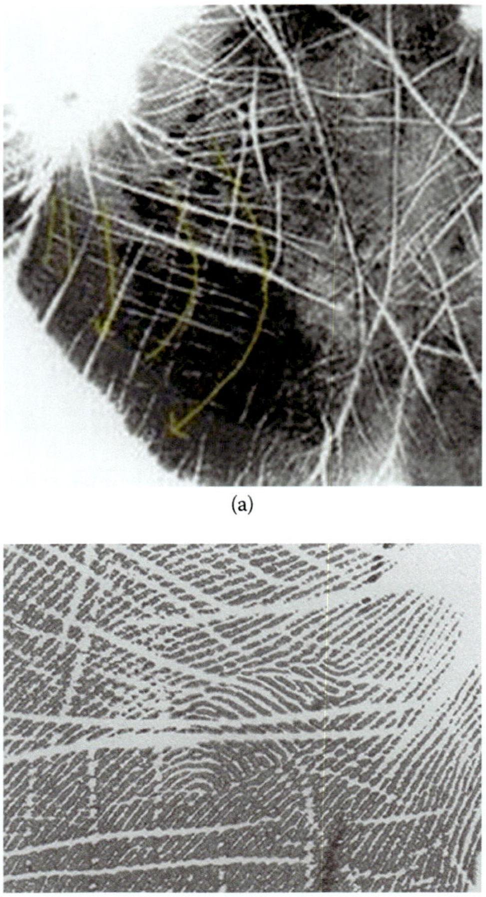

(a)

(b)

FIGURE 4.20 Examples of vestiges found in the thenar. (Courtesy of Linda Manigault.)

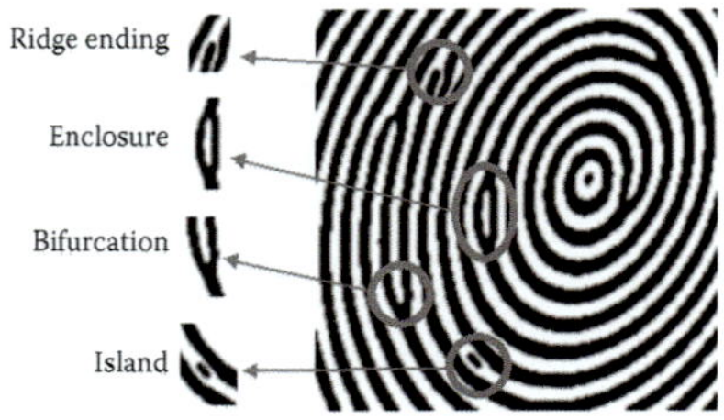

FIGURE 4.21 Characteristics commonly found within the friction ridge details. (Courtesy of Ioan Truta.)

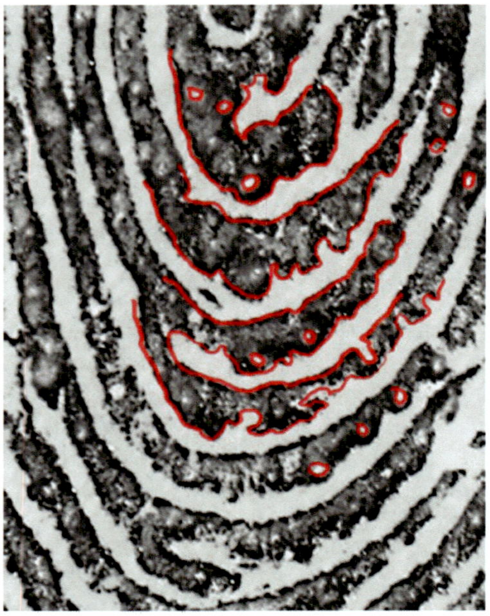

FIGURE 4.22 An example of level 3 detail, as found in a latent impression. (Courtesy of Ioan Truta.)

4.10.1 Individual Characteristics

The analysis of an impression is also focused upon the recognition of the individual characteristics found within the specific friction ridge pathways. These characteristics, or minutia points, are what the examiner will use to formulate a determination on the potential source of the impression. Figure 4.21 demonstrates the type of characteristics commonly found within friction ridge detail that may used by the analyst to further examine the impression during a comparison to a known exemplar. In addition to these details, referred to as level 2 characteristics, the individual friction ridges have a shape as determined by the presence of sweat pores. The placement of these pores along the ridge will result in a specific formation along the edges of the ridge, or the presence of a pore within the ridge, referred to as level 3 characteristics. These characteristics are also considered individual, due to their permanent position within the ridge. However, during a comparison, they may not be considered without the presence of level 2 characteristics, as they may not always be produced in the latent impression due to the conditions of the skin, amount of residue, and elasticity of the skin. Figure 4.22 is an example of level 3 detail, as found in a latent impression. Often, due to their fragile nature, latent impressions will have distortion that the examiner must also be able to interpret. Distortion may be rotational, lateral or pressure in nature.

The determination of sufficiency is based upon the culmination of data as observed by the examiner. The amount of levels 1, 2, and 3 detail observed during the analysis may result in one of three determinations: insufficient ridge detail for further examination, sufficient ridge detail for exclusionary purposes, or sufficient ridge detail for identification. The difference between the two determinations of sufficient ridge detail may be founded in the overall quality and quantity of information observed. Pattern type and limited characteristics may be enough to exclude a person as being the source of an impression, but not be enough form a conclusion of identity. Standards within a jurisdiction will imply any minimum thresholds that may be applicable. An examiner's own knowledge and experience are often the standard for decisions.

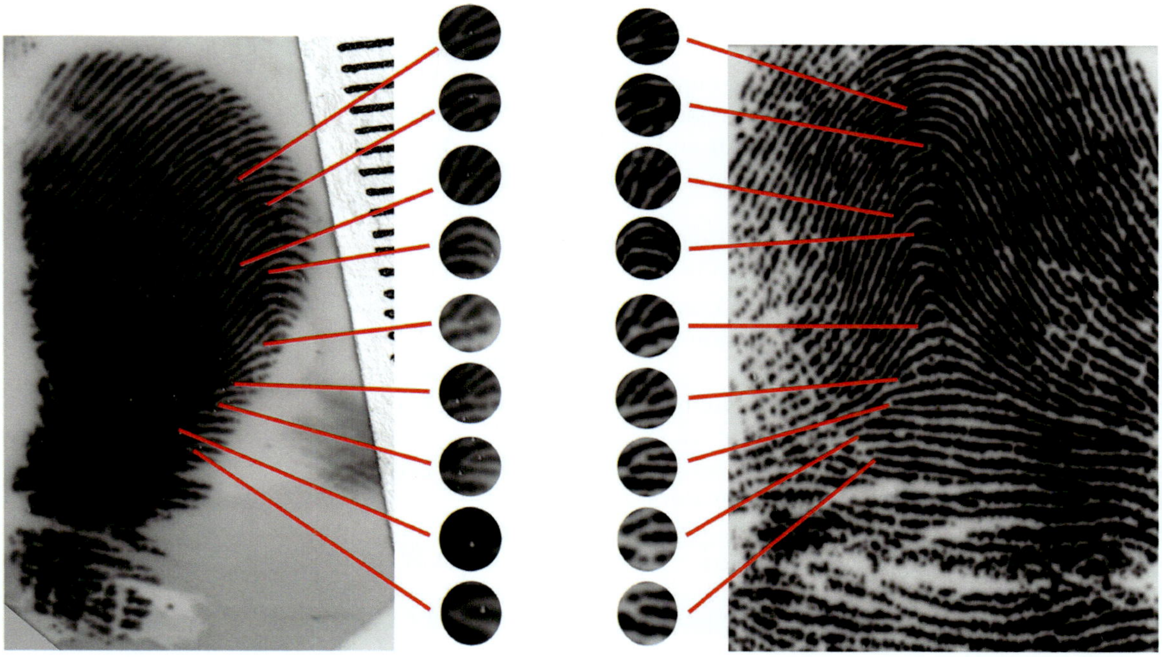

FIGURE 4.23 Example of charted identification, highlighting several comparison points. (Courtesy of Andrew Reitnauer.)

Once a determination has been made regarding the sufficiency of an impression to compare to a known exemplar record, the examiner will perform this examination. A thorough examination of all applicable friction ridge skin exemplars available will be performed in order to determine if a conclusion may be reached regarding identity. Once a thorough examination has been performed, a conclusion will be reached at the evaluation phase. There are three conclusions that may be reached through the comparison of an impression to the exemplar record on an individual: identification, exclusion, and inconclusive.

If an impression and an exemplar record have been found to have a sufficient amount of corresponding information, without the presence of an unexplainable dissimilarity, a conclusion of identification may be reached. This conclusion states that the chances that another person has created the unknown impression is a practical improbability based upon the information present. If an impression and an exemplar record are compared and are found to have dissimilarities that cannot be explained, then the person may be excluded as being the source of the impression. Level 1 detail, pattern types and ridge counts, may be used alone to exclude, but they may never be used without the presence of level 2 characteristics to reach a conclusion of identification. Following the comparison, if one of these two conclusions cannot be reached, due to missing exemplar information, or other explainable reason, the examiner may reach an inconclusive conclusion. The reason for this decision should be explained, and if applicable, new exemplar records requested for the required anatomical source. Figure 4.23 is an example of a charted identification, highlighting several comparison points.

4.11 CONCLUSION

For centuries, fingerprints have been used as a means of personal identification, from their early use in pottery, through the signing of legal documents, to their applications today. Over the past century, advancements have been made regarding the development of latent impressions at crime scenes and on items of physical evidence. These advancements have allowed examiners the opportunity to analyze, compare, and form conclusions to the source of an impression. With the technological advancements continuing to be made, examiners have a growing selection of development techniques to process evidence. The recognition of evidence and the features of an impression have allowed examiners a scientific method in order to reach a sound conclusion, based on the properties of the traditional scientific fields. Laboratories have recognized the need for quality assurance, and the identification of human factors that can influence forensic scientists; courts have also recognized the standards for admissibility of expert testimony. As the fingerprint discipline continues to evolve as a field of forensic science, the reliability of the examination of friction ridge skin will continue as a primary means of identification.

BIBLIOGRAPHY

Agarwal, M., Herlihy, R., and Reitnauer, A. A comparative study of the development of blood impressions on dark-colored substrates using phloxine B and acid yellow 7. *Fingerprint Whorld*. 36(140), pp. 98–111. July 2010.

Ashbaugh, D. *Quantitative-Qualitative Friction Ridge Analysis*. Boca Raton, FL: CRC Press. 2000.

Babitsky, S., Mangraviti, J., and Todd, C. *The Comprehensive Forensic Services Manual*. Falmouth: SEAK. 2000.

Dror, I.E. Practical solutions to cognitive and human factor challenges in forensic science. *Forensic Sci. Policy Manage*. 4, pp. 105–113. 2014.

Faulds, H. On the skin—furrows of the hand. *Nature*. 22, p. 605. October 1880.

Fingerprint Sourcebook. https://www.gov.uk/government/publications/fingerprint-source-book

Galton, S.F. *Finger Prints*. New York, NY: Macmillian and Company. 1892.

Hepburn, D. The papillary ridges on the hands and feet of monkeys and men. *Sci. Trans. Royal Dublin. Soc. 5* (Series II), pp. 525–537.

http://www.forensic-evidence.com/site/EVID/LegalPhotog.html.

IAI Twins Study. 2007. http://www.theiai.org/twinsresearch/twins_2007.php.

Kiely, T.F. *Forensic Evidence: Science and the Criminal Law*. Second Edition. Boca Raton, FL: CRC Press. 2005.

Klaatsch, H. Zur Morphologie der Tastballen der Saugetiere. *Morph. Jahrb. Bd*. 14, pp. 407–435.

National Academy of Science. *Strengthening the Forensic Sciences in the United States: A Path Forward*. National Academy Press. 2009.

Pilla, A. and Reitnauer, A. Validation study of the recovery of a DNA profile following traditional latent print processing techniques. *NEDIAI Newslett*. 3. 2010.

Reh, L. Die Schuppen der Saugetiere. *Jenaische Zeitschr. Fur Naturwiss. Bd*. 29, pp. 151–220.

Resolutions & Legislative Committee. 1997. *IAI Resolution* 97–9. https://www.theiai.org/member/resolutions/1997/RES97_9.PDF.

Table of Reagents Program. Chesapeake Bay Division of the International Association for Identification. www.CBDIAI.org

Triplett, M. *Fingerprint Dictionary: An Examiner's Guide to the Who, What, Where of Fingerprint Identification*. Bellevue, WA: Two Rings Publishing. 2010.

Whipple, I. The ventral surface of the mammalian chiridium. *Z. Morphol. Anthropol*.

Wilder, H.H. One the disposition of the epidermic folds upon the palms and soles of primates. *Anat. Anzeiger. Bd*. 13.

Will West. http://82141360.weebly.com/will-west-case.html.

CHAPTER 5

Forensic Biology

Samar Ahmed and Amarnath Mishra

CONTENTS

Body fluids include blood, semen, saliva, urine, sweat, nasal secretions, tears, human milk, and so on, that are found in various crime scenes, such as murder, rape, accidents, robbery, sexual offenses, and so forth. After the examination, these biological fluids play an important role in connecting the criminal with the crime.

5.1 BLOOD

Blood is the fluid connective tissue. It consists of a fluid part called plasma and a cellular part consisting of red cells (erythrocytes), white cell (leucocytes), and thrombocytes (platelets or discs) (Figure 5.1).

5.1.1 Locating Bloodstains in Crime Scenes

Locating the bloodstain in a crime scene is usually not a difficult task unless, as in some cases the stain may have changed color and thus becomes hard to identify. The search for the location of a stain is carried out in the following ways:

1. Examination under strong oblique light. This is done when investigating the area and any articles of clothing.
2. Use of colored lights, red, green, and yellow, sometimes prove useful.
3. UV rays are very useful to locate bloodstains. Examination is done in the dark under the rays. UV rays can detect stains successfully even when the stain has been washed.
4. Luminol: A chemical used to locate bloodstains. Areas suspected of carrying bloodstains are sprayed with luminal, and the resultant reaction is florescence. Areas with positive fluorescence are areas with bloodstains.

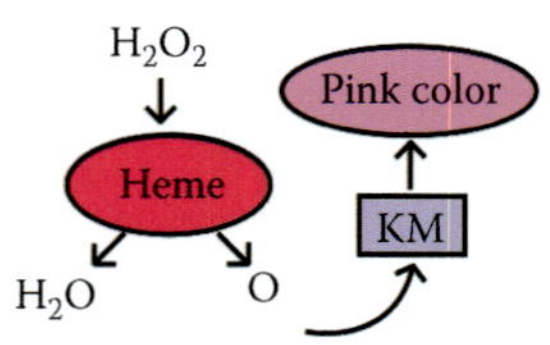

FIGURE 5.1 Diagrammatic representation of blood.

5.1.2 Collecting Bloodstains

When collecting bloodstains the forensic specialist should do the following:

1. Establish the location of the evidence and the position of the article with respect to other stationery objects at the scene. Data should be noted in copies, notes, sketches, and photographs.
2. Note the direction, size, and number of stains.
3. Note condition of stains: whether they are dry, sticky, wet, etc.
4. Note whether the stains are contaminated or exposed to natural elements or heat.
5. Write the method of collection: whether the stains were scraped, cut, lifted, dislodged, or collected in the form in which it is being sent.
6. Pack the bloodstain from various sources separately in suitable bottles or cellophane envelopes of appropriate size.
7. Preserve the continuity of the chain of possession and distinct identity of the evidence through proper packing, labeling, and sealing and through observing other legal formalities.

5.1.3 Collection of Bloodstains According to Form

The following techniques are used during the collection of bloodstains in different forms.

5.1.4 Liquid Blood

- Liquid blood is found at a scene in the form of blood pools: two samples, each about 5 mL, are collected in clean vials. In one, *sodium fluoride, oxalate*, or *citrate* is added, and the other is kept without any preservative.
- If the blood in the pool has dried, about 3 g of dried blood is collected.
- If the blood in the pool is a sticky mass, a piece of cloth is stained in the center of the pool, dried and packed as usual along with 3 g of dried blood.

5.1.5 Wet Stains

- A clean piece of rag or filter paper is taken and pressed against the stains. The stains are transferred to the rag; if the stains are partially dry, the piece is moistened, preferably with saline water, and pressed against the stains.
- If the stains are on a non-absorbent surface, it is allowed to dry and collected; if the stain contains sufficient liquid blood, it is collected in the same way as liquid blood.
- If the stains are on an absorbent surface, it is allowed to dry, and the article is collected.

5.1.6 Dry Stains

- On cloth, take possession of the cloth bearing the dry stain; the number, position, and sizes of stains are properly recorded.
- If the blood is found in the nail, it is collected by swabbing with the help of cotton or washing with saline.
  - If blood is found in the hair, it is collected by combing the hair; if a sufficient quantity is not obtained, hairs are cut and collected.
  - When the bloodstain is found on grass, one should tie the grass with a thread, cut the tuft, dry it, and pack it in an envelope or glass jar.

5.1.7 Washed Blood

- If the blood at the scene of a crime or on the cloth has been washed, it is still possible for the laboratory staff to detect traces of blood from the washed material.

5.2 EXAMINATION OF BLOODSTAINS

5.2.1 Physical Examination

In natural light examination of exhibits for brown or reddish-brown stains, powder or crystals of reddish-brown color, the areas should be demarcated. In case of absence of clear and visible stains, washed stains should be examined under 230–269 nm frequency UV light.

1—Presumptive Tests

- These suspected bloodstains; contaminated materials should be tested for positive for blood.

5.2.2 Tetramethyl Benzidine (TMB) Test

NOTE: TMB is carcinogenic. Use of gloves is required.

5.2.3 Reagent Preparation

Acetate Buffer

Sodium acetate	5.0 g
Glacial acetic acid	43.0 mL
Deionized water	50.0 mL

Working Solution

TMB	0.4 g
Acetate buffer	20.0 mL

Mix, filter, and store in brown-colored bottle in refrigerator.

Procedure

1. Place a cutting or swabbing of the stain on filter paper or spot test paper.
2. A drop of TMB solution is placed on the stain, followed by a drop of 3% hydrogen peroxide.
3. An immediate blue-green color is a positive test for peroxidase activity, indicative of hemoglobin. This is not a confirmatory test for blood.

Standards and Controls: A known bloodstain and unstained control must be tested.

5.2.4 Phenolphthalein Test (Kastle-Meyer Test)

Reagent Preparation

Stock Solution	Phenolphthalein	2.0 g
–	Potassium hydroxide	20.0 g
–	Distilled water	100 mL
–	Zinc dust	20.0 g

Mix, add a few boiling chips, and boil under reflux for 2–3 hours or until the solution has lost its pink color. Cool and decant into a bottle containing some zinc to keep it in the reduced form.

Working Solution

Solution #1:	Ethanol	10 mL
Solution #2:	Phenolphthalein stock	2 mL
–	Distilled water	10 mL
–	Ethanol	2 mL
Solution # 3:	3% Hydrogen peroxide	10 mL

Procedure

1. A small cutting, swabbing, or extract of the suspected bloodstain is placed on filter paper or spot test paper.
2. Two or three drops of ethanol are placed on the stain.
3. Two drops of working phenolphthalein solution are added to the stain.
4. After waiting to insure that no color develops at this stage, two or three drops of 3% hydrogen peroxide are added.
5. An intense pink color is a positive test for peroxidase activity, indicative of hemoglobin. This is not a confirmatory test for blood.

Standards and Controls

- A known bloodstain and unstained control must be tested (Figure 5.2).

5.2.5 Leucomalachite Green Reaction

Procedure

- Step 1: Add 1–2 drops of LMG reagent. If there is a color change, then the test is inconclusive.
- Step 2: Add 1–2 drops of H_20_2. If a color change appears deep blue-green, then the test is positive.

Limitations

- *Sensitivity* is 1:1000
- *Specificity:* Not specific to human peroxidase and thus can render false positive with vegetable peroxidases.

FIGURE 5.2 Illustrates a positive Kastle-Meyer test.

5.2.6 Luminol

5.2.6.1 Theory

The iron in hemoglobin acts as a catalyst to cause a reaction between luminol and H_2O_2. Luminol loses nitrogen and hydrogen and gains oxygen. The results in 3-aminophthalate that is energized and emits light.

5.2.6.2 Procedure

Spray the luminol directly onto the stain in question in the dark to see the luminescent reaction that can last for 15 seconds. If the stain emits a light, then the test is positive for possible presence of blood (Mozayani et al. 2011).

2—Confirmatory Tests

- Stains positive for the presumptive test should be further examined by the following tests.

5.2.7 Takayama Test

Reagent Preparation

Standard glucose solution (100 g/100 mL)	3 mL
10% Sodium hydroxide	3 mL
Pyridine	3 mL
Distilled water	7 mL

Reagents should be made fresh daily.

Procedure

1. Place material to be tested on a microscopic slide and cover with a coverslip.
2. Add a drop of Takayama reagent and allow to flow under the coverslip.
3. Warm slide gently on a hot plate at 65°C for 10–20 seconds.
4. Allow to cool and observe under microscope at 100×.
5. The appearance of pink needle-shaped crystals of pyridine hemochromogen (pyridine ferroprotoporphyrin) is a positive reaction for heme.

5.2.8 Teichmann's Test

Reagent Preparation: Mix and store in stoppered bottle.

Potassium chloride	0.1 g
Potassium bromide	0.1 g
Potassium iodine	0.1 g
Glacial acetic acid	100 mL

Procedure

1. Place material to be tested on a microscopic slide and cover with a coverslip.
2. Let the reagent flow under the coverslip.
3. Warm the slide gently on a hot plate at 65°C for 10–20 seconds.
4. Allow to cool and observe under microscope at 100×.
5. The appearance of brown rhombohedron-shaped crystals of ferroprotoporphyrin chloride is a positive reaction for heme.

5.2.9 Spectrophotometric Estimation

Reagent Preparation

- Solution 1: → 0.2% sodium lauryl sulfate in water
- Solution 2: → 0.2% mercaptoethanol in 1% NH_3 solution

These reagents will keep for approximately 4 days.

Procedure

- To a 1 cm long stained thread, add 10 mL of Solution 1.
- Incubate at 37°C for 15–20 minutes.
- Add 10 mL of Solution 2 and mix.
- Transfer liquid to a microcapillary cuvette.
- On a spectrophotometer, monitor the reaction at 560 mm against a reaction blank until absorption reaches maximum.
- When the reaction is complete, after 5–10 minutes, scan the sample between 600 and 500 nm. Two peaks, which are clearly defined at 558 nm and 529 nm, indicate the presence of hemoglobin derivatives.

Standards and Controls

- Known bloodstains of various ages must be tested; oxyhemoglobin exhibits absorption peaks at 576 and 538 nm. The apparent shift is thought to be due to the formation of reduced hemoglobin derivatives.

3—Detection of Origin of Bloodstains (Human versus Non-Human)

5.2.10 Precipitin Test

This test is used to determine if the blood is of human or animal origin. The idea is that animals injected with human blood form antibodies against the blood. Animal blood collected in a beaker is used to isolate antigens. Blood serum is also isolated to collect the antibodies.

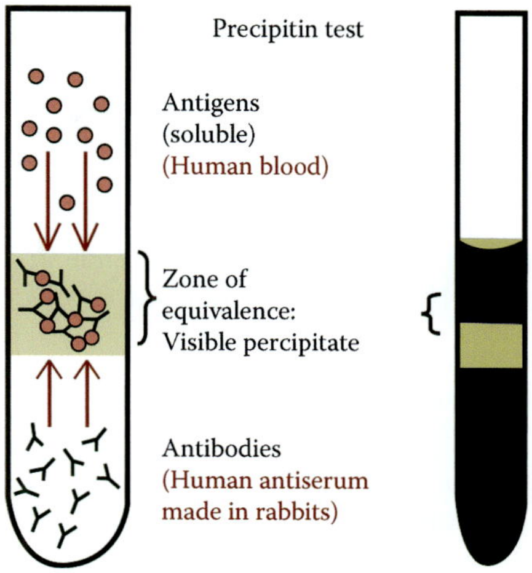

FIGURE 5.3 Diagrammatic representation of the precipitin test.

In the case of human blood, the antibodies recovered from the animal blood interact with the antigens in the human blood and clump. The most common precipitin test is the precipitin ring test. Human blood is layered on top of the animal serum containing the human blood antibodies. The interaction between the antibodies and the antigens forms a cloudy ring at the interface of the two liquids (Figure 5.3).

5.3 SEMINAL FLUID

Seminal fluid is an important biological fluid, which is ejaculated from the male reproductive organ. Human semen is a white or slightly yellow, thick, and viscous liquid having a characteristic odor. It is slightly alkaline in nature (pH = 7.32–7.70); its semitransparent relative density is 1.028.

An average male releases 2.5–6 mL of seminal fluid during one ejaculation containing 100–200 million spermatozoa. After ejaculation, human semen coagulates immediately due to the conversion of fibrinogen into fibrin. After 15–20 minutes, the action of the enzyme fibrinolysin causes it to reliquify.

5.3.1 Composition of Semen

Chemically, semen is a complex mixture of organic and inorganic compounds. Important constituents of semen, from an identification point of view, are proteins including enzymes (acid phosphatase), blood group factors, choline, fructose, citric acid, uric acid, and zinc. The composition varies from one individual to the other.

Semen is composed of the following:

- Seminal plasma (90%)—Secretion of seminal vesicle epididymis prostate gland and Cowper's gland.
- Spermatozoa (10%)—Each mL of semen contains about 100 million spermatozoa that are motile for about 45 minutes to 3 hours after ejaculation.

5.3.2 Structure of Spermatozoa

The spermatozoon has three parts: head, neck and tail.

The head contains the chromosomes. It is flat, oval, and flexible. The diameter of head ranges from 2.5–3.5 μ. The anterior aspect of the head is covered with a cytoplasmic sheet that is known as the *acrosome*.

The neck is very delicate and small, whereas the tail is an elongated part containing fibrin.

Seminal stain is important evidence in case of rape, attempted rape, sodomy, and in civil cases viz. disputed paternity cases (Figure 5.4).

5.3.3 Collection of Semen

In practice, a seminal stain can be presented in a number of forms and the collection methodology varies according to the form; it can be presented as the following:

1. Dry stain from thigh collected by a wet cotton or swabbing.
2. Suspected portion of cloth where stain is collected by cutting the fabric then drying and preserving it.
3. Pubic hair, in which case the hair is plucked or cut and placed in a small container.
4. Stains on smooth surface can be collected by scraping with knife or any sharp instrument and placed into a glass container.

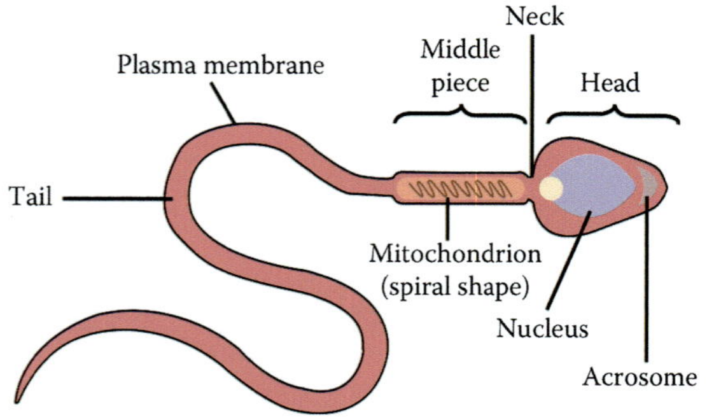

FIGURE 5.4 Diagrammatic representation of the structure of spermatozoa.

5.3.4 Examination of Semen and Seminal Stains

5.3.4.1 Physical Examination

Color: Thick, yellowish white, glary, opalescent secretion having a characteristic odor known as seminal odor.

Texture: On touch, seminal stains are starchy.

Appearance: Garments sent for forensic examination are usually dirty, having variety of stains; in natural light some stains are reddish colored, while others are brown, yellow, or faint gray in color. These are often mixed with stains of blood vaginal discharge, urine and semen; so as to restrict the investigation to seminal stains only, preliminary examination is done under filtered UV light. The fluorescence of the seminal stains is of a bluish-white color, and such stains should be selected for further examination.

5.3.5 Presumptive Test

5.3.5.1 Acid Phosphatase Test (Sodium-α-Naphthyl Phosphate Test)

This method is best on the presence of an enzyme *acid phosphatase* in semen. Acid phosphatase is present in semen and other body fluids, and in fresh vegetables, fungi and bacteria. Polyacrylamide gel electrophoresis staining with umbelliferyl phosphate reagent distinguishes seminal acid phosphatase from other acid phosphatase in other fluids. The enzyme is also present in semen in much higher concentration than in other body fluids. This is can be used as a very good screening test for the examination of seminal fluid.

Reagent Preparation: NaCl (230 g), glacial acetic acid (5 mL), sodium acetate anhydrous or trihydric Na acetate (20 g), Brentamine Fast Blue B salt (0.5 g), Ca-α-naphthyl phosphate (0.5 g), Teepol or aerosol 1% sol (10 mL) and distilled water (900 mL) are the constituents of the reagent. A buffer is made by dissolving NaCl, glacial acetic acid, and Na-acetate in distilled water. Brentamine Fast Blue B salt is dissolved in a small amount of this buffer. A fine suspension of Ca-α-naphthyl phosphatase is prepared by grinding the same in Teepol or aerosol with a pestle and mortar. The resulting suspension is added to the remaining amount of buffer. The Brentamine solution is then added to the Ca-α-naphthyl phosphate solution, and the mixture is then filtered and stored in an amber-colored bottle.

Procedure: A sheet of filter paper is thoroughly moistened with normal saline and pressed over the area to be examined for a couple of minutes. The filter paper is lifted off and the reagent is spread to it in about one minute.

The area corresponding to the seminal stain appears *purple-red color.*

5.3.5.2 Florence Test

The test is based on the formation of choline per iodide crystal due to the chemical reaction between choline present in semen and iodine in the test reagent. A florence test is a very delicate test; a negative test may be obtained if choline content is low or stain is decomposed. A positive test may be obtained with other body tissue extract containing choline.

Fluorescent Reagent

- The fluorescent reagent is composed of KI (1.66 g), I_2 (2.56 g) and H_2O (30 mL).

Procedure

- Add stain, distilled water, and HCl.
- Put the extract on a microscopic slide and add fluorescent reagent.
- Dark brown crystals of choline periodide will appear under the microscope.

5.3.5.3 Barberio Test

A Barberio test depends upon presence of spermine in semen. Barberio reagent is a saturated aqueous or alcoholic solution of picric acid. This test is based on the formation of spermine picrate crystal due to the chemical reaction between spermine present in semen and the picric acid added as the reagent. The disadvantage of this test is the pleomorphic nature of the crystal, which sometimes takes the form of a deposit without any structure. This test renders positive results even without the presence of spermatozoa because of the presence of prostatic secretion, thus manifesting importance in cases with azoospermia.

Procedure

A small portion of stain is extracted with distilled water and then concentrated by evaporation on a water bath. A drop of concentrated extract is mixed with a drop of *Barberio reagent* on a microscopic slide and examined microscopically after covering with coverslip. Formation of *spermine picrate crystal* indicates the presence of semen. The spermine picrate crystals are yellow in color, needle-shaped rhombic, star and lens-shaped.

Stain + Barberio reagent → Crystal of spermine picrate

5.3.5.4 Puranen Test

A portion of stain is extracted with a little amount of distilled water and treated with 5% solution of naphthol yellow S. Characteristic yellow crystal of spermine flavinate are seen. These crystals are yellow and lenticular in shape.

Stain + Naphthol yellow S (5%) → Yellow lenticular crystal of spermine flavinate

5.3.5.5 Thin Layer Chromatography

TLC test is used to test for spermine and choline present in semen. This technique was developed by Yano in 1970.

- Solvent System: 100 mL of HCl solution kept in a developing jar for about 2 hours to make it fully saturated with solvent vapor.
- Developing Reagent: Two different reagents are needed for choline and spermine, the Dragendorff reagent and potassium iodoplatinate reagent.

1. *Dragendorff reagent* is composed of two solutions:
- Solution 1, which is composed of Bismuth subnitrate (0.25 g), distilled water (40 mL), and glacial acetic acid (100 mL)
- Solution 2, which is composed of KI (8 mL) and distilled water (20 mL)
- Both the solutions are stored separately in amber-colored bottles. Immediately before use one mL of the each of the two solutions is mixed with 4 mL of glacial acetic acid and 20 mL of distilled water.

2. *Potassium iodoplatinate reagent* is composed of KCl 10% w/v, (2 mL) KI 4 %W/V (50 mL), and distilled water (20 mL).

Procedure

- About 1–2 cm of stain, area is cut out and soaked with 0.2 mL HCl and extract is used as test sample.
- 0.1% w/v aqueous solution of *choline chloride* and 0.1w/v HCl solution of *spermine phosphate* are used as a control sample.
- A glass plate measuring 20 × 20 cm is layered with a mixture of silica gel G and water (1:2) in amount to make the layer 0.25 mm thick. The plate is air-dried and then activated at 110°C for 90–120 minutes.
- A drop of sample is spotted on the plate, then the plate is placed in a developing jar and left for 20 minutes.
- The plate is taken out dried with hair dryer and cooled; lower 2/3 of the plate is sprayed with Dragendorff reagent for the diction of choline spot and upper 1/3 of the plate is sprayed with *potassium iodoplatinate* for the detection of spermine.
- The TLC method is used for the detection of choline and spermine, especially in the case of azoospermia and oligospermic.

5. Lactate Dehydrogenase Chemical (LDHC): Sperm-specific LDH isoenzyme can be separated from other LDH by polyamide gel electrophoresis.

Advantages

- Stain is stable in tropical condition for over 4 weeks.
- Isoenzyme pattern of human semen is differentiated easily from that of commonly encountered animals.

5.3.6 Confirmatory Test

Microscopic Examination

- A small portion of the stained area is cut from fabric and moistened with a few drop of 0.01 N-HCl and kept about for 30 minutes.
- Individual threads are then teased by the help of needle.
- 1 or 2 drops of liquid are then spread out on a microscopic slide and smear is prepared on it; the slide is then allowed to dry and stained by one of the following staining dye and examined under a microscope.
  - Hematoxylin and eosin
  - Malachite green and eosin
  - Aniline blue and eosin
  - Methylene blue and eosin
- The smear is slightly heated and then stained with methylene blue, then left for 15 minutes. The slide is washed in running water and then counterstained with eosin, again washed under running water and air-dried; the slide is then ready for microscopic examination.
- In microscopic examination 1/3 or 2/3 of head is observed with pinkish color but 1/3 portion (tail) of spermatozoa is also observed under microscope without any stain (Figure 5.5).

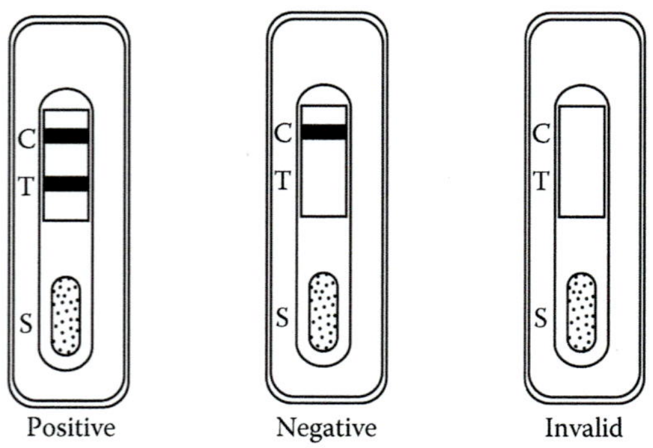

FIGURE 5.5 Represents PSA test for semen detection.

5.4 SALIVA EXAMINATION

Saliva in a crime scene is an important trace evidence which is found either expectorated or in a combination of stains and secretion in sexual or violent activity.

Examination of saliva stains lies in two separate assignments:

- Localization of the stain
- Stain detection/identification

5.4.1 Localization of the Stain

Locating the saliva stain in a crime scene is problematic because, unlike blood, there are no internal constituents in saliva that are visible.

5.4.2 Stain Detection/Identification

In 1928, the German investigator B. Mueller proposed using alpha-amylase as a marker to validate the presence of saliva in a crime scene. The problem with alpha-amylase was that it is an enzyme that has not evolved with the human evolution and remains very similar in all living beings. There are also at least four variants in humans alone, only two of which are in saliva, whereas the other two are excreted by the pancreas. This renders testing for alpha-amylase a presumptive test rather than a sure test for the presence of human saliva.

Crime labs use a reagent (chemical) called Phadebas to conduct this presumptive test for alpha-amylase. This test is relatively cheap, quick, and highly sensitive to any alpha-amylase enzymatic activity. However, it is important to keep in mind that this test alone cannot confirm the presence of human saliva, because this presumptive test will give a positive result if the alpha-amylase enzyme from *any organism* is present.

Laboratory tests for saliva remained presumptive until the late 1980s, when a group of researchers in Japan succeeded in developing a monoclonal antibody that is specific for the alpha-amylase variant that is present in human saliva in particular. Therefore, instead of testing for enzymatic activity, now we can detect the alpha-amylase molecule itself, and specifically, the alpha-amylase from human saliva. This ushered in the development of test kits that are now being used in forensic laboratories around the world to screen for human saliva (known to many as Lateral Flow Immunochromatographic Strip Test or Rapid Stain Identification [RSID] Saliva kits).

5.4.3 PCR Stain Examination

With the advent of innovative molecular biological techniques becoming the norm in the forensic laboratory, it is plausible to imagine the eventual replacement of the serological testing methods traditionally used to identify questioned stains with molecular biological techniques.

Molecular biology techniques maybe used when the sample is not enough or in contaminated samples. (For this purpose mRNA can be of use.)

After isolation of the nucleic acid, PCR assays are done for the detection of blood- and semen-specific genes then using tissue-specific transcripts for a variety of stains.

5.5 HAIR EXAMINATION

5.5.1 Sampling

- Spread the exhibit on a clean white surface under proper illumination.
- With hand magnifier, carefully locate any loose hair/fiber and collect.
- If any hair or fiber is found adhering to the exhibit, it can be either picked up using forceps or may be transferred to adhesive tape.
- If the exhibit happens to be a container or an object with crevices, a vacuum sweeper with an appropriate filter can be used to collect the hair/fiber.
- Samples collected in the above manner should be individually packed in cellophane or paper folders and labeled; proper noting should be made on the worksheet for their exact location on the exhibit.
- Each sample should be preliminarily examined under a microscope to note color and texture and to determine whether it is a hair, fiber, or indistinguishable at that magnification.
- Care should be taken to note the presence of root bulb or sheath of cells in the hair samples. They should be properly preserved for determination of sex or serological/DNA examination.

Examination of hair can help in the determination of species or origin, sex, site (part of the body), genetic markers, and source by comparison. Different morphological and histological characteristics of hair can be examined under microscope/stereomicroscope by temporary or permanent mount, scale casting, cross-sectioning, and micrometric analysis.

5.5.2 Temporary Mount

- Make a temporary mount of the hair sample on a clean slide with the distilled H_2O or glycerin. Cover with a coverslip.
- Examine under a microscope from one end of the hair to the other for general appearance, length, color, and treatment-dye or bleach presence or absence of root, tip and shaft characteristic, and contamination, if any.

5.5.3 Permanent Mount

If the item is a hair, it may also be cleaned in xylene and mounted on a microscopic slide as follows:

- Place hair on slide in a drop of xylene and add permanent mounting medium.
- Place a coverslip on the hair, allowing the medium to spread under coverslip that is encasing hair.
- Label the slide appropriately and allow it to dry for 48 hours.
- Following permanent mounting of the hair, it can be examined for different morphological characteristics and micrometry.

5.5.4 Standards and Controls

Animal Hair: Sufficient samples of hair from different species should be maintained in a laboratory for reference and comparison purposes.

Human Hair: Hairs of unknown origin may be compared with hairs of known origin to determine the possibility of a common source. For comparison purposes, an adequate number of standards (at least 10 strands collected at random) should be examined (Figure 5.6).

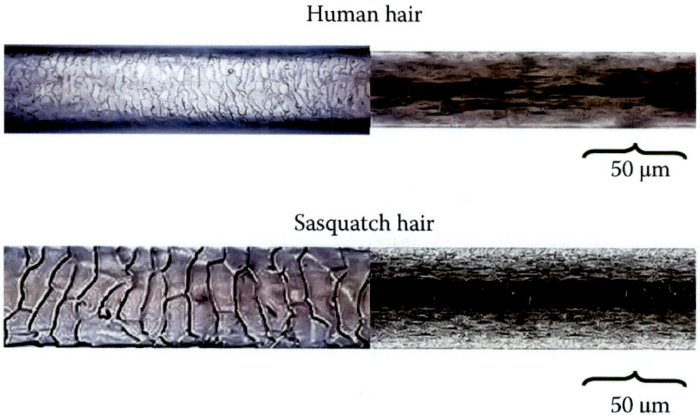

FIGURE 5.6 Human hair and animal hair.

TABLE 5.1 Comparison between Human Hair and Animal Hair

Feature	Human Hair	Animal Hair
Color	Relatively consistent along shaft	Often shows profound color changes and banding
Cortex	Occupying most of the width of shaft greater than medulla	Usually less than width of medulla
Distribution of pigment	Even, slightly more toward the cuticle	Central or denser towards medulla
Medulla	Less than one-third width of shaft Amorphous, mostly not continuous when present	Greater than one-third width of shaft Continuous, often varying in appearance along shaft, defined structure
Scales	Imbricate, similar along shaft from root to tip	Often showing variation in structure along shaft from root to tip

Source: Adapted from Gaensslen RE, *Sourcebook in Forensic Serology, Immunology, and Biochemistry*, National Institute of Justice, Washington, DC, 1983.

BIBLIOGRAPHY

Gaensslen RE. 1983. *Sourcebook in Forensic Serology, Immunology, and Biochemistry*. Washington, DC: National Institute of Justice.

James SH. 1983. Bloodstain pattern interpretation. In: Eckert WG and James SH, eds. *Interpretation of Bloodstain Evidence at Crime Scenes*, 11–67. New York, NY: Elsevier Science.

Mozayani A and Noziglia C (eds.). 2011. *The Forensic Laboratory Handbook 15 Procedures and Practice*. New York, NY: Springer Science+Business Media, LLC. doi: 10.1007/978-1-60761-872-0_2.

Quarino L, Hess J, Shenouda M, Ristenbatt RR, Gold J, and Shaler RC. 1993. Differentiation of a-amylase from various sources: An approach using selective inhibitors. *FSS*, 33(2): 87–94.

CHAPTER 6

Forensic Genetics

Anna Barbaro

CONTENTS

6.1 INTRODUCTION

For many years, DNA analysis has been used in different areas, such as medical genetics, biotechnologies, microbiology, agriculture—and obviously in forensics, where it's the most commonly used method for solving crimes and controversial evidential biological relationships.

In 1953, Watson and Crick from Cambridge University (UK) described for the first time the double helix structure of DNA. In 1962, they received the Nobel Prize for their discovery, and even then they probably could not imagine the future great usefulness of their finding.

DNA is found in all nucleated cells: in human cellular nucleus there are 22 pairs of autosomal chromosomes and one pair of sex chromosomes (XX in female and XY in male). During conception each individual receives one-half of its genetic material from its father and one-half from its mother.

The DNA molecule is a polymer consisting of several nucleotides: a nucleotide is made by a phosphate group, a deoxyribose and a nitrogenous base bound to the deoxyribose by an N-glycosidic connection. Bases are purines (adenine, cytosine) and pyrimidines (guanine and thymine).

A gene is a segment of DNA with a coding or non-coding function, and within chromosomes there are up to 100,000 paired genes. The gene location on the chromosome is called locus. Each diploid human cell contains around 6 pg DNA; hence, 1 ng DNA has around 333 copies of each locus.

Each gene may have variants called alleles: a locus is polymorphic if it has many alleles, so that at least 2% of its population is heterozygous. This means each individual (except those who are twins) has a unique genome that cannot be altered by any known treatment.

6.2 HISTORY

In 1985, Prof. Alec Jeffreys from Leicester University found that some regions in the human genome contain short DNA sequences that repeat next to each other at a given locus. Differing from individual to individual, these sequences are referred to as a variable number of tandem repeats, or VNTR. Jeffreys developed a technique to examine length variation of VNTR regions: DNA is cut by restriction enzymes in order to produce some that are separated by electrophoresis on agarose gel and then transferred to a cellulose membrane for subsequent detection by radioactively labeled probes (Southern blotting). Fragments obtained are so variable in size that it is extremely unlikely that unrelated individuals have the same VNTR pattern. Analyzing these restriction fragment length polymorphisms (RFLPs), Jeffreys made possible the first human identity test, which he called DNA fingerprinting.

The test was first used in 1985 in an immigration case, where it allowed a British citizen from Ghana to prove his identity and avoid the expulsion from the United Kingdom. In 1987, DNA testing was applied to identify the murderer of two young girls, Lynda Mann and Dawn Ashworth, who were raped and killed in Narborough Leicestershire (UK) in 1983 and 1986, respectively. The test was able to exonerate 17-year-old Richard Buckland, a kitchen porter from a local psychiatric hospital who was well known for his learning disabilities and history of sexual behavior, and who knew Dawn Ashworth and had confessed to killing her. DNA fingerprints were then used to identify the real perpetrator through a *mass DNA screening*: investigators analyzed biological samples taken from over 4000 men (between 17 and 34 years old) belonging to villages close to the homicide areas and who at the time of the murders did not have any alibi. A young man named Colin Pitchfork was arrested in September 1987, and convicted of murders because his DNA matched with semen stains found on the girls' bodies. He became the first murderer in the world to be accused due to a DNA test. Unfortunately, this method, while powerful in its ability to differentiate individuals, required large amounts of un-degraded DNA (not always available with forensic samples) and was laborious and time consuming.

In 1988, forensic DNA analysis was admitted for the first time in a U.S. courtroom in a case of sexual assault (*State of Florida v. Tommy Lee Andrews*). In 1989, the validity of the DNA was challenged during the trial against Joseph Castro, convicted for the murder of his pregnant neighbor and her infant daughter, but then acquitted by the court notwithstanding the unfavorable results of a DNA test.

The defense asserted that the testing laboratory had not performed the analysis according to the standards procedure, so incriminatory results showing that the blood found on the suspect's watch was from the mother were ambiguous. This had a significant impact on the credibility of DNA testing and underlined the relevance of a correct analysis procedure in order to assure the reliability of DNA test results and their effective usability in court.

6.3 APPLICATIONS OF DNA TYPING

Today, forensic laboratories conduct hundreds of DNA tests, since modern methods greatly expanded the sources of evidence that can be tested and reduced the amount of material necessary to obtain conclusive results.

The main practical applications of forensic DNA typing include the following:

1. Personal Identification

Except particular cases (e.g., genetic diseases), DNA is the same in all biological samples from an individual, so a DNA test is the primary method for identifying and distinguishing among individuals, in particular in cases of disaster victim identification (DVI).

2. Forensics Caseworks

DNA from evidence found at a crime scene can be compared with one of the victim's/suspect's to identify the donor in order to establish if a suspect is guilty or not.

3. Biological Relationship

Each person inherits DNA from parents, so DNA typing is commonly used to establish paternity and maternity as well as to reconstruct family relationships.

6.4 ANALYTICAL PROCEDURES

Forensic DNA typing is a multistep process that includes several phases, discussed in the following sections.

6.4.1 DNA Extraction

DNA may be extracted from a wide range of forensic samples, such as biological fluids (e.g., blood, saliva), oral swabs, hairs, fluid stains, cadaveric tissues, and bones but also contact traces.

DNA extraction consists in DNA purification from the other cell components and generally involves the following:

- Cellular lysis (by chemical and physical methods) in order to release DNA
- Protein removal (by protease) and lipid removal (by detergents or surfactants)
- Precipitation of DNA free from the other cellular components

The most common procedures are as follows:

- *Organic extraction* is a liquid-liquid extraction procedure involving several steps of purification by phenol-chloroform and final DNA precipitation by ice-cold ethanol or isopropanol (sometimes by increasing the ionic strength with sodium acetate).
- *Spin columns* purification relies on the nucleic acid binding to a solid phase (silica or other) under special pH and salt conditions.
- *Magnetic beads* DNA isolation technology involves polymer-coated magnetic beads that in the presence of chaotropic salts can bind to DNA.

The ability to maximize DNA recovery from forensic samples in order to obtain a high quantity of high-quality DNA, free of inhibitors, is relevant for further applications, including polymerase chain reaction (PCR) sequencing and microarray analysis.

Different DNA extraction kits are available commerically, and some have been suitable for biorobot automation for several years now (e.g., EZ1 by Qiagen, Automate Express by Applied Biosystems). Automated procedures can reduce labor time and cost, minimizing contamination issues because all reagents are included in special prefilled, sealed cartridges that are placed on the instrument. After initial pre-lysis, all purification steps are performed, automatically eliminating human error in reagent/sample preparation and handling.

6.4.2 DNA Quantification

DNA quantification is an important step in forensics in order to confirm that samples contain enough DNA for further typing; this is because scarce DNA quantity may result in partial profiles, while too much DNA template may produce artifacts.

The traditional quantification method is the measurement of absorbance at 260 nm by a spectrophotometer: a value of 1 corresponds to a concentration of 50 µg/mL for double-stranded DNA. Proteins absorb at 280 nm, so the absorptions ratio at 260:280 is useful to evaluate the sample contamination: a value of 1.8 is an indication of purity. This procedure is not species-specific, because not only human DNA absorbs at the same wavelength.

Alternative methods have been developed over the years (Slot Blot, Ethidium Bromide, Picogreen), but now the most widely used method is real-time PCR (qPCR). This procedure combines PCR with fluorescence detection and involves the use of special probes targeting a specific region of the human DNA; it allows monitoring the detection of amplification products accumulated cycle by cycle.

The quantity of DNA in the sample can be estimated by a comparison with a calibration curve produced by known standards. Real-time PCR involves the use of an internal control (IPC) to check for the presence of inhibitors and for any DNA template degradation in the sample. The method is species-specific, highly sensitive, and allows quantification of a very small DNA quantity that is relevant when working with aged or degraded samples (Figure 6.1).

Several commercial kits for real-time quantification of forensic samples are available and guarantee in a short time reliable and accurate results. Some of them allow also the detection of the male component present in the total DNA, which is very useful when working with mixed samples (e.g., sexual assault cases).

6.4.3 Polymerase Chain Reaction

The polymerase chain reaction (PCR) was developed in April 1983 by Kary Mullis and some members of the Human Genetics group at the Cetus Corporation. For this invention, Mullis received the Nobel Prize in 1993. PCR is a sensitive and rapid procedure that permits us to obtain millions of copies of DNA; it consists of repeated cycles of heating and cooling required for the enzymatic replication of the DNA. Each cycle has three steps:

- *Denaturation*: The two complementary DNA strands are denatured by heat.
- *Annealing*: The sample is cooled to allow primers (short synthetic DNA fragments) to anneal to the complementary regions adjacent to DNA target segments.
- *Extension*: Temperature is raised to enable DNA polymerase to add nucleotides (dNTPs). This allows extending the primers and obtaining a copy of the DNA template.

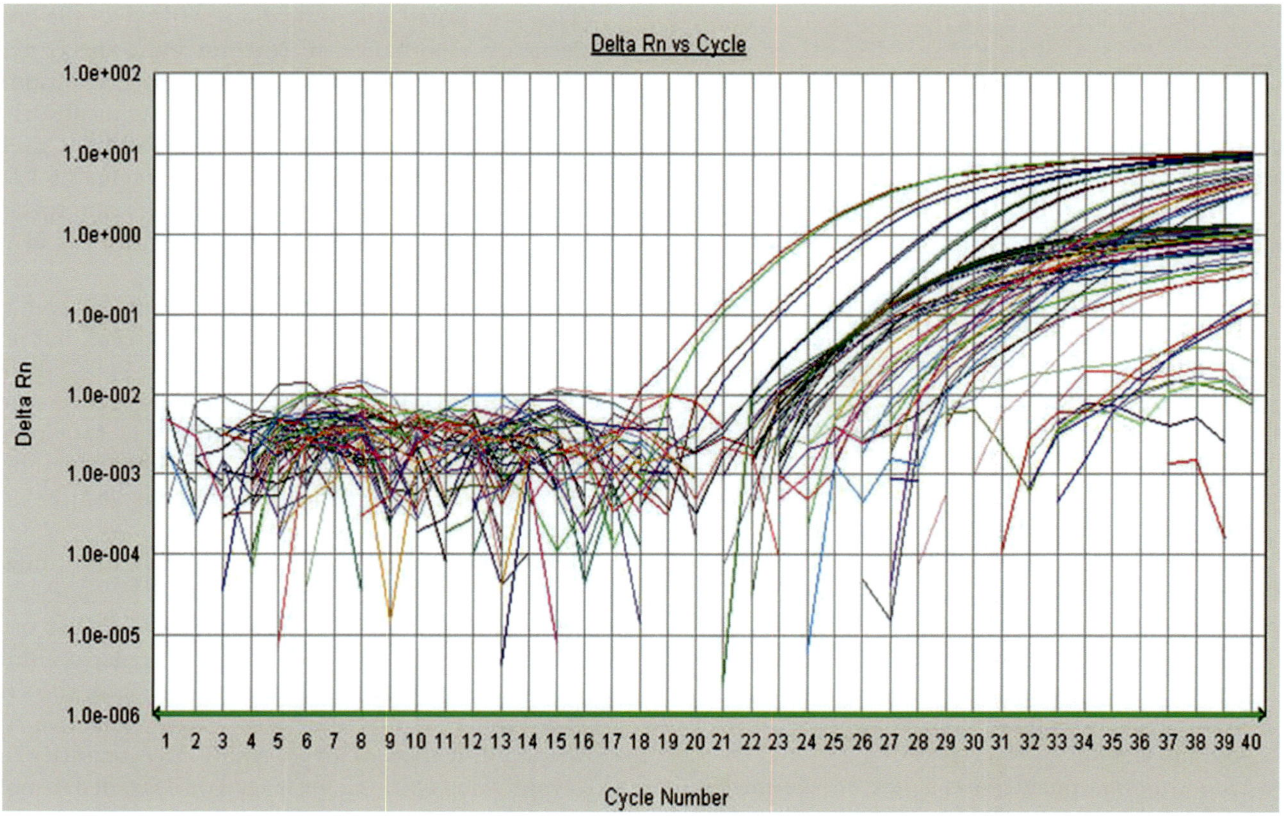

FIGURE 6.1 Real-time amplification plot.

The PCR result is an exponential accumulation of the target sequence equal to 2^n (n = number of amplification cycles). Thus after 30 cycles, approximately a billion copies of the target DNA template is produced (Figure 6.2).

Many commercial kits containing all PCR components (buffer, primers, Taq polymerase) and allowing multiplex PCR analysis of several loci are now available. To facilitate laser detection on automatic instruments, all loci with alleles overlapping in size are labeled with different colors of fluorescent dyes.

6.4.4 Capillary Electrophoresis (CE)

Capillary electrophoresis (CE) consists in ions separating according to their electrophoretic mobility within a special medium (millimeter capillaries or micro/nanofluidic channels) in the presence of a high voltage. This is the choice method for DNA fragment detection but also for DNA sequencing by semiautomatic sequencers.

PCR products are injected into silica capillaries filled with a special polymer and then, when the voltage is

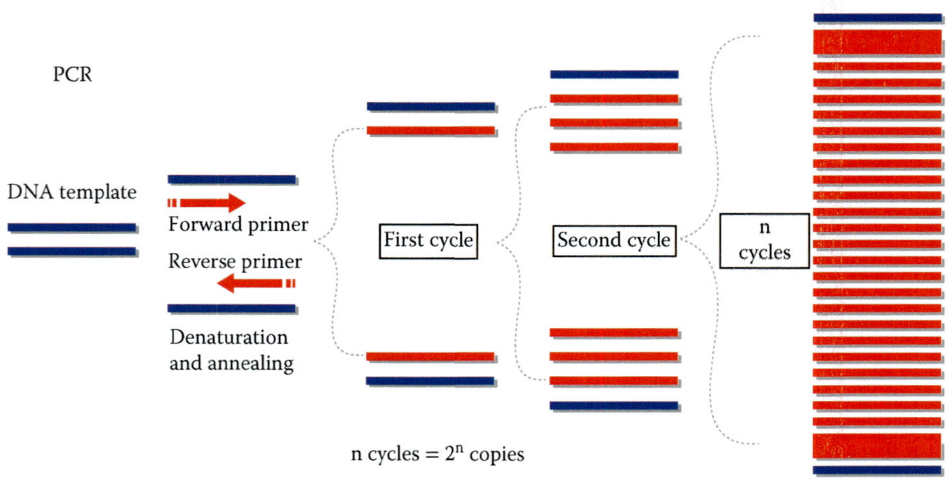

FIGURE 6.2 Polymerase chain reaction (PCR) process.

applied, they migrate with different speed, according to their size; shorter fragments move faster than longer fragments. When DNA fragments amplified with fluorescent dye-labeled primers pass in front of the detection cell, the laser leads the dye to fluoresce. The fluorescence is captured by a charge-coupled device (CCD) camera that converts the fluorescence signal into electronic information then processed by the instrument software.

An internal size standard (labeled with a dye different from the ones of PCR primers) is placed within each sample to create a calibration curve useful to normalize mobility differences among different injections. Alleles are finally designated by comparison to external allelic ladders.

6.5 AUTOSOMAL FORENSIC MARKERS

6.5.1 Short Tandem Repeats

Many repeated DNA traits are placed in almost every chromosome, especially close to the centromeric area. Minisatellites (VNTRs) have generally core repeats between 9 and 80 bp, while microsatellites (short tandem repeats, or STRs) contain 2–6 bp repeats and are typically placed in the non-coding intron region (Figure 6.3). STR classification is based on the length of the core repeat units, on the number of adjacent units, and obviously on the total length of the overall repeated region. The number of repeats is variable among individuals; this provides a wide variety of alleles (generally more than 10 alleles for the commonly used STRs) in a population and obviously a high degree of discrimination when multiple STR loci are examined. Hundreds of STR systems have been mapped throughout the human genome: they are useful in several fields such as genetic mapping, linkage analysis, and human identity testing.

STRs show some advantages—such as easy amplification by PCR, high heterozygosity, low mutation rate (10^{-3}), and a smaller size than VNTRs—that made them suitable for forensic applications where sample degradation is a common problem.

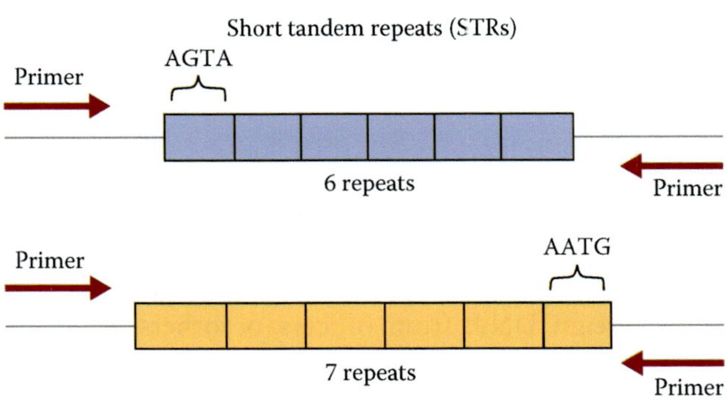

FIGURE 6.3 Example of STR structures.

In October 1993, the DNA Commission of the International Society of Forensic Genetics (ISFG) developed and recommended the STR nomenclature that is widely used: alleles are named by the number of repeats which they contain; intermediate alleles are designated by the number of complete repeat units and the number of base pairs of the partial repeat unit.

Many commercial multiplexes (Table 6.1), including primers for STR markers selected for forensics, have been developed over the years, allowing initially simultaneous amplification of a few loci to large multiplexes which are now commonly used in forensic laboratories (Figure 6.4).

Laboratories often require simple, rapid, and high-throughput work flow, especially to process reference samples for DNA databases. To serve this purpose, some amplification kits that have been developed that employ a reaction mix optimized to enable direct amplification of single-source samples (e.g., saliva) on swabs or paper substrates. The procedure is simple and rapid because it does not require any DNA extraction, and a fragment of the sample may be added directly to the reaction mix.

This method reduces extraction and purification costs, minimizing the risk of errors and contamination during different steps.

6.5.2 Mini STRs

DNA degradation is a common problem in forensics, since biological evidence may remain exposed for a long time to harsh environmental conditions (e.g., heat, humidity, ultraviolet radiations) or to microorganisms, especially in the case of missing person investigations. Degradation may affect the analysis or, depending on its extent, may cause typing failure.

Chemical reactions affecting DNA include oxidation (leading to base modification), hydrolysis (leading to base loss), and single- and double-strand breakage. Bacterial enzymes (commonly from microorganisms in the gastrointestinal tract or from the environment) cleave DNA to generate a pool of small fragments, generally in the average range of 80–200 base pairs (bp) that, falling within most markers of primer target regions, may compromise PCR efficiency.

In addition, forensic samples may contain substances that inhibit or inactivate PCR. Inhibitors include heme from blood, melanin from skin and hairs, tannins from leather, dyes (such as the indigo dye in denim fabrics), and humic acid from soils. In cases where DNA is limited in quantity or in quality (degraded or inhibited samples), conventional STR analysis produces only partial DNA profiles because of allele or locus dropout, especially for the larger STR loci. The problem is more evident when large multiplex PCR are used due to the wide size range of PCR products generated.

TABLE 6.1 Main Commercial Multiplexes Available for STR Detection by Sequencers

Applied Biosystems	Year	No. Loci	Promega	Year	No. Loci
AmpFlSTR Blue	1996	3	Gamma STR	1997	4
AmpFlSTR Green I	1997	3	PowerPlex 1.1	1997	8
Profiler	1997	9	PowerPlex 1.2	1998	10
Profiler Plus	1997	10	PowerPlex 2.1	1999	9
COfiler	1998	7	PowerPlex 16	2000	16
SGM Plus	1999	11	PowerPlex ES	2002	9
Identifiler	2001	16	PowerPlex Y	2003	12
Profiler Plus ID	2001	10	PowerPlex S5	2007	4
SEfiler	2002	11	PowerPlex 16 HS	2009	16
Yfiler	2004	17	PowerPlex ESX 16	2009	16
MiniFiler	2007	8	PowerPlex ESX 17	2009	17
SEfiler Plus	2007	11	PowerPlex ESI 16	2009	16
Sinofiler	2008	15	PowerPlex ESI 17	2009	17
Identifiler Direct	2009	16	PowerPlex CS7	2009	7
NGM	2009	16	PowerPlex 18D	2011	18
Identifiler Plus	2010	16	PowerPlex Y23	2012	23
NGM Select	2010	17	PowerPlex 21	2012	21
GlobalFiler	2012	24	PowerPlex Fusion	2012	24
YFiler plus	2014	27	PowerPlex ESX/ESI Fast	2014	16/17
NGM Detect	2016	18	PowerPlex Fusion 6C	2015	27
Qiagen	**Year**	**No. Loci**	**Qiagen**	**Year**	**No. Loci**
Nonaplex ESS	2010	9	Hexaplex ESS	2010	10
ESSplex	2010	12	HDplex kit	2010	11
ESSplex Plus	2011	12	Triplex AFS QS	2010	2
ESSplex SE QS	2010	13	Triplex DSF	2010	3
Decaplex SE	2010	10	Argus X-12	2009	12
Idplex Plus GO	2010	16	Argus Y-12	2009	12
Idplex Plus	2010	16	Argus X-12 QS	2010	12
Investigator 24plex GO	2015	24	Investigator 24plex QS	2015	24
HealthGene Technologies	**Year**	**No. Loci**	**HealthGene Technologies**	**Year**	**No. Loci**
SureID® 21G	2015	21	SureID® 27Y	2015	21

Partial DNA profiles generally may not provide a discrimination power sufficient to include or exclude a potential contributor to the sample. Recovery of information from these difficult samples is often enhanced by analyzing smaller markers called mini-STRs. Reduced-size amplicons are created by moving the forward and reverse PCR primers close to the STR repeats regions in order to obtain small PCR products. Mini-STRs were used during the identification of the World Trade Center victims. Most bone samples were analyzed by conventional STR analysis, but many samples were in such bad condition (because of heat, fire, or bacterial degradation) that scarce or no results were obtained. At that time, John Butler and Bruce McCord from the National Institute of Science and Technology (NIST) were developing miniaturized STRs primers. Their use improved the 9/11 remains analysis, and in fact today, they are commonly used in the identification of missing person remain (DVI) and in cold case analysis.

In addition, mini-STR typing is generally more sensitive than traditional STR analysis. This helps obtain results from samples with little DNA quantity, such as biological traces arising from casual handling of objects ("touch DNA"); this implies that now it is possible to detect foreign DNA from officers or others who may have handled an item years ago.

Another relevant advantage is the mini-STRs compatibility with samples processed using commercial STR

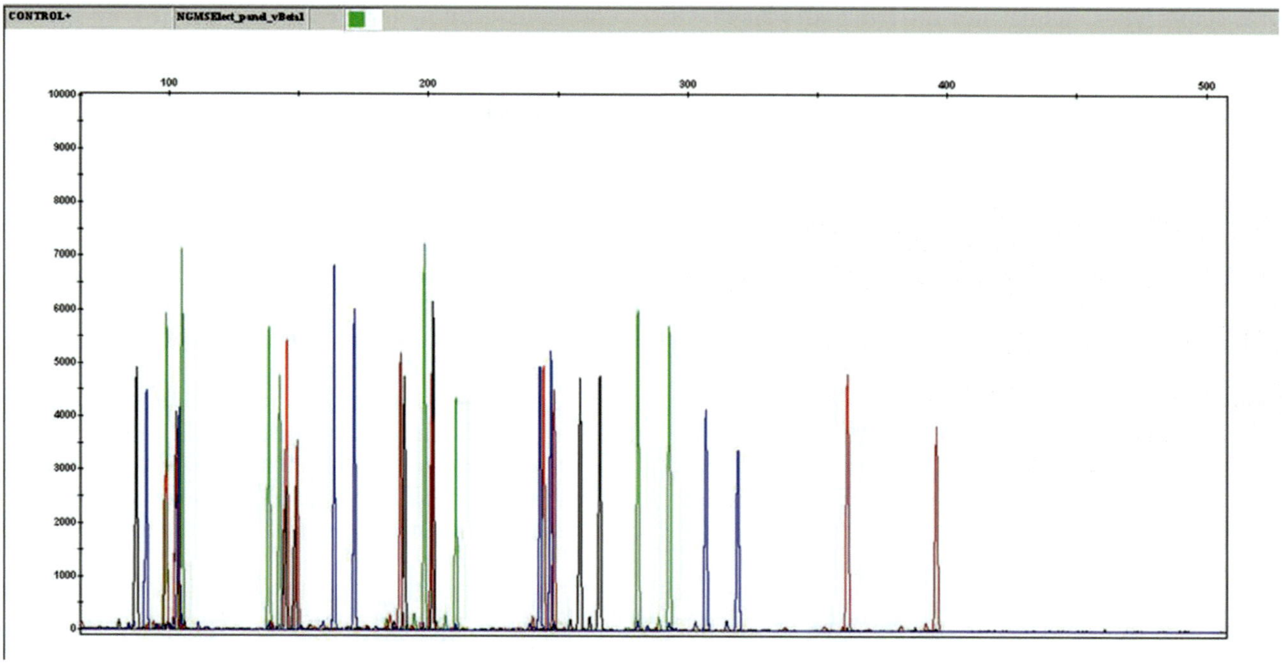

FIGURE 6.4 Control DNA 007 analyzed by Applied Biosystems "AmpFlSTR NGM Select."

multiplexes, included those of convicted offenders stored in national databases. The first commercial multiplex, "AmpFlSTRs Minifiler," was introduced in 2007 by Applied Biosystems.

In 2009, the European DNA community recommended the expansion of the European Standard Set (ESS), which included seven loci (TH01, vWA, FGA, D21S11, D3S1358, D8S1179, and D18S51), by adding some short amplicons (mini- and midi-STRs) that are more successfully amplified in compromised samples. This also may decrease the chance of obtaining false positive matches during cross-border DNA data exchanges, especially in case of partial profiles.

Thus, Europe adopted five new loci: D2S441, D10S1248, D22S1045, D1S1656, and D12S391. In 2012, the FBI proposed, for profile inclusion in the U.S. national database CODIS (Combined DNA Index System), the expansion of the traditional 13 core STR loci (D3S1358, D5S818, D7S820, D13S317, D8S1179, VWA, TH01, D16S539, D18S51, D21S11, FGA, TPOX, and CSF1PO), internationally recognized as standard routine markers in human identification, by including more loci.

In the last few years, several multiplexes, including the above new markers, have been commercialized, allowing the analysis of up to 27 markers (Schumm et al., 2013).

A review of the multiplexes most commonly used over the years is shown in Table 6.1.

6.6 FORENSIC MARKERS IN SEXUAL CHROMOSOMES

6.6.1 Y-Chromosome: Y STRs

STRs useful for forensic DNA analysis have been found in human sex chromosomes (X-Y).

The Y chromosome (ChrY) contains 86 genes, which code for only 23 distinct proteins. It includes about 58 million bp, consisting in approximately 2% of the total DNA in a male cells.

Around 300 million years ago, the X and Y chromosomes were homologues and comparable in size and genetic content: then the Y-chromosome underwent a series of deletions/mutations, reducing it to its current size (around 50 megabase).

ChrY recombines with the ChrX only in small segments of pseudo-autosomal regions at the telomeres. The non-recombining region of the ChrY is named NRY and contains euchromatin (with functional genes) and heterochromatin (transcriptionally not active). The analysis of Y-chromosome short tandem repeats (Y-STRs) has become a very useful tool in evolutionary studies as well as in forensic caseworks. Haplotypes (physically linked loci) from this region are transmitted unchanged through many gtenerations, except for occasional rare mutations. This implies ChrY is inherited in a paternal manner: males who are related through the same male lane have the same or similar

Y-STR haplotypes, while non-related males have different Y-STR haplotypes.

So, Y-STR typing can be used as a supplement to the traditional autosomal typing, but obviously alone it's not enough to identify an individual.

Male-specific systems aid in cases involving the analysis of mixtures or degraded DNA samples (generally producing partial autosomal STR profiles) by providing additional information and statistical discriminating power.

Main applications of Y-STR analysis in forensics:

1. Sexual assault cases
   a. In sexual mixed samples (e.g. vaginal swabs), the male component can be masked due to the high concentration of female sample: female DNA does not contain Y-STR, so the male component is easily detected without the need for a differential extraction.
   b. To determine the number of males present in a mixture (e.g., in cases of multiple perpetrator rape).
   c. Deposition of semen by an azoospermic or oligospermic males.
2. Criminal paternity
   a. When an alleged father is not available for the test, his male relatives can be used as a reference.
   b. Y-STRs can be used as a supplement to autosomal STR analysis to prove paternity.
3. Disaster victim identification and/or missing persons
4. A male individual can be identified by typing a male relative (such as a father, son, brother, uncle, etc.) who can be used as a reference.
5. Ancestry
6. Since Y-STRs are inherited through the paternal line, they are identical in all males belonging to the same family (except for occasional changes occurred through generations). Because of this, their analysis may be useful in genealogical tests.
7. Mixed samples
   Y-STRs are useful for the analysis of mixed samples from sexual or not sexual caseworks, especially in case of not balanced mixed samples where the male component is in small quantity compared to the female DNA ("masking effect"). Y-STR typing can clearly identify the male donor who contributed to the evidence.

Many Y-STR loci have been described and proved to have utility in forensic genetics. In 1997, an international multicenter study recommended the use of nine core loci for standard forensic haplotyping (the minimal haplotype loci, MHL or minHt): DYS19, DYS389I, DYS389II, DYS390, DYS391, DYS392, DYS393, and DYS385a/b.

In January 2003, the Scientific Working Group on DNA Analysis Methods (SWGDAM) recommended in the United States the use of all MHL loci (minimal haplotype loci) plus DYS438 and DYS439.

With the establishment of the core loci, manufacturers started to develop several commercial multiplexes that allow for the analysis of a large number (23–27) of Y-STR loci (Table 6.1).

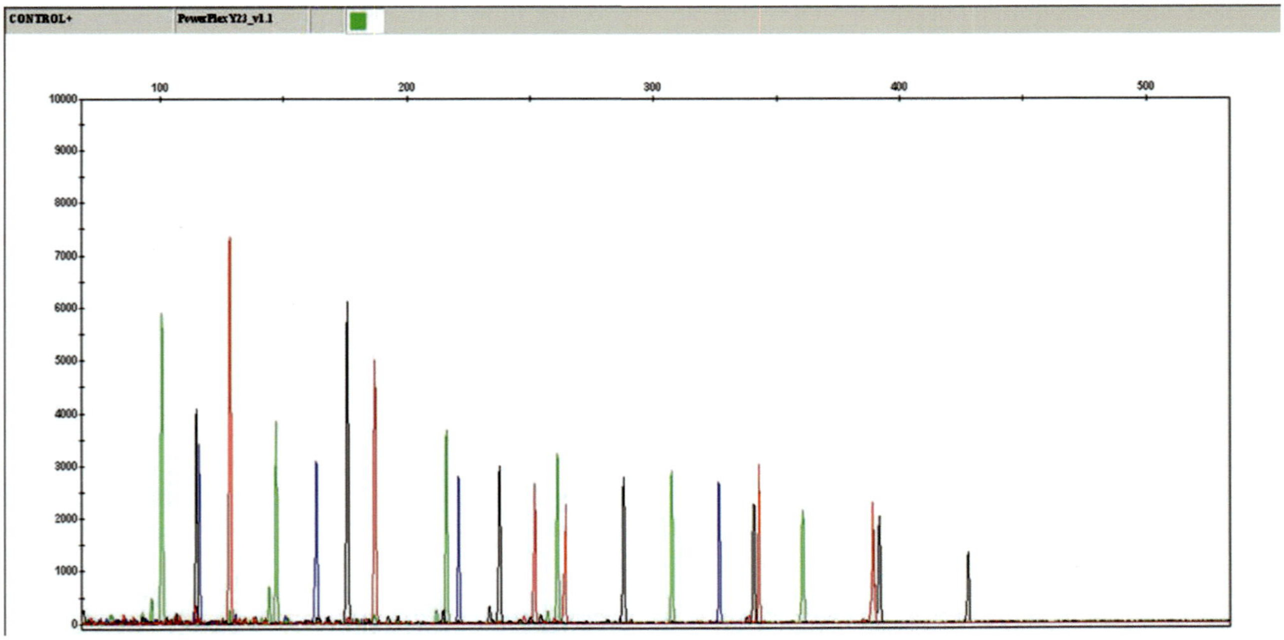

FIGURE 6.5 Control DNA 2800 analyzed by the Promega "PowerPlex Y23."

An example of a Y-STR haplotype obtained by a commercial multiplex is shown in Figure 6.5.

A Y-STR database consists of haplotype frequencies instead of allele frequencies. This is because Y-STR loci are inherited as a block of linked haplotypes; therefore, estimates of the multilocus frequency cannot be done by the product rule but by the counting method, which is based upon the evaluation of how many times a particular multilocus haplotype is observed in a particular database.

Obviously, the ability to obtain a reliable and accurate estimate depends on the ethno-geographic composition of the database, the number of individuals and the Y-STR loci included. In 2000, an online open-access reference database (YHRD) was created with the aim to store Y haplotypes from many populations all over the world (www.yhrd.org).

6.6.2 X-Chromosome: X STRs

Some STRs are located on the X chromosome (ChrX). The X chromosome spans more than 153 million base pairs and include around 2000 genes, many of them not related to sex, others perhaps related to sexual dimorphisms. Females have two X chromosomes, but only one ChrX is active per cell; males have only one X chromosome, so the ChrX markers appear in hemizygosity and their haplotype is transferred to their daughters.

In contrast to ChrY markers, which do not recombine during meiosis, the two female X chromosomes are prone to recombination: all ChrX markers are located on the same chromosome within an area of 240cM, so the use of these markers requires an exact knowledge about their genetic localization. Due to recombination, X markers provide a multilocus system, while the Y chromosome and mtDNA are linked haplotypes.

The peculiarity of X chromosome ChrX was first observed in 1890 by Hermann Henking. The idea to apply X-chromosomal markers in forensics came from experiences in the field of clinical genetics during the second half of the 20th century, and the use of X markers has increased greatly in the last 10 years because of their usefulness in completing the analysis of autosomal and Y-chromosomal markers in difficult cases such as complex family relationships.

When testing the duo mother/daughter, X markers are similar to autosomal markers and they do not provide any advantage. However, mother/son or father/daughter kinship tests are more efficiently performed using X markers.

Paternity cases involving the common trio constellation of mother, offspring and alleged father are usually solved with autosomal STRs alone. On the contrary, X-STR markers are used in deficient paternity cases, where the alleged father is missed and only his close relatives are available (e.g., his mother) or in case of DNA-analysis of multiple females supposed to have the same father. In these cases, autosomal DNA markers cannot exclude paternity, since two sisters can inherit different alleles from the father even if they are full siblings. On the contrary, daughters of the same father inherit the same paternal ChrX hence the analysis of two alleged sisters can attribute or exclude the common paternity. In complex cases involving close relatives as alleged fathers, the analysis of X chromosome markers may give more information in comparison with autosomal STRs.

In addition, X-STRs have been proven to be powerful for assigning pedigree members over long distances in order to rejoin families, for example in case of wars and mass disasters victims' identification or also of worldwide migration, even if obviously they fail if X-chromosomal lines are interrupted by a father/son relationship.

Forensic laboratories have introduced the analysis of X-STR markers in their routine: more than 50 X-STRs have been found and the most informative selected for analysis by in-house or commercial PCR multiplexes (Table 6.1). An example of an X-STR haplotype obtained by a commercial multiplex is shown in Figure 6.6.

The X-chromosome is also a good source of information for population genetic studies; compared with autosomes, the ChrX has lower recombination/mutation rates and smaller effective population size resulting in a faster genetic drift.

Due to the linkage disequilibrium frequency estimate cannot proceed by the product rule but by the counting method, evaluating how many times a particular haplotype is observed in population samples.

This means that an X-STR database consists of haplotype frequencies rather than allele frequencies. A free online database (www.chrx-str.org) accessible for the forensic community was created in order to provide a reference database for X-STRs and includes published population data from several countries.

Gender identification is routinely performed by the analysis of the amelogenin gene that occurs on both the X- and Y- chromosomes. In 1993, K. Sullivan developed for the first time a PCR primer set targeting a 6 bp deletion on the X- chromosome. When analyzed by electrophoresis, female DNA amplified by these primers shows only one peak, while male DNA produces two peaks (because males are XY). The ratio between X and Y peaks can be helpful in mixtures interpretation in order to understand the ratio of the contributors.

Gender misidentification may have bad consequences when working with caseworks samples, thus, for some years, primers for the amplification of the amelogenin gene are commonly included in the multiplex routinely used by forensic laboratories.

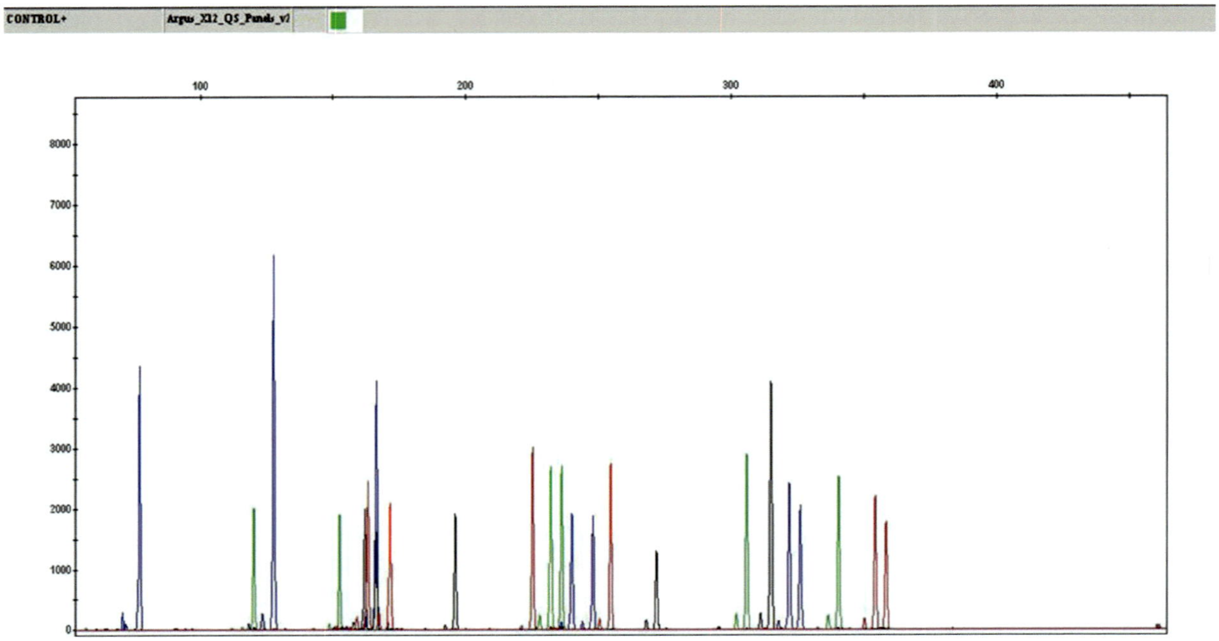

FIGURE 6.6 Control DNA 9947A analyzed by the Investigator Argus "X-12 QS."

6.7 ALTERNATIVE DNA MARKERS

6.7.1 Single-Nucleotide Polymorphism

A single-nucleotide polymorphism (SNP) is a single base change in a DNA sequence: it occurs when a single nucleotide (A, T, C, or G) in the genome is replaced by any of the other three bases (Figure 6.7). SNPs represent the most common form of natural genetic variation in the human genome (approximately 90%) and are considered the major genetic source of phenotypic variability: approximately 7 million SNPs occur with a minimum allele frequency (MAF) of 5% in the genome, and other 7 million with a MAF of 1%. The rate of SNPs varies along human chromosomes: X-Y chromosomes have less genetic variation than autosomes because the number of chromosomes is fewer than for autosomes.

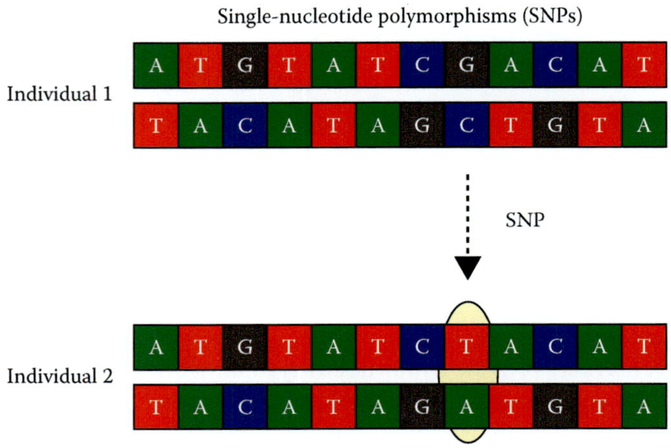

FIGURE 6.7 SNP structures.

The most common type of SNPs has alleles A-G in a strand and T-C in the opposite strand. Even if an SNP could theoretically have three or four alleles, almost all common SNPs have only two alleles: the minor allele is the one showing the lowest frequency at a locus.

There are variations in SNP distribution between human populations, so an allele that is common in one geographical or ethnic group may be less frequent or rare in another one. Regardless, the amount of variation is reduced by the linkage disequilibrium between closely linked SNP markers; this creates haplotype blocks separated from each other by recombination hotspots.

SNPs are initially produced by rare spontaneous mutations, and then they reach an appreciable population frequency by genetic drift and selection. The mutation rate is low (approximately 10^{-8} per base pair per generation), so the probability of a further mutation at the same locus are practically nonexistent. SNPs may be found within coding or non-coding regions of genes, or in the intergenic regions between genes and in both nuclear and mitochondrial DNA.

Only about 3%–5% of the DNA sequence codes for proteins, hence most SNPs are outside of the coding sequences. Due to degeneracy of the genetic code, an SNP within a coding sequence may not always produce a change in the aminoacidic sequence of a protein, but often the mutation is "silent" and the same polypeptide sequence is produced (*synonymous SNP*). On the contrary, a *nonsynonymous SNP* produces a variation in a polypeptide sequence; in particular, a *missense* change produces a different aminoacid while a *nonsense* change results in a premature stop codon. SNPs not placed in the coding regions may have consequences for gene splicing, transcription factor binding or the sequence of non-coding RNA.

Variations in DNA sequence can predispose individuals to diseases or influence their response to therapies, environmental factors (e.g., bacteria, viruses, toxins, or chemicals) or to drug effects. In addition, SNPs may affect phenotypic expression, even if it depends also on the presence of multiple polymorphisms and their positions within a given region.

During the last few years, many research efforts made in the public (Human Genome Project) and in private (SNP Consortium) sectors allowed generation of high-density SNPs maps in order to provide a framework for further research studies and forensic applications.

SNPs exhibit many *advantages*, such as abundance in the genome, low mutation rates (10^{-8}), reduced amplicon sizes, high-throughput genotyping, potential for phenotypic trait prediction, and ancestry studies. On the contrary, *disadvantages* include low polymorphism and discrimination power, a requirement to analyze a large number of SNPs in order to reach a significant discrimination power (PD) and difficulties with body fluid mixture detection (due to the fact they're generally biallelic).

According to Budowle and van Daal (2008), SNPs may play a useful role in several forensic applications, such as the following:

1. *Individual identity test*: A panel of 52 SNPs has been developed for human identification (Sanchez et al., 2006). The SNP's low polymorphism implies that a high number of markers should be analyzed in order to reach the same discrimination power obtained by the traditional analysis of 10–15 autosomal STRs.
2. *Lineage test, family reconstruction*: A set of linked SNPs (Y-SNPs, mt-SNPs) have been found useful as haplotype markers to identify persons by kinship analyses.
3. *Ancestry study*: Informative SNPs for establishing high probability of a person's geographical ancestry (AIMs).
4. *Phenotypic identification*: SNPs are selected in order to establish individual phenotypic characteristics such as skin color, hair color or eye color, with the aim to produce an identikit useful for investigative purposes.

In 2010, S. Walsh from Erasmus University (the Netherlands) developed the IrisPlex system that consists of a highly sensitive assay able to predict, according to a statistical model, the blue and brown human eye color from DNA samples with over 90% precision. In 2014, she introduced the HIrisPlex system, capable of predicting both eye and hair color.

DNA-based phenotypic prediction analysis is relevant in all cases where there isn't any suspect or when the suspect DNA does not match the evidence or any other profile in a DNA database. Phenotypic prediction is also useful in missing person cases or for analyzing old/ancient DNA in anthropological or evolutionary studies.

Since 2014, France has allowed the analysis of phenotypic SNP on crime scene samples when the traditional STR profile does not match with samples included in the database.

The most commonly used method for analyzing SNPs is the SNaPshot® reaction. This is a primer extension-based method that enables rapid and robust multiplexing of up to 10 SNPs. The reaction involves the single-base extension extension of an unlabeled oligonucleotide at the 3' end of the base immediately adjacent to the SNP by dideoxynucleotides (dNTP) labeled with different fluorescent dyes. Unlabeled, no complementary oligonucleotide sequences with different lengths act as mobility modifiers, so extended SNaPshot primers differing by size and color are separated by capillary electrophoresis.

6.7.2 Mitochondrial DNA

Mitochondrial DNA (mtDNA) is a valuable tool in forensic analysis; it's placed inside mitochondria, the organelles in the cytoplasm that convert chemical energy from food into adenosine triphosphate (ATP). It is a closed circular molecule of 16,569 bp, containing 37 genes, 13 of them involved in oxidative phosphorylation; there are from 50 up to several thousand copies of mtDNA per cell. The non-coding region "displacement (D)-loop" is a 1200 bp segment with a mutation rate 10 times higher than the coding regions: it contains three hypervariable regions called HVI, HVII, and HVIII, respectively (Figure 6.8).

The HVI (16024–16365) and HVII (73–340) regions are the most analyzed regions in forensics, while HVIII (438–574) is less studied because it has minor variability. The first human mitochondrial DNA sequence, called the *Cambridge Reference Sequence* (CRS), was published in 1981 by S. Anderson and the Sanger group while they were working at Cambridge University. The original sequence unfortunately included some errors, and in 1999 a revised version (rCRS) was published by R. Andrews: luckily the most-used sequences were identical in the original CRS and the revised one.

The rCRS now represents the reference sequence to which all the other sequences obtained from tested samples are compared, and then differences are recorded, resulting in a specific individual mtDNA profile.

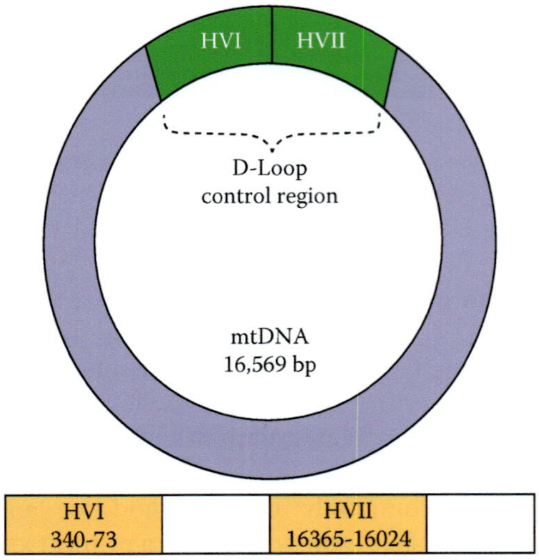

FIGURE 6.8 Structure of human mitochondrial DNA.

A common problem in mtDNA analysis is *heteroplasmy,* a phenomenon consisting in the existence of multiple mtDNA types (haplotypes) within an individual. Generally, the two types differ at only one base. This event may complicate the analysis and should be taken into consideration during data interpretation in order to avoid false exclusions. For years, the international forensic community (i.e., ISFG) published guidelines for a correct mtDNA analysis and data interpretation.

Mitochondrial DNA is maternally inherited because in human sperm, mitochondria are generally placed at the base of the tail, which is lost during fertilization. In addition, mitochondria accidentally gone beyond are destroyed by the egg cells. This means that, excluding a mutation, all maternally related persons (e.g., mother, daughter, sister) have identical mtDNA sequences.

In this way, any maternal relative sample can be used as a reference sample even if the donor and the evidence are separated by many generations. This implies that mtDNA cannot be used for identification purposes, since different persons share the same mitochondrial haplotype. The ability of recovering mitochondrial DNA from scarce or degraded samples is greater, since the mtDNA is available in more copies than nuclear DNA, and it's less prone to nuclease activity, due to its circular form. Consequently, mtDNA plays an important role in missing person investigations, mass disasters or in the analysis of samples containing limited/degraded biological material and generally not giving successful results by nuclear DNA typing (e.g., hair shafts, bones, teeth, decomposed samples).

MtDNA analysis is also useful in the medical field for the study of human diseases caused by deleterious mutations in gene-coding regions of the mtDNA; in addition, molecular anthropologists and evolutionary biologists can examine either the genetic variation in humans and the relatedness between different populations, rather than only the possible relationships between human and other species.

6.8 NEW METHODOLOGIES

6.8.1 Next-Generation Sequencing

DNA sequencing involves determining the order of the four deoxyribonucleotide bases: adenine (A), guanine (G), cytosine (C), and thymine (T). The most widely used sequencing method was developed by Frederick Sanger in 1977, and is based on the primer-extension procedure by selective incorporation of dideoxynucleotides (ddNTPs) during DNA replication in vitro catalyzed by the DNA polymerase.

Since its introduction, sequencing has played an important role in many DNA applications such as diagnostics, virology, and biotechnology: in fact, it was successfully used to complete the Human Genome Project, and genome projects of other species. Over the years, automatic sequencers used to detect sequencing products have improved, but unfortunately the analysis chemistry had remained relatively unchanged, causing some disadvantages as a high-cost, time-consuming, low-throughput procedure.

In the past few years, a new era of DNA sequencing has started: Next-generation sequencing (NGS) consists in a high-throughput DNA sequencing different from Sanger procedure. The principle is similar to capillary electrophoresis (CE) sequencing; DNA polymerase catalyzes the incorporation of fluorescently labeled deoxynucleotides (dNTPs) into a template strand; at the incorporation point, during each cycle, nucleotides are identified by the fluorophore excitation. The main difference between traditional and the new sequencing method is that NGS utilizes massively parallel sequencing to generate more than sounds of sequence information, and the final product is directly detected without any electrophoresis.

The procedure relies on the preparation of NGS libraries in a cell-free system by two PCR steps in the first step, specific primers per each target sequence are used. The length of the target regions is relevant for obtaining optimal results. During the second PCR step, adapters are incorporated into the amplicons by either legating the adapters to the PCR products or by using PCR primers with the adapter sequences at the 5' end of the base. Sequences obtained are then aligned by special software to the appropriate reference sequence.

Protocols are available for whole-genome sequencing, mRNA-Seq, targeted sequencing custom-selected regions or protein-binding regions. The procedure can be applied in various fields such as disease diagnosis, agricultural genomics, microbiological research, ancient DNA analysis and obviously forensics for the first time.

In 2007, Applied Biosystems and Illumina introduced the second-generation sequencing system based on the oligonucleotide ligation and a two-base encoding system. In 2010, Applied Biosystems started the commercialization of the Ion Torrent, a low-cost and rapid sequencer that uses semiconductor technology instead of fluorescence or chemiluminescence. The Ion Torrent semiconductor sequencing chip contains approximately 7 million sensors and allows the completion of a sequencing run in less than 2 hours: it translates chemically signals (A, C, G, T) into digital information (0, 1), reducing analysis costs and time.

Forensic DNA analysis requires accuracy and reproducibility, especially when analyzing difficult samples (low copy number, degraded or mixed samples). Generally, STR typing provides enough discrimination power for forensic applications; however, it has, unfortunately, some limitations, such as partial loss of information from degraded DNA samples and in particular the inability to analyze in a single reaction multiple different genetic polymorphisms. The high throughput and low cost of NGS technology may overcome these problems, allowing the analysis of a single NGS assay of multiple STR loci in autosomes than in sex chromosomes (X-Y), mitochondrial DNA, and relevant SNPs (i.e., the ones related to ancestry and physical traits)—even if combining either mtDNA or mRNA markers in multiplex PCR nuclear markers appears difficult due to the large variation in target copy numbers.

NGS technology may potentially increase efficiency, reducing samples consumption and the time required for multiple analysis. Regardless, another important advantage of NGS is that DNA fragments can be designed as short as possible because they not need to be separated by CE, and this will improve the chance of typing degraded DNA/RNA samples.

In 2014, Thermo Fisher introduced the first two commercial SNP multiplexes designed for the Ion PGM System: the *AmpliSeqIdentity Panel* that amplifies 124 autosomal SNPs (including most of the SNPforID) together with individual identification SNPs (IISNPs) and 34 Y-chromosome SNPs, and the *AmpliSeqAncestry Panel* that includes most of the ancestry-informative markers (AIMs). New assays have been developed recently to detect the same STRs routinely analyzed by capillary electrophoresis allowing comparison.

Even if some NGS studies and papers have been published in the last years, before the introduction of NGS as routine in forensics, more work is required to solve several problems concerning either technical aspects (i.e., low-template library preparation) than data processing, in order to satisfy the forensic community needs.

6.8.2 Rapid DNA Analysis

The ability to perform in a short time an accurate analysis of a suspect's DNA has the potential to reduce crimes and to increase public safety, especially on country borders, allowing fast research of profiles against a DNA database while the suspect is still in custody. Toward this end, in 2006 the FBI started a Rapid DNA initiative and in 2010 created a Rapid DNA Program Office to direct the development of commercial instruments able to produce within 2 hours a complete DNA profile compatible with previous CODIS profiles with the aim to integrate these new instruments within the DNA labs. Thus, in the few last years, new systems have been commercialized (e.g., RapidHIT, DNAscan, Rapid DNA Analysis System) that combine all laboratory steps (DNA purification, amplification, separation/detection) in cartridges containing all the reagents and materials needed to perform each reaction: analysis is completed in around 2 hours, greatly reducing time-to-results. The final output (autosomal DNA profile) is compatible with identification databases.

Initially designed only for direct oral swabs analysis, these new instruments now can proceed to analyze some forensic samples as well, and different commercial kits routinely used in forensic labs have been modified and validated for the use with rapid instruments. These systems are easy to use also by non-technical personnel and allow the operator to perform a DNA analysis in a mobile station or in the local police station, helping law enforcement to reduce time and cost of the investigation.

Due to the high interest and expansion of rapid DNA analysis, in 2014, the FBI released an "Addendum to the Quality Assurance Standards for DNA Databasing Laboratories performing Rapid DNA Analysis and Modified Rapid DNA Analysis Using a Rapid DNA Instrument" as a supplement to the "Quality Assurance Standards for DNA Databasing Laboratories" (September 1, 2011).

6.9 DATA INTERPRETATION

Before using DNA results for comparison purposes, it's necessary to evaluate the quality of profiles obtained in order to identify any potential artifact. The first step consists in evaluating if a profile is single or mixed. A DNA profile is from a single source if there are one or two alleles at all loci and/or the peak height ratio for all heterozygous loci are within the expectation, while a sample is generally considered a mixture if three or more alleles are found in one or more loci and the peak height ratio for one or more loci are below the values empirically determined by the laboratory.

The peak height ratio is the ratio between the height of the lowest peak (in raw fluorescence units, or RFUs) and the height of the highest peak, expressed as a percentage. In single-source samples, at heterozygote, loci the value is normally ≥70%, while in the case of mixed samples, an allelic imbalance is commonly observed and the peak height ratio is significantly lowered. So, more peaks in one or more loci and a significant peak imbalance are indicative of a mixture. The minimum number of contributors in a mixture is evaluated on the locus that exhibits the main number of peaks. Since generally the peak area reflects the quantity of DNA in the sample hence in case of mixtures it will be possible to determine the contribution of each donor (e.g., 1:1, 1:3, 1:5) by assessing the ratio between the peak areas. Several software packages (e.g., STRMix, LRMix, DNAMix, Forensim, Genoproof Mixture, Gene Mapper IDX) may support mixture interpretation. Regarding altitude, to be accepted, peaks should be greater than 150 RFU, but in the case of degraded samples and/or low DNA amount, the minimal value may be lowered to 50 RFU, according to international scientific community suggestions. Regarding shape, peaks should be regular, but in case of problems such as they appear split or with aberrant morphology, then it's difficult to recognize a true peak (Figure 6.9).

Another issue is DNA quantity; forensic evidence (i.e., contact traces found on objects) often contains a low number of cells that result in a low content of DNA. The term "low copy number" (LCN) indicates a DNA quantity less than 100 pg, while low template (LT) is generally used to indicate less than 200 pg. The amplification of samples containing low DNA levels may result in partial profiles (due to allelic or locus dropout), considerable allelic peak imbalance in a heterozygous locus (peak height ratio generally <60%), and artifact presence due to stochastic effects. With low DNA or in case of

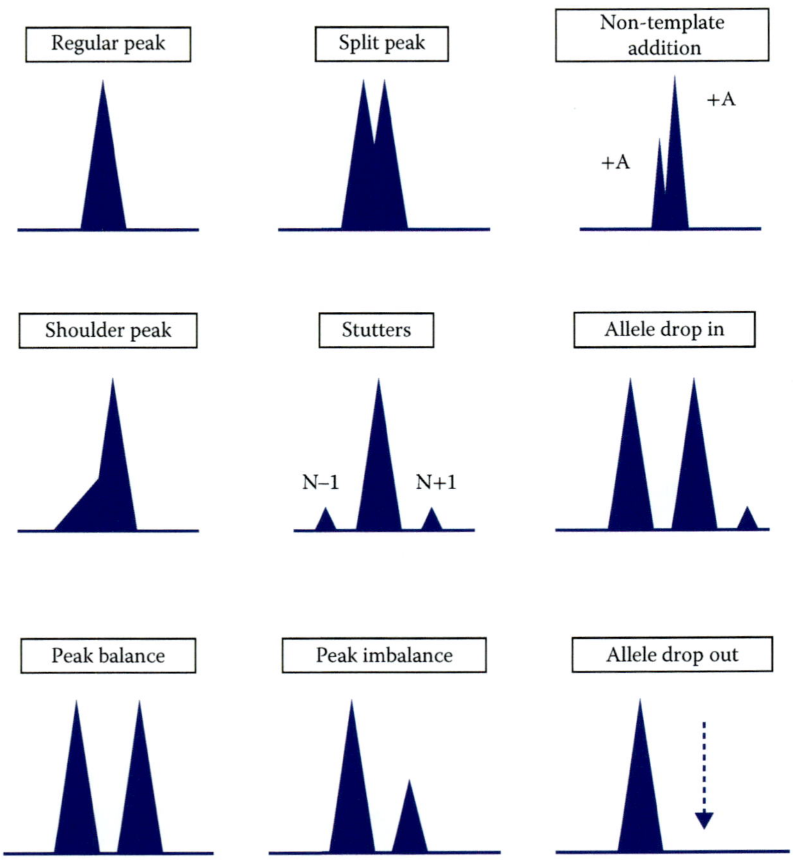

FIGURE 6.9 Example of peaks.

highly degraded samples, or when a high number of loci is examined, the possibility of artifacts is greater than in normal samples.

False peaks may include PCR products (e.g., stutter, non-template dependent nucleotide addition, non-specific amplification product) as well as analytical artifacts (e.g., spikes, raised baseline, pull-up due to incomplete spectral separation, peaks due to fluorescence accessory). Stutters, non-template-dependent nucleotide additions, dissociated dyes, and incomplete spectral separation are reproducible; spikes and raised baseline are generally non-reproducible. Stutters are peaks that are usually one repetition ($n - 1$) shorter than the corresponding peak and in fewer cases one repetition longer ($n + 1$); a stutter peak area is generally less than 15% of the main allele. Sometimes, in special conditions, the peak area may increase and simulate a real allele. Stutters complicate the interpretation of mixed DNA profiles and may become difficult to understand if a peak is or not a true allele coming from a minor contributor. Hence, each laboratory should develop internal criteria to determine if instrumental data represent either a real DNA peak or instrument noise.

Particular care should be taken during the analysis of LCN; since regular procedures cannot be applied to low DNA samples, laboratories should develop and validate internal procedures for reliable analysis and correct data interpretation.

Low DNA analysis analysis generally requires enhanced assay sensitivity obtained by increasing the PCR cycle number, reducing PCR reaction volume, adding a post-PCR sample cleanup increasing instrumental sample injection time. This may produce artifacts and contamination. Due to stochastic variations, PCR results from a single analysis can be unreliable, so replicate PCR amplifications are required in order to develop a "consensus profile" (Butler, 2010). A stochastic threshold must be established by a laboratory validation study and used during data interpretation to evaluate data reproducibility.

Peak sizing attribution is generally performed by special software (e.g., GeneMapper) including as reference specific panels and bin sets containing the size in bp of all alleles per each locus. Allelic peaks in the sample are usually compared with the corresponding ones in the allelic ladder, the external size standard containing all alleles of all loci. The software calls "OL" (off the ladder) all peaks not found in the corresponding ladder position, such as rare alleles not included in the ladder or, sometimes, false peaks. Consequently, after the evaluation of the technical aspects, DNA typing results must be verified also by review of peak designation and other software-generated information, either in the samples or in the quality controls (QCs).

6.10 BIOSTATICAL EVALUATIONS

6.10.1 Criminal Caseworks

Forensic scientists are generally required to analyze crime scene samples in order to establish whether or not they are from the same donor and in particular if evidence DNA matches the suspect's profile. If profiles don't match, that individual did not contribute to the sample; if they match, the suspect may have contributed to the evidence sample. In some cases, the possibility that a suspect's close relative (typically a brother) is the potential evidence contributor should be considered, therefore it's relevant to analyze also a reference sample from that relative.

According to the SWGDAM Guideline (2010), there are the following typical situations:

- DNA typing results are inconclusive or not interpretable.
- DNA profiles from two samples are different ("NOT match"), so it's possible to conclude they are from different sources.
- DNA profile from the samples are indistinguishable (they "match"), so they may have a common source.

Statistics should be calculated also in mixture cases if an individual cannot be excluded as a contributor of a mixture.

6.10.1.1 Random Match Probability

The random match probability represents the chance that a DNA profile of a random person in a given population matches the evidence profile. A DNA profile frequency indicates how frequent is a DNA profile in a specific population. It's obtained by calculating the genotype frequency per each locus and then multiplying the frequency across all loci. RMP is given by the reciprocal of profile frequency. Rare genotypes provide stronger evidence. Allele frequencies for different population groups are obtained collecting samples from anonymous donors belonging at least to three generations of the specific populations tested. Different population databases may sometimes produce slightly different results.

6.10.1.2 Likelihood Ratio

A likelihood ratio (LR) is a ratio between two probabilities of the same evidence under two mutually exclusive hypotheses: the hypothesis that the defendant is the source of the DNA profile (prosecutor hypothesis), versus the hypothesis that an unknown unrelated individual from the population is the donotr (defendant hypothesis). Interpretation of the strength of the statis-tical value can be variable, and it should be considered in a context with the other case circumstances.

TABLE 6.2 Evett's Verbal Predicates for Likelihood Ratios

Likelihood Ratio (LR)	Verbal Predicates
1 < LR ≤ 10	Limited evidence to support
10 < LR ≤ 100	Moderate evidence to support
100 < LR ≤ 1000	Moderately strong evidence to support
1000 < LR ≤ 10,000	Strong evidence to support
10,000 < LR	Very strong evidence to support

LR values of more than 100 are strong evidence to support the prosecutor hypothesis; for LR less than 1 the equivalent is a support for the defender hypothesis. In order to associate verbal predicates to LR values for providing a clearer support to the court, a qualitative verbal scalesù (Table 6.2) was developed by Evett and Weir (1998) and Evett et al. (2000).

6.10.1.3 Combined Probability of Exclusion/Combined Probability of Inclusion (CPE/CPI)

CPE/CPI are used to calculate the probability that a randomly selected person from a given population would be excluded/included as a contributor to a mixture. CPE can be used to conservatively interpret complex DNA mixtures. This gives an estimate of population size whose genotype shows at least one allele not found the DNA mixture: an individual can be excluded if he has an allele per each locus that is not detected in the mixture.

Multiple calculations may be done for the same mixture component when different assumptions regarding the number of contributors are made. A CPE/CPI approach assumes that all alleles are present: so analysis of low levels of DNA cannot be correctly performed because some alleles may be lost.

Very often forensic laboratories work with compromised samples: degraded or low DNA samples produce partial profiles (due to allelic or locus drop out) in addition drop-in phenomena may also occur. In these cases DNA profile of the tested sample may not match the one of the alleged contributor, because the classical conservative model of statistical evaluation "match vs no-match", gives respectively a value of 1 or 0.

With the aim to overcome problems related to the evaluation of complex samples, in 2012 the DNA Commission of the International Society of Forensic Genetics (ISFG) published a recommendation to include in statistical evaluation also the probability of drop in/drop out. This provides a probabilistic model, where the probability of the evidence of "match vs. no-match" can assume any value between 1 and 0.

6.10.2 Paternity Test

In traditional paternity tests, DNA profiles of the trio (alleged father, mother and child) are compared in order to evaluate if the alleged father can be the true biological father. Paternity analysis may be performed in absence of the mother. Each person receives one allele from the mother and the other one from the father; hence, if an allele in the child is not of maternal origin, then it has to come from the biological father. This evaluation is done per all loci analyzed in a multilocus profile.

If the tested man (alleged father) does not exhibit the obliged paternal alleles, then the result of the analysis is an *exclusion*. The international scientific community has established three incompatibilities as a minimum to affirm the alleged father is not the biological father. Generally, 15–17 markers are enough to reach a sufficient number of incompatibilities; alternatively, it's required to extend the analysis to additional loci, including SNPs or markers on sex chromosomes.

Regardless, in the case of inconsistency for 12 loci, the calculation of a paternity index for mutation is required. Some authors (Lindner et al., 2014; Sun et al., 2012; Jacewicz et al., 2004; Brandt-Casadevall et al., 2003) have described cases where three genetic incompatibilities were observed between the alleged father and the child, even if the man was the real biological father. On the contrary, if the tested person has per each locus the obligate paternal allele, the result is an *inclusion*, and a paternity index (PI) should be calculated. PI value represents the relative probability that the alleged father and not an unrelated, random man transmitted the obligate allele to the child.

PI (sometimes indicated as L) is given by the formula X/Y, where X indicates the probability that the alleged father has the obligate allele and Y is the chance that an unrelated man in the population has the same allele. An X value is 1 if the alleged father is homozygous for the allele of interest, while it is 0.5 if the alleged father is heterozygous.

When analyzing many loci, the paternity index is calculated per each locus and all resulting values are to determine the total value "combined paternity index" (CPI), which is a measure of the strength of the genetic evidence (likelihood ratio, or L). The CPI value can range from 0 to infinity: therefore, if CPI is between 0 and 1, the genetic evidence is favorable to non-paternity; if CPI >1, it's more consistent with the paternity hypothesis.

The likelihood ratio (L) is converted into a "probability of paternity" ("W" from the German word *Wahrscheinlichkeit*, "probability") by the formula $W = L/(1+L)$ and the contrary, $L = W/(1 - W)$. A 100% value of probability is mathematically impossible, but generally, when analyzing multiple polymorphic markers, significant values around 99.99% or more are obtained.

Each country has established a threshold value for affirming that the tested man is the true biological father: the CPI value is generally 1000 in Europe and 100 in the United States. The probability of paternity calculation values useful to affirm paternity is "practically proven"; the probability is variable between countries, but all are generally beyond 99%. For immigration cases, the U.S. Department of State requires as a minimum probability of paternity a value of 99.5%.

Another approach throughout the United States, and similar to the probability of exclusion, is the "random man not excluded" (RMNE), which represents the part of the population that shows all the obligate alleles and therefore could not be excluded as contributors. The RMNE value for a single locus is given by the formula $1 - (1 - p)^2$.

In case of multiple loci analysis, RMNE values are multiplied over all loci, and the combined final value is the "combined random man not excluded" (CRMNE), which is equivalent to the CPI. CRMNE is generally less than 1, and it is analogous to 1 – CRMNE or power of exclusion (PE) that represents the probability of excluding a falsely accused man.

Statistical calculations are done by using a database containing allele frequencies of the relevant populations. Databases are created by testing unrelated people belonging to a selected population for at least three generations. Several software packages (free in some cases) are available to forensic experts (e.g., DNA View, GenoProof, Familias, Pater) in order to perform paternity calculations. According to Hummel (1997), statistical values can be translated in verbal predicates useful for clearly explaining the result obtained (Table 6.3).

Identical evaluations can be done in the case of maternity testing. Laws regulating private paternity or maternity tests differ between countries; in some cases the analysis is forbidden, in others it can be performed not only on living persons but also as a prenatal test.

Generally, a buccal swab or a blood sample can be collected for the paternity test. In the case of deficiency paternity, testing the analysis of close relatives of the tested person may be useful to reconstruct the family branch in order to verify if the person is biologically related to a family. In criminal cases, paternity tests are generally performed after sexual assaults or to identify human remains (i.e., mass disasters), where it is necessary to compare remains to DNA profiles (reverse paternity test) with those of the family members (Figure 6.10).

Parentage tests on siblings (sisters, brothers), aunts, uncles, or sometimes grandmothers, grandfathers, grandchildren are often required to test if people are really blood relatives. Less frequently, the reconstruction of entire family trees is required; the case of the Romanov family, whose remains were found in a mass grave in Ekaterinsburg (Russia) is well known. DNA identification performed in 1994 by Prof. Peter Gill from the Forensic Science Service (UK) allowed verification

TABLE 6.3 Hummel's Verbal Predicates for Paternity Tests

Probability of Paternity%	Verbal Predicates
>99.73	Paternity practically proven
>99–99.73	Paternity highly likely
>95–99	Paternity very likely
>90–95	Paternity likely
>80–90	Certain indication of paternity
>70–80	Indication of paternity
>20–30	Indication of potential non-paternity
>10–20	Indication of non-paternity
>5–10	Paternity unlikely
>1–5	Paternity very unlikely
>0.27–1	Paternity highly unlikely
<0.27%	Paternity practically excluded

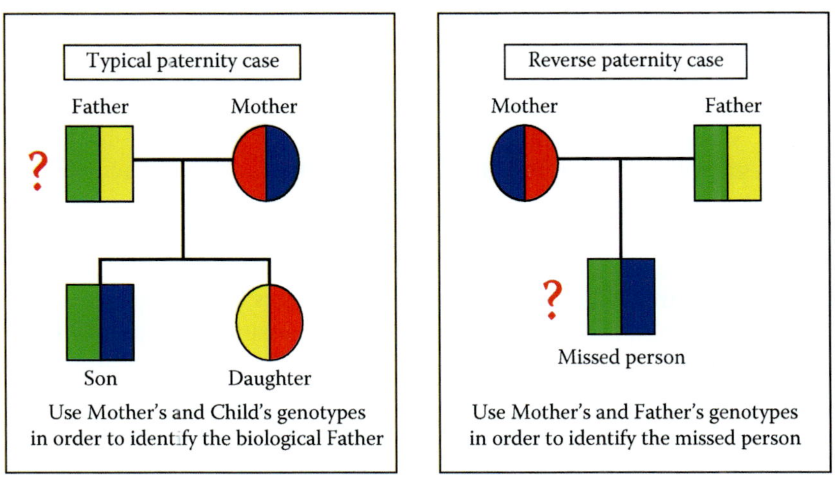

FIGURE 6.10 Examples of paternity tests.

TABLE 6.4 Example of DNA% Shared in Typical Familial Relationships

Relationship	Shared DNA
Full Siblings	50%
Parents–Child	50%
Half Siblings	25%
Uncle/Aunt–Nephew/Niece	25%
Grandparents–Grandchildren	25%
First Cousins	12.5%
Half Cousins	6.25%

that Anna Anderson was not the Princess Anastasia as previously thought.

When in a family tree, the distance between individuals increases, minor is the number of genes shared (Table 6.4). In these cases, the analysis of sexual chromosomes (Y or X) or of mtDNA can assist in the reconstruction of relationships through female or male lines.

6.11 DNA ADMISSIBILITY IN THE COURT

Forensic DNA analysis is an area that requires careful inspection; in fact, although DNA analysis in most courts is generally admissible in principle, in many cases judges found DNA evidence was not acceptable because analysis was not performed in accordance with internationally accepted principles/rules. In fact, DNA analysis is a multistep technical process that needs to be performed by a qualified expert who must have the scientific education, training, and experience proportional with the analysis required and eventually the testimony provided. The international community (e.g., SWGDAM, DAB, ENFSI, ISFG) has developed guidelines and recommendations for the application of correct DNA typing procedures and for data interpretations; these instructions should be followed by forensic laboratories to ensure that accurate and reliable results are obtained and correctly interpreted.

One of the most important issues in forensics is the accidental transfer of DNA. Contamination can occur during any step of the process (collection, preservation, handling, or analysis). Common sources of contamination include not only investigators at the crime scene and laboratory personnel but also samples, reagents, and consumables. Modern new sensitive procedures, while increasing the ability to detect low DNA quantities, also increase the possibility of detecting contaminants. Forensic laboratories should develop internal procedures in order to minimize the risk of contamination (e.g., analysts should wear personal protection such as gloves and hair caps, use sterile mono-use items such as tweezers and scalpels, or, when this is not possible, use items that are accurately sterilized); and also to detect and register any eventual contamination that may happen. Each laboratory should set up an exclusionary database with all personnel DNA profiles, which is useful to detect/exclude any potential contamination.

According to *Locard's Exchange Principle*, "every contact leaves a trace"; consequently, sometimes DNA found at crime scenes may be from a person who came in contact with the scene at a previous time and therefore has no relation to the criminal event (secondary or tertiary transfers). The quantity of DNA in a contact trace depends on the number of associated cells, hence it's highly variable between individuals. Some people are "good shedders" and lose epithelial cells more than others; and some factors such as sweating (that is related to humidity, temperature, stress), personal habits (i.e., washing hands several times), and personal activities can influence the quantity of DNA available in a trace. In addition, the touched substrate type (porous, not-porous, rough, smooth), the contact length (10 sec, 1 minutes, etc.), and the contact type (repeated or single touch) can also affect it.

Furthermore, the elapsed time between trace deposition and DNA collection, together with the effect of the exposition to the environment consistently influence DNA persistence and may produce sample deterioration. (Loewe, 2002; Phipps and Petricevic, 2007; Kumar, 2015). This means that detecting a genetic profile at a crime scene is not always equivalent to determining a person's guilt. Evidence may have been touched or contaminated with exogenous DNA from individuals not related to the crime, such as DNA from persons not related to the criminal event. Often, problems that are related to data interpretation because of peak assignments or biostatistical interpretation may be complicated, especially in the presence of partial or mixed profiles.

The reliability of the results should be maintained by a stringent quality management program, which includes proficiency testing, validation studies, and quality control procedures. Quality control (QC) refers to tests performed by a laboratory to ensure that DNA-typing results and interpretation meet data from specified known standards, while quality assurance (QA) involves other measures that are taken in order to monitor, verify, and document the laboratory activity and performance.

Laboratory accreditation is crucial for high-quality DNA testing; in particular, the ISO/IEC 17025 Guide (2005) refers to a set of standards internationally established to ensure high quality in laboratories. The Guide specifies the "general requirements for the competence of testing and calibration laboratories. It covers testing and calibration performed using standard methods, non-standard methods and laboratory-developed methods" (par. 1.1 ISO/IEC Guide). A laboratory certified according to ISO/IEC 17025 requirements has the technical expertise required to perform the analysis and quality management system that is essential to ensure the accuracy of analytical data and the traceability of measurements. This means it meets all international standards and produces reliable results that are interpreted by a qualified staff. In fact, it's internationally established that only laboratories with this accreditation can send their DNA profiles to a national DNA database.

In the past few years, DNA databases have become one of the most efficient tools to provide information about unknown criminals. Today, almost 6 million DNA profiles from suspects and convicted offenders are stored in European databases and there have been more than 1 million hits.

DNA databases originally created for sex offenders have been extended to include almost any type of criminal offender, because often, crimes are committed by repeat offenders. With this perspective, the great value of a DNA database is its ability to connect crimes in order to identify criminals that sometimes are not directly suspected and to prevent further crimes.

In April 1995, the National Criminal Intelligence DNA Database (NDNAD) was set up in the UK. In the United States, the creation of a national database was established in 1994 by the DNA Identification Act the Combined DNA Index System (CODIS) was officially activated in October 1998. According to FBI statistics, as of April 2017, CODIS has already produced more than 373,099 matches, which has assisted investigators in more than 358,069 cases (www.fbi.gov).

BIBLIOGRAPHY

Addendum to the Quality Assurance Standards for DNA Databasing Laboratories performing Rapid DNA Analysis and Modified Rapid DNA Analysis Using a Rapid DNA Instrument (12/1/2014).

Bär W., Brinkmann B., Budowle B., Carracedo A., Gill P. et al. (1997), DNA recommendations. Further report of the DNA Commission of the ISFG regarding the use of short tandem repeat systems, *Forensic Sci Int.* 87 (3): 179–184.

Bär W., Brinkmann B., Lincoln P., Mayr W., Rossi U. et al. (1992), Editorial: Recommendations of the DNA Commission of the International Society for Forensic Haemogenetics relating to the use of PCR-based polymorphisms, *Forensic Sci. Int.* 55: 1–3.

Bär W., Brinkmann B., Lincoln P., Mayr W., Rossi U. et al. (1993), Editorial: Statement by DNA Commission of the International Society for Forensic Haemogenetics concerning the National Academy of Sciences report on DNA Technology in Forensic Science in the USA, *Forensic Sci. Int.* 59 (1): 1–2.

Barbaro A., Fernandez-Formoso L., Phillips C., Carracedo A. and Lareu M.V. (2013), Casework application of a standalone pentaplex assay of extended-ESS STRs, *Leg. Med.* 15 (4): 217–221.

Bill M., Gill P., Curran J., Clayton T., Pinchin R. et al. (2005) PENDULUM-a guideline-based approach to the interpretation of STR mixtures, *Forensic Sci. Int.* 148: 181–189.

Blanco-Verea A., Brion M., Ramos-Luis E., Lareu M.V. and Carracedo A. (2008), Forensic validation and implementation of Y-chromosome SNP multiplexes, *Forensic Sci. Int. Genet. Suppl. Ser.* 1: 181–183.

Børsting C. and Morling N. (2015), Next generation sequencing and its applications in forensic genetics, *Forensic Sci. Int. Genet.* 18: 78–89.

Bouakaze C., Keyser C., Amory S., Crubézy E. and Ludes B. (2007), First successful assay of Y-SNP typing by SNaPshot minisequencing on ancient DNA, *Int. J. Legal Med.* 121 (6): 493–499.

Brandt-Casadevall C., Gené M., Piqué E., Borrego N., Gehrig C. et al. (2003), Presence of two mutations between father and child in two cases of paternity testing, *Progr. Forensic Genet. 9*. 1239: 647, ICS, Elsevier.

Brion M., Sanchez J.J., Balogh K., Thacker C., Blanco-Verea A. et al. (2006), Analysis of 29 Y-chromosome SNPs in a single multiplex useful to predict the geographic origin of male lineages, *Int. Congr. Ser.* 1288: 13–15.

Buckleton J., Triggs C.M. and Walsh S.J. (2005), *Forensic DNA Evidence Interpretation*. Boca Raton, FL: CRC Press, p. 534.

Budowle B. and van Daal A. (2008), Forensically relevant SNP classes, *BioTechniques*. 44: 603–610.

Butler J. (2005), *Forensic DNA Typing–Biology, Technology, and Genetics of STR Markers*. Burlington, MA: Academic Press, Elsevier.

Butler J.M. (2011), *Advanced Topics in Forensic DNA Typing Methodology*. Burlington, MA: Academic Press, Elsevier.

Butler JM. (2015), *Advanced Topics in Forensic DNA Typing: Interpretation*. Burlington, MA: Academic Press, Elsevier.

Butler J.M., Kline M.C. and Decker A.E. (2008) Addressing Y-chromosomes short tan dem repeat (Y-STR) allele nomenclature, *J. Genet. Geneal.* 4 (2): 125–148.

Butler J.M. and Levin B.C. (1998), Forensic applications of mitochondrial DNA, *Trends Biotechnol.* 16 (4): 158–162.

Chung D.T., Drabek J., Opel K.L., Butler J.M. and McCord B.R. (2004), A study on the effects of degradation and template concentration on the amplification efficiency of the STR miniplex primer sets, *J. Forensic Sci.* 49: 733–740.

Coble M.D. and Butler J.M., (2005) Characterization of new miniSTR loci to aid analysis of degraded DNA, *J. Forensic. Sci.* 50: 43–53.

de Knijff P., Kayser M., Caglia A., Corach D., Fretwell N. et al. (1997), Chromosome Y microsatellites: Population genetic and evolutionary aspects, *Int. J. Legal Med.* 110 (3): 134–140.

DNA Advisory Board. (2000), Quality assurance standards for forensic DNA typing laboratories, *Forensic Sci. Commun.* 2(3). Available at: https://archives.fbi.gov/archives/about-us/lab/forensic-science-communications/fsc/july2000/quality-assurance-standards-for-forensic-dna-testing-laboratories.

DNA-Database Management Review and Recommendation, ENFSI DNA Working Group, April (2010).

Evett I.W., Jackson G., Lambert J.A., and McCrossan S. (2000), The impact of the principles of evidence interpretation on the structure and content of statements, *Sci. Justice.* 40(4): 233–239.

Evett I.W. and Weir B.S. (1998), *Interpreting DNA Evidence.* Sunderland, MA: Sinauer Associates, 278 pages.

FBI Quality Assurance Standards for DNA Databasing Laboratories. (2011). Available at: https://www.fbi.gov/file-repository/quality-assurance-standards-for-dna-databasing-laboratories.pdf/view

Gill P. (1994), Identification of the remains of the Romanov family by DNA analysis, *Nat. Genet.* 6: 130–135.

Gill P. (2001), An assessment of the utility of single nucleotide polymorphisms (SNPs) for forensic purposes. *Int. J. Legal Med.* 114 (4–5): 204–210.

Gill P., Brenner C., Brinkmann B., Budowle B., Carracedo A. et al. (2001), DNA Commission of the International Society of Forensic Genetics: Recommendations on forensic analysis using Y-chromosome STRs, *Forensic Sci. Int.* 124 (1): 5–10.

Gill P., Brenner C.H., Buckleton J.S., Carracedo A., Krawczak M. et al. (2006), DNA commission of the International Society of Forensic Genetics: Recommendations on the interpretation of mixtures, *Forensic Sci. Int.* 160: 90–101.

Gill P., Gusmao L., Haned H., Mayr W.R., Morling N. et al. (2012), DNA commission of the International Society of Forensic Genetics: Recommendations on the evaluation of STR typing results that may include drop-out and/or drop-in using probabilistic methods, *Forensic Sci. Int. Genet.* 6: 679–688.

Gill P., Werrett D.J., Budowle B. and Guerrieri R. (2004), An assessment of whether SNPs will replace STRs in national DNA database: Joint considerations of the DNA working group of the European Network of Forensic Science Institutes (ENFSI) and the Scientific Working Group on DNA Analysis Methods (SWGDAM), *Sci. Justice.* 44: 51–53.

Gjertson D.W., Brenner C.H., Baur M.P., Carracedo A., Guidet F. et al. (2007), ISFG: Recommendations on biostatistics in paternity testing, *Forensic Sci. Int. Genet.* 1 (3): 223–231.

Gusmao L., Butler J.M., Carracedo A., Gill P., Kayser M. et al. (2006), DNA Commission of the International Society of Forensic Genetics (ISFG): An update of the recommendations on the use of Y-STRs in forensic analysis, *Forensic Sci. Int.* 157: 187–197.

Hares D.R. (2012), Expanding the CODIS core loci in the United States, *Forensic Sci. Int. Genet.* 6: e52–e54.

Hill C.R., Kline M.C., Coble MD. and Butler J.M. (2008), Characterization of 26 miniSTR loci for improved analysis of degraded DNA samples, *J. Forensic Sci.* 53: 1.

Houck M.M. and Siegel J.A. (2006), *Fundamentals of Forensic Science.* Burlington, MA: Academic Press, Elsevier.

Hummel K. (1997), Erblich-polymorphe Eigenschaften des Blutes zur Klärung strittiger Blutsverwandtschaft und fraglicher Identität—Hierzu benutzte biometrische—Buch neu kaufen—Kovac, Dr. Verlag.

Guide ISO/IEC 17025:2005 (2005),. General requirements for the competence of testing and calibration laboratories.

Jacewicz R., Berent J., Prosniak A. and Dobosz T. (2004), Non-exclusion paternity case with a triple genetic incompatibilities, *Progr. Forensic Genet. 10.* 1261: 511–513, ICS, Elsevier.

Jeffreys A.J., Wilson V. and Thein S.W. (1984), Hypervariable "minisatellite" regions in human DNA, *Nature.* 314: 67–73.

Jeffreys A.J., Wilson V. and Thein S.L. (1985), Individual-specific "fingerprints" of human DNA, *Nature.* 316: 76.

Kayser M., Caglia A., Corach D., Fretwell N., Gehrig C. et al. (1997), Evaluation of Y-chromosomal STRs: A multicenter study, *Int. J. Legal Med.* 110 (3): 125–133, 141–149.

Kayser M., de Knijff P., Dieltjes P., Krawczak M., Nagy M. et al. (1997), Applications of microsatellite-based Y chromosome haplotyping, *Electrophoresis.* 18: 1602–1607.

Kayser M., Kruger C., Nagy M., Geserick G., de Knijff P. et al. (1998), Y-chromosomal DNA-analysis in paternity testing: Experiences and recommendations, *Adv. Forensic Genet.* 7: 494–496.

Kidd K.K., Pakstis A.J., Speed W.C., Grigorenko E.L., Kajuna S.L. et al. (2006), Developing a SNP panel for forensic identification of individuals, *Forensic Sci. Int.* 164: 20–32.

Kiely T.F. (2006), *Forensic Evidence: Science and the Criminal Law.* London: CRC Press/Taylor & Francis.

Kumar P., Gupta R., Singh R., and Jasuja OP. (2015), Effects of latent fingerprint development reagents on subsequent forensic DNA typing: a review. *J. Forensic Leg. Med.* 32:64–69.

Lindner I., von Wurmb-Schwark N., Meier P., Fimmers R. and Büttner A. (2014), Usefulness of SNPs as supplementary markers in a paternity case with 3 genetic incompatibilities at autosomal and Y chromosomal loci, *Transfus. Med. Hemother.* 41 (2): 117–121.

Lowe A., Murray C., Whitaker J., Tully G., and Gill P. (2002), The propensity of individuals to deposit DNA and secondary transfer of low level DNA from individuals to inert surfaces. *Forensic Sci. Int.* 129: 25–34.

Morling N., Allen R.W., Carracedo A., Geada H., Guidet F. et al. (2002), Paternity Testing Commission of the International Society of Forensic Genetics: Recommendations on genetic investigations in paternity cases, *Forensic Sci. Int.* 129 (3): 148–157.

Mullis K. (1990), The unusual origin of the polymerase chain reaction, *Sci Am.* 262 (4): 56–61, 64–65.

Parson W., Gusmao L., Hares D.R., Irwin J.A., Mayr W.R. et al. (2014), DNA Commission of the International Society for Forensic Genetics: Revised and extended guidelines for mitochondrial DNA typing, *Forensic Sci. Int. Genet.* 13: 134–142.

Phipps M. and Petricevic S. (2007), The tendency of individuals to transfer DNA to handled items. *Forensic Sci. Int.* 168(2–3):162-168.

Roewer L., Krawczak M., Willuweit S., Nagy M., Alves C. et al. (2001), Online reference database of European Y-chromosomal short tandem repeat (STR) haplotypes, *Forensic Sci Int.* 118: 106–113.

Sambrook J. and Russel D.W. (2001), In vitro amplification of DNA by the polymerase chain reaction, Chapter 8, Sambrook J. and Russel D.W. (eds.), *Molecular Cloning: A Laboratory Manual.* New York, NY: Cold Spring Harbor..

Sanchez J.J., Phillips C., Børsting C., Balogh K., Bogus M. et al. (2006), A multiplex assay with 52 single-nucleotide polymorphisms for human identification, *Electrophoresis.* 27: 1713–1724.

Sanders J. (2000), *Forensic Casebook of Crime.* London: True Crime Library, Forum Press. p. 229.

Schneider M., Bender K., Mayr W., Parson W., Hoste B. et al. (2004), STR analysis of artificially degraded DNA—Results of a collaborative European exercise, *Forensic Sci. Int.* 139: 123–134.

Schumm J.W., Gutierrez-Mateo C., Tan E., and Selden R. (2013), A 27-locus STR assay to meet all United States and European law enforcement agency standards. *J Forensic Sci.* 58 (6): 1584–1592.

Schumm J.W., Wingrove R.S. and Douglas E.K. (2004), Robust STR multiplexes for challenging casework samples, *Prog. Forensic Genet.* 10: 547–549.

Scientific Working Group on DNA Analysis Methods (SWGDAM). (2000), Short tandem repeat (STR) interpretation guidelines, *Forensic Sci. Commun.* 2, 90 pages.

Sobrino B. and Carracedo A. (2005), SNP typing in forensic genetics, *Forensic DNA Typing Protoc.* 297: 1064–3745.

Southern E.M. (1975), Detection of specific sequences among DNA fragments separated by gel electrophoresis, *J. Mol. Biol.* 98: 503–517.

Sulem P., Gudbjartsson D.F., Stacey S.N., Helgason A., and Rafnar T. et al. (2007), Genetic determinants of hair, eye and skin pigmentation, *Nat. Genet.* 39: 1443–1452.

Sullivan K.M., Mannucci A., Kimpton C.P., and Gill P. (1993), A rapid and quantitative DNA sex test: Fluorescence-based PCR analysis of X-Y homologous gene amelogenin, *BioTechniques.* 15 (4): 637–641.

Sun H.Y., Li H.X., Zeng X.P., Ren Z., and Chen W.J. (2012), A paternity case with mutations at three CODIS core STR loci, *Forensic Sci. Int. Genet.* 6 (1): 61–62.

SWGDAM MtDNA Interpretation Guidelines for Mitochondrial DNA Analysis by Forensic DNA Testing Laboratories (2013). Available at: https://www.swgdam.org/publications

Szibor R. (2007), X-chromosomal markers: Past, present and future, *Forensic. Sci. Int. Genet.* 1: 93–99.

Szibor R., Krawczak M., Hering S., Edelmann J., Kuhlisch E. et al. (2003), Use of X-linked markers for forensic purposes, *Int. J. Legal Med.* 117: 67–74.

The International HapMap Consortium. (2007), A second generation human haplotype—Map of over 3.1 million SNPs, *Nature.* 449: 851–861.

Thorisson G.A. and Stein L.D. (2003), The SNP Consortium website: Past, present and future, *Nucleic Acids Res.* 31 (1): 124–127.

Tomas C., Sanchez J.J., Castro J.A., Børsting C., and Morling N. (2008), Utility of X-chromosome SNPs in relationship testing, *Forensic Sci. Int. Genet. Suppl. Ser.* 1: 528–530.

Walsh S, Lindenbergh A, Zuniga S.B, Sijen T, de Knijff P. et al. (2011), Developmental validation of the IrisPlex system: Determination of blue and brown iris colour for forensic intelligence, *Forensic Sci. Int. Genet.* 5: 464–471.

Wang N., Akey J.M., Zhang K., Chakraborty R., and Jin L. (2002), Distribution of recombination crossovers and the origin of haplotype blocks: The interplay of population history, recombination and mutation, *Am. J. Hum. Genet.* 71: 1227–1234.

Watson J.D. and Crick F.H.C. (1953), A structure for deoxyribose nucleic acid, *Nature.* 171: 737–738.

Weiner M.P. and Hudson T.J. (2002), Introduction to SNPs: Discovery of markers for disease, *BioTechniques*. 10 (Suppl. 4–7), 12–13.

Wiegand P. and Kleiber M. (2001), Less is more—Length reduction of STR amplicons using redesigned primers, *Int. J. Legal Med.* 114: 285–287.

Willuweit S., Roewer L. (2007), Y chromosome haplotype reference database (YHRD): Update, *Forensic Sci. Int. Genet.* 1 (2): 83–87.

Zarrabeitia M.T., Mijares V. and Riancho J.A. (2007), Forensic efficiency of microsatellites and single nucleotide polymorphisms on the X chromosome, *Int. J. Legal Med.* 121 (6): 433–437.

CHAPTER 7

Forensic Facial Recognition

Shelina Khalid Jilani and Stephen Driver

CONTENTS

7.1 INTRODUCTION

Facial recognition is the ability to establish a suspect's identity based upon his or her facial characteristics. Automatic facial recognition software and methods have been widely studied due to their role not only in an investigation, but also, for example, in visual surveillance and the duplication of government-issued identification documents such as drivers' licenses and passports (Jain et al., 2007, 2011).

Facial recognition is a form of biometrics that has developed into an accepted forensic tool capable of positively identifying an individual. It is a niche field of forensic science, within which constant technological advancements and expertise are being deployed.

Early face recognition algorithms made use of simple geometric models; however, the process has now matured, using sophisticated representations and matching processes.

The task of an investigating officer or forensic scientist when investigating a crime is to establish the identity of the unknown subject or the victim.

In comparison to automated facial recognition, facial comparison is a far more demanding role for a forensic scientist, since she/he must be able to work with CCTV footage and captured images that are retrieved under nonidentical conditions. Variances in image quality, lighting conditions, viewpoint and camera lens all play an important role for digital images. They are point of consideration when a scientist carries out comparative facial analysis. A proficient examiner must be able to help in the identification of an unknown individual based solely on the facial characteristics and features observed. The key factor in this process of identification is the establishment of unique individual markers such as tattoos, piercing, scars as a result of trauma, or birthmarks and moles.

While algorithmic systems work by identifying a face under "real time" the aim of facial comparison appears slightly later during an investigation. The purpose of carrying out facial comparisons can either be for verification of a known control, "is this John?" or it may be the comparison between an unknown subject and a known control.

The use of photographic evidence has been admissable in British courts for nearly 50 years (Tolson, 1864). While, the use of CCTV footage was first used in the 1980s to aid in information about a theft which took place in a retail store (Fowden and White, 1982).

7.2 WHY USE FACIAL RECOGNITION FOR IDENTIFICATION?

Biometrics is the automatic recognition of an individual using distinguishable traits. Whereas, an expansive definition is any automatically measurable, robust and distinctive physical characteristic or personal trait that can be used to identify an individual or verify the claimed identity of the individual. Biometric-based techniques have quickly emerged from the field of forensic science; they are one of the most promising identifying options in recent years. Instead of authenticating people and allowing them access to domains via personal identification numbers (PINs), passwords, and security questions, biometric-based techniques examine one's behavioral and physiological characteristics in order to ascertain one's identity (Jain et al., 2006; Jafri and Arabnia, 2009.) PINs and passwords are easily lost and/or stolen, and security question answers as well as keys can be duplicated or misplaced; however, physiological characteristics cannot be lost or easily duplicated.

"Measurable" refers to a characteristic or trait that is easily presented, located, and converted into a quantifiable digital format by a sensor of a system. Such measurability allows for the process of matching to occur, which automates the initial process of facial recognition. "Robust" relates to the extent to which a characteristic or trait has the ability to change over time. The changes subject to individual characteristics and traits can be a result of aging, illness, or the environment, such as chemical exposure and injury (Woodward et al., 2003). A biometric technique which is considered to be highly robust will not be subject to significant change over time; however, a less robust biometric based technique will be more easily prone to change. "Distinctiveness" measures the variability and change in the biometric pattern among the general population. It is generally accepted that the higher the degree of distinctiveness, the more unique and specific the identifying marker. A lower score in distinctiveness suggests the likelihood of the identifying marker being very prevalent within the general population and not very unique and specific.

Identification and verification are the two key goals of biometric techniques, particularly for facial recognition. Identification is the establishing of a criminal's or a victim's identity (Woodward et al., 2003). The technique will make an attempt to answer the question "Who is X?" with the help of previously stored data and determine if there is a match to allow the identification of the criminal or a victim known as "X." Verification is a different concept than identification, as with verification the recognition system compares a newly inputted characteristic to previously collected and stored data from the same person to verify the individual's identity. With such a one-to-one search style, the technique will either verify the identity of a criminal/victim or fail to verify the individual's identity.

While the concept of recognizing an individual as a criminal or a victim based solely on their facial features, appears intuitive, facial recognition as a biometric technique allows for a more automated process to occur, and is constantly evolving with technological advancements.

Facial recognition offers a variety of advantages when compared to other biometric-based techniques. Following is a discussion of a few of the advantages belonging to this biometric-based technique.

Face recognition is a passive process which requires no participation by the user, and facial images can be gained with the use of a camera placed at a distance, which is particularly beneficial for security and surveillance purposes. Data acquisition is less challenging in comparison to the other biometric-based techniques, which are fraught with problems. For example, techniques that require the fingers and the palm can be rendered useless if the epidermis is damaged as a result of trauma or scarred as a result of injury. However, with facial recognition, data can be gathered discreetly, and therefore facial recognition software is a non-intrusive technique.

The application of facial recognition systems are extensive, and with a constant evolution in science and technology it is feasible to await a facial recognition system that will be able to identify a criminal and/or a victim with minimal information. Such a system would take into account various situations and overcome issues such as image resolution and facial aging, as well as be able to supplement accurate identification with a forensic artist's sketch of the individual. In recent years, there have been many uses of technology in places such as banks, supermarkets, airports, and educational institutes. In many cases, CCTV systems and identification systems have been installed for the safety and accurate identification of people within these establishments.

In previous years, primary users of facial recognition software have been computer vision researchers, academics, police officers, and forensic scientists. In recent years, some government agencies have now begun to use the biometric system for security reasons to eliminate any terrorist threat. The U.S. government began a program called U.S.-Visit (United States Visitors and Immigrant Status Indicator Technology), now referred to as the Office of Biometric Identity Management (OBIM), which is for foreign travelers who gain entry into the United States. When foreign travelers receive their visa for entry into the United States, they must submit a fingerprint and have their photograph taken. The biometric data (fingerprint and photograph) is then checked against a database of known criminals and suspected terrorists.

7.3 A HISTORICAL INSIGHT INTO FACIAL RECOGNITION

Facial recognition has always remained a major focus of research because of its non-invasive nature.

There are two categories of facial recognition: two-dimensional (2D) facial recognition and three-dimensional (3D) facial recognition. 2D facial recognition involves comparing a 2D picture with an image stored within a database (for example). However, with such a form of facial recognition, limitations do exist, as the picture in question should show the individual's face in the direction of the camera. In addition, changes in lighting conditions and individual factors such as a change in hair color and/ or style may affect the ability of the computer to retrieve the correct individual's data, causing a failure in facial recognition.

The contemporary facial recognition category known as 3D facial recognition allows for images to be captured and produces a 3D view of the suspect (for example) with the aid of facial points that cannot be modified significantly over time, including distance between the eyes and shape of the nose. Changes in the lighting conditions or deviations within the surrounding environment do not affect the facial points, which are seen as a great advantage for 3D facial recognition systems.

It is important to mention that it is a great challenge to create an automated software that equals the ability of a human to recognize people and faces. Although humans are programmed with the ability to recognize faces, humans have yet to master the ability to recognize an extensive number of unknown faces, and this is where computerized programs and software excel. A computer-generated software/program is almost limitless in its ability to generate data from "memory." This, coupled with its high computational speed, means that computerized facial recognition software has the capacity to generate results much more quickly than human facial recognition.

The first attempt to identify an individual by comparing a set of facial photographs was reported in the British Courts in 1864. The case of *R v. Tolson* (1864) was a case in which Mary Tolson was charged with bigamy, and a photograph that she claimed showed a likeness of her first husband was admitted in order to prove his identity against the person referred to in the marriage register.

In 1882, the first known systematic method of facial recognition was developed and introduced by French criminologist and anthropologist Alphonso Bertillon (Bertillon, 1986, n.d.). The criminal identification system was a system which identified people by measurements of the head and body, individual marks, tattoos, scars, and other personal characteristics. This identification system was later renamed Bertillonage in honor of the French criminologist (Figure 7.1).

The taken measurements were made into formulas that referred to a single unique individual, and recorded on cards which also had a photographic frontal and side profile portrait of the suspect, currently referred to as a mug shot (Figure 7.2). The cards were systematically filed and cross indexed so they could be easily retrieved. In 1884, Bertillon used this method to aid in the identification of 241 multiple offenders. Because of this mass identification of multiple offenders, the system was quickly picked up by multiple police forces in Great Britain, Europe, and the United States. However, although the Bertillonage system was widely accepted by multiple police forces, it later started to become difficult to implement. The measuring instruments required maintenance, the process was deemed too labor-intensive and there was the need of rigorous training for the individuals who took the measurements. Differences in measurements became apparent: trained officers would take measurements in different ways, and when the same individual was measured multiple times, different measurements were recorded. Moreover, age was not considered a factor which could affect the results. Not until later was it discovered that measurements could alter as the criminal aged.

With a lack of technological advancements prior to the 20th century, the identification of criminals was potentially based only upon Alphonso Bertillon's method of identification. However, as improvements in technology and scientific instruments occurred, the first research paper was published in 1966 by Woody Bledsoe, Helen Chan Wolf, and Charles Bisson on a system named Man Machine, which required an operator to locate and extract facial features such as the nose, ears, mouth, and eyes from a photograph. The features were then put into a computer to allow it to conduct an automated matching process. This automated process calculated the distances and ratios to a common pre-identified reference point, which were then compared to reference data.

As the speed of technological improvements steadily increased and showed substantial growth, making scientific instruments more effective, a different form of facial recognition software was produced. The new software explored another dimension of utilizing morphological features for the purpose of identification. In 1971, Goldstein, Harmon, and Lesk used 22 specific morphological features—"specific subjective markers" such as hair color, lip thickness, and eyebrows—to identify people based on facial photographs (Goldstein et al., 1971). To conduct the identification task, the markers were given to trained individuals and were also input into a computer. It was concluded by Goldstein, Harmon, and Lesk that six various facial features are required to identify an individual in a database of 255 participants, and they predicted that 14 facial features are required to identify an individual in a gallery of 4×10^6 faces. Goldstein et al.'s facial recognition software was not recognized as the first fully automated facial recognition software, since it required an operator to function the software, and the measurements of the morphological features were taken manually. Hence, the software was classed as being semiautomated.

FIGURE 7.1 Mugshot of Alphonse Bertillon with accompanied measurements for identification. (From Image of Bertillon system (n.d.), http://www.nlm.nih.gov/visibleproofs/media/detailed/iii_c_138.jpg.)

In 1987, mathematicians Larry Sirovich and Michael Kirby developed the first face recognition algorithms at Brown University. They applied principal component analysis (PCA), a standard linear algebra technique, to solve the recognition problems of their previous researchers' software/techniques difficulties. This technique was hailed a milestone. PCA is a statistical method and one of the most successful techniques that has been used in facial recognition. The main purpose of PCA is to minimize the large dimensionality of the data space to smaller intrinsic dimensionality of feature space, which is required to describe the data economically. The key theme with utilizing PCA for face recognition is to express large 1D vector of pixels produced from the 2D facial images into compact principle components of the feature space, called eigenspace projection.

Eigenspace is calculated by identifying the eigenvectors of the covariance matrix derived from a set of facial images known as vectors (Sirovich and Kirby, 1987; Delac et al., 2005). Once the eigenspace has been calculated, various decisions for the application of the results can be considered. Vectors known as eigenvectors are computed by PCA and are in the direction of the largest variance of the training vectors, referred to as eigenfaces. Each eigenface can be viewed as a feature, so when a particular face is projected onto the "face space," its vector within the face space describes the importance of each of the features within the face. The face is expressed in the face space courtesy of its eigenface coefficients. As previously stated, Kirby and Sirovich were among the first to apply PCA to facial images; they successfully demonstrated that PCA is an optimal compression scheme that reduces the mean squared error between the original images and their reconstructions for any given level of compression. Furthermore, the study demonstrated that less than

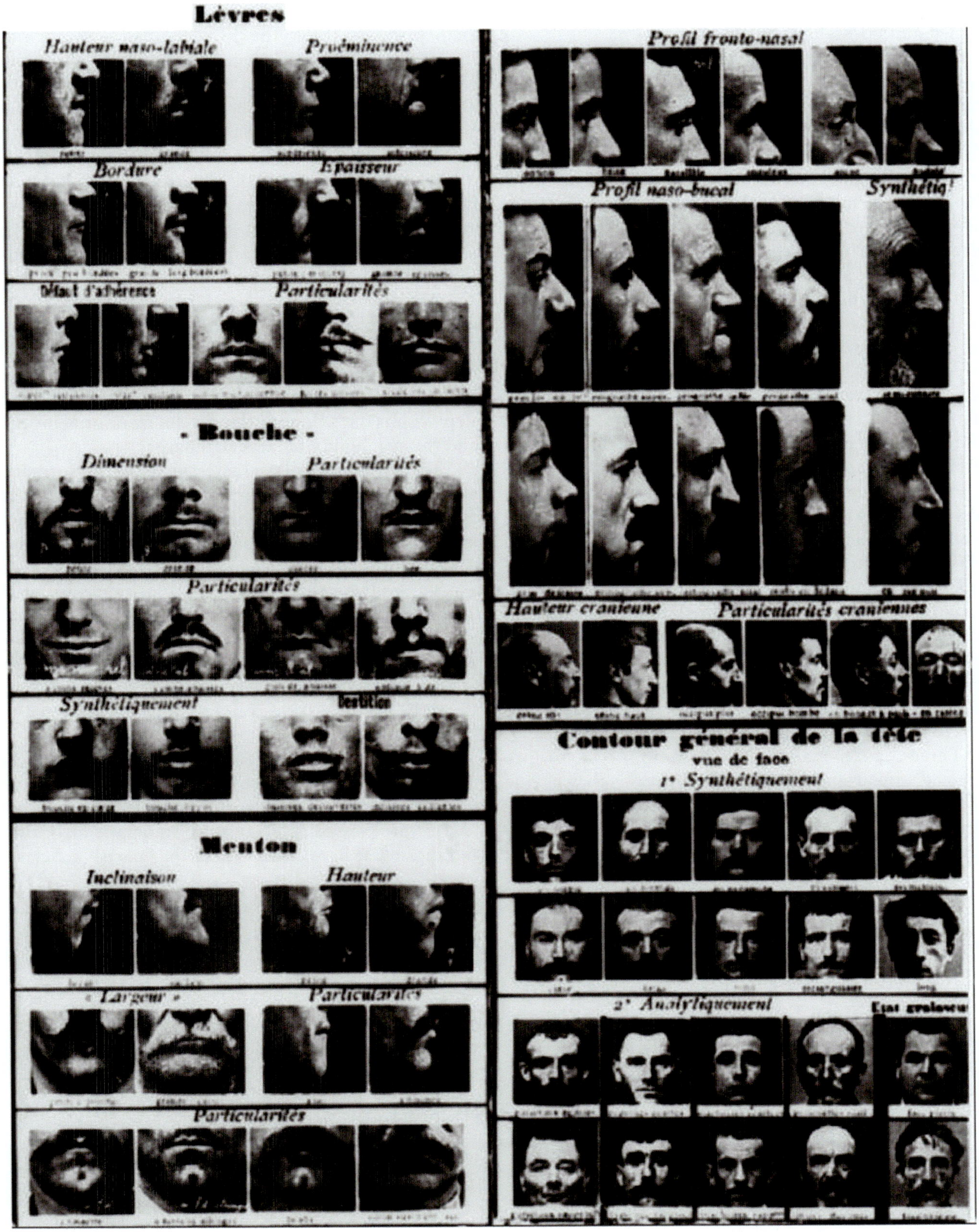

FIGURE 7.2 Photographic collection of variances in surface morphology from front and profile images. (From Alphonso Bertillon Biography: http://www.nlm.nih.gov/visibleproofs/galleries/biographies/bertillon.html, http://flavorwire.files.wordpress.com/2011/11/forensic_bertillon_card.jpg.)

100 values were required to accurately code a suitable aligned and normalized face.

Computational models of face recognition give insight into theoretical understanding in addition to practical applications. Two-dimensional face recognition using eigenfaces is one of the oldest computational methods of face recognition. Turkand Pentland published the groundbreaking "Eigenfaces for Recognition" in 1991. The eigenfaces method works by analyzing face images and computing eigenfaces, which are faces composed of eigenvectors (principal components). The comparison of eigenfaces is used to identify the presence of a face and its identity (Turk and Pentland, 1991).

The method of eigenfaces is based on an information theory approach, with a five-step process. First, the system needs to be prepared by inputting a set of training images of faces. The face images are made into smaller sets of characteristic features called eigenfaces, which can be considered the principal components on the initial training set of face images. Recognition is enabled by projecting a new image into the subspace spanned by eigenfaces (facespace) and then classifying the face by matching its position in facespace with the positions of the known individual. Within this framework it was possible to automatically learn and later recognize new faces (Turk and Pentland, 1991). Recognition under broadly varying conditions is achieved by training on limited characteristic views, including a front view, a 45-degree view, and a side view. The approach has many advantages over its previous predecessors because of its speed, simplicity, and insensitivity to small and/or gradual changes in face images.

Three-dimensional face recognition systems are expected to be robust to the types of issues that plague 2D face recognition systems. The most crucial requirements in support of producing reliable face recognition systems are (1) large facial image databases and (2) a testing procedure effective enough to assess the system. In September 1993, the FERET (Facial Recognition Technology) was introduced to the field of forensic facial recognition, which was sponsored by the U.S. Department of Defense. The FERET program addressed both issues of providing a large database of facial images and establishing FERET tests (Phillips et al., 1999). The aim of the FERET program was to create an automatic face recognition database that would be competent enough to be able to assist intelligence and security personnel in the process and performance of their duties (Figure 7.3).

As research within facial recognition became an active area of study, the research carried out within the field was propelled by other educational sectors of study, including computer vision, psychology, and neuroscience. The reason for active research and rapid progression within the field was the development of algorithms and the availability of large databases.

To achieve a robust assessment of performance, algorithms are typically evaluated against varying categories of facial images. The varying categories of facial images are created by separating facial images dependent on different lighting conditions, presence of vision glasses, and the time between acquisition date of the image on the database and the image presented to the algorithm. The separation of facial images based on the points mentioned allows for a better understanding of face recognition in general as well as the associated strengths and weaknesses linked with each category of facial images.

Facial recognition algorithms consist generally of two parts: (1) face detection and normalization, and (2) face identification. Algorithms that consist of both "parts" are classed as being fully automatic algorithms, and those that have either one of the "parts" are classed

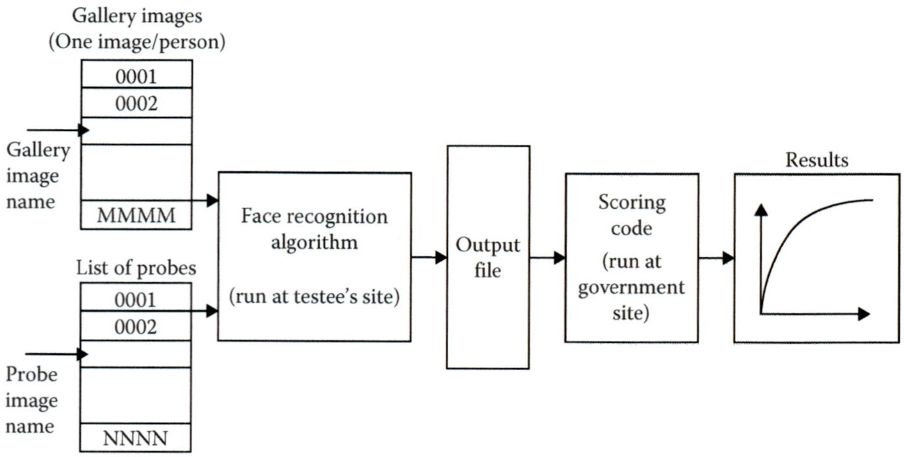

FIGURE 7.3 A schematic showing the process of facial recognition carried out by the FERET system. (From Phillips, P.J. et al., *IEEE Trans. Patt. Anal. Mach. Intelligen.* 22, 1090–1104, 2000. With permission.)

as being partially automatic algorithms. The evaluation of the FERET program, called Sep 96 FERET, evaluated both fully and partially automatic algorithms. Partial algorithms are given a facial image and the coordinates of the center of the eyes, whereas fully automatic algorithms are only given facial images.

In 1996, the FERET Verification Testing Protocol for face recognition algorithms was devised to provide an independent and accurate assessment of reliability and accuracy of existing facial recognition systems; it also served the purpose of promoting research in facial biometrics. A target set containing a gallery of "known individuals" and a probe set up of an "unknown individual" was presented to participating software programs in 1996.

Two versions of tests were carried out; the first assessed automatic facial location and the other provided eye coordinates to examine the recognition performance on manual input systems. Enrollment and test data were collected according to strict guidelines. A scoring procedure was formulated based on ROC graphs. False match rate and false non-match rate were plotted on log–log scales.

To achieve a recognition probability rate of >90%, the system will exhibit a higher false alarm rate. The best system has a 10% false alarm rate, with others varying from 30% to 60% (Phillips et al., 1999; Rizvi et al., 1998). Over 6 months, the >90% recognition rate using the same FERET protocol exhibited a reduction in general false alarm rates. The best of the systems exhibited <2% false alarm rate, while others demonstrated a variety ranging between 20% and 30%. This gave the recognition system an increased recognition probability with no significant incline in false alarm rate.

Further tests were performed until March 1997, when the U.S. Department of Defense published details of the results and the entire project. Because of the FERET program, specific strengths and weaknesses associated with each algorithm were identified. A key drawback and disadvantage associated with face recognition algorithms appeared to be sensitivity to disparities in illumination caused by a change in sunlight intensity throughout the day. Changes in illumination resulted in a significant drop in performance.

Furthermore, it was demonstrated that the position of the "target face" also played a vital role in affecting the performance rate of the system. A 15-degree difference in position between the query image and the stored database image created substantial difference in the recognition threshold, whereas a difference of 45 degrees rendered the system ineffective for the purpose of recognition. Despite the limitations from luminosity and face position, the process of identification demonstrated by the FERET program was proven to be successful and provided results which were useful to many sectors of study and work. With substantial improvement in the development of facial algorithms for computerized recognition since the FERET program, the capabilities of modern technology have always been tested and will continue to be verified, until a program is developed that is able to overcome all the issues affected by the facial recognition software.

7.4 FAMILIAR FACE RECOGNITION

The face is a primary source of recognition and association in social interactions which are carried out on a daily basis. The human face discloses a great deal of information to the perceiver and is able to recognize emotions, intentions, mood, and attentiveness as well as to determine the identity of an individual.

As humans, we can recognize numerous faces throughout our lifetime. And with only a glance, upon seeing a familiar face after many years we are able to recognize the individual; this is a robust skill which is truly fascinating.

In the field of forensic science, once a questioned facial image is obtained it is required to be assesed, for the purpose of identification. At times, the media is utilized as a way to gain information and help law enforcement agents with identifying an "unknown" facial image.

When a crime is investigated, the identity of an unknown suspect is sought via means such as CCTV analysis and witness statements. The police will often question witnesses who may have been onlookers to the crime and try and get them to assist the police in many ways in establishing the identity of the suspect. When a witness is asked to attempt the identification of a suspect via photographs, identification parades, and possibly even facial composites, the process is said to be prone to errors. In contrast, the majority of us manage to recognize the faces of people who are familiar to us in our everyday lives or on television, irrespective of variations shown between different appearances of the same person. Error-prone unfamiliar face memory is transformed to generally very reliable performances with known faces.

There is neuropsychological evidence to suggest that there are somewhat different processes which underlie the recognition of unfamiliar faces and the recognition of familiar ones. People with prosopagnosia display difficulties in facial recognition, and sometimes this is due to an injury to the brain. Such people say they are unable to recognize even their closest relative's face. However, some prosopagnosia patients can manage to match images of unfamiliar faces, although using laborious and somewhat time-consuming processes.

Young et al. investigated residual deficits in face processing among a group of 34 brain-injured war veterans.

Amid this group, Young and his research colleagues found one man who was impaired at familiar facial recognition but unimpaired at unfamiliar face matching, and another war veteran who was impaired in unfamiliar face matching but recognized familiar faces quite normally. The pattern of "double dissociation" is consistent with the idea that different brain areas and processes are involved in the task of recognizing familiar faces and matching unfamiliar ones. Evidence for dissociation amid familiar and unfamiliar face processing is the observation that familiar face recognition appears to be dependent upon various kinds of information from unfamiliar recognition.

Lander and Butcher's (2001) research suggest that representations of familiar faces capture something about their characteristic patterns of motion as well as their static form. Even within the static form, there appears to be varied emphases on the visual representations of familiar and unfamiliar faces. Research by Ellis et al. (1979) first demonstrated that unfamiliar face recognition was subjugated by external features belonging to the face, such as hair.

People generally find it difficult to recognize faces they've only seen once, if the hairstyle is altered or concealed in any way. However, when faces are familiar, their internal features are more important in facial recognition. Research by O'Donnell and Bruce in 2001 demonstrated that the eyes in particular seemed to be better represented in recently familiarized faces.

For an unfamiliar face, within Western Europe, for example, hair is generally visible and variable in color and style. Thus, it is fair to suggest that outer features of the face generally convey the most information that is beneficial and is utilized for matching and memory. Hairstyle usually varies from one occasion to another, as hair is a transient feature. Thus, it is of no surprise that the visual memory system can place emphasis on internal features.

Consistent with this, a study by Megreya and Binderman in 2009 highlighted that when face recognition was tested in Egypt, adults showed better memory for internal features for unfamiliar and familiar faces because of the head scarf. It may be a processing preference due to culture, meaning that one's attention will naturally be drawn toward the internal features (eyes, nose, and mouth) when external features are concealed.

Burton et al. suggested that representations of a familiar face are built by averaging together individual occurrences of seen faces (Burton et al., 2005). The differential weighting of internal features during familiarization, and for cultures where external features are not often viewed, will possibly arise as a result of selective attention, weighting areas of the face differently. The research carried out by Burton and his colleagues has demonstrated that people are faster in their ability to recognize familiar faces when shown an average of 20 different photographic images of them, than when shown an individual at a single instance.

An extension to this research was carried out by Jenkins and Burton in 2008, where the results showed that, on average, when famous facial target images were used as a probe to match against a database of stored images, specifically celebrities, performance increased from 51% correct matching when using individual images as probes, to 100% correct when the averages were used as probes. As a result, both Jenkins and Burton suggested that images should be used on identity documents such as passports to help improve both human and computerized methods of using such images.

7.5 STAGES IN FACIAL RECOGNITION

When we meet a person we are familiar with and know quite well, the recognition of that individual is fairly effortless and does not require much processing. The ability for us to recognize a person we are fairly well acquainted with, seems effortless however involves a process which has been studied as part of research through systematic recordings of everyday behavior.

Young et al. (1993) collected a large sample of information in relation to instances of errors and difficulties in person recognition in a study they named, "The Faces That Launched a Thousand Slips." The participants were asked to keep notes of any difficulties they experienced when recognizing people over a period of 8 weeks. A total of 922 recorded incidents were analyzed from the preset time period. According to the information provided by the study, on average almost one incident per day displayed difficulty in recognition.

The incidents were grouped into particular types, with the most common type being person misidentification. Approximately 25% of all incidents recorded occurred when somebody appeared to be familiar, but the participant failed to remember why that person in particular was familiar. At such times, the issue of failure to initially recognize was resolved by a protracted process.

In general, there are three main stages in person recognition, each equally as important in the process as the other. Stage 1 is to match the inbound "visual pattern" to a previously stored visual representation of what the person in question looks like. If it's possible to match the incoming visual pattern to a stored visual representation of what a person looks like, then it is acceptable to classify the recognition as "familiar" (Wilkinson and Rynn, 2012). Stage 2 of person recognition involves retrieving information to state why the person in question has been identified as familiar; for example, "Where do you know this person from?" and "How do you know them?" Stage 3 involves the retrieval of the name belonging to the person in question. It has not yet been possible to identify whether in the stages of person recognition one can jump from Stage 1 straight to Stage 3, where the retrieval of the person's name occurs. There has been research carried out to demonstrate that there appears to be no direct route from "visual pattern matching" to name recall.

In 1990, Brennen et al. conducted an experiment in which the participants were required to answer a series of questions about celebrities from definitions; for example, What is the name of the person who played James Bond in *Skyfall*? (Wilkinson and Rynn, 2012; Byers, n.d.). The research demonstrated how all three experiments reported that tip-of-the-tongue states (TOTSs) were induced in participants by reading item-specific information.

In Experiments 1 and 2, subjects participating in the research attempted to name famous people. Both Experiments 1 and 2 showed that, in a TOTS, seeing a picture of the face of the questioned person did not facilitate naming, whereas the initials of the person's name did. In Experiment 3, a similar result was obtained with a landmark naming task.

It is a common issue that at times a person may not be able to accurately recognize a person and may mistakenly misidentify a person because the incoming visual pattern may get matched with the wrong stored person representation. In a forensic context, the issue of mistakenly misidentifying a person is nothing out of the norm. A police officer or a member of the public who becomes a witness to a crime can mistakenly identify a criminal as potentially a person whom they may know or have "come across," and this may be caused by a certain resemblance the witness sees. Many contextual factors also come into play. Even if a person who seems familiar is correctly identified, the details of why the person in question is familiar may be misremembered. The ability to remember who is familiar can involve the use of episodic information such as "I think I saw her there," or it can be a lot more general "semantic information," such as "She is the person who stars in that program."

The simple process of person recognition does not allow differentiating between the two kinds of information one may have of why a face is familiar. In a forensic context, the differences between episodic and semantic information are important. For example, one might see a short section of CCTV footage in relation to a robbery, and the person within the CCTV footage may be a person one may "know." While the issue of remembering information for the purpose of person identification may or may not be present, recalling names, even of familiar people, can be error-prone and difficult. In a forensic context, when the police are investigating a crime, images produced from the CCTV camera or facial composites may potentially trigger a less specific cue to an identity, which should be considered as a significant lead even when names of the potential criminal are not known or recalled.

7.6 FACIAL RECOGNITION AND THE AFFECTING FACTORS

There is a wide variation seen in facial recognition ability: from those unable to recognize highly familiar people, to those individuals who can recognize someone who they have seen only once, some years earlier.

In facial recognition there are many factors which can affect the ability of an individual to recognize a face. The key affecting factors include but are not limited to individual factors, contextual factors, and lighting and color.

Recent years have shown a renewed interest in the theoretical and practical implications of individual differences in facial recognition. With any form of test, a reasonable sample of participants will naturally reveal a range of performance scores. Some researchers try and determine the reason for variation, putting it down to the person's ability to recall a person or to a specific factor in face processing. A study carried out by Woodhead and Baddeley demonstrated a wide range of results in the participant's ability to discriminate familiar faces from different faces at or near chance ($d' = 0$) to performances that were nearly perfect ($d' = 6.8$). Woodhead and Baddeley (2009) later tested a group of participants who were reasonably good and relatively poor recognizers again later; they found that a significant difference in face recognition abilities remained, and the group of participants also varied in their recognition memory ability for non-face pictures. However, there appeared to be no difference in the participant's verbal memory.

When there is no memory component involved in the ability of an individual to face match, differences are observed. In 2006, Megreya and Burton (2009) carried out research and used a face-matching task that was initially introduced by research carried out by Bruce et al. in 1999, where participating individuals were asked to decide which, of any, of the 10 faces shown in an array matched a good-quality target photograph (Henderson et al., 2001; Bruce et al., 1999). It is feasible to state that the error rates on such a performance task are generally high, but also fairly variable, as Megreya and Burton found the participant's mean performance as 82% correct with a standard deviation of 12%.

Megreya and Burton (2009) examined what factors correlated with performance in the array-matching task. It was found that there were significant positive correlations between unfamiliar face matching and recognition memory for unfamiliar faces, in addition to the matching task correlating with a number of additional tasks of visual memory and processing. The matching task did not correlate, however, with the participant's abilities to recognize recently familiarized faces and famous faces—unless these were turned upside down. Since we know that when faces are inverted, participants must rely on analyzing faces in a more piecemeal way, rather than the typical configural way of processing.

Prosopagnosic people, who have difficulties in recognizing familiar faces in their day-to-day life, seem to have specific deficits in processing configural rather than local facial features. Research carried out by Russell et al. in 2009 studied volunteers who were particularly good at recognizing faces, and classified them as the "super recognizers." They usually scored very high on the Cambridge Face Matching as well as the Cambridge Face Memory Tests, which are tests of unfamiliar face processing. However, super recognizers are not mainly skilled at tasks of inverted face recognition. This puts forward that skill in recognizing familiar faces and remembering unfamiliar faces in some tasks relies on expertise in configural processing, but that other tasks concerning faces, particularly matching unfamiliar faces, correspondingly require the ability to analyze local features well.

In relation to contextual factors, we are often surprised to meet people unexpectantly and fail to recognize them completely. Context plays a major role in facial recognition; therefore it can help facial recognition as well as hindering it. It is also well researched that appropriate contextual information can facilitate recognition of faces that are familiar, in a manner that accelerates familiarity decisions. Research carried out in 1986 by Bruce and Valentine was the first type of facial recognition research which demonstrated that faces from closely associated pairs such as Laurel and Hardy were judged familiar more quickly if they immediately followed an image of the associated partner's face. Research of such caliber suggests that the representations of different people in memory are somewhat interconnected in some way.

Contextual factors are very important for the recognition of familiar faces. In a criminal context, it can be deemed highly imperative that people are able to remember and recall what, where, and when they see someone. A witness to a crime of any sort must know that the person seen in an identification parade and brought forward in front of the witness may be one of several individuals who may fit the descriptive brief the witness gave to the police.

While familiar people's identities and therefore faces are usually bound by places where we encounter them ("That's the man who catches the same train as I do"), we know very little about them and ultimately know little about how well we are able to recall specific episodes involving particular people.

It is feasible to conclude that we are good at familiar face recognition. Anyone, including witnesses and the police, who claims to recognize a person in a CCTV image or any other form of digital imagery within any context, as somebody they know, should be taken very seriously. This is because ultimately it is the fate of a person and a decision that is not taken very lightly by professionals within the law and criminal defense field.

Because of the very real and serious implications that are involved with facial recognition in a criminal context, obtaining good image quality, facial composites, and custody images and then broadcasting the images nationally and at times internationally (depending on the level of crime that's been committed) is pivotal in any criminal case investigation. It is imperative that when an individual becomes a witness to a crime, he or she would normally know the suspect as a result of the crime rather than knowing them prior to the criminal event. We are not perfect, and it is nothing out of the norm that one can confuse two people and be unable to provide accurate names or locations or be easily misled by context.

Lighting conditions and color may also affect the ability of an individual to recall and recognize another individual.

A study carried out how Russell et al. in 2006 directly compared discrimination ability for faces that differed in shape, and surface appearance such as pigmentation, or both. Faces were created using a 3D face model; however, they were presented to the participants in a 2D manner. It was found that photographic negation had a minimal effect on matching performance for faces that only differed in shape; however, it created a large decrement, from approximately 78% down to 64%, when faces varied in pigmentation.

The performance rate was better with faces that differed in shape and pigmentation in general; however, performance was still affected by negation. The research concluded that negation interrupts our ability to use pigmentation cues to identity. Although we may not observe a face in a photographic negative under "normal circumstances," we may encounter a face which is subject to light from unusual directions.

Pigmentation cues should not be confused with color information. Under specific lighting conditions, including when lighting is dim, there will be no color information seen in a face. It is an incorrect assumption to think that color would aid better identification in comparison to monochrome colors; however, in tests carried out in research, the effects of color are usually either nonexistent or highly informative.

Research carried out by Bruce et al. in 1999 included four experiments which looked into the matching of unfamiliar target faces taken from high-quality video against an array of photographs. In Experiment 1, targets were present in 50% of arrays. Accuracy was poor and worsened when viewpoint and expression differed between target and array faces. In Experiment 2, targets were present in every array, but performance remained highly error prone. In Experiment 3, short video clips of the targets were shown and replayed as often as necessary, but performance levels were only slightly better than in Experiment 2. Experiment 2 showed that external face features dominated matching. The results urge caution in the use of video images to identify people who have committed crimes.

While there is an advantage for CCTV in that it allows identification of the color of clothing simultaneously, it has little advantage for faces. In CCTV footage which is subject to dim lighting or night conditions, color is not present and the only difference between potential colors is created by the darkness or lightness among the tones; however, in relation to facial recognition, the lack of light can almost mask facial features and potentially unique characteristics such as moles and distinctive scars. Furthermore, a lack of appropriate lighting conditions coupled with factors such as camera distance will all result in affecting accurate facial recognition. Since at a distance a face may appear smaller and relatively coarse details be visible.

7.7 FACIAL MAPPING AND FORENSIC IMAGERY ANALYSIS

Digital imagery, which includes photographs and CCTV footage, is used to help the judicial system. Facial recognition at times forms part of circumstantial evidence; therefore, with imagery analysis, facial recognition can be submitted as evidence. "Imagery" refers generically to "photographs" that can be custody images of a known suspect or surveillance images which are taken discreetly. Imagery typically contains wave fronts of emitted or reflected energy, which is captured by a camera system and then recorded by optical disk, film, or any other media source.

Lately, the use of imagery and CCTV for the purpose of security has led to a substantial increase in the use and support of digital imagery and digital forensics in the investigation of a crime or the prosecution of a criminal. Subsequently, this has led to the requirement of experts in forensic imagery analysis who consequently help in facial recognition and identification.

Facial comparison, formally known as facial mapping, is a manual process carried out by forensic imagery analysts who analyze facial characteristics and features of individuals captured from digital imagery. Forensic imagery analysts are able to compare the morphological features of a criminal or group of criminals captured on CCTV or other forms of digital imagery to the individual or group of individuals who are alleged to be the person/s on the captured CCTV footage or photograph.

Although the face is considered a key factor for identifying individuals, posture, gait, height, and build are also crucial factors that are required for the accurate identification. The expertise of a forensic imagery analyst is not limited to the face; clothing, footwear, and vehicle analysis is also possible and dependent on the crime, can all be used as circumstantial evidence that will assist the investigating team and ultimately the judicial system. Forensic imagery analysts are able to differentiate between recognition and identification in the work they carry out. Analysts classify recognition as when there are observable similarities between the person on the captured CCTV and/or digital imagery and the person who has been identified prior to the analysis, to the extent that the analyst is capable of positively stating that the individuals under comparison are one and the same.

Identification leaves no room for assumption and occurs when there is no doubt that the individual captured on the CCTV or digital imagery is that individual who has been positively identified. Identification is possible due to the presence of "unique identifying markers," which are features on an individual as a result of individual differences in lifestyle, diet and possibly environmental factors. Unique identifying markers can be scars, moles, birthmarks, and body art such as tattoos. A positive identification between the individual captured on the CCTV who exhibits these markers in the same location, position, and form as that of the previously positively identified individual is an accurate result.

Scars can be a result of past wounds and injuries which have required medical assistance, and as a result, a scar has been formed. Tattoos are generally very specific to an individual because they can represent one of many things, including affiliation with a gang in prison, display of love for a loved one, as well as a form of symbolic gesture. The uniqueness of the type of tattoo and the location, all aid in positive identification.

Birthmarks are benign skin irregularities, which are specific and exclusive to an individual, as somebody who has a photograph of him/herself in their pocket. It is not farcical to class birthmarks as being "facial fingerprints" because of their distinctiveness.

It is important to mention that although facial recognition is fundamentally associated with the unique identifying markers present on the face of a person, it's important to keep in mind that they are not limited to the face and can be found anywhere on the body. Recognition may have some probative value but only as support to the evidence, whereas identification can stand as proof on its own.

Trained forensic imagery analysts are able to view digital imagery and CCTV free from issues of cognitive preconception which can't affect the reliability of the results. An untrained eye will naturally anticipate that the person captured on the offense digital imagery and CCTV is the same person who has been positively identified by the police or a witness, and hence unconsciously will form an opinion with a strong certainty.

However, a competent practitioner will be free of bias and will take a very neutral stand to any proposition posed from either the prosecution or defense.

Many techniques have been developed in order to achieve safe and reliable facial mapping results. All the techniques have been designed to accomplish one goal, and that is to try and exclude the suspect individual by looking for significant facial differences, also referred to as negative (nonmatching) indicators. There are currently four main methods in use for facial comparison: holistic comparison, morphological analysis, photo anthropometry and superimposition. Subject to the image quality in use, an appropriate selection for the type of facial comparison method can occur. However, the order in which these techniques are applied varies.

Moreover, the selection of an appropriate method is also dependent on the training of the forensic imagery analyst, the experience of the analyst as well as the purpose of the examination. Irrespective of the method chosen for the purpose of comparison, the repeatability and accuracy if the conclusions that can be drawn from the image comparison are directly related to the quality of the images.

As a general rule of thumb, the lower the quality of the image used for the purpose, the weaker the conclusion that can be drawn. Ideal images for facial comparison are high in resolution and have adequate focus of the facial features of interest inclusive of facial blemishes and moles. The images also have minimum image distortion, sufficient lighting and little to no obscuration of features. In general, optimal images are taken under the same lighting conditions where factors such as resolution and subject pose can be controlled and, more importantly, consistently repeated. However, it is also possible that images which are captured under non identical conditions are deemed sufficient to carry out comparative analysis.

In facial mapping, when a comparison is made between two images, it's imperative to have a minimal time interval between the two images. It is not always possible to have images that don't have a big time interval between them; this is usually the case with multiple robberies from one organized crime group, who possibly commit a crime in a more spaced timescale. Having said that, facial comparison can be undertaken utilizing suboptimal images; however, in such circumstances the forensic analyst is completely trained and is able to fully evaluate the images accurately.

As mentioned previously, there are four main methods in use for facial comparison, which are holistic comparison, morphological analysis, photo anthropometry, and superimposition. Holistic facial comparison exploits a basic human ability, which is where all facial features are examined simultaneously and compared to another facial image. Holistic comparison is a common practice; however, it is not alarming that a forensic analyst assessing facial features during a review is not able to explicitly explain the basis of his or her conclusions.

The advantages associated with holistic facial comparison include the fact that it can be attempted on any image and does not require an identical subject facial pose or orientation and angle. Another advantage is the fact that no contemporaneous document of the process is required for facial review, therefore not requiring any specialized equipment. The process of holistic facial comparison is generally quick and requires minimal training. A major associated disadvantage with holistic facial comparison is the fact that studies have highlighted that this process has low and variable accuracy rates.

Morphological comparison is recommended as a primary method for facial comparison and is based on the assessment and correspondence of the appearance, shape presence, and location of facial features. These features incorporate global (overall face), local (anatomical structures like the nose and their components like the nasal bridge), and discriminating characteristic facial marks such as moles and scars. The primary action is to study the facial features to see if there is any obvious difference. If a profound difference is observed between the nose (for example) between the unknown subject in the questioned imagery and the known control, then it is fair to conclude that both the people are not one and the same. Transient features such as hair, including style and color, should not be taken as a distinguishing factor. If there is no clear difference in the facial features, then the analyst can progress onto analyzing the facial landmarks (such as the glabella and nasion point) of the individual. In conjunction with the facial landmarks, the forensic imagery analyst must also consider the underlying facial muscles that are responsible for expression.

Morphological comparison is performed very carefully, and the facial landmarks are used as guides to help the analyst search for significant and/or insignificant differences, which in turn can help in the establishment of a suspect's identity. The shape of the feature and proportionate size are all taken into consideration. Morphological facial comparison is a systematic method in which the facial features of a subject's face, are described and compared. Further to this, features can be subdivided into additional categories. For example, a comparative comment can be made on components such as the helix, anti-helix, tragus, and the lobe. All the components can be addressed individually or in combination. Conclusions drawn because of morphological comparison are based on subjective assessment and interpretation of the observations.

Morphological comparison is regarded as sensitive to image quality. Loss in quality caused by low resolution, distortion, or blurring can reduce if not eliminate the detailed feature's visibility. As a result, the ability to identify similarities and dissimilarities becomes reduced and therefore introduces great uncertainty. The overall effect of this will be the inability to either positively identify or eliminate a suspect individual.

Among the advantages related to morphological comparison is that, with appropriate training, an analyst can obtain the best results from images that share a similarity in angle, pose, and orientation. It is easy to explain the results to an untrained individual who is not competent in the area. Another advantage of morphological facial comparison is that a feature list can be drawn, and it is considered to be a more reliable method of facial comparison. A disadvantage associated with this method of facial comparison is the fact that a limited number of research studies have been completed on the accuracy and reproducibility of this method, in addition to the fact that to carry out morphological analysis, one must be competent in the knowledge of surface anatomy and be trained.

The third type of facial comparison method is called photogrammetry, which is derived from facial anthropometry a study of facial measurements (FISWG Guidelines for Facial Comparison Method, 2012). Facial measurements are recorded from an image and then are taken from a second image; both sets of data are compared, and conclusions are based on subjective thresholds for acceptable differences between the sets of measurements. However, given the uncontrolled conditions under which the images are taken (surveillance, CCTV) and depending on their quality, photogrammetry can make it difficult to define a threshold boundary of similarity or dissimilarity in measurements to support a respective conclusion of identification or elimination of an individual. It is advised that to carry out photogrammetry, one must use original imagery for the purpose of facial mapping. Reproductions of originals will invariably be subject to a loss of detail and resolution, which in turn will affect the results produced.

An advantage of photogrammetry is the fact that no expensive specialized equipment is required, and generally an itemized facial features list is utilized. A major disadvantage of using photogrammetry for facial mapping, other than it being a method that requires advanced training and accuracy, is that large-scale studies on the use of anthropometric comparison, based on approximately 30 facial landmarks and high-resolution images, have demonstrated that photo-anthropometry has limited discriminating powers (FISWG; Thompson and Black, 2007).

However, FISWG has identified the following imaging conditions that must be met in order to gain reliable results when using photogrammetry as a method for facial comparison/ mapping:

- Same viewpoint
- Minimal distortion
- Minimal compression artifacts
- Known focal length
- Sufficient resolution and focus to resolve features/landmarks of interest
- Same lighting
- Minimal obscuration
- Known lens distortion
- Known subject distance
- Known angle of head tilt (if present)
- Same image aspect ratio
- Same pose
- Short time interval between photographs
- Similar expressions

Photogrammetry is extremely sensitive to image quality: any distortion or damage to image resolution and/or blurring can affect the chance of getting reliable results. A decline in image quality will subsequently reduce the accuracy of the measurements recorded. Adding to this is the determination of a specific pose and expression of the subject that can be greatly reduced by the effects of the blurring, and so on, which further introduces error and uncertainty. The greater effect of this all is a reduction in accuracy of analysis with the potential of improperly including or excluding a subject individual in relation to a crime (Figure 7.4).

Superimposition is the last of the four methods used for facial comparison. Superimposition can be used in conjunction with morphological analysis, as it can add to the value of the results obtained. Superimposition is the process of creating two images that are aligned, and then comparing them visually with the assistance of video techniques such as fade and transitions.

As with any other method of work, a high level of care and training should be taken when attempting superimposition, taking particular care with image enlargement and scaling. This is vital, as differences can be present among any two sets of images, such as orientation, pose and angle. A discussion of a few of the superimposition techniques follows.

A *fade* is where one image is progressively replaced by another image by gradually changing the transparency of the image layers such that the entirety of both the images are observed at reduced transparency concurrently.

Matching is where an analyst will align two different faces against each other to determine if there is any match. It is important to mention that this method of superimposition is able to highlight anomalies very easily, and since human faces are largely symmetrical, however, if a low-resolution set of images are being compared in this way, then this method can be difficult. A "wipe" is when a straight line passes across the screen gradually revealing the underlying image such that both parts of both the images in use at full opacity can be observed simultaneously.

FIGURE 7.4 Photogrammetry image created by Shelina Jilani and Stephen Cole, Acumé Forensics. (All consent has been given for the purpose of this photogrammetry.)

FIGURE 7.5 Superimposition image created by Shelina Jilani and Stephen Cole, Acumé Forensics. (All consent has been given for the purpose of this superimposition.)

As mentioned previously, facial features can be used in helping to determine the identity of an individual. There may be various additional factors that may be required, such as clothing, gait, height, and build, that can all be considered and examined prior to drawing a conclusion. The advantages of superimposition as a method is outweighed by its disadvantages; for example, the conditions under which one can achieve reliable results are very restrictive. Further, superimposition cannot be used as an independent comparison method. To carry out superimposition analysis, the analyst must be highly trained, as there is a chance that with the use of some image transition tools an inexperienced user can be misled.

It is rare that the identification report would be used as a stand-alone piece of evidence in court. Forensic facial mapping is rarely used as a singular piece of evidence against a suspect; however, it is used alongside other circumstantial evidence with the aim to come to an accurate decision within the court. Although the camera does not lie, it can mislead an untrained eye and lead to an inaccurate conclusion.

Imagery such as photographs and CCTV footage is the only permanent record of events that have taken place, and therefore it is important to make sure the imagery is made available to the court when necessary. The camera merely records the events that are unfolding before it; the events that are recorded are of evidential value only if what is recorded is properly captured and accurately interpreted (Figure 7.5).

7.7.1 Summary

The use of expert evidence to assist facial identification from CCTV can be useful to the court, however it is clear that research is required for the evalution of techniques. While experts may be employed by both the prosecution and defense, the opinions presented are subjective. As a result, research is required to further the neiche disiciple of facial mapping and aid the jury's understanding with emperical evidence. However, it remains unclear at present if any facial comparison technique will be subject to scientific testing and peer review in order for any method to be conclusively assigned as reliable or unrelaible.

7.8 FACIAL COMPOSITES AND ELECTRONIC FACIAL IDENTIFICATION TECHNIQUES

A composite image is a pictorial likeness produced from a witness's recall of a suspect for the purpose of achieving a likeness. The composite image is intended to be an aid to the investigation of crime alongside other corroborating evidence. The term "composite" is commonly used by practitioners when referring to any facial or full-bodied image, irrespective of the technique used to produce it. This is especially important to understand when dealing with the courts and media.

Police officers often rely on a witness to provide a comprehensive account of the incident. In some circumstances, the witness has to convey a description of the perpetrator based only on a brief encounter. The pertinent question is, "How is it possible to accurately convey the perpetrator's face when the image exists only as a memory in the witness's mind?" This corresponds well to the typical circumstances under which a trained police officer will subsequently work with the victim (or other witnesses to a crime) in an attempt to produce a facial likeness or facial composite of the perpetrator.

Unless the witness is a gifted artist, it is unlikely that he or she will be able to provide a reliable sketch of the offender. Typically, assuming that the attacker is unknown to the witness, he or she will first be asked to provide a detailed verbal description of the attacker and to recount the incident in as much detail as possible. When the interview is complete, an attempt is then made to produce a likeness under the guidance of a specially trained operator.

While sketch artists are still widely used in the United States, this process will most likely (in the United Kingdom, at least) use some form of computerized facial composite system. A facial composite system is therefore a tool designed to allow the expression of the facial appearance retained in the witness's memory in some tangible form, such as a digital image or computer printout. The desired outcome is that the generated composite be of sufficient accuracy that subsequent display to members of the public will result in direct recognition and that the details of the suspect will be supplied to the police.

In many cases, a generated composite may not be accurate enough to produce a definite "hit" but will nonetheless provoke members of the public who recognize basic similarities to provide the names of possible suspects. In most cases, it is the combination of the composite with other basic information such as age, build, and the type of crime that results in the provision of suspect names.

The process by which a witness and a composite operator arrive at a final facial composite is a complex interplay of computer imaging and human cognitive function, and the final result depends on a number of factors. The overall success of the composite process is, first and foremost, reliant on the witness's ability to retain some memory of the face in question. Undoubtedly, some people are better equipped to perform this task than others.

Other factors such as the witness's state of mind (i.e., they may be in various degrees of shock as a result of the crime), the period of time over which the crime took place, the proximity of the perpetrator to the witness during the crime, and the time elapsed between the crime and the composite construction will also affect the memory. From a scientific and technological perspective, there are critical aspects to consider in the design of an effective composite system. It should provide sufficient flexibility of use and image quality to meet the needs of different witnesses and operators and should be constructed, as much as possible, to match their normal cognitive processes.

Although systematic methods for remembering faces have been outlined by Penry, the inventor of the original Photo-FIT system, it is unreasonable and impractical to expect that potential witnesses and victims will be well trained in these techniques. Rather, the emphasis must be on the design of composite systems and associated interview techniques, which allow the best evidence to be produced by ordinary members of the public. The relative weakness of human beings at the process of recall and description of faces, as contrasted with their remarkable capacity for face recognition, is well documented. In simple terms, to first recall and then accurately describe a face, even that of a family member or a close relative, is cognitively difficult for many people.

Until recently, the facial composite systems used by international police forces were exclusively based on a construction process in which individual facial features (eyes, nose, mouth, eyebrows, etc.) are selected one at a time from a large database and then electronically "overlaid" to produce the composite image. Such systems are often referred to as *feature-based* since they rely on the selection of individual features in isolation. However, after a long period of research and development, work conducted largely within British universities has produced systems that are based on a rather different principle and are finding increasing use by police forces.

These systems may be broadly described as holistic or global in that they primarily attempt to create a likeness to the suspect through an evolutionary mechanism in which a witness's response to groups of complete faces (not just features) converges toward an increasingly accurate image. This section will feature a system which had its origins in research undertaken by Kent University and the Open University and is now commercially established under the name E-FIT-V, which may best be described as a hybrid system in that it attempts to exploit holistic information while retaining some of the feature-based processing employed in most systems of the previous generation and which are effective under certain conditions.

7.8.1 Historical Background to Suspect Composite Construction

Prior to the introduction of Identi-Kit (Figure 7.6) in the early 1960s, police forces did not routinely attempt to portray a suspect's likeness for subsequent release to the media. Some forces occasionally did use an artist's impressions (Figure 7.7) taken from witness interviews to illustrate a few examples. However, the police artists did not receive any form of interview training, and resulting arrests were minimal. Sketch artists have been used to produce suspect composites since the 1950s, and continue to be used by some UK and overseas forces to the present day. It is acknowledged that a fully trained police sketch artist who has been interview trained will be able to produce a good likeness of the suspect, dependent on the recall ability of the witness, and the FBI still use and train sketch artists in preference to the use of computer software systems.

Smith & Wesson, an American company most famous for their manufacture of firearms, created the Identi-Kit system, originating from an invention by Hugh C. Macdonald of the Los Angeles Police Department, who had developed sets of facial features on transparencies to save time sketching descriptions of criminals in 1940 wartime Europe. It was in use the United States and in the United Kingdom throughout the early 1960s, until the introduction of Photo-FIT in 1970. The first recorded use of Identi-Kit in the United Kingdom is documented as the Cecil Court antique shop murder.

On March 3, 1961, Elsie Batten, a shop assistant, was found stabbed to death in an antique shop owned by Louis Meyer in Cecil Court, off London's Charing Cross Road WC2. The detective sergeant assigned to the case was Raymond Dagg, who interviewed Louis Meyer and a neighboring shop assistant, who told him they had seen a suspicious youth of Indian appearance at the shop a few days earlier.

But how could the witnesses describe the suspect? Raymond Dagg decided to use the new Identi-Kit system and compiled a facial composite of the suspect from shop owner Louis Meyer's recollection and then independently from the other witness. The two pictures were so similar in appearance that it was decided to publish them in the press.

On March 8, 1961, only a week later, a policeman from a nearby station at West End Central saw Edwin Bush in Old Compton Street in Soho and recognized him from the Identi-Kit pictures. He arrested Bush on suspicion of being responsible for the murder of Elsie Batten, who was 59. Remarkably, Bush had a copy of the Identi-Kit pictures from the newspaper in his pocket. He was later picked out at an identification parade by one of the two witnesses and then later confessed to the murder. Edwin Bush was convicted for murder and was executed on July 6, 1961 in Pentonville Prison. This was the first time Identi-Kit was used to solve a case by Scotland Yard.

Identi-Kit was a software that was replaced by Photo-FIT, a software created by Jacques Penry, a photographer who was fascinated by facial morphological anatomy and published his book *How to Read Character from the Face* in 1939. Penry claimed that there was a link between a person's personality and their human physique. He also claimed that he could deduce a person's character instantly from their facial appearance. He argued that using the Penry system of facial classification could rid the society of "criminals, mental deficits, neurasthenics and vocational misfits."

In 1968, Jacques Penry presented his Photo-FIT system (Figure 7.8) to the Home Office in London. The kit consisted of narrow paper strips showing a photograph of various facial features such as eyes, nose, mouth, and so on, with approximately 40 of each accompanied with

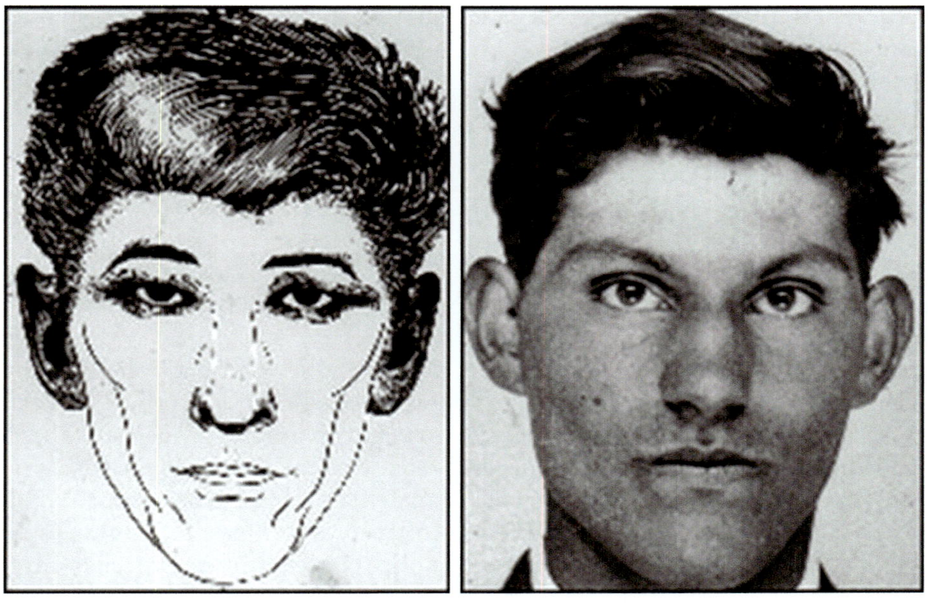

FIGURE 7.6 Identi-Kit image versus image of Edwin Bush.

FIGURE 7.7 Three sketches taken from witness interviews of alleged offender.

an index and various transparent overlays for beards, glasses, wrinkles and so on. The various elements were then combined in a purpose-made frame to represent the suspect person's facial appearance.

Photo-FIT was first used in relation to the murder of James Cameron in Islington in October 1970 (Figure 7.8). The Photo-FIT of the suspect was shown on "Police 5" on October 22, 1970, and the image was recognized by a shop assistant who remembered a man who had bought an umbrella from his shop in Victoria with a check that had bounced. He remembered the man had produced a firearms certificate to verify his identity. John Ernest Bennett was subsequently identified and arrested in Nottingham. He was later convicted of the murder.

Photo-FIT continued to be used by police forces throughout the United Kingdom until the introduction of a computer composite software in 1988 called E-FIT, which allowed an operator to call on a library of photographic facial features stored in the computer's memory to construct a realistic suspect's image.

Because of this software, an early arrest was made of Colin Ireland, who was convicted of a series of murders of gay men in London. On July 21, 1993. Ireland gave himself up to the police after seeing a "Wanted" poster showing an E-FIT image of him. He initially gave a false explanation of his contact with one of the victims but later changed his story and confessed to his crimes when told his fingerprints had been found at the scene of another murder in the series. He was jailed for life for the murders in December 1993 and remained imprisoned until his death in February 2012, at the age of 57.

7.8.2 Historical Background to Holistic Composite Systems

Although there are many differences in details in the various commercial composite systems available, until 5 years ago, all commercial systems operated with the same feature-based philosophy whereby the individual features of the face are selected from databases of examples, which had been suitably categorized. The commercial systems E-FIT, Pro-FIT, Identi-Kit, COMPHOTOFIT, and Faces all fall into this category. One of the earliest innovations that aimed to partly address the limitations associated with a finite database of candidate features was the experimental system developed by Brunelli and Mich (1996) named Spotit!

This system relied on a PCA model for each class of feature, achieving a reduction in the dimensionality of the problem and providing a basis from which novel features could be constructed. The "pre-face" image or starting point in this system was the mean face into which the facial features are set/blended. Seven sliders then control the appearance of each facial feature, where each slider corresponds to a principal component or mode of variation. The ranges of composites that can be produced using this technique are fundamentally limited by the finite size of the sample used in the PCA.

However, Brunelli and Mich included a tool that allowed the operator to manually distort the shape of a chosen feature. In this sense, there is an unlimited set of feature shapes that can be achieved. One of the major weaknesses would appear to be that the

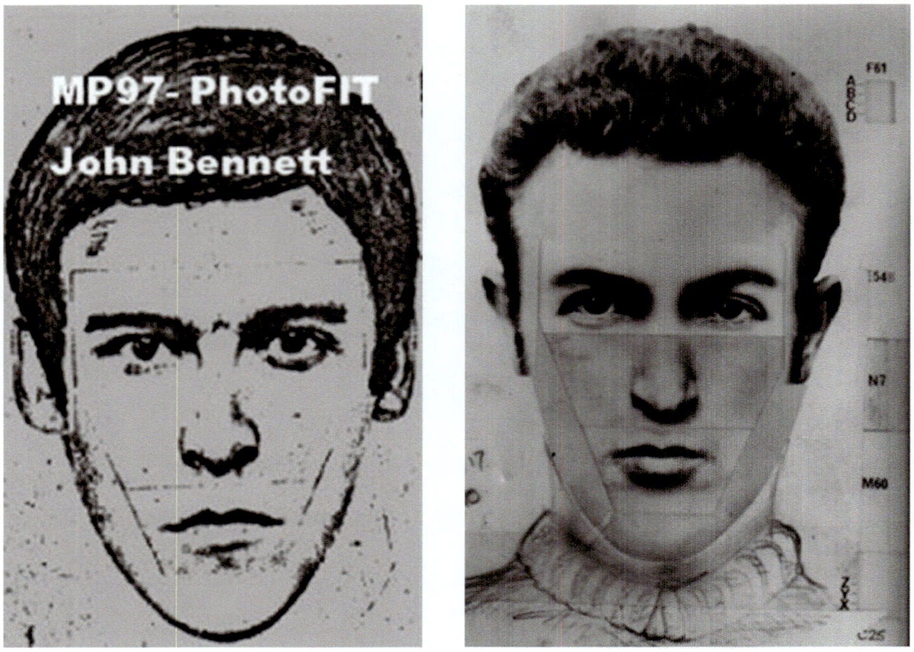

FIGURE 7.8 Photo-FIT image of John E. Bennett.

sliders incorporated in the interface control changes in appearance defined on a mathematical premise, and as such do not correspond to a specific perceptual meaning (e.g., "a turned-up nose"). Therefore, any prospective witness/operator will find it difficult to locate the optimum slider positions required for a good likeness of the target face.

An "intelligent" search procedure is required to overcome the difficulty of selecting the most appropriate features from an almost unlimited sample. Genetic algorithms (GAs) offer a conceptually pleasing solution to the search problem. Evolutionary techniques based on Darwinian theory that simulate complex structures, textures, and motions for use in computer graphics and animation were described as early as 1991. DiPaolo, also working in the computer graphics arena, describes such an algorithm for facial appearance, based on an aesthetic selection process in which faces are represented by genotypes comprising 25 parameters.

However, the first recorded use of a GA for generating facial composite imagery for police use was by Caldwell and Johnston. The GA is initialized with a population of 20 faces, which are constructed from individual facial features in a style reminiscent of earlier systems. Faces are displayed to the operator, who is required to assign a fitness score to each face depending on its similarity to the target. Parent faces are chosen from the initial population according to their associated fitness score and bred with each other using the standard principles of crossover and mutation.

Attempts have been made to incorporate information concerning the configuration of facial features into feature based systems such as E-FIT, and the effectiveness of these ad hoc "pseudo holistic" approaches have been examined (Caldwell and Johnston, 1991). However, a more elegant and possibly more effective approach is to model facial variation as a whole.

The earliest work in this direction was that of Hancock (2000), who describes a developmental system that utilized both global PCA face models and a GA. Critically, this design appears to be the first to allow composite images to be created by adjusting global/holistic properties of facial appearance, in a way that is not too demanding of the witness. Unlike previous systems, this approach is truly global, relying on whole-face templates (the principal components) rather than a database of facial features. In this context, the principal components are often referred to as eigenfaces, which had been explored in the computer vision literature and originated with the seminal work of Sirovich and Kirby in 1987. Hancock used two separate PCA models, one for face shape and another for pixel intensity values. Using two independent models overcomes problems associated with head pose and blurring that would otherwise degrade the composite images.

The operator was presented with a selection of 18 faces to which fitness ratings must be assigned on a scale of 0 to 10. The genetic algorithm selects faces with a high rating (fitness proportionate selection) as parents. Parameters defining an offspring's appearance were selected at random from the parents (uniform crossover) and a mutation applied to some of the parameter values. This procedure was performed 18 times to form a new generation of faces. Hancock's original PCA model was built on a limited sample of 20 female faces.

The system has been subsequently refined and developed by Frowd and Hancock in a series of publications and is now known as Evo-FIT. The EFIT-V system with which this chapter is primarily concerned was conceived independently (the research system operated under the name EigenFIT and assumed commercial form under the name, EFIT-V, in 2007).

This system also employs PCA model building and evolutionary search techniques, though it differs somewhat in basic approach and functional details. The EFIT-V system is built on two core elements: the construction of a statistical appearance model of human faces and a stochastic search algorithm. In the following section, the core elements of the EFIT-V system are explained (Figure 7.9).

7.9 EFIT-V: OPERATIONAL PROCEDURE

It has been outlined how EFIT-V combines stochastic search methods with systematic tools for altering facial appearance to form an essentially hybrid system. At the time of this writing, the EFIT-V system has been used by approximately 45 police forces. EFIT-V is designed to be flexible so that the approach to face construction can be adapted to witnesses and their abilities. For this reason, no rigid operational procedure is recommended. However, the following sequence of events is typical of an EFIT-V interview.

An initial interview is first conducted. Current ACPO (Association of Chief Police Officers) guidelines recommend an interview based on the cognitive model initially devised by Geiselman and Fisher. We note in passing that alternative interview models are being researched which may better suit the methodology of systems such as EFIT-V.

On system start-up, a PACE-compliant form is displayed into which details that identify the composite are entered. Fields are provided for the witness's forenames, surname, date of birth, and also the operator's rank and number. This information is combined with the current date to generate a unique reference number that can be used to identify the composite for future reference.

In an attempt to accurately seed the starting point for the stochastic search, witnesses are asked to select from a sample of basic face shapes displayed on the screen. An "unsure" option exists in which case the first faces are generated as variations from the average face shape.

The witness then proceeds to select the hairstyle, or in the event that this was not visible, the headwear worn by the suspect. From a perceptual point of view, it is sensible to ask the witness to select an appropriate hairstyle first, as the external features are more salient in unfamiliar faces and there is evidence to suggest that facial features should be selected in order of decreasing significance. The user can scroll through the available hairstyles using a slider, with each increment in the slider position displaying nine more hairstyles in the familiar three-by-three configurations. Hairstyles are mapped onto a blank head-shape so that the witness may view the hair in some context. A filter is provided to sort the hairstyles into categories describing the length and color.

Thus, the number of candidate hairstyles that the witness must examine can be greatly reduced by marking the appropriate checkboxes provided in the filter.

At this point, the stochastic search begins and a first generation of nine faces is presented. The witness is asked to select a face from the nine which best resembles the suspect. If unable to do so because none bears sufficient resemblance, the witness may request to see another group until a face appears that constitutes a satisfactory starting point. Virtual faces that exhibit a poor likeness to the target may be removed from view.

This step declutters the field of view, making it easier for the witness to form an opinion on the suitability of the remaining visible faces. Once the witness has made a choice, nine more faces comprising the first generation then replace the initial population and the process of selecting a face is repeated. In this mode, the user has the option to lock the shape of a particular facial feature that exhibits a good likeness to the corresponding feature on the target face. This is achieved by choosing a region in an iconic face located on the right-hand side of the interface and then selecting one of the nine virtual faces.

Placing the cursor over a feature in the iconic face and using a single click of the left mouse button turns that region from gray to blue, indicating that the shape of the chosen feature will be fixed through subsequent generations. Deselecting a region of the iconic face reintroduces shape variation in the previously locked feature. If required, more than one feature may be fixed at any given instant. The available choices of features that can be locked are the eyebrows (left/right pair), eyes (left/right pair), nose, mouth, and face shape or any combination of these.

Typically, after a witness has selected the preferred face from five or six generations, he or she will be prompted to provide feedback on the composite image

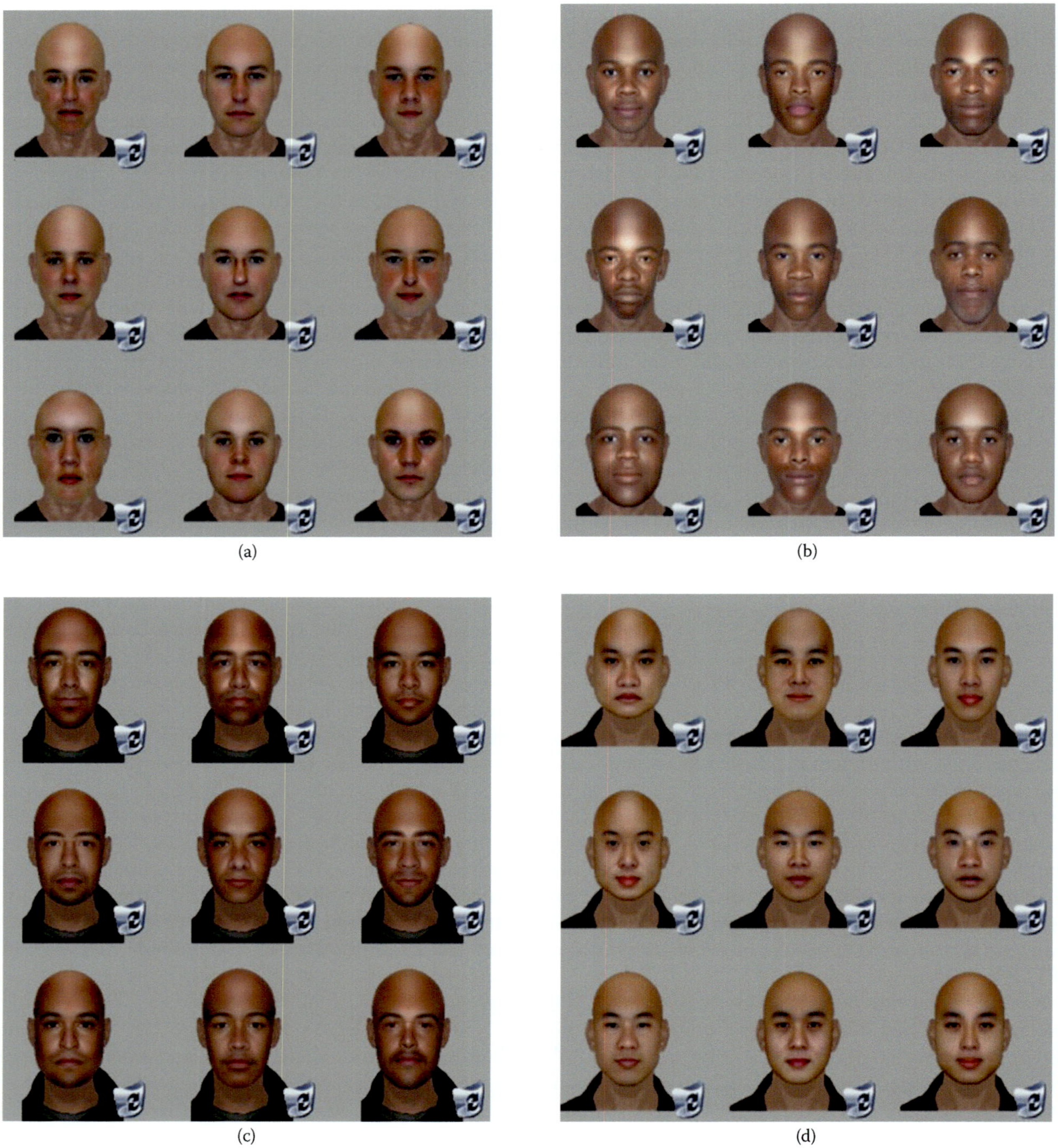

FIGURE 7.9 Random generation of faces in EFIT-V through sampling a statistical model of facial appearance. (Examples are shown for each of the class models *White Male, Black Male, Hispanic Male*, and *Oriental Male*.) (Used with permission from Chris Solomon).

so far and whether there are any definite characteristics or features that they would like to alter. The operator will then respond using the array of systematic tools at their disposal in an attempt to "progress" the composite toward a better likeness.

This step is important in the use of EFIT-V since the operator should resist any attempt to create a "final" product at this stage but only use the information provided by the witness to progress the composite likeness and confirm whether or not the modified composite now represents a better likeness. If the witness confirms an improved likeness, the system immediately reverts to the evolutionary mode and takes this likeness as the starting point for the subsequent stochastic variations. Again, the witness is then asked to select the best example from a sequence of generations, three to six being typical.

Further systematic changes may be requested at this stage, including the use of paintwork using an associated graphics package such as Adobe Photoshop or Corel PaintShop. Paintwork can be added to EFIT-V images at any time and the system used subsequently in the normal way, but it is generally advisable to defer certain forms of artistic enhancement to late in the process due to the problems of image registration.

An Undo function and a Load function are available. Typically, these are used when the witness feels that a poor choice of face has been made, or a face has been selected unintentionally and another image is preferred and has great likeness to the suspect. Once an acceptable likeness has been obtained, the current stallion image (best likeness) is saved both as a graphics file and as a file internal to EFIT-V, which can be loaded into the program at any point in the future.

A complete audit trail is kept by EFIT-V so that the time, date, personnel involved, and all steps in the construction process are saved to the hard disk of the computer. The entire contents can also be burned directly to CD from within EFIT-V as an exhibit for subsequent evidential procedures.

A meaningful evaluation of the effectiveness of any facial composite system is surprisingly complex. From a policing perspective, the primary goal is very simple—namely the provision of a correct name for the suspect. Secondary goals also exist, namely speed and ease of use, which can have direct financial implications for police forces.

The attempt to reach the primary goal is affected by many factors:

- The inherent capability of the composite system to create good likenesses (i.e., its imaging capability).
- Its inherent methodology (i.e., the degree to which the system matches the cognitive processes and needs of the witness and operator).
- The capability and skills of the police operator. Although standardized training courses exist, operator skill and experience vary widely.
- The capability, willingness, and emotional state of the witness.
- The nature of the crime or offense. There is, for example, some provisional evidence that offenses in which the witness has time or presence of mind to consciously attempt to commit the face to memory result in a different encoding of the face compared to offenses in which no conscious attempt is made (e.g., a distraction burglary in which the victim will have no reason to consciously attempt to remember the face of the perpetrator at the time of the incident).
- The effective use of the composite once it has been created. In simple terms, a composite image may represent a good likeness to the target subject, but if the subsequent procedures do not result in a sufficient or appropriate cross section of the police or public seeing the image, it will fail in its basic objective. This aspect and its impact on success rates is often strangely overlooked.

The supply of relevant supplementary information along with the composite image can affect the ability and willingness of someone to offer a name. For example, an image supplied with supplementary information such as "a white male aged 30–35 years, with a strong northern accent and scruffily dressed" is likely to have better chances of success than the image alone.

As a commercial system, the evaluation of the effectiveness of EFIT-V to date has largely been gauged by feedback from police forces using the system routinely rather than through academic studies. At the E-FIT user conference in 2009, West Yorkshire police reported a 40% naming rate over an 18-month period from May 2008 to November 2009 that encompassed more than 1000 interviews. This indicates that when the factors mentioned above are properly considered, performance can be excellent. Functional developments of the system have also been driven by the real-life requirements of operators and witnesses and by advances in our understanding of facial and image processing as well.

Figure 7.10 shows an array of famous faces, all of which were created by trainees on various training courses delivered in 2010. These images were not produced under conditions of strict forensic validity, but were produced from memory and indicate EFIT-V's inherent ability to produce accurate likenesses of a subject. A novel use of EFIT-V has recently been reported by Cheshire police. An elderly man suffered a fatal cardiac arrest in Davenham, Cheshire, but the police were unable to identify him. The forensic service's postmortem photographs of the man were not considered suitable for public release and likely to cause distress.

Accordingly, EFIT-V was used to create a likeness to the subject, a procedure lasting only 1 hour, which was then printed in the local press. The man was subsequently identified. Figure 7.11 highlights the process required to undertake EFIT-V.

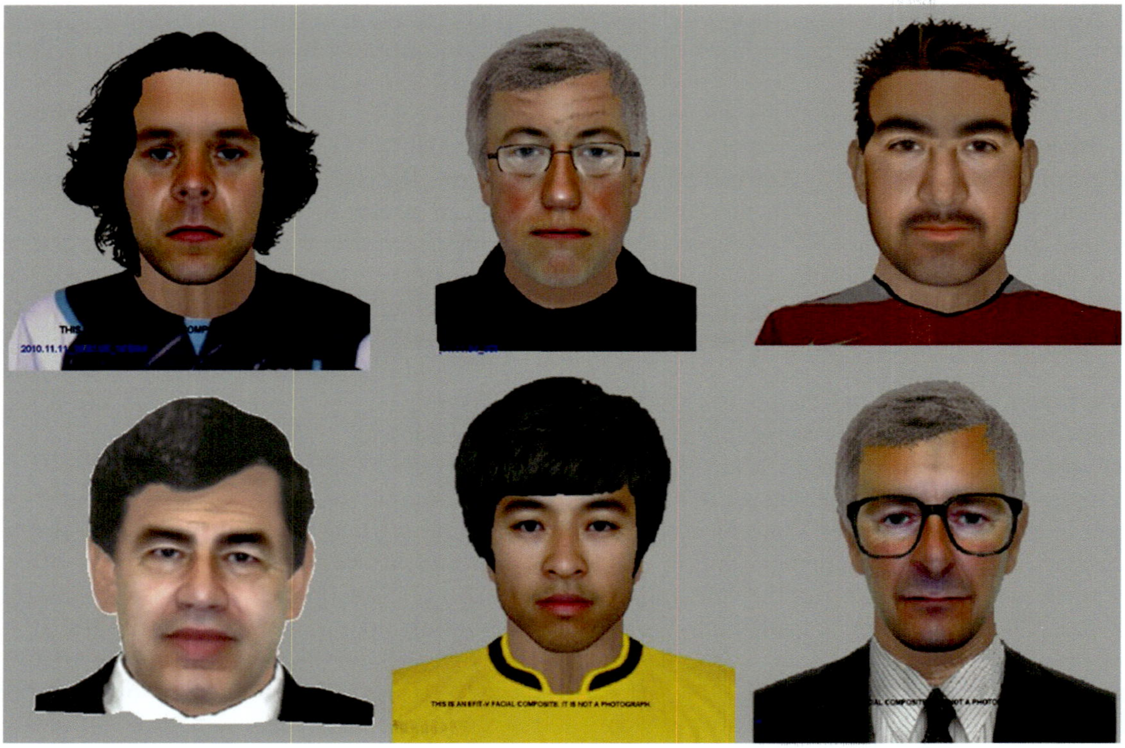

FIGURE 7.10 Construction of famous faces from memory using the EFIT-V system. The images above were created during training of police operators. Proceeding from the top row, left to right, the target subjects are Carlos Tevez (footballer), Alex Ferguson (football manager), Eric Cantina (former footballer), Gordon Brown (former Prime Minister), Bruce Lee (martial artist), and John Major (former Prime Minister). (Used with permission from Chris Solomon).

FIGURE 7.11 EFIT-V Image process created by Stephen Driver and Shelina Jilani, Acumé Forensics.

BIBLIOGRAPHY

A. Bertillon. *Signaletic Instructions Including the Theory and Practice of Anthropometrical Identification.* R.W. McClaughry (Trans.). Chicago: The Werner Company, 1896.

A. Bertillon (n.d.) *Alphonse Bertillon Biography.* Available at: http://www.nlm.nih.gov/visibleproofs/galleries/biographies/bertillon.html

W. W. Bledsoe. *A Man Machine Facial Recognition System: Some Preliminary Results.* Technical Report 12. Panoramic Research Inc., Palo Alto, CA, 1965.

V. Bruce, Z. Henderson, K. Greenwood, P. Hancock. A.M. Burton and P. Miller. Verification of face identities from images captured on video. *Journal of Experimental Psychology: Applied,* 5(4):339–360, 1999.

R. Brunelli and O. Mich. SpotIt! an interactive identikit system. *Graphical Models and Image Processing: GMIP,* 58(5):399–404, 1996.

A.M. Burton, R. Jenkins, P.J.B. Hancock and D. White. Robust representations of face recognition: The power of averages. *Cognitive Psychology,* 51:256–284, 2005.

C. Caldwell and V.S. Johnston. Tracking a criminal suspect through facespace with a genetic algorithm. In *Proceeding of the 4th International Conference on Genetic Algorithms*, Burlington, MA, Morgan Kaufmann, pp. 416–421, 1991.

Criminal Law Web: *R. v. Tolson* [1886–1890] All ER Rep 26; [1886–90] All ER Rep 26, May 11, 1889. http://www.law–lib.utoronto.ca/bclc/crimweb/rvtolson.html

K. Delac, M. GrGic and P. Liatsis. Appearance based statistical method for face recognition. *47th International Symposium ELMAR—2005*, Zadar, Croatia, pp. 151–158, June 8–10, 2005.

S. DiPaolo. Investigating face space. *SIGGRAPH Presented Paper (sketch)*, 2002.

H.D. Ellis, J.W. Shepard and G.M. Davies. Identification of familiar and unfamiliar faces from internal and external features—Some implications for theories of face recognition. *Perception*, 8:431–439, 1979.

FISWG Guidelines for Facial Comparison Method. Section 6, Version 1.02012.02.02, 2012.

S.J. Gibson, C.J. Solomon, M.I.S. Maylin and C. Clark. New methodology in facial composite construction: From theory to practice. *International Journal of Electronic Security and Digital Forensics*, 2:156–168, 2009.

A.J. Goldstein, L.D. Harmon and A.B. Lesk. Identification of human faces. *Proceeding of IEEE*, 59(5):748–760, May 1971.

P.J.B. Hancock. Evolving faces from principal components. *Behaviour Research Methods, Instruments and Computers*, 32(2):327–333, 2000.

J.B. Hancock, A.M. Burton and V. Bruce. Face processing: Human perception and principal components analysis. *Memory and Cognition*, 24(1):26–40, 1996.

A.M. Harris and G.K. Aguirre. Prosopagnosia. *Current Biology*, 17: R7–R8, 2007.

Z. Henderson, V. Bruce, and A.M. Burton. Matching the faces of robbers captured on video. *Applied Cognitive Psychology*, 15:445–464, 2001.

J.H. Holland. *Adaptation in Natural and Artificial Systems*. Ann Arbor, MI: University of Michigan Press, 1975.

Image of Bertillon System, n.d., http://www.nlm.nih.gov/visibleproofs/media/detailed/iii_c_138.jpg

L.D. Introna. Disclosive ethics and information technology, disclosing facial recognition systems. *Ethics and Information Technology*, 7(2):73–86, June 2005.

R. Jafri and H.R. Arabnia. A survey of face recognition techniques. *Journal of Information Processing Systems*, 5(2):44–55, June 2009.

A. Jain, R. Bolle and S. Pakanti (eds.). *Biometrics: Personal Identification in Networked Security*. Berlin: Springer Science & Business Media, 2006.

A.K. Jain, P. Flynn and A. Ross (Eds.), *Handbook of Biometrics*. Springer, 2007.

A.K. Jain, B. Klare and U. Park. Face Recognition: Some Challenges in Forensics. *9th IEEE International Conference on Automatic Face and Gesture Recognition*, Santa Barbara, CA, pp. 726–732, 2011.

R. Jenkins and A.M. Burton. 100% Accuracy in automatic face recognition. *Science*, 319:345, 2008.

M. Kirby and L. Sirovich. Application of the Karhunen-Loeve procedure for the characterization of human faces. *IEEE Transactions on Pattern Analysis and Machine Intelligence*, 12:103–107, 1990.

K. Lander, V. Bruce and E. Hill. Evaluating the effectiveness of pixilation and blurring on masking the identity of familiar faces. *Applied Cognitive Psychology*, 15:101–116, 2001.

I. Marques and M. Grana. *Face Recognition Algorithms*. June 16, 2010.

A.M. Megreya and M. Binderman. Revisiting the Processes of internal and external features of unfamiliar faces: The headscarf effect. *Perception*, 28:1831–1848, 2009.

C. O'Donnell and V. Bruce. Familiarisation with faces selectively enhances sensitivity to changes made to the eyes. *Perception*, 30:755–765, 2001.

P.J. Phillips, H. Moon, S.A. Rizvi and P.J. Rauss. *The FERET Evaluation Methodology for Face-Recognition Algorithms*. Technical Report NISTIR 6264, pp. 1–20, January 7, 1999.

P.J. Phillips, H. Moon, S.A. Rizvi and P.J. Rauss. The FERET evaluation methodology for face-recognition algorithms. *IEEE Transactions on Pattern Analysis and Machine Intelligence*, 22(10): 1090–1104, 2000.

G. Porter and G. Doran. An anatomical and photographic technique for forensic facial identification. *Forensic Science International*, 114:97–100, 2000.

R v Fowden and White (1982), Crim LR 588.

R v Tolson (1864), 4 F & F 103.

S. Rizvi, P. Phillips and H. Moon. *The FERET Verification Testing Protocol for Face Recognition Algorithms*. National Institute of Standards and Technology. Technical Report 6281, 1998.

K. Sims. Artificial evolution for computer graphics. *Computer Graphics*, 25(4):319–328, 1991.

L. Sirovich and M. Kirby. Low-dimensional procedure for the characterization of human faces. *Journal of the Optical Society of America A*, 4(3):519–524, 1987.

C. Solomon, S. Gibson and M. Maylin. A new computational methodology for the construction of forensic, facial composites. *Computational Forensics*, 5718:67–77, 2009, Springer-Verlag LNCS.

T. Thompson and S. Black. Facial recognition and imagery analysis. In *Forensic Human Identification. An Introduction*, Chap. 16. Boca Raton, FL: BAHID, CRC Press, pp. 257–270, 2007.

T. Thompson and S. Black. Osteology. In *Forensic Human Identification. An Introduction*, Chap. 11, Boca Raton, FL: BAHID, CRC Press, 2007.

M. Turk and A. Pentland. Eigenfaces for recognition. *Journal of Cognitive Neuroscience*, 3(1):72–86, 1991, Massachusetts Institute of Technology.

C. Wilkinson and C. Rynn. Familiar face recognition. In *Craniofacial Identification*. C. Wilkinson and C. Rynn (Eds.), Chap. 1. Cambridge: Cambridge University Press, pp. 1–9, 2012.

D. Woodward, C. Horn, J. Gatune and A. Thomas. *Biometric: A Look at Facial Recognition.* RAND, p. 1, 2003.

A.W. Young, F. Newcombe, E.H.F. De Haan, M. Small and D.C. Hay. Face perception after brain injury: Selective impairments affecting identity and expression. *Brains*, 116:941–959, 1993.

CHAPTER 8

Forensic Odontology

Alan Diego Briem Stamm and María Cecilia Pastor Carson

CONTENTS

8.1 INTRODUCTION

The forensic discipline is concerned with the application of science and technology to detect and investigate crime and administration of justice, requiring the coordinated efforts of a multidisciplinary team. Typically, this effort involves the cooperation and coordination of law enforcement officials, forensic pathologists, forensic anthropologists, forensic odontologists, criminalistics, and other specialists as deemed necessary. Human identification is one of the most challenging subjects that man has been confronted with.

Forensic odontology has become an integral part of forensic medicine. With the passage of time, the role of forensic odontology has increased, as very often teeth and dental restorations are the only means of identification. Forensic odontology has played a key role in identifying people in mass disasters (aviation, earthquakes, tsunamis), crime investigations, ethnic studies, and in identifying decomposed and disfigured bodies, like those of drowned persons, fire victims, and victims of motor vehicle accidents. Other areas of application include criminalistics, in cases involving abuse of children and elderly. Bite marks also help in detection of culprits. Forensic odontology also renders its service in investigating dental malpractice and archeology. The scope of forensic dentistry is broad and ever-challenging. Each case is different, and even the seemingly routine case may test the dentist's ingenuity in applying his dental knowledge.

The various methods employed in forensic odontology include tooth prints, radiographs, photographic study, rugoscopy, cheiloscopy, and molecular methods. Investigative methods applied in forensic odontology are reasonably reliable, yet the shortcomings must be accounted for to make it a more meaningful and relevant procedure. Most dental identifications are based on restorations, caries, missing teeth and/or prosthetic devices, such as partial and full removal prostheses, which are compared with antemortem records. The establishment of forensic odontology as a unique discipline has been attributed to Dr. Oscar Amoedo (the father of forensic odontology), who identified the victims of a fire accident in Paris, France, in 1898.

What follows is a discussion of different topics covered by the forensic odontology specialty, promoting the work of dental experts in the multidisciplinary team identification, according to international standards and globalizing philosophies.

8.2 IDENTIFICATION

Identification of individuals is not always straightforward and easy, especially in medicolegal cases where the individuals are either unable to give accurate answers or are purposefully misleading. Living individuals for whom identification is required are criminals attempting to elude custody, amnesia victims, comatose victims, victims of disfiguring trauma, or people requiring identity confirmation following identity theft. Deceased individuals that may require identity confirmation include the homeless, illegal/undocumented immigrants, burnt, or decomposed bodies (Figure 8.1), and disfigured, skeletal remains of individuals [1,2].

The most common methods for establishing a positive identification are visual, fingerprint, DNA, and dental comparison [1]. A corpus identification, in which a relative or close friend identifies the individual by viewing the body, is also accepted as positive identification. However, corpus identification is not beyond human error and is not possible when the body is in advanced stages of decomposition or severely damaged by trauma such as fire or mutilation [3,4]. The identification process is characterized by the utilization of appropriate techniques and means to discover an identity, and can be developed either by skilled technicians (judiciary or police authorities) or by professionals with differentiated and specific knowledge in the area of biology (forensic medicine or dentistry), with a practically unlimited array of appropriate techniques and means to achieve human identification [4–6].

The information provided by the multidisciplinary team can lead police investigators to possible identities for the unknown individual. Comparisons between possible identities and the unknown individual can direct investigators to a presumptive or positive identification [7,8]. Presumptive identification may also be made based on tattoos, circumstantial evidence, personal effects, or facial reconstruction. This type of identification is not scientifically confirmed, but can be accepted as final when foul play is not suspected and no other reason for doubt exists [3,7].

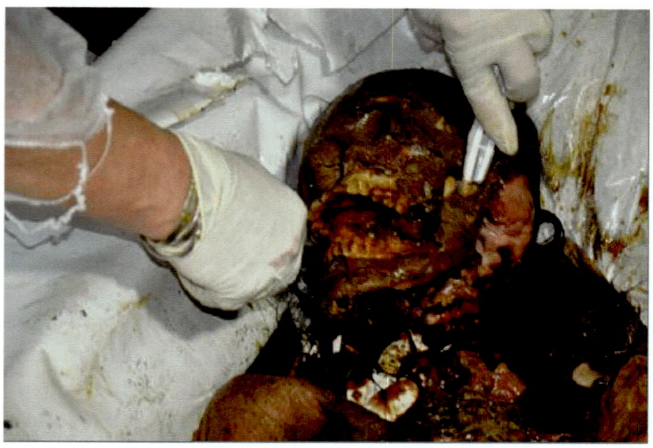

FIGURE 8.1 Putrefying corpse.

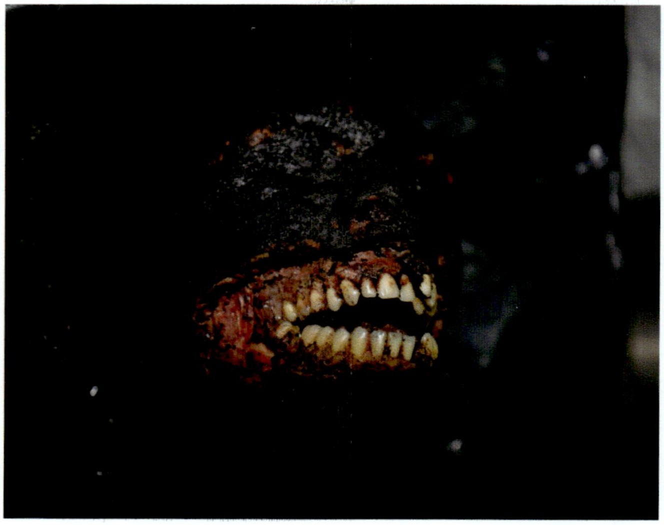

FIGURE 8.2 Carbonized corpse.

Postmortem identification represents one of the great branches of study and research in forensic dentistry and medicine, considering that both sciences deal with a same material—the human body at different stages, such as ripped, lacerated, carbonized (Figure 8.2), macerated, putrefied, skeletonized—always with a single objective, that is to say, to establish human identity [1,3,7].

8.3 GLOBALIZATION IN FORENSIC SCIENCES

As expressed by Prof. Dr. Cyrill Wecht, "Forensic Science has no geographic boundaries. By its very nature it is global in nature." Throughout the world, various groups are making great strides to develop the potential of forensic science [8]. The promotion of teams has been recommended for these procedures (disaster victim identification, or DVI), always under protocols and standards recognized internationally. Since the teeth and their restoration can resist highly unfavorable conditions, forensic odontology has played a key role in the identification of great number of victims (Figure 8.3).

Different groups in the world are working toward developing forensic odontology and its standard methodologies, defining criteria for forensic practice, and conducting research in various aspects of forensic science [7,9]. Although the application of forensic science may vary by political jurisdiction and laws, the science of forensic science needs to be universally grounded in theory, principles, and methods [9,10]. Concepts of science, quality, and performance all begin with a sound, comprehensive education in the sciences—forensic science is no different.

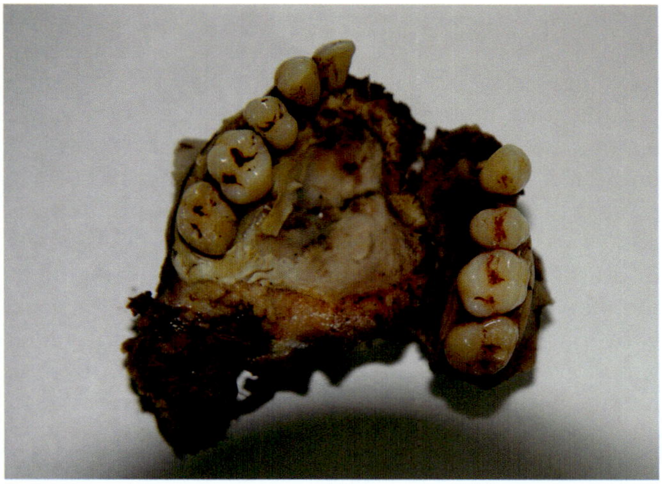

FIGURE 8.3 Resistant tooth tissues.

Crime, especially high levels of crime, affects the health of the people of any country, and the more extreme this is, the sicker and unhealthier the people will be. The UNODC (United Nations Office on Drugs and Crime) did a study, beginning with the estimate that in 2010 there were 468,000 intentional homicides. Traumatized survivors of the victims of deaths caused by criminal incidents are 20 times the number of dead annually. This means that annually about 100 million people around the world are traumatized as a direct result of violent crime [9–11].

Other forms of violent death are also contributing to the decimation of the world's population. Among these are traffic accidents, drowning, falls, fires, and deliberate acts of violence against oneself or others. The World Health Organization (WHO) estimates that on average, over 1.6 million people lose their lives to random acts of violence worldwide. On average, 2233 people commit suicide around the globe every day—roughly one person every 40 seconds. In the last 45 years, suicide rates have increased by 60% worldwide. Suicide is now among the three leading causes of death of those aged 15–44; and WHO estimates that during the last two decades, suicide rates have been increasing globally to a mortality rate of 16 per 100,000. All these fatalities usually end up in the jurisdiction of forensic sciences [11]. In 2013, there are some, but relatively few, examples of sustained provision over many years of forensic medicine training in one center for a number of medical practitioners from another country. And if it is true for forensic medicine, it is even more so for the related disciplines of odontology, anthropology, and toxicology. It is time for existing, laudable, but ad hoc efforts to be raised to a more organized level [12]. Again quoting Prof. Dr. Wecht,

> *Forensic scientists must be willing and prepared to play an important and highly sensitive role in death investigation that has international significance and far reaching political ramifications. Utilization of universal knowledge and skills in resolving such controversial matters and thereby helping to achieve social justice should be an acknowledged objective of individual forensic scientists as well as national and international forensic scientific professional organizations.* [9]

INTERPOL guidelines [13] recommend that the location of each body, body part, and piece of property is recorded with reference to a known point by experienced police officers. Pathologists and odontologists may be included in the scene teams to identify body parts and dental structures, particularly where severe body fragmentation has occurred. In a compact well-controlled disaster site it is easy to manage the recovery process but this is not the usual occurrence, particularly in large-scale natural disasters. More regularly in such incidents, the 2004 Asian tsunami being a good example, victims are spread over a large area and survivors begin collecting the deceased before authorities arrive at the scene [14,15].

8.4 FORENSIC ODONTOLOGY

Forensic odontology is often considered to be the area of overlap between the dental and legal professions. Occasionally, the forensic odontologist deals with legal issues on behalf of the dental profession. But, most often, the odontologist answers questions posed by the justice system and provides answers to legal authorities and expert opinions in courts of law. Significantly, much of the odontologist's work is on behalf of grieving family members who have lost a loved one and need to have closure to come to terms with their grief [16,17]. All people possess an identity during their lifetime, and the dignity of confirming and maintaining this identity after death is a strong, compelling societal need. Forensic odontology assists society in accomplishing this through comparison of AM (antemortem, before death) and PM (postmortem, after death) data to identify the corpse. There are also legal requirements for confirmation of a deceased person's identity, including religious issues, matters surrounding the estate, remarriage of a surviving partner, and insurance or financial affairs [17]. Of particular legal importance is a case in which a person is the victim of violent crime. Identification of the victim's body becomes circumstantial evidence during the police investigation into cause of death, and is later used in the prosecution of the person responsible for the death [16–19].

Worldwide, dentists qualified in forensic science are giving expert opinion in cases related to human identification, bite-mark analysis, craniofacial trauma, and malpractice. Human identification relies heavily on the quality of dental records; however, forensic odontologists can still contribute to the identity investigation in the absence of dental records through profiling the deceased person using features related to teeth. Along with other healthcare providers, dentists encounter cases of injuries which could be non-accidental [20]. Detection, interpretation, and management are important from a legal and humanitarian point of view. Dentists should be aware of the legal impact these cases have, and should refer them to the appropriate authorities for suitable action. Dental identification is a comparative technique, where the PM dental records are analyzed and compared against AM records to confirm identity and establish the degree of certainty that the dental records obtained from the remains of a decedent and the AM dental records of a missing person are for the same individual [18,19]. Currently, the identification is carried out manually by comparing extracted features from a PM dental record to extracted fractures from a database of AM records. Several individual teeth may be missing or filled after a decedent's AM record is taken, hence, dental features need to be recorded based on the contour/shape of individual teeth rather than the contour of the whole jaw [18].

The new millennium has brought new challenges of terrorism, natural disasters, and a high rate of crime in Latin America and other places in the world have also had a marked increase in crimes. Dental hard tissues are extremely resistant to fire and are usually the only remains after an extended period of burial. Since the late 1890s, forensic dentistry has gradually established itself as important, often indispensable, in medicolegal cases, in particular for identification of the dead [21,22]. The specialty of forensic dentistry generally covers three basic areas:

1. Identification of human remains
2. Litigation relating to malpractice
3. Criminal proceedings, primarily in the areas of bite-mark evaluation and abuse cases especially child abuse

The teeth and dental restorations are the strongest elements in the human body and survive the destructive influences of fire and exposure to the elements. Methods to identify the deceased must be reliable and accurate. The comparison of AM to PM dental records is a widely accepted and dependable method of forensic identification. Considerable discussion in the forensic odontology literature has addressed the validity of the concept of uniqueness in human dentition. Thompson observed in 1897: "There are so many variations of peculiarities of the teeth and of artificial operations upon them, that there is but a remote chance of the same case ever being exactly supplicated. Every practicing dentist can testify to that fact." While this statement reflects the generally accepted convention, it provides no actual evidence in support of uniqueness [23]. This contention was not challenged scientifically for many years. Keiser-Nielsen [24] pointed out that no physical feature is in fact unique. He also correctly explained that a dental identification does not rely on the presence of a single feature, but on the presentation of the features evident on 32 teeth in the complete adult dentition [25,26]. He posited that the multiplication of combined occurrences allows an odontologist to be confident that duplications in other individuals are unlikely to occur. To highlight the individuality of a given dentition, he cited the case with four missing teeth and four restored teeth, which would give 736,281,000 possible combinations, leading him to conclude that it would be just about impossible to observe two identical combinations [27,28].

Dental identification is one approach to human identification. Other approaches include visual identification, which is known to be unreliable due to a high rate of false positives; comparison of medical records and data, such as serial numbers on prosthetic joints and breast implants; fingerprints, if AM data are available; and DNA analysis [29–31]. The contours and extensions of dental fillings and crowns, for example, produce unique identifying traits when they are depicted as two-dimensional shadows on radiographs. These are used in forensic comparisons. The decrease in caries rate and the subsequent decline in the use of amalgam restorations over the past few decades have resulted in loss of these important identifiers in some cases [32]. These situations create a challenge for the forensic odontologist [33,34]. Still, radiographs show many other anatomical features, such as root shape, surrounding bone trabeculae, root canal filling materials, retentive pins and posts, pulp size and shape, and periodontal and periapical inflammatory disease that can be of significant value in identification cases [33,35,36].

Dental identification assumes a primary role in the identification of remains when PM changes, traumatic tissue injury or lack of a fingerprint record invalidate the use of visual or fingerprint methods. The identification of dental remains is of primary importance when the deceased person is skeletonized (Figure 8.4), decomposed, saponified (Figure 8.5), mummified (Figure 8.6), burned, or dismembered.

The principal advantage of dental evidence is that, like other hard tissues, it is often preserved after death [33,37]. Even the status of a person's teeth changes throughout life and the combination of decayed, missing and filled teeth is measurable and comparable at any fixed point in time. The fundamental principles of dental identification are those of comparison and exclusion. For example, dental identification is used when AM records for the putative deceased person are available and circumstantial evidence suggests the identity of the decedent [35,37].

There are two types of discrepancies: those that can be explained and those that cannot. Explainable discrepancies normally relate to the time elapsed between the

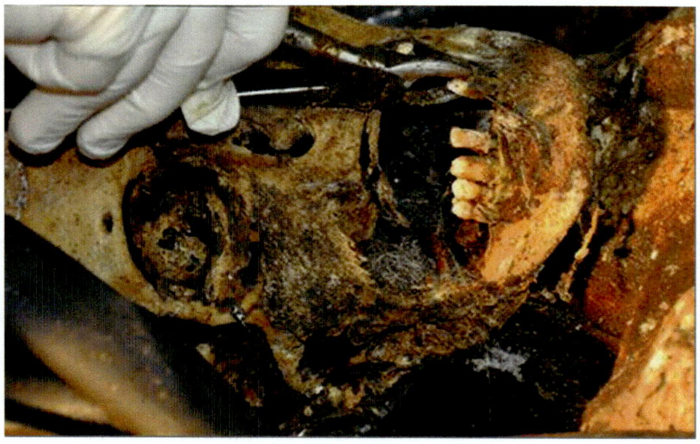

FIGURE 8.4 Skeletonized corpse.

FIGURE 8.5 Saponified corpse.

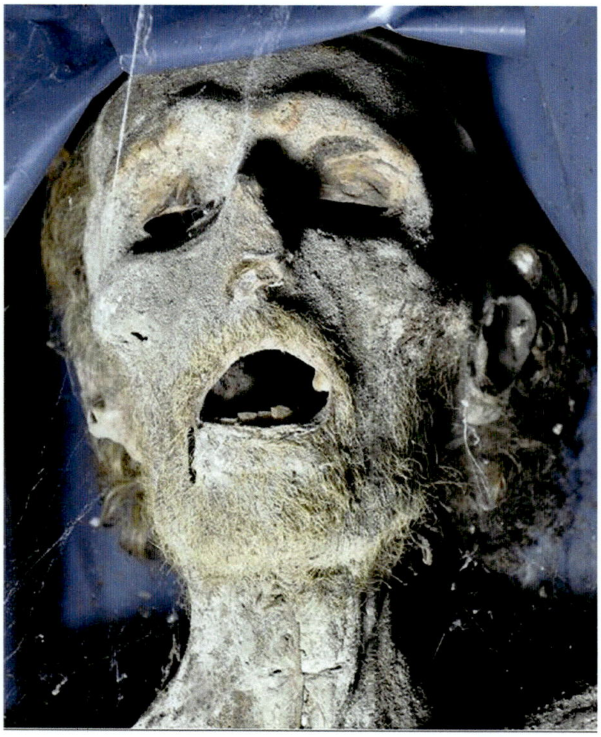

FIGURE 8.6 Mummified corpse.

AM and PM records [38]. Examples include that teeth extracted or restorations placed were found in postmortem records only. If a discrepancy is unexplainable—for example, a tooth is not present on the AM record but is present on the PM record—then an exclusion must be made [37,38]. If there are no AM dental records, a PM dental profile will typically provide information characteristics of the victim:

- 1—Age
  - In children: The patterns of tooth eruption, the root length, and tooth wear are assessed
  - In young adults: The third molar development
  - In middle-aged and older adults: Periodontal disease progression, excessive wear, multiple restorations, extractions, bone pathosis, and complex restorative work are assessed; recently, dentine composition and cement deposition have been examined in relation to age determination
- 2—Ethnic
  - Can be assessed from skull shape and form
  - Other characteristics, such as cusps of Carabelli, shovel-shaped incisors, and multicusped premolars
- 3—Gender can be assessed from the following:
  - Skull shape and form (no gender differences regarding teeth morphology)
  - Presence or absence of Y-chromatin in teeth
  - DNA analysis
  - Mandibular canine's size
- 4—Socioeconomic status can be assessed through the quality, quantity, and presence or absence of dental treatment
- 5—Occupation, dietary habits, and dental or systemic diseases; the presence of erosion can suggest alcohol or an eating disorder, while stains can indicate smoking or use of tetracycline; unusual wear patterns may result from pipe stems or cigarette holders;

A range of conclusions can be drawn following a comparison of AM and PM records. The American Board of Forensic Odontology (ABFO), however, recommends these to be limited by four conclusions [39]:

1. Positive identification: The AM and PM findings match in sufficient detail, without any unexplainable discrepancy, to establish that they are from the same individual.
2. Possible identification: The AM and PM data have consistent features, but, because of the quality of either the PM remains or AM evidence, it is not possible to establish identity positively.

3. Insufficient evidence: The available information is insufficient to form the basis for a conclusion of any sort.
4. Exclusion: The AM and PM data are clearly inconsistent.

Natural teeth are the most durable organs in the bodies of vertebrates, and humankind's understanding of their own past and evolution relies heavily upon remnant dental evidence found as fossils. Teeth can persist long after other skeletal structures have succumbed to organic decay or destruction by some other agencies, such as fire. Much of forensic odontologists' expertise is based on clinical experience, fundamental research and advances in knowledge in relation to dentistry in general [40]. Dental identification of humans occurs for a number of different reasons, and in a number of different situations, like for the body of a victim of violent crime, fire, traffic accident, and workplace accident [41]. A body can be disfigured to such an extent that identification by a family member is neither reliable nor desirable. Bodies of people who have been deceased for some time prior to discovery and those found in water also present unpleasant difficulties in identification. Through the specialty of forensic dentistry, a dentist can play a small but significant role in this process. By identifying the victims of crime and disaster through guidelines and standards, a dentist can assist those involved in crime investigation [42–44].

8.5 HISTORY OF FORENSIC ODONTOLOGY

> *Forensic odontology has been with us since the beginning when, according to the Old Testament, Adam was convinced by Eve to put a "bite mark" in an apple. The earliest dental identification began with the Agrippina and the Lollia Paulina case. Shortly after her marriage in the year 49 AD to Claudius, Emperor of Rome, Agrippina began plotting to secure her position. Because she feared that the rich divorcee Lollia Paulina might still be a rival for her husband, Agrippina soon decided that it would be safer if Lollia Paulina was dead. To be safer Agrippina sent her own soldiers to kill Lollia Paulina; the soldiers were further instructed to bring back her head. Cutting off the head after inflicting death was not uncommon in those days, the only positive proof of death being visual. Agripinna stared at the severed head, unable to recognize the distorted face; she parted the lips with her fingers, looking for Lollia Paulina's teeth, which were known to have certain distinctive characteristics. Only then was she satisfied that it was Lollia Paulina. It marks the first use of dental identification of which there is record.*
>
> —Senn and Stimson, 2010

Charles the Bold in 1477 was identified by dental characteristics, while Paul Revere identified General Joseph Warren through a fixed-wire silver bridge in 1776 [45–49]. Nathan Keep identified Dr. Parkman from the fit of dentures on study models in 1849, and Napoleon the IV in 1879 [46,47]. In 1870, Ansil L. Robinson was charged with the murder of his mistress, Mary Lunsford. Evidence against Robinson included an attempt to match his teeth to the bite marks on the victim's arm [50]. Forensic odontology was used to identify victims of a fire in the Vienna Opera House in 1878, but the modern era of forensic odontology is said to have commenced with the identification of the victims of the Bazar de la Charité fire that occurred on May 4, 1897, in Rue Jean-Goujon, Paris. Dr. Oscar Amoëdo returned to Cuba in 1889 after studying at New York Dental College. He was then sent as a delegate to the International Dental Congress in Paris in 1890 [51,52]:

> *He decided to stay in Paris and became a dental instructor and teacher, eventually becoming a full professor. While in Paris, he wrote 120 scientific articles. A tragic fire at a charity event stimulated his interest in dental identification and the field of forensic odontology. While he was not involved with the identification of the victims from the fire, he knew many of the victims who survived and interviewed them. His accounts of the fire were presented in a paper at the International Medical Congress of Moscow and were published in English in 1897. Dr. Amoëdo wrote a thesis entitled "L'Art Dentaire en Medicine Legale," which earned him a doctorate and served as the basis of his book by the same name published in 1898.*

The book he wrote was the first comprehensive text on forensic odontology, and he is considered by many to be the father of forensic odontology (Figure 8.7).

In 1895, Dr. Pablo Valencia recognized a corpse that he could demonstrate as belonging to Joseph Martí. This description was later found by a letter addressed to Horatio

FIGURE 8.7 Dr. Oscar Amoëdo, father of forensic odontology. (From http://www.ecured.cu/index.php/Oscar_Amoedo_Vald%25C3%25A9s.)

S. Rubens Gonzalo de Quesada; it says, "Bazán also confirms the description of the missing upper incisor expose at autopsy, as he extracted the tooth, therefore, seems almost certain that the loss of Martí is reality." Then in 1907, remains were analyzed in the cemetery of Santiago de Cuba, where the physician J. Montero Zambrano conducted a study of the skull and teeth done which coincided with the analysis of Dr. Zayas Bazán, who was the dentist of José Martí; it was concluded that the body found was that of the caudillo José Martí [46]. Among the most prominent contemporary cases is that of the Argentine pilot Lt. Benjamin Matienzo (1891–1919), a military and aviation pioneer who in Argentina on June 20, 1919, in an attempt to cross the Andes, fell and crashed in the mountains. His remains were found months later; he had survived the fall, but in search of help, died of cold and starvation. His positive identification was possible by comparison of his dental remains to his dental record [46].

In 1937 in Chantilly, a murderer was convicted on the evidence of the bite marks that the victim inflicted during her struggle for life [45,47]. Wayne Clifford Boden was a Canadian serial killer and rapist active from 1969 to 1971. He earned the nickname "the Vampire Rapist" because he had the penchant of biting the breasts of his victims, a method of operation that led to his conviction due to forensic odontological evidence [45]. Ondontological evidence has also assisted in the PM identification of Charles Gardel (Figure 8.8), Josef Mengele (Figure 8.9), and Ernest "Che" Guevara [46].

> *Strom (1954) and Gustafson (1962) reported on the identification of victims of the Second World War trough forensic odontology. Teare (1951) discussed the identification of the 28 victims of a plane crash in 1950, Frykholm (1956) described a Swedish shipping accident in 1950 where 15 were killed and Mercer, Reid, and Uttley (1954) and Warren (1955) a rail accident in New Zealand in 1953 where 151 perished. Bradley & Miller (1955) described the use of odontology in the identification of victims of a plane crash in Canada. The odontology aspects of the identification of the 118 victims of a fire aboard the SS Noronic in Toronto.*
>
> —Senn and Stimson, 2010

FIGURE 8.8 Charles Gardel. (From www.todotango.com/gardel/.)

FIGURE 8.9 Joseph Mengele. (From http://seuhistory.com/etiquetas/josef-mengele.)

After the end of World War II, there were rumors that Adolf Hitler had escaped with his wife Eva Braun [19]. Actually they had died together in 1945; however, their bodies had been burned and then buried by Russian soldiers [19]. Due to lack of AM and PM records, it was a challenge to dispel the rumors they were still alive. Finally, pieces of Hitler's mandible were found that revealed remnants of a bridge as well as unusual forms of reconstruction to the mandible, with evidence of periodontal disease [53]. Adolf Hitler's identity was confirmed when the work matched the records kept by his dentist, Hugo Blaschke [53].

The fire on board the *Scandinavian Star* was one of the world's worst ferry disasters. Dental identity could be established in 107 cases (68%) [54]. Forensic odontologists successfully identified tsunami victims in South-East Asia in December 2004; more than 92% of the non-Thai victims have been identified, out of which about 80% were identified by dental information. This high success rate of dental identification in Thailand was a matter of surprise for many forensic experts [55].

8.6 THE TEETH

Teeth are parts of the human organism that are not easily decayed. Located inside the mouth, they are thus more protected from decaying after a person's death [56]. Teeth are the hardest substance in the body and this fact, combined with their location—relatively protected behind the soft tissues of the cheeks (Figure 8.10) [57], lips and jawbones—are the reasons why they are so useful in identification, a fact that was brilliantly described by the forensic anthropologist from Spain, Prof. Dr. Jose Reverte Coma, expressing "the mouth can be considered as the black box of the body" [58].

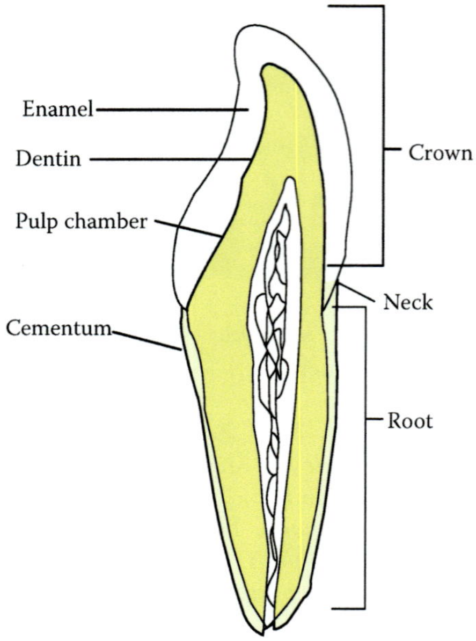

FIGURE 8.10 Tooth structure in cross section. (Adapted from McLanaghan Thesis 2003.)

Even in the fire that burns so hot because of aviation fuel after a plane crash, a victim's teeth can remain intact when other body parts are destroyed due to this protection by bone and swelling of the tongue during the intense heat. Dental work such as crowns, fixed bridges, and removable dentures can also survive intense physical and chemical forces and aid in identification. To aid in identification, the patient's name should always be inserted into the acrylic of dentures and appliances at the time of fabrication [56,59].

Because the teeth are subject to genetic variation, the examination of the mouth will usually commence by a description of dental anomalies such as missing teeth, misplaced or rotated teeth, unusually shaped or sized teeth, and supernumerary teeth. The status of each tooth with respect to restorations that have been placed will be recorded. The exact design and style of each restoration may not only reveal the country in which the dentist was trained [60,61]. Therefore, teeth based identification is one of reliable tools for PM identification On average, humans have 32 teeth; each tooth has five surfaces, meaning that inside a mouth there are 160 tooth surfaces with various conditions. Tooth development begins during the sixth week of embryonic life with the formation of the primordial tooth buds. Tooth development is slightly, but significantly, more advanced in girls than in boys, even before puberty. The deciduous dentition begins eruption between six to nine months of age, starting with the anterior teeth and progressing posteriorly. These 20 "baby" teeth are usually completely erupted by 2 to 2 1/2 years of age. The permanent dentition begins emerging at 6 years of age with the four first molars. Between the ages of 6 and 12, the permanent anterior teeth emerge [60]. Around age 12, the second molars erupt. The final four permanent teeth to emerge, out of the total 32, are the third molars, also called "wisdom" teeth. These teeth are the most unstable. Typically, they erupt around age 18 to early 20s. Sometimes these teeth are congenitally absent or are unusual in appearance (e.g., they may appear as peg teeth). The completed definitive tooth is naturally divided into two regions: a root and a crown. "The transition from crown to root takes place at the cervix or neck of the tooth in a sinuous outline, and is called the cement enamel jun. The completed definitive tooth is naturally divided into two regions: a root and a crown. The transition from crown to root takes place at the cervix or neck of the tooth in a sinuous outline, and is called the cement enamel junction or the cervical line" [60]. Human teeth are composed of four tissues: the soft tissue of the pulp and three calcified tissues called dentin, enamel, and cement [59]. The crown consists of an outer layer of enamel and an inner layer of dentin. Dental enamel is the hardest tissue in the human body. Enamel functions as a resistant outer structure, allowing the tooth to withstand the abrasive force of mastication (chewing). Dentin is slightly harder than bone but considerably softer than enamel. Once the enamel is destroyed, dentin is rapidly penetrated by dental decay. Cement covers the root and provides a place of attachment for connective tissue fibers which secure the root to the surrounding bony socket, known as the alveolus. Dental pulp is a connective tissue located in the pulp cavity of a tooth [59]. There are two types of dental pulp: coronal pulp in the central pulp chamber of the crown and radicular pulp in the pulp canals of the root Forensic recording of dental characteristics involves dividing each tooth into five surfaces; mesial (front), distal (back), lingual (toward the tongue), vestibular (toward the cheek), and occlusal (biting), and recording the status of each of these surfaces both graphically on an odontogram and descriptively in words [62–64]. Information recorded includes the presence or absence of the tooth; the presence of anatomical variations both of the teeth and surrounding structures; the location and material of any restorations; evidence of any habits or personal behaviors and other features that could contribute to the identification of the individual [64]. Given that an adult dentition has a maximum of 32 teeth, and each tooth is divided into 5 surfaces, this provides 160 points of potential comparison. Comparisons are made of entire dentitions, individual teeth and individual surfaces [62,64]. The use of a minimum number of concordant points to establish identity has been advocated as a method to guarantee reliability of the dental identification process. This use of comparative points is similar to that historically used in fingerprint analysis, where matches were attested by a predetermined number of corresponding ridge details, variously anywhere between 10 and 16 [65]. For dental comparisons, Keiser-Nielsen [24] and Sognnaes [66] recommended a minimum of 12 points of similarity to increase accuracy, while Stimson [67] proposed 8. In these discussions, "points" referred to the matching of entire teeth not single surfaces [19].

8.7 ODONTOGRAMS

Odontograms (Figure 8.11) are symbolic systems graphs where dental variables are recorded. In dentistry, the first mode of nomenclature tooth was introduced in 1861 by Adolph Zsigmondy as a necessary "coshorthand system for recording fast data" [68].

The Two Digit System or the FDI system (named for the conference where it was first introduced, the Federation Dentaire Internationale in 1970) divides the dental arcade into four quadrants: upper right, upper left, lower left, and lower right. Prefix numbers are assigned to each quadrant: 1, 2, 3, and 4 in permanent dentition and 5, 6, 7, and 8 in deciduous dentition, respectively. Added to this prefix is a number, 1 through 8 for permanent dentition and 1 through 5 for deciduous for the specific tooth. Each central incisor is assigned 1 and counting each tooth, moving posteriorly, each third molar is assigned 8 [68]. Therefore, in this system, the upper right canine would be designated as 13. INTERPOL has proposed, for the case of identification of disaster victims, the use of the FDI system designed for such an odontogram, including spaces for describing treatments of all kinds of information both AM and PM [69].

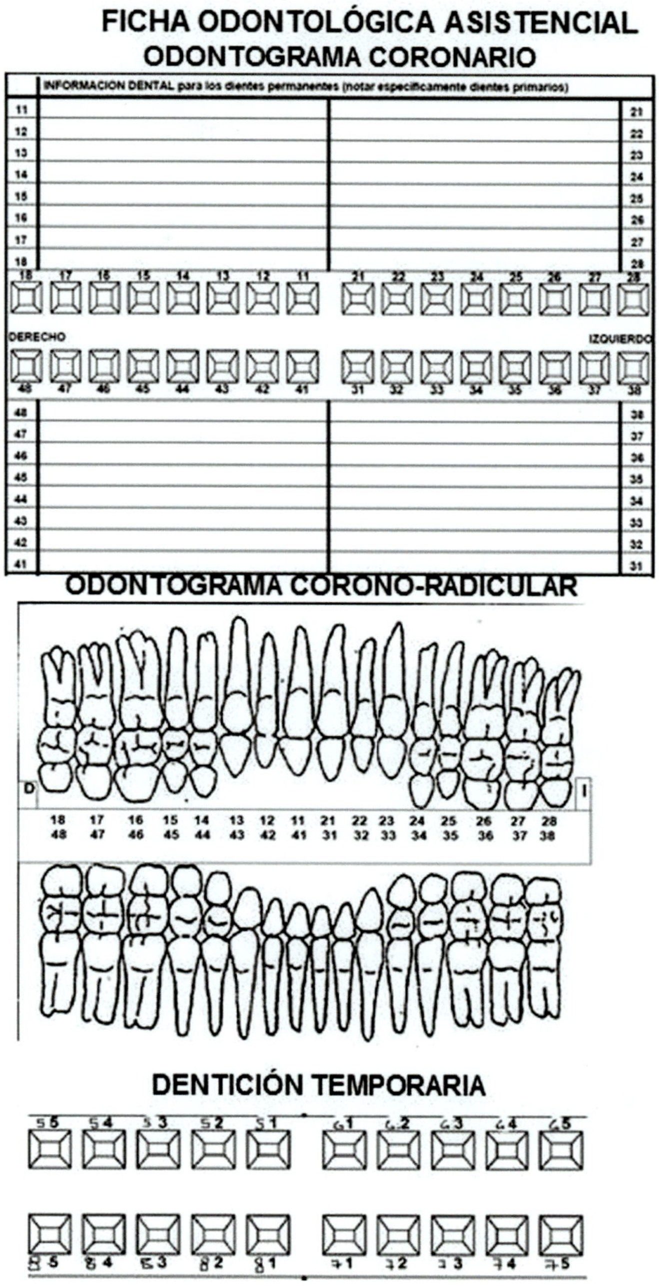

FIGURE 8.11 Odontogram.

8.8 FORENSIC RADIOLOGY

The use of radiological investigation is well accepted in forensic odontology practice. They provide an objective assessment and recording of the hard tissues of the teeth and jaws as well as surgical or restorative features that may be of interest to the examiner. Furthermore, they provide a visual image, that can be used to demonstrate intricate details to a lay audience [70–72]. A non-destructive method , radiography also plays a vital role in forensic dentistry to uncover the hidden facts which cannot be seen by means of physical examination. Dental examination and comparison between antemortem and postmortem dental records and radiographs (Figure 8.12) produce results with a high degree of reliability and relative simplicity [73,74].

Panoramic radiographs (Figure 8.13) are also helpful to determine the age of the individual by assessing the stage of eruption [73].

X-ray equipment is a great advantage in both internal and dental examinations, particularly when an estimate of a victim's age is required, and also to discover fractures or other unique identification information. X-ray examination is also a very effective method of locating and identifying evidential material such as bullets or bomb fragments. X-ray equipment, preferably portable, should always be made available in the mortuary [41,73,74]. The use of radiographs is characteristic of techniques that involve observation of morphologically distinct stages of mineralization. Age estimations are also based on the degree of formation of root and crown structures, the stage of eruption, and the intermixture of primary and adult dentitions [75]. The size

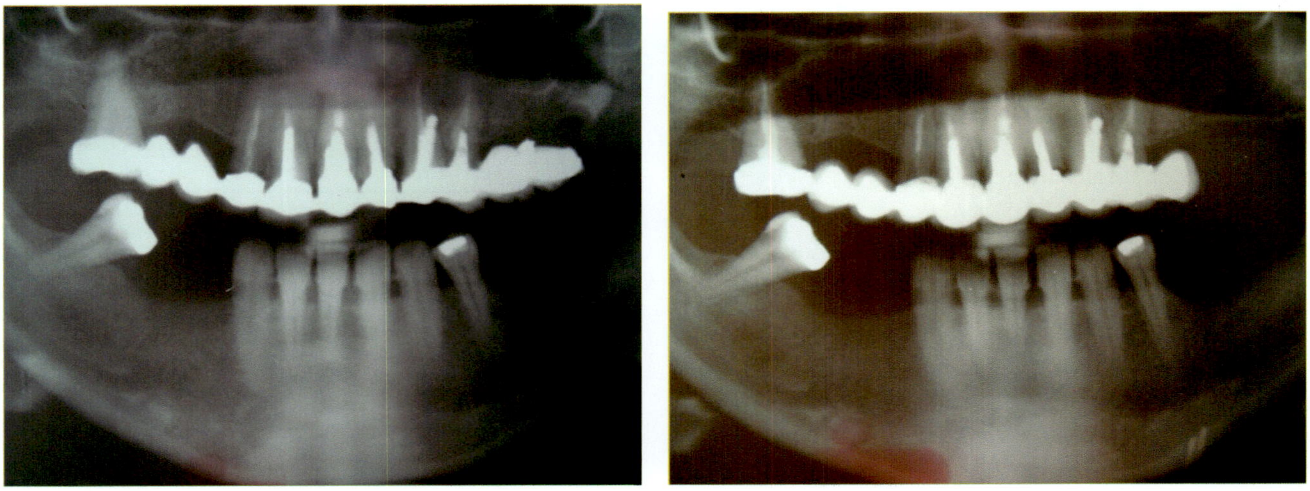

(a) (b)

FIGURE 8.12 Comparison through radiographic study. (a) Antemortem and (b) postmortem.

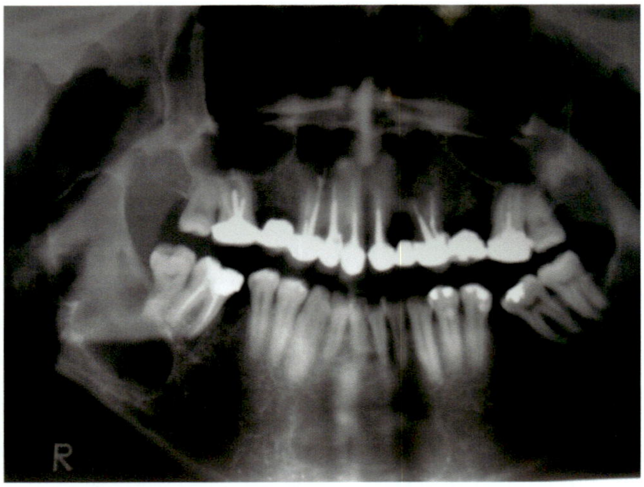

FIGURE 8.13 Orthopantomography.

of dental pulp cavity is reduced as a result of secondary dentin deposit. The measurements of this reduction can be used as an indicator of age [41,76]. Using radiographs, the pulp length and width are measured. These ratios are found to be significantly correlated with age. Results show the strongest correlation with age to be in ratio between the width of the pulp and the root. This indicates that the rate of deposition of dentine on the mesial and distal walls is more closely related to age than that on the roof of the pulp cavity. However, the limitation of the technique is that the correlation between age and the ratios between pulp and the root length has been found to be significant for only maxillary cuspids and premolars [41,77]. Advances in computer technology coupled with improvement in sensor technology over the past 25 years have resulted in the adoption of digital radiography systems in dental practice. These now include the ability to image orthopanoramic, cephalographic, and computed tomographic images for nearly instant delivery to clinical workstations [78]. This stands in marked contrast to film-based dental radiography, particularly in forensic applications, and holds many advantages for the forensic dentist. The dentist-investigator is able to speedily discern whether or not features that might serve to confirm or refute a suspected identification are visible and order reimaging if needed while the specimen is available. In addition, postmortem and antemortem images can be rapidly transmitted across great distances without any loss of fidelity, questions of orientation (left versus right side), or acquisition date and other provenance issues. In the past, film-based images were first reproduced or copied onto additional film substrates and then hand-delivered (mail, courier, etc.) for comparison [41,77,79]. Loss of detail and possible loss of the original image were not uncommon [80]. Older, film-based images can, by the use of optical scanning hardware and software, be converted to an electronic image (data set) which can be treated similarly to original digital radiographs (transmission, optimization, storage, etc.) [81,82].

Digital radiographic imaging software also allows the investigator to optimize or enhance the image as viewed onscreen, resulting in visualization of greater detail in the captured image—again increasing the likelihood of an identification or exclusion. Many investigators are working to perfect comparative systems (digital image subtraction, image rectification, point-to-point analysis, etc.) to assist the forensic dentist in analyzing radiographic images [83]. Several sophisticated computer applications are now available for use in collating and comparing large amounts of dental data [84]. These applications are effective at sorting large numbers of antemortem records to reduce the number of potential matching postmortem records to only a few. This allows the forensic odontologist to complete the manual comparison of the actual charts and radiographs to determine if a match exists [83–85]. Although there are many avenues available to authorities to arrive at the identity of unknown human remains, dental identification is rapid, reliable, readily available in most situations, and relatively inexpensive in comparison. For example, DNA requires time-consuming testing and collection of samples. Fingerprinting requires that the unknown remains retain soft tissue suitable for lifting print exemplars as well as the availability of fingerprint records on file. Nowhere is this more evident than in cases involving multiple fatalities. DVI (disaster victim identification) or MFI (multiple fatality incident) situations tax the resources of the medical examiner. In today's fast-paced world, rapid identification is expected, if not demanded, by the next of kin and the press. "Digital radiography coupled with computer-aided methods of comparing the postmortem dental information gathered in the morgue to ante mortem dental information provided by the families of the missing and law enforcement allows rapid resolution and identification" [85]. This would require reliable automatic segmentation techniques that can extract the contour of each individual tooth for latter retrieval purposes to allow for retrieval based on teeth shapes.

The objective of the new perspective research is to automate the process of forensic odontology using image processing and pattern recognition techniques [84,85]. There are several advantages for automating this procedure. An automatic system can perform identification on a large-scale database while a manual or semiautomatic system is useful for verification on a small data set. Also, automating this process will come up with an ordered list of closest matches that we may refer to in order to decide the best match [86]. Accordingly, this will facilitate for forensic odontologists to only manually verify through this best match short list instead of manually searching a large number of AM records. In order to achieve this goal, we need to automate the process of segmenting the dental radiographs and to separate each individual tooth. For automated identification, the dental records are usually available as radiographs. An automated dental identification system consists of two main stages: feature extraction and feature matching. During feature extraction, certain salient information of the teeth such as contours, artificial prosthesis, number of cuspids, frontal sinus (Figures 8.14 and 8.15), and so on, is extracted from the radiographs [86,87].

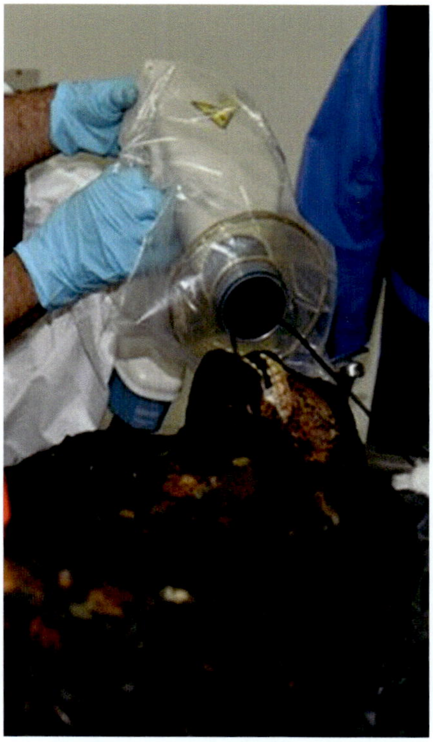

FIGURE 8.14 Obtaining X-rays through the NOMADTM equipment.

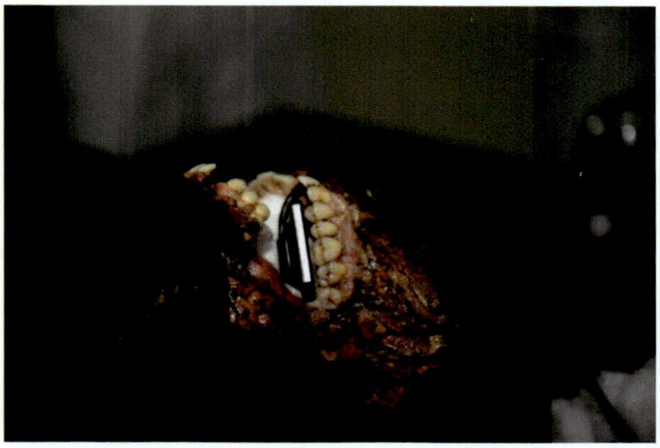

FIGURE 8.15 Electronic sensor positioned in the oral cavity to perform radiographic imaging.

8.9 BITE-MARK ANALYSIS

Bite-mark evidence recovery and analysis is the most complex and demanding role that the forensic dentist plays in the criminal justice system. Complex issues when bite marks are found on human skin, such as in cases of sexual homicide, sex assault and rape, and in domestic violence cases of abuse, require a high level of training and expertise. Unfortunately, there are no areas of this aspect of the discipline that the dental hygienist can be involved in, primarily because of the urgency of the cases that require an almost immediate deployment of the odontologist. Also, there is a legal requirement that warrants, court orders, and legal consent for the seizure of evidence from suspects only include specific personnel possessing specialized training and skills [88].

Typically, police personnel, usually forensic identification officers, collect bite-mark evidence from the bitten victims of crime [89].

> *This includes recording the injuries using high resolution forensic photographs, making casts of the bite site and swabbing the skin's surface for salivary DNA. Interestingly, bite marks, sucking and/or kissing can leave saliva behind as the suspect's mouth comes in contact with the victim's skin. This saliva can be a source of DNA evidence, which can be analyzed in conjunction with the physical comparison of the shapes and sizes of the teeth to the marks found on the victim's skin.*
>
> —Giannelli, 2008

The photographs of the bite mark that are recovered by the police are submitted to specially trained forensic odontologists for examination and interpretation. The forensic significance (quality) of the injuries depicted in the evidence is determined according to whether there are sufficient details visible from the teeth marks to allow comparison to any suspect's teeth (Figure 8.16).

In sex crimes, bite marks on women are characteristically seen on the nipples, breasts, thighs, neck, and legs. For male victims, bite marks are seen more on the arms, shoulders, back, and hands [90,91]. Bite marks to the hands, arms, and shoulders on male suspects may be caused by the teeth of a victim who has bitten in self-defense [90].

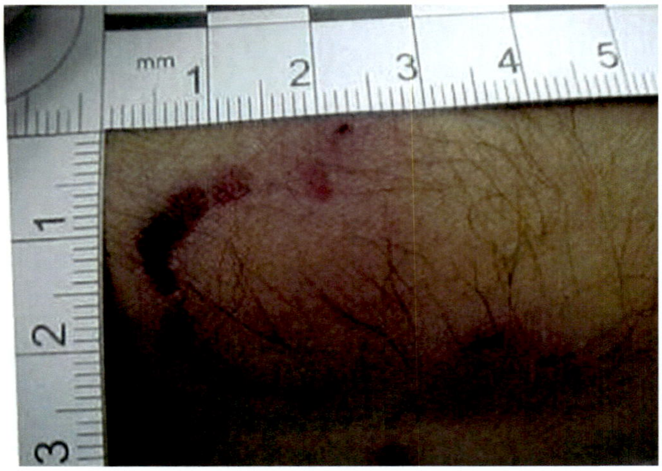

FIGURE 8.16 Bite marks.

If the marks from teeth record a large amount of detail and the evidence is well documented, there is a strong likelihood that the odontologist's conclusions will play a role in the identification of the perpetrators of these crimes [92].

Suspects may be identified through the assessment of bite-mark injuries in cases of abuse (of children, spouses, elderly) and in women during sexual attacks. Bite marks can be found on the following:

- The victim (by the attacker)
- The attacker (suspect) when a victim attempts to defend him- or herself
- An object found at the crime scene

The first published issue of forensic bite marks hinged on a piece of cheese found at the crime scene. A representative human bite is described as an elliptical or circular injury that records the specific characteristics of the teeth. Alternatively, it may be composed of two U-shaped arches that are separated at their bases by an open space [92]. The injuries caused by teeth can range from bruises to scrapes and cuts or lacerations. It is possible to identify specific types of teeth by their class characteristics. For example, incisors produce rectangular injuries and canines produce triangular injuries. Other characteristics include fractures, rotations, attritional wear, congenital malformations, and so on. When these are recorded in the injury, it may be possible to compare them to identify the specific teeth (person) that caused the injury [92,93]. Evidence collection from the bite victim that dentists should be familiar with include the following:

1. Documentation: Make a descriptive record of the injury, including the physical appearance, color, size, and orientation of the injury, location on the body, relative contour and elasticity of the site, and types of injuries.
2. Photographs: Take photographs, both color and black-and-white films. A reference scale (ruler) should be placed in the same plane as the injury and visible in the photographs to enable subsequent measurements.
3. Saliva swab: (a) Saliva will have been deposited on the skin during biting and this should be collected and analyzed. (b) A buccal swab or a sample of whole blood must be collected from the victim at this time to assess the victim's DNA. This will enable analysis of any mixtures that are found in the sample from the bite.
4. Impression: Fabricate an impression of the bitten surface to record any irregularities produced by the teeth.

The following evidence was recovered during examination of the bite-mark suspect:

1. Clinical examination: The extra- and intra-oral structures are examined and are noted on a dental chart. Special attention is focused on the status of the dental health, occlusion and mandibular articulation, tooth mobility, periodontal pocketing, dental restorations, diastemate, fractures, caries, and so on, and the function of masticatory muscles.
2. Photographs: Full-facial and profile photographs are produced in addition to frontal and lateral views of the teeth in occlusion.
3. Impressions: It is necessary to produce extremely accurate study casts of the teeth that record all characteristics of the dentition.
4. Bite simple: A sample of the suspect's bite is recorded in centric occlusion using a wax.
5. Salivary sample: Saliva is also taken for DNA testing [93].

The most common methods to determine if the suspect's teeth caused the bite mark include techniques to compare the following:

- The suspect's study casts with the actual or photographs of the bite mark
- The suspect's teeth pattern of dental cast using tracing with photographs of the bite mark
- The suspect's test bites with the actual bite mark

The conclusions are often based on the expert's level of personal experience.

Factors that may affect the accuracy of bite-mark identification include the following:

1. Time-dependent changes of the bite mark on living bodies
2. Effects of where the bite mark was found
3. Damage on soft tissue
4. Similarities in dentition among individuals
5. Poor techniques, photography, impressions

Also, dental profiles of the suspect are subject to change over time, for example, loss of teeth, or teeth attack by dental caries.

The suspect's DNA profile obtained from saliva or blood with salivary DNA surrounding the bite-mark area proves to be a more reliable form of identification. Even if the dentist cannot match the available evidence to someone's existing dental records, he or she can provide important clues to identity that may help the investigators. For example, the dentist can make estimates about age, socioeconomic class, and history based on examination of the teeth. By collating this evidence with evidence from other forensic examiners, investigators can narrow down the identity possibilities [92,94].

The characteristics of human bites are superficial abrasion and/or a subsurface hemorrhage looking like an arch. These marks are caused by the incisors, canines, and premolars. The abrasions and/or hemorrhage caused by the canine are in the shape of points. If the perpetrator has dentures, additional specific marks can be expected [93]. These marks differ between bridges, crowns, and dentures. Crowns and bridges may have a ceramic surface and partial denture braces to fix at the teeth. These peculiarities can be responsible for specific wounds and additional markers for identification [92,93].

Depending on the part of the body and the constitution of the skin. the bite mark can be distorted. Frequently, this can be the reason for problems when analyzing bite marks. To prevent mistakes by the pattern-associated comparison, it is recommended to simulate bites at similar body parts using the study casts of the suspect or using a digital technique for a step-wise dynamic comparison [95]. Sheasby and MacDonald [96] recommend a classification to emphasize the need of a scientific approach for the interpretation of the types of distortion. They introduce the terms of primary and secondary distortion. Primary distortion is defined by the dynamics of the bite. Secondary distortions have three categories: time-related distortion when a bite changes with time elapsed subsequent to the bite being made, posture distortion, and photographic distortion [92–94].

8.10 MASS DISASTERS

Forensic dental response teams provide invaluable assistance in cases of mass disasters in which large numbers of deceased victims must be identified. Similar to personal identification above, but on a larger scale that includes additional complications, disaster victim identification (DVI) involves transcription of AM dental records, PM examination and recording, and reconciliation of these records to identify each victim to give back their name [97,98]. Natural or man-made disasters leave behind many casualties that include not only the deceased victims but also the next of kin who are left to grieve the loss of a loved one. The forensic dental response team should formulate itself in a way that allows for adequate training and accumulation of the needed resources and equipment. In fact, dealing appropriately with AM records is the single most challenging area in any DVI response, since it involves accurately and precisely preparing the records for potential comparisons [99].

Standardization of the DVI forms and terminology is required to ensure accuracy in the comparisons. AM records vary widely in their completeness and the amount of included detail, so the team faces the daunting task of summarizing all the incoming data [100]. The U.S.-based WinID3 (Windows Identification) program allows both the Universal/National System used in the United States and the Federation Dentaire International (FDI) tooth numbering. An INTERPOL-sponsored program is called DVI System International, from PlassData in Denmark [13]. The latter was being beta-tested during INTERPOL's tsunami response in Thailand. It has now developed into one of the world's best DVI databases, since it can also handle data from DNA as well as most medical records and physical descriptors, such as scars, birthmarks, and tattoos [13,99,100].

The International Criminal Police Organization (INTERPOL) was established as the International Criminal Police Commission in 1923, and aims to assist international and cross-border criminal police cooperation [14]. Global police communication services, operational data services, and databases for police, operational police support services and training and development are the commission's core functions. Approximately 186 of the 195 countries of the world are members of INTERPOL. The INTERPOL DVI guidelines and associated forms, published originally in 1984, are recognized by the vast majority of countries outside the United States as the best practice method for data collection in multiple fatality incidents to facilitate identification of victims [16,101,102].

These guidelines divide the DVI process into five phases. Phase 1 details activities at the scene; Phase 2 is the procedures in the mortuary; Phase 3 covers AM information retrieval; Phase 4 involves reconciliation; and Phase 5, personal and incident debriefing. These processes are aimed at collecting data that will result in the maximum number and certainty of identifications in a timely manner but also provide information that may assist in any investigation into the incident [98,103,104].

Many authors have discussed problems that regularly arise in the dental aspects of DVI. Pretty and Sweet [21] summarized it well when commenting that mass disasters are complex situations that are both physically and emotionally demanding. Many of the problems that are encountered are met on a daily basis by odontologists in their identification work but become magnified just by the increased number of victims [105,106]. A number of these problems are outside the direct control of odontologists. Brannon and Kessler [107] classified these as external problems, and included such things as the condition of the remains, the quality of the AM dental records, and dysfunctional administrative structures. In contrast, their list of internal problems—which included stress, inexperience, and recognition of newer dental materials—would appear to be influenced by the lack of clear procedural guidelines [104,108]. For the odontology component in each of the phases of DVI, it is recommended that these guidelines should include roles and procedures, and should also address all issues that can be anticipated to relate to the involvement of odontologists in a DVI incident, including team membership criteria, team notification details, management structures, organizational responsibilities, logistics, team size and composition, and payment issues [105,108,109].

A number of authors [110,111] have commented that the condition of the remains critically impacts on the potential for successful dental identification. The nature of the collapse of the twin towers of the World Trade Center on September 11, 2001 meant that the remains were severely fragmented, commingled, pulverized, and incinerated but also that recovery had to be delayed for quite some time leading to additional degradation of remains. More than 20,000 body fragments were recovered from the approximately 2800 individuals reported missing, highlighting the difficulty that identification specialists faced. This impacted the techniques that were able to be used and the majority of identifications that were able to be completed were done by DNA analysis. In the 4 years after the incident, only 1594 of the victims were formally identified and 53% of these were by DNA alone. "Genetic information also contributed in many of the other identifications" [99,112–114]. Unsolved cases are mostly due to insufficient AM or PM data. In such circumstances, forensic workers mostly have to rely on time- and money-consuming DNA identification procedures.

In order to avoid these difficult and lengthy identification procedures, radio frequency identification (RFID) tags can be incorporated into the strongest and most protected human body part: the tooth. In case of absence of teeth, it can be incorporated into dentures also. RFID is a wireless electronic communication technology. RFID technology was first introduced in 1940, during World War II, and used to identify airplanes belonging to the Royal Air Force. During the 1980s and 1990s, with the advances in information technology and the possibility of producing low-cost tags, the interest in RFID was renewed. It forms part of a technology known as "automatic identification and data capture" and is used to identify, locate, and track people, animals, and property [115].

Positive identification of the denture is usually done with a tiny, discreet identification code which is embedded in the denture base [116]. The standard requirements for denture markers are that they should be biologically inert when incorporated into the denture, inexpensive, easy and quick to apply, possible to retrieve after an accident, acid resistant, and able to survive elevated temperatures [116,117]. The marking must also be aesthetically acceptable, visible (readable) and durable without jeopardizing the strength of the prostheses. In addition, the marking should be permanent and resistant to everyday cleansing and disinfecting agents [118,119]. In countries where unique identification numbers are given to each individual, dentures may be marked with that number to enable positive identification. There are two main methods in marking dentures, namely the surface method and the inclusion method. In the surface method, the marks are located on one of the denture's surface and can be done by scribing or engraving the denture itself. In this technique, letters or numbers are engraved with a small round dental bur on the fitting surface of the maxillary complete denture. This engraving can cause detrimental effects, such as food debris getting lodged, leading to bacterial infection [116,119].

Another surface-marking technique, embossing, comprises initials of the name and the surname of the patient that are scratched with a dental bur on the master cast. This technique produces embossed lettering on the fitting surface of the denture and has been associated with malignancy, possibly due to continued tissue irritation, and may not be an ideal method for denture marking. A better way is to cover the embossed marking on the denture framework with the denture base acrylic and process it to a finished state; hence, it causes no irritation to the tissue.

8.11 IDENTIFICATION THROUGH SOFT TISSUES

In some particular circumstances, often related to a criminal investigation, there can be other data that are important to the process of human identification. Some of these data result from soft oral and perioral tissue prints [120]. In fact, lips, as well as the hard palate, are known to have features that can lead to a person's identification. The study of lip prints is known as cheiloscopy; the study of hard palate anatomy to establish someone's identity is called palatoscopy [121].

8.11.1 Rugoscopy or Palatoscopy

One of the techniques used by forensic odontology in the hard task of identifying a person is the palatal rugoscopy, which refers to the study, recording, and classification of ridges located in the mucous of the palate or roof of the oral cavity. The method of identification most used is the visual recognition of fingerprints, but when the characteristics of the body do not allow its implementation, such as in the case of advanced decomposition, carbonization, or skeletonization, the palatal rugae can provide important information about the identity of the investigated subject.

The use of human palatal rugae has also been suggested as an alternative method of identification. It has been reported that even when non-odontological methods of identifying a victim are more limited, the palatal rugae are important evidence that can be recovered in a practical and simple way, playing their anatomical cost patterns directly from the hard palate or mucosal surface of prosthetic elements [120]. This method allows identification by direct comparison of the models of the maxilla in which tissues are duplicates of the hard palate, AM and PM, so the odontological finding is essentially confirming subject-specific information [122].

Palatal rugoscopy is the study, recording, and classification of palatal rugae [121,122]. These rugae originate between the 12th and 14th weeks in intrauterine life, remaining unchanged throughout life. Because of their protected location, the rugae are elements of interest that constitute identificatory resistance to external agents (Figure 8.17).

This makes them especially valuable in identifying both living subjects and fresh corpses [123]. Rugae are not damaged from trauma due to their internal position in the oral cavity and are insulated from heat by the tongue and buccal fat pads. In one study, it was reported that no two palates are alike in their configuration and that the palatal print did not change. In twins also, the

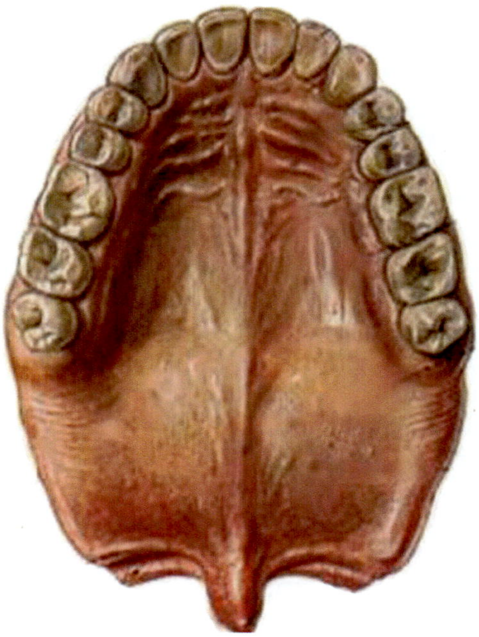

FIGURE 8.17 Anatomy of the hard palate. (From http://www.hpchile.cl/forense/images/stories/pals.jpg.)

studies indicated that the patterns may be similar but not identical. Rugae were first described by Winslow in 1732. The earliest illustration of palatal rugae was probably by Santorini in 1775, wherein he put a drawing depicting three wavy lines crossing the midline of palate. The first palatal classification system was put forth by Goria in 1911. The first suggestion for the use of palatal rugae as a method of personal identification was suggested by Harrison Allen in 1889. The term "palatal rugoscopy" was proposed in 1932 by a Spanish investigator named Trobo Hermosa [124]. Once formed, rugae may experience changes in their size due to growth of the palate, but retain their embryological shape. Palatal rugae appear around the third month of intrauterine life from the covering of connective tissue in the palatal process of forming maxillary bone. Palatal rugoscopy can have a major role in human identification. Cast models and AM intraoral photographs can be found in dental records and serve as the first protocol to perform the identification process [124]. Furthermore, for at-risk populations (for example, astronauts and firemen), this first record can be preventively arranged and archived for the possible need of identification. Researchers have found the task of classification a difficult aspect of rugae studies. The subjective nature of observation and interpretation within and between observers poses a problem. Today, there are several known palatal rugae classifications. However, according to several authors, Argentine odontologist Juan Ubaldo Carrea's classification is considered very practical. This author divides palatal rugae into four different types (Figure 8.18) [125].

Palatal rugae are classified only according to their form, and no formula (rugogram) is developed. Limson and Julian [143] compared the rugosities of university students by an impression with irreversible hydrocolloid and cast models in plaster type II. The rugae were highlighted with well-sharpened graphite pencils. The rugae were photographed and the models were scanned, achieving a 92%–97% success rate. The authors claimed that this error rate of 3%–8% can be reduced by using an intraoral scanner, with a direct transfer to the computer [126,127]. Some identification methods are available for edentulous victims, such as comparing the anatomy of the paranasal sinuses and comparing the bone patterns observed in radiographs. In addition to this, the victim's own dentures can also be used, which are found inside the mouth or in their home. Among the evidence from an edentulous victim, the palatal rugae are considered to be one of the unique morphological features. Ohtani et al. [128] studied the possibility of identifying edentulous individuals by comparing the rugae in denture molds against models obtained from impressions taken from the patients. Impressions were taken from the mucosal surfaces of complete dentures with alginate impression materials, and 146 maxillary casts were made from hard dental plaster. They then compared the rugae patterns to identify the pairs (dentures and plaster models). The median percentage of correct matches was 94%, and the error rate was attributed to three factors: poorly demarcated eminences of rugae, change of palatal height in some cases, and non-complex rugae patterns. Using palatal rugoscopy, Castellanos et al. [129] reported the identification of the body of an adult woman in a city in Colombia.

It is often difficult to obtain dental arch impressions of corpses that arrive at the forensic medicine institutes to be compared with the AM data of the alleged victim. As the experts or technicians are not familiar with dental impression materials and there is no dental laboratory structure, photographs are more practical. AM models can be obtained from the victims' dentists and then compared with the PM photographs using free image-editing software. There are several ways to analyze palatal rugae. Intraoral inspection is probably the most used and also the easiest and the cheapest. However, it can create difficulties if a future comparative exam is required. A more detailed and exact study, as well as the need to preserve evidence, may justify oral photography or oral impressions and [130]. Calcorrugoscopy (Figure 8.19), or the overlay print of palatal rugae in a maxillary cast, can be used in order to perform comparative analysis.

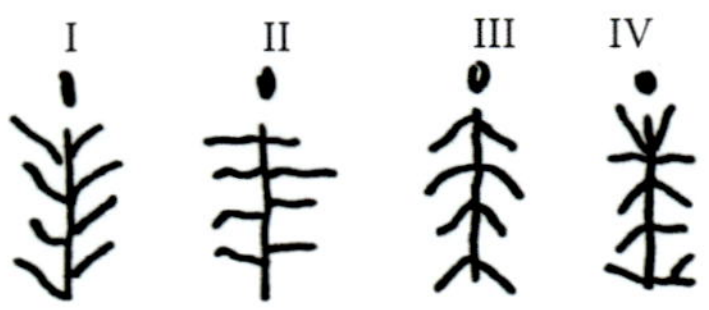

FIGURE 8.18 Carrea's system. (From Briem Stamm AD, *Forensic Oral Pathol J.*, 3, 13–17, 2012.)

FIGURE 8.19 Calcorrugoscopy.

Other more complex techniques are also available. By using stereoscopy, for example, one can obtain a three-dimensional image of palatal rugae anatomy. It is based on the analysis of two pictures taken with the same camera, from two different points, using special equipment. Another technique is the stereophotogrammetry, which, by using a special device called the Traster Marker, allows for an accurate determination of the length and position of every single palatal ruga [127,131,132]. However, due to its simplicity, price, and reliability, the study of maxillary dental casts is the most used technique [133,134].

Palatoscopy is a technique that can be of great interest in human identification. In fact, contrary to lip prints, it is possible to have AM data established, such as records found in dental practice in different forms (dental casts, old prosthetic maxillary devices, and intraoral photographs). However, palatoscopy might not be so useful in crime scene investigations in the linking of suspects to crime scenes. In fact, this kind of evidence is not expected to be found in such circumstances [125,135,136]. Another aspect of palatoscopy that one must consider is the possibility of rugae pattern forgery [137]. In a case report, Gitto et al. [138] described a method where palatal rugae were added to a complete denture in order to improve speech patterns in some patients. This process can lead to false identity exclusion due to misleading AM data.

8.11.2 Cheiloscopy

Cheiloscopy (from the Greek words *cheilos*—lips and *skopein*—to look at [120]) is the name given to lip print studies [139–141]. The importance of cheiloscopy is linked to the fact that lip prints are unique to one person, except in monozygotic twins [159]. Like fingerprints and palatal rugae, lip grooves are permanent and unchangeable [120,143,144]. It is possible to identify lip patterns as early as the sixth week of intrauterine life [120]. From then on, lip groove patterns rarely change, resisting many afflictions, such as herpetic lesions. In fact, only those pathologies that damage the lip, like burns, seem to rule out cheiloscopic study [120]. Lips are two (Figure 8.20) [145] highly sensitive mobile folds, composed of skin, muscle, glands, and mucous membranes.

They surround the oral orifice and form the anterior boundary of the oral cavity. Anatomically, whether covered with skin or mucosa, the surface that forms the oral sphincter is the lip area. There is an upper lip (from under the nose and extending laterally toward the cheek from the nasolabial sulcus) and a lower lip (bound inferiorly by a prominent groove, the labiomental sulcus); the two lips are joined at the corners of the mouth—the commissures—and separated by the buccal frenum [120,143]. There are two different kinds of lip coverings: skin and mucosa. When the two meet, a white

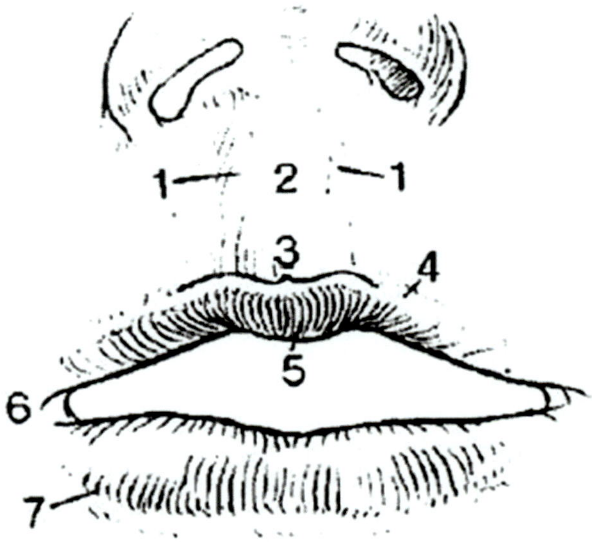

FIGURE 8.20 Lip anatomy. (From *Atlas of Human Anatomy, Head and Neck Section*, Netter F., Copyright 1996, Elsevier Health Sciences.)

wavy line is formed—the labial cord—which is quite prominent in people of African descent. Where identification is concerned, the mucosal area holds the most interest. This area, also called Klein's zone, is covered with wrinkles and grooves that form a characteristic pattern: the lip print [120,142].

This biological feature was first described by Fisher in 1902 [120]; however, it was only in 1930 that Diou de Lille developed some studies which led to lip print use in criminology. In 1932, Edmond Locard, one of France's greatest criminologists, acknowledged the importance of cheiloscopy. In 1950, Le Moyne Snyder, in his book *Homicide Investigation*, mentioned the possibility of using lip prints in the matter of human identification [146]. Sometime later, Santos in 1960, suggested that the fissures and the crisscross lines in the lips could be divided into different groups (simple and compound), and each group could be further divided into eight subtypes [147].

The first cheiloscopic expertise was demonstrated in Poland in 1966, when a lip print was revealed on window glass at the scene of a burglary. The examination was carried out and the expert concluded that the trace of lips revealed at the scene did not belong to the suspect [148]. Renaud in 1972, studied 4000 lip prints and confirmed the singularity of each one [149]. Two years later, Suzuki and Tsuchihashi developed another study which resulted in a new classification for lip prints. This study, conducted over a long period of time, enabled the researchers to confirm not only lip print singularity, but also lip response to trauma; in fact, they observed that after healing, the lip pattern was equal to that before the injury occurred. It was during the period 2000–2010, that cheiloscopic studies were carried out by several researchers in India and other countries [150–152]. Different aspects of lip prints like stability, sex determination [153,154] and various morphological lip print patterns among different populations were studied. A study on PM changes of lip prints [155,156] was also carried out to find out the changes in anthropometric measurements of the lip region before and after fixation. All these studies were in agreement with the Japanese research and thus helped in concluding that cheiloscopic studies can be implemented as an auxiliary method of identification [155].

Fingerprints are developed by a number of methods which rely on the fact that sweat and body oils which have been transferred from the body to an object react with a number of reagents to become visible [120]. Fingerprint powders adhere to sweat and body oils, iodine when heated reacts with sweat, ninhydrin reacts with the amino acids in sweat, heated cyanoacrylate (Super Glue) reveals latent prints, and sweat fluoresces when illuminated by a laser. Alvarez et al. [157] tested developing the latent lip prints using a similar method. According to these researchers, the vermilion borders of the lips (Figure 8.21) have minor salivary and sebaceous glands.

These glands are associated with hair follicles, sweat glands in between, and secreting oils. With these secretions and continual moisturizing, it makes the latent lip prints (Figure 8.22) [158] available at most crime scenes.

In a study by Castello et al. [159] on luminous lip prints, Nile Red was considered as a potential developer for latent lip prints. They used a property of luminescence for latent lip print development. Luminescence is an especially useful property for the search of invisible evidence at the scene of a crime.

Cheiloscopy is interesting mostly in identifying the living, since it can be the only way to link a person to

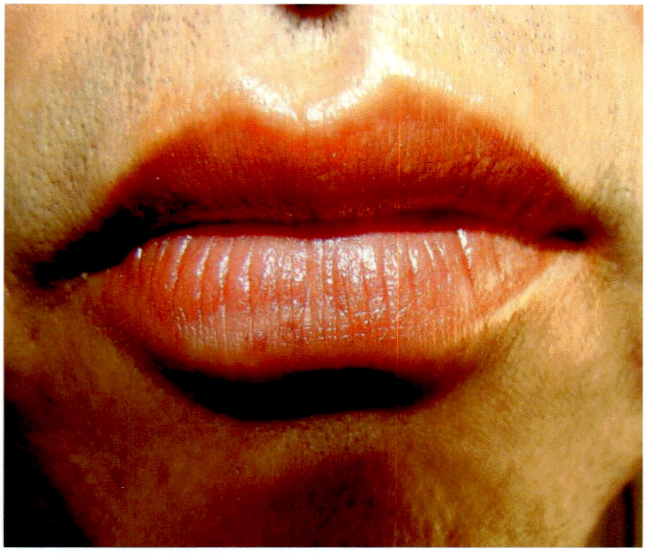

FIGURE 8.21 Grooves of the lips.

FIGURE 8.22 Latent lip print. (From Odontostomatology Laboratory Expertise [L.P.O.] directed by PhD Gabriel Fonseca, Cordoba, Argentina.)

someone or to a specific location. However, although lip prints have previously been used in a court of law, their use is not consensual, and some authors believe further evidence is needed to confirm their uniqueness [120,154,156]. In fact, lip print use is controversial and rare. The FBI has used this kind of evidence only in a single case in order to obtain a positive identification. Today, new research allows for cheiloscopy use in a court of law in the United States [160,161]. Recent studies also point out other possibilities, namely, DNA detection in latent lip prints: some researchers are trying to relate characteristic lip patterns with a person's gender [162]. Another aspect that might be interesting to study is the possibility of using identifiable lip prints obtained from the skin of assault and murder victims, in a similar way to what has already been done with latent fingerprints [161]. The lip print is produced by a substantially mobile portion of the lip. This fact alone explains the reason why the same person can produce different lip prints, according to the pressure, direction, and method used in taking the print [120]. If lipstick is used, the amount can also affect the print. This problem, however, can be solved if recordings are made until all the substance is used [120,151,156]. Manual register of the overlay is another problem, due to the possibility of some subjectivity [120]. Another factor to be considered is the existence of some pathological conditions (lymphangiomas, congenital lip fistula, lip sclerodermia, Melkersson-Rosenthal syndrome, syphilis, lip cheilitis, among others). One must also consider the possibility of PM changes of lip prints from cadavers with various causes of death. Utsuno et al. [155] have studied these changes and concluded that a satisfactory identification rate was achieved. However, this study was carried out under a laboratory environment, and what happens to lip prints obtained from cadavers exposed to the natural environment is still not known. In Argentina,

Bernardoni et al. [163] conducted a study on 100 fresh corpses using the so-called Fraile's method, originally conceived of by a senior chief of police of the province of Chaco (Argentina), Charles Fraile, for fingerprint analysis in corpses with a high state of decomposition. The results allowed the confirmation of the compatibility of adaptation and the analysis of lip prints using Fraile's method on fresh corpses, allowing crisp reproduction and display of labial furrows morphotypes in 95% of cases.

8.12 CONCLUSION

Forensic dentists may play a major role in identification in an increasingly globalized world. Forensic dentistry has varying applications that require different levels of readiness both technically and emotionally on the part of multidisciplinary team members. The applications include identification and age estimation of living or deceased individuals from their teeth, jaws, or facial bones; analysis of bite marks to identify perpetrators and victims of violent and sexual attacks; cases of family violence (marital, child, and elderly abuse and neglect), and last but not least, to help in archeological and anthropological studies of populations. Recent tragedies and past and present situations have increased awareness concerning the importance of forensic dentistry in identification of victims. However, forensic dentistry is not yet fully introduced into the dental curriculum as a subject.

Moreover, the likelihood of future disasters due to terrorism, earthquakes and other causes requires the world's dental profession to prepare for an expanded role in bioterrorism response and criminal and civil proceedings. Dentistry has an important role in the recognition of abuse among persons of all ages. Dentists have a major role to play in keeping accurate dental records and providing all necessary information so that legal authorities may recognize malpractice, negligence, fraud or abuse, and identify unknown humans. Currently, there is no agreement among forensic dentists about the uniqueness of the dentition or behavior of human skin during biting, for example. Although these issues have never been proven scientifically, much research is needed to prove suspicions that human dentition is unique. Forensic dentistry is an important science and must be treated as such.

BIBLIOGRAPHY

1. Arbenz GO. Identidade e identificação—Conceitos gerais. In: *Medicina Legal e Antropologia Forense.* Rio de Janeiro: Atheneu, 1998, pp. 105–127.
2. Smith S. The development of forensic medicine and law-science relations. *J Public Law.* 1988; 3:305–6.
3. Bernstein M. Forensic odontology. In: Eckert WG. (editor). *Introduction to Forensic Sciences.* 2nd ed. Boca Raton, FL: CRC Press. 1997, pp. 304–51.
4. Müller K, Saayman G. Clinical forensic medicine: Completing the form J88—What to do and what not to do. *S Afr Fam Pract.* 2003; 45:39–43.
5. Curran WJ. Titles in the medicolegal field: A proposal for reform. *Am J Law Med.* 1975; 191:1–11.
6. Manly, RS, Shiere FR. The effect of dental deficiency on mastication and food preference. *Oral Surg Oral Med Oral Pathol.* 1950; 3:674–85.
7. Bernitz H. The challenges and effects of globalisation on forensic dentistry. *Int Dent J. 2009;* 59(4):222–4.
8. Wecht CR. Relationships of the medical examiner. *Marshall Law Rev.* 1965; 14:427.
9. Craig I. A critical look at the evidence. *J R Soc Med.* 1993; 86:56–60.
10. National Institute of Justice, Office of Justice Programs, U.S. Department of Justice. *Mass fatality incidents: A guide for human forensic identification.* June of 2005. Available from: https://www.ncjrs.gov/pdffi les1/nij/199758.pdf (accessed April 2013).
11. World Health Organization. *Prevention of violence: A public health problem.* World Health Assembly Resolution WHA49.25: WHO, 2010.
12. World Health Organization. *Prevention of violence: A public health problem.* World Health Assembly Resolution WHA49.25: WHO, 2013.
13. INTERPOL. Thailand tsunami victim identification information management centre history. 2004. Available from: \\http://www.interpol.int/Public/asiandisaster/background/TTVI_History.aspS (accessed February 2004).
14. Grupo de Evaluación de INTERPOL sobre el Maremoto. La respuesta del equipo de identificación de víctimas sobre el maremoto del sudeste asiático entre diciembre de 2004 y febrero de 006 [citado March 27, 2011]. Available from: http://www.interpol.int/Public/Disaster Victim/TsunamiEvaluation20100330ES.pdf.
15. Briem Stamm AD. Standards, protocols and globalization in forensic odontology. *Forensic Oral Pathol J.* 2011; 2(4):9–12.
16. Sweet D. Interpol DVI best-practice standards—An overview. *Forensic Sci Int.* 2010; 201(1–3):18–21.
17. John MK. Justice through forensic odontology. *Dental Asia.* Nov/Des 2006: 30–34.
18. Avon SL. Forensic odontology: The roles and responsibilities of the dentist. *J Can Dent Assoc.* 2004; 70:453–8.
19. Senn DR, Stimson PG. *Forensic Dentistry.* Boca Raton, FL: CRC Press. 2010.

20. Chandra Shekar BR, Reddy CV. Role of dentist in person identification. *Indian J Dent Res.* 2009; 20(3):356–60.
21. Pretty IA, Sweet D. A look at forensic dentistry—Part 1: The role of teeth in the determination of human identity. *Br Dent J.* 2001; 190:359–366. May 2001; 48(3):487–96.
22. Leung CK. Forensic odontology. *Hong Kong Med Diary.* 2008; 13:16–20. Available from: http://www.fmshk.org/database/articles/03db05_1.pdf [accessed on March 24, 2012].
23. Borrman H, Dahlbom U, Loyola E, René N. Quality evaluation of 10 years patient records in forensic odontology. *Int J Legal Med.* 1995; 108:100–4.
24. Keiser-Nielsen S. Dental identification: Certainty V probability. *Forensic Sci.* 1977; 9(2):87–97.
25. Adams BJ. Establishing personal identification based on specific patterns of missing, filled, and unrestored teeth. *J Forensic Sci.* 2003; 48:487–96
26. Ulucam E, Alicioglu B, Cikmaz S, Yilmaz A, Sut N. The morphometric analysis of crista phallica in identification of sexes. *Int J Morphol.* 2009; 27:977–80.
27. Vale GL. Dentistry, bite marks, and the investigation of crime. *J Calif Dent Assoc.* 1996; 24:29–34
28. Brannon RB, Morlang WM. Tenerife revisited: The critical role of dentistry. *J Forensic Sci.* 2001; 43(3):722–5.
29. McDowell JD, Kassebaum DK, Stromboe SE. Recognizing and reporting victims of domestic violence. *J Am Dent Assoc.* 1992; 123(9):44–50.
30. Tsang A, Sweet D. Detecting child abuse and neglect—Are dentists doing enough? *J Can Dent Assn.* 1999; 65:387–91.
31. Deplama AM. Gathering the forensic evidence. *RDM.* 2005; 25(2):79–103.
32. Adams BJ. The diversity of adult dental patterns in the United States and the implications for personal identification. *J Forensic Sci.* 2003; 48(3):497–503.
33. Sweet D, Di Zinno JA. Personal identification through dental evidence—Tooth fragments to DNA. *J Calif Dent Assoc.* 1996; 24(5):35–42.
34. Appelbaum KL. Commentary: The art of forensic report writing. *J Am Acad Psychiatry Law.* 2010; 38:43–5.
35. Acharya AB. Teaching forensic odontology: An opinion on its content and format. *Eur J Dent Educ.* 2006; 10(3):137–41.
36. Goodman P. A universal system for identifying permanent and primary teeth. *J Dent Child.* 1967; 34:312–5.
37. Scott B. Forensics experts lending aid. *Access.* 2001: 12–15.
38. Bell GL. Dentistry's role in the resolution of missing and unidentified persons cases. *Dent Clin North Am.* 2001; 45:293–308.
39. American Board of Forensic Odontology. *Guidelines for the use of dental information in missing person and unidentified body cases.* 1993. Available from: www.abfo.org (accessed November 2013).
40. Valenzuela A, Marques T, Exposito N, Martín-De Las Heras S, García G. Comparative study of efficiency of dental methods for identification of burn victims in two bus accidents in Spain. *Am J Forensic Med Pathol.* 2002; 23:390–3.
41. Pretty IA, Addy LD. Associated post-mortem dental findings as an aid to personal identification. *Sci Justice.* 2002; 42:65–74.
42. Merlati, G, Savio, C, Danesino, P, Fassina, G, Menghini, P. Further study of restored and unrestored teeth subjected to high temperature. *J Forensic Odontostomatol.* 2004; 22:34–9.
43. Pretty IA, Webb DA, Sweet D. The design and assessment of mock mass disasters for dental personnel. *J Forensic Sci.* 2001; 46(l):74–9.
44. Sarode SC, Zarkar GA, Kulkarni MA. Role of forensic odontology in the world's major mass disasters: Facts and figures. *Dent Update.* 2009; 36:430–2, 435–6.
45. Gustafson G. *Forensic Odontology.* New York, NY: American Elsevier Publishing. 1996.
46. Luntz LL. History of forensic dentistry. *Dent Clin North Am.* 1977; 21:7–17.
47. Singh K, Anandani C, Bhullar RK, Agrawal A, Chaudhary H, Thakral A. Teeth and their secrets—Forensic dentistry. *J Forensic Res.* 2012; 3:1.
48. Forbes E. *Paul Revere and the World He Lived In.* Boston, MA: Houghton Mifflin. 1943.
49. Ring ME. Paul Revere—Dentist, and our country's symbol of freedom. *NY State Dent J.* December 1976; 42(10):598–601.
50. Pierce LJ, Strickland DJ, Smith ES. The case of *Ohio v. Robinson.* An 1870 bite mark case. *Am J Forensic Med Pathol.* 1990; 11:171–7.
51. Amoëdo O. The role of the dentists in the identification of the victims of the catastrophe of the "bazar de la charite." *Dent Cosmos.* 1897; 39:905–12.
52. Amoëdo O. *L'Art Dentaire en Medicine Legale.* Paris: Masson et Cie. 1898.
53. Highfield R. Dental *Detective Work Gets to the Root of Hitler Mystery.* London: Daily Telegraph. 1999.
54. Solheim T, Lorentsen M, Sundnes PK, Bang G, Bremnes L. The "Scandinavian Star" ferry disaster 1990—A challenge to forensic odontology. *Int J Leg Med.* 1992; 104: 339–45.
55. Schuller-Götzburg P, Suchanek J. Forensic odontologists successfully identify tsunami victims in Phuket, Thailand. *Forensic Sci Int.* 2007; 171:204–7.
56. Rogers SL. *The Testimony of Teeth: Forensic Aspects of Human Dentition.* Springfield, IL: Thomas Books. 1988.
57. McLanaghan Thesis (2003).

58. Reverte Coma JM. *Antropología Forense*. Madrid: Ministerio de Justicia. 1999.
59. Türp JC Alt KW. Anatomy and morphology of human teeth. In: Alt KW, Rösing FW, Teschler-Nicola M. (editors). *Dental Anthropology: Fundamentals, Limits, and Prospects*. New York, NY: Springer-Verlag/Wien. 1998, pp. 71–91.
60. Jurel SK. Role of dentist in forensic investigations. *J Forensic Res*. 2012; 3:148.
61. Bowers CM. *Forensic Dental Evidence an Investigator's Handbook*. 1st ed. San Diego, CA: Elsevier Academic Press. 2006.
62. Puerini SJ. Forensic odontology and the postmortem identification process. *Med Health R I*. 2005; 88:308–9.
63. Miles, AEW. The dentition in the assessment of individual age in skeletal material. In: Brothwell DR (editor). *Dental Anthropology*. New York, NY: Macmillan Company. 1963, p. 191.
64. Hillson S. *Teeth*. New York: Cambridge University Press. 1986.
65. Molnar S. Sex, age, and tooth position as factors in the production of tooth wear. *Am Antiq*. 1971; 36:182–7.
66. Sognnaes RF. Dental science as evidence in court. *Int J Forensic Dent*. 1976; 3(9):14–6.
67. Stimson PG, Mertz CA (eds.). *Forensic Dentistry*. Boca Raton, FL: CRC Press. 1997.
68. Fonseca GM, Salgado Alarcón G, Cantín M. Lenguaje odontológico forense e identificación: obstáculos por falta de estándares. *Rev Esp Med Legal*. 2011; 37(4):162–8.
69. INTERPOL. *Guía para la identificación de víctimas de catástrofes*. 2009. Available at: http://www.interpol.int/Public/DisasterVictim/guide/guideES.pdf (Accessed February 12, 2014).
70. Nomir O, Abdel-Mottaleb M. Human identification from dental x-ray images based on the shape and appearance of the teeth. *IEEE Trans Inform Forensics Sec*. 2007; 2(2):188–97.
71. Chen H. Automatic forensic identification based on dental radiographs. Ph thesis, Michigan State University, 2007.
72. Hinchliffe J. Forensic odontology, Part 1. Dental identification. *Br Dent J*. 2011; 210:219–24.
73. Jain AK, Chen H. Matching of dental x-ray for human identification. *Pattern Recognit*. 2004; 37:1519–32.
74. Lee SS, Choi JH, Yoon CL, Kim CY, Shin KJ. The diversity of dental patterns in the orthopantomography and its significance in human identification. *J Forensic Sci*. 2004; 49:784–6.
75. Stavrianos C, Kokkas A, Anderopoulos E, Eliades A. Applications of forensic dentistry: Part 1. *Res J Med Sci*. 2010; 4:179–86.
76. Yang F, Jacobs R, Willems G. Dental age estimation through volume matching of teeth imaged by cone-beam CT. *Forensic Sci Int*. 2006; 159S:S78–S83.
77. Lamendin H, Cambray JC. Étude de la translucidité et des canalicules: Intérêt en odonto-stomatologie légale. *Revue d´Odonto-Stomatologie* 1978; 2:111–9.
78. Williems G. A review of the most commonly used dental age estimation techniques. *J Forensic Odontostomatol*. 2001; 19:9–17.
79. Dias PEM, Beaini TL, Melani RFH. Age estimation from dental cementum incremental lines and periodontal disease. *J Forensic Odontostomatol*. 2010; 28(1):13–21.
80. Lichtenstein JE, Fitzpatrick JJ, Madeweel JE. The role of radiology in fatality investigations. *Am J Radiol*. 1988; 150:751–5.
81. Zhou J, Abdel-Mottaled M. A content-based system for human identification based on bitewing dental x-ray images. *Pattern Recognit*. 2005; 2132–42.
82. Jain K, Chen H, Minut S. Dental Biometrics Human Identification Using Dental Radiographs, *Proceedings of 4th International Conference on Audio and Video-Based Biometric Person Authentication (AVBPA)*, Guildford. 2003, pp. 429–37.
83. Piotrowski M, Szczepaniak PS. Active Contour Based Segmentation of Low-Contrast Medical Images, *International Conference on Advances in Medical Signal and Information Processing-MEDSIP'2000*, Bristol. 2000, pp. 104–9.
84. Hu S. Hoffman EA, Reinhardt M. Automatic lung segmentation for accurate quantization of volumetric x-ray CT images. *IEEE Trans Med Imaging*. June 2001; 20(6):490–8.
85. Gonzalez R, Wood R. *Digital Image Processing*. Reading, MA: Addison Wesley. 1993.
86. Pham D, Jonasson G, Kiliaridis S. Assessment of trabecular pattern on periapical and panoramic radiographs: A pilot study. *Acta Odontol Scand*. 2010; 68:91–7.
87. Martin-de las Heras S, Valenzuela A, Ogayar C, Valverde AJ, Torres JC. Computer-based production of comparison overlays from 3D-scanned dental casts for bite mark analysis. *J Forensic Sci*. 2005; 50:127–33.
88. Francescani C, Baram M. *Did 'bite mark' expert fabricate evidence?* ABC News. February 2008. Available from: http://abcnews.go.com/print?id=4311309 (accessed September 14, 2008).
89. Giannelli P. Bite Mark Analysis, Case Research Paper Series in Legal Studies 08–06, Case W. *Res. Univ. Sch. of Law*. 2008.
90. Bowers C. Problem-based analysis of bite mark identifications: The role of DNA. *Forensic Sci Int*. 2006; 159S:104–9.

91. Heras S, Valenzuela S, Valverde A, Torres J, Luna-del-Castillo J. Effectiveness of comparison overlays generated with dental printer software in bite mark analysis. *J Forensic Sci.* 2007; 52:151–6.
92. Rawson R, Ommen R. Statistical evidence for the individuality of the human dentition. *J Forensic Sci.* 1984; 29:245.
93. De Valck E. Major incident response: Collecting ante-mortem data. *Forensic Sci Int.* 2006; 159S:S15–S9.
94. Pretty I, Sweet D. Digital bitemark overlays – An analysis of effectiveness. *J Forensic Sci.* 2001; 46:1385–9.
95. Thali MJ, Yen K, Schweitzer W, Vock P, Boesch C, Ozdoba C, Schroth G, Ith M, Sonnenschein M, Doernhoefer T, Scheurer E, Plattner T, Dirnhofer R. Virtopsy, a new imaging horizon in forensic pathology: virtual autopsy by postmortem multislice computed tomography (MSCT) and magnetic resonance imaging (MRI)—A feasibility study. *J Forensic Sci.* 2003; 48(2):386–403.
96. Sheasby DR, MacDonald DG. A forensic classification of distortion in human bite marks. *Forensic Sci* Int. 2001;122(1):75–78.
97. Petju M, Sutterayongprasert A, Thongpud R, Hassuri, K. Importance of dental records for victim identification following the Indian Ocean tsunami disaster in Thailand. *Public Health.* 2007; 121(4):251–7.
98. Torpet LA. DVI system international: Software assisting in the Thai tsunami victim identification process. *J Forensic Odontostomatol.* 2005; 23:19–25.
99. Sweet D. Solving certain dental records problems with technology—The Canadian solution in the Thailand tsunami response. *Forensic Sci Int.* 2006; 159(Suppl. 1):S20–3.
100. Hoffenblad C. *DVI System International 2.3 User Manual.* Denmark: Plass Data Software A/S. 2005.
101. James H. Thai tsunami victim identification—Overview to date. *J Forensic Odontostomatol.* 2005; 23:1–18.
102. De Valck E. Considerations 20 years after the publication of the article "The dentist as an expert in disasters—Dental identification in the disaster with the Zeebruge Ferry." *Rev Belge Med Dent* (1984). 2009; 64(4):197–9.
103. Tan PH, Wee KP, Sahelangi P. Remembering the Musi–Sil-kAir Flight MI 185 crash victim identification. *Ann Acad Med Singapore.* 2007; 36(10):861–6.
104. Pachar JV, Bryan K. El sistema de apoyo internacional para la gestión forense de cadáveres en situaciones de desastre. La experiencia de Haití, 2010. *Cuad Med Forense.* 2010; 16(1):81–5.
105. Facts and Details. Dead and missing from the Great East Japan earthquake and tsunami of March 11, 2011.
106. Dental Health Magazine. The Dental Industry and Japan Catastrophe. Edición del 12 de Abril de 2011.
107. Brannon and Kessler, 1999.
108. Zohn HK, Dashkow S, Aschheim KW, Dobrin LA, Glazer HS, Kirschbaum M, Levitt D, Feldman CA. The odontology victim identification skill assessment system. *J Forensic Sci.* 2010; 55(3):788–91.
109. Brannon RB, Kessler HP. Problems in mass-disaster dental identification: A retrospective review. *J Forensic Sci.* 1999; 44(1):123–7.
110. Clark DH. Dental identification problems in the Abu Dhabi air accident. *Am J Forensic Med Pathol.* 1986; 7 (4): 317–321.
111. Nuzzolese E, Di Vella G. Future project concerning mass disaster management: a forensic odontology prospectus. *Int Dent J.* 2007; 57 (4): 261-266.
112. Budimlija Z, Prinz M, Zelson-Mundorf A, Wieserma J, Baterlink E, Mackinnon G. World Trade Center human identification project: Experiences with individual body identification cases. *Croat Med J.* 2003; 44(3): 259–263.
113. Brkic H, Strinovic D, Slaus M, Skavic J, Zecevic D, Milicevic M. Dental identification of war victims from Petrinja in Croatia. *Int J Legal Med.* 1997; 110:47–51.
114. Millet C, Jeannin C. Incorporation of microchips to facilitate denture identification by radiofrequency tagging. *J Prosthet Dent.* 2004; 92:588–90.
115. Richmond R, Pretty IA. The use of radio-frequency identification tags for labeling dentures—Scanning properties. *J Forensic Sci.* 2009; 54(3):664–8.
116. Borrman HI, DiZinno JA, Wasén J, René N. On denture marking. *J Forensic Odontostomatol.* 1999; 17:20–6.
117. Marella GL, Rossi P. An approach to person identification by means of dental prostheses in a burnt corpse. *J Forensic Odontostomatol.* 1999; 17:16–9.
118. Alexander PM, Taylor JA, Szuster FS, Brown KA. An assessment of attitudes to, and extent of, the practice of denture marking in South Australia. *Aust Dent J.* 1998; 43:337–41.
119. Iqbal MK, Kim S. A review of factors influencing treatment planning decisions of single-tooth implants versus preserving natural teeth with nonsurgical endodontic therapy. *J Endod.* 2008; 34:519–29.
120. Caldas IM, Magalhaes T, Alfonso A. Establishing identity using cheiloscopy and palatoscopy. *Forensic Sci Int.* 2007; 165(1):1–9.
121. Sharma P, Saxena S, Rathod V. Comparative reliability of cheiloscopy and palatoscopy in human identification. *Indian J Dental Res.* 2009; 20(4):453–7.

122. Thomas CJ, van Wyk CW. The palatal rugae in identification. *J Forensic Odontostomatol.* 1988; 6(1):21–5.
123. Perrella M, Costa F, Vessecchi S, Moccelin E, Daruge E. *Identificação por rugoscopia palatina e dactiloscopia.* Available from: http://www.ibemol.com.br/forense2000/071.asp.
124. Berketa JW, James H, Marino V. Radiographic recognition of dental implants as an aid to identifying the deceased. *J Forensic Sci.* 2010; 55(1): 66–70.
125. Briem Stamm AD. Análisis comparativo de rugas palatinas empleando el método de Carrea en personal de Gendarmería Nacional en Formosa, Argentina. FOPJ. 2012; 3(6):13–7.
126. Limson KS, Julian R. Computerized recording of the palatal rugae pattern and an evaluation of its application in forensic identification. *J Forensic Odontostomatol.* 2004; 22(1):1–4.
127. Buchtová M, Tichy F, Putnová I, Míšek I. The development of palatal rugae in the European pine vole, *Microtus subterraneus* (Arvicolidae, Rodentia). *Folia Zoo.* 2003; 52(2):127–36.
128. Ohtani M, Nishida N, Chiba T, Fukuda M, Miyamoto Y, Yoshioka N. Indication and limitations of using palatal rugae for personal identification in edentulous cases. *Forensic Sci Int.* 2008; 176:178–82.
129. Aparicio Castellanos DC, Henr'quez Higuera LF, Hurtado Avella AM, Pedraza Gutiérrez AP, Casas Martínez JA. Identificación positiva por medio del uso de la rugoscop'a en un Municipio de Cundinamarca (Colombia): Reporte de caso. *Acta Odontol Venez.* 2007; 45(3):e1–6.
130. Kapali S, Townsend G, Richards L, Parish T. Palatal rugae patterns in Australian Aborigines and Caucasians. *Aust Dent J.* 1997; 42(2):129–33.
131. Hoggan BR, Sadowsky C. The use of palatal rugae for the assessment of anteroposterior tooth movements. *Am J Ortho Dentofacial Orthop.* 2001; 119:482–8.
132. Burris BG, Harris EF. Identification of race and sex from palate dimensions. *J Forensic Sci.* 1998; 43(5):959–63.
133. Kashima K. Comparative study of the palatal rugae and shape of the hard palate in Japanese and Indian children. *Aichi Gakuin Daigaku Shigakkai Shi.* 1990; 28:295–320.
134. Hermosilla VV, San Pedro VJ, Cantín IM, Suazo GIC. Palatal rugae: Systematic analysis of its shape and dimensions for use in human identification. *Int J Morphol.* 2009; 27:819–25.
135. Gopichand PV, Kaushal S, Kaur G. Personal identification using lip prints (cheiloscopy)—A study in 500 Punjabi females. *J Indo Pac Acad Forensic Odontol.* 2010; 1:20–2.
136. Grimaldo-Carjevschi M. Rugoscopía, Queiloscopía, Oclusografía y Oclusoradiografía como métodos de identificación en Odontología Forense: Una revisión de la literatura. *Acta Odontol Venez.* 2010; 48(2).
137. Hemanth M, Vidya M, Shetty N, Karkera BV. Identification of individuals using of the palatal rugae: Computerized method. *J Forensic Dent Sci.* 2010; 2(2):86–90.
138. Gitto CA, Esposito SJ, Draper JM. A simple method of adding palatal rugae to a complete denture. *J Prosthet Dent.* 1999; 81(2): 237–9.
139. Negré Muñoz MC. Nuevas aportaciones al revelado de huellas labiales: Los lisocromos en Queiloscopia. *Thesis Doctoral, Universitat de Valencia*, 2004.
140. Suzuki K, Tsuchihashi Y. A new attempt of personal identification by means of lip print. *J Indian Dent Assoc.* 1970; 42(1):8–9.
141. Coward RC. The stability of lip pattern characteristics over time. *J Forensic Odontostomatol.* 2007; 25(2):40–56.
142. Suzuki K, Tsuchihashi Y. Two criminal cases of lip print. *Acta Criminol Jpn.* 1975; 41:61–4.
143. López Palafox J. Aplicaciones ignoradas en Odontología forense. Interés de la Queiloscopía en la averiguación de delitos (1st Part). *Maxillaris* 2001; 529.
144. Ball J. The current status of lip prints and their use for identification. *J Forensic Odontostomatol.* 2002; 20:436.
145. Netter F. *Atlas of Human Anatomy, Head and Neck Section.* New Jersey, NJ: Elsevier Health Sciences. 1996.
146. Snyder LM. *Homicide Investigation.* Springfield, IL: Thomas. 1950, p. 65.
147. Santos M. Queiloscopy, A supplementary stomatological means of identification. *Int Microform J Leg Med.* 1967; 2:66.
148. Kasprzak J. Possibilities of cheiloscopy. *Forensic Sci Int.* 1990; 46:145–51.
149. Renaud M. L'identification chéiloscopique en médicine légale [Cheiloscopic identification in forensic medicine]. *Nouv Presse Med.* 1973; 2: 2617-2620.
150. Saraswathi TR, Gauri M, Ranganathan K. Study of lip prints. *J Forensic Dent Sci.* 2009; 1:28–31.
151. Sivapathasundharam B, Prakash PA, Sivakumar G. Lip prints (Cheiloscopy). *Indian J Dent Res.* 2001; 12:234–7.
152. Sharma P, Saxena S, Rathod V. Cheiloscopy: The study of lip prints in sex identification. *J Forensic Dent Sci.* 2009; 1:24–7.
153. Patel S, Paul I, Astekar MS, Ramesh G, Sowmya GV. A study of lip print in relation to gender, family and blood group. *Int J Oral Maxillofac Pathol.* 2010; 1(1):4–7.

154. Augustine J, Barpande SR, Tupkari JV. Cheiloscopy as an adjunct to forensic identification: A study of 600 individuals. *J Forensic Odontostomatol.* 2008; 27:44–52.
155. Utsuno H, Kanoh T, Tadokoro O, Inoue K. Preliminary study of post mortem identification using lip prints. *Forensic Sci Int.* 2005; 149:129–32.
156. Castello A, Alvarez M, Verdu F. Just lip prints? No: There could be something else. *FASEB J.* 2004; 18:615–6.
157. Castelló A, Alvarez M, Miguel M, Verdú F. Long-lasting lipsticks and latent prints. *Forensic Sci Commun.* April 2002; 4. Available from: http://www.fbi.gov/hq/lab/fsc/backissu/Apr2002/verd.html.
158. Odontostomatology Laboratory Expertise (L.P.O. directed by PhD Gabriel Fonseca, Cordoba, Argentina.
159. Castello A, Alvarez M, Negre MC, Verdu FA. Revelado de huellas labiales invisibles con reactivos fluorescentes. *Cuad Med Forense.* 2003; 34:43–7.
160. Bowers CM, Bell GL. *Manual of Forensic Odontology.* 3rd ed. Ontario, CA: American Society of Forensic Odontology. 1997, pp. 16–8.
161. *The People of the State of Illinois, Plaintiff-Appellant, vs Lavelle L. Davis*, Defendant-Appellee. Appellate Court of Illinois, Second District, Case No. 94-CF-76, November 20, 2007, p. 67.
162. Schulz MM, Wehner HD, Reichert W, Graw M. Ninhydrin-dyed latent fingerprints as a DNA source in a murder case. *J Clin Forensic Med.* 2004; 11:202–4.
163. Bernardoni M, Sauer S, Briem Stamm A. Análisis experimental del comportamniento de huellas labiales en cadáveres frescos usando el Método Fraile. Gac Int Cien Forense. 2013; 3:19–24.

CHAPTER 9

An Introduction to Digital Audio Forensics

Michael Dixon

CONTENTS

9.1 OVERVIEW

Watching TV programs and films, it is easy to think that audio enhancement is a simple process where conversations can be easily isolated from a noisy nightclub background. The reality is very different, requiring specialized knowledge of audio software, hardware, and legal processes.

Real-world audio enhancement usually involves recordings made in less than ideal conditions and with less than ideal equipment. Hidden omnidirectional microphones that pick up sound from all directions recording in lossy file formats are usual. This results in quiet voices hidden within a broad spectrum of background noise. Enhancement can indeed sometimes yield dramatic improvements in the intelligibility of the voice in a recording. However, the improvements are usually more discrete, such as balancing the listening volume of the two voices in a conversation, or the removal of mains hum or background hiss.

The history of audio forensics probably goes back to its use by the military as far back as World War II, when sound spectrographs were used to try to identify enemy voices in radio transmissions. In 1974, the Watergate affair featured an erased recording. Over 18 minutes of recorded material had deliberately been erased; a team of six scientists were chosen to examine the recording in what was probably the first forensic authentication case in history.

In the past, analog, and later, digital signal processing (DSP) hardware was used to process audio, to filter out background noise, and so on. Today, this is almost exclusively carried out using software.

9.2 HUMAN VOICE

Human beings have an audible frequency range of about 20 Hz–20,000 Hz, with most of its sensitivity around 300–10,000 HZ. The average male speaking voice has a fundamental frequency of between 85–155 Hz, and the average woman's speaking voice is 165–255 Hz. A very deep male voice could be as low as 65 Hz, while a high female soprano singer might be 1000–1280 Hz and a high-pitched scream could be around 3000 Hz.

Used in telephony, the range 300–3400 Hz is the most important range for speech recognition. Reducing this range can noticeably reduce intelligibility, but increasing it doesn't have much added effect. The dynamic range is about 96 dB; this is the quietest to loudest range.

9.3 AUDIO ENHANCEMENT

The main goal of forensic audio enhancement is to make the spoken voices in a recording more discernible. This can be done by removing unwanted background noise, amplifying voices, hiss removal, mains hum removal, and so on. The human voice has a random waveform, whereas the unwanted background noise in a recording can be a nonrandom repeating noise pattern. This nonrandom noise can be removed to make the vocal part of the recording clearer. It is much more difficult to remove unwanted background noise when it is random and within the voice frequency range without also removing elements of the voice in the recording.

9.4 AUTHENTICATION/OTHER

In addition to enhancement, forensic audio analysis is also used to authenticate recordings as genuine. Comparing frequency range, background noise, and amplitude levels throughout a recording can, in expert hands, show if the recording has been edited. Forensic audio analysis has been used to invalidate the ostensible location of a 999 (emergency) call made on a mobile phone. The recording was recreated using the same handset in the same location and the background noises compared, proving that the call was not made at the alleged location.

Electrical network frequency (ENF) analysis is recorded simultaneously with the audio; a 49–51 Hz bandpass filter can isolate it and compare it to a database. ENF can also affect some battery-operated recorders (50 Hz in Europe, 60 Hz in the United States) fluctuations database.

Voiceprints, or voice spectrography, is an analysis of the frequencies in a voice. It is used to compare a voice in a recording to that of a known subject to ascertain if both recordings are of the same person.

9.5 AUDIO FUNDAMENTALS

9.5.1 Waveform Measurements

Several measurements describe waveforms:

Amplitude—This is the change in pressure from the peak of the waveform to the trough. High-amplitude waveforms are loud; low-amplitude waveforms are quiet. Peak amplitude is the maximum value in the waveform.

Cycle—Describes a single oscillation of the waveform.

Frequency—This is measured in hertz (Hz) and is the number of cycles per second. Higher frequencies have a higher musical pitch.

Phase—Measured in 360 degrees, this indicates the position of a waveform in a cycle. Zero degrees is the start point and 360 is the end point. It is used to describe two sound waves relative to each other; when the crests and troughs align the waveforms are said to be in phase.

Wavelength—Measured in units such as meters/centimeters, it is the distance between two points with the same degree of phase. As frequency increases, wavelength decreases.

9.5.2 Sample Rate

Sample rate indicates the number of samples taken of an audio signal each second and determines the frequency range of the audio file. The higher the frequency of the sample rate, the closer the shape of the digital waveform will be to that of the original analog waveform (Table 9.1).

TABLE 9.1 Sample Rates

Sample Rate	Quality Level	Frequency Range
8000 Hz	Telephony	0–4000 Hz
11,025 Hz	AM radio, lower-quality PCM, MPEG audio	0–5512 Hz
22,050 Hz	Near FM radio	0–11,025 Hz
32,000 Hz	Above FM radio, MiniDV	0–16,000 Hz
44,100 Hz	Audio CD	0–22,050 Hz
48,000 Hz	Standard DVD, Digital TV	0–24,000 Hz
96,000 Hz	DVD-Audio, HD-DVD	0–48,000 Hz

9.5.3 Nyquist-Shannon Sampling Frequency

This is a frequency equal to half the sample rate, and it determines the highest reproducible audio frequency for that rate. Audio CDs use a sample rate of 44,100 Hz because the resulting Nyquist-Shannon frequency is 22,050 Hz—just above the 20,000 Hz limit of human hearing.

9.5.4 Bit Depth

This determines the dynamic range of the audio. When sound is sampled, each sample is assigned the amplitude value closest to the original wave's amplitude. A higher bit depth allows more possible amplitude values and therefore a greater dynamic range (Table 9.2).

TABLE 9.2 Bit Depth

Bit Depth	Quality Level	Amplitude Values	Dynamic Range
8-bit	Telephony	256	48 dB
16-bit	CD	65,536	96 dB
24-bit	DVD	16,777,216	144 dB
32-bit	Best	4,294,967,296	192 dB

9.5.5 Audio File Formats

Uncompressed CD quality audio at 44,100 samples per second and 16 bits per sample requires around 88 KB per second, 5 MB per minute. That figure doubles to 10 MB per minute if in stereo.

The main uncompressed format is *PCM* (pulse code modulation); file formats storing this are as follows:

- *Waveform Audio File Format (WAV)* encoding *LPCM* (linear pulse code modulation)
- *Audio Interchange File Format (AIFF)* encoding *PCM*

Both the above formats can use compression, however.

9.5.6 Lossless Compressed File Formats

These formats create smaller file sizes without reducing the audio quality. Lossless formats include the following:

- *FLAC* (Free Lossless Audio Codec): 50%–60% reduction in file size
- *ALAC* (Apple Lossless Audio Codec): 40%–60% reduction in file size

9.5.7 Lossy Formats (Compressed)

Lossy formats reduce file size by throwing away some of the audio information; they achieve much higher compression rates than lossless formats because of this. The loss of information within the file is not always easily heard in music files.

- *MP3*—MPEG-1 Layer 3
- *AAC*—Advanced Audio Coding
- *WMA*—Windows Media Audio

9.5.8 Upsampling/Downsampling

Often audio files are recorded at low quality with low sample rates and bit depths. While working on audio files, it is required that the sample rate and bit depth be higher than that of the original recording. This is achieved by upsampling: converting the sample rate to a higher rate by interpolation, the audio equivalent of resizing an image in a photo-editing application. If the opposite is required—a reduction in the sample rate—this is known as downsampling.

9.5.9 File Formats for Forensic Work

Audio requiring any kind of forensic audio work should always be saved using an uncompressed file format. While any kind of enhancement is being conducted, a high bit depth should be used: 32-bit resolution, if possible. However, this will need to be downsampled for distribution.

9.6 HEADPHONE TYPES

9.6.1 Open-Back Headphones

Sometimes referred to as vented, this design has an open back to the earcup. This design gives a character to the sound that is often described as having an open, more natural sound stage. One reason for this is that there are fewer reflections than with a closed back (or sealed) design. Open-back headphones are often regarded as providing a more accurate sound than the closed-back variety—audiophile headphones are normally open-back design. A disadvantage of the open-back design is that the source sound is able to leak out and the external, ambient sound leak in. This lack of isolation from external noise means open-back headphones are not suitable for listening in noisy environments.

9.6.2 Closed-Back Headphones

The earcup is closed in this design, which reduces the effect of external ambient noise. Typical applications for the closed-back headphone design are DJ and studio monitoring. Closed-back headphones are also useful in situations where the listener needs to prevent noise leakage, for example, in an office or while traveling.

Full-size closed-back designs (often called circumaural) encompass the ears, providing excellent isolation from outside noise. A smaller earpad closed design that sits on top of the ear will often sound more like traditional open-back headphones because the sound can leak in and out.

The trade-off for the benefits of isolation from external noise with the closed-back design is that the earcups reflect and resonate the sound made by the headphone drivers. The reflection of sound waves can cause closed-back headphones to sound boxy, with a small soundstage. However, this design usually has better low-frequency reproduction than do open-back designs.

9.6.3 Noise-Canceling Headphones

Noise-canceling headphones reduce ambient external noise by using small microphones located inside the earpiece and active electronics within the headset. The principle is that the ambient external noise is inverted and then summed with a signal from the audio source. The result is that the ambient noise from outside is effectively cancelled out. Such headphones are better at canceling lower rather than higher frequencies. The active electronics inside noise-canceling headphones require power to operate in noise-canceling mode, but can be run passively without power in a non-noise-canceling mode.

9.6.4 Earbud Headphones

Earbud headphones are small in size and are placed directly outside one's ear canal, without fully sealing one's ear. Probably the most popular type of headphones they are small, lightweight, easily transportable, and, normally, relatively cheap. This type of headphone is not very efficient and leaks ambient sound in.

9.6.5 Sound-Isolating Earphones

Also known as ear canal headphones (ECHs) or in-ear monitors (IEMs), these earphones are placed into the ear canal and effectively seal one's ear. They are small, lightweight and very portable. This type of earphone is usually of a higher audio quality than earbud headphones and is good at blocking ambient noise.

9.6.6 Speakers

Studio standard monitor speakers can be used instead of headphones and can make it easier to listen to conversations and decipher words. However, loudspeakers can be used only in quiet listening rooms where environmental ambient noise is not an issue.

9.7 WAVEFORM EDITORS

9.7.1 Overview

Digital audio editing software or waveform editors are the main tools used in audio forensics and enhancement. These both allow the amplitude or frequency of an audio file to be viewed graphically and provide tools to adjust the waveform. There are software packages specifically designed for audio forensics, with audit trails and simplified toolsets for common tasks. However, with user knowledge of the processes involved, the same results can be obtained using non-forensic-specific software. There are many free or open-source audio-editing software packages that are suitable for most forensic audio work.

Whatever software package is used, it should at least have the basic features listed as in the following sections.

9.7.2 Level Meters

These are used to monitor the amplitude of audio during playback or recording (Figure 9.1).

Waveform display shows a waveform as amplitude against time. Usually, the x-axis shows time, and the y-axis shows amplitude. This type of display is very useful for identifying where the areas of activity are within an audio file, such as periods of conversation. It shows when clipping (waveform distortion when the signal exceeds the maximum dynamic range) has taken place, the signal strength, the signal compared to the noise floor, and much more (Figure 9.2).

Spectral frequency display shows a waveform by its frequency content against time. The x-axis shows time, and the y-axis shows frequency. This display is useful for analyzing the audio frequency content for building high-pass, low-pass and band-pass filters. Most of these types of displays are customizable as to color content; usually the lighter colors indicate a higher amplitude of the particular frequency indicated (Figure 9.3).

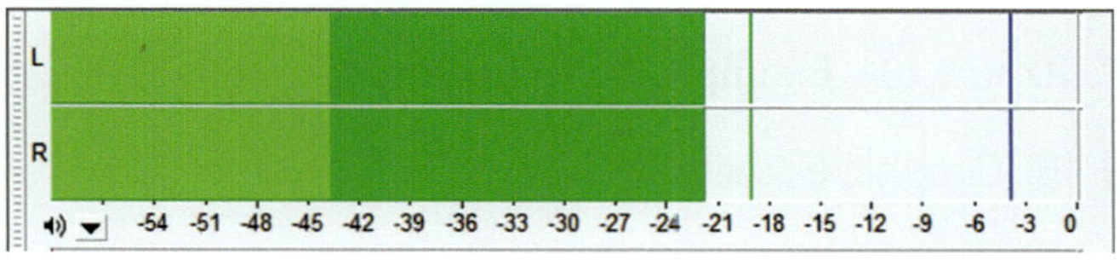

FIGURE 9.1 Waveform display.

The ability to decrease or increase the amplitude (amplify) of the waveform is essential. This is one of the most important tools in audio forensics. Conversations are often recorded covertly, with the result that one side of the conversation is much louder than the other. One speaker is usually nearer to the recording device, or one person is on a telephone but the other speaker can still be heard. The ability to selectively amplify sections of the waveform is very useful in correcting the differences in amplitude in these situations (Figures 9.4 and 9.5).

9.7.3 Clipping

When a signal is recorded too loudly for the recording device, the signal is cut or clipped at the maximum level. A clipped signal can often be recovered to some extent by most software packages. Digital clipping occurs when a signal's amplitude exceeds the bit depth maximum level (Figure 9.6).

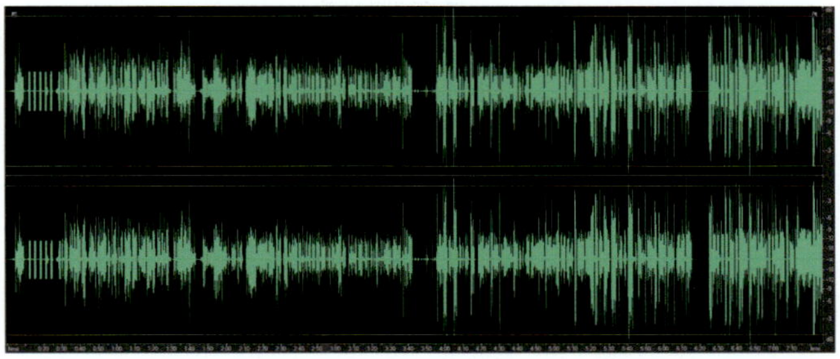

FIGURE 9.2 Spectral frequency display.

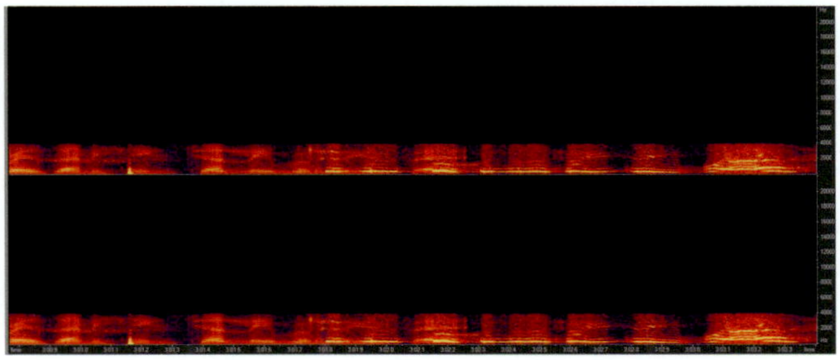

FIGURE 9.3 Amplification.

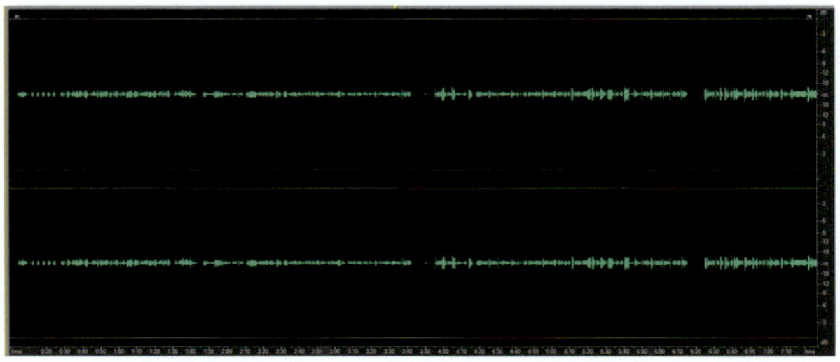

FIGURE 9.4 Original waveform.

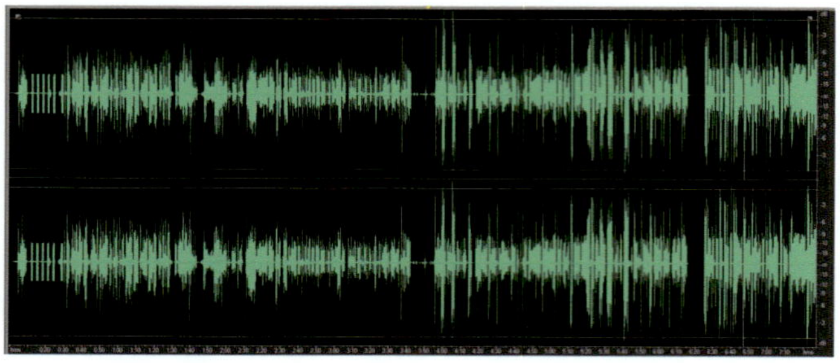

FIGURE 9.5 Plus 12 DB amplification.

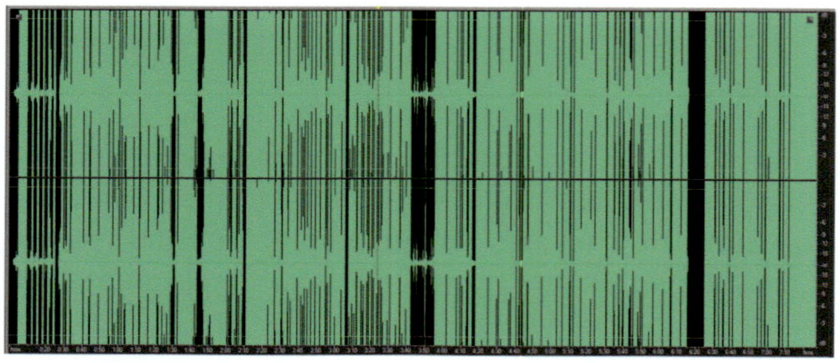

FIGURE 9.6 A clipped waveform.

9.8 FILTERS

9.8.1 Band Pass

A band-pass filter passes a range of frequencies through while removing all other frequencies. This is useful for removing a background noise whilst preserving the frequencies containing the voice content of an audio file (Figure 9.7).

9.8.2 Low Pass

This filter passes low frequencies and removes high frequencies. A low-pass filter is useful for removing unwanted high-frequency noise, such as a hiss (Figure 9.8).

9.8.3 High Pass

This filter passes high frequencies and removes low frequencies. A high-pass filter is useful for removing unwanted low frequencies, such as rumbles (Figure 9.9).

9.8.4 Band Stop

A band-stop filter attenuates frequencies within a specified range. Also known as a notch filter, band stop is the opposite of band pass. A 49 Hz–11 Hz band stop can be used to remove mains hum in countries where transmission occurs at 50 Hz (Figure 9.10).

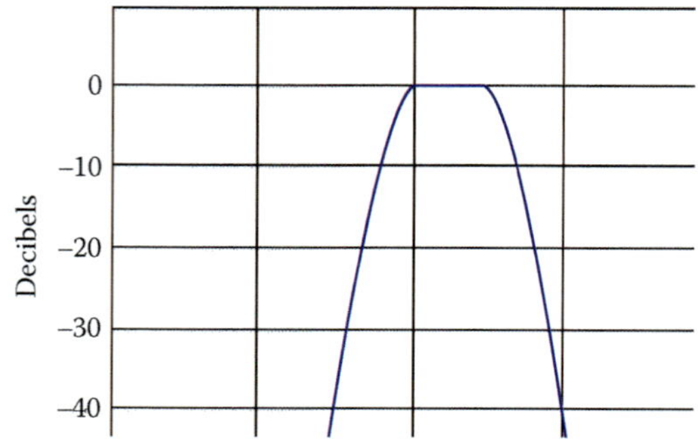

FIGURE 9.7 7000 Hz to 16,000 Hz band-pass filter.

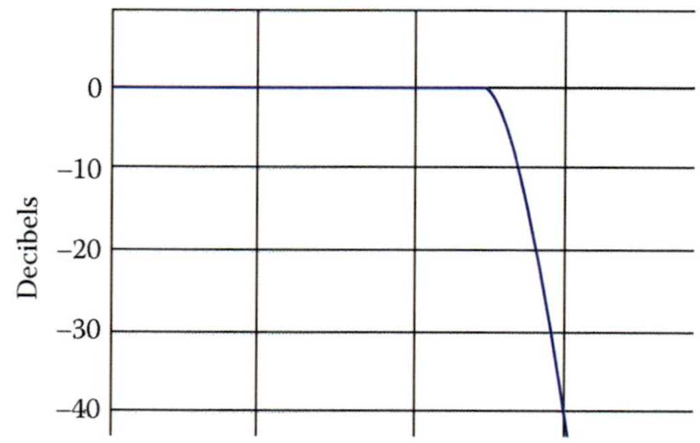

FIGURE 9.8 Low-pass filter.

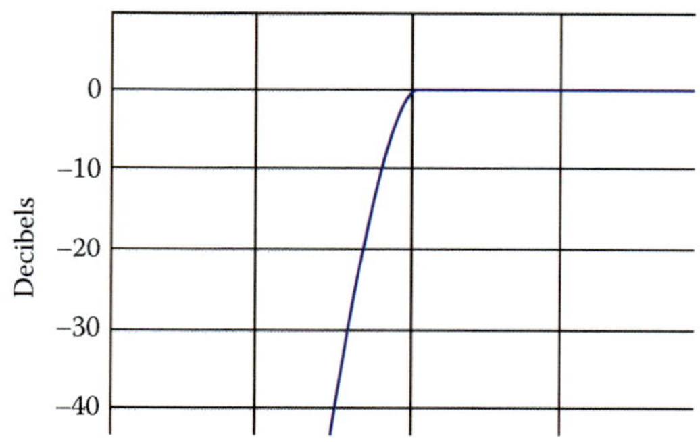

FIGURE 9.9 High-pass filter.

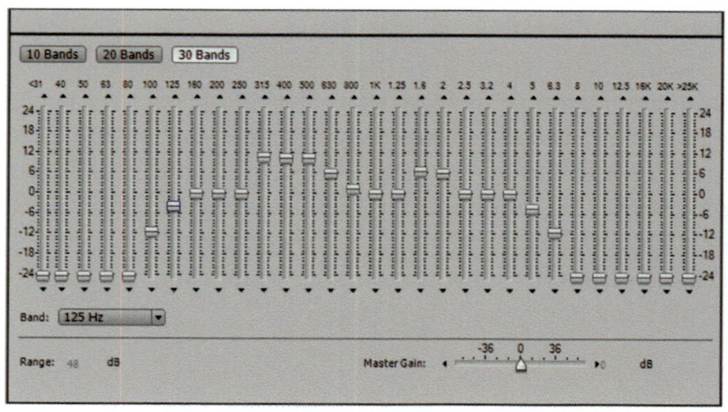

FIGURE 9.10 Example of typical software equalizer.

9.8.5 Graphic Equalizers

A graphic equalizer boosts or cuts specific frequencies, and its controls allow the audio amplitude to be adjusted at specified frequencies. More control bands allow better isolation of specific frequencies and are therefore more useful for audio forensics.

9.8.6 Noise Reduction Filters

Sound engineers will record the ambient background noise of a location to later add to the dialogue to create a natural sound to the silence. Noise reduction filters do the opposite: the silence of an audio track is sampled and used to create a filter to remove it. The sampled area of waveform to be used for the noise reduction filter must not contain any voices; otherwise, they will be removed along with the unwanted ambient sounds. These filters work well in removing AC mains hum and its harmonics as well as other nonrandom noise or combinations of noise.

Adaptive noise reduction filters automatically learn the noise content and remove it in real time. The filters can be set to preserve an important bandwidth, such as voice content, while actively removing noise outside this range. They are also used remove variable background noise, such as wind.

9.8.7 Audit Trail

It is important to keep a record of each step of the enhancement process if the software doesn't do this automatically. If the enhanced audio file is to be used in court, it must be able to be recreated, process by process, from the original audio file. This audit trail can be simply screen grabs of the audio filter setting along with notes of the procedures.

9.8.8 Summary

There isn't often a magic bullet in the real world of forensic audio enhancement. Results are achieved by using a mix of the above filtering processes along with selective amplification and critical listening. Experience and timescale play a large part in achieving good results.

9.9 USEFUL TERMINOLOGY

9.9.1 Amplitude

Amplitude represents the volume of an audio signal. There are different standards for measuring amplitude, but the decibel (dB) is the most common.

9.9.2 Band-Pass Filter

A filter that allows a selected range of audio frequencies to pass through but attenuates all other frequencies.

9.9.3 Bit Depth

The bit depth is the number of bits used to represent audio signals amplitude: 8-bit resolution provides 256 possible amplitude levels and a 48 dB dynamic range, while 16-bit resolution provides 65,536 levels and a 96 dB range.

9.9.4 Clipping

Clipping is when a signal is recorded too loudly for the recording device, the signal is cut or clipped at the maximum level. Digital clipping occurs when a signal's amplitude exceeds the bit depth maximum level.

9.9.5 Codec

Codec (compressor/decompressor) is the data compression schemes used by the audio file formats.

9.9.6 DAT

Digital audio tape (DAT) is a digital medium developed by Sony in the 1980s.

9.9.7 Decibel (dB)

In audio, the decibel (dB) is a logarithmic unit of measurement used for amplitude.

9.9.8 Dynamic Range

Dynamic range is the audio amplitude range, from quietest to loudest.

9.9.9 Equalization (EQ)

Equalization refers to increasing or decreasing the amplitude of specific audio frequencies relative to the amplitude of other audio frequencies.

9.9.10 Frequency

Frequency is measured in hertz (Hz) and is the number of cycles per second. Higher frequencies have a higher musical pitch.

9.9.11 Hertz (Hz)

Hertz refers to cycles per second; it is a unit of measurement that describes the frequency of a sound.

9.9.12 Normalize

Normalize is to adjust the highest peak of a waveform so it nearly reaches the digital maximum, the same amount of gain is used to raise or lower all other peaks accordingly. Typically, audio is normalized to 100% to achieve maximum volume.

9.9.13 Pulse Code Modulation (PCM)

PCM is used to digitally represent analogue signals.

9.9.14 Phase

Phase is the position of one sound wave relative to other sound waves.

9.9.15 Root Mean Square (RMS)

RMS is a mathematical formula used to determine the average amplitude of an audio signal.

9.9.16 Signal-to-Noise (S/N Ratio)

Signal-to-noise ratio describes the difference between the highest signal level before distortion and the average level of the noise floor.

9.9.17 Sample Rate

Sample rate indicates the number of samples taken of an audio signal each second and determines the frequency range of the audio file. The higher the frequency of the sample rate, the closer the shape of the digital waveform will be to that of the original analogue waveform.

9.9.18 Sound Wave

Sound travels through air as longitudinal waves and is measured in hertz (Hz). Humans can hear sound waves with frequencies of 20 to 20,000 Hz.

9.9.19 Waveform

Waveform is a term that describes the visual representation of an audio signal, usually displayed as amplitude across time. In acoustics, waveform refers to a sound wave of a specific frequency.

CHAPTER 10

Forensic Toxicology

Amarnath Mishra and Nino Nardareshvili

CONTENTS

10.1 INTRODUCTION

Time passes, but the need for toxicological understanding persists. As much as we might wish for the end of poverty, ignorance, hunger, and exposure to hazardous chemicals, and as much as we work toward these goals, the challenges are formidable, and the end is not in sight. Chemicals and finished products made from chemicals continue to play an ever-present part in our lives. Although it is not evident that the benefits of chemicals always outweigh their risks, there is little doubt that a wide spectrum of chemicals and drugs has enhanced both the duration and quality of our lives. That said, some of them in certain situations are clearly harmful to certain people. Among the fruits of toxicologists' labors is information on how best to eliminate, reduce, or prevent such harm.

The term "forensic toxicology" covers any application of the science and study of poisons to the administration of justice. The subject is usually associated with work for the police, the coroner, and the criminal law courts. However, the analysis and identification of medicines and the maintenance of agricultural, industrial, and public health are also aspects of forensic toxicology.

Accidental self-poisoning and attempted suicide cases are generally the responsibility of the clinical toxicologist, who may work in conjunction with a poison control center. A small proportion of these cases is referred to the forensic toxicologist, either because of an allegation of deliberately harmful poisoning or because the patient dies and a coroner's inquest is ordered. The defining difference between the clinical toxicologist and the forensic toxicologist is the judicial element. The clinical toxicologist is primarily concerned with the identification of drugs and poisons as an aid to the diagnosis and treatment of acute and chronic poisoning. If the patient dies, the analytical data obtained by the clinical toxicologist may well be sufficient for use by the pathologist and the coroner in determining the cause of death in cases where there are no suspicious circumstances. In other cases, including those where the patient recovers but claims to have been poisoned by a third party, it is usual for the investigation to be referred to a forensic toxicologist. Although the above indicates that the forensic toxicologist is generally involved in cases of suspected poisoning, more recently other roles have developed in areas such as doping in sports (of both humans and animals) and workplace drug-testing biological systems. Forensic toxicology deals with the application of toxicology to cases and issues where those adverse effects have administrative or medicolegal consequences.

Toxicology is the study of the adverse effects of drugs and chemicals on and where the results are likely to be used in court. Forensic toxicology is a completely modern science, based on published and widely accepted scientific methods and practices, used to analyze drugs in biological materials and interpret those results. Many of the methods it employs have been derived from innovations in clinical medicine and academic laboratories throughout the world. Thousands of articles related to forensic toxicology methods, instrumentation and interpretation are published in hundreds of peer-reviewed journals every year, increasing our understanding of the benefits, risks, and dangers associated with use and abuse of illicit and recreational drugs, medications, and alcohol.

Forensic toxicologists work with pathologists, medical examiners, and coroners in helping to establish the role of alcohol, drugs, and poisons in the cause of death. The toxicologist identifies and quantifies the presence of drugs and chemicals in blood and tissue samples. This is done using state-of-the-art chemical and biomedical instrumentation capable of detecting small amounts of toxic materials, positively identifying them, and accurately measuring how much is present. Accuracy, validity, and reliability are essential, as this information is used in the determination of the cause and manner of death. Those determinations are the prerogative of the medical examiner or coroner; however, the toxicologist is a key member of the team of experts who assist in that determination, consulting on pharmacology, drug kinetics and interactions, metabolism, adverse and idiosyncratic reactions, drug tolerance, postmortem artifacts, drug stability, and other factors. The pathologist considers this information in the context of the investigative and medical history of the case as well as the findings of disease or other medical conditions at autopsy. Accurately establishing the appropriate cause and manner of death has serious implications for public health and public safety, and forensically reliable toxicology is an essential component of that process.

Forensic toxicologists perform analysis of drugs and alcohol in biological samples—typically blood and urine, but increasingly in other matrices such as oral fluid and hair—to determine the timing, extent, and impairment resulting from different patterns of drug and alcohol use. The toxicologist uses state-of-the-art analytical methods, such as those found in many research and hospital laboratories, to isolate drugs from complex biological samples, prepare them for analysis through extraction and purification, then determine the identity and amount of drug present. Following the analytical phase, the forensic toxicologist provides interpretation of the result with respect to whether the dose represents typical therapeutic use, recreational use, or potential abuse, and he or she can provide opinions about the likely effects of these patterns of use. This can include performance enhancement that occurs following the use of stimulants, and impairment from recreational or prescription medication use and misuse. Forensic toxicologists review and testify in cases of impaired driving involving alcohol and drugs, and address diverse issues such as transportation safety, drug-facilitated crimes, competency, intoxication, and diminished capacity. Forensic toxicologists frequently testify in court to both their findings and their interpretation.

Enforcing these rules requires periodic off-season, random and event-focused drug testing for performance-enhancing drugs and other medications that appear on the organizations' prohibited substances lists. Forensic toxicologists in this field use many of the same high-performance analytical methods to detect current and historical use of banned substances, including stimulants, anabolic steroids, and diuretics.

Use of drugs by people in the workplace has significant safety and economic consequences. Forensic toxicologists perform testing of urine samples in regulated and inspected laboratories. Testing for five major classes of abused drugs and their metabolites, these scientists employ highly uniform and well-defined techniques and methods to minimize the risk of errors, ensuring that employees are treated fairly and that testing is done to the highest forensic standards. The majority of workplace drug testing is not covered directly by accreditation programs, however. These unregulated programs can perform tests using other matrices such as oral fluids, sweat, and hair.

10.2 DETECTION AND MEASUREMENT OF DRUGS AND ALCOHOL IN BLOOD AND URINE

This is very important for the qualitative and quantitative analysis of drugs and alcohol in blood and urine samples. There are basic drug test types and their approximate detection times are given in Table 10.1.

10.2.1 Time Duration of Drugs in the System

Alcohol—3–5 days in urine, up to 90 days in hair and around 10–12 hours in blood
Amphetamines—1–3 days in urine, up to 90 days in hair and around 12 hours in blood
Barbiturates—2–4 days in urine, up to 90 days in hair and 1–2 days in blood
Benzodiazepines—3–6 weeks in urine, up to 90 days in hair and 2–3 days in blood
Cannabis—7–30 days in urine, up to 90 days in hair, 2 weeks in blood
Cocaine—3–4 days in urine, up to 90 days in hair, 1–2 days in blood
Codeine—1 day in urine, up to 90 days in hair, 12 hours in blood
Heroin—3–4 days in urine, up to 90 days in hair, up to 12 hours in blood
LSD—1–3 days in urine, up to 3 days in hair, 2–3 hours in blood

TABLE 10.1 Basic Drug Test Types and Their Approximate Detection Times

	Urine	Blood	Hair	Saliva
Marijuana—Single Use	1–7+ days	12–24 hrs	Doubtful	
Marijuana—Regular Use	7–100 days	2–7 days		
Amphetamines	1–3 days	24 hours		Not validated
Cocaine	1–3 days	1–3 days		(0–24 hours?)
Heroin, Opiates	1–4 days	1–3 days	Months	
PCP	3–7 days	1–3 days		

MDMA (ecstasy)—3–4 days in urine, up to 90 days in hair and 1–2 days in blood
Methamphetamine (crystal meth)—3–6 days in urine, up to 90 days in hair, 24–72 hours in blood
Methadone—3–4 days in urine, up to 90 days in hair, 24–36 hours in blood
Morphine—2–3 days in urine, up to 90 days in hair, 6–8 hours in blood

10.3 TESTING OF OPIUM/CRUDE MORPHINE/POPPY STRAW

10.3.1 Presumptive Tests (Color Tests)

Positive results of these tests are only a presumptive indication for the presence of opium alkaloids. It is mandatory for the analyst to confirm such results by use of an alternate technique.

10.3.1.1 Marquis Test

Take a small amount of suspected sample in a test tube and add about 10 drops of water, then crush the sample with a glass rod. Place a few drops of water solution through filter paper/supernatant liquid on a spotting plate and add a few drops of Marquis reagent. The development of a purple-violet color indicates the presence of opium/crude morphine.

Preparation of Marquis Reagent: 8–10 drops of 40% formaldehyde solution is added to 10 mL of conc. sulfuric acid.

10.3.1.2 Ferric Salt Test

Take a small amount of suspected material on a spot plate and add about 2 drops of water; triturate the sample until the water becomes a brown color. Take 1 drop of brown liquid to another part of the spot plate and add 1 drop of reagent. The appearance of a brown-purple color indicates the positive test for the presence of meconic acid. This meconic acid is present in raw and prepared opium, but it will not be detected in crude morphine.

Preparation of Ferric Salt Reagent: Dissolve 1 g of ferric sulfate in 20 mL of water.

10.3.2 Alternate Test for Meconic Acid

10.3.2.1 Ferric Chloride Test

Dissolve an appropriate sample of opium in water and add a drop of dilute hydrochloric acid followed by a few drops of 10% solution of ferric chloride. A red color will appear. Divide this solution into two parts. Take the first part, add dilute hydrochloric acid to it in excess, and warm. The red color of the solution remains there. Take the second part and add a solution of mercuric chloride. The color of the solution is not affected.

Preparation of Mercuric Chloride Reagent: Dissolve 5 g mercuric chloride in 100 mL of water.

Dilute Hydrochloric Acid: About 10% W/W of HCl in water.

10.3.2.2 Porphyroxine Test

Take a small amount of suspected material on a spot plate and add 2 drops of water. Triturate it with glass rod. Take 1 drop of brown liquid from this mixture to another part of the plate, add 1 drop of 2 N hydrochloric acid, and heat gently. Appearance of red color indicates the presence of porphyroxine.

10.3.3 Thin-Layer Chromatography

Stationary Phase: Activated silica gel (with or without fluorescing substance) TLC (thin-layer chromatography) plates of 0.25/0.20 mm thickness.

Mobile Phase/Solvent Systems

System A: Toluene, Acetone, Ethanol, and Conc. Ammonia (45:45:7:3)
System B: Ethyl acetate, Methanol, and Conc. Ammonia (85:10:5)
System C: Ethanol, Chloroform, Dioxane, Petroleum ether, Benzene, Ammonium hydroxide, and ethyl acetate (5:10:50:15:10:15:5)
System D: Ethanol, benzene, ammonium hydroxide and dioxane (5:50:5:40)

Visualization Methods

1. UV light at 254 nm
2. Dragendorff's reagent spray
3. Acidified potassium iodoplatinate reagent spray

Preparation of Dragendorff's Reagent: Mix together 2 g of bismuth subnitrate, 25 mL of glacial acetic acid and 100 mL of water to produce solution (1); dissolve 40 g of potassium iodide in 100 mL of water to produce solution (2). Mix 10 mL of solution (1), 10 mL of solution (2), 20 mL of glacial acetic acid, and 100 mL of water.

Preparation of Acidified Potassium Iodoplatinate Reagent: Dissolve 0.25 g of platinic chloride and 5 g of potassium iodide in water to 100 mL. For the acidified version, 2 mL of concentrated hydrochloric acid is added.

For screening of opioids viz. morphine, codeine, thebaine, paperverine, and narcotine, TLC is used.

In TLC for separation of morphine, codeine, thebaine, paperverine and narcotine, keeping standard in

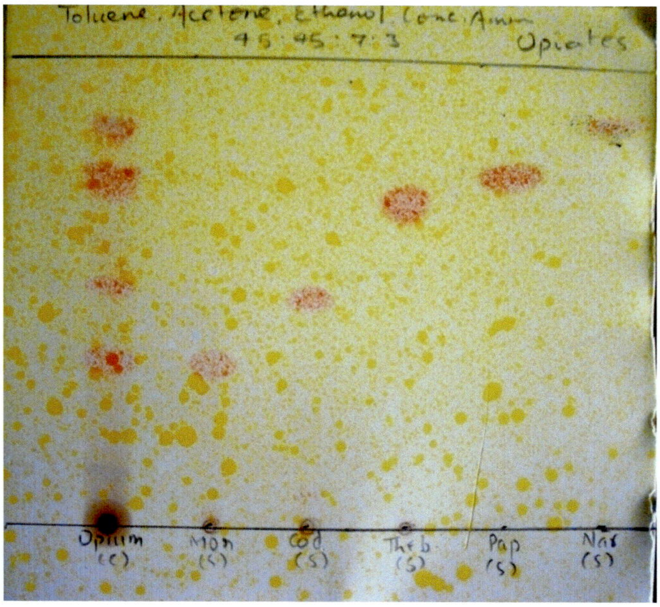

FIGURE 10.1 TLC plate showing the separation of different analytes (using Toluene: Acetone: Ethanol: Conc. Ammonia) (45:45:7:3, v/v/v/v).

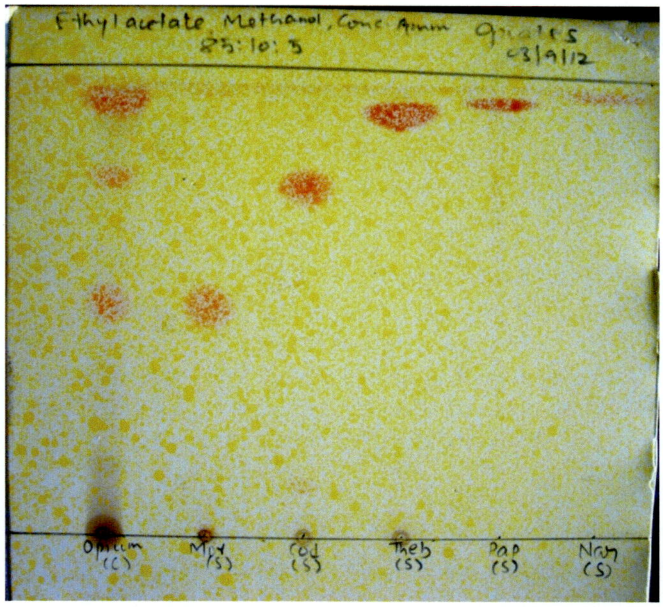

FIGURE 10.2 TLC plate showing the separation of different analytes (using Ethyl acetate: Methanol: Conc. Ammonia) (85:10:5, v/v/v).

first row and samples in second to sixth rows, the plate was run using solvent system Toluene: Acetone: Ethanol: Conc. Ammonia in 45:45:7:3, v/v/v/v ratio, which is shown in Figure 10.1.

The developed plate was sprayed with Dragendorff's reagent spray. Appearance of yellow/orange/red-orange/brown-orange spots indicated the presence of opiates, namely morphine, codeine, thebaine, paperverine, and narcotine.

In TLC for separation of morphine, codeine, thebaine, paperverine, and narcotine, keeping standard in first row and samples in second to sixth rows, plate was run using solvent system Ethyl acetate: Methanol: Conc. Ammonia in 85:10:5, v/v/v ratio, which is shown in Figure 10.2.

The developed plate was sprayed with Dragendorff's reagent spray. Appearance of yellow/orange/red-orange/brown-orange spots indicated the presence of opiates, namely morphine, codeine, thebaine, paperverine, and narcotine.

In TLC for separation of morphine, codeine, thebaine, paperverine, and narcotine, keeping standard in first row and samples in second to sixth rows, plate was run using solvent system Ethanol: Benzene: Amm. Hydroxide: Dioxane in 5:50:5:40, v/v/v/v ratio, which is shown in Figure 10.3.

The developed plate was sprayed with Dragendorff's reagent spray. Appearance of yellow/orange/red-orange/brown-orange spots indicates the presence of opiates, namely morphine, codeine, thebaine, paperverine, and narcotine.

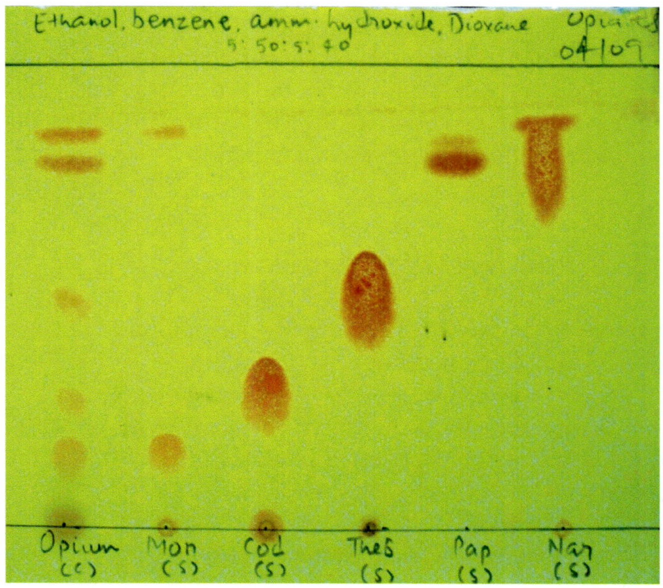

FIGURE 10.3 TLC plate showing the separation of different analytes (using Ethanol: Benzene: Amm. Hydroxide: Dioxane) (5:50:5:40, v/v/v/v).

10.4 TEST FOR DIACETYL MORPHINE/HEROIN/SMACK/BROWN SUGAR

10.4.1 Presumptive Tests (Color Tests)

Positive results of these tests are only a presumptive indication for the presence of heroin. It is mandatory for the analyst to confirm such results by use of an alternate technique.

10.4.1.1 Marquis Test

Take a small amount of suspected sample on a spotting plate and add a few drops of Marquis reagent. The appearance of a purple-violet color indicates the presence of heroin.

Preparation of Marquis Reagent: 8–10 drops of 40% formaldehyde solution is added to 10 mL of conc. sulfuric acid.

10.4.1.2 Mecke's Test

Take a small amount of suspected sample on a spotting plate and add a few drops of reagent. The appearance of a deep green color indicates the presence of heroin.

Preparation of Mecke's Reagent: 0.25 g of selenious acid is dissolved in 25 mL of conc. sulfuric acid.

10.4.1.3 Frohde Test

Take a small amount of suspected sample on a spotting plate and add a few drops of reagent. The appearance of purple, becoming a gray-purple color, indicates the presence of heroin.

Preparation of Frohde's Reagent: 50 mg of molybdic acid or sodium molybdate is dissolved in 10 mL of hot conc. sulfuric acid. The resulting solution should be colorless.

10.4.1.4 Nitric Acid Test

Take a small amount of suspected sample on a spotting plate and add a few drops of conc. nitric acid. The appearance of a yellow color, which turns to green on standing, indicates the presence of heroin.

10.4.2 Thin-Layer Chromatography

Sample Preparation: Take appropriate amount of suspected sample in methanol.

Stationary Phase: Activated silica gel (with or without fluorescing substance) TLC plates of 0.25/0.20 mm thickness.

Mobile Phase/Solvent Systems

System A: Ethyl acetate, Methanol, and Conc. Ammonia (85:10:5)
System B: Chloroform and Methanol (90:10)
System C: Diethyl ether (water saturated), Acetone, and Diethylamine (85:8:7)

Other Solvent Systems

System 1: Ammonia, Benzene, Dioxane, and Ethanol (5:50:40:5)
System 2: Acetic acid, Ethanol, and Water (30:60:10)
System 3: Chloroform, Dioxane, Ethyl acetate, and Ammonia (25:60:10:5)
System 4: Ethyl alcohol, Chloroform, Dioxane, Petroleum ether (30°–60°), Benzene, Ammonia, and Ethyl acetate (5:10:50:15:10:5:5)
System 5: Ethyl acetate, Benzene, and Ammonia (60:35:5)
System 6: Ethyl acetate, *n*-Butyl ether, and Ammonia (60:35:5)

Visualization Methods

1. UV light at 254 nm
2. Dragendorff's reagent spray
3. Acidified potassium iodoplatinate reagent spray

Preparation of Dragendorff's Reagent: Mix together 2 g of bismuth subnitrate, 25 mL of glacial acetic acid, and 100 mL of water to produce solution: (1) dissolve 40 g of potassium iodide in 100 mL of water to produce solution; (2) mix 10 mL of solution (1), 10 mL of solution (2), 20 mL of glacial acetic acid, and 100 mL of water.

Preparation of Acidified Potassium Iodoplatinate Reagent: Dissolve 0.25 g of platinic chloride and 5 g of potassium iodide in water to 100 mL, and add 2 mL of concentrated hydrochloric acid to make it acidic.

10.5 TEST FOR CANNABIS

10.5.1 Microscope Examination

The following microscopic features (trichomes) broken or as such are found on the surface of the fruiting and flowering tops of cannabis, which are the characteristic features of cannabis product.

1. Nonglandular hair (trichomes), numerous, unicellular, rigid, curved, with a slender-pointed apex, and an enlarged base, usually containing a cystolithic hair but frequently broken and the cystolith freed (especially in cannabis resin)
2. The glandular trichomes occur in three forms:
   a. Sessile glands with one-celled stalk (generally on the lower epidermis)
   b. Long multicellular stalk form (generally on the bracteoles surrounding the female flowers). The head in both forms is globular, consisting of 8 to 16 cells. It is frequently detached (especially in cannabis resin)
   c. Small glandular trichome, with one-celled stalk (for the diagram/figures, please see "Recommended Methods for Testing CANNABIS, U.S., New York 1987")

10.5.2 Color Tests

Positive results of color tests are only the presumptive indication of the possible presence of cannabis products. It is necessary for the analyst to confirm the presence of cannabis product by the use of an alternative technique.

10.5.2.1 Fast Blue B Salt Test

10.5.2.1.1 Filter Paper Method

Fold two filter papers to form fluted funnels. Keep these paper funnels on each other. Place a small amount of suspected sample into the corner of the upper funnel of the paper and add 2 drops of solution 1. Allow the liquid to penetrate to the lower filter paper funnel. Discard the upper filter paper and dry the lower filter paper. Now add a very small amount of the solid Fast Blue B reagent to this lower paper and add 2 drops of solution 2. A purple-red-colored stain on the filter paper indicates the presence of cannabis product.

Reagents

- *Solid reagent*: Dilute and mix Fast Blue B Salt with anhydrous sodium sulfate in the ratio of 1:100.
  - **Solution 1**: Petroleum ether
  - **Solution 2**: A 10% w/w aqueous solution of sodium bicarbonate

10.5.2.1.2 Test Tube Method

Take a small amount of suspected material in a test tube; add to it a very small amount of the solid reagent and 1 mL of solution 1. Shake well for 1 minute and add 1 mL of solution 2. Shake the test tube for 2 minutes, and allow this test tube to stand for 2 minutes. A purple-red color in the lower layer of chloroform indicates the presence of cannabis product.

Reagents

- *Solid reagent*: Dilute and mix Fast Blue B Salt with anhydrous sodium sulphate in the ratio of 2.5:100.
  - **Solution 1**: Chloroform
  - **Solution 2**: 0.1 N aqueous sodium hydroxide solution

10.5.2.1.3 Duquenois-Levine Test

Take a small amount of suspected material in a test tube and shake with 2 mL reagent for 1 minute, add 2 mL of conc. HCl and shake it well. Allow it to stand for 10 minutes and then add 2 mL of chloroform. The appearance of violet color in chloroform layer (lower layer) indicates the presence of cannabis.

Reagent: 5 drops of acetaldehyde and 0.4 g of vanillin are dissolved in 20 mL of 95% ethanol.

10.5.2.2 Alternate Test

Extract the sample with petroleum ether. Filter and evaporate to dryness. Add 2 mL of Duquenois reagent to dissolve the residue. Add 2 mL conc. HCl. Shake and keep for 10 minutes. Transfer the solution into a test tube add 2 mL of chloroform and shake. Purple color in the chloroform layer indicates the presence of tetrahydrocannabinols.

Reagent: 5 drops of acetaldehyde and 0.4 g of vanillin are dissolved in 20 mL of 95% ethanol.

10.5.2.3 Test for Differentiation between Bhang, Ganja, and Charas

Extract the suspected material of cannabis in ethanol. Take a drop of extract in a cavity of a spot tile or in a micro tube, add 2 drops of chromogenic reagent 1 and mix thoroughly, followed by the addition of 2 drops of reagent 2.

Bhang gives a green color, ganja a blue color, while charas gives a violet color.

Reagent 1: p-Aminophenol (1 mg) in ethanol (10 mL)

Reagent 2: Caustic potash (1 g) in distilled water (10 mL)

10.5.2.4 Thin-Layer Chromatography

1. **Stationary Phase**: Activated silica gel (with or without fluorescing substance) TLC plates of 0.25/0.20 mm thickness.

   Mobile Phase/Solvent Systems:
   System A: Petroleum ether and Diethyl ether (80:20)
   System B: Cyclohexane, Di-isopropyl ether and Di-ethylamine (52:40:8)
   System C: *n*-Hexane, Dioxane, and Methanol (70:20:10)
   Visualization: Fast Blue B Salt
2. **Stationery Phase:** Silica gel G, TLC plate modified with 10% solution of silver nitrate by dipping or spraying and dried.
   System D: Toluene, using nonsaturated condition (development in open chamber)
   Silica gel G, TLC plate modified with 10% solution of diethylamine by dipping or spraying immediately before use
   System E: Xylene, hexane, and diethylamine (25:10:1)

10.6 TEST FOR COCAINE

10.6.1 Color Test

Positive results of color tests are only the presumptive indication for the presence of cocaine. It is necessary for the analyst to confirm the presence of cocaine by an alternative technique.

10.6.1.1 Scott's Test

Step 1: Take an appropriate amount of suspected material in a test tube, add 5 drops of solution 1 and shake well. A blue color develops at once if cocaine is present. If blue color has not appeared, add more test sample. If blue color is still not developing, then it indicates that the sample does not contain cocaine.

Step 2: Add 1 drop of solution 2, and shake. The blue color will disappear and a clear pink-colored solution will appear. If the blue color does not disappear, add a second drop of solution 2.

Step 3: Add several drops of solution 3 and shake. The appearance of a blue color in the chloroform layer indicates the presence of cocaine.

Reagents

Solution 1: 2% Cobalt thiocyanate in water, diluted with 96% glycerin in 1:1
Solution 2: Conc. hydrochloric acid
Solution 3: Chloroform

10.6.1.2 Ethyl Benzoate Test

Take appropriate amount of suspected sample and moisten it with nitric acid. Evaporate to dryness. Add a few drops of alcoholic potash. Odor of ethyl benzoate indicates the presence of cocaine.

10.6.2 Thin-Layer Chromatography

Developing Solvent Systems

System A [1]: Chloroform, Dioxane, Ethyl acetate, Ammonia (29%) (25:60:10:5)
System B [1]: Methanol, Ammonia (29%) (100:1.5)
System C [1]: Cyclohexane, Toluene, Diethylamine (75:15:10)
System D [2]: Ethyl acetate, Benzene, Ammonium hydroxide (60:35:5)
System E [2]: Chloroform, Ethyl acetate, Ammonium hydroxide (40:10:10 drops)

Visualization Methods

1. UV light 254
2. Acidified potassium iodoplatinate reagent
3. Dragendorff's reagent

Preparation of Solution for TLC

An appropriate sample of exhibits and standard are dissolved in methanol.

10.7 TEST FOR BENZODIAZEPINE

10.7.1 Thin-Layer Chromatography

Stationary Phase: Activated silica gel (with or without fluorescing substance) TLC plates of 0.25/0.20 mm thickness.

Solvent/Mobile/Developing System

Solvent System A: Chloroform and Acetone 80:20
Solvent System B: Chloroform and Methanol 90:10
Solvent System C: Cyclohexane, Toluene, and Diethylamine 75:15:10

Sample Preparation: The solutions of exhibit powder/tablet/capsules and standard may be prepared in methanol.

Visualization

The plates must be dried prior to visualization at 120°C for 5 minutes in an oven or by using a hot-air blower to remove all traces of diethylamine from the plate.

Visualization Methods

1. UV light at 254 nm
2. 2 N Sulfuric acid/heat/UV light at 366 nm
3. Acidified potassium iodoplatinate reagent

Preparation of Acidified Potassium Iodoplatinate Reagent: Dissolve 0.25 g of platonic chloride and 5 g of potassium iodide in sufficient water to produce 100 mL. This is potassium iodoplatinate reagent; for the acidified version, add 5 mL of concentrated hydrochloride acid to 100 mL of iodoplatinate solution.

Method: First observe the plate under UV light at 254 nm. Spray the plate with 2 N sulfuric acid and heat it in a oven at 80°C for 5 minutes. Observe the fluorescent spot on plate under UV light at 366 nm. Spray the plate with acidified iodoplatinate reagent. Appearance of purple color indicates the presence of benzodiazepines.

For screening of benzodiazepam drugs *viz.* alprazolam, chlorazepam, diazepam, lorazepam, and nitrazepam, TLC is used.

In TLC, for separation of alprazolam, chlorazepam, diazepam, lorazepam and nitrazepam, keeping standard in first row and sample in second row, plate was run using solvent system Ethyl Acetate, Methanol: Conc. Ammonia in 85:10:5, v/v/v ratio, which is shown in Figure 10.4.

The developed plate was first observed under UV light at 254 nm. The developed plate was sprayed with acidified iodoplatinate reagent. Appearance of purple color indicated the presence of benzodiazepines, namely alprazolam, chlorazepam, diazepam, lorazepam, and nitrazepam.

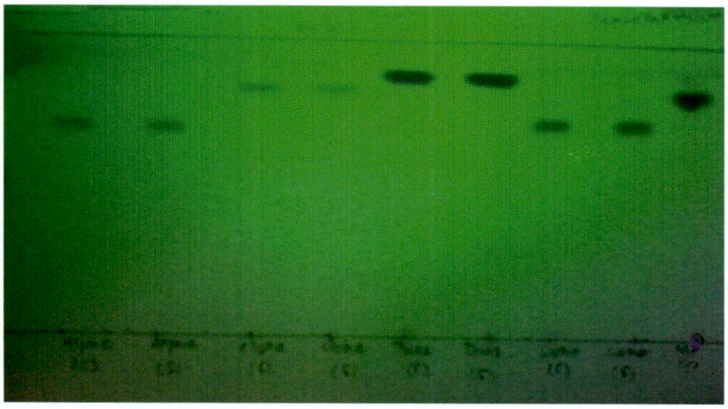

FIGURE 10.4 TLC plate showing the separation of different analytes (using Ethyl Acetate, Methanol: Conc. Ammonia) (85:10:5, v/v/v).

10.8 ANALYSIS OF ALCOHOL IN LIQUORS/DRINKS

10.8.1 Introduction

Liquor is normally known as a mixture of water and alcohol. The term "alcohol" is often used for ethyl alcohol. Country-made liquor is an alcoholic product, usually prepared from fermentation of carbohydrates present in cereals, jaggery, fruits, mahua, palm, molasses, and so on. The liquors are sold on the market in various brands and covered under the Excise Act. The possession, sale, and transportation of liquor is allowed only as per the Rules and Regulations of Excise and Prohibition. Many times, these liquors are smuggled from one state to another state, illegally possessed, and transported without proper valid documents. These samples are seized by the police and submitted to the forensic laboratory for their examination. The liquor is examined in the laboratory for two purposes: first, for excise purposes, where mainly the presence of alcohol plays an important role and accordingly the examination of liquor samples for the qualitative and quantitative analysis is the main purpose of the investigation. Second, the liquor is examined for quality control/duplicate samples, which are being sold in the market in which the examination is carried out for parameters other than alcohol contents. The alcohol contents are also reported in percentage of proof spirit, percentage of alcohol (weight by volume), and percentage of alcohol (volume by volume).

10.8.1.1 Qualitative Analysis of Liquor

10.8.1.1.1 Test for Ethyl Alcohol

The following tests are to be carried out for the detection of ethyl alcohol in the exhibits.

1. **Iodoform Test**: Take about 1 mL or appropriate of sample (distilled or as such depending upon the nature of sample and concentration of ethanol) and add about 1 mL of 5% sodium hydroxide solution and then add iodine solution (20 g potassium iodide + 10 g iodine in 100 mL water) drop-wise with shaking until the liquid becomes persistent dark brown in color. Keep it for 2–3 minutes. If the iodine color disappears, add more drops of iodine solution until the liquid is the persistent brown color of iodine. Add a few drops of dilute sodium hydroxide solution to remove extra iodine. Add an equal volume of water; keep it for 10 minutes. Yellow crystalline precipitate indicates the presence of ethanol.
2. **Dichromate Test:** To about 1 mL or appropriate amount of sample (distilled or as such, depending upon the nature of samples and concentration of ethanol) is added about 0.2 mL of 2% potassium dichromate solution, followed by about 1 mL of conc. sulfuric acid. The yellow color of the dichromate changing to green or blue indicates the presence of ethanol.

10.8.1.1.2 Test for Methanol

1. **Chromotropic Acid Test:** Take about 1 mL or appropriate amount of sample (distilled or as such, depending upon the nature of sample and concentration of methanol) in a test tube; add about 2 mL of potassium permanganate solution (3 g potassium permanganate and 15 mL of phosphoric/orthophosphoric acid in 100 mL distilled water) and shake well. Now add a few crystals of sodium bisulfate and shake till the disappearance of color (potassium permanganate color) of the solution. Add about 1 mL of chromotropic acid (5% of aqueous solution of sodium salt of chromotropic acid) and add conc. sulfuric acid slowly with the inner sidewall of the test tube to the extent of 15 mL. Appearance of violet color indicates the presence of methanol.
2. **Schiff's Reagent Test:** Take about 4.5 mL of sample (distilled or as such, depending upon the nature of sample) in a test tube and add 0.5 mL of ethanol (if the concentration of ethanol is high in the sample, the sample is fortified accordingly so that 5 mL volume should contain only 0.5 mL ethanol. Add 2 mL of 3% potassium permanganate solution and 2 mL of phosphoric acid. Keep it for 10 minutes. Add 1 mL of 10% oxalic acid followed by 1 mL of concentrated sulfuric acid. The contents are cold at room temperature. Now add 5 mL of Schiff's reagent, keep it for half an hour, and observe the color. The appearance of purple color indicates the presence of methanol. The parallel experiments may also be carried out with the control sample, containing

0.5 mL solution (0.5% methanol in rectified spirit/ethanol) mixed with 4.5 mL of water, and a blank sample having 5 mL water. The color that appeared in the test sample may be matched with the color of the control/standard sample of methanol which is equivalent to 2 mg of methanol. Thus the semiquantitative examination of methanol may be carried out.

10.9 CONTROLLED SUBSTANCES

10.9.1 Scope and Application

The following methods are used to identify controlled substances. Controlled substances are commonly found both in liquid and solid samples, varying in size from a few milligrams to multi-kilogram submissions, while the concentration can vary from a few parts per million to almost 100% purity. Because of the great diversity of controlled substances as well as variations in size and concentration, we have established performance-based methods (guidelines) and not rigid step-by-step instructions for the analysis of controlled substances. These procedures allow the individual scientist the flexibility to choose the best methods with which to analyze controlled substance submissions. A subdiscipline included in this manual is methamphetamine quantitation. Since these subdisciplines require additional training and proficiency testing above what is required for controlled substances analysis, only qualified analysts who have been trained in these areas will be able to perform subdisciplines.

10.9.2 Analytical Reference Standard

An analytical reference standard is a dilution or extraction standard that is created to allow for the analysis of the standard by a particular instrument or method (e.g., dilution of cocaine with methanol for GC/MS analysis). This standard can be produced using either a primary or a secondary standard (positive control).

10.9.3 Database

A listed compound found in the schedule of controlled substances.

10.9.4 Control Sample

A comparison standard for verifying or checking the findings of an experiment. A positive control contains the analyte of choice for the method or test being evaluated. A positive control is used to evaluate a positive result. A negative control does not contain the analyte of choice and is used to verify a negative result.

DAILY For procedures covered by this document, "daily" refers to testing conducted within 72 hours.

10.9.5 Method Blank

A method bank is a analytical control consisting of all reagents and solvents that is carried through the entire analytical procedure. The method blank is used to define the level of laboratory background contamination.

10.9.6 Standard—Primary

A primary standard is a commercially purchased compound that is traceable back to a manufacturer. Its identity is confirmed by verifying its composition by comparing FTIR or GC/MS results with literature or a previously confirmed primary standard. If a certificate of analysis is accompanied with the standard, then that also can be used as a verification source. The resulting documentation of this comparison will be maintained in the Standard Verification Logbook.

10.9.7 Standard—Secondary

A secondary standard is a laboratory-produced sample or casework sample that has been compared to a primary standard. A secondary standard must be compared to a primary standard by utilizing GC/MS, GC/FTIR, or FTIR. The resulting documentation of this comparison will be maintained in the Standard Verification Logbook.

10.9.8 Modification

A change—an alteration or amendment that introduces new elements into the details, or cancels some of them, but leaves the general purpose and effect of the subject-matter intact.

10.9.9 Instrument Blank

A volume of clean solvent that is analyzed on an instrument to ensure that the instrument is working properly and/or there are no contamination issues associated with the instrument.

10.9.10 Solvent

A liquid substance that is used to dissolve or dilute another substance.

10.10 SAFETY

Refer to the Forensic Services Division Safety Manual and the appropriate Material Safety Data Sheets (MSDS) for general safety tips and hazard information regarding the use of reagents and solvents, the handling of gas cylinders and overall safety guidelines.

Everyone should be aware that the majority of the chemicals used in the chemistry section have one or more hazardous properties.

Many exhibits of evidence contain potential hazards (razor blades, syringes, and broken glass) and/or are potentially infected with biological hazards. It is important to take the appropriate precautions to reduce the risk of injury to oneself and to others who may handle the evidence in the future.

10.11 SAMPLING PLAN

10.11.1 Scope

The principal purpose of sampling is to answer a relevant question about the population by examining a portion of the population. Therefore, a sampling plan needs to be used only when multiple items are grouped together as one exhibit. If you are analyzing only a single item, then a sampling plan is not needed. Two types of sampling plans can be incorporated to help make this determination: statistical and non-statistical. The sampling strategy will guide the analyst to the proper plan to use. Both plans set a minimum number to be analyzed, which can always be exceeded. In cases where a relevant question about the population is not needed, the analyst could itemize the population in a way that no more than one entity is tested. When an agency combines multiple items with residue into one exhibit, the analyst may choose to examine only one item, either by itemizing it separately or by making the report clearly reflect what has been examined.

In most controlled substance cases, a non-statistical approach may suffice. This type of sampling plan must provide an adequate basis for answering the question applicable to the law (e.g., Is there a controlled substance present in the population?).

A statistical-based approach will be applied to cases with multiple visually consistent items (except marijuana and commercially prepared pills, capsules and tablets) that meet or exceed a weight enhancement. Statistically selected units must be analyzed and must have both presumptive and confirmatory-level testing. The statistical approach will return a sample size (n) needed to test from a known population (N) that will give us a predetermined level of confidence that a significant portion of the population is the same. The hypergeometric sampling plan allows us to state with 95% confidence that at least 90% of the total population is the same.

For the non-statistical method (square root method), the number returned is the number of items that need a presumptive test. A confirmatory test will then have to be done on at least one of the items.

For the statistical method (Hypergeometric Plan), the number returned is the number of items that need both a presumptive test and a confirmatory test.

When the sampling strategy dictates a sampling plan and it is not executed, it should be documented in your notes or in a conversation log as to why you did not use a sampling plan.

10.12 MINIMUM EXAMINATION REQUIREMENTS

10.12.1 Physical Examination

After removing the sample from its packaging (if appropriate), a thorough physical characterization of an exhibit should be conducted, and the following observations should be noted, if applicable: type of material, color, size, shape, amount, morphology, significant markings, odor, and texture.

Every attempt should be made to preserve evidence. No more than half the available sample should be used in most cases, and the physical combination of evidence items will not be permitted.

If it becomes necessary to use the entire sample, the extracted sample remaining after the analysis may be sealed and returned with the evidence. If no sample can be maintained after analysis, then the analyst shall record this in the note packet with a statement such as "evidence consumed in analysis."

In some cases, representative sampling may be desirable on evidence that is visually consistent.

At some point during the physical examination of the item, a weight must be determined (except when dealing with residue amounts). Gross weight measurements are made by weighing the entire item (packaging and contents). Net weight measurements are determined by weighing only the contents of an item. Gross weight measurements are acceptable for samples that are below the state and federal sentencing guidelines. Net weight measurements should be used when the sample has the potential to exceed these sentencing enhancements. Items that contain a small amount of material that clings to the packaging can be considered residue and reported as such. The balance should be cleaned and tared prior to weighing a sample.

TABLE 10.2 Categories of Analytical Techniques

Category A	Category B	Category C
FTIR	Gas chromatography	Color test
GC/FTIR	HPLC	UV
GC/MS	Microcrystalline test	X-ray
Cannabis only: Macroscopic examination Microscopic		Pharmaceutical identifiers

10.13 CATEGORIZING ANALYTICAL TECHNIQUES

Techniques for the analysis of drug samples can be broken down into three categories, based on their discriminating power. Table 10.2 lists examples of such techniques in order of decreasing discriminating power from A to C.

BIBLIOGRAPHY

Anthony CM, David Osselton M, and Brian W (Eds). *Clarke's Analysis of Drugs and Poisons*, 3rd edition (2004). London: British Pharmacopoeia.

Butler William P. (1967) *Methods of Analysis for Alkaloids, Opiates, Marihuana, Barbiturates & Miscellaneous Drugs*. Washington, DC: Department of Justice, p. 59.

Clarke EGC (1986) *Isolation and Identification of Drugs*, 2nd edition. London.

ENFSI (European Network of Forensic Science Institutes) (2003) Guidelines on Representative Drug Sampling. *Version 1-1*.

Frank RS, Hinkley SW, and Hoffman CG (Mar 1991) Representative sampling of drug seizured in multiple containers. *Journal of Forensic Scientist*, Vol 36, No. 2:350–57.

Garratt DC. *Quantitative Analysis of Drugs*, 3rd edition (1964). New York, NY: Springer, pp. 476–501.

Georgia Bureau of Investigation (Dec 27, 2004) Chemistry Operations Manual—Sampling. *Revision 10*.

Huestis M, Mitchell J, and Cone E (Oct 1996) Urinary excretion profiles of 11-nor-9-carboxy-delta-9-tetrahydrocannabinol in humans after single smoked doses of marijuana. *Journal of Analytical Toxicology*, Vol 20:441–52.

Huestis M, et al. (2007) Cannabinoid concentrations in hair from documented cannabis users. *Forensic Sci Int.* 2007; *Vol 169(2–3): 129–136.*

Klemenc S (2000) Noscapine as an adulterant in illicit heroin samples. *Forensic Science International*, Vol 108:45–9.

Anderson et al. *Recommended Methods for Testing Opium/Crude Morphine: Manual for Use by National Narcotics Laboratories* (1987) New York, NY: United Nations.

CHAPTER 11

Clinical Forensic Medicine

Child Sexual Abuse

Dalia M. Al-Saif and Lori D. Frasier

CONTENTS

11.1 INTRODUCTION

Child sexual abuse (CSA) is defined as "the involvement of dependent, developmentally immature children and adolescents in sexual activities that they do not fully comprehend, to which they are unable to give informed consent or that violate the social taboos of family roles" (Finkelhor, 1994; Pereda et al., 2009a,b; Stoltenborgh et al., 2011). It involves pedophilia, rape, and all forms of incest.

It is one of the most important international public health problems that affects all societies, regardless of cultural, religious, or economic background. The international combined prevalence is 11.8%, and it is highest for girls in Australia and boys in Africa, and lowest for both in Asia and Europe (Stoltenborgh et al., 2011; Pereda et al., 2009). Variations in prevalence among countries and continents could be attributed to different ethnicities with their different cultural beliefs and values that affect the rate of disclosure and reporting (Kenny and McEachern, 2000). The predominant victims are girls—between 10% and 20% of their peer population—while male victims constitute less than 10%, with a male to female ratio of 1:2.5–3.

CSA has long-term consequences of physical health symptoms, including those regarding general health, GI, gynecologic pain, cardiopulmonary symptoms, and obesity. Those with a history of CSA were found to be 1.35–2.12 times more likely to have health problems. CSA is also associated with psychological disturbances that might appear later in life. Anxiety disorders, eating disorders, depression, posttraumatic stress disorders, sleep disorders, and suicidal attempts were all significantly correlated with a history of CSA.

Concerns about CSA can arise after an alarming sexualized behavior or statement from the child. It might surface subsequent to a custody or parental visitation argument. The child should be presented to the medical care provider, who can provide medical evaluation of the child to evaluate the child's health and, in acute cases, assess for injuries, collect evidence, and test for short-term consequences of sexual abuse like sexually transmitted infections and pregnancy. Sometimes the main role of the expert is to provide a virginity check, as virginity is of considerable importance in certain cultures.

Assessment of an alleged case of child sexual abuse consists of a well-structured forensic interview, medical history, medical examination, and a proper interpretation of findings. The role of an expert is to correlate the provided history of incident with physical findings to attain a reliable diagnosis of the condition.

11.2 FORENSIC INTERVIEW

Sexual victimization of children is usually surrounded with secrecy and mostly lacks corroborative evidence like physical signs, medical findings, or non-victim witnesses; hence, most of the time, children are the only source of information. Children from the age of 4 years can be considered as informative witnesses. The quality of information obtained from them is dependent on the techniques used by the interviewer and the response of the child to these techniques. Several approaches to collecting data from children were researched and best-practice guidelines were structured to ensure good quality of these data. Different child forensic interview protocols organized these guidelines with the aim of increasing adherence to them. These protocols are used to interview children regarding allegations of different types of abuse and even for child witnesses of violence.

The following discussion examines factors that affect collection of information from children and research-proven best techniques of eliciting such information.

11.2.1 Memory of the Child and Techniques to Elicit Information

A child's disclosure of a sexual abuse is delayed most of the time due to several factors, including those related to the child, the perpetrator, and the interaction between them. This delay affects the child's memory and the reactions of the child in the forensic interview. Some understanding of memory is needed for better practice of forensic interview guidelines.

11.2.2 Script versus Episodic Memory

Specific details of any incident, like time and place, are vital for that incident to be legally supported. In the case of child victimization, these details are highly dependent on the child's memory.

Child sexual abuse is often a repeated event over a long period of time. Children and even adults tend to incorporate repeated incidents into a general scheme that is known as script memory (Goodman et al., 2002). Retrieving an instance of a repeated event activates all similar instances, leading to overlapping and confusion. Children might disclose good-quality, forensically vital details but fail to specify time and place of occurrence, which divests these details of any legal importance. Also, rare but crucial information could be masked by the repeated other details and not even mentioned by the child. For example, the child could be asked to specify the place of the incident, and he/she might choose to mention the most common one but fail to tell about a rare but important one where physical evidence could be allocated. This can result in contradictions in the child's account, which can mislead the investigators and affect the credibility of the child.

Interviewers are recommended to shift the child's recollections from script memory to episodic memory by asking the child to give details of a single incident. The child is asked whether this type of incident occurred many times or only one time. If there were many times, the child is then asked to talk about the first incident, the last one, or the most remembered one. The child is requested to give all that he/she knows about this single event.

A technique that is suggested in repeated abuse is to ask the child about specific information in the incident in the context of all incidents (e.g., "Did he hit you at any time?"). Children are more receptive to suggestions by adults if asked about a particular incident than if asked in general.

11.2.3 Recall versus Recognition Memory

Research has shown that more details could be obtained from children by tapping recall memory, where the child freely narrates what happened without any influence from the interviewer. This is best conducted with invitation prompts using open-ended questions (e.g., "Tell me all that happened, from the beginning till the end"). Data obtained after this type of prompt are more legally important, as they come from the child freely without being introduced by someone else. These prompts yield more central and accurate details of the alleged assault, especially in older children, and it has been found to be effective in delayed interviews. Young children present difficulties responding to such questions; however, research has shown that they could still give many forensically important details without the need for more focused questions.

Invitations could be cued by data already mentioned by the child to get more details (e.g., "Tell me all about the touch" if the touch was already mentioned by the child in the general invitation). Cued invitations were found to be more useful with older children (Lamb et al., 2007).

Direct inquiries using the WH questions (what, where, who, and how) can bring about specific details of place, persons, acts, and so on. Specifying a time using the When question is a difficult task for children, especially in a repeated event and with a delayed interview. This can be replaced by one of the other WH questions by anchoring the detail in question to a well-recognized event like a school vacation or a birthday party (e.g., "What grade of school were you in at that time?"). Asking about the number of incidents ("How many times?") is also a difficult job, and the child can be asked a general question of whether it was one time or many times.

Invitations that provoke free-recall memory and end up with a free narrative could be confusing and lead to mixing up several acts within an event. Time segmentation is suggested, where the narrative is segmented into parts and details of each section are obtained separately (e.g., "Tell me everything that happened since he entered the room till he went out of the room").

Prompts tapping recognition memory include option-posing prompts (e.g., "Did he touch you over or under your clothes?" or "Did she slap you?"). The child is offered choices to search his or her memory for the true one without allowing the child to freely give information. This type of questioning is risky, owing to the children's suggestibility (especially young age groups of 6 years or less) if introduced early in the interview and if repeated. Offering choices to children gives them the opportunity to pick any of the choices, which affects the reliability of information, as the choice could be the easiest rather than the true one. This suggestibility of children increases with long delays before the forensic interview. It can allow for contradictory information, which is encountered less in free-recall narrative.

Option-posing prompts should be delayed till all invitation prompts are exhausted, and if used, should be paired with an invitation (e.g., when the child chooses one answer, it is followed by, "Tell me all about it").

Suggestive prompts ("He was lying over you, wasn't he?") are even more risky and should be discouraged and limited to situations where the information is important for the safety of the child or it was proven by another corroborative evidence but the child denies it.

A multipart prompt where the interviewer includes two or more demands in a single question is commonly used by forensic interviewers, even trained ones. An example: "Did he touch your private parts or hurt your body?" Children rarely ask for clarifications of such questions. They would rather choose to answer with few words, which affects the amount of details that are central to the allegation. These prompts should be discarded from any forensic interview with children.

Facilitators (e.g., *Aha, OK,* repeating what the child says in a neutral way) were shown to encourage the continuation of the narrative provided spontaneously by the child.

11.2.4 Source-Monitoring Errors

When a child is asked about an event, there might be mixing of real incidents with other sources of information, which could be TV shows, stories, or witnessed events.

Previous interviews with the child, whether by the police, social workers, schoolteachers, or even a curious caregiver, can introduce information that later might mix up with reality. Psychological therapy, although of benefit, can introduce fabrication following memory-recovery practices that therapists use. Source-monitoring errors are exacerbated after using suggestive prompts and with repeated exposure to information introduced by others.

Such testimony could appear as an implausible, fantastic description of the event, raising suspicions regarding its reality. However, the interviewer should be nonjudgmental and broad minded as these details might have true explanations that carry a real forensic importance.

The interviewer needs to differentiate between these sources by directly asking the child whether what has been said did truly happen to him/her. This inquiry should be used cautiously, as it might give the child the feeling that he not believable, which could discourage further disclosure. This direct questioning is not applicable to young children at 3 years of age or younger. Children can be asked about their feelings and what they heard, smelled or saw during the incident, as these cannot be fabricated if not truly experienced by the child. Children who participated in an event rather than witnessing it are more able to give accurate details and their suggestibility is lowered.

At the same time, interviewers need to open their minds to other explanations for what is mentioned by a child. An example is touching private parts, which could be an innocent touch during toilet training. The child might give implausible information that seems to be fantastic and imaginary; getting more details could reveal the truthfulness of these data. Inconsistencies in a child's account could be solved by asking more details and showing the child that the interviewer is confused and needs further explanation.

11.2.5 Child Responses in the Forensic Interview

Children behave emotionally different during the forensic interview, and the higher the number of abuse allegations, the less the child is upset during the interview. A research study showed that most children showed neutral expressions and very few cried during disclosure. Crying was found to be more associated with sexual abuse than with other types of abuse.

Reluctance and denial are recognized responses during a child's forensic interview. Children use different methods to redirect the interviewer into neutral subjects that are not related to the abuse by providing answers unrelated to the question. Some children say that they don't want to talk about it. These responses are explained by shame, embarrassment, assuming responsibility, and committing to the perpetrator's request for secrecy, especially if the perpetrator is emotionally connected with the child. Older children are more likely to disclose events, and their disclosures were found to be more accurate. However, this is balanced by their socio-emotional development and knowledge of consequences of disclosure that stand ahead of disclosure. Interviewers are faced with difficulties with such children, and they try to overcome this reluctance by shifting to more suggestive option-posing questions and fewer supportive utterances.

In fact, these children need more support, and an extended rapport-building phase is needed to overcome this reluctance. Empathetic comments (like "I wonder if it makes you nervous to be questioned by a stranger") help overcome anxiety, in contrast to attempts to minimize the child's feelings (like, "Don't be embarrassed to say this").

Confrontation and forced extraction of information doesn't help with a reluctant child. Sometimes, ending the interview would be the best choice, where another session could reveal more data.

A child's reluctance could be attributed to cultural issues and thus training, experience and cultural sensitivity of the interviewer could enhance rapport-building with the child and make him or her more comfortable with people different from themselves, which results in increased disclosure.

11.2.6 Interview Settings

The forensic interview should be conducted in a place that maximizes the child's concentration and enhances disclosure. Reduction of distracting objects is recommended. The presence of accompanying caregivers should be discouraged. The caregiver could be the suspect, and disclosure is more free in the absence of the perprator. Children 6 years or younger might suffer separation anxiety in unfamiliar situations. The caregiver needs to encourage the child to be alone, and the child might need to know where the caregiver is so the child can periodically check. With insisting children, the caregiver could stay in the interview room but sit behind the child so the caregiver's expressed emotions wouldn't be seen by the child.

The use of anatomical aids like anatomically detailed dolls and diagrams is a controversial issue. It has the advantage of clarification and consistency of what the child says, distancing the child from showing his own body parts, and communicating with a shy child. However, they have the disadvantage of distracting the child, upsetting the child and caregiver by the private parts of the doll. Also young children don't understand the doll presentation of themselves or another person. These aids have been found to increase the number of true reports, but at the same time there is an increase in false reports. They are suggestive methods where the interviewer is introducing the private parts of the doll or the drawing and asking the child if anybody touched them. These methods carry the same risk of suggestive questions and could challenge a criminal case. For those interviewers who find them of help, it is recommended to use them as demonstration aids, late in the interview, and only after exhausting all other ways of extracting data from the child.

Electronic recording of the forensic interview, whether audio or video, is a vital tool in any forensic interview setting. It has been found to be more accurate than a verbatim transcript that can miss many of the forensically important central details of the incident. They are widely used and recommended in many forensic interview settings.

11.2.7 Forensic Interviewing Protocols

Research-proven best practice guidelines of the forensic interview are organized into different protocols. RATAC (Rapport, Anatomy, Touch, Abuse, Closure) and NICHD (The National Institute of Child Health and Human Development) are among the well-known protocols and are followed by many forensic interviewers and accepted in many jurisdictions.

11.2.8 NICHD Protocol

The NICHD is the most researched forensic interviewing protocol where the behavior of the interviewers was reviewed to test for its applicability. It was found to be applicable across countries. It is of value in interviewing children with low verbal abilities and was modified to be appropriate in obtaining forensic information from child witnesses of violence.

The interviewer gender has its effect on the interaction with the child during the forensic interview; however, this effect diminished following the NICHD protocol guidelines. This protocol increases the use of open-ended questions and elicits more details from the alleged victims. The NICHD protocol helped produce children's statements that were of higher quality. Also it has been found to increase the accuracy in judging the credibility of the child, which enhances the delivery of justice.

This section will discuss the stages of the forensic interview based on best-practice guidelines that are followed in the NICHD protocol.

Before starting the interview, it is recommended to inquire about the child's background to assess development and linguistic abilities and to know more about the surrounding environment for better understanding of the situation.

11.2.9 NICHD Phases of the Forensic Interview

1. *Introduction*: The interview starts with introducing the interviewer and the place of the interview to the child. The role of the interviewer should be explained, allowing any further inquiry from the child. The child should be aware of any video or audio recording and any witnesses, whether inside or outside the room.

   The child is then given some rules to be followed through the interview. He/she is instructed to tell only true things that really happened to him/her, not to guess, to correct any mistake said by the interviewer, and to indicate any lack of understanding so the interviewer can rephrase the question in a simple way. These rules have been found to decrease confusion and suggestibility.
2. *Rapport-building*: This is an icebreaker phase where children are asked to talk about themselves (e.g., "I want to know you better, tell me things you like to do"). This can relieve anxiety and encourage more talk in the following stages.
3. *Training in episodic memory*: The child is then asked to narrate a neutral event that is not related to the alleged abuse. This narrative event practice increases the rapport and helps assess the child's verbal and cognitive abilities. The developmental age of the child affects memory, suggestibility, language, and emotional maturity; each of these plays a role in the child's response to questions from adults. The interviewer should use age-appropriate questions for better and less suggestible responses by children.

   The interviewer should choose a neutral event to talk about, like a birthday party or a recent event that the child remembers well. It is better to be close in time and similar to but not the same time and setting in which the alleged assault took place. The interviewer should use a neutral voice tone and facial expressions, as less neutral expressions might lead to biases during the interview. Expressing emotions during the training phase and shifting to blunt emotions in the allegation phase could discourage the child narrative.

Techniques tapping the child's recall memory are used, starting with general invitations followed by gradual use of the more focused cued invitations and time segmentation.

The response of the child during this stage predicts the amount of detail that might be given in the substantive (allegation) phase. Children who have been trained in the use of open-ended questions in this stage respond with 2.5 times more information in the subsequent phases of the interview. This emphasizes how sensitive the child is to the interviewer's expectations. If the child didn't respond well in this stage, it is better to stop the interview, as hasty introduction of the allegation phase would lead to more reluctance.

4. *Transition to substantive issues*: After the narrative event practice, the child is smoothly moved into getting the allegation narrative. The interviewer asks the child to tell the reason of his presence with the interviewer. A reluctant child could gradually be asked more specific questions but only after exhausting general invitations (e.g., "Now that I know you better, tell me why are you here today"; "Your mother is concerned that something might have happened to you, tell me about it"; "Did anybody hurt you? Tell me more about it"; "I have heard that your uncle bothered you, tell me about it").
5. *Investigating the incident*: If the child responded well following the general invitations, the interviewer then asks the child to provide more information (e.g., "Tell me more about that"). Children might respond with silence, say they don't know or shift the topic back into a neutral one. The interviewer needs to draw the child back without forced extraction of information. Questions should start as general, and gradually focused questions are used, like a zooming camera, while maintaining the general picture of the whole incident. Examples of these focusing questions are follow-up inquiries (e.g., "Then what happened?"), cued invitations (e.g., "You mentioned earlier that he punched you on face, tell me all about this"), temporal cues (time segmentation, for example, "You said that he took off his clothes; tell me all that happened just after he took off his clothes"), and direct questions (e.g., "Where did that occur?").
6. *Break*: During the break the interviewer can review and document the obtained information, looking for missing data.
7. *Eliciting information that you expected but not mentioned by the child*: Information already known by the interviewer could be used in the option-posing style as a final resource if no data was obtained using the open-ended prompts. These risky questions should be paired with general invitations (e.g., "Did he touch you under your clothes? Tell me all about it").
8. *Close the interview by thanking the child* for providing information and asking if there is anything more the child wants to add or to ask the interviewer about.
9. *Neutral topic*: At the end of the interview, the child is shifted into a neutral topic. The interviewer spends a couple of minutes drawing the child away from the allegation by talking about something unrelated, like what the child is planning to do after leaving.

11.2.10 Extended Forensic Interview

Disclosure is a process rather than an event, and an extended forensic interview is offered where children are given the opportunity to release additional information at more than one session.

This process is advised with children who are reluctant, frightened, or too young to give details. More than one forensic interview decreases the risk of suggestibility and allows for a better understanding of the child's language and the observation of how the child interacts with caregivers and family members. Concern about memory contamination by several interviews is overcome by ensuring adherence to guidelines where free recalls are encouraged rather that suggestive prompts given. Benefits of extended evaluations for resolving suspicious abuse cases outweigh the risks.

It should be acknowledged that different professionals can conduct the forensic interview and that no single forensic interview is perfect; even well-experienced forensic interviewers are faced with difficult interviews. They need to apply their experience and background knowledge to overcome the difficulties and to end up with a legally sound forensic interview. An interview should use the best methods of extracting information that don't negatively affect the emotions of the interviewed child. Following best-practice guidelines in a well-structured protocol together with regular peer reviews is recommended to reach this goal.

11.3 MEDICAL HISTORY

Physicians who are evaluating suspected cases of child sexual abuse need to elicit some information from children with the main goal of maintaining their health and protection. Taking the medical history could help the examiners refer the child to other medical services or to initiate specific treatments. Physicians should be familiar with the principles of the forensic interview to avoid contaminating the child's memory and to end up with legally accepted information that can be used later in the court in conjunction with the forensic interview.

Information should be collected from previous interviews from legal authorities or social services. Parents or caretakers are interviewed separately. Detailed background family and social history should be obtained. This clarifies the living situation and those who spend time with and take care of the child. Custodial issues should be made clear. It is important to inquire about the behaviors of the child and any changes that can be traced and correlated with the timing of abuse. Examples are sleeping and eating patterns, behavioral changes, developmental regression, and sexualized behavior or sexually spoken words.

A history of past medical or surgical history as well as any previous accidental falls, anogenital surgery or procedures should be obtained, as they could explain later findings during the medical examination. Specific signs such as genital discharge or itching should be probed to determine the possibility that the child contracted a sexually transmitted infection.

The child should be talked to separately, as the presence of parents could influence the emotion of the child and hence affect the disclosure. This could be difficult with young children, but parents should be encouraged to leave the child at this stage. A clear reliable history could be obtained even from very young children who have the verbal ability to narrate an incident, and hence age shouldn't be used as a barrier from obtaining a history from the child. The medical history provides an opportunity for the examiner to build trust with the child and to relieve the anxiety that is experienced by some children. The child needs to be informed about the role of the examiner and the special part of the examination involving private parts of the body that are not examined in routine pediatric assessment.

Specific questions including the exact details of the incident are important for predicting the presence of findings in the examination. For example, anal or rectal bruising or tears were significantly more prevalent in children who provided a history of anal penetration.

The timing of the incident (or of the last one, if many incidents were disclosed) is also important for predicting the presence of injuries, interpreting healed findings, and for deciding on collecting forensic evidence. Questions should include specifics of the incident that may lead to the possibility of finding evidence of the assailant's body fluids. There should be an inquiry about whether there was pain or bleeding during the incident and whether there are presenting symptoms of painful urination or bowel movement. The presence of bleeding at the time of assault and the timing of examination after the assault are predictors of abnormal anogenital examination. Time between the assault and the examination is inversely related to the number and severity of the detected injuries. Examination within 72 hours detected more injuries than delayed examinations. Bruises, in contrast, can be more apparent with time. Adolescents should be asked about menstruation, tampon use, previous speculum examination, depression, eating disorders, or any other mental health problems.

The child should be prepared for the medical examination by the examiner explaining every step and assuring the child that the examination is noninvasive and painless. The child is given the opportunity to ask any question during all stages of the medical evaluation. The physician should ask for an explanation of any observed physical finding during the examination.

The child and parents should understand that at the end of the medical evaluation, no one can tell if the child has been abused or that the findings were consistent with the provided history. It is also important to explain that a normal examination does not rule out abuse. The decision about the amount of information to be told to the child depends on the child's age and ability to understand the given information.

The medical history is not recorded in the same manner as the forensic interview and hence, physicians are highly encouraged to maintain good documentation of the obtained history with all detailed behaviors of the child during the interview and interactions with caretakers. These documents could be released during legal proceedings and would be the only source of information of what the child disclosed in the clinic.

11.4 MEDICAL EXAMINATION

There is a universal agreement among experts that a reliable history provided by the child following a well-structured forensic interview represents the most important element in the evaluation of suspected child sexual abuse. However, in many situations such history is unobtainable, either because the child is nonverbal or avoids telling what happened for several reasons. Some of those reasons are discussed in the preceding section regarding the forensic interview. Such cases emphasize the importance of other corroborative evidence such as findings in the body of the child. The detection of physical findings that are consistent with the provided history will further strengthen the case. It should be emphasized, however, that absence of positive physical findings should not be used as a proof of lack of sexual assault, as the findings following examination of sexual assault cases most of the time are normal.

A body of research has been conducted to reach a consensus on the findings that could be used as an evidence of trauma following sexual assault. Different study designs and samples have led to variable findings; some of them were constant among studies, which allowed for interpretation.

Medical examiners who are involved in cases of alleged child sexual abuse should have a good knowledge of the normal anatomy and development of the anal and genital areas. These are not part of the routine pediatric assessment; hence, many physicians are not familiar with them. Examination of the anogenital area is particularly important for medical examiners, as it is the target for sexual assault.

11.4.1 Anatomy and Variations of Female External Genitalia

Female external genitalia consists of the **mons pubis**, which is a hair-bearing (in adolescence) rounded eminence of skin with an underlying pad of fat that overlies the pubic bone.

Labia majora (single: *labium majus*) extend downward and backward from the mons as two longitudinal skin folds enclosing fat together with superficial and deep fascia. The skin of the outer side is hair-bearing while the inner is smooth and non-hair-bearing. The labia meet anteriorly at the anterior commissure and posteriorly become parallel to each other, fusing with other skin to form the posterior labial commissure (Figure 11.1).

Inner to the labia majora are two smaller non-hair-bearing skin folds that are devoid of fat, the **labia minora** (single: labium minus). Each of them split anteriorly and joins with the other one to enclose the clitoris (erectile tissue). They extend obliquely downward, laterally, and backward to meet posteriorly with a fold of skin stretching between them, the **posterior fourchette**. There is a great diversity in the size and symmetry of labia minora. **Labial adhesions** (agglutination) are partial or complete fusion of the labia minora that could obscure the view of inner vulvar structures (Figure 11.2a).

Labia adhesion was thought to result from trauma in sexual abuse; however, its frequent presence in children screened for non-abuse has led to consideration of its innocent nature. It results from skin irritation that could be related to infection or friction. It is mostly seen in fair-skinned girls, owing to their thin skin that is more vulnerable to irritation. This adhesion usually breaks down spontaneously with age as estrogen levels increase, and that's the basis of its treatment with the application of a small amount of estrogen

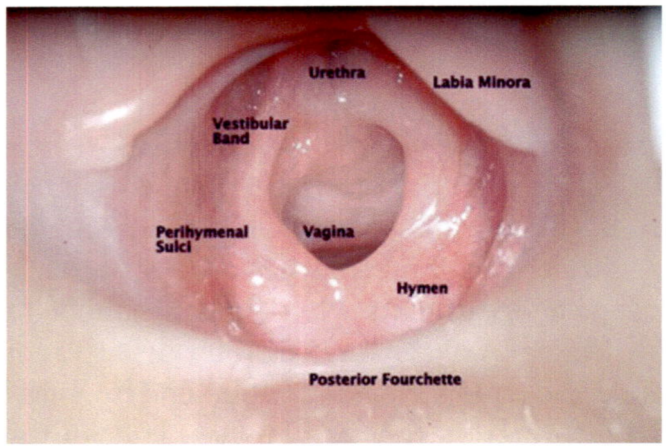

FIGURE 11.1 An example of prepubertal genital anatomy with major figures labeled.

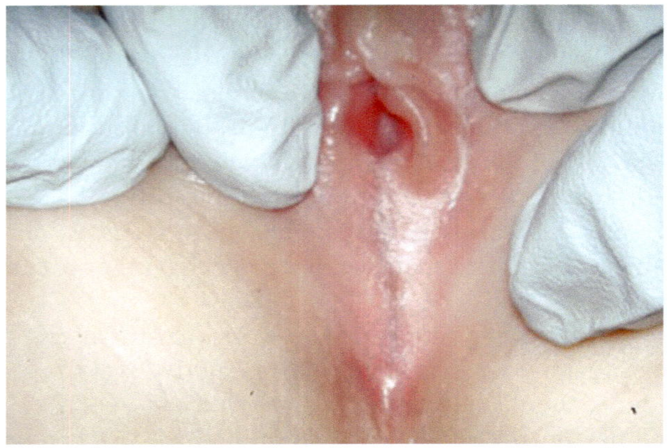

(a)

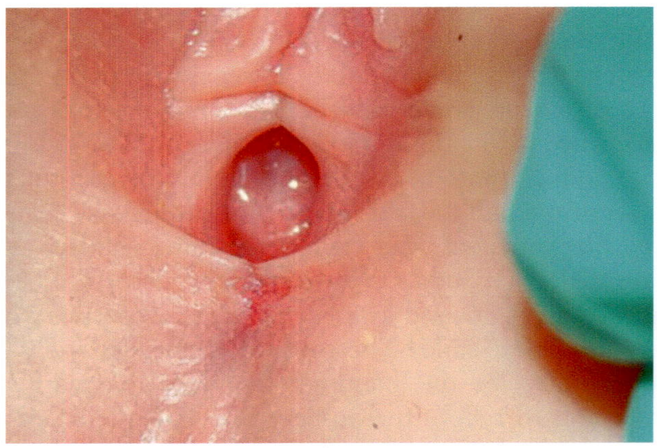

(b)

FIGURE 11.2 (a) Labial adhesion. Note how the inner vulvar structures are obscured by the adhesion. (b) Friability of the posterior fourchette likely represents dehiscence of the labial adhesion.

The posterior fourchette could present with several conditions that can be confused with the trauma of sexual abuse. These include *friability of the fourchette* that

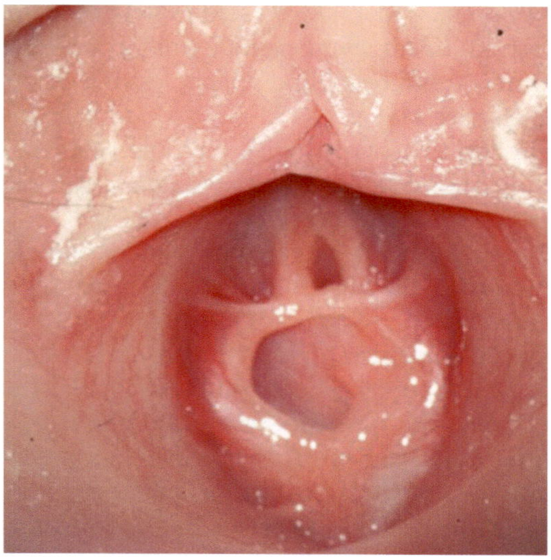

FIGURE 11.3 Periurethral bands.

dehisces easily with traction on labia majora. It should not be confused with trauma, and the posterior fourchette needs to be assessed prior to any manipulation of vulva. A **midline avascular area** in the posterior fourchette is a congenital finding that might be mistaken for a scar. Together with the friable fourchette, these areas were observed in cases with minor posterior adhesions of labia minora and thought to be a result of dehiscence of these adhesions (Figure 11.2b).

The **midline raphe** is a midline area of raised tissue that results from fusion of the two halves of the perineum and could extend from the posterior fourchette along the perineum to the anal opening.

The cleft between the labia minora is the **vestibule**. It contains the **external urethral opening** as a short sagittal cleft with slightly raised margins anteriorly and the **vaginal introitus** that covers the **hymen** posteriorly. Ducts of **greater vestibular glands** (Bartholin's glands) open lateral to the hymen. The concave boat-like area between the vestibule, just between the vaginal introitus and the stretched posterior fourchette, is the **fossa navicularis**.

Erythema of the vestibule is a normal finding resulting from congestion of capillaries. While *increased vascularity* results from dilatation of other vessels, both are observed in normal children.

Vestibular (or *periurethral*) **bands** are extensions of tissue that connect the vestibule with its structures like the urethra or hymen. **Periurethral** bands are very common and found in children of all ages. Some these bands might have a semilunar shape, giving the view of pockets on both sides of the urethra. Bands could be multiple and bilateral and could also be found posterior to urethra as *perihymenal* bands (Figure 11.3).

These bands, although common in newborns, are more frequently observed in older age groups. This is attributed to the redundant tissues at the neonatal period that resolve with age, giving a better view of the vestibule (Berenson 1993). Bands in the posterior vestibule give the view of an irregular fossa navicularis.

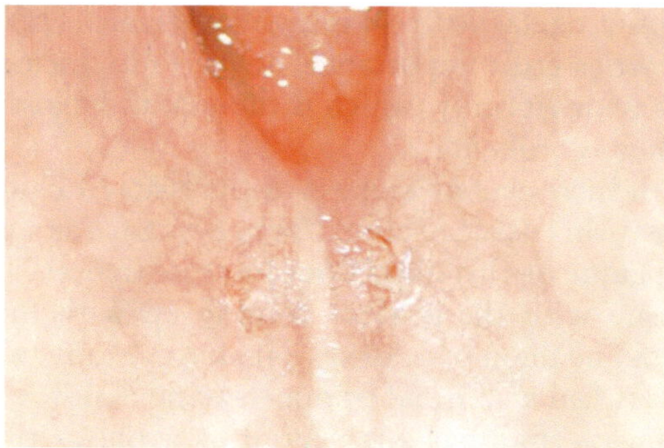

FIGURE 11.4 Linea vestibularis.

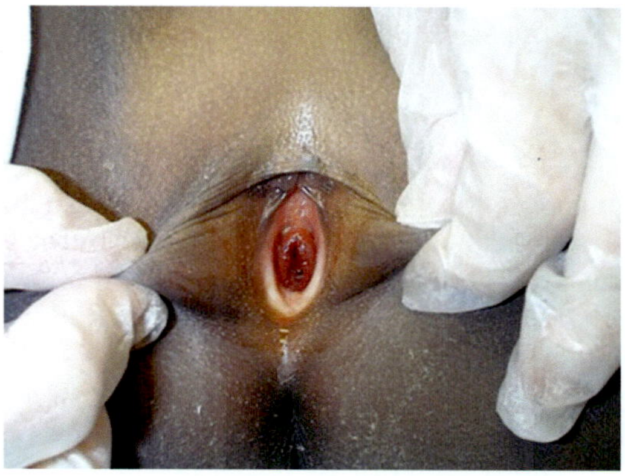

FIGURE 11.5 Urethral prolapse.

The *linea vestibularis* is a congenital white line or spot on the posterior vestibule. It is a congenital finding that could persist or become more prominent with age (Figure 11.4).

A **patulous** or **dilated urethra** is a normal anatomical variation, where the urethral opening looks large. The urethra may spontaneously dilate when traction is applied to the labia majora for visualization of the internal structures. **Urethral prolapse** appears as a red mass anterior in the vestibule and is a non-specific finding that should not be mistaken for trauma (Figure 11.5).

11.4.2 The Hymen

The hymen is a folded mucous membrane of endodermal origin that is attached to the vaginal wall and partially or completely covers the vaginal introitus. Vascular supply is rich near its attachment but scarce close to the edge and the amount of elastic fibers is highly variable. This small tissue carries great importance, owing to its ancient correlation with virginity, which is thought to be lost when the hymen is broken.

With increased awareness of the issue of child sexual abuse, this tissue regained its importance as a potential indicator of this abuse. Several researchers studied this tissue with the goal of coming up with findings that could be diagnostic of sexual abuse. Many findings were classified as normal or non-specific. Knowledge of these normal findings is essential to avoid attributing them to trauma.

When evaluating findings on the hymen, the convention of the clock face is used to locate findings on the hymen, with the 12 o'clock anterior near the urethra and the 6 o'clock posterior toward the anus.

11.4.3 Types and Configurations

The hymen is a constant finding in all newborn girls. Its absence is associated with other anomalies of the genital tract like vaginal agenesis. The most common types of hymen that have been described include the following.

Annular: Hymenal tissue that presents circumferentially (360 degrees) around the introitus. It could be smooth or redundant with folded tissue. The opening could be central, anterior or posterior (Berenson et al., 1991; Mor et al., 1986).

Crescentic: A posterior rim of hymen that is attached anteriorly at 1 o'clock and 11 o'clock with absent tissue below the urethra (Figure 11.6).

Fimbriated: A redundant hymen, which is folded on itself. Some studies use this terminology to describe a fringed hymen with several clefts that give it a ruffled appearance (Figure 11.7).

Septated: A band of tissue that extends from one side of the hymen to the other, either vertically or horizontally, making a septum that divides the hymenal orifice into two openings. This could be associated with a septated vagina, and it is suggested to pass a feeding tube between both openings to exclude this variation. One of the openings could be a blind pouch, leaving a single real opening (Figure 11.8).

Cribriform: A hymen with multiple small openings that result from congenitally incomplete canalization of the vaginal introitus.

Microperforate: A hymen with a small opening. The configuration of the hymen in this case is usually sleeve-like (Figure 11.9).

Carancula hymenalis (myrtiform caruncle): Found in sexually active girls where remnants of the hymen are present in between transections.

Imperforate hymen: Absent opening, a variation that presents a medical problem at puberty with failure of escape of menstrual blood, leading to hematocolpos. This is surgically corrected. It is thought that this type of hymen still has a small undetectable opening that allows the passage of discharge through prepubertal and premenarchal stages, while a real imperforate hymen, a rare finding, would be problematic since early childhood.

Prevalence of hymenal configurations differs between studies with the annular, crescentic, and fimbriate (with its two definitions) representing the majority.

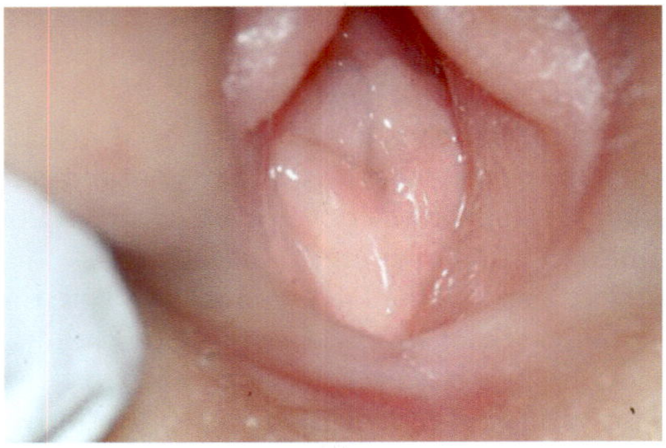

FIGURE 11.7 Fimbriated hymen.

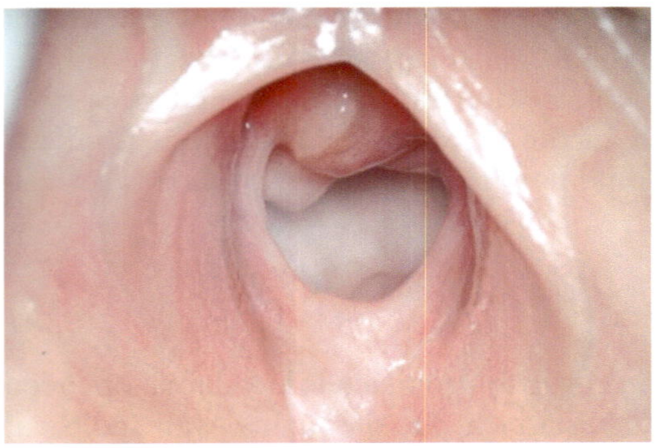

FIGURE 11.6 Crescentic hymen.

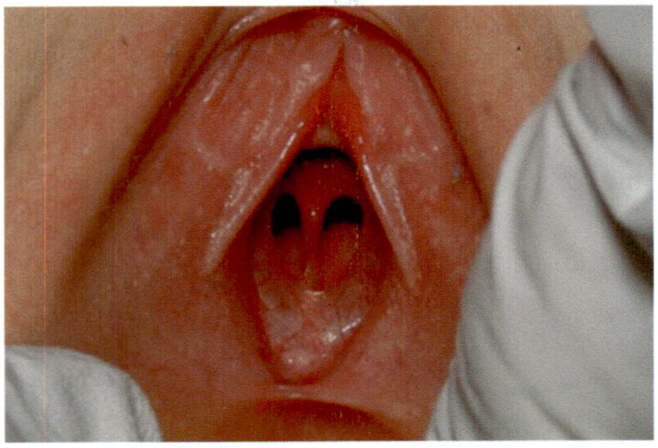

FIGURE 11.8 Septated hymen.

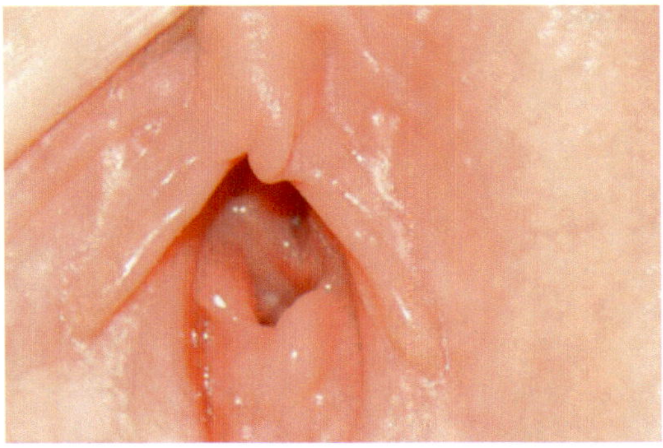

FIGURE 11.9 Microperforate or sleevelike hymen.

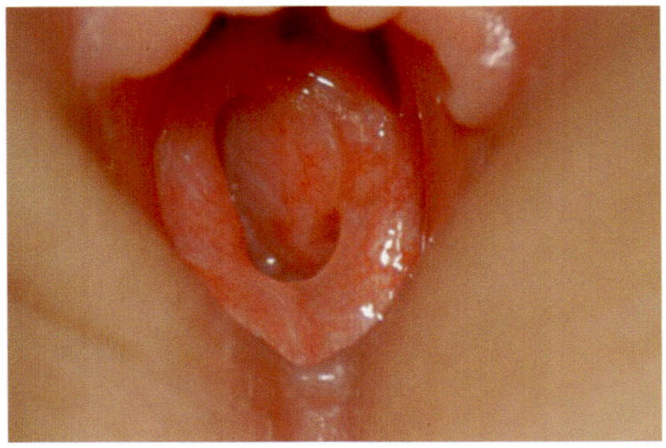

FIGURE 11.10 External hymenal ridge.

11.4.4 Anatomical Variations of the Hymen and Vagina

External hymenal (vestibular) ridges are longitudinal elevations of hymenal tissue that extend from the urethra anteriorly or fossa navicularis posteriorly to the rim of the hymen. They could be present at both sites. These ridges might persist, disappear, or appear for the first time in the follow-up examination of non-abused children (Figure 11.10).

Longitudinal internal vaginal ridges are fibrous-like solid elevations that extend longitudinally in the vaginal walls and are covered with normal vaginal mucosa. They are different from the horizontal rugae of the vagina and can be single or multiple in the anterior, posterior, or lateral vaginal walls. These ridges could end before the hymen or extend to reach the rim of the hymen. Their extension to the hymen might lead to misinterpretation of absent hymenal tissue at this site. Ridges of the vagina are more often seen in older children than in newborns, as the hymen decreases, giving a better view of the vaginal content. An oblique rather than a direct view of the hymen is used to see these ridges.

Ridges in the midline anteriorly and posteriorly are more wide and prominent and called vaginal columns. The anterior midline columns are related to the urethra, as it is present at the same site.

Bumps (mounds) are solid elevations at the rim of the hymen, with the base measuring at least the same as its length. They could be multiple and on any location of the hymenal rim. Bumps could result from the intersection of external ridges or internal longitudinal vaginal ridges with the hymenal rim or present independently. A bump can give a false view of a notch just next to it. The base of this pseudo notch doesn't extend beyond the base of the bump (Figure 11.11).

Tags are flaps of hymenal tissue that extend from the rim of the hymen. Their length is more than their width. They might be multiple and could exist independently or similar to bumps as an extension of external or internal vaginal ridges. They may result from cleavage of a hymenal septum.

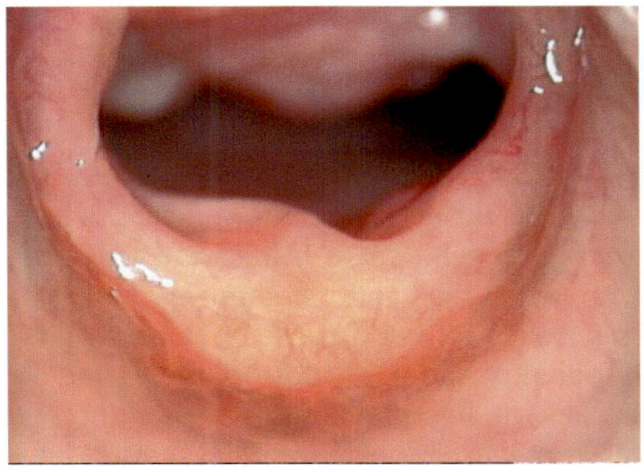

FIGURE 11.11 Bump caused by intersection of the intravaginal ridge with the hymen.

Notches are concave-like irregularities of the hymenal rim. They are classified according to their depth into superficial notches that extend to half or less of the width of the hymen at the site where it is located. Deep notches extend to more than half of the hymenal width. Anterior and lateral notches were found normally in non-abused children, while posterior deep ones were not observed in any of the normative studies. Clefts that extend to the base of the hymen are found normally in the ventral half of the hymen but none were noticed in the posterior half in normative studies.

A **cyst**, which is a fluid-filled elevation, could be found in the rim of the hymen, tip of a tag, or on any side of the vestibule.

Hymenal erythema or the presence of a **prominent vessel** that is more than twice the width of surrounding vessels in an area where it is not normally expected to find such a vessel (Figure 11.12).

The shape and configuration of the hymen together with some of the anatomical variants change dynamically with age, and an understanding of the physiological influence of hormones on the hymen can lead to a better appreciation of these changes.

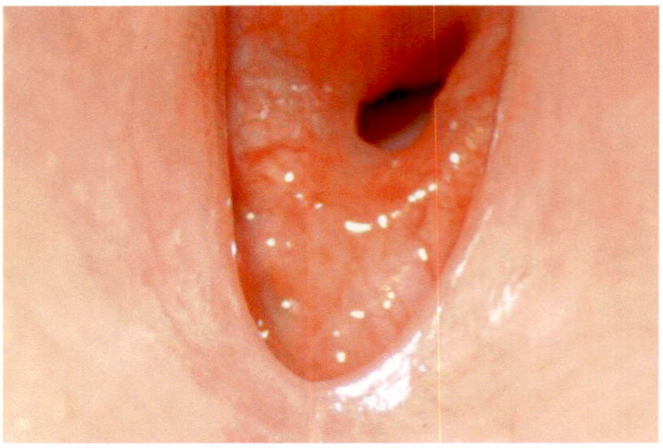

FIGURE 11.12 Prominent vessel on the surface of the hymen, also a normal finding.

11.4.5 Physiological Changes of Female External Genitalia

External genitalia of the female undergo physiological changes in different ages under the influence of hormones, particularly estrogen. Changes in serum estrogen can be explained with the hypothalamus–pituitary–gonadal axis. This axis is activated in the body of the girl during the gestational period. Gonadotropin-releasing hormone (GRH) from the hypothalamus activates the release of follicular-stimulating hormone (FSH) and luteinizing hormone (LH) from the pituitary, which in turn exerts an effect on the ovaries to release estrogen.

In late pregnancy, maternal estrogen increases and applies negative feedback on the axis, leading to the inhibition of endogenous secretion of estrogen.

On delivery, there is a withdrawal of maternal estrogen effect on the axis, leading to reactivation and estrogen secretion from the body of the newborn girl. In the first few days of life, maternal estrogen that is still present in the body together with a surge of endogenous estrogen act upon the internal and external genitalia.

The effect of estrogen on external genitalia is reflected on the hymen that appears pink, pale, and redundant. Abundant hymenal tissue is folded on itself to accommodate the increased amount of tissue. Its edges could fold backward, obscuring the view of the vestibule. High estrogen could have an effect on the uterine lining, leading to spotting of blood that is noticed in the first days of life in some newborn girls (mini menstruation).

High estrogen levels fade up at the age of 2–4 years and result in a decreased amount of hymen tissue. At this stage, the hymen is thin and translucent, with lacy vessels and attenuation of the posterior rim. Folds of the hymen disappear and the tissue smooths out with rolled edges, returning back. Some notches might disappear.

It was observed that annular hymens change configuration into crescentic shape, and this was found mostly in annular hymens that show an anterior notch at 12 o'clock. This was explained with the evolution of hymenal tissue that disappears anteriorly starting with these notches, which are more frequently observed at the anterior and lateral areas in non-abused children. Vertical and horizontal diameters of the hymen were found to increase with age and could be attributed to this decrease in hymenal tissue.

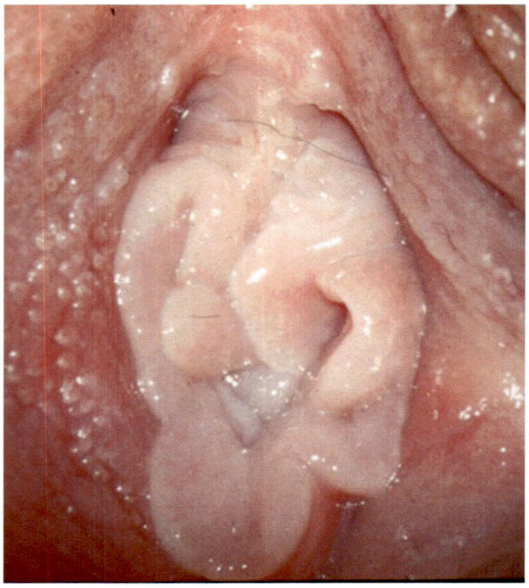

FIGURE 11.13 Estrogenized adolescent hymen.

A similar effect of increased estrogen on genitals is observed again toward puberty. Labia minora are enlarged and become paler. The hymen turns pale, thick, redundant and more elastic. Elasticity was measured in one study with a speculum and found to be an early sign of puberty. It increases with age and is well correlated with later stages of puberty (Figure 11.13).

11.4.6 Anatomy of the Anal Canal and Perianal Area

The anal canal is about 2.5–4 cm in length and extends from the rectal ampulla to end at the anal opening. The upper part is lined with the columnar epithelium, an extension of the rectal epithelial tissue. The mucous membrane of this part folds longitudinally to form the **anal columns**; furrows between the columns are called **anal sinuses**. At the lower end of anal sinuses are semilunar, valve-like horizontal folds of mucous membrane that join together, making the **dentate line**. Just below this line is the anal transitional zone where the columnar epithelium transforms into the squamous epithelium that lines the lower part of the anus. The anal canal is lined with the **internal anal sphincter** that is an extension of the muscular coat of the colon. Superficial to it is the **external anal sphincter** with its deep, superficial and subcutaneous parts. This is responsible for voluntary control over the anal opening and gives the anus its puckered, corrugated look. The area surrounding the anal opening is called the **anal verge**, and it is the area of interest in the examination of sexual assault cases with anal involvement.

11.4.7 Anatomical Variations of the Perianal Area

Erythema is a normal finding in the perianal area, particularly in children who are still in diapers. It can extend up to 3 cm around the anal opening.

Pigmentation is also observed in children screened for non-abuse. Its prevalence is greater in blacks, and it is expected to be a darker color.

Skin tags are protrusions of anal verge tissue, which interrupts the symmetry of the perianal skin folds. It is normally found in the midline anterior and posterior but can be found in any location.

The **smooth area in the anal verge** is where anal folds are absent and are explained with the congenital anomaly of superficial division of the external anal sphincter just underlying this smooth part (Figure 11.14).

Venous congestion is a purplish discoloration surrounding the anal opening that appears after a period of separation of gluteal folds to view the anus. It increases parallel to the time taken in the examination and disappears with release of gluteal folds. It results from pooling of venous blood that fails to return back from the pelvis and shouldn't be confused with real bruises that are traumatic in nature (Figure 11.15).

Intermittent dilatation of the anal sphincter is a normal reflex to the stimulation of the sphincter by separating the gluteal folds. It results from the inhibition of reflex closure of the anus (McCann et al., 1989).

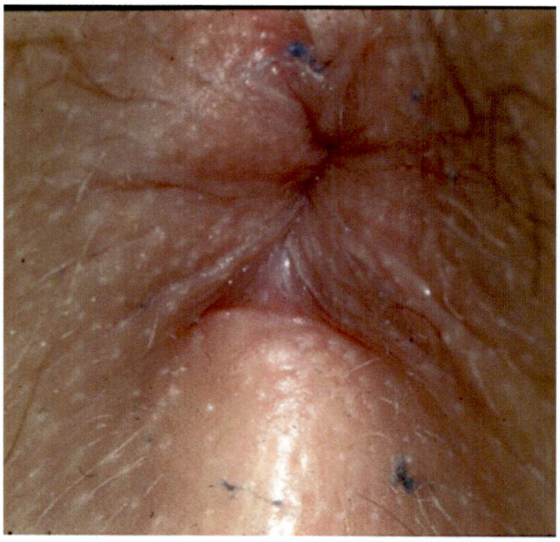

FIGURE 11.14 Smooth area in the anal verge.

A normal variant that could be mistaken for an injury is an **extension of the dentate line** that could be seen upon dilatation of the anal sphincter. A follow-up exam would show persistence of such a finding (Figure 11.16).

Failure of midline fusion can have the appearance of anal laceration. Its persistence in the follow-up examination would reveal its congenital nature (Figure 11.17).

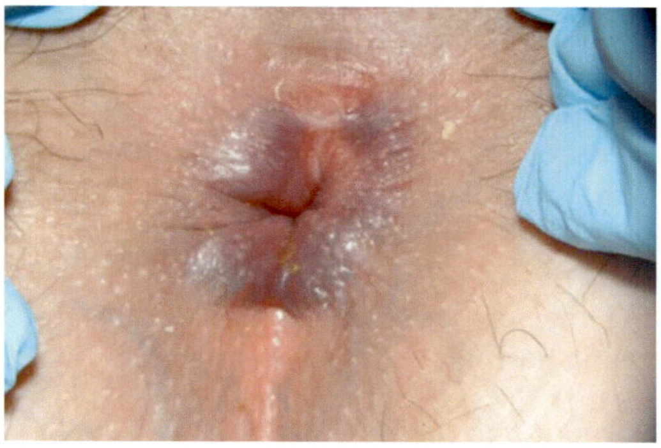

FIGURE 11.15 Perianal venous congestion.

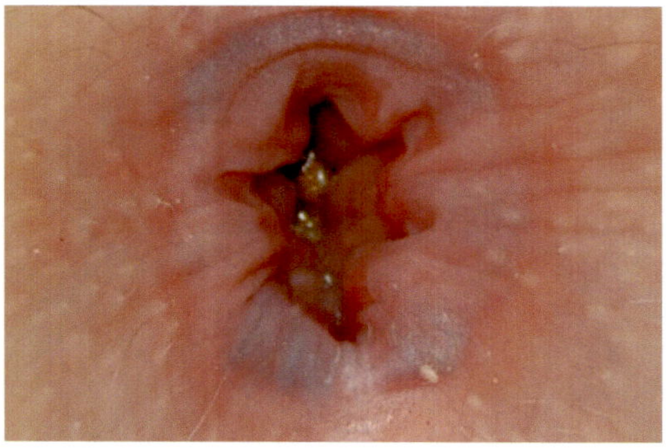

FIGURE 11.16 Extension of the dentate line.

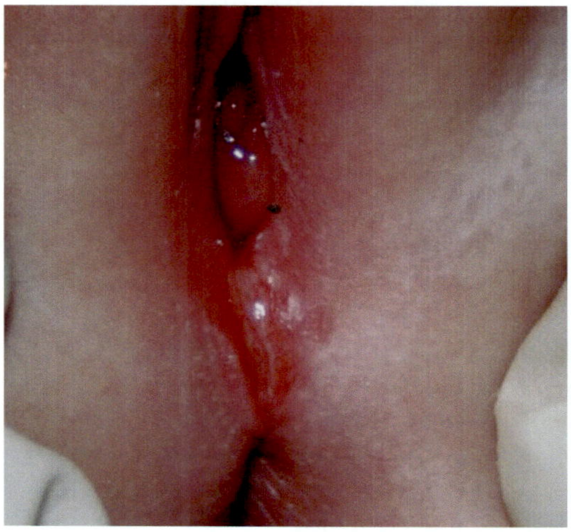

FIGURE 11.17 Failure of midline fusion.

11.4.8 Positions and Techniques of the Anogenital Examination

Several positions and methods were used by examiners with the goal of reaching the best view of the anogenital area. **Supine lithotomy position** is used to better view the mons, labia, and posterior fourchette. It can be modified to **frog leg position** in children of young age groups in which the knees are abducted and the feet are approximated to each other. The child could be examined in the lap of the caregiver.

Gentle **separation of labia** can expose the vestibule; but **labial traction**, where the examiner pulls the labia majora between the index finger and thumb outward and downward, was proven to be superior to labial separation in viewing the vestibule, fossa navicularis, the hymen, and content of the vaginal canal.

Prone knee-chest position is managed with the child in a kneeling position with approximation of the chest to the knees and the side of the face on the bed. The knees are separated in 90 degrees of flexion. The gluteal folds are separated to visualize the introitus. This position is the best to examine the hymen, especially the posterior part, which drops down under the effect of gravity. It smooths the irregularities and only real findings persist, the false notches next to bumps disappear.

Combining the three methods of labial separation, traction, and prone position increases the chance of detecting injuries to the genitalia, especially the hymen. Although not needed in all cases, data collected through the three methods may be necessary in certain cases.

The prone knee-chest position is used also to examine the perianal area. Some children do not tolerate this position, and a supine knee-chest position is another option, where the knees are approximated to the chest while the child is lying supine.

A redundant hymen with edges that are folded backward or collapsed, obscuring the opening, was found to open with **water floatation**. In adolescence, when the hymen is less sensitive, a **Q-tip** or a large swab can be used to evaluate the hymen's rim. This could be covered with balloon latex for contrast.

The use of the **Foley catheter** was also studied and found to be superior in its ability to provide a wider view of the hymenal rim. It is inserted and inflated with air and then pulled against the hymen to show the whole edge. It needs to be manipulated to several directions to demonstrate hymenal edge at the opposite side. A Foley catheter is needed to evaluate the redundant hymen of adolescent girls, as it represents difficulty owing to its folded nature. It is well tolerated by girls at this age group. Injuries to the hymen were detected more frequently with this method.

Toluidine blue is a dye that is used in histological slides. It stains nuclei of cells and needs a broken skin or mucous membrane to expose such nuclei. It is applied after collection of evidence and the excess is removed with gauze that is dampened with warm water. It is useful to demonstrate small breaks in the tissues. Such breaks can be misinterpreted as trauma if there is a breakdown of skin due to infection or irritation. Toluidine blue uptake must be interpreted with caution.

11.4.9 Anogenital Findings and Evidence of Sexual Assault

Although not inevitable, documenting injuries in suspected cases of child sexual abuse represents an important factor in legal proceedings. Such findings, when present, strengthen the case. The diagnosis of anogenital injury requires the presence of either acute findings or an evidence of previous trauma. Acute findings resulting from blunt trauma include hematomas, bruises (ecchymoses), abrasions, and lacerations. Swelling and redness are other acute signs of injury but are subtle and can result from other causes like irritation or infection (Adams et al., 2001). It was found that children who present with genital injuries have more nongenital injuries than those who are free of genital injuries.

Vulvar injuries are mostly presented as ecchymosis, abrasions, or lacerations in the fourchette, fossa navicularis, and/or labia minora. The resistance that these parts present at the entrance of the introitus explains their greater involvement. Injuries are more documented in the less estrogenized tissues, while high estrogen levels increase tissue elasticity and protect tissues (Adams et al., 2001).

Hymenal injuries include lacerations, either partial or complete, reaching the hymenal attachment with the vaginal wall. The are mostly located at the posterior part of the hymen between 5 o'clock and 7 o'clock. Lacerations might present with minor bleeding and pain and acute signs of trauma like redness and swelling are noted at the edges of the laceration (Figures 11.18 and 11.19).

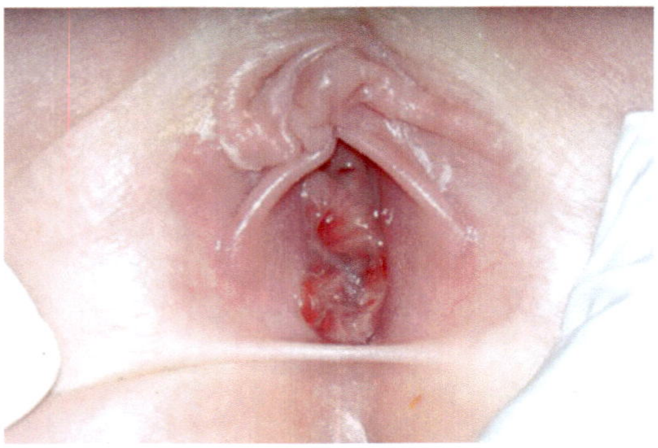

FIGURE 11.18 Acute injury due to sexual assault in a young child. Attempted penetration results in superficial bruising on the hymenal surface. This type of injury will usually heal without any residual findings.

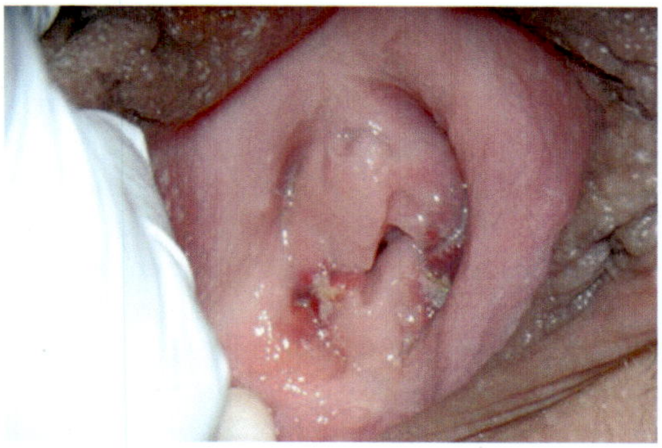

FIGURE 11.19 Lacerations of the hymen from penetrating trauma at 4 o'clock and 8 o'clock in an adolescent.

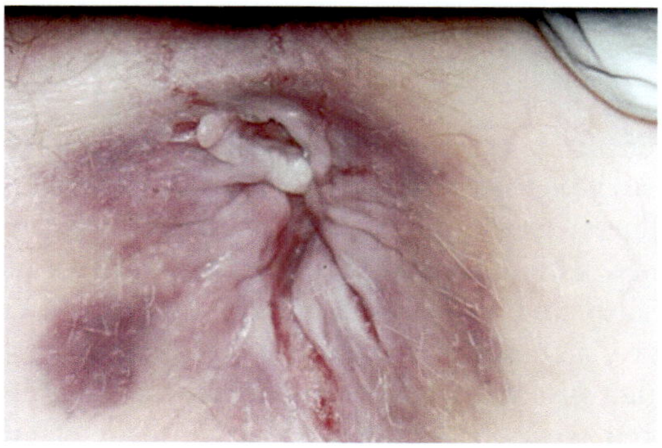

FIGURE 11.20 Perianal lacerations and bruising in a sexually assaulted mentally disabled child.

Violent rape can lead to extensive lacerations that reach the vagina and perineal body and result in an extensive hemorrhage.

A swab or Foley catheter might be used to better locate a laceration in an adolescent that is hidden between the folds of a redundant hymen. If acute, the laceration could bleed again after manipulation, as a preformed blood clot might detach.

Acute perianal injuries that result from forced sexual assault include erythema, swelling, bruises, abrasions, fissures, and lacerations. Although these findings can be used as an evidence of sexual abuse, there are other explanations for their presence. Erythema of the anal verge and thickening of anal folds are examples of the non-specific findings that can be misdiagnosed as being of traumatic nature.

Bruises, abrasions, fissures, and lacerations are of traumatic origin, whether from sexual abuse or not. Accidental injuries like falling astride, impacting bicycle crossbars or playground equipment, and pedestrian accidents can all result in similar injuries as those resulting from sexual abuse.

Anal fissures are superficial linear splits in the skin. They can result from sexual abuse but are also commonly seen in children who complain of constipation and pass hard stools. They can result from diseases like skin gut disease or Crohn's disease.

Lacerations are deeper splits of skin in the perianal area that reach the subcutaneous tissue (Myhre et al., 2013). Their diagnosis is obvious if located outside the midline, while they could be confused with a congenital midline failure of fusion if located in the midline. A follow-up examination is needed to confirm the diagnosis. Myhre found that both fissures and lacerations are significantly associated with anal abuse with penetration (Figure 11.20).

Several factors should be considered before diagnosing anogenital injuries as resulting from CSA. Discussion of some of the aspects is presented in the following sections.

11.4.10 Consensual versus Non-Consensual Sexual Intercourse

The presence of anogenital injuries does not specify the sexual act as being non-consensual. Similar injuries to the hymen, fossa navicularis, and posterior fourchette were documented in girls after consensual sexual intercourse. However, a study showed that the non-consensual group had a higher prevalence and different pattern of anogenital injuries. Lacerations of the posterior fourchette and fossa navicularis, abrasions of the labia, ecchymosis of the vagina and cervix together with the involvement of the perineum and anus were seen more in the non-consensual group. The increased involvement of the fourchette, fossa and labia in this group is explained by their being the most resistant parts at the entry of any attempted penetration. The hymen was found to be more involved in the consensual group. The assaulted group had more nongenital injuries. Tissue responses to consensual and non-consensual intercourse are affected by many factors, and a significant difference was correlated with knowing the offender and with prior reporting of sex within 72 hours.

11.4.11 Previous Sexual Activity

Previous sexual activity has an effect on the presence of anogenital injury, as it was found that self-reported virgins presented with more anogenital injuries following sexual intercourse but with the same pattern as non-virgins. Another study found hymenal tears but not other genital injuries to be found more in self-reported virgins. Also the age at which the first vaginal penetration occurred is crucial to the finding of hymenal trauma. Adams et al., (2001) did not find this correlation between the age and the presence of genital injuries. This could be explained by the adolescent age group that was selected in the study.

11.4.12 Accidental Anogenital Injuries versus Sexual Assault

Children often present to the hospital with anogenital injuries where the caregivers provide a history of an accident. These cases might pose a challenge to the medical examiner, as injuries to such areas are rare and should raise a suspicion of sexual assault. Findings from a sexual assault versus an accident could be very similar. Therefore, a detailed history of the event should be obtained and compared with the findings in order to determine the plausibility of the provided history. Accidents that could lead to genital injuries include falls in general, falls on a bicycle crossbar, and activities around a playground or pool.

Sexual abuse injuries mostly involve the posterior genital structures—the posterior hymen, posterior fourchette, and fossa navicularis—and hence the involvement of these structures is highly suggestive of sexual abuse.

Straddle injuries occur when the child falls astride with a hard object coming between the legs and compressing the soft tissues of the anogenital areas with the bony pelvis. Various objects were documented, with monkey bars being among the most common. This compression could result in hematomas, abrasions, and lacerations that involve the anterior, lateral, or posterior part of the external structures rather than interior vaginal introitus. The labia and pelvic skeleton protect the hymen from these accidental injuries, and hence injuries are seen more in the labia majora and minora, posterior fourchette, and fossa navicularis. It is unusual to involve the hymen or vagina even with higher-force straddle falls, such as from inline skating (Figures 11.21 and 11.22).

Straddle injuries are usually unilateral and rarely involve the perianal area. Anotched posterior fourchette was found in girls reporting a straddle injury. A clear history should be provided to correlate with the findings to reach a plausible explanation of the injuries.

Accidental impalement of the vagina and anus could be part of a straddle fall or occur independently where an object penetrates the vagina or anus. This type of accident is rare, and it can result in injuries to the vagina, hymen, posterior fourchette, or fossa navicularis, with little injury to the labia minora. If penetrating the anus, it causes perianal lacerations, anal tears, and accidental rectal penetration. The posterior distribution of these injuries is similar to injuries resulting from sexual assault and might present a difficulty unless a good explanation is provided for these findings (Figure 11.23).

Injuries considered to be unique to sexual assault with penetration were documented in *motor vehicle accidents*. Pedestrians run over by a vehicle were reported to have bruises, lacerations, and abrasions of the anogenital area similar to those resulting from sexual assault. Four cases were reported with injuries to the posterior fourchette, fossa navicularis, vestibule, labia majora and minora, as well as radiating anal lacerations, hematomas, posterior laceration of the hymen, and vaginal lacerations following a low-velocity motor vehicle passing over their trunks. These findings are identical to those of sexual assault and found to heal in a similar way. There could be associated injuries to the intra-abdominal organs and/or fractures of the limbs. Proposed mechanisms for such injuries are increased intra-abdominal pressure that pushes the genitals outside, resulting in shearing forces that tear the skin. Although other body injuries can explain their presence, a thorough investigation should be done for the possibility of previous sexual assault, as healed clefts of the hymen could be similarly present following assault and accidents.

It must be emphasized that a good protocol-based forensic interview of the child is an invaluable tool to allocate findings to accidental injuries or assault. Details of the history can be correlated with physical findings, and a plausible explanation should be reached before excluding sexual assault as a cause. Also an inquiry about accidental injuries is needed to exclude them as a cause of healed injuries or suspicious non-acute findings.

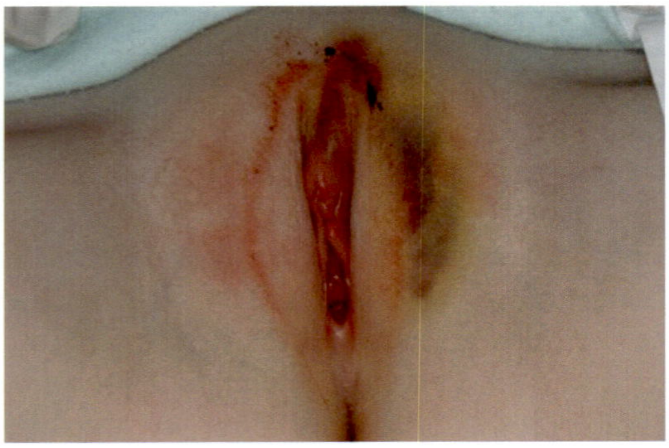

FIGURE 11.21 Labial hematoma in a child that was caused when she fell on a bar at the playground.

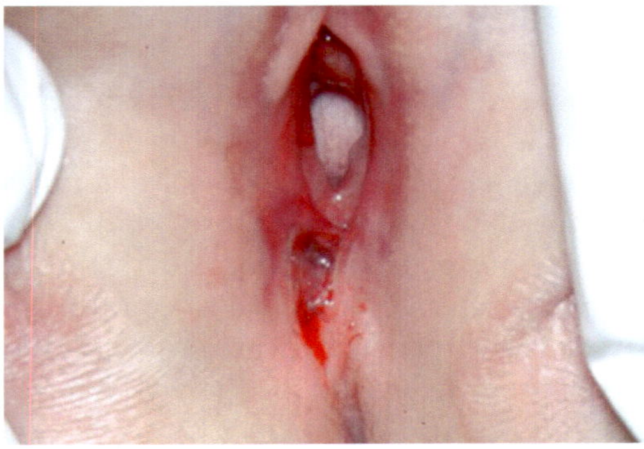

FIGURE 11.22 Posterior fourchette and perineal injury caused when a child fell on the arm of a metal chair. Note the hymen is not injured.

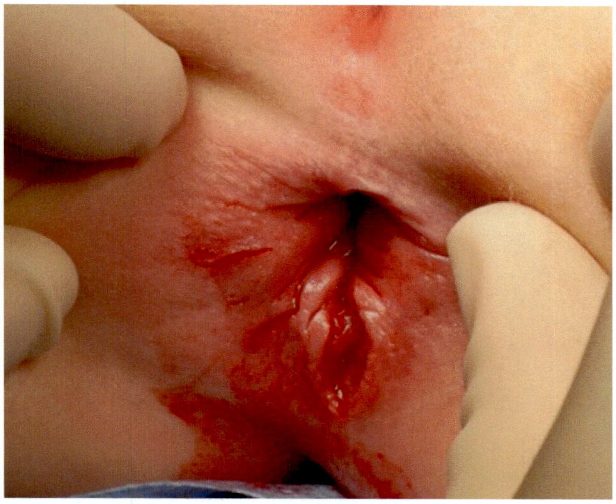

(a)

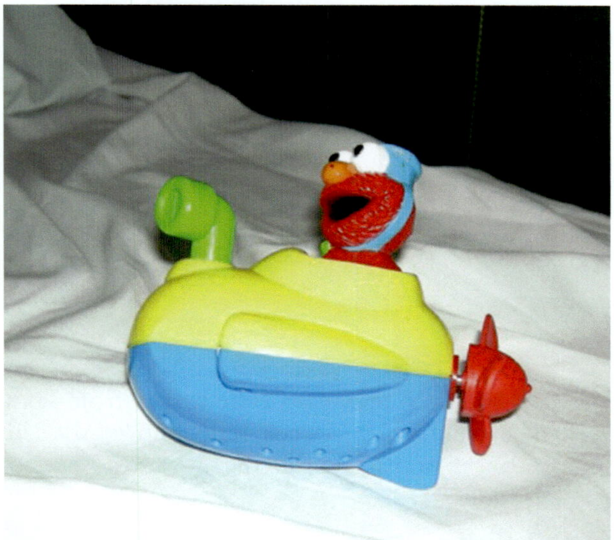

(b)

FIGURE 11.23 (a) Anal laceration caused accidentally when a child fell on a toy while bathing. (b) Toy that the child fell on.

Sports such as gymnastics, aerobics, swimming, biking, horseback riding, and other vigorous sports were not found to be associated with anogenital injuries and shouldn't be used to explain their presence.

11.4.13 Tampons and Hymenal Findings

The influence of tampon use on the hymen emerges as a legal issue when some attribute hymenal findings to their use while others refute any relation. Emans et al., (1994) found that the diameter of the hymen is wider in tampon users but the cause-and-effect relationship was not established, and it could be that the wider diameter is the cause for choosing this menstrual hygiene method rather than a result of its use. Authors concluded that complete clefts could not be attributed to the use of tampons, to sports, or even to speculum examination, owing to the elasticity of the hymen, which can accommodate distention without any injury.

Adams (2004) found that most tampon users who are not sexually active have no deep notches or clefts and only those few with complete clefts in the posterior hymenal rim have reported painful insertion of tampons.

Goodyear stated that tampon use cannot be excluded as a cause of hymenal clefts, especially since they were documented in some of Emans' cases who were non-sexually active tampon users, and the correlation compared with pad users was nearly significant.

A girl should be asked about any incident of difficult tampon insertion or speculum examination before the examiner concludes that a cleft is a result of sexual assault.

11.4.14 Healing of Anogenital Injuries

The healing of anogenital injuries has its implications in the medicolegal assessment of suspected child sexual abuse. The importance of understanding healing arises from the fact that it has been used by medical examiners as an explanation for the lack of injuries in cases presenting with an alleged sexual abuse. They indicate that the absence of physical findings doesn't preclude a previous injury. Examiners were advised not to delay the examination of suspected cases, as the healing process is rapid and could be complete. Examination within the first 72 hours would result in better detection of injuries. Children who provide a history of pain or bleeding at the time of assault were found to be normal most of the time if examined after a few weeks. Anal injuries, including bruising, lacerations, and scars were detected more often in early examination, within 7 days of the assault.

Another medicolegal importance of healing is that many of the healed injuries are attributed to non-intentional (accidental) injuries. It was found that accidental injuries heal in exactly the same way as those of abuse, and hence differentiating between them presents a challenge to the examiner. This emphasizes the importance of asking about previous incidents of accidental falls or injuries that the child experienced. Accidental injuries that result in persistent healed injuries should be painful, bloody, and memorable rather than being occult and missed by the child or the caregiver.

Longitudinal studies followed cases of accidental and abusive anogenital injuries to study the time of healing and the sequel of such injuries. Researchers found that hematomas and superficial lacerations of the labia majora and minora heal completely, without any evidence of previous trauma. Some injuries to the labia healed with labial adhesions, a finding that is seen even in non-abused children, and hence considered a non-specific finding that cannot be used as a proof of previous injury.

Injuries to the posterior fourchette, even deep ones, heal completely or with a minor vascular change as a faint midline irregular avascular appearance. These are similar to and sometimes cannot be distinguished from the midline avascular area. Tensive lacerations of the posterior fourchette heal with tissue distortion.

Injuries to the vulva and vagina healed with bridging synechiae and adhesions. Perihymenal and hymenal swelling, petechiae, hematomas, and abrasions of the hymen heal completely, while perihymenal tears healed with vascular changes of the perihymenal mucosa. Fusion of the labia minora to the hymen was also documented in three abuse cases and only one non-abused case, and it was thought to be a result of a healed scar from previous injury.

Partial tears to the hymen could end up with a smooth-edged normal hymen or with a superficial notch that could be peaked. The edges of this partial laceration turn from jagged edges into a smooth one. These resultant notches are similar to superficial notches normally found and cannot be differentiated from them. Hence, this finding cannot be used as a proof of previous hymenal injuries. These notches are more difficult to detect in estrogenized redundant hymen of newborn or pubertal girls. Lacerations exceeding half the width of the hymenal tissue were found to heal with deep notches.

A consistent finding that is diagnostic of healing of a previous penetrating injury is a complete transection of the hymen. A tear of the hymen that reaches the base at the attachment to the vaginal wall was found to heal with a full thickness cleft. The presence of such clefts in the posterior hymen was not found in non-abused cases and hence is considered an indication of previous trauma to the hymen. Transections can hide between folds of a redundant hymen in adolescents but can be detected with a cotton-tipped applicator (Figure 11.24).

Scarring of the hymen was not documented apart from extensive hymenal lacerations that healed with a scar and contractures. These scars can be found adjacent to the hymen as adhesions between the hymen and the vestibule but not on the hymen itself (McCann et al., 1992). Berkowitz (2011) reported a case of extensive lacerations through the hymen, posterior fourchette, perineal body, and 2–3 mm of anus. Healing was with decreasing hymenal opening and a scar covering the genital area, ending with a hymen with no opening and hematocolpos. Adhesions around the hymen were reported in prepubertal children with allegation of sexual assault.

Berenson (2000) reported a sexual abuse case with hymenal perforation where the hymenal edges were intact and a single small well-demarcated fenestration was found in the middle of the hymenal tissue. Hostetler et al. (1994) reported the same finding in three girls who presented as cases of sharp-penetrating genital injuries. This fenestration was thought to result from a healed hymenal injury.

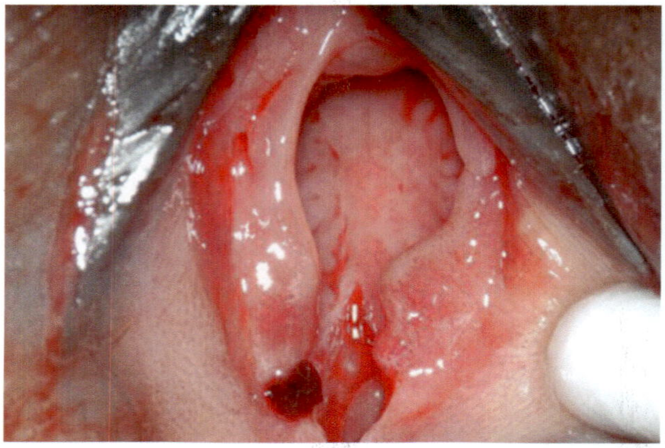

(a)

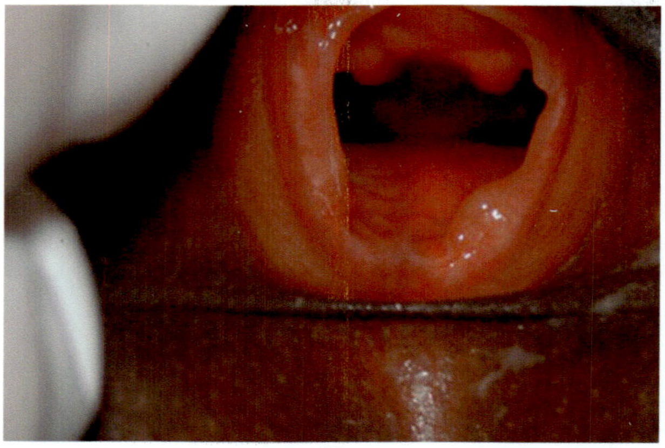

(b)

FIGURE 11.24 (a) Acute tear of the hymen from sexual assault in a child. (b) Six-week follow-up of the child demonstrating a transection at the site of the previous deep laceration.

Anal injuries heal in a similar manner, with superficial lacerations, abrasions, fissures, hematomas, and swelling, healing rapidly and completely. Healed lacerations and tears might present as wedge-shaped scars or distortions of the anal folds. These findings fade with time and appeared less at puberty. Some lacerations healed with a narrow fibrotic line that is easily interpreted if outside the midline. However, if located in the midline, it could be confused with congenital midline variations like midline raphe. Any midline finding should be interpreted cautiously, as it could be congenital. Anal tags were found following injuries to the anal area, and scarring and pigmentation were also noticed after surgical repair of anal injuries. McCann (2003) found that all perianal injuries that occurred after a single sodomy healed rapidly

In general, anogenital injuries heal quickly (days to weeks) and most of the time with no or non-specific findings. Variations in the timing of healing depend on many factors, including the depth and severity of injury and the healing ability of the injured child. Absence of findings in a child with alleged sexual abuse doesn't preclude abuse, and in fact, the anogenital area is expected to be free of injury, owing to the rapidity of the healing process.

11.4.15 Lack of Anogenital Injuries

The detection of injuries during the medical examination of a suspected child sexual abuse case would present strong corroborative evidence that strengthens the case, especially if correlated with a clear history that is provided by the child. However, these injuries are not inevitable, and their absence is more common. Injuries were absent in 52% of sexually active girls (Adams et al., 2004). A review of 21 studies involving children examined for an alleged sexual assault found that these injuries are absent in 26%–73% of girls and 17%–82% of boys. Older studies have shown a higher rate of injuries, and this was explained by the fact that previously, only severe cases of sexual assault sought medical evaluation. Additionally, the classification of abnormal findings has changed, as more research into normal findings has emerged, such that many abnormal findings were reclassified into non-specific or normal. This reclassification lowered the rate of detected injuries (Bays and Chadwick, 1993). One study found that injuries were mostly absent, even in cases with repeated episodes of sexual assault with penetration. Adams found that the majority of legally proven cases of child sexual abuse were found to be free of injuries.

This area of forensics sparks much debate among medical and legal professionals, who both believe in the effect of finding injuries on the legal outcome of the case. The greatest controversy was regarding the methods of confirming child sexual abuse other than physical examination in order to set a sample for studying the presence or absence of injuries in abused cases. While some chose behavioral screening, parental interviews, and child interviews, Adams chose legal outcome as a more accurate indicator to prove the occurrence of sexual assault. However, even this method was biased, as stated by Adams, because most of those cases ended up with plea bargains so that no one would know what really happened.

Reasons that were suggested for lacking anogenital injury in cases assessed for sexual assault include the following:

1. Sexual assaults involved acts that were not expected to leave any finding, like fondling.
2. Children lacked the concept of penetration and could refer to the mere genital touch as penetration. Sexual assault is not confined to penetration past the hymen but involves any penetration, even labial, that doesn't leave any finding.
3. Adolescents have an elastic hymen that allows distention without leaving any injury, and this explains the lack of correlation between a history of penetration and lack of findings. Adolescents who were involved in consensual sexual acts and therefore were expected to better understand the concept of penetration were found to have no injuries (Anderst et al., 2009). However, this elasticity is not a feature of the preadolescent hymen and hence cannot explain a lack of hymenal injuries with penetration in this age group.
4. The anus can accommodate the passage of large stools without injury and is expected similarly to allow penetration without leaving any sign.
5. Healing is rapid, and previous injuries might leave no evidence that can be traced. Most of the cases are examined late and hence most potential findings are expected to subside.
6. False allegations should be considered as an explanation of absent findings. Causes of false allegation include custody disputes, delusional psychotic parents, sexual play between children and age-appropriate sexual exploration.

In conclusion, it is important to know that the presence of anogenital injuries means that a trauma had occurred either sexually (consensual or non-consensual), or accidentally. It is of equal importance to know that the presence of injures is not inevitable after a sexual act, even a non-consensual one, and that their absence doesn't negate the incident of sexual contact. An accurate history of the event and an accurate assessment of physical findings are the main factors that allow reaching a just decision.

11.4.16 Hymenal Orifice Diameter, Posterior Rim of the Hymen, and Evidence of Sexual Assault

The significance of hymenal orifice diameter measurements as a tool in diagnosing child sexual abuse was among the first researched findings. A "gapping hymenal orifice" was the term used when the vagina was easily seen without labial separation or traction and was documented in non-abused girls. Studies have reached variable conclusions, with some finding that it is a useful tool, while others negate its importance. Measurements that were suggested to be used as criteria for a normal hymenal orifice diameter varied widely among studies. The positions and techniques of the examinations differed among studies and have their effect on the measurements.

It was found that the vertical diameter increases with BMI (body mass index) and that both vertical and horizontal diameters increase with age. The diameter was found to change with the position of the child, the examination method, the degree of the perihymenal muscular relaxation, the hymenal configuration, and the degree of tissue estrogenization. One study found that the correlation between sexual abuse and increased diameter was found to be significant only in cases where other findings were observed, like lacerations of the hymen or the presence of posterior hymenal clefts at 5 to 7 o'clock. However, the presence of any of these findings is enough for diagnosis, regardless of the hymenal orifice diameter.

A horizontal hymenal orifice diameter of 6.5 mm or more was found of high specificity but low sensitivity, and that of 11.5 mm or more was more specific to abuse cases. This increase in the specificity was at the expense of sensitivity.

The variability of results from different studies diminished the importance of this tool in diagnosing previous sexual assaults. A more reliable method was used, which is measuring the posterior rim of the hymen at 6 o'clock. This method was hindered by the difficulty in estimating, using photos, the point of hymenal attachment to the vaginal wall. The light reflex that is present in the photographs was used as an estimate to locate this point. This measurement was also found to change with the examination method and the degree of relaxation, but McCann found no changes with the examination method.

A measurement of 1 mm or more was found in the non-abused children. Those non-abused children with less than 1 mm diameter were more found to have longitudinal intravaginal ridges, which could explain the lower hymenal rim measurements. Lower measurements were documented in abused cases; however, only a few of them were reported. The rarity of this finding lowered its sensitivity and questioned its usefulness alone as a diagnostic tool of child sexual abuse. Narrowing of the hymen could be of significance only if compared to the rest of the hymen.

The term "attenuation of the hymen" is used to describe a narrow hymenal rim. However, attenuation of tissue should be used as evidence only if the same tissue, previously examined, appeared to attenuate upon a second examination, an unexpected situation in the majority of child sexual abuse cases. Adding to that, attenuation is a normal physiological process in which lowered levels of prepubertal estrogen lead to a decrease in the overall hymenal tissue that was found in longitudinal studies of non-abused children.

In conclusion, hymenal measurements should not be used alone as a diagnostic tool for previous penetration. The continuity rather than the width of the posterior hymenal rim should be assessed where a clear rim of hymenal tissue is always present in the posterior part of a normal hymen between 3 o'clock and 9 o'clock.

11.4.17 Notches

Notches were well documented in normative studies. Their depth and location were given importance, to be used as evidence of a sexual assault. Superficial and deep notches are normally found in the anterior half of the hymen at and/or above 3 to 9 o'clock as a part of the normal evolution of the annular hymen into a crescent. Superficial notches formed part of the normal irregularity of the posterior hymenal rim. However, deep notches and complete clefts that extend to where the hymen attaches to the vaginal wall were not found in the posterior hymen of any normative study, and only in sexually active girls in control studies, which makes them an important sign indicating previous trauma to the hymen. Lateral deep notches and clefts at 3 o'clock or 9 o'clock in adolescents were found significantly more in sexually active girls.

It is difficult to rely on measurements as small as 1 mm (lower measurement of a normal hymen) to determine whether a notch is superficial or deep, and hence it is emphasized again that it is better to assess the continuity of the posterior rim of the hymen that was a consistent finding in all non-abused children.

11.4.18 Anal/Perianal Findings and Evidence of Sexual Assault

While acute findings of anal sexual abuse are obvious, controversy arises in the determination of findings that result from chronic ongoing abuse. **Skin tags** were classified as a normal finding—especially if located in the midline—as they were commonly found in non-abused children. However, longitudinal studies have shown skin tags developing in the healing process of anal injuries.

Scars were noticed as fine fibrous lines in the area of a healed laceration. They were found in the midline, crossing the midline, and outside the midline. With time, these scars become less apparent, and midline scars become hidden between anal folds. While it is easy to interpret scars that are outside the midline to be a result of trauma, apparent midline, scars be difficult to distinguish from median raphe wedge-shaped scars that were described in older studies. None were found in a longitudinal study that followed four cases with anal lacerations.

Hyperpigmentation was noticed after surgical correction of an anal trauma resulting from sexual abuse.

Anal dilatation is a non-prominent feature of acute abuse. Its association with chronic abuse has been studied. It can be external where the anal canal can be seen, or total where both the external and internal anal sphincters dilate, enabling the examiner to see the rectal ampule (Myhre et al., 2013). Dilatation was found in 49% of prepubertal children who were selected for non-abuse.

There is an association between the prone knee-chest position and the dilatation of the anal sphincter. The anal tone is a reflex that increases with increased abdominal pressure. Decreasing abdominal pressure, as happens in the knee-chest position, decreases the tone resulting in anal dilation.

Anal dilatation with stool in the rectal ampule is common and is produced by the distention of the rectum. This distention results in inhibition of the reflex that is responsible for keeping the anus closed. It also modifies the response of the anal muscles to stimulation and the voluntary effort to contract the external sphincter. With distention, the contraction can be sustained for only a brief period of time, which explains the intermittent dilatation.

Other effects on anal dilatation include anesthesia, injuries, and diseases of the nervous system or smooth/striated muscles.

Attempts to measure the antero-posterior (AP) and horizontal diameters of the anal opening during dilatation showed that almost all children in a non-abused group have a maximum AP measurement of less than 20 mm. Nearly half of them had stool in the rectal ampule. This dilatation was intermittent in two-thirds of the cases. Lower measurements were documented in the absence of stool.

A dilated anus could have a round or oval shape. Marked irregularities in anal dilatation are rare, and moderate irregularity could result from intermittent opining and closing of the sphincter. Neuromuscular diseases can show similar irregularity.

Although immediate total dilatation with AP diameter of 20 mm or more without stool in the ampule is of concern (Myhre et al., 2001), total anal dilatation is still an indeterminate finding, and more research is needed before reaching a conclusion about its association with anal sexual abuse (Myhre et al., 2013).

The presence of **anal warts** as a suspicious finding of sexual abuse is discussed with sexually transmitted infections (STIs).

11.4.19 Conditions Mimicking Sexual Abuse

The diagnosis of CTA based on physical findings can be challenging. Many conditions might present with features that are similar to those resulting from sexual abuse. These conditions include infectious, neoplastic, inflammatory, congenital, or genetic diseases. The examiner should have knowledge about the existence of such conditions. While a good social and medical history of the child with a review of systems could reach the accurate diagnosis easily, some conditions are more confusing and need more investigation before giving a final diagnosis of sexual abuse, with its legal and social consequences. Some of these situational difficulties in diagnosis are discussed in this section, as follows:

1. A condition that mimics signs and symptoms of abuse might coexist with sexual abuse, making the diagnosis more difficult. An example is a vaginal foreign body that is common in girls and is frequently composed of small bits of toilet paper. However, larger objects can be self-inserted by the child or inserted by a sexual perpetrator. Such foreign bodies can cause a copious vaginal discharge that may raise a concern of abuse. A concurrent infection could be a complicating issue. However, repeated insertion of foreign bodies into the vagina by a child and the presence of an infection could raise a concern of previous sexual contact.

   Perianal fissures are features of lichen sclerosus that can make defecation painful, potentially resulting in encopresis. Both fissures and encopresis are suspicious findings that raise the concern of sexual abuse.
2. A known disease could present with features that mimic features of sexual abuse and lead to confusion. An example of this is Crohn's disease, with fissuring, scars, and fistulae in the anogenital area.
3. Rarely, both infectious conditions and injuries, whether accidental or resulting from sexual abuse, can end up with scars. These scars can be so similar as to make it difficult to recognize their origin. The location of some scars can be used as a clue to their origin, while geometric scars are more likely to be of a traumatic nature.
4. The presence of a pathological condition does not rule out sexual abuse, as both can coexist. Lichen sclerosus, for example, is characterized by atrophic skin that is easily broken. Fissures or lacerations could occur following sexual abuse in a child who has atrophic skin, which leads to visible injuries that would be undetectable in an otherwise healthy skin. However, normal activities and toileting can also lead to injuries in lichen sclerosus. Differentiating the trauma of sexual abuse in the face of lichen sclerosus is extremely difficult (Figure 11.25).
5. Some infectious conditions could result either from sexual contact or innocent contact. This is discussed in the section on sexually transmitted infections.

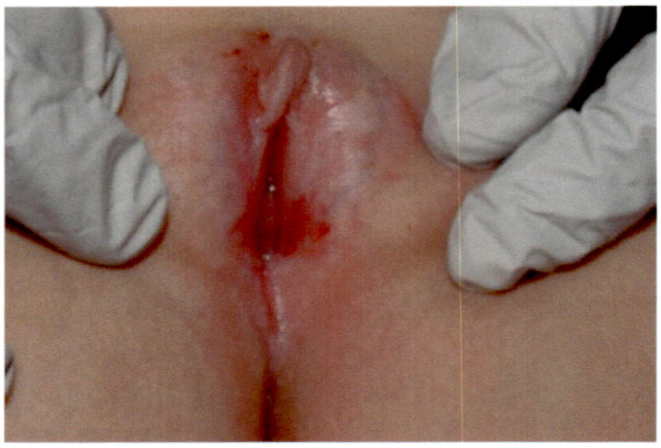

FIGURE 11.25 Lichen sclerosus in a prepubertal child.

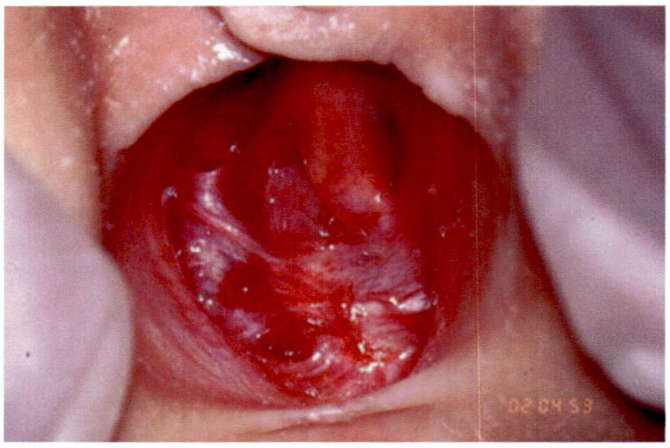

FIGURE 11.26 Vascular malformation/hemangioma leading to extreme redness and swelling of the vaginal area. The condition was followed for several weeks and did not change.

6. Location of the skin condition could be the reason for suspicion, as in the case of Mongolian spots or vascular malformations if located in the vaginal or perianal area (Figure 11.26).

The workup for any suspicious case should involve a prior knowledge of mimicking conditions and their different presentations (Table 11.1). A detailed history from the child and the caregiver could easily unveil the true condition. Proper examination by experienced clinicians with appropriate referral is needed in certain situations; a skin biopsy confirms the diagnosis. A follow-up examination is needed to differentiate congenital and acquired conditions. Referral to social services should be started if all attempts fail at reaching a diagnosis for a suspicious skin condition.

11.4.20 Forensic Evidence

Forensic evidence is powerful evidence in cases of child sexual abuse, especially if it correlates with the history provided by the victim and the physical findings. However, the procedure of its recovery could be uncomfortable and stressful both to the child and the examiner, mainly if the examiner lacks proper training. Studies show a low rate of recovered evidence from child cases (<25%). This was explained by the delayed nature of their presentation that ends up with losing evidence in most of the cases. Also it has been found that the exchange of biological material between the perpetrator and the victim is minimal in young children.

The decision on whether to collect evidence depends on several factors. Screening tools have been suggested

TABLE 11.1 Anogenital Conditions Mimicking Features of Sexual Abuse.

Congenital
Mongolian spots
Vascular malformations
Epidermal nevus
Hemangioma of infancy
Inflammatory
Psoriasis
Crohn's disease
Bullous pemphigoid
Seborrheic dermatitis
Contact dermatitis
Kawasaki syndrome
Behçet's disease
Pemphigus vulgaris
Lichen sclerosus
Perianal pseudo verrucous papules and nodules (PPPN)
Neoplastic
Darier's disease
Langerhans cell histiocytosis
Bowenoid papulosis
Rare neoplasms
Infectious
Vulvovaginitis
Pinworms
Human papillomavirus
Molluscum contagiosum
Herpes simplex virus
Epstein–Barr virus
Perianal and vaginal streptococcal infections
Viral exanthems of any kind
Anatomic
Urethral prolapse
Hematologic
Hemorrhagic disease of the newborn
Idiopathic thrombocytopenic purpura (ITP)
Henoch–Schönlein purpura (HSP)

to determine which cases are eligible for evidence collection. These tools are based on obtaining information, some of which is known only by the child. This can be misleading, as children might provide unreliable answers. Hence, screening tools require skills and training before application, and any decision on evidence collection should not be based on history only.

The probability of recovering forensic evidence from a child suspect of sexual abuse is governed by different dynamics that represent the principle elements for assessing the need for evidence collection:

1. The type of assault: A history of genital/genital or genital/anal contact or ejaculation is predictive for the detection of forensic evidence. However, lack of reporting such type of contact should not preclude evidence collection. There have been reported cases where semen was recovered from children who mentioned only digital contact.
2. The presence of physical injuries could be predictive for the recovery of evidence, according to the American Academy of Pediatrics (AAP). Pain and bleeding were significantly associated with positive evidence. However, with the introduction of DNA technology, long intervals could pass where the injuries would heal and leave no physical signs, while DNA could still be recovered. Hence, collection of evidence is appropriate even in the absence of physical injuries.
3. The time of the last contact determines the necessity of immediate examination and evidence collection. The evidence should be collected as close as possible to the time of the last contact. Evidence could be lost from the body by degradation of some seminal components in body orifices. It can drain from the vagina or wash from the mouth.

There is a debate regarding the time limit for evidence collection in the case of suspected child sexual abuse. While the AAP recommends 72 hours as the time limit (American Academy of Pediatrics Committee on Adolescence, 1994; American Academy of Pediatrics Committee on Child Abuse and Neglect, 1999), recent studies suggest lowering this limit to 24 hours, as there is minimal recovery of evidence, including DNA, beyond this time limit. These suggested time limits depend on the age of the child and the type of the collected evidence. In prepubertal children, the body rarely retains evidence beyond 24 hours, while evidence was recovered more from clothes and bed linens after that time interval. Therefore, there should be a meticulous search for these items.

As the age of the child increases, the possibility of recovering evidence from the body after longer time periods increases. Adolescent cases act as adults where evidence could persist up to 96 hours. The vagina was found to be the most common source of evidence in this age group.

A possible explanation for low detection of evidence from the vagina in prepubertal girls is that sexual assault in this age group rarely involves vaginal intercourse, owing to the relatively small size of the hymen and vagina.

It should be acknowledged that the need for a timely forensic assessment should depend not only on the chance of recovering evidence but also on many other factors. Documenting and treating injuries, post-exposure prophylaxis for certain STIs and pregnancy prophylaxis, child safety and the emotional needs of the family and the child as provided by the available community resources should all be considered. Thus, 72 hours could be used as the time limit to assess these children, although most evidence would be lost after 24 hours.

1. Actions taken by the child after the assault could affect the possibility of recovering evidence. Bathing, changing clothes, washing the body, and wiping can all lower the chance of finding evidence. However, there are reported cases where evidence was recovered even after bathing and wiping.
2. The age of the perpetrator is a predictive factor; those older than 18 years were more often linked with positive evidence recovery.
3. Female victims are more likely to have positive forensic evidence than male victims.

11.4.21 Collection of Forensic Evidence

Collected evidence includes semen, saliva, and blood. DNA can be extracted from blood, sperm, and shed epithelial cells in the saliva and skin. These samples are obtained with swabbing the body orifices like the mouth, vagina, and anus or by swabbing the stains that are present on the skin of the victim. Evidence can also be obtained from clothes, bed linens, or any other surface that may have had contact with biological material from the perpetrator.

Forensic evidence kits that include items needed in the procedure of evidence collection have been developed according to different jurisdiction systems. Standardizing the procedure of forensic evidence collection is needed for legal acceptance. Protocols of these kits include collection of clothes and sample collection from possible points of contact with the perpetrator. Number of swabs, areas to be swabbed, and the technique of collection are instructed in the protocol of each kit. However, the kits are not used uniformly across cases, and discretion in its application occur. While all children can be sampled for oral, anal, and skin evidence, only pubertal girls can have a vaginal or endocervical sample, which can retain evidence for a longer time. Prepubertal girls are not tolerant to collecting such a sample, as their hymens are too sensitive to be touched by a sampling swab.

Given the different factors that can affect a decision on whether to collect evidence and what to collect at which time interval, it should be acknowledged that depending solely on those as discrete indicators for the presence or absence of trace evidence or DNA of the perpetrator could lead to missed identification of some cases. Therefore, any decision to collect evidence should be dealt with on a case-by-case basis. As a general guide and to ensure effective evidence collection, examiners need to collect as soon as possible after the last contact, and not necessarily stop after 24 hours. The examiner should consider obtaining evidence in cases with an inadequate history or unconsciousness. Evidence collection should proceed even if the physical examination was normal, and other items that might have evidence should be looked for.

It is suggested that an examination of children younger than 10 years could be delayed if the child is asymptomatic, presents after 24 hours from the assault, denies genital contact or ejaculation, and in the case of a young familial perpetrator.

Proper collection and storage should be coordinated with police, and chain of custody should be maintained throughout the process of collection, storage, and transfer to the laboratory.

11.5 SEXUALLY TRANSMITTED INFECTIONS AND EVIDENCE OF CHILD SEXUAL ABUSE

Several microorganisms are sexually transmitted. Some have gained forensic importance owing to their potential use as evidence of child sexual abuse. *Neisseria gonorrhoeae, Chlamydia trachomatis, Trichomonas vaginalis*, syphilis, HIV, human papillomavirus, and herpes simplex virus are some of the STIs that are encountered in children who are evaluated for sexual abuse. The prevalence of STIs in these children is different in various studies but generally low.

Tests that are used to detect causative organisms in children should be selected cautiously. While in adults, the main purpose of testing is screening and treatment of the infection, which needs a highly sensitive test, children do need the same sensitivity but with high specificity also. Tests that are highly sensitive but with low specificity can lead to false positive results, with disastrous legal consequences for the child, the suspect, and the family unit, if the suspect was a family member.

Before reaching a diagnosis of sexual abuse by the presence of an STI that is strongly associated with sexual contact, there should be an exclusion of other explanations for its presence. An infection from a previous unrelated sexual abuse should also be considered. In general, obtained samples should be retained for repeated tests and for testing other STIs.

Trying to link a child with a positive test to a suspect who is also positive for the same microorganism requires the isolation of genetically identical organisms. This should be interpreted considering many factors that differ with the type of the organism.

The prevalence of STIs in children is low, and hence not all children who are evaluated for sexual abuse need to be investigated for STIs. The AAP and Centers for Disease Control and Prevention (CDC) guidelines recommend testing children in the following situations:

- The child has signs or symptoms indicative of an STI.
- The child has findings indicative of penetration.
- The suspect is known to have STIs.
- STIs are highly prevalent in the community.

Girls often present with vaginal malodorous discharge and sometimes bleeding. A foreign body might be discovered in the vagina, which is, most of the time, toilet paper. Although exploration could be an explanation for their presence, these girls need to be tested for STIs, as sexual abuse has been reported in some cases with foreign bodies.

Detection of an STI in a child without a disclosure of any sexual contact should be suspicious and needs to be reported and properly investigated. At the same time, there should be an open mind to other innocent modes of transmission.

11.5.1 *Neisseria gonorrhoeae*

Neisseria gonorrhoea (NG) is Gram-negative intracellular diplococcus that remains alive in body fluids and is transmitted through sexual contact. It can infect the eyes, pharynx, or anogenital area. Anogenital infection is mostly asymptomatic in adolescents and adults, while mostly symptomatic in children with purulent discharge, itching and redness of the urethra, vagina, or anal area. The type of the epithelium and pH of the vagina that differs in the two age groups explains this difference in the presence of symptoms. Asymptomatic infections have been reported in children but are rare. Prepubertal girls have a low risk of ascending infection and complications following the infection.

The incubation period is in the range of 2–7 days but may reach 3 weeks in children. This has a legal implications in tracing the suspects who were in contact with the child in that time period, in the case of a single recent contact.

Although sexual contact is the most common mode of transmission, innocent transmission should be excluded before reaching a diagnosis of child sexual abuse. Vertical transmission from an infected mother to a newborn during childbirth can result in genital, respiratory, or eye infection. It can persist for the immediate neonatal period up to 1 month after birth. There are reported cases of rare non-sexual transmission. Some research has demonstrated the survival of the microorganisms on inanimate objects for periods of time that are sufficient for transmission and infecting others. Fomites, linens, and toilet seats are some of these objects. NG has been isolated from artificially inoculated toilet seats but not in random swabbing of the seats. It has also been found that some neonates were infected with NG while their mothers were negative for it. Non-sexual transmission was the explanation of the NG epidemics that ceased once the source of infection was discovered and eliminated.

Regardless of the proposed non-sexual transmission, sexual contact remains the main mode of transmission. An NG infection that is detected beyond the neonatal period should raise a strong suspicion of sexual contact and a thorough investigation and reporting to child protective services should be done.

Recent CDC reports recommend a nucleic acid amplification test (NAAT) as the preferred test for the diagnosis of NG infection. It has the advantage of non-invasive sampling that uses the first-catch urine to detect the organism. It is so sensitive as to detect a single strand of DNA or RNA of the organism and hence does not need swabbing to collect more organisms that are required for cultures. It can detect the infection in symptomatic and asymptomatic cases. There is no need to repeat the NAAT for confirmation of the test in adolescents or adults.

Culture is still the method of choice to detect NG in boys, and the rectum and pharynx in boys and girls. Cross reactivity with other normal flora that is found in the pharynx and rectum (e.g., *N. meningitidis*) can give false positive NAAT results. A swab with specific features is inserted 2–3 cm in the rectum and 1–2 cm in the urethra and rotated to obtain a good sample for culture. Meatal discharge can be collected for culture with no need to swab the urethra. Culturing the organism is also needed to determine the sensitivity of the organism in cases of treatment failure.

Serotyping determines the genetic sequence of organisms in an attempt to create a linkage between them. This has been used in epidemiological settings, and it has the potential to be used in forensic settings to link the victim with the suspect as a proof of sexual contact. However, interpreting such typing needs the consideration of several factors: the probability of two unrelated strains having the same DNA genotype, the frequency of a particular genotype in a random sample of NG isolates, genotypic differences that are needed to determine lack of relation, and the level of genetic variations that occurs in isolates from the local population. Serotyping is not standardized for use in a forensic setting and is not validated for use in providing evidence in court.

11.5.2 *Chlamydia trachomatis*

Chlamydia trachomatis (CT) is identified by the presence of Gram-negative intra-cytoplasmic inclusion bodies. Worldwide, it is the most prevalent STI. Its prevalence is attributed to the asymptomatic subclinical nature of infection that lasts for a long time. Children with CT, unlike infection with NG, are commonly asymptomatic. Sexual contact is the most common mode of transmission. Vertical transmission from an infected mother can persist asymptomatic for up to 2–3 years, which makes a determination of sexual contact more difficult in this age group.

NAAT is recommended by the CDC in testing for CT in the first-catch urine sample from girls. Culture is the method of choice for the detection of the infection in the rectum and pharynx in boys and girls and for detecting the infection in boys. Meatal discharge is enough for culturing the organism. Culture is also needed for the sensitivity of the organism for treatment purposes.

Comparing serovars is complex, and although it can be used for epidemiological purposes, its relevance in the forensic setting needs knowledge of the local prevalence of these types. It is of potential benefit only after considering other factors that affect the interpretation, similar to the situation with NG.

11.5.3 Screening for NG and CT in Cases of CTA

The risk of sexual transmission of NG and CT to child victims of sexual abuse has not been studied; there is a low prevalence of NG and CT in this age group. A study showed that only 16 cases turned out to be positive for NG or CT out of 2008 children investigated for the possibility of sexual abuse within 72 hours post assault. Almost all were symptomatic with acute vulvovaginitis. This lowers the need for screening asymptomatic children (Simmons and Hicks, 2005). If indicated, such screening should be done before starting treatment. With initial assessment in the case of a single recent contact, the examiner should look for signs of infection such as discharge and redness. A first voided urine, or one hour after the last voided one, should be obtained for NAAT for both NG and CT in girls. Swab the pharynx and rectum, and the urethra in boys, for culture if the infection is suspected (Papp et al., 2014).

As the organisms might not appear on the first test owing to the incubation period, a repeated test—if indicated—should be done on the 2-week follow-up examination. The unlikely ascending infection and complication in children warrants a delayed treatment till the follow-up testing.

In cases of an extended sexual abuse over a long time period or a single abuse that occurred a long time before the examination, giving sufficient time for the organism to appear, a single test is enough.

11.5.4 Syphilis

Treponema pallidum, the organism responsible for syphilis, is a spirochete that is transmitted sexually. Other modes of transmission include vertical transmission from an infected mother. Rare cases with innocent transmission via oral lesions through kissing and touching were reported. However, whenever the infection is detected in a child beyond the neonatal period, sexual abuse should be highly suspected, and the child needs to be thoroughly investigated.

There are several manifestations of syphilis as a primary chancre or skin rash. Condyloma lata can be confused with genital warts.

Testing for the presence of treponema involves probable serological tests (specific FTA-ABS and non-specific RPR/VDRL) and definitive tests (dark field microscopy and skin biopsy). A child who has disclosed sexual contact or a suspected victim of sexual abuse needs a test of the serum at the initial presentation and at 6 weeks, 3 months, and 6 months to let time for seroconversion and the appearance of antibodies. The first sample is used to compare with the others.

11.5.5 HIV

The risk of sexual transmission of HIV depends on many factors: the infection of the perpetrator, the type of contact, the amount of transmitted material and the presence of tissue injury. A single vaginal penetration has a risk of 0.0001–0.003, while a single anal penetration poses a 0.005–0.032 risk of HIV transmission.

After excluding other modes of transmission; non-transfusional, non-vertical HIV in a child should be suspicious for sexual abuse. In cases with disclosure of sexual abuse, the child should be tested for HIV if there is a concurrent STI, the child has injuries following the assault, the suspect is known to have HIV or has high-risk behavior, in the case of multiple perpetrators, or if HIV is common in the community.

Testing the serum for the infection should be as close to the assault as possible. Other samples at 6 weeks, 3 months, and 6 months after the incident should be taken. Phylogenetic analysis of the HIV strains and their potential use in determining the source of infection is being researched. This has the potential to provide a direct link between the suspect and the abused victim.

11.5.6 Human Papillomavirus (HPV)

Genital warts or (condyloma acuminata) can be transmitted sexually, but the examiner should be open-minded to other modes of transmission. Autoinoculation from other body areas of the child and innocent hetero-inoculation from the parent or caregiver during toileting or diaper change cannot be differentiated from sexual contact. The virus can be transmitted vertically from an infected mother and it may persist up to 5 years after birth. The predictive value of anogenital warts as an evidence of sexual abuse increases with the age of the child.

Genital warts are diagnosed clinically by the detection of flesh-colored flat papules that can make clusters. They can be found in the perianal area, labia, penile shaft, or scrotum. Warts are painless but if irritated can be itchy and bleed. The body of the child should be examined for the presence of extra-genital warts, and the caregiver should also be examined for their presence. The differentiation between innocent and sexual transmission by the caregiver can never be reached. Although certain types of HPV are more found in genital areas, the same types were also recorded in children, so typing cannot be used to determine the mode of transmission.

The difficulty in liking an HPV infection to sexual abuse is attributed to the subclinical infection in some cases and the long persistence after vertical transmission. The variable incubation period that might reach weeks to years can present a difficulty in tracing the suspect.

11.5.7 Herpes Simplex Virus (HSV)

Herpes simplex type 1 is mostly non-genital, while type 2 is commonly a genital infection. However, typing cannot be used to differentiate between a sexual and non-sexual mode of transmission, as either type can infect both sites.

Unroofed vesicles should be swabbed and cultured for the detection of the virus. The typical vesicular eruption of HSV might not present in children. Thus, any eruption, ulceration or skin lesion in the anogenital area of the child should be swabbed. Polymerase chain reaction (PCR) for detection of HSV in the vesicles has been used in adults to increase the retrieval of the virus.

As with HPV, vertical, hetero- and autoinoculation in addition to sexual contact cannot be differentiated, and investigating the child is needed before reaching a diagnosis of sexual abuse.

11.5.8 *Trichomonas vaginalis* (TV)

TV is diagnosed by the presence of motile flagellate in the wet mount sample of the vagina. Vertical transmission is rare but can persist up to 9 months. The presence of TV is strongly associated with sexual contact. If detected in the child's urine, it could be fecal contamination with *Pentatrichomonas hominis*, a non-pathogenic intestinal flagellate appearing similar to TV.

11.5.9 Bacterial Vaginosis

Bacterial colonization is commonly encountered in the vagina of an abused child but also found in non-abused children; hence, its presence should be interpreted cautiously (Kohlberger and Bancher-Todesca, 2007). *Gardnertella vaginalis*, enterobacteriaceae, bacteroids, and ureaplasma are part of the long list of bacteria that colonizes the vagina in prepubertal and pubertal girls. Their presence is not diagnostic of sexual abuse (Table 11.2).

TABLE 11.2 Implications of Commonly Encountered Sexually Transmitted (ST) or Sexually Associated (SA) Infections for Diagnosis and Reporting of Sexual Abuse among Infants and Prepubertal Children

ST/SA Confirmed	Evidence of Sexual Abuse	Suggested Action
Gonorrhea[a]	Diagnostic	Report[b]
Syphilis[a]	Diagnostic	Report[b]
Human Immunodeficiency Virus[c]	Diagnostic	Report[b]
Chlamydia trachomatis[a]	Diagnostic	Report[b]
Trichomonas vaginalis	Highly suspicious	Report[b]
Anogenital warts (condylomata acuminata)[a]	Suspicious	Report[b]
Genital herpes[a]	Suspicious	Report[b,c]
Bacterial vaginosis	Inconclusive	Medical follow-up

Source: Adapted from Kellogg N, American Academy of Pediatrics Committee on Child Abuse and Neglect. *Pediatrics*, 116, 506–512, 2005.

[a] If not likely to be perinatally acquired and rare non-sexual, vertical transmission is excluded.

[b] Reports should be made to the agency in the community mandated to receive reports of suspected child abuse or neglect.

[c] If not likely to be acquired perinatally or through transfusion, unless there is a clear history of autoinoculation.

BIBLIOGRAPHY

Adams JA. Normal studies are essential for objective medical evaluations of children who may have been sexually abused. *Acta Paediatr.* 2003;92(12):1378–80.

Adams JA. Medical evaluation of suspected child sexual abuse. *J Pediatr Adolesc Gynecol.* 2004;17(3):191–7.

Adams JA. Guidelines for medical care of children evaluated for suspected sexual abuse: An update for 2008. *Curr Opin Obstet Gynecol.* 2008;20(5):435–41.

Adams JA. Medical evaluation of suspected child sexual abuse: 2011 update. *J Child Sex Abus.* 2011;20(5):588–605.

Adams JA, Botash AS, Kellogg N. Differences in hymenal morphology between adolescent girls with and without a history of consensual sexual intercourse. *Arch Pediatr Adolesc Med.* 2004;158(3):280–5.

Adams JA, Girardin B, Faugno D. Adolescent sexual assault: Documentation of acute injuries using photocolposcopy. *J Pediatr Adolesc Gynecol.* 2001;14(4):175–80.

Adams JA, Harper K, Knudson S, Revilla J. Examination findings in legally confirmed child sexual abuse: It's normal to be normal. *Pediatrics.* 1994;94(3):310–7.

Adams JA, Kaplan RA, Starling SP, Mehta NH, Finkel MA, Botash AS et al. Guidelines for medical care of children who may have been sexually abused. *J Pediatr Adolesc Gynecol.* 2007;20(3):163–72.

Adams JA, Knudson S. Genital findings in adolescent girls referred for suspected sexual abuse. *Arch Pediatr Adolesc Med.* 1996;150(8):850–7.

Adams JA, Starling SP, Frasier LD, Palusci VJ, Shapiro RA, Finkel MA et al. Diagnostic accuracy in child sexual abuse medical evaluation: Role of experience, training, and expert case review. *Child Abuse Negl.* 2012;36(5):383–92.

Altchek A, Wasserman B, Deligdisch L. Prepubertal distal longitudinal vaginal folds. *J Pediatr Adolesc Gynecol.* 2008;21(6):351–4.

American Academy of Pediatrics Committee on Adolescence. Sexual assault and the adolescent. *Pediatrics.* 1994;94(5):761–5.

American Academy of Pediatrics Committee on Child Abuse and Neglect. Guidelines for the evaluation of sexual abuse of children: Subject review. *Pediatrics.* 1999;103(1):186–91.

Anderst J, Kellogg N, Jung I. Reports of repetitive penile-genital penetration often have no definitive evidence of penetration. *Pediatrics.* 2009;124(3):e403–9.

Asati DP, Singh S, Sharma VK, Tiwari S. Dermatoses misdiagnosed as deliberate injuries. *Med Sci Law.* 2012;52(4):198–204.

Bays J, Chadwick D. Medical diagnosis of the sexually abused child. *Child Abuse Negl.* 1993;17(1):91–110.

Bechtel K. Sexual abuse and sexually transmitted infections in children and adolescents. *Curr Opin Pediatr.* 2010;22(1):94–9.

Berenson AB. Appearance of the hymen at birth and one year of age: A longitudinal study. *Pediatrics.* 1993;91(4):820–5.

Berenson AB. A longitudinal study of hymenal morphology in the first 3 years of life. *Pediatrics.* 1995;95(4):490–6.

Berenson AB. Normal anogenital anatomy. *Child Abuse Negl.* 1998;22(6):589–96; discussion 97–603.

Berenson AB, Chacko MR, Wiemann CM, Mishaw CO, Friedrich WN, Grady JJ. A case-control study of anatomic changes resulting from sexual abuse. *Am J Obstet Gynecol.* 2000;182(4):820–31; discussion 31–4.

Berenson AB, Chacko MR, Wiemann CM, Mishaw CO, Friedrich WN, Grady JJ. Use of hymenal measurements in the diagnosis of previous penetration. *Pediatrics.* 2002;109(2):228–35.

Berenson AB, Grady JJ. A longitudinal study of hymenal development from 3 to 9 years of age. *J Pediatr.* 2002;140(5):600–7.

Berenson A, Heger A, Andrews S. Appearance of the hymen in newborns. *Pediatrics.* 1991;87(4):458–65.

Berenson AB, Heger AH, Hayes JM, Bailey RK, Emans SJ. Appearance of the hymen in prepubertal girls. *Pediatrics.* 1992;89(3):387–94.

Berkowitz CD. Healing of genital injuries. *J Child Sex Abus.* 2011;20(5):537–47.

Black CM, Driebe EM, Howard LA, Fajman NN, Sawyer MK, Girardet RG et al. Multicenter study of nucleic acid amplification tests for detection of *Chlamydia trachomatis* and *Neisseria gonorrhoeae* in children being evaluated for sexual abuse. *Pediatr Infect Dis J.* 2009;28(7):608–13.

Boos SC. Accidental hymenal injury mimicking sexual trauma. *Pediatrics.* 1999;103(6 Pt 1):1287–90.

Boos SC, Rosas AJ, Boyle C, McCann J. Anogenital injuries in child pedestrians run over by low-speed motor vehicles: Four cases with findings that mimic child sexual abuse. *Pediatrics.* 2003;112(1 Pt 1):e77–84.

Bottoms BL, Goodman GS, Schwartz-Kenney BM, Thomas SN. Understanding children's use of secrecy in the context of eyewitness reports. *Law Hum Behav.* 2002;26(3):285–313.

Boyle C, McCann J, Miyamoto S, Rogers K. Comparison of examination methods used in the evaluation of prepubertal and pubertal female genitalia: A descriptive study. *Child Abuse Negl.* 2008;32(2):229–43.

Cantlon J, Payne G, Erbaugh C. Outcome-based practice: Disclosure rates of child sexual abuse comparing allegation blind and allegation informed structured interviews. *Child Abuse Negl.* 1996;20(11):1113–20.

Carnes CN, Nelson-Gardell D, Wilson C, Orgassa UC. Extended forensic evaluation when sexual abuse is suspected: A multisite field study. *Child Maltreat.* 2001;6(3):230–42.

Cederborg AC. Factors influencing child witnesses. *Scand J Psychol.* 2004;45(3):197–205.

Chen LP, Murad MH, Paras ML, Colbenson KM, Sattler AL, Goranson EN et al. Sexual abuse and lifetime diagnosis of psychiatric disorders: Systematic review and meta-analysis. *Mayo Clin Proc.* 2010;85(7):618–29.

Christian CW. Timing of the medical examination. *J Child Sex Abus.* 2011;20(5):505–20.

Christian CW, Lavelle JM, De Jong AR, Loiselle J, Brenner L, Joffe M. Forensic evidence findings in prepubertal victims of sexual assault. *Pediatrics.* 2000;106(1 Pt 1):100–4.

Closson FT, Lichenstein R. Vaginal foreign bodies and child sexual abuse: An important consideration. *West J Emerg Med.* 2013;14(5):437–9.

Colvin CW, Abdullatif H. Anatomy of female puberty: The clinical relevance of developmental changes in the reproductive system. *Clin Anat.* 2013;26(1):115–29.

Dalton SR, Hossler E, Maroon M, Pride H, Shabanowitz R. Secondary syphilis and suspected child abuse. *J Am Acad Dermatol.* 2013;69(4):640–2.

Darville T. Chlamydia trachomatis infections in neonates and young children. *Semin Pediatr Infect Dis.* 2005;16(4):235–44.

Daval-Cote M, Liberas S, Tristan A, Vandenesch F, Gillet Y. Gonococcal vulvovaginitis in prepubertal girls: Sexual abuse or accidental transmission? *Arch Pediatr.* 2013;20(1):37–40.

de Barbeyrac B, Benali L, Clerc M, Garapon S, Bébéar C, Gromb S. *Chlamydia trachomatis* infection in children: Do not forget perinatal acquisition: A case report of a 7-year-old girl, *C. trachomatis* infected, presumed sexually assaulted. *J Forensic Leg Med.* 2010;17(2):96–8.

de Barbeyrac B, Benali L, Clerc M, Garapon S, Bébéar C, Gromb S. Authors reply to: Min Karen L et al. A response to: *Chlamydia trachomatis* infection in children: Do not forget perinatal acquisition. [2010;17:450]. *J Forensic Leg Med.* 2011;18(4):187.

DeMattia A, Kornblum JS, Hoffman-Rosenfeld J, Trees DL, Tumpey AJ, Laraque D. The use of combination subtyping in the forensic evaluation of a three-year-old girl with gonorrhea. *Pediatr Infect Dis J.* 2006;25(5):461–3.

Dendrinos ML, Quint EH. Lichen sclerosus in children and adolescents. *Curr Opin Obstet Gynecol.* 2013;25(5):370–4.

Dion J, Cyr M. The use of the NICHD protocol to enhance the quantity of details obtained from children with low verbal abilities in investigative interviews: A pilot study. *J Child Sex Abus.* 2008;17(2):144–62.

Edgardh K, Ormstad K. The adolescent hymen. *J Reprod Med.* 2002;47(9):710–4.

Ehrnst A. Challenges in virological diagnosis of HIV -1 transmission from sexual abuse—HIV-1 genetic links are mandatory. *Am J Reprod Immunol.* 2013;69(Suppl. 1):116–21.

Emans SJ, Woods ER, Allred EN, Grace E. Hymenal findings in adolescent women: Impact of tampon use and consensual sexual activity. *J Pediatr.* 1994;125(1):153–60.

Everson MD. Bizarre, improbable, and fantastic elements in children's accounts of abuse. *Child Maltreat.* 1997;2:134–49.

Faller KC. Anatomical dolls: Their use in assessment of children who may have been sexually abused. *J Child Sex Abus.* 2005;14(3):1–21.

Faller KC, Cordisco-Steele L, Nelson-Gardell D. Allegations of sexual abuse of a child: What to do when a single forensic interview isn't enough. *J Child Sex Abus.* 2010;19(5):572–89.

Finkelhor D. The international epidemiology of child sexual abuse. *Child Abuse Negl.* 1994;18:409–17.

Floyed RL, Hirsh DA, Greenbaum VJ, Simon HK. Development of a screening tool for pediatric sexual assault may reduce emergency department visits. *Pediatrics.* 2011;128(2):221–6.

Fontes LA, Plummer C. Cultural issues in disclosures of child sexual abuse. *J Child Sex Abus.* 2010;19(5):491–518.

Frasier LD. The pediatrician's role in child abuse interviewing. *Pediatr Ann.* 1997;26(5):306–11.

Gardner JJ. Descriptive study of genital variation in healthy, nonabused premenarchal girls. *J Pediatr.* 1992;120(2 Pt 1):251–7.

Girardet R, Bolton K, Lahoti S, Mowbray H, Giardino A, Isaac R et al. Collection of forensic evidence from pediatric victims of sexual assault. *Pediatrics.* 2011;128(2):233–8.

Goodman GS, Batterman-Faunce JM, Schaaf JM, Kenney R. Nearly 4 years after an event: Children's eyewitness memory and adults' perceptions of children's accuracy. *Child Abuse Negl.* 2002;26(8):849–84.

Goodyear-Smith F. What is the evidence for non-sexual transmission of gonorrhoea in children after the neonatal period? A systematic review. *J Forensic Leg Med.* 2007;14(8):489–502.

Goodyear-Smith FA, Laidlaw TM. Can tampon use cause hymen changes in girls who have not had sexual intercourse? A review of the literature. *Forensic Sci Int.* 1998;94(1–2):147–53.

Gray H. *Anatomy of Human Body.* Philadelphia, PA: Lea & Febiger 1918.

Hammerschlag MR, Guillén CD. Medical and legal implications of testing for sexually transmitted infections in children. *Clin Microbiol Rev.* 2010;23(3):493–506.

Hariton TN. Sexual assault in prepubertal girls: "It is normal to be normal" – or is it? Evidence of vaginal penetration in prepubertal girls. *Med Sci Law.* 2012;52(4):193–7.

Hariton TN. Response to "signs of recent or healed injury to the genitalia in prepubertal girls describing penile-vaginal contact are uncommon." *Med Sci Law.* 2013;53(2):119–20.

Hariton TN. Response to Alfonso O. Lopez's letter to the editor "Criminal defense perspective and articles regarding sexual assault in prepubertal girls." *Med Sci Law.* 2013;53(2):116.

Hariton TN. Response to Dr John Stirling's letter to the editor "Evidence of sexual assault in prepubertal girls." *Med Sci Law.* 2013;53(2):113–4.

Heger AH, Ticson L, Guerra L, Lister J, Zaragoza T, McConnell G et al. Appearance of the genitalia in girls selected for nonabuse: Review of hymenal morphology and nonspecific findings. *J Pediatr Adolesc Gynecol.* 2002;15(1):27–35.

Heppenstall-Heger A, McConnell G, Ticson L, Guerra L, Lister J, Zaragoza T. Healing patterns in anogenital injuries: A longitudinal study of injuries associated with sexual abuse, accidental injuries, or genital surgery in the preadolescent child. *Pediatrics.* 2003;112(4):829–37.

Hershkowitz I, Fisher S, Lamb ME, Horowitz D. Improving credibility assessment in child sexual abuse allegations: The role of the NICHD investigative interview protocol. *Child Abuse Negl.* 2007;31(2):99–110.

Hershkowitz I, Orbach Y, Lamb ME, Sternberg KJ, Horowitz D. Dynamics of forensic interviews with suspected abuse victims who do not disclose abuse. *Child Abuse Negl.* 2006;30(7):753–69.

Hlavka HR, Olinger SD, Lashley JL. The use of anatomical dolls as a demonstration aid in child sexual abuse interviews: A study of forensic interviewers' perceptions. *J Child Sex Abus.* 2010;19(5):519–53.

Hornor G. Common conditions that mimic findings of sexual abuse. *J Pediatr Health Care.* 2009;23(5):283–8.

Hostetler BR, Muram D, Jones CE. Sharp penetrating injuries to the hymen. In: Muram D, editor. *J Pediatr Adolesc Gynecol.* 1994;7: 94–6.

Ingemann-Hansen O, Charles AV. Forensic medical examination of adolescent and adult victims of sexual violence. *Best Pract Res Clin Obstet Gynaecol.* 2013;27(1):91–102.

Ingram DM, Everett VD, Ingram DL. The relationship between the transverse hymenal orifice diameter by the separation technique and other possible markers of sexual abuse. *Child Abuse Negl.* 2001;25(8):1109–20.

Jenny C. Emergency evaluation of children when sexual assault is suspected. *Pediatrics.* 2011;128(2):374–5.

Jenny C, Crawford-Jakubiak JE, Committee on Child Abuse and Neglect, American Academy of Pediatrics. The evaluation of children in the primary care setting when sexual abuse is suspected. *Pediatrics.* 2013;132(2):e558–67.

Joanne A. Time Limits for Conducting a Forensic Examination: Can Biological Evidence be Recovered 24, 36, 48, 72, 84 or 96 Hours Following a Sexual Assault? May 19, 2005.

Jones LW, Bass DH. Perineal injuries in children. *Br J Surg.* 1991;78(9):1105–7.

Jones JS, Dunnuck C, Rossman L, Wynn BN, Genco M. Adolescent Foley catheter technique for visualizing hymenal injuries in adolescent sexual assault. *Acad Emerg Med.* 2003;10(9):1001–4.

Jones JS, Rossman L, Hartman M, Alexander CC. Anogenital injuries in adolescents after consensual sexual intercourse. *Acad Emerg Med.* 2003;10(12):1378–83.

Katz C, Hershkowitz I. The effect of multipart prompts on children's testimonies in sexual abuse investigations. *Child Abuse Negl.* 2012;36(11–12):753–9.

Kellogg N. The evaluation of sexual abuse in children. *Pediatrics.* 2005;116(2):506–12.

Kempe H. Sexual abuse, another hidden pediatric problem: The 1977 C. Anderson Aldrich lecture. *Pediatrics.* 1978;62: 382–9.

Kenny MC, McEachern AG. Racial, ethnic, and cultural factors of childhood sexual abuse: A selected review of the literature. *Clin Psychol Rev.* 2000;20(7): 905–22.

Kimberley N, Hutson JM, Southwell BR, Grover SR. Vaginal agenesis, the hymen, and associated anomalies. *J Pediatr Adolesc Gynecol.* 2012;25(1):54–8.

Kimberly W, Stuart B. Sexually transmitted diseases treatment guidelines, 2010. *MMWR.* 2010;59(RR-12):90–5.

Kimberly A. Workowski M. Sexually transmitted diseases treatment guidelines, 2006. *MMWR Recomm Rep.* 2006;55(RR-11):1–94.

Kohlberger P, Bancher-Todesca D. Bacterial colonization in suspected sexually abused children. *J Pediatr Adolesc Gynecol.* 2007;20(5):289–92.

Lamb ME, Garretson ME. The effects of interviewer gender and child gender on the informativeness of alleged child sexual abuse victims in forensic interviews. *Law Hum Behav.* 2003;27(2):157–71.

Lamb ME, Orbach Y, Hershkowitz I, Esplin PW, Horowitz D. A structured forensic interview protocol improves the quality and informativeness of investigative interviews with children: A review of research using the NICHD Investigative Interview Protocol. *Child Abuse Negl.* 2007;31(11–12):1201–31.

Lamb ME, Orbach Y, Sternberg KJ, Hershkowitz I, Horowitz D. Accuracy of investigators' verbatim notes of their forensic interviews with alleged child abuse victims. *Law Hum Behav.* 2000;24(6):699–708.

Lamb ME, Sternberg KJ, Orbach Y, Hershkowitz I, Horowitz D. Differences between accounts provided by witnesses and alleged victims of child sexual abuse. *Child Abuse Negl.* 2003;27(9): 1019–31.

Lo MK, Say PJ, Healy C. A response to: *Chlamydia trachomatis* infection in children: Do not forget perinatal acquisition [2010;17:96–98]. *J Forensic Leg Med.* 2010;17(8):450–1.

Lopez AO. Criminal defense perspective and articles regarding sexual assault in prepubertal girls. *Med Sci Law.* 2013;53(2):115.

McCann J, Miyamoto S, Boyle C, Rogers K. Healing of hymenal injuries in prepubertal and adolescent girls: A descriptive study. *Pediatrics.* 2007;119(5):e1094–106.

McCann J, Miyamoto S, Boyle C, Rogers K. Healing of nonhymenal genital injuries in prepubertal and adolescent girls: A descriptive study. *Pediatrics.* 2007;120(5):1000–11.

McCann J, Voris J, Simon M. Genital injuries resulting from sexual abuse: A longitudinal study. *Pediatrics.* 1992;89(2):307–17.

McCann J, Voris J, Simon M, Wells R. Perianal findings in prepubertal children selected for nonabuse: A descriptive study. *Child Abuse Negl.* 1989;13(2):179–93.

McCann J, Voris J, Simon M, Wells R. Comparison of genital examination techniques in prepubertal girls. *Pediatrics.* 1990;85(2):182–7.

McCann J, Voris J. Perianal injuries resulting from sexual abuse: A longitudinal study. *Pediatrics.* 1993;91(2):390–7.

McCann J, Wells R, Simon M, Voris J. Genital findings in prepubertal girls selected for nonabuse: A descriptive study. *Pediatrics.* 1990;86(3):428–39.

Mor N, Merlob P, Reisner SH. Tags and bands of the female external genitalia in the newborn infant. *Clin Pediatr (Phila).* 1983;22(2):122–4.

Mor N, Merlob P, Reisner SH. Types of hymen in the newborn infant. *Eur J Obstet Gynecol Reprod Biol.* 1986;22(4):225–8.

Myhre AK, Adams JA, Kaufhold M, Davis JL, Suresh P, Kuelbs CL. Anal findings in children with and without probable anal penetration: A retrospective study of 1115 children referred for suspected sexual abuse. *Child Abuse Negl.* 2013;37(7):465–74.

Myhre AK, Bemtzen K, Bratlid D. Perianal anatomy in non-abused preschool children. *Acta Paediatr.* 2001;90(11):1321–8.

Myhre AK, Berntzen K, Bratlid D. Genital anatomy in non-abused preschool girls. *Acta Paediatr.* 2003;92(12):1453–62.

Myhre AK, Myklestad K, Adams JA. Changes in genital anatomy and microbiology in girls between age 6 and age 12 years: A longitudinal study. *J Pediatr Adolesc Gynecol.* 2010;23(2):77–85.

Narang T, Kanwar AJ, Kumaran MS. Condyloma lata in a preschooler: The dilemma of sexual abuse versus non-abuse. *Indian J Sex Transm Dis.* 2013;34(2):135–7.

A National Protocol for Sexual Assault Medical Forensic Examinations Adults/Adolescents. Washington, D.C.: U.S. Department of Justice 2013.

Newton AW, Vandeven AM. The role of the medical provider in the evaluation of sexually abused children and adolescents. *J Child Sex Abus.* 2010;19(6): 669–86.

Orbach Y, Hershkowitz I, Lamb ME, Sternberg KJ, Esplin PW, Horowitz D. Assessing the value of structured protocols for forensic interviews of alleged child abuse victims. *Child Abuse Negl.* 2000;24(6): 733–52.

Orbach Y, Lamb ME. Assessing the accuracy of a child's account of sexual abuse: A case study. *Child Abuse Negl.* 1999;23(1):91–8.

Orbach Y, Lamb ME. Enhancing children's narratives in investigative interviews. *Child Abuse Negl.* 2000;24(12):1631–48.

Orbach Y, Lamb ME. The relationship between within-interview contradictions and eliciting interviewer utterances. *Child Abuse Negl.* 2001;25(3): 323–33.

Ornstein A, Hatchette T. Human papillomavirus and anogenital warts in children. *CMAJ.* 2012;184(3): 321.

Palusci VJ, Cox EO, Shatz EM, Schultze JM. Urgent medical assessment after child sexual abuse. *Child Abuse Negl.* 2006;30(4):367–80.

Papp JR, Schachter J, Gaydos CA, Van Der Pol B. Recommendations for the laboratory-based detection of *Chlamydia trachomatis* and *Neisseria gonorrhoeae*—2014. *MMWR Recomm Rep.* 2014; 63(RR-02):1–19.

Paradise JE. Predictive accuracy and the diagnosis of sexual abuse: A big issue about a little tissue. *Child Abuse Negl.* 1989;13(2):169–76.

Parnis D, Du Mont J. Examining the standardized application of rape kits: An exploratory study of post-sexual assault professional practices. *Health Care Women Int.* 2002;23(8):846–53.

Pereda N, Guilera G, Forns M, Gómez-Benito J. The international epidemiology of child sexual abuse: A continuation of Finkelhor (1994). *Child Abuse Negl.* 2009;33(6):331–42.

Pereda N, Guilera G, Forns M, Gómez-Benito J. The prevalence of child sexual abuse in community and student samples: A meta-analysis. *Clin Psychol Rev.* 2009;29(4):328–38.

Pillai M. Genital findings in prepubertal girls: What can be concluded from an examination? *J Pediatr Adolesc Gynecol.* 2008;21(4):177–85.

Pokorny SF, Murphy JG, Preminger MK. Circumferential hymen elasticity: A marker of physiologic maturity. *J Reprod Med.* 1998;43(11):943–8.

Poole DA, Dickinson JJ. Evidence supporting restrictions on uses of body diagrams in forensic interviews. *Child Abuse Negl.* 2011;35(9):659–69.

Price J. Injuries in prepubertal and pubertal girls. *Best Pract Res Clin Obstet Gynaecol.* 2013;27(1):131–9.

Price HL, Connolly DA. Children's recall of emotionally arousing, repeated events: A review and call for further investigation. *Int J Law Psychiatry.* 2008;31(4):337–46.

Roberts KP, Powell MB. Describing individual incidents of sexual abuse: A review of research on the effects of multiple sources of information on children's reports. *Child Abuse Negl.* 2001;25(12):1643–59.

Salhan B, Omisore OT, Kumar P, Potter J. A rare presentation of imperforate hymen: A case report. *Case Rep Urol.* 2013;2013:731019.

Sayfan L, Mitchell EB, Goodman GS, Eisen ML, Qin J. Children's expressed emotions when disclosing maltreatment. *Child Abuse Negl.* 2008;32(11):1026–36.

Saywitz K, Camparo L. Interviewing child witnesses: A developmental perspective. *Child Abuse Negl.* 1998;22(8):825–43.

Shapiro RA, Makoroff KL. Sexually transmitted diseases in sexually abused girls and adolescents. *Curr Opin Obstet Gynecol.* 2006;18(5):492–7.

Siegfried EC, Frasier LD. Anogenital skin diseases of childhood. *Pediatr Ann.* 1997;26(5):321–31.

Simmons KJ, Hicks DJ. Child sexual abuse examination: Is there a need for routine screening for *N. gonorrhoeae* and *C. trachomatis*? *J Pediatr Adolesc Gynecol.* 2005;18(5):343–5.

Sjöberg RL, Lindblad F. Delayed disclosure and disrupted communication during forensic investigation of child sexual abuse: A study of 47 corroborated cases. *Acta Paediatr.* 2002;91(12):1391–6.

Snell R. *Clinical Anatomy, by Regions.* 9th ed. Philadelphia, PA: Lippincott Williams & Wilkins 2012.

Springman RE, Wherry JN, Notaro PC. The effects of interviewer race and child race on sexual abuse disclosures in forensic interviews. *J Child Sex Abus.* 2006;15(3):99–116.

Stefanaki C, Barkas G, Valari M, Bethimoutis G, Nicolaidou E, Vosynioti V et al. *Condylomata acuminata* in children. *Pediatr Infect Dis J.* 2012;31(4):422–4.

Sternberg KJ, Lamb ME, Hershkowitz I, Yudilevitch L, Orbach Y, Esplin PW et al. Effects of introductory style on children's abilities to describe experiences of sexual abuse. *Child Abuse Negl.* 1997;21(11):1133–46.

Stirling J. Evidence of sexual assault in prepubertal girls. *Med Sci Law.* 2013;53(2):112.

Stoltenborgh M, van Ijzendoorn MH, Euser EM, Bakermans-Kranenburg MJ. A global perspective on child sexual abuse: Meta-analysis of prevalence around the world. *Child Maltreat.* 2011;16(2):79–101.

Thackeray JD, Hornor G, Benzinger EA, Scribano PV. Forensic evidence collection and DNA identification in acute child sexual assault. *Pediatrics.* 2011;128(2):227–32.

Tobey AE, Goodman GS. Children's eyewitness memory: Effects of participation and forensic context. *Child Abuse Negl.* 1992;16(6):779–96.

Varese F, Smeets F, Drukker M, Lieverse R, Lataster T, Viechtbauer W et al. Childhood adversities increase the risk of psychosis: A meta-analysis of patient-control, prospective- and cross-sectional cohort studies. *Schizophr Bull.* 2012;38(4):661–71.

Victor V. Re: The development of forensic interview training models: A reply to Lamb, Orbach, Hershkowitz, Esplin, and Horowitz (2007). *Child Abuse Negl.* 2008;32(11):1003–6.

Vitale V, Cigliano B, Vallone G. Imperforate hymen causing congenital hydrometrocolpos. *J Ultrasound.* 2013;16(1):37–9.

Watkeys JM, Price LD, Upton PM, Maddocks A. The timing of medical examination following an allegation of sexual abuse: Is this an emergency? *Arch Dis Child.* 2008;93(10):851–6.

Whaitiri S, Kelly P. Genital gonorrhoea in children: Determining the source and mode of infection. *Arch Dis Child.* 2011;96(3):247–51.

Woods CR. Gonococcal infections in neonates and young children. *Semin Pediatr Infect Dis.* 2005;16(4):258–70.

Yavagal S, de Farias TF, Medina CA, Takacs P. Normal vulvovaginal, perineal, and pelvic anatomy with reconstructive considerations. *Semin Plast Surg.* 2011;25(2):121–9.

Yordan EE. The hymen and tanner staging of the breast. In: Yordan RA, editor. *J Pediatr Adolesc Gynecol.* Spring 1992;5(2):76–9. doi: 10.1016/S0932-8610(19)80071-3.

Young KL, Jones JG, Worthington T, Simpson P, Casey PH. Forensic laboratory evidence in sexually abused children and adolescents. *Arch Pediatr Adolesc Med.* 2006;160(6):585–8.

CHAPTER 12

Forensic Entomology

Adrienne Brundage, Jason Byrd, and Lerah Sutton

CONTENTS

12.1 INTRODUCTION

Entomology is the scientific study of insects, and the science itself is a specialized area of zoology. Entomology as a science is extremely broad in its interpretation. Technically, any form of scientific study in which there is a focus on insect-related inquiries can be defined as entomology. Despite human interaction with insects throughout human societies from prehistory to today, the scientific study of insects experienced a slow and irregular start. In the 1st century BC, Aristotle published a text, *Historia Animālium*, in which Book 4 detailed animals without blood, the non-vertebrates. In that book, he includes insects as class Entoma. The current class, Insecta, is the Latin translation of Aristotle's *Entomon*. The 11th century demonstrated a written record of the understanding that some predatory insects can protect crops (Needham et al., 2000). Entomology as a studied discipline did not start until the 16th century (Saltini, 1989). In the 17th and 18th centuries, entomology matured as a science, with many works being published that encompassed systematics, developmental biology, anatomy, and physiology.

Scientists have struggled with both the estimation of total number of insect species, and total number of insects as a percentage of biomass on earth. Approximately one million insect species have been described. However, scientists now estimate that 5.9–7.8 million species may exist (Stork et al., 2015). Insects make up 75%–80% of the world's known species. The extreme success of insects is due to their adaptability. Species of insects can fly and swim, have adapted to high-altitude freezing conditions, brine pools, subterranean life in the absence of light, and as parasites. The insects of interest to forensic entomologists are those that have adapted to the carrion ecosystem. These insect species are attracted to decomposing human and animal tissue, which they colonize with their eggs and larvae, who feed on the remains and develop in a predictable manner with a rate that is largely based on temperature influences.

Simply stated, forensic entomology can be defined as the scientific study of insects and their arthropod relatives that interacts with legal matters. Of course, expansion of the term "entomology" to include "arthropod relatives" is contrary to the basic definition of the word. However, the fact remains that entomologists are frequently consulted on cases involving non-insect arthropods. In many cases, the entomologist may choose to consult with a subject matter expert about the particular organism in question. Doing so may be a preferred approach, but empirical research on the organism in question may provide enough data for the entomologist to present the information in court as an expert witness.

This chapter will discuss the overall utility of insects in a legal investigation and how entomological knowledge may be applied in a variety of cases. In some instances, photographic documentation may provide some useful information to the forensic entomologist. However, the standard procedure is to collect live and preserved entomological samples at the crime scene during the overall scene investigation. This type of physical evidence collection should be supplemented by making additional collections during the autopsy. This chapter will provide step-by-step instructions for collection and documentation at the crime scene and during autopsy. This chapter is designed to brief the reader on the scope and application of forensic entomology, and provide a step-wise procedure for the scene investigator to follow, including proper packaging and shipment to a qualified forensic entomologist.

12.2 HISTORY AND ENTOMOLOGICAL RESEARCH

Forensic entomology is not a new concept. Though its utility in death investigations, civil litigation, and other criminal cases may be relatively new by comparison, using insects to answer certain scientific questions has been in practice for hundreds of years. In general, there are three major subfields of forensic entomology: urban, stored product, and medicolegal. Urban cases often relate to termite infestations and stored product usually relates to commercial food contamination. But the medicolegal aspect dates back as early as 13th-century China from its use—and subsequent write-up—in a local death investigation by Sung Tz'u in *The Washing Away of Wrongs* (McKnight, 1981). In the 19th century, other countries began to publish on the topic as well. European scientists produced two milestone publications, one in 1855 by Bergeret and another in 1894 by Mégnin. Canadian scientists Johnston and Villeneuve published on the topic in 1897. Scientific research in the United States was conducted and published concurrently with the European studies and continued into the 20th century, but none of the material was utilized in a courtroom setting until the 1970s and 1980s (Villet et al., 2010). It was not until the late 1980s and after that police and other investigators began making regular use of entomology evidence in death investigations and their subsequent criminal trials. This awareness was bolstered by trainings and workshops on the utility of entomological evidence. Entomologists began presenting their empirical research and casework at major forensic conferences, which helped to show the value of entomologists as expert witnesses and case consultants (Anderson, 2005).

Early research into forensic entomology took a much different focus than the ongoing research of today. In fact, it was not truly focused on forensic science casework until the late 20th century. Initially, entomology research that had a medicolegal application looked only at decomposition-related studies—and even then, it did not specifically address vertebrate remains. Rather, these early entomology studies looked at the succession patterns of insects as they related to decomposition of organic plant material such as trees. In some cases, they focused on changes in insects within different landscapes such as lakes or sand dunes (Vincent et al., 1985; Graham, 1925; Forbes, 1925; Chapman et al., 1926). The initial focus of this research did not have a forensic application but instead was intended to gain more information on individual arthropod species, since little taxonomic information was available at that time (Dorsey, 1940). Carrion food sources were used to attract insects of interest to the research site, and researchers then described the unique larval and adult specimens they observed. This information was also used to explain the history and life cycle of insect species as well as in attempts to suppress certain species that had a negative impact on livestock (Davis, 1915; Cole, 1942; Deonier, 1940).

Concurrently with the insect succession studies, research endeavors were addressing taxonomy, ecology, morphology, physiology, and other descriptive studies of several insect families and orders that would come to be forensically important in later decades. The morphological and physiological research was more broadly focused on entire orders of flies, beetles, and springtails (Motter, 1898; Folsom, 1902; Davis, 1915; Illingworth, 1926; Steele, 1927; Dorsey, 1940), whereas the taxonomy research focused more closely on two Diptera families: Sarcophagidae and Calliphoridae (Aldrich, 1916; Knipling, 1939; Hall, 1948). Shortly thereafter, the link between insect succession, development, and temperature began to be better understood. One of the first to associate temperature with developmental rate was Kamal's study on Diptera aged at constant temperature (Kamal, 1958). A study by Howden in 1950 looked at beetle succession on carrion, which was one of the first studies of its kind ever conducted (Howden, 1950). These two studies would be the harbingers of future research in forensic entomology.

In the 1960s, entomology research quickly gained a forensic science focus with particular regard to insect succession throughout decomposition. Studies conducted by Jerry Payne included various ecological systems, including aquatic systems and burials, and were also the first to introduce utilize pigs and suitable substitutes for humans in decomposition research. His work—particularly his 1967 dissertation—is arguably the first true research on forensic entomology as it is practiced today (Payne, 1965, 1967, 1968; Payne and Crossley, 1966; Payne et al., 1968; Payne and King, 1969, 1970, 1972). From the 1970s to the turn of the century, forensic entomology research was a burgeoning discipline, with studies being published on topics ranging from mosquitoes in medical research to fly egg identification using new microscopy techniques. The importance of field research was recognized with the opening of the Anthropological Research Faculty, also known as the "Body Farm," at the University of Tennessee, where the founders would begin to draw a tangible link between human decomposition and forensic entomology (Rodriguez and Bass, 1985).

Though the research foundation for forensic entomology was laid primarily in the mid-20th century, from the 1980s and beyond forensic entomology became recognized as a useful application to criminal proceedings. Along with this recognition came the necessity for better and more plentiful research into all the various aspects of entomology that could be used—and subsequently testified to—in a criminal investigation. Numerous publications were produced between 1980 and the early 2000s that addressed temperature effects on insect development, collection and rearing procedures, insect succession models for decomposition, use of pigs as models for humans, statistical error rates, weather and climate data, and even the application of DNA to forensic entomology cases. In the United States and in many other countries worldwide, forensic entomology is well established as an important component of a death investigation. New applications even include wildlife and animal death investigations (Anderson, 1999). Two major forensic entomology textbooks are widely utilized, both of which have seen a second edition published within the last 10 years (Catts and Haskell, 2008; Byrd and Castner, 2010). To attempt to fully explain all the research upon which the current state of forensic entomology has been built would be too lofty an undertaking for this chapter, but the scope of forensic entomology continues to grow year after year, with new students and researchers producing groundbreaking studies and applications that better utilize insects in forensic investigations.

12.3 AREAS OF FORENSIC ENTOMOLOGY

The broad field of forensic entomology is commonly broken down into three general areas: medicolegal, urban, and stored product pests. Although most forensic entomologists focus in medicolegal entomology, some focus only in urban or stored product areas, while a few entomologists may work in more than one area on a routine basis.

12.3.1 Urban

The urban aspect of forensic entomology deals with the insects that affect human society and its environment. Generally, urban forensic entomologists are called upon to identity the insect pests responsible for infestations of public, commercial, and private dwellings (Figure 12.1).

FIGURE 12.1 Damage to a dwelling from a termite infestation. (Photo courtesy of Chris Baranski.)

FIGURE 12.2 Cowpea beans infested with weevils, a common stored product pest. (Photo courtesy of CSIRO.)

These scientists develop control and eradication plans, and identify the causes that led to an infestation. This casework can sometimes result in criminal or civil litigation. The urban forensic entomologist casework generally involves roaches, biting and non-biting flies, and bedbugs. Most of the questions answered are centered on control issues, but urban forensic entomologists are commonly requested for expert opinion on artefacts on human and animals that either may be insect derived or patterns of injury. There is some overlap with the medicolegal aspect of forensic entomology, as urban insect pests may feed on both the living and the dead. Urban pests may produce problems for the forensic investigator because their feeding and scavenging may produce antemortem, perimortem, or postmortem artifacts that may be misinterpreted as injuries.

12.3.2 Stored Product

Many food products can become infested or contaminated by insect pests (Figure 12.2). Such contamination may result from improper handling, packaging, or storage. Some infestations may be accidental, while others may be a case of intentional contamination. Additionally, some reported cases of contamination may be allowable, as the U.S. federal government sets allowable limits for insect contamination of food products. These limits are defined dependent on the food item in question, so the stored product forensic entomologist must be familiar with the food item and the allowable limits of insect matter. Simply because an insect is found in a food item does not necessarily imply liability. Stored product entomologists may be called upon to assist in control and eradication measures, and their work has general overlap with urban forensic entomology on common pest species. They may also be able to determine when a particular investigation or contamination event occurred. They often provide testimony in criminal and civil court actions to assist the trier of fact in assigning liability and assessment of monetary damages.

12.3.3 Medicolegal/Medicocriminal

When many people use the term "forensic entomology," they are indeed referring to medicolegal forensic entomology. This area of forensic entomology focuses on the insects that inhabit decomposing human and animal remains. Commonly, the medicolegal forensic entomologist is called upon to determine a minimum postmortem interval, or establish a time of colonization of the remains utilizing the recovered insect species. Expert opinions may be offered on the postmortem movement of remains, time of burial versus minimum time of death, postmortem treatment of remains such as freezing or concealment, recovery of victim DNA from the digestive system of insect larvae, and possibly a qualitative toxicological assessment of the insect larvae. This area of forensic entomology is the most widely practiced, and is the specialization of the majority of currently board certified forensic entomologists.

12.4 WHAT CAN INSECTS TELL US ABOUT THE SCENE?

The estimated time of insect colonization, cause and manner of a person's death, the season of insect colonization and the colony's postmortem movement, and evidence of neglect of a living person can all potentially be determined through medicolegal forensic investigation.

12.4.1 Time of Colonization

Knowledge of insect biology and life history allow an investigator to tell a great deal about a crime scene. The primary question asked of a forensic entomologist is time of colonization estimation (TOC). TOC is often associated with the minimum postmortem interval (PMI), or time of death, due to the life history and habits of colonizing insects (Amendt et al., 2007; Benecke, 2004; Smith, 1986). Forensically important insects are generally in the ecological group of decomposers—those organisms that utilize the nutrients bound up in dead matter (Price, 1997). Decomposers efficiently find and exploit dead matter, and those that reply upon ephemeral resources such as remains of humans and animals excel at resource location (Price, 1997; Cain et al., 2008). Due to this resource location efficiency, colonizing insects with unobstructed access to bodies may arrive at a newly dead organism within minutes after death (Catts and Haskell, 2008; Hall, 1995, Byrd and Castner, 2010) (Figure 12.3). Therefore, estimation of colonizing insect age (TOC estimation) may be used as an indicator of how long that body has been available for insect colonization, and, by extension, how long that body has been dead (PMI) (Byrd and Castner, 2010; Davidson, 1944).

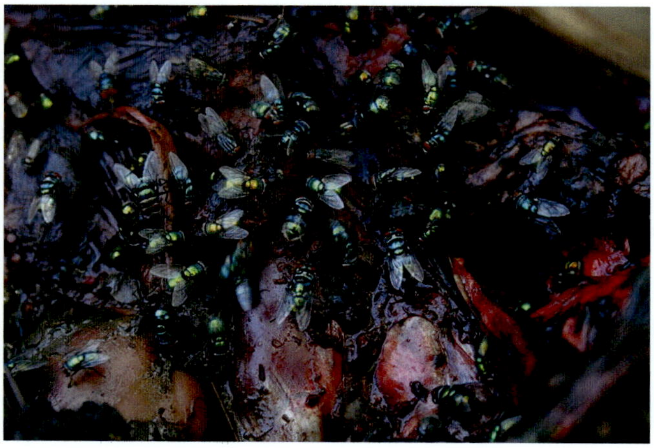

FIGURE 12.3 Blowflies are often the first insects to colonize human and animal remains after death. They are especially quick to colonize areas of trauma. (Photo courtesy of Paul Venter.)

TOC estimation relies on knowledge of basic insect physiology. Insects are poikilothermic, meaning their growth and development is affected by ambient temperature (Davidson, 1944), and each insect species has a lower and upper threshold, below or above which the insect no longer grows (Price, 1997). Between these thresholds, lower ambient temperatures lead to slower insect growth, while higher ambient temperatures lead to faster insect growth. This growth pattern may be described by a mathematical formula (Michaud and Moreau, 2011; Higley et al., 1986; Byrd and Castner, 2010).

It is possible to use this mathematical formula to estimate the PMI, given some obvious assumptions. If we assume the insects observed on a body arrived right after death, and their growth was primarily dictated by ambient temperature, then it is possible to calculate the time needed for an observed colonizing insect to reach the observed developmental stage at the observed ambient temperature. This calculated time is the time of colonization, which, under most circumstances, we may assume is equal to the postmortem interval (Smith, 1986; Byrd and Castner, 2010; Catts and Haskell, 2008). If the arrival time of insects is different from time of death (i.e., the body was blocked from insect activity, insects arrived before death, substances were used to repel insects, etc.) then the time of colonization does not equal time of death, and should not be used as such (Byrd and Castner, 2010; Tomberlin et al., 2011).

12.4.2 Case Study: Time of Colonization

The neighbors of an elderly male resident of a mobile home community called for a welfare check after noticing papers piling up on the resident's front porch. Officers responding to the call found the mobile home near dumpsters at the back of the park. It had no air conditioning, the windows were open, and the resident was found in the late stages of decay, lying near the center of the living room. The advanced stages of decay and the witness statements led the pathologist to estimate several weeks had passed since the decedent had died. Insect activity, however, told a different story. Large, third instar (third stage) larvae were found in the head region of the decedent. Adult flies were active all over the mobile home. The ambient temperature of the trailer was the same as outdoors, due to the lack of air conditioning, and the open windows allowed for easy access to the body. Flies of the same species were found in the dumpster, indicating that the flies colonizing the body were likely present at the moment the resident died, and had unfettered access to his body. Calculation of time of colonization (TOC) using ambient temperatures indicated a time of death of 5 days prior to discovery. Further investigation corroborated this TOC estimation.

12.4.3 Extension of Time of Colonization Estimation

The insects that colonize a body are not static; they arrive in blending waves made up of different species, depending on time of year, temperature, location, and state of decomposition of the body (Price, 1997; Michaud et al., 2015). This is known as insect succession (Price, 1997). Knowledge of the order in which insects arrive at carrion, and the time they take utilizing that carrion as a resource, allows investigators to estimate TOC (and, by extension, PMI) to include the life of several successive waves of insects.

12.4.4 Case Study: Time of Colonization Extension

The nearly skeletonized body of a middle-aged female was found in a park. The lack of tissue made PMI estimation by pathologists nearly impossible. Investigators noticed many small, flat, and "hairy" beetle larvae feeding in the tissue, and numerous pupal casings around the body. Analysis of this evidence indicated the pupal casings belonged to a species of blowfly, common in the area, that is known to colonize fresh bodies. The flattened beetle larvae were dermestid beetles, known to feed on dry remains. Using ambient temperature, entomologists were able to calculate the TOC estimation using both the time it took the initial colonizers to arrive at and colonize the body, develop through their larval stages, pupate, and emerge into adults, and the time necessary for the second grouping of insects, the dermestid beetles, to arrive and colonize the body (Figure 12.4). This allowed for an extension of the TOC estimation and gave a range for the possible time of death.

FIGURE 12.4 Dermestid beetles feeding on soft tissues still present on a human skull. (Public domain photo (CCO 1.0)).

12.4.5 Cause and Manner of Death

Insect colonizers tend to oviposit and feed on tissue that is easily accessible and in a state ready for eating. This means that insects showing up quickly after death will colonize an animal in the areas of the body easy to locate, protected from elements and danger, and easy for the offspring to feed upon. These areas include natural bodily openings, such as the eyes, ears, nose, mouth, and genitalia. This also includes unnatural bodily openings, such as perimortem wounds (Byrd and Castner, 2010; Smith, 1986; Campobasso, 2001). Larvae hatching from eggs oviposited in any of these areas will feed on the tissues in the general vicinity of the egg mass, and then move into new areas. Early maggot masses can therefore be expected only in areas of natural bodily opening (e.g., the head and genitals). If maggot masses are found in any other area, especially those likely to be inflicted with wounds during a struggle, then there was likely a wound of some sort in that area that allowed for larval penetration. The presence of wounds may indicate a death from something other than natural causes, or give indication of events that happened just before death (Smith, 1986).

Similarly, certain diseases such as diabetes may cause festering wounds on appendages, especially the feet. These wounds will attract colonizing insects in the same manner as a decomposing body (James, 1947; Smith, 1986). Presence of maggot masses in these areas in concert with medical history may give some clue as to diseases present in the decedent around the time of death.

12.4.6 Case Study: Cause and Manner of Death

The body of a young man was found by the roadside in an advanced state of decay. Autopsy technicians noted that the flesh of the head was nearly gone, as was the flesh of the left hand and right foot. Large maggot masses were present in the head, hand, and foot regions, and accounted for the consumption of tissue. While insects were expected to colonize the head region, they are unable to feed on the hands or feet without the presence of wounds. Large maggot masses in these areas indicated wounds on these appendages right around the time of death.

12.4.7 Season of Colonization and Postmortem Movement

All arthropods, including insects, have a distribution range based on a variety of factors. These may include availability of food, dispersal ability, and climate. This results in different species of decomposers living in different areas at different times of the year. Knowledge of the range and distribution of various insects is important when it comes to forensics, since it can indicate the potential location of death. For example, Brundage, Bros, and Honda (2011) showed that forensically important flies showed significant habitat differences within a single county, with different communities maintained in urban, rural, and riparian habitats. This suggests that animals killed and colonized in urban areas will have very different species of flies feeding on the remains than those killed and colonized just a few miles away in rural or riparian habitats. Similarly, Gruner, Slone, and Capinera (2007) showed significantly different species composition of flies colonizing animal remains in winter, spring, summer, and fall. This indicates that remains found in the same area at different types of year will be associated with different insect species. Knowledge of the types of forensically important insects common to different regions and different seasons can allow an investigator to determine potential location of death and colonization, differentiate the place of death from a potential dump site, and narrow down the season during which the animal remains decomposed.

Insects may also indicate the movement of remains after death through evidence of insect colonization left over at the original death site. Diptera larvae exploit carrion for a relatively short time. After they have finished feeding upon the remains, they leave those remains and find a protected place in which to pupate. This area may be directly underneath the body, in the vicinity of the body, or farther away across smooth surfaces (Byrd and Castner, 2010). The presence of numerous pupal casings or pupating flies in a particular area indicates that at one time a body was present, and may give evidence that a carcass was once in the area, even if it is long gone (Figure 12.5).

Similarly, fly larvae may continue to feed on purged fluids from a decomposing animal long after the majority of the tissue has been removed through scavenger feeding or movement of the body to conceal a crime (Haglund and Sorg, 1996). Maggots that were once associated with remains may feed on fluids that have seeped into the ground, soaked into bedding (Kelly et al., 2009) or other material, or were dropped from suspended bodies (Haglund and Sorg, 1996; Fisher et al., 2006). These larvae may be analyzed in the same way as those removed directly from the carcass, and used to construct a TOC estimation of the purged fluids.

FIGURE 12.5 Puparia of blowflies (Calliphoridae) under leaf litter and on top of soil. These insects have dispersed from the body as larvae and formed pupae in a protected location. (Photo courtesy of Lerah Sutton.)

12.4.8 Case Study: Season of Death

The skull of an unknown male was discovered disarticulated from a body in a heavily wooded area during early fall. The skull was completely devoid of flesh, and had the remains of a paper wasp nest inside the skull cavity. No indication of time of death was present near where the skull was found. Entomologists studied the wasp nest. This particular species of wasp was known to build its nests in enclosed, dry areas during spring, and inhabit those nests for the duration of spring, summer, and fall, leaving only when winter proper arrived. Nests were then abandoned and not reused again. The fact that a wasp nest was present in the skull indicated that the skull had to be completely clean of tissue during the spring, to allow for building of the nest. The fact that the nest had no living wasps or larvae associated with it when discovered indicated that it was not a recently built nest, but had been built at least the year before. This told investigators that the skull had to be clean and dry at least a year and a half before discovery to allow for the wasp nest to be used and abandoned. Therefore, the owner of the skull likely did not die during the summer months, but likely the sometime before spring the year prior to discovery. The skull would have had to be fully devoid of tissue before nest construction. This added at least a year to the minimum time of death.

12.4.9 Evidence of Neglect

Insects colonizing a body are most commonly used to determine time of death (Byrd and Castner, 2010). However, they do have the ability to colonize festering wounds of still-living humans and animals (James, 1947). An investigator can use the same techniques as discerning time of colonization or postmortem interval to calculate a time of neglect: the primary difference is that the first two terms describe insects that colonized a body after death, while the latter describes insects that colonized a living human. The science is the same. An investigator can use the ambient temperature and knowledge of the insect life cycle to estimate the age of the larvae collected from a still-living patient. Assuming that the insects colonized an open wound, the age of the insect indicates how long that insect has been feeding on the patient. If the insect is large enough to see, or is feeding on apparent areas (rather than internally or in areas that are not easily visible), then it can be inferred that the patient was neglected for as long as the insect was feeding. This gives the investigator an estimated time of neglect.

Time of neglect may cause some problems when trying to determine TOC for PMI estimation, however. It is important to keep in mind that many of the same species that colonize dead animals have the ability to colonize open wounds, and may be present before the animal was dead (James, 1947). If these insects did colonize a patient before death, then using the full insect age will lead to an incorrect PMI estimation. This is one of the reasons forensic entomologists use the term "time of colonization" to describe the insect age calculations. Use caution when attempting these estimations unless it is known for certain that the insects colonized after death and not before.

12.4.10 Entomotoxicology

Insects that colonize a body after death are feeding directly on tissue, and whatever substances happen to be in that tissue. The old adage "you are what you eat" applies quite literally in these cases (Campobasso, 2001). Any and all substances present in decomposing tissue are ingested by colonizing insects, and these decomposers lack the physiology to excrete many of these substances (Pounder, 1991; Campobasso, 2001). The chemicals end up being stored in the insect body, and can be extracted through common toxicological methods. It is therefore possible to test for the presence of chemicals in a decomposed or mummified animal by testing the insect colonizers rather than the animal tissue itself, using common toxicology techniques (Gosselin et al., 2011).

One important limitation to this technique is it is unable to determine an exact amount of substance presence in animal tissues (Tracqui et al., 2004). As the colonizers feed, they will intake varying amounts of the substance, and bioaccumulate the chemical in tissues. There is no known correlation between the amount of chemical present in a living human, and the amount of chemical stored in insect tissues during colonization (Tracqui et al., 2004). We cannot quantify the chemical using this method, only answer the yes-or-no question "Was this chemical present in the decedent?" with certainty.

12.4.11 Case Study: Entomotoxicology

The mummified body of a male was found in a deeply wooded area at the end of a harsh winter. The body was clothed in hiking gear associated with warmer temperatures, indicating the decedent had not been prepared for the cold. Investigators postulated that the remains belonged to someone who had gotten lost during warmer months. However, witnesses stated that the decedent had been seen in early December, and was not known to hike in the snow. Pupal casings around the body were collected and tested for the presence of alcohol and drugs. All casings came back positive for both ethanol and heroin, indicating that the decedent had both of these substances in his body at the time of his death. Investigators theorized the decedent was not in his right mind when entering the woods, which explained his lack of protective clothing.

As with all forensic sciences, forensic entomology is simply the application of a science to a practical situation. These cases and scenarios illustrate the most common use of insects in casework, although the applications are truly endless. Any practical application simply takes advantage of the knowledge we have gained about insects through general study.

12.5 DNA ANALYSIS

One aspect of forensic entomology that cannot be overlooked is the use of DNA. As DNA analysis has become ubiquitous in forensic investigations (James 1947), its use is becoming more and more common in all aspects of forensic science, including forensic entomology (Wells et al., 2007). The most common usage of DNA is for positive identification of insects associated with remains (Wells and Stevens, 2008; Benecke, 1998). The correct identification of colonizing insects is important for TOC analysis, yet morphological characteristics may be obscured due to poor collection techniques or damage during processing. DNA analysis allows investigators to potentially identify insect species without the need for morphological characteristics (Meiklejohn, et al., 2011, Rolo et al., 2013).

Additionally, DNA analysis allows investigators to test for the presence of human DNA on or in an insect specimen, thereby determining if that specimen had fed upon human remains, or had been associated with human remains prior to collection (Wells et al., 2001). It may also indicate the movement of human DNA by insect movement, rather than by human or animal movement (Durdle, van Oorschot, and Mitchell, 2009). Both of these circumstances are important, as they may change the timeline of a decedent.

DNA use is an area of ongoing investigation, and while common in forensic science laboratories, it is still rare in forensic entomology. Both cost and time are barriers to the full adoption of molecular methods for identification, and until these methods become cheaper and easier to use on a regular basis, they will be outmatched by morphological identification techniques.

12.6 BASIC INSECT ANATOMY

Insect anatomy is the foundation of entomology. Arthropods in general have evolved strategies to live successfully under a variety of conditions, and a strong understanding of external and internal anatomy of the insects involved in decomposition gives the investigator a good basis to understand insect behavior.

The overall body form of an insect is cylindrical and elongate, and is broken up into three major body regions: the head, the thorax, and the abdomen. The head is made of sclerotized, or hardened, segments fused to form a capsule. It is rigid to protect the brain and give strength to the mouthparts, and houses the sensory center of the organism. The sensory center consists of olfactory input through the antennae, and visual input through the eyes (Gullan and Cranston, 2009).

Visual input allows the insect to see movement of prey or enemies, potential oviposition sites, potential food, and it assists in mate location. Most insects have two types of eyes: the simple eyes and the compound eyes. The compound eyes, when present, take up the bulk of the insect head, and consist of many individual units or lenses working together to form a single image. Single lenses, called the simple eyes, are present at the vertex of the head in some organisms, and give the insect information about light and dark. Working together, the compound and simple eyes allow flies and other insects to find carrion (Gullan and Cranston, 2009; Nation, 2011).

Insect antennae act as the center for olfaction (Gullan and Cranston, 2009). The antennal structures are found anterior on the head, and come in a variety of forms, from long and thin to robust with many tiny hairs. The antennae pick up on airborne molecules, including products of decomposition, which allow the insect to locate potential resources from great distances. Insects use the relative abundance of volatiles to locate decomposing matter that is out of visual range (Gullan and Cranston, 2009).

The insect mouthparts come in a variety of forms, depending on the evolved use. Some insects have chewing mouthparts with large mandibles, which allow that insect to feed on a variety of substrates. Other insects have piercing and sucking mouthparts, which allow the insect to pierce through skin or the surface of a plant and feed on the internal fluids. Still others have sponging mouthparts, which enable the insect to extrude digestive juices into the environment and soak up the resulting digested substance (Nation, 2011). Some insects have siphoning mouthparts which act like a straw and allow the insect to feed on freely available liquids like water and nectar, while others have specialized mouth hooks, in place of the mouthparts, that can scrape food in the environment for eating. The types of mouthparts found in forensically important insects vary based on the type of tissue each insect is feeding upon. Those insects that feed during the early stages of decomposition tend to have sponging mouthparts as adults and mouth hooks as larvae. Those that feed during the later stages of decomposition, when tissue tends to be tougher, tend to have chewing mouthparts (Mullen and Durden, 2002).

The thoracic region of the adult insect has three pairs of legs, and often has wings. The legs are five-segmented, and adapted for a myriad of other behaviors common to the individual insect. There are usually two pairs of wings, and the wings tend to be slender with veins throughout for strength. These veins and the open areas between the veins (called cells) are used to identify many insect species. Some insects may not have wings at all, or have lost their wings through evolution or behavior. Other insects have modified wings for protection and flight. Beetles have two pairs of wings, but the first pair is hardened into a protective covering for the hind wings. Flies have one pair of well-developed wings, while the hind wings are reduced into knob-like organs that are used for balance during flight (Nation, 2011).

The abdomen is generally cylindrical, and varies from 9 to 11 visible segments. Each segment bears a pair of holes on the lateral surfaces called the spiracles, which allow for oxygen to diffuse into the internal trachea. The abdomen does not usually have any appendages, and primarily serves to house the internal organs. The terminal end of the abdomen houses the genitalia and other specialized structures. Some female genitalia are heavily sclerotized and used for defense as stingers (Gullan and Cranston, 2009).

The internal organs of the insect are housed within a hollow body cavity called the hemocoel. This cavity contains all the organs, including the heart and brain, and the digestive, reproductive, nervous, and respiratory systems. The organs are bathed in a nutrient-rich hemolymph, which fills the hemocoel with fluid. The hemolymph combines some of the functions of vertebrate blood and lymph, delivering nutrients, removing metabolites, and carrying out basic immune functions (Nation, 2011). Circulation of hemolymph is maintained mostly by a system of muscular pumps moving the hemolymph through compartments separated by membranes. Insects have an open circulatory system: hemolymph is not confined to vessels. Instead, it sloshes around the hemocoel and bathes the organs with nutrients and hormones while removing wastes and assisting in immune functions (Mullen and Durden, 2002). Most insect hemolymph doesn't carry oxygen, and therefore does not have the characteristic red color caused by hemoglobin. The heart is a simple dorsal tube, closed at the posterior end, and dotted with openings called ostia. The ostia allow hemolymph to enter the dorsal vessel, and the vessel pumps the hemolymph forward toward the brain. The hemolymph then flows backward in the hemocoel, assisted by muscle contractions in the ventral diaphragm (Mullen and Durden, 2002).

Oxygen is provided to the tissues from the environment via the respiratory system. Air enters the insect via the openings found on the lateral or posterior surfaces of the body, called spiracles. Spiracles are attached to a network of tracheal tubes that branch throughout the body, ultimately contacting all the internal organs and tissues (Mullen and Durden, 2002; Gullan and Cranston, 2009).

The digestive system is responsible for the breakdown of foods and the excretion of waste products. It begins with the foregut, which receives the ingested food, and is responsible for the initial digestion through muscular grinding. Chemical digestion primarily takes place in the midgut, where enzymes break down carbohydrates and proteins into absorbable units, which are absorbed through the midgut lining. Whatever is left over after absorption moves into the hindgut, where excess water and ions are absorbed. Waste products are excreted into the environment (Mullen and Durden, 2002; Nation, 2011).

The insect nervous system is in charge of conveying and integrating information about the internal and external environments. It consists primarily of the brain, found along the dorsal region of the head capsule, and a ventral nerve cord, which travels ventrally from the brain along the thorax and abdomen. The nerve cord is studded with ganglia, thickened regions of tissue that contain nerve cells. Each ganglion is the nerve center for its associated segment, and sends information from that segment back to the brain for processing (Nation, 2011).

12.7 THE INSECT LIFE CYCLE

The bulk of forensic entomology relies on an understanding of the reproduction of insects and the resulting life cycle. Reproduction in most insects involves two sexes: a male and a female. The female reproductive system is responsible for producing and storing eggs, providing eggs with nutrition, receiving and storing the sperm, fertilizing the eggs, and depositing the eggs into the environment. The male reproductive system is responsible for producing sperm and presenting it to the female for egg fertilization (Nation, 2011).

The primary forensically important insects are the Diptera, or the true flies, due to their ability to quickly locate and colonize remains. The dipteran life cycle is therefore considered the most important life cycle to understand (Smith, 1986; Catts and Haskell, 2008). The Diptera exhibit a complete metamorphosis, meaning they start out as eggs, hatch into the first of several larval instars, pupate, and eclose into adults. Most dipteran females lay eggs, and are termed oviparous. Others retain the eggs internally until they hatch, and deposit early instar larvae into the environment. These are called ovoviviparous or larviparous. A very few groups retain the developing larvae in their bodies until the larvae are ready to pupate. These are called pupiporous flies (Nation, 2011). The larvae tend to inhabit aquatic or semiaquatic environments during these immature stages. The number of larval stages, termed instars, varies with species. In general, flies have three or four larval instars before pupation. Once the larval stage has finished feeding, the immature fly will enter the dispersal, or wandering stage (Mullen and Durden, 2002). This dispersal stage takes the larvae 15–20 feet away from the carrion and to a protected place in which to pupate (Catts, 1992). The dispersing larvae will crawl under things in the environment, or dig a few centimeters down into the soil, where the outer cuticle of the larva hardens into a protective shell, ultimately called the pupal case. Inside this pupal casing, enzymes transform the larvae into an adult (Nation, 2011).

12.7.1 Calculating Time of Colonization

Dipteran larvae do not produce their own heat (Nation, 2011). Instead, they rely upon the ambient temperature, which determines how quickly or slowly they grow (Davidson, 1944). Warmer ambient temperatures result in a quick life cycle, while slower ambient temperatures result in an extended life cycle. It is this property that allows forensic entomologists to apply insect development data to determine a TOC estimation on remains. This also makes temperature the most important density independent factor for insects (Beck, 1983; Byrd, 1998).

Temperature has a significant effect on dipteran metabolic and developmental rate (Nation, 2011). Every insect has thermal activity and death thresholds: both lower and upper limits, below or above which they can no longer function (Nation, 2011; Beck, 1983; Block, 1982). These thermal thresholds are naturally different for different species, and often associated with life history and climate. There is a distinct variation among species when it comes to temperature thresholds. The lower limits are better known than the upper limits, and become important when mathematically calculating a TOC estimation (Block, 1982). Experimentally determined developmental thresholds for forensically important flies are usually between 6°C and 10°C. If published thresholds are not available, a the general rule of thumb is to use a lower developmental threshold for cold-weather species, and a higher threshold for warm-weather species (Ames and Turner, 2003; Davies and Ratcliffe, 1994; Anderson, 2000).

Each stage of insect growth requires a certain amount of heat above a minimum temperature and below a maximum temperature (Hagstrum and Milliken, 1988; Davidson, 1944), which may be represented by a linear model. These linear models describe units of heat-time called degree day or degree hour models. In these cases, development is recorded as the temperature above the minimum developmental threshold multiplied by either days or hours (i.e., a unit of time) (Yang et al., 1995; Michaud and Moreau, 2011; Higley et al., 1986).

The model allows us to calculate the time it takes a fly to develop using ambient temperature and this formula:

$$(\text{Average ambient temperature} - \text{Minimum threshold}) \times \text{Unit of time}$$

The average ambient temperature over a given period of time (days or hours) is calculated, and the developmental threshold of an insect species is subtracted (6°C or 10°C, usually). The results are multiplied by a unit of time (number of days or hours). The result is called a "degree day" (DD) (if the unit of time used was a day) or a "degree hour" (DH) (if the unit of time used was an hour). These are the two most common units of time seen in this type of model, simply because weather stations often record ambient temperature in daily or hourly intervals.

The formula may be used to calculate how many degree days (DD) or degree hours (DH) are necessary for an insect to get through various stages in its life cycle, as well as how many degree days have accumulated over time. The DD/DH necessary for an insect to get through its life cycle is determined in the lab. The data are recorded as hours needed for a species to develop at a given temperature, and these data may be converted into DD or DH simply by using the formula. These developmental data may be found in scientific publications and accessed online. Each developmental stage, from egg to adult, may be calculated in this manner.

Once the DD or DH necessary for insect development is known, it is possible to calculate the time necessary for the DD to accumulate at recorded ambient temperatures. The species threshold temperature is used in the same DD formula, but the average temperature is a weather station recording over a given period of time. Once all this information is calculated, the DD necessary for an insect species to develop is applied to the total DD accumulated (ADD) over a period of time to determine how long it would take an insect to develop to an observed life stage given the recorded ambient temperature.

Take, for example, the case of an unknown decedent found by the side of the road. Investigators discover this body covered in third instar maggots. The maggots are actively feeding, and there is no indication that the flies were kept from immediately colonizing the body after death. A forensic entomologist would first need to collect the maggots for identification. Then, the entomologist would need to find developmental data on that species of maggot in the literature. This data would be recorded as number of hours necessary for development at a standard temperature. Using this information, the entomologist could calculate the number of degree days necessary for the maggots to reach the beginning and end of the third instar. This range would allow the investigator to account for the fact that the exact age of the maggot remains unknown – it is not possible to tell if the maggot was at the very beginning of the third instar, or nearing the very end of the third instar, so a range of possible developmental times is necessary. The entomologist would then find out the historical ambient temperature by finding data from local weather stations. These data are reported in average daily or hourly temperatures, and made available through governmental databases. The number of degree days or degree hours that accumulated in the environment could then be calculated, and the time necessary for the colonizing fly to reach the observed stage of development determined.

12.7.2 Insect Succession and Extended Time of Colonization

Insect that feed on bodies are broken up into different ecological groups: necrophagous species, which feed primarily upon animal and human remains; omnivorous species can feed upon both remains and other organisms colonizing those remains; predators and parasites feed on necrophagous or omnivorous species; adventive species use the remains as an extension of their primary environment; and incidental species are associated with remains simply due to happenstance (Roberts and Márquez-Grant, 2012; Price, 1997). The most useful of these groups are the necrophagous species, since they are feeding directly on the remains themselves. However, some information may be gleaned from the other ecological groups (Price, 1997; Smith, 1986). Necrophagous insects arrive on and in a corpse in a relatively predictable sequence, and form the ecological succession of insects. This succession is influenced by the environment, season, and the decompositional state of the remains. The insects arrive in blending waves, called seres, of organisms, each comprised of different species attracted to a particular state of decay (Goff, 1993; Smith, 1986).

The number of seres that colonize a body depends on the placement of the remains. Exposed corpses yield approximately eight seres, while buried remains yield only three (Mégnin, 1894). This difference is due to the availability of decomposing tissue, along with the ability of those insects to reach tissue that is blocked from easy access. While some insects will readily colonize tissue placed in the open air, they may not be able to reach that same tissue buried just a few inches below the soil surface. Buried bodies therefore have a lower number of colonizing insects, and take a longer period of time to decompose that those in the open air (Mégnin, 1894).

Different insects are attracted to different stages of generalized decomposition. While stages of decomposition are not necessarily discrete and are notoriously imprecise, historically scientists have broken up decomposition of animal remains into five major stages: fresh, putrefaction, active decay, butyric fermentation, and dry decay (Haglund and Sorg, 1996). Each of these stages attracts one or more seres of insects and other arthropods in a predictable sequence. From the moment of death, the insect fauna of an animal body begins to change. Any ectoparasites (insects feeding on the living animal tissue) associated with the body leave relatively quickly as the body cools and the blood ceases to circulate (Mullen and Durden, 2002). Myiasis-causing flies may or may not die—it is dependent upon if they are obligate parasites of living tissue, or facultative parasites that can feed on both living and dead tissue. Botflies, for example, are dependent upon a living host, and if the host dies, the botfly dies. *Cochliomyia* sp., on the other hand, can feed on living or dead hosts, and may just continue to feed after the animal dies (Mullen and Durden, 2002; Smith, 1986).

Insects in the necrophagous group are attracted to the body within minutes of death, and are therefore associated with the fresh stage of decay. The first adults tend to be observed on a fresh corpse within an hour after death, as long as there is adequate access to the body (Smith, 1986). Some investigators report arrival time to be as early as 15 seconds after death, although this timing has yet to be adequately studied (Catts and Haskell, 2008). Eggs and first instar maggots tend to appear with the onset of autolysis, and this early sere is characterized by the presence of adult flies and fly eggs. Eggs will be found near natural bodily openings, on wounds, and sometimes in protected folds of skin or coverings. Those eggs will hatch to first instars quickly in warm environments, but there will not be a large maggot mass on the body; the tissue will still look fresh. Primarily, blowflies, houseflies, and flesh flies will make up the earliest seres observed (Midgley et al., 2010; Schoenly and Reid, 1987). Larvae grow according to ambient temperature, and move throughout the body. This movement will spread bacteria and digestive enzymes as the larvae feed on tissues. The larvae move in a mass, benefiting from communal heat and shared digestive secretions. Larvae first feed between muscles, then on the muscle fibers themselves as the maggots grow and the digestive juices get to work. The rate of decay increases, and the odors emitted from the body attract more blowflies, flesh flies, beetles, and mites. They are joined by parasitic wasps that lay their eggs inside maggots and later inside pupae. This second sere is characterized by putrefaction of tissue, and the presence of blowflies and flesh flies primarily (Byrd and Castner, 2010).

Once the body enters active decay, several generations of maggots are present on the body. Some of the maggots will be well into the third instar, and will begin to disperse from the remains to find pupation sites. These maggots will burrow into the soil or crawl under nearby objects for safety. This later decompositional stage no longer proves attractive for early sere members, which make way for those insects that prefer later stages of decay. Predatory maggots are much more abundant at this stage, and may be feeding upon other species in the maggot mass, along with predatory beetles that feed on both larvae and animal tissues (Watson and Carlton, 2005). Parasitic wasps are also common, attacking the huge maggot masses and developing pupae. Active decay attracts a new sere characterized by carpet beetles and grease moths. As active decay moves into butyric fermentation, two additional seres are attracted: first, a sere consisting of small flies known as cheese skippers and beetles arrive at the body. The second sere consists of dump flies, phorid flies, and clown beetles (Smith, 1986). As the carrion is stripped of most of its soft tissue, the remaining tissue begins to dry out, making the body less palatable to the mouth hooks of maggots. Beetle adults and larvae feed on skin and ligaments, while certain late-stage flies, such as the cheese fly, arrive to feed on whatever moist flesh remains. Predators and parasites are still prevalent at this stage, feeding on the straggling maggots or other soft-bodied insects in the vicinity (Schoenly, 1992; Smith, 1986).

Once the remains have completely dried out, the body attracts insects that can feed on keratinized hair and skin. This dry stage of decomposition is highly attractive to a new sere consisting primarily of mites and beetles. This stage tends to last for a long while, since the business of feeding on dried-out tissue takes a great deal of time and digestive enzymes. The beetles will remain on the bones as long as the skeleton is undisturbed and has dried tissue (Schoenly, 1992). After the dried tissue has been cleaned by the beetles, moths, and mites, only the bones' empty pupal casings remain. There is no longer any major insect activity, and any further decomposition is accomplished by bacteria and physical factors.

By way of comparison, a buried animal has fewer seres with lower species diversity (Payne, 1968). Freshly buried animals tend to attract flies that must burrow through the top layers of soil to reach the remains. Active decay may attract root-eating beetles, and dry decay is populated by rove beetles (Payne, 1968; Smith, 1986). Since early successional experiments, there have been many, many attempts to characterize the number of seres that show up on bodies of different sizes. It is difficult to positively identify the seres, however, and entomologists have agreed upon only a broad definition of these blending waves. Use of insect succession for TOC estimation is therefore dependent largely upon the types of flies and beetles present in the area, and their likelihood of arriving at fresh versus decaying flesh (Smith, 1986).

12.7.3 Adventive and Incidental Species

A myriad of other insect and arthropod species may be associated with decomposing carrion simply by chance. These organisms use the body for shade, shelter, or as a vantage point for predation. These arthropods could just as easily use any object in the environment, and do not have any intrinsic forensic significance. However, their presence may indicate an extended postmortem interval (e.g., the presence of a spider web on a body indicates an extended PMI). As a group, the organisms that may be found on carrion but do not have any direct forensic application are called adventive species (Smith, 1986; Byrd and Castner, 2010; Catts and Haskell, 2008).

Any mobile terrestrial or airborne arthropod may accidentally land on or in the vicinity of carrion. These specimens may be collected along with the forensically important organisms, but they do not have any forensic value, due to their unpredictable arrival and accidental nature. These organisms are called incidental species as a group since they don't use the body for anything at all, and are often identified and ignored during a forensic case (Smith, 1986; Byrd and Castner, 2010).

12.7.4 Important Insects in Decomposition

Diptera are commonly known as the true flies, and are one of the largest and most diverse orders. The order name literally means "two winged," and refers to the fact that the hind pair of wings is greatly modified and reduced. There are approximately 120,000 species worldwide, with around 20,000 found in North America. Diptera are considered the most important order to human and animal health, due to their vector capabilities, and are the most important in forensics, since they often compose the bulk of the first sere.

12.8 WORKING A CASE AT THE CRIME SCENE

The application of entomology and the types of cases encountered can be extensively varied, but the standard procedures for working any case on scene are generally the same. Some basic equipment and information is required at all scenes and can be obtained with relative ease. At every scene, a kit will be needed for proper collection and storage of the insects. Once the insects are properly collected, they should be sent to an entomologist who will identify and analyze them at a later date. Temperature data is also of vital importance to entomological analysis. Since it is uncommon for an entomologist to be present on every scene—though very helpful when possible—making a collection kit ahead of time and learning some of the basics of how to collect forensically significant insects can make the collection process simple and straightforward.

12.8.1 Assembling a Collection Kit

The first step toward being prepared to collect insect evidence on scene is assembling a collection kit. While there are some prefabricated kits commercially available for purchase, many of the required items can be easily and inexpensively obtained at local stores, though some items may need to be ordered ahead of time. Essential collection kit items include the following:

- Insect net
- Thermometer
- Collection vials
- Preservation chemicals
    - A mixture of kerosene, alcohol, and acetic acid (KAA)
    - 80% ethyl alcohol (EtOH)
    - Ethyl acetate
- Featherweight forceps
- Kill jar
- Plastic spoons
- Plastic containers
- Aluminum foil
- Vermiculite
- Food source
    - Beef liver
    - Canned cat food
- Labels
    - Plain paper
    - Self-adhesive
- Pencil
- Trowel
- Gloves
- Ruler or scale
- Camera
- Shipping containers
- Entomological Death Scene Form (Figure 12.6)

Forensic Entomology Data Form

Date: ______	Collector: ______
Case Number: ______	Agency: ______
Location : (*GPS coordinates, nearest physical address, city, state, country*)	
Decedent: ______	Age: ______ Sex: ______
Last Seen Alive: ______	Date/Time Found: ______
Date Reported Missing: ______	Time of Insect Collection: ______
Site Description:	
Condition of the remains: ☐ whole ☐ partial	If partial, what part is present:
Presence of trauma: ☐ yes ☐ no ☐ unknown	Evidence of scavenging: ☐ yes ☐ no ☐ unknown

Evidence of possible traumatic injury sites: (*Comment and/or draw below*)

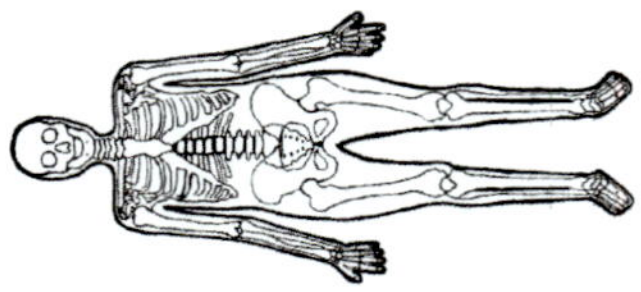

Type of body/remains concealment:
☐ none ☐ plastic bag ☐ container, type: ______ ☐ burial, depth: ______
☐ other: ______

Location(s) of insect activity: (*check all that apply*)
☐ head ☐ mouth ☐ eyes ☐ ears ☐ anus ☐ genitals ☐ chest ☐ abdomen
☐ wound(s), location(s): ______ ______ ☐ other: ______

Location on body of insect specimen collection: (*check all that apply*)
☐ head ☐ mouth ☐ eyes ☐ ears ☐ anus ☐ genitals ☐ chest ☐ abdomen
☐ wound(s), location(s): ______ ☐ other: ______

Approximate stage of decomposition:
☐ fresh ☐ bloated ☐ active decay ☐ advanced decay ☐ skeletonized
☐ saponification ☐ mummification ☐ dismemberment ☐ other: ______

Body exposure: (*check all that apply*)
☐ open air ☐ burial ☐ fully clothed ☐ partially clothed ☐ nude
☐ full sun ☐ partial shade ☐ full shade ☐ debris, type: ______
☐ other: ______
Portion of body clothed and description of clothing :

Location of body and insect collection site: (*check all that apply*)
☐ indoor ☐ outdoor ☐ aquatic ☐ rural ☐ urban/suburban

Indoor: ☐ house ☐ shed or outbuilding *Was structure closed to outside insect access?* ☐ yes ☐ no ☐ unknown *Was structure temperature controlled?* ☐ yes, temperature: ______ ☐ no ☐ unknown	Outdoor: (*check all that apply*) ☐ forest ☐ field ☐ pasture ☐ brush ☐ grass ☐ roadside ☐ pavement ☐ trash container ☐ vacant lot ☐ other: ______
Aquatic: (*check all that apply*) ☐ pond ☐ lake ☐ creek ☐ river ☐ canal ☐ ditch ☐ gulf ☐ swampy area ☐ salt water ☐ fresh water ☐ brackish water ☐ standing water ☐ running water ☐ other: ______ Water temperature: ______ *Was the body floating on water surface?* ☐ yes ☐ no ☐ unknown	Notes on the collection site or body condition:

Scene temperatures: (*complete all that apply*)
ambient:______ ambient (1 ft):______ body surface:______ ground surface:______
under-body interface:______ maggot mass:______ soil temperature (1 inch):______
soil temperature (3 inches):______ A/C or Heat:______ ceiling fan: on/off
Note: Record all temperatures periodically each day at the side for 3-5 days after recovery.

Method of insect preservation for soft-bodied specimens:
☐ hot water kill and 80% ethanol ☐ 80% ethanol ☐ other:______

Number of preserved samples:	Number of live samples:
How are live samples being maintained? ☐ room temperature at: ______ ☐ other: ______	Where were the specimens sent?

FIGURE 12.6 Entomological Evidence Data Form used to document the conditions at the crime scene when collecting insect evidence. (Courtesy of Richard Merritt.)

12.8.2 Collecting Evidence on Scene

Once the collection kit is assembled, the process of collecting entomological evidence on scene should be simple. Since blowflies go through several developmental stages on scene associated with the decomposition process of a body, it is important to collect a representative sample from each life stage present. This includes adults, eggs, larvae, and pupae. Adult beetles and beetle larvae (grubs) may also be collected and sent to an entomologist, but they don't offer as much insight into the TOC window as do blowflies. Temperature data must be collected on scene in order to ascertain the developmental stage of the insect and for comparison to historical weather data, which will also be used in entomological analysis. Collection on scene can be split into six steps as indicated in the following sections.

1. Visual observations and photographs of scene.
   a. This should always be the first step in entomological evidence collection on scene, because the act of collecting insects may, in some cases, alter the appearance of the scene due to the invasive nature of insect collection. Photographs of the scene itself should be taken, including botanical habitat and tree cover, to indicate the amount of sun or shade that was present over the body throughout the process of decomposition if the scene is outdoors. If the scene is indoors, be sure to photograph windows, doors, or other areas where light or airflow may enter the scene. This step can be supplemented by filling out the Entomological Death Scene Form (Figure 12.6), which will list all information necessary to document. Environment, weather conditions, state of decomposition, and any other significant findings should be noted before any collection begins. Photographs of the insects themselves should also take place before collecting them. These photographs should be associated with written descriptions of the insects or other arthropods noted on scene. These descriptions can be general in nature (i.e., nonscientific), but should be as detailed as possible to give the entomologist a complete account of the death scene from the point of view of the on-scene investigator. Sketches with compass directions or other diagrams can be included to supplement the photographs, and any trauma, dismemberment, wrapping, or other artifacts on the remains should be noted, as these may alter insect activity and development.

12.8.2.1 Collection of Temperature and Meteorological Data

2. Because insects undergo temperature-dependent development, it is paramount that accurate temperature data is collected on scene. The warmer it is, the faster the insects will develop. Likewise, the colder is it, the slower they will develop. As such, it is important to identify the closest weather station that collects temperature data in order to obtain historical data that will be used in the entomological analysis. For temperature data collection on scene, several different measurements must be taken.
   a. *Ambient air temperature.* This temperature should be taken at about 4 ft. from the ground surface in the shade. If indoors, note the setting of the thermostat (if present) as well as the recorded ambient temperature (Figure 12.7).
   b. *Body surface temperature.* This should be taken from the upper surface of the remains by placing the temperature probe just on the surface of the remains. If the body is wrapped, placing the probe on the outer surface of the wrapping is appropriate (Figure 12.8).
   c. *Body–ground interface temperature.* This temperature should be measured by placing the thermometer directly in between the body and the surface upon which it is resting (e.g., soil, floor). Be sure not to puncture the body or introduce any new trauma in the process of taking this temperature measurement (Figure 12.9).
   d. *Maggot mass temperature.* Place the temperature probe slightly into the center of the maggot mass to obtain an accurate reading.

FIGURE 12.7 Recording ambient air temperature at the scene. (Photo courtesy of Lerah Sutton.)

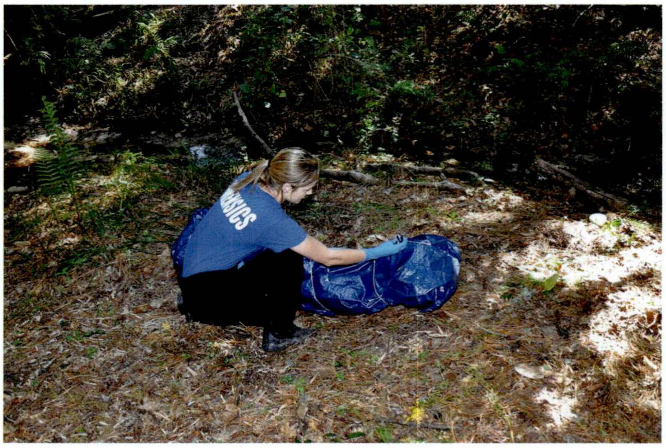

FIGURE 12.8 Recording upper body surface temperature. (Photo courtesy of Lerah Sutton.)

FIGURE 12.10 Recording ground surface temperature. (Photo courtesy of Lerah Sutton.)

FIGURE 12.9 Recording body–ground interface temperature. (Photo courtesy of Lerah Sutton.)

If there is more than one area of the body in which maggots are feeding, this step should be repeated at every area of collection.

e. *Ground surface temperature.* This reading should be taken several feet away from the body along the surface of the ground—either floor or soil. If the scene is outdoors, an additional reading should be taken by inserting the probe a few inches into the soil (Figure 12.10).
f. *Under-body soil temperature.* In an outdoor scene, a soil sample may be requested from underneath the body, in which case a soil temperature should be taken by inserting the temperature probe a few inches into the soil directly under where the remains were located. This should not be done until all other documentation and evidence processing has been completed and the body has been removed.
g. *Daily ambient air temperature.* If possible, the ambient air temperature should be recorded on scene for 3–5 days after the body has been removed. This will allow an entomologist to compare the data obtained from the nearest weather station to the temperatures collected on scene and to then correlate the historical data with the on-scene temperature collection. This type of temperature data can prove very important in courtroom testimony when standard error is calculated. If temperature data can be collected on scene several times throughout the day, that is ideal, but a daily maximum and minimum will suffice.
h. *Storage temperature.* If insect collection did not occur until after the body was removed from the scene, or if additional insect collection took place at autopsy, the temperature of the storage location should also be noted along with the length of time the body was stored before collection took place.
i. *Historical weather data.* This information can be obtained after leaving the scene by contacting the National Weather Service or other certified weather-recording entities. By using GPS coordinates or other location information recorded on scene, locate the nearest weather station to the death scene. Document its station number and its distance from scene. Daily maximum and minimum temperatures should be obtained from the weather station for comparison to scene data, and hourly data should also be obtained when available. Precipitation, humidity, cloud cover, wind speed, or other necessary weather information should be obtained when useful or requested by the consulting entomologist.

12.8.2.2 Collection and Preservation of Insects on Scene

3. A representative sample of all life stages and species of insects observed on scene should be documented, collected, and preserved for subsequent analysis.
   a. Collecting insects for a preserved sample should begin with adult insects—generally flies found over or around the body, though beetles may also be present. About 50 adult flies should be collected, if possible, but a representative sample of each species present should be collected if collecting 50 is not feasible. For beetles, 10–15 adults should be collected. Adult flies should be collected using an insect net. When they are present over a body, a sweeping motion should be used over the body to trap insects in the net. This motion should be done quickly enough to prevent the net from dragging over the body itself but not so quickly as to scatter the adult flies. Another option for collection if adult flies are not abundant over the body is to hold the net with the base of the ring down and the enclosed mesh portion of the net up toward the sky. To a fly, "up" is always "out" (Figure 12.11). Moving very slowly in a downward motion toward the surface of the body will allow the net to appear as part of the natural environment to a fly. Once the opening of the net is near the insects of interest, gently rustle the net, which will cause the adults to fly up and into the net. When flies are trapped in the net, there are two options for killing the adults. The first is to fold the mesh portion of the net over the hoop to prevent their escape and insert it into a kill jar charged with ethyl acetate. Tighten the lid over the mesh of the net and leave the adults in the jar for several minutes. Once they have stopped moving they can be placed into a dry vial or one with alcohol. The second method is to continue holding the tip of the net up and reach inside the net with a vial of preservation solution (alcohol or KAA). Place the opening of the vial directly underneath the insects in the net and gently tap the insects from outside the net, causing them to fall into the preservation solution (Figure 12.12). It is not necessary to keep adult insects alive for shipment to an entomologist, so either method of preserving the adults is sufficient. Adult beetles may be collected with soft-touch forceps and placed into a kill jar or directly into preservation solution. If a live adult collection is requested, do not mix beetles with flies, as beetles are often predators and will eat the other evidence.
   b. After collecting the preserved adults, larval samples should be obtained. The maggots are generally the most important components of entomological collection analysis, so a complete and representative sample is vital. Fifty to sixty individuals of each observed species should be collected from each colonized area of the body. Different species may be distinguished based on shape, color, or size. When possible, they should be collected separately. The largest maggots are usually the oldest larvae and should be collected first, as they were likely the first to colonize

FIGURE 12.11 When capturing flying adult insects in a net, holding the tail of the net up and toward light will prompt the insects to crawl or fly upward, thereby trapping them in the net more effectively. (Photo courtesy of Lerah Sutton.)

FIGURE 12.12 Adult blowflies may be collected by placing them directly into a killing solution from within the insect net. (Photo courtesy of Lerah Sutton.)

FIGURE 12.13 Placing soft-bodied larvae into near-boiling water to preserve them before packaging in a vial of preservation fluid such at EtOH. (Photo courtesy of Lerah Sutton.)

FIGURE 12.15 A post-feeding blowfly larvae that has wandered away from the body to enter the pupal stage. (Photo courtesy of Lerah Sutton.)

FIGURE 12.14 Place preserved larvae into a vial of EtOH with featherweight forceps. (Photo courtesy of Lerah Sutton.)

the remains. Obtaining a preserved sample of maggots on scene is very important, because it allows an entomologist to determine the age of the maggots at the time of the death scene investigation. To do this, maggots must be properly preserved on scene to prevent decomposition or degradation of the sample during shipment to an entomologist. One option is to place the larvae, which have been collected with featherweight forceps, into very hot (i.e., nearly boiling) water for about 15 seconds and then place them into a vial of EtOH (Figure 12.13). If hot water is not readily available on scene, placing the larvae into a solution of KAA for several seconds will be an adequate substitute for hot water. After immersion in KAA, the maggots should be transferred into a vial of EtOH (Figure 12.14). Soft-bodied insects should not be kept in KAA for an extended period of time or shipped in this solution, as it is a fixative: exposure to KAA for too long will result in maggots that are brittle and difficult to work with. If there is a maggot mass with large numbers of maggots, they may be collected using a plastic spoon as an alternative to individually picking them up with forceps. Beetle larvae (grubs) should be collected and preserved the same way as the fly larvae, but only 10–20 individuals of each observed species are needed.

c. The oldest insects on scene are often the fly pupae, and a sample of 50–60 should be collected from on or around the remains. Pupae are small, rigid, and brown to black in color. They may look similar to roach egg casings or mouse droppings but can be distinguished by their segmented casings. Maggots will migrate away from a body before pupating (Figure 12.15), so the area surrounding the remains should be searched for pupae. In an outdoor environment, maggots may burrow down an inch or two into loose soil or under rocks or limbs; thus, it may be necessary to use a trowel to dig a few inches into topsoil to uncover pupae. Indoors they may be found under rugs or baseboards. Pupae should be collected using featherweight forceps (Figure 12.16). A preserved sample of pupae may be collected by placing them directly into EtOH, but a live sample is preferred.

FIGURE 12.16 Pupae may be easily collected with featherweight forceps. (Photo courtesy of Lerah Sutton.)

12.8.2.3 Packaging and Shipment of Live Insects on Scene

4. As with the preserved samples, a representative sample of all observed insect species should be collected and kept alive for shipment to an entomologist. The collection methods are the same whether the samples are to be preserved or kept alive, but the packaging methods differ. One major difference is that a live adult sample of flies is not necessary for shipment to an entomologist unless specifically requested.
    a. After collecting maggots with featherweight forceps, the live sample should be placed into a "maggot motel." This motel is assembled by taking a plastic storage container and placing some vermiculite or loose soil into the bottom of it. A small sheet of aluminum foil should be formed into a pouch—tightly enough so the maggots feel sheltered but not so tight as to prevent their eventual migration for pupation—and a food source placed inside the pouch. The maggots should then be gently placed directly onto the food source and the pouch should be placed on the vermiculite (Figure 12.17). Close the lid onto the plastic container and poke small air holes in the lid, ensuring they are not so large that the maggots or flies will escape during shipment.
    b. Pupae will be searched for and collected in the same way for a live sample as a preserved one (if requested). For their packaging, fill a plastic container with vermiculite and place the pupae into it, sealing the lid and poking small air holes (Figure 12.18). Neither foil nor a food source is necessary for a live pupae collection, as they have already finished the feeding stage of their life cycle.
    c. If collecting live samples of beetles, ensure that both their larvae and adults are packaged separately from the larvae or adults of flies. Beetles can be predacious and may eat the fly evidence, which would severely hinder entomological analysis.

FIGURE 12.17 A plastic container with a tight-fitting lid can be used to package live larvae with a food source for shipment to an entomologist. (Photo courtesy of Lerah Sutton.)

FIGURE 12.18 Post-feeding larvae and pupae can be packaged in a small plastic container with vermiculite for shipment to an entomologist. (Photo courtesy of Lerah Sutton.)

12.8.2.4 Labeling Collected Specimens

5. Both preserved and live samples should be labeled inside and out (Figure 12.19). Plain paper labels must be written in pencil and placed either inside the vial of EtOH or inside the maggot/pupae motel. Write duplicate

FIGURE 12.19 All entomological samples should be labeled inside on plain paper and outside on a self-adhesive label. All labels should be written in pencil. (Photo courtesy of Lerah Sutton.)

information—again in pencil—on self-adhesive labels and place them on the outside of the vials and plastic containers. Include case number, agency, location/address of the scene, date, time of collection, name (or initials) of collector, location of collection on body or scene, and contents of the sample on both types of labels. Do not fill labels out in ink, as the alcohol will cause the ink to run and be illegible to the entomologist performing the analysis.

12.8.2.5 Shipment of Evidence to an Entomologist

6. Once all adults, larvae, and pupae have been collected in their preserved and live forms as appropriate, it is time to send the samples to an entomologist. It is a good idea to make contact with a consulting entomologist prior to going on scene, so he or she can tell you what type of samples are preferred and other types of information that must be collected on scene. Carefully place the properly labeled vials and plastic containers into shipping containers, ensuring that the "up" side of the box is clearly indicated for the postal service of choice to prevent the samples from getting damaged during transport. Be sure to include a fully filled-out entomological death scene form with the samples and any crime scene photos as appropriate. Note the total number of each type of sample included. The faster the samples are able to reach an entomologist, the better, since live samples must be removed from their shipment packaging and placed into rearing facilities. It is best to contact the consulting entomologist upon shipment to let him or her know live samples will be arriving so the proper facilities can be prepared in a timely manner. Also ensure that contact information for the investigator who performed the collection is included with the samples, so that the entomologist may contact the investigator with questions or requests for additional information.

12.9 WORKING WITH AN ENTOMOLOGIST

12.9.1 Laboratory Identification and Analysis

Once the collected specimens are received by the forensic entomology laboratory, there are several items which should be addressed promptly. First, the insects that were collected alive must be placed into a larger container and provided a suitable food source. The container with the larvae and their food source must then be placed inside another larger container with a substrate that allows for natural larval dispersal and burrowing. Ideally, the living larvae are in a temperature-controlled environment so that their growth can be carefully monitored. The soft-bodied larvae that were preserved at the scene must then be placed in KAA, or blanched in hot water if this was not completed at the scene.

Once proper rearing and preservation has been accomplished, the entomologist will then seek to make an identification of the collected insects to the lowest taxonomic level possible. Having the identifications completed will provide the taxonomic identification necessary for the entomologist to be able to gather growth and development data from the relevant literature. Once the life history information is gleaned from the relevant literature, meteorological data is obtained from a local recording station. Having the meteorological data will allow for a comparison of the climate at the crime scene versus the recording station location. This information is then utilized to determine the probable age of the collected insects. The age of the insects equates TOC and/or the minimum PMI.

12.9.2 Case Report Information

For medicocriminal casework, basic case report information should include the identification of the insects collected; the location, or station identification, for the meteorological data; and the entomologist's estimation of insect age. For urban and stored product forensic entomology case reports, the insect identification is included, as well as any health or disease transmission concerns, and the source of infestation. The published case report is what the forensic entomologist will submit to the investigative agency. In turn, this is what will form the basis of the deposition and expert witness testimony.

12.10 CONCLUSION

Entomological evidence will not be present in all legal investigations. In the cases where entomological evidence is present, it will likely not provide all the answers the investigator may seek to obtain. However, in the cases where entomological evidence is found and recovered, an analysis of such evidence will provide information that may not be obtained otherwise. That information, even if slight, is another piece of the investigation that may be useful in the later stages of a legal investigation. The collection of entomological evidence is not difficult, expensive, or time consuming. Therefore, there is little reason for investigating agencies to omit the collection of entomological evidence from their crime scene protocols. Utilizing the equipment and methods detailed in this chapter, the investigator should have the basic skills needed to process a crime scene for entomological evidence, and be able to gather the needed environmental information. With the collected insects, environmental data, and adequate photography of the scene, the investigator should be able to package and ship the materials to a qualified forensic entomologist. Having provided the needed information, the investigator should receive a report of analysis from the entomologist detailing the species identification and estimated minimum time of colonization in a comprehensive report.

BIBLIOGRAPHY

Aldrich, J.M. 1916. *Sarcophaga and Allies in North America*. La Fayette, IN: Thomas Say Foundation.

Amendt, J., C. P. Campobasso, E. Gaudry, C. Reiter, H. N. LeBlanc, and M. J. R. Hall. 2007. Best practice in forensic entomology—Standards and guidelines. *International Journal of Legal Medicine* 121:90–104.

Ames, C. and B. Turner. 2003. Low temperature episodes in development of blowflies: Implications for postmortem interval estimation. *Medical & Veterinary Entomology* 17:178–186.

Anderson, G. S. 1999. Wildlife forensic entomology: Determining time of death in two illegally killed black bear cubs. *Journal of Forensic Sciences* 44 (4):856–859.

Anderson, G. S. 2000. Minimum and maximum development rates of some forensically important Calliphoridae (Diptera). *Journal of Forensic Sciences* 45 (4):824–832.

Anderson, G. S. 2005. Effects of arson on forensic entomology evidence. *Canadian Society of Forensic Sciences Journal* 38 (2):49–67.

Beck, S. D. 1983. Insect thermoperiodism. *Annual Review of Entomology* 28 (1):91–108.

Benecke, M. 1998. Random amplified polymorphic DNA (RAPD) typing of necrophageous insects (Diptera, Coleoptera) in criminal forensic studies: Validation and use in practice. *Forensic Science International* 98 (3):157–168.

Benecke, M. 2004. Neglect of the elderly: Forensic entomology cases and considerations. *Forensic Science International* 146:S195.

Block, W. 1982. Cold hardiness in invertebrate poikilotherms. *Comparative Biochemistry and Physiology Part A: Physiology* 73 (4):581–593.

Brundage, A., S. Bros, and J. Y. Honda. 2011. Seasonal and habitat abundance and distribution of some forensically important blowflies (Diptera: Calliphoridae) in Central California. *Forensic Science International* 212 (1–3):115–120. doi: 10.1016/j.forsciint.2011.05.023.

Byrd, J. H. 1998. Temperature dependent development and computer modeling of insect growth: Its application to forensic entomology. PhD Dissertation, Entomology, University of Florida.

Byrd, J.H. and J. L. Castner. 2010. *Forensic Entomology the Utility of Arthropods in Legal Investigations*. Edited by Byrd, J. H. and J. L. Castner. 2nd ed. Boca Raton, FL: Taylor & Francis.

Cain, M. L., W. D. Bowman, and S. D. Hacker. 2008. *Ecology*. Edited by Cain, M. L. Sunderland, MA: Sinauer Associates.

Campobasso, C. P. 2001. Factors affecting decomposition and Diptera colonization. *Forensic Science International* 120 (1–2):18–27.

Catts, E. P. 1992. Problems in estimating the postmortem interval in death investigations. *Journal of Agricultural Entomology* 9 (4):245–255.

Catts, E. P. and N. H. Haskell. 2008. *Entomology and Death: A Procedural Guide*. Edited by Catts, E. P. and N. H. Haskell. Second edition. Clemson, SC: Joyce's Print Shop.

Chapman, R. N., C. E Mickel, J. R. Parker, G. E. Miller, and E. G. Kelly. 1926. Studies in the ecology of sand dune insects. *Ecology* 7 (4):416–426.

Cole, A. C. 1942. Observations of three species of Silpha (Coleoptera: Silphidae). *American Midland Naturalist* 28 (1):161–163.

Davidson, J. 1944. On the relationship between temperature and rate of development of insects at constant temperatures. *Journal of Animal Ecology* 13 (1):26–38.

Davies, L. and G. G. Ratcliffe. 1994. Development rates of some pre-adult stages in blowflies with reference to low temperatures. *Medical and Veterinary Entomology* 8:245–254.

Davis, W. T. 1915. Silpha surinamensis and *Creophilus villosus* as predaceous insects. *Journal of New York Entomological Society* 23:150–151.

Deonier, C. C. 1940. Carcass temperatures and their relation to winter blowfly populations and activity in the Southwest. *Journal of Economic Entomology* 33:166–170.

Dorsey, C. K. 1940. A comparative study of the larvae of six species of Silpha (Coleoptera, Silphidae). *Annals of the Entomological Society of America* 33 (1):120–139.

Durdle, A., R. A. H. van Oorschot, and R. J. Mitchell. 2009. The transfer of human DNA by *Lucilia cuprina* (Meigen) (Diptera: Calliphoridae). *Forensic Science International Genetics Supplement Series* 2 (1):180–182.

Fisher, R. S., W. U. Spitz, and D. J. Spitz. 2006. *Spitz and Fisher's Medicolegal Investigation of Death : Guidelines for the Application of Pathology torime Investigation.* Springfield, IL: Charles C Thomas Publisher.

Folsom, J. W. 1902. Collection of the grave. *Psyche: A Journal of Entomology* 9 (315):363–367.

Forbes, S. A. 1925. The lake as a microcosm. *Illinois Natural History Survey Bulletin* 15 (9):537–550.

Goff, M. L. 1993. Estimation of post-mortem interval using arthropods' development and successional patterns. *Forensic Science Reivew* 5:81–94.

Gosselin, M., S. M. R. Wille, M. del Mar Ramírez Fernandez, V. Di Fazio, N. Samyn, G. De Boeck, and B. Bourel. 2011. Entomotoxicology, experimental set-up and interpretation for forensic toxicologists. *Forensic Science International* 208 (1):1–9.

Graham, S. A. 1925. The felled tree trunk as an ecological unit. *Ecology* 6 (4):397–411.

Gruner, S. V., D. H. Slone, and J. L. Capinera. 2007. Forensically important Calliphoridae (Diptera) associated with pig carrion in rural north-central Florida. *Journal of Medical Entomology* 44 (3):509–515.

Gullan, P. J. and P. S. Cranston. 2009. *The Insects: An Outline of Entomology*. New York, NY: John Wiley & Sons.

Haglund, W. D. and M. H. Sorg. 1996. *Forensic Taphonomy: The Postmortem Fate of Human Remains.* Boca Raton, FL: CRC Press.

Hagstrum, D. W. and G. A. Milliken. 1988. Quantitative analysis of temperature, moisture, and diet factors affecting insect development. *Annals of the Entomological Society of America* 81 (4):539–546.

Hall, D. G. 1948. *The Blowflies of North America.* Baltimore, MD: Thomas Say Foundation.

Hall, M. J. M. 1995. Trapping the flies that cause myiasis: Their responses to host-stimuli. *Annals of Tropical Medicine and Parasitology* 89 (4):333–357.

Higley, L. G., L. P. Pedigo, and K. R. Ostlie. 1986. DEGDAY: A program for calculating degree-days, and assumptions behind the degree-day approach. *Environmental Entomology* 15 (5):999–1016.

Howden, A. E. T. 1950. *The succession of beetles on carrion.*

Illingworth, J. F. 1926. Insects attracted to carrion in Southern California. *Proceedings of the Hawaiian Entomological Society* 6:397–401.

James, M. T. 1947. *The Flies that Cause Myiasis in Man.* Washington, DC: U.S. Government Printing Office.

Kamal, A. S. 1958. Comparative study of thirteen species of sarcosaprophagous Calliphoridae and Sarcophagidae (Diptera) I. Bionomics. *Annals of the Entomological Society of America* 51 (3):261–271.

Kelly, J. A., T. C. van der Linde, and G. S. Anderson. 2009. The influence of clothing and wrapping on carcass decomposition and arthropod succession during the warmer seasons in Central South Africa. *Journal of Forensic Sciences* 54 (5):1105–1112.

Knipling, E. F. 1939. A key for blowfly larvae concerned in wound and cutaneous myiasis. *Annals of the Entomological Society of America* 32 (2):376–376.

McKnight, B. 1981. *The Washing Away of Wrongs: Forensic Medicine in Thirteenth-Century China.* Ann Arbor, MI: University of Michigan Center for Chinese.

Mégnin, P. 1894. *La Faune des cadavres: Application de l'entomologie à la médicine légale.* Paris: Masson & Gauthier-Villars.

Meiklejohn, K. A., J. F. Wallman, and M. Dowton. 2011. DNA-based identification of forensically important Australian Sarcophagidae (Diptera). *International Journal of Legal Medicine* 125 (1):27–32.

Michaud, J.-P. and G. Moreau. 2011. A statistical approach based on accumulated degree-days to predict decomposition-related processes in forensic studies. *Journal of Forensic Sciences (Blackwell Publishing Limited)* 56 (1):229–232.

Michaud, J.-P., K. G. Schoenly, and G. Moreau. 2015. Rewriting ecological succession history: Did carrion ecologists get there first? *Quarterly Review of Biology* 90 (1):45–66. doi: 10.1086/679763.

Midgley, J. M., C. S. Richards, and M. H. Villet. 2010. The utility of coleoptera in forensic investigations. *Current Concepts in Forensic Entomology*, 57–68. Netherlands: Springer.

Motter, M. G. 1898. A contribution to the study of the fauna of the grave: A study of on hundred and fifty disinterments, with some additional experimental observations. *Journal of the New York Entomological Society* 6 (4):201–231.

Mullen, G. R. and L. A. Durden. 2002. *Medical and Veterinary Entomology*. New York, NY: Academic Press.
Nation, J. L. 2011. *Insect Physiology and Biochemistry*. Boca Raton, FL: CRC Press.
Needham, J., G.-D. Lu, and N. Sivin. 2000. *Science and Civilization in China: Volume 6 Biology and Biological Technology, Part 6 (Medicine)*. Cambridge: Cambridge University Press.
Payne, J. A. 1965. A summer carrion study of the baby pig *Sus scrofa* Linnaeus. *Ecology* 46 (5):592–602.
Payne, J. A. 1967. A comparative ecological study of pig carrion decomposition and animal succession with special reference to the insects. PhD Dissertation, Clemson University.
Payne, J. A. 1968. Arthropod succession and decomposition of burried pigs. *Nature* 219 (5159):1180–1968.
Payne, J. A. and D. A. Crossley. 1966. Animal species associated with pig carrion. *Oak Ridge National Laboratory–Technical Monograph* 1432:1–65.
Payne, J. A. and E. W. King. 1969. Lepidoptera associated with pig carrion. *Journal of the Lepidopterists' Society* 23:191–195.
Payne, J. A. and E. W. King. 1970. Coleoptera associated with pig carrion. *Entomologist's Monthly Magazine* 105 (1265–1267):224–232.
Payne, J. A. and E. W. King. 1972. Insect succession and decompostition of pig carcasses in water. *Journal of the Georgia Entomological Society* 7 (3):153–162.
Payne, J. A., F. W. Mead, and E. W. King. 1968. Hemiptera associated with pig carrion. *Annals of the Entomological Society of America* 61 (3):565–567.
Pounder, D. J. 1991. Forensic entomo-toxicology. *Journal of the Forensic Science Society* 31:469–472.
Price, P. W. 1997. *Insect Ecology*. New York, NY: John Wiley & Sons.
Roberts, J. and N. Márquez-Grant. 2012. *Forensic Ecology Handbook: From Crime Scene to Court*. Vol. 9. New York, NY: John Wiley & Sons.
Rodriguez, W. C. and W. M. Bass. 1985. Decomposition of buried bodies and methods that may aid in their location. *Journal of Forensic Science* 30 (3):836–852.
Rolo, E. A., A. R. Oliveira, C. G. Dourado, A. Farinha, M. Teresa Rebelo, and D. Dias. 2013. Identification of sarcosaprophagous Diptera species through DNA barcoding in wildlife forensics. *Forensic Science International* 228 (1–3):160–164. doi: 10.1016/j.forsciint.2013.02.038.
Saltini, A. 1989. *Storia delle scienze agrarie*. Bologna: Edagricole.
Schoenly, K. and W. Reid. 1987. Dynamics of heterotrophic succession in carrion arthropod assemblages: Discrete seres or a continuum of change? *Oecologia* 73 (2):192–202.
Schoenly, K. 1992. A statistical analysis of successional patterns in carrion-arthropod assemblages: Implications for forensic entomology and determination of the postmortem interval. *Journal of Forensic Sciences* 37 (6):1489–1513.
Smith, K. G. V. 1986. *A Manual of Frensic Entomology*. Ithaca, NY: Cornell University Press.
Steele, B. F. 1927. Notes on the feeding habits of carrion beetles. *Journal of the New York Entomological Society* 35 (1):77–81.
Stork, N. E., J. McBroom, C. Gely, and A. J. Hamilton. 2015. New approaches narrow global species estimates for beetles, insects, and terrestrial arthropods. *Proceedings of the National Academy of Sciences* 112 (24):7519–7523.
Tomberlin, J. K., R. Mohr, M. E. Benbow, A. M. Tarone, and S. Van Laerhoven. 2011. A roadmap for bridging basic and applied research in forensic entomology. *Annual Review of Entomology* 56 (1):401–421. doi: 10.1146/annurev-ento-051710-103143.
Tracqui, A., C. Keyser-Tracqui, P. Kintz, and B. Ludes. 2004. Entomotoxicology for the forensic toxicologist: Much ado about nothing? *International Journal of Legal Medicine* 118 (4):194–196.
Villet, M. H., C. S. Richards, and J. M. Midgley. 2010. Contemporary precision, bias and accuracy of minimum post-mortem intervals estimated using development of carrion-feeding insects. In *Current Concepts in Forensic Entomology*, 109–137. Netherlands: Springer.
Vincent, C., D. K. McKevan, M. Leclercq, and C. L. Meek. 1985. A bibliography of forensic entomology. *Journal of Medical Entomology* 22:212–219.
Watson, E. J. and C. E. Carlton. 2005. Succession of forensically significant carrion beetle larvae on large carcasses (Coleoptera: Silphidae). *Southeastern Naturalist* 4 (2):335–346.
Wells, J. D., F. Introna, G. Di Vella, C. P. Campobasso, J. Hayes, and F. A. H. Sperling. 2001. Human and insect mitochondrial DNA analysis from maggots. *Journal of Forensic Sciences* 46 (3):685–687.
Wells, J. D. and J. R. Stevens. 2008. Application of DNA-based methods in forensic entomology. *Annual Review of Entomology* 53 (1):103–120.
Wells, J., R. Wall, and J. Stevens. 2007. Phylogenetic analysis of forensically important Lucilia flies based on cytochrome oxidase I sequence: A cautionary tale for forensic species determination. *International Journal of Legal Medicine* 121 (3):229–233.
Yang, S., J. Logan, and D. L. Coffey. 1995. Mathematical formulae for calculating the base temperature for growing degree days. *Agricultural and Forest Meteorology* 74 (1–2):61–74. doi: 10.1016/0168-1923(94)02185-M.

CHAPTER 13

Forensic Veterinary Science and Medicine

Víctor Toledo González and Francisco Carvallo Chaigneau

CONTENTS

13.1 INTRODUCTION

In recent years, we have been bombarded by a number of so-called forensic science TV programs involving homicides, suicides, and robberies. One or two professionals routinely analyze these cases, and the culprits are found and arrested within 30 minutes—the magic of television!

In reality, this is nearly impossible, because the evidence gathered cannot be analyzed by a mere three people, let alone the case be resolved by a single professional. The field of forensic science is not an activity for general practitioners either.

The forensic analysis group (as seen in the field) is multidisciplinary and consists of specialists involved in the corresponding areas in which they are competent. Many disciplines are intertwined to analyze one or more evidence samples, thus allowing one source to determine the "how" and "who" of a wrongfully committed act. Unfortunately, despite the technological capacity that we possess in our day, it is not always possible to reach such conclusions.

In recent years, humanity has become aware of the environmental damage our species has wrought upon the planet. The brutal urban expansion (demographic and technological) to natural areas by displacing native flora and fauna is an excellent example of this. This new consciousness has led people to organize protests and demonstrations against road projects as well as energy and natural resource exploitation. We are still encroaching into wildlife habitation, however, and the question of how to deal with our new neighbors arises. As a direct result, cases of animal abuse and cruelty (which may be a manifestation of future criminal behavior in young children) are on the rise.

Social demand is calling for the discussion of these issues, requiring a higher degree of knowledge, training, and specialization by those who must enforce the law than is currently seen. However, one such specialization (that of the veterinary forensic experts) was not considered due to the lack of professionals trained in recognized institutions. This discipline would ensure reasonable protection and hope for wildlife welfare and conservation, companion animal welfare, and dignified treatment of animals intended for human consumption. Such discipline, which considers animals as active members in the development of a society, necessary and just.

Thus was born the imperative that professionals involved in animal care and trained under classical concepts of each profession (holistic veterinarians, marine biologists, biologists, etc.) integrate and perfect these concepts in a forensic context to deal with animal legal issues and criminology. These professionals have responded to such concerns (by analyzing new evidence of animal origin) for some time, but their findings were discarded without being used by prosecution.

More recently, the concept of forensic veterinary science has evolved. These disciplines deal with cases concerning unlawful acts involving animals (committed by or against them) but under a objective prism and scientific approach that allows us to answer the same "who, how, and why" questions. Investigators so involved must operate under strict moral, ethical, and bioethical standards. Such work must be closely linked to the work of all entities involved in the justice system, thus allowing using new valid evidence to be considered in judicial proceedings that involve animals as well as people. Clearly, such work must also be supported in the very laws of the region or country in question (considering how altruistic social development and its subsequent religious practices can be) without losing the objectivity and autonomy of judicial exercise.

It is noteworthy that this area is more developed in some countries, but is still constantly improving. This largely corresponds to more personal rather than institutional efforts by individuals who have decided to contribute their expertise in an effort to combat this widely recognized challenge. Success may alter our reality, bringing about a slightly better and more just world where humans and wildlife might live in peace and harmony.

13.2 AREAS OF FORENSIC MEDICINE AND VETERINARY SCIENCE

In general we could say that there are two major areas in which forensic veterinary science could contribute greatly: Animal abuse cases and cases of wrongful acts against wildlife.

We will review veterinary forensics, animals involved in forensic cases, where and when a forensic veterinarian may act, and the implementation of some criminology techniques (in concise detail) to help make possible a type of expert research involving animals.

13.3 FORENSIC VETERINARY SCIENCE AND DEVELOPMENT

In simple terms we could say that forensic veterinary science is *justice based on scientific research*, in cases where an animal's life or well-being is compromised, and when it directly or indirectly affects human endeavors.

The human forensic discipline is much more developed than its animal counterpart, and is widely recognized around the world. Consequently, for decades professionals in the human forensics field have been able to obtain and perfect academic degrees not available to veterinary practitioners. Although some institutions have begun generating that knowledge for veterinarians, such sharing is a recent development. Therefore, the development of forensic veterinary science (and any specialization) seen in the field presently is usually due to self-training.

To date, in many countries the classically trained veterinary professional's work has been enough to collaborate and provide services in this area. However, the future goal is to have professionals who will be constantly refining and specializing aspects of forensic veterinary science. These professionals could take greater advantage and learn from the (non-veterinary) techniques acquired through multidisciplinary investigation without loss of traditional veterinary knowledge.

To further this discipline, the following is required:

1. Forming multidisciplinary working groups for the development of a database to compare animal evidence (whole animals, parts of it, or by-products found in places where a crime has occurred)
2. Generating and publishing scientific research to validate evidence or investigative proceedings in a court of law
3. Generating debates and conversations among professionals involved in forensic science in general, and practitioners of veterinary forensics in particular, thus allowing the establishment of agreements on standardization of procedures and protocols, which in turn allows the globalization and collaboration of different institutions at the national and international level
4. Generating multidisciplinary consulting alongside specialization

Cooper and Cooper (2007) indicate that the skill sets of the veterinary forensics investigator may be applied to such areas as criminal and civil cases, insurance claims, malpractice, industrial disputes, drafting environmental impact governmental requirements, inspection of pet shops, zoonosis, animal abuse (domestic, consumption, or wildlife), animal welfare, smuggling, investigation, and so on. This is not yet a complete list, and the work of forensic veterinary experts can be as varied as the situations that may arise when an animal is a victim. This list is varied, and contains concepts that will be reviewed later.

13.4 MEDICINE, FORENSIC SCIENCE, AND CRIMINALISTICS

Before going further, it must be stated that when speaking of forensic medicine as applied to both humans and animals, it is meant that the study is performed on the animal (living or dead) and must be performed by a medical specialist in forensic sciences (an expert on pathology or a clinical veterinary medicine). Forensic science, on the other hand, works with all others aspects of evidence (ranging from footprints to DNA) and those working in it are well qualified in one of the basic sciences such as anatomy, chemistry, biology, or a similar field.

Furthermore, criminology is defined as the study of the signs of a criminal act in order to determine all possible information concerning the circumstances of the crime. In this way, answers to such questions as how the crime was committed and who the perpetrator was can be obtained. It must be noted that criminology can be divided into three fundamental parts:

1. Forensic or criminalistic techniques
2. Criminal tactics
3. Methodological techniques

The first uses the achievement of art, basic science, and technical trades in the research process. Its application allows for an objective analysis of the evidence and the resulting applications by an expert researcher. Criminal tactics studies, on the other hand, focus on the principles of research planning, the general theory of distinctive versions, and learning the legal basis of the research as used in each case (*modus operandi*). Finally, the methodology of classical scientific inquiries may be applied. This may include observation, experimentation, measurement, classification, comparison, and /or modeling.

In this context, we could say that animals can participate in a criminal act in the role of offender, victim, tangential face (the animal no participle directly in conflict but it may can provide indirectly some evidences on what had happened [maybe contain hair of aggressor, etc.]), or as an agent (in some cases used as a biomarker or biosensor). A few authors have written about this, but in 2007 Cooper and Cooper, in *Introduction to Veterinary and Comparative Forensic Medicine,* wrote about it, indicating that animals can participate in a criminal act as per the following.

The animal in the role of offender (the cause) may cause a range of injuries ranging from the physical harm of bites of varying degrees, abrasions or lacerations (Figures 13.1 and 13.2), and allergic reactions (in cases of hypersensitivity) to the psychological harm to humans or other animals and/or transmission of diseases that may or may not be zoonotic (diseases naturally transmitted between vertebrate animals and humans, a definition offered by the World Health Organization, WHO). In this case, the animal may be the perpetrator or the victim. It is also noteworthy that in this context, zoonosis can be classified as evidence in three groups:

- Those that are equally dangerous for humans and animals (e.g., rabies or anthrax)
- Those that rarely occur or produce mild effects in animals, but cause serious disease in humans (e.g., brucellosis, hydatidosis, herpes virus)
- Those that can cause outbreaks in domestic and wild animals but are rarely of great significance

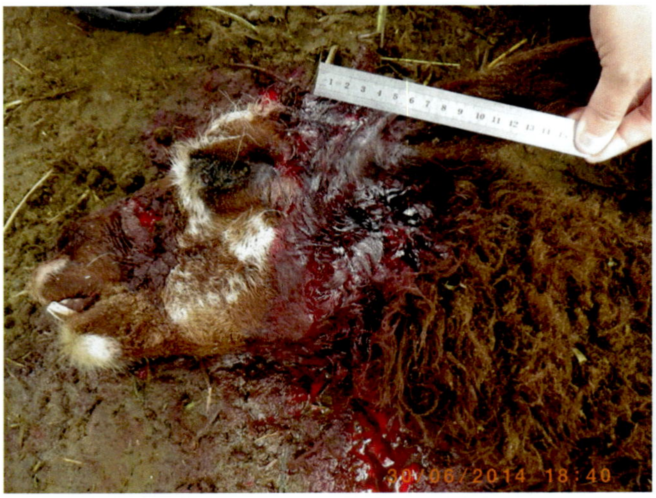

FIGURE 13.1 Alpaca attacked by dogs. Wounds in the neck area with abundant blood loss. (Víctor Toledo González Property.)

to humans in terms of health (Newcastle disease, spongiform encephalopathies, transmittable diseases/TSEs).

Other common zoonoses are rabies, toxocariasis, leishmaniasis, leptospirosis, brucellosis, and others in **dogs**; toxoplasmosis, pasteurellosis, and others in **cats**; avian influenza, chlamydophilosis, psitacosis, salmonellosis, fiardiasis, and others in **birds**; salmonellosis in **reptiles**; rabies, salmonellosis, hydatidosis, brucellosis, bovine tuberculosis, leptospirosis, anthrax, *E. coli*, and others in **farm livestock**; rabies, hantavirus syndromes, rat bite fever (Haverhill fever), and lymphocytic choriomeningitis in **rodents**; anisakiasis in **fishes**, and so on.

Importantly, many zoonotic diseases can be transmitted via food, as in the case of salmonellosis, brucellosis, tuberculosis, and transmissible spongiform encephalopathy.

The **animal victim** may suffer a series of injuries and insults caused by humans rather than by natural causes.

Animals can suffer physical damage such as trauma, heat, cold, immersion in water (or other toxic liquids), and intoxications. In addition, they may suffer psychological damage, including deprivation of company or unsuitable social grouping, taunting, teasing and/or threatening, and sexual damage. Some of these symptoms are not clearly understood in veterinary clinical exercises.

In some cases, certain anomalous behaviors of the animal patient were observed that reflected improper conduct of the owner (even symptoms of abuse normally associated with violence). This reinforces the theory of the need for forensic specialists who have the veterinary expertise required in events like this.

Sometimes the victims are wild animals. By-products of human progress and population growth or the entry

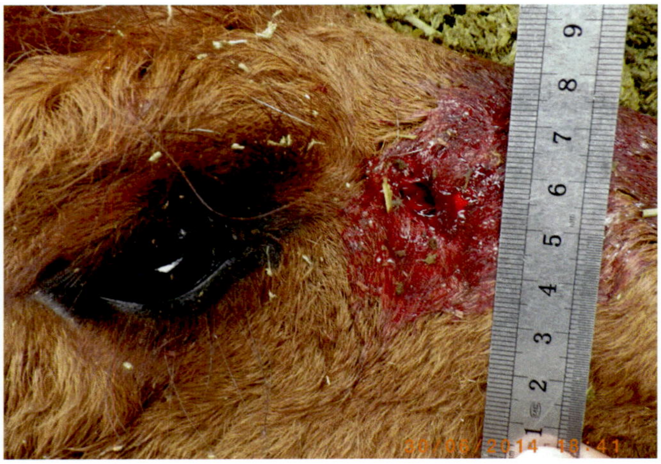

FIGURE 13.2 Bite wound close to the eye. (Víctor Toledo González Property.)

of exotic animals (invasive species) into a place can lead to displacement of other native species as a result of the ensuing struggle for food or land. In extreme cases, this may lead to the extinction of a whole species.

Animals also play a role in other philosophies, up to and including various occult and satanic rituals. As such, they may be subjected to various types of abuse or bizarre methods of slaughter in furtherance of these beliefs.

Still other animals may be victims of **neglect**. This occurs in cases where the animals are not provided with the necessities needed to meet their basic requirements of life, such as nutrition and housing. The first problem mainly consists of the questions of what is a sufficient quantity and quality of food to stay healthy, and access to drinking water of good quality. As for accommodation, it should be appropriate to the needs of the species concerned. Shelters should incorporate natural environmental elements and allow social interaction for when animals form a group. Also, in regard to malnutrition it is imperative to consider both ends of the spectrum: both very thin and obese animals are malnourished. Both extremes can cause metabolic, physical, and behavioral changes or alterations. To determine the body condition of animals, two tables that had a score ranging from 1 to 5 were used, with 1 being for the slimmest animal and 5 being the most obese. The other table ranges from 1 to 9, but has the same purpose. Since this score is used only on live animals, it is recommended to use the terms "good," "proper," or "emaciated animal" during the postmortem examination.

Also, abused animals can suffer **non-accidental trauma** (Figures 13.3 through 13.6), resulting in injuries with or without fracture, wounds caused by the impact of bullets or projectiles, flaking skin to conceal identification marks and property damage, traps and snare damage (which sometimes can cause skin peeling or even amputation of some part of the body), deaths from overdose

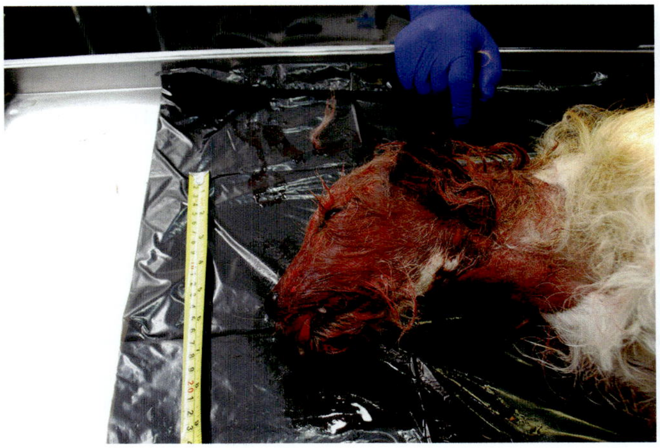

FIGURE 13.3 Dog thrown from a building. (Víctor Toledo González and Federico Cifuentes Ramos Property.)

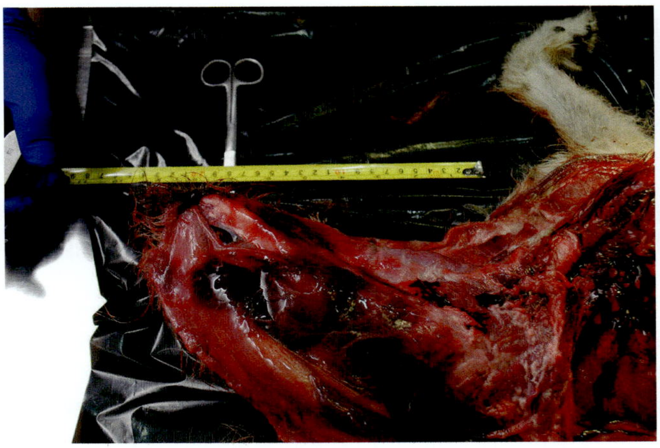

FIGURE 13.4 It's possible to show the large bruise on his right side was hit by the product dropped to the cement floor. (Photo: Víctor Toledo González and Federico Cifuentes Ramos Property.)

of drugs and anesthetics, veterinary malpractice or those practicing illegally, and/or thermal injuries. Among the latter, we mention direct exposure to flame or hot surfaces (e.g., cigarettes, lighters, fire marks for identification), burns for electrocution (something becoming more common in high-voltage towers), microwave radiation, hyperthermia related to excessive ambient temperature (e.g., animals locked in cars or boxes for an extended trip without ventilation), excess radiant heat (e.g., near heat sources like stoves, fireplaces, etc., but without direct contact), hypothermia, and frostbite.

The role of **animals as agents or biomarkers** can provide valuable information on what is happening around them and therefore can affect us directly or indirectly.

An ideal biomarker would be a simple organism to study, one about which we have a well-known understanding of its physiology and behavior in all possible habitats.

FIGURE 13.5 Dog hanged in central courtyard of a group of houses. The dog was fed by the residents but some of them did not agree. (Carlos Muñoz Quezada and Víctor Toledo González Property.)

Animals (dead or alive) have always been natural models in various fields of forensic science. Examples include birds killed by poisoning from heavy metals resulting from industrial activity, livestock contaminated with heavy metals resulting from volcanic eruptions (natural disasters), animals poisoned by pesticides and herbicides, fish poisoned by mining tailings, and sick pets as a result of environmental pollution. Case animals are examined, and through laboratory tests or clinical examination indicate the presence of toxic or harmful elements in human and/or animal health items. In this context, these animals act as true sentinels of the environment.

The use of birds as environmental sentinels is not a new development: many decades ago, caged canaries were taken down into coal mines to detect traces of toxic gas that could be potentially dangerous to miners.

Another example of environmental monitoring involving animals concerns anthracosis (the deposition of carbon in the respiratory tract and associated lymph nodes). This is well documented in humans but has also been recognized in dogs, cats, and other animals that live in urban environments where air pollution is prevalent.

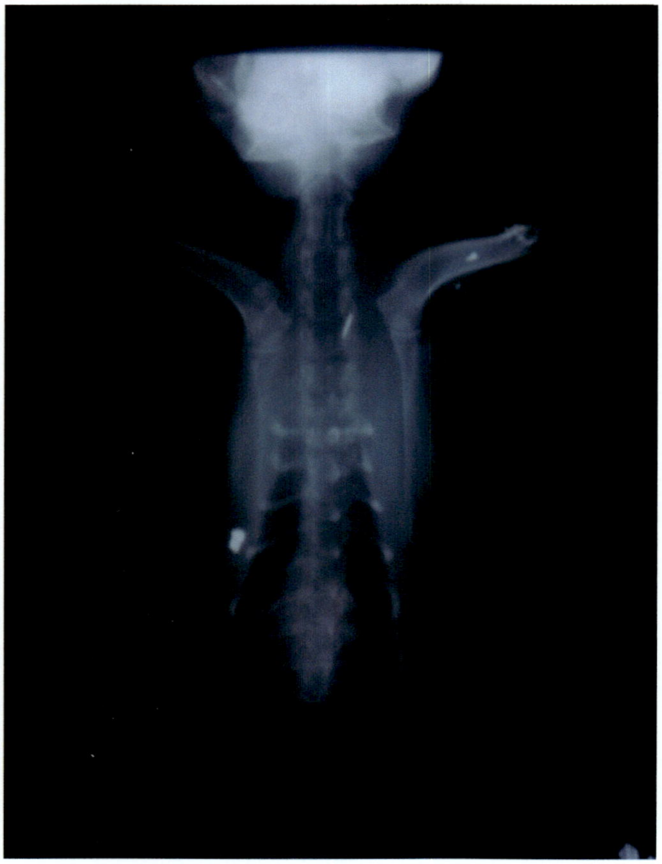

FIGURE 13.6 Bullet into respiratory cavity. (Carlos Muñoz Quezada and Víctor Toledo González Property.)

13.5 LEGISLATION

In the last 30 years, animal law has seen particular growth in, and revision of, relevant legislation. This has been paired with concern for better enforcement, especially, but not exclusively, in the developed world. In other countries, such as in Latin America, animal law has remained fairly static while people are grappling with overwhelming problems of poverty and governance. At times, the modernization of animal law has resulted from social pressure.

The animals likely to be affected by litigation can be categorized as domesticated species (dogs, cats, pets in general, and production animals); non-domesticated species that are kept in captivity for conservation, education, entertainment (zoos); and wild species.

According to Cooper and Cooper (2007), concern for animal welfare that gives rise to investigations and litigation are the welfare of domestic (pets and livestock) or other captive animals; farm animal welfare (farm, market, slaughter); the transport of animals, species protection and laws regulating the taking and killing of wild animals and their exploitation; the keeping of animals and regulation through licensing; commercial activities involving pedigreed animals such as horses and other performance or traction animals; the welfare of non-domesticated species; the illegal movement/smuggling of animals; and illegal possession of animals.

Particularly in regard to animal control regulations in wildlife, further concerns that give rise to investigations and litigation include insurance claims regarding injuries (death or damage caused by animals or to animals); civil law claims dealing with trespass, nuisance, or negligence; strict liability for animals; malpractice (professional negligence); disciplinary proceedings resulting from professional misconduct; abuse of humans and animals; and accidents and occupational health and safety, among others.

Some laws (falsely labeled as animal protection) protect only the emotional integrity of the people involved, and not that of the animals—an example of which can be seen in human–animal relationships in traditional sports. Moreover, in some countries whose legislation contains penalties for cruelty or mistreatment, there is no clear definition as to what constitutes an act of cruelty or abuse. This is clearly a legal vacuum allowing for the payment of only very small fines. It is also worth considering that in some countries animals are without rights, and remain movable property much like a TV or car.

Following such logic, a person having ordinary rights and obligations may question whether newborn babies have such obligations. What about animals? Do they have obligations?

The discussion is a lengthy one, and opinions differ, but one aspect that is clear is that animals should be treated with dignity and respect. Compassionate treatment should be given to all living beings that live in such close proximity to humans. Many animals also have functions of great importance in that those animals are the source of work or food for many. Compassion should be applied in all such cases, as well as other situations, including when animals are used in the rehabilitation of children with various syndromes (hippotherapy, etc.); animals used to guide the blind; rescue animals (saving human lives no matter the person's religion, color, or political position); and animals who replace the child who could not be born. Another thing that is clear is that the road ahead is difficult and will require sensitizing authorities to the issues at hand, in the hope of getting responsible animal ownership, protection, and welfare written into legislation.

13.6 ANIMALS IN FORENSIC CASES

13.6.1 Circuses

In many circuses, animals both small and large are still used as part of the entertainment. Many of the conditions in which these animals are found are not suitable for their mental, psychological, and/or physical well-being. This conditions them to a degree of stress that can manifest into something much worse. Many television programs have shown elephants fleeing from handlers, demolishing everything in their path. Some of these cases may have been averted had the animals not been confined in small spaces with unsanitary feed, tied with worn ropes, and with obvious pathological alterations (e.g., estereotipes). These basic needs could be inspected during routine quarantines performed when circuses enter new countries or even states. Such quarantines already take place to scan for potentially sick animals that could spread infections (including zoonotic diseases) and could therefore be combined with animal welfare inspections. During these inspections (and subsequent quarantines, if any), official documentation required for animals could be checked more thoroughly than presently. It is here, then, where the forensic veterinary expert could act in tandem with official auditors to safeguard animal welfare and public health.

13.6.2 Zoos

Zoos operate under four well-defined mission activities: education, research, conservation, and recreation. However, many of them reach only the last two goals. Clearly, the former are not necessary in most zoos for the maintenance and reproduction of the species. Perhaps worse is the lack of necessary buildings provided to the animals in most zoos. The list is neverending but is comprised of such things as giraffes burned by improperly positioned or damaged wires or stressed animal escapes. In this last case, the animal is generally controlled by firearms with subsequent death of it. Obviously, the human element is always present when an event occurs, whether in response to acts of animal abuse, neglect, lack of knowledge, or inadequate habitat constructions for them. Whatever the cause, it is clear that the animals habitually get the short end of the stick.

It would be unfair to not mention that there are good zoos worldwide, concerned about the animals' well-being. These are not the norm, however, and most of them are privately owned. Many seized animals, thanks to the work of the veterinary expert, end up being adopted by such zoos. Others animals that are adopted by these zoos may be animals rescued from circuses, who are adopted temporarily in order to begin a rehabilitation program. Unfortunately, many of these animals have been mistreated or in captivity for prolonged periods, and are not able to survive on their own. Therefore, they are condemned to life in captivity with no possibility of returning to their natural environment. Fortunately, some of them can be released back to their natural environment after rehabilitation, giving satisfaction to their caregivers.

13.6.3 Competition Animals

In my country (Chile) and in many others, there is a plethora of "sports" that use animals. Blood horse racing, Chilean races (consisting of a contest of speed between two horses in a natural terrain), the rodeo, the "*amansadura*" (taming horse), greyhound racing, dog sledding, dog fighting, cockfighting, and so on. We can agree or not about the morality of such activities, but the fact remains that they do exist. The problems with such activities (from a veterinary forensic view) are the practices that go on behind closed doors in some of these "sports."

We have seen greyhounds with muscular deformities and the use of anabolic doping in racehorses or dogs. We have seen how bait dogs are killed, just as in a cockfight. In all cases, there is a common component that is illegal in many places: gambling! The only illegal aspect in many places, while animals are abused in the plain sight of all, leaving many people to feel they have no legal power to stop these "customs."

13.6.4 Massive Disasters

In countries that have a high rate of disasters such as earthquakes, floods, and volcanic eruptions, the medical specialization of veterinarians who come to help animals affected by natural events is necessary. In Chile some years ago, the eruption of the Llaima volcano caused the deposition of heavy metals in many farm animals and pets. In this region, many families depend on their animals for what they produce, so this disaster meant so much pain for them.

It is important to emphasize that the role of the veterinary professional in disasters and other emergencies can vary widely, from the large-scale and often distressing duties that were carried out following the 2004 tsunami to the more mundane (but no less important) rescue of stranded and/or displaced animals both large and small. All such endeavors are prime examples of the roles veterinarians may play in the legal/forensic component.

13.6.5 Dog and Forensic Jobs

Dogs (as well as other species) are used in various aspects of crime investigation. For example, a dog following of scent is used for tracking or detection of incendiary devices and narcotic drugs. Dogs also play a role in disaster relief.

On the other hand, it is necessary to point out the importance of having dogs in the search for bodies in mass disasters, such as avalanches, through the detection of blood. This work has the potential to be dangerous, and during the course of their work, dogs may themselves be injured or killed.

13.6.6 Animals in Natural Disasters

Canines have been used for many years to assist those who are blind, deaf, or similarly afflicted. More recently, they have begun to be utilized to provide assistance to those prone to epileptic seizures, and a recent report shows interest in the possible role of dogs protecting women from domestic abuse. In the past, adults have been the primary recipients of these benefits, but interest is steadily increasing toward providing such services to children.

The use of other animals has also provided a degree of assistance to humans by encouraging physical, emotional, and social well-being (e.g., hippotherapy, dolphin therapy). All of these uses raise ethical and legal considerations, however, and currently interest in the extent to which the welfare of such animals may be compromised has been on the rise.

13.6.7 Human–Animal Relationships

According to Cooper and Cooper (2007) and others, the close relationship that can exist between humans and their animal companions has long been recognized. Such relationships could also be strongly influenced by religious and cultural attitudes. Affinity with one's animals may be present in situations where livestock is kept for commercial or research purposes (such as farming), but it is far more pronounced in situations with pets or companion animals.

In some cases, such relationships may be negatively affected by aggression or neglect on the part of the human, though, and as a consequence the animal may suffer or (in extreme circumstances) die. Many decades ago, a correlation between people who practice cruelty to animals and their commission of human crime was observed (e.g., Ted Bundy and Jeffrey Dahmer, two American serial killers who in their youth had committed acts of animal cruelty). This research demonstrates the important role of the veterinary profession in recognizing and preventing family violence. In this regard, one may also cite social worker Stuart James Hutton, who suggested in 1983 that evidence of animal abuse of any kind can be a useful indicator of early diagnosis of abuse to other family members.

On the other hand, the terms "bestiality" and "zoophilia" describe the sexual act between a person and an animal. Such practices have been documented by people from around the world throughout history, and persist even in modern times. These terms do not consider the damage done to the victim, however, and so the term "sexual abuse" should be used, as it is when speaking of human beings used involuntarily for sexual gratification. Regardless of what term is used to describe such atrocities, the physical damage inflicted on an animal can lead to injuries to the genitals, lower digestive tract, rectum, and anus. These lesions may be severe and lead to the animal's death. Depending on animal size, type of sexual act performed, and the gender of the animal, the trauma may be observed in external genitalia, anus, perianal area, vagina, or the uterus. In male specimens, the bands surrounding the penis and scrotum may also be affected.

13.7 INTERNATIONAL AND CULTURAL CONSIDERATIONS

There are wide variations among countries as to how animals are treated and the extent to which the authorities recognize violations of the law, even though the importance of animal welfare is being increasingly promoted on a global scale. As such, the expert opinion may vary if the circumstances of the alleged infringement are different from what was expected, and this is usually what happens when consulting in other countries or cultures. The biggest problem for veterinarians and other professionals concerning animal welfare cases is the lack of an objective definition of the subject. This makes decision making difficult for the courts, and for experts to relate findings and opinions with what is right according to the law, in contrast to the strong feelings and sensitivity of those involved.

The issue continues to evolve, and veterinarians aspiring to work in legal, disciplinary, or other hearings need to be aware of current discussions and dissensions if their statements are to be of optimum value for those who must arbitrate. It should be noted as well that in many countries, it is the obligation of the veterinarian to report cases of abuse (just as human doctors are required to do).

Specific procedures in veterinary forensics promote research in these situations in order to clarify the facts where alleged abuse of animals is suspected. Collaboration and encouragement is given to the application of existing legal rules (even touting new rules) related to the status of animals, behaviors of people toward them, and the public impact that causes offense to social sensitivity.

13.8 FORENSIC TECHNIQUES

Among the various possible techniques criminologists perform in the veterinary field, are discussed in the following.

13.8.1 Forensic Odontology

In human forensic work, forensic odontology is a very well-developed discipline largely concerned with, where legal implications may arise regarding the identification of cadavers and human remains; estimation of age in both the living and dead; identification and interpretation of bite wounds and lip imprints; and description and investigation of dental and oral lesions, especially those due to trauma.

Although the importance of animal bites (both in human and veterinary work) has long since been established, comparative aspects have generally not attracted the same level of interest. Consequently, those who are involved in such work must often extrapolate from human odontology or make do with what has been published in veterinary, pathological, and zoological literature. Such literature is essential reading insofar as it highlights the comparative aspects where dentition is concerned. References to the odontology of some species may also be found in specialized journals, such as those that include reports of anomalies affecting the teeth in dolphins. Particular attention may have to be paid to gross postmortem features in wildlife cases where it is alleged that dogs have been used illegally for hunting. A detailed example of how such studies could assist in forensic cases is provided in a paper by Simpson (2006). This research focuses on patterns and significance of bite wounds in otters.

Apparently, lip-print identification (cheiloscopy) is not widely used in animal forensics, but does seem to have potential. Such methods have parallels, as in, for example, the identification of gorillas using their unique nose prints.

The analysis of bite marks is a specialized field and has been admissible in a court of law for quite some years. In the case of animal work, reference can usefully be made to texts concerning human forensic medicine, such as the use in some cases of scanning electron microscopy, digital imaging, histology, contrast medium enhanced radiography, and computerized axial tomography.

Dental examination plays a crucial and informative role in *postmortem* forensic work, which explains why it is widely used by archaeologists to identify and age the skeletal remains of animals. A single tooth can assist in the speciation of both domesticated and wild animals (cetaceans are a particularly good example of the latter).

Today, pets such as cats and dogs are not solely designated to a role in functional values (care, work, etc.), as it was for decades for the family and social circle. In modern times, the values given to animals include emotional and psychological factors. It must be noted, though, that these new attributes are assigned by society and pertain to obvious personal benefits. However, the increase of integration into family life can be seen as a process of adaptation between the two species, and with this increase in household dogs being reported, there is likewise a proportionate increase in the percentage of dog attacks of varying magnitude of humans and other animals. Much of the evidence caused by dogs today (found in crime scenes, or CSs, such as teeth, bites, secretions, etc.) are not considered legal during court proceedings in Chile. Perhaps more importantly, this evidence is analyzed by forensic scientists lacking veterinary training, who base these studies on a collection of forensic information that is limited or even nonexistent. This (unsurprisingly) eventually results in an inefficient process and incomplete research. Therefore, it is essential to have a worldwide database of existing dog bites with which to compare those present in a CS, allowing for the identification of the species of the aggressor at the very least.

Bites resulting in litigation proceedings increasingly occur. Reports indicate that the main victims of dog bites are children. The most affected ages vary between studies: 0–15, <6, 5–9, 7–12, and 7–9 years. The attacks are often fatal to children (especially the little ones), and the number of attacks against children is significantly higher than those against adults. Likewise, attacks of the elderly very often result in death. Obviously, this correlation can be explained by the difficulty in defending oneself while living in such age groups. While death may occur, more commonly the main consequences arising from dog bites are injuries and scars from the attacks. In addition, the potential for infectious disease transmission, psychological scars, disabilities, economic costs of medical and psychological treatment, and costs of sick leave must be considered. Most dog attacks that occur seem to be without provocation to the casual observer. In reality, most attacks occur when an animal is disturbed while eating, because they do not like to be under threat or feel that their territory is being invaded. Many surveys conclude that the highest risk is given for large-breed dogs such as the German shepherd, pit bull terrier, rottweiler, and chow, but all dogs should be considered potentially dangerous—even small dogs like the Jack Russell terrier, which can inflict severe bites.

Overall, the most common methods for the determination of the origins of a human bite include techniques to compare the morphology of the teeth (shape, size, and position of the teeth, together with the shape of the dental arches), with similar traits and characteristics present in life-size photographs of the injuries, with transparent overlays.

Given the existence of the large number of animal species in Chile, and considering that the domestic dog is involved in the largest number of cases associated with bites (mild or severe), patterns of bites were compared according to skull shape and by morphologic and morphometric analysis of dental semi-arcs of the domestic dog (*Canis lupus familiaris*) for medicolegal purposes. Plaster dental models and impressions of bite marks were obtained of three pure breeds—boxer, Dalmatian, and German shepherd—via plaster dental models. Measurements taken included the maximum external distance between upper and lower canine, and maximum external distance between upper and lower incisors. These results show that only the maximum distance between upper canine would allow statistically significant identification of a breed

($p \leq 0.05$) in cast models. In a blind study as well as from a morphometric point of view, Dalmatians were identified with a high rate of sensitivity and specificity in comparison to the boxer and German shepherd, impeding a high grade of identification between these two latest breeds. The morphological study, however, allowed identification and individualization of 100% of dogs (Figures 13.7 through 13.9). It may be concluded, therefore, that both morphological and morphometric methods are useful and complementary tools in the identification and individualization of a potentially aggressive dog.

While using alginate and plaster is not a problem as a forensic technique, it should be noted that some authors suggest the use of other materials such as vinyl polysiloxane (silicone) for printing, and plastic or resin for casting. These materials provide better quality and durability, unlike alginate impressions, which are not reusable and must be processed immediately. Also, the use of plaster may result in the existence of bubbles, thus increasing the possibility of the model fracturing.

The high correlation between measurements made on plaster models and the traces of bite wounds would use these models as a means of fixing the teeth of a specimen at the time of the assault or of discovery of a corpse. However, the values obtained allow, at the least, a narrowing of the search range. Pretty and Sweet (2001) indicate that there are a minimum number of points of agreement or features that are required for positive identification. In many cases, a single tooth can be used to identify whether it contains enough unique features. The Chilean study reinforces the need for complementary morphological and morphometric studies to identify not only dog breeds but, more importantly, to identify a specific individual.

FIGURE 13.7 Semidental arcade for a boxer. (Photo: Víctor Toledo González Property.)

FIGURE 13.8 Semidental arcade for a Dalmatian. (Photo: Víctor Toledo González Property.)

FIGURE 13.9 Semidental arcade for a German shepherd. (Photo: Víctor Toledo González Property.)

13.8.2 Bloodstains

In many cases where there is aggression between or against animals, bloodstains will be present on the victim and/or perpetrator. Bloodstains may also be found in the vicinity of the crime. Fresh blood is quite easy to identify as such, and may also be collected by just about anyone. If the bloodstains are several hours or even days old, however, the more sophisticated techniques utilized by the forensic veterinarian may be needed for identification.

The first thing that must be determined when blood is present is whether that blood is human or animal. Samples of human blood can be injected into a rabbit, and it will be expected to form antibodies against the human blood. After that, the blood found at the event site (depending on time elapsed) can be challenged against the serum sample obtained from the rabbit. If the corresponding blood is of human origin, the rabbit serum will show a precipitation reaction (band) indicating the presence of human blood. Likewise, if no such reaction occurs, then the blood is of animal origin.

Poaching of wild animals, illegal slaughterhouses, satanic rituals utilizing animals in their rites, pets with gunshot wounds, and even the entertainment industry are some cases where we could find and gather evidence via bloodstains. The forensic veterinarian will have techniques to gather this type of evidence, even if the crime scene has been cleaned in an attempt to destroy evidence.

Approximately 8% of the weight of a live human body is blood. This rule applies to animals as well;

therefore, the techniques used in humans are compatible for use in cases of animals.

The mammalian erythrocyte possesses biconcave nuclei, which do not contain DNA. Therefore, in order to obtain samples one must utilize the presence of DNA in other blood cells (neutrophils, leukocytes, etc.). The erythrocytes of birds do contain a nucleus, however.

In cases pertaining to wildlife hunting, slaughterhouses, satanic rituals that use animals in their rites, or the shooting of domestic animals as entertainment, blood splatters may be found. This type of evidence may be collected even in cases where the perpetrator has cleaned the crime scene in an attempt to obscure the crime.

Through blood splatter patterns (distribution of blood splatter), we can answer the question of how the victim came to be at the scene of the crime and from where he came. From this, one may reconstruct past events and determine how the crime was committed.

Arterial damage results in a "jet" of blood, containing a high volume per latid, and amount and trajectory of the jet will depend on the impact force used on the animal and/or the weapon or object used to commit the crime. The splatters found on walls can also be used to determine approximate time of death, by observing how far splatters have leaked toward the floor.

Bloodstains on jute and textiles that have been wet are often of a greenish color, light brown, or somewhat diffuse. If samples have not been wet, they can be darker in color, such as dark red or black. In metals (excluding stainless steel, which will always have a red color), the color varies under the influence of oxide or other substances likely to support corrosion.

In water, color intensity alone can be observed in correspondence with the concentration of blood.

As you can see, the techniques utilized in the investigation of blood vary greatly.

13.8.2.1 Stains on Hard Surfaces

Scraping smooth surfaces or hardwood with a sharp knife allows residue of dried blood to be collected. If the bloodstained item is small and transportable, package it in a paper bag or envelope. Dilution and contamination potential is minimized by eliminating the use of water as the collection medium. Do not use a plastic container in place of a paper packet, because the static charge from the plastic will cause the blood flakes to disperse and stick to the sides of the container. This technique can be combined with the tape-lift method by scraping the stain near the tape's sticky side. The static charge will cause the flakes to stick to the tape. The tape can then be placed on vinyl acetate.

For dried bloodstains on a non-absorbent surface, fingerprint-lifting tape may be placed over the stain and lifted off. The stain is transferred to the adhesive side of the tape, which may then be secured on a clear piece of acetate for submission to the laboratory.

13.8.2.2 Stains on Soft Surfaces

When the surfaces are porous and/or not conducive to scraping (carpets or other), a sample must be cut and removed from the tainted piece. If such a sample cannot be taken, white blotting paper or filter paper may be placed under the disputed item, then drops of saline should be added to the stain until transferred to the tissue paper in sufficient amounts to assure that the material can be analyzed. It is then left to dry prior to packaging and shipping. In this case, the sample can be sent in very well-sealed paper, along with notes indicating the technique used.

Wrapped in Bloody Clothes: If animals are found wrapped in clothes or in conditions that avoid exposure to drafts or fans, the first thing you should do is remove evidence such as hairs, fibers, gunshot residue, and so on, present in the clothes or dry the blood sample to fix it to fabric (textile). Excessive heat can affect the quality of the sample, so caution should be used. Finally, these samples should be stored in cartons wrapped in wrapping paper separately. The paper should be thick so as to prevent breakage, and tight to ensure no waste of evidence such as fabric patches or blood granules. Also, the paper should not be pliable. Cuttings should be packaged in separate paper envelopes.

If the item is small and transportable, then package it in a paper bag (or plastic bag to prevent contamination of other objects). Bring it to a secured location, take it out of the bag, and allow the evidence and the bag to thoroughly air-dry.

Any materials such as knives, axes, or blunt objects gathered for evidence should be stored in hard cardboard or timber boxes. Boxes should be secured during transport to prevent the breakdown of waste material stains.

If the samples are small they may be placed in petri dishes or tubes that do not contain anticoagulants.

If possible, the investigator should also collect samples from unstained areas of the item for negative controls.

Wet Absorption: A sterile swab, gauze pad, or threads are slightly moistened with sterile distilled water. An effort should be made to concentrate the stain in a localized portion of the swab or pad. For example, when using a swab, the stain should be concentrated on the tip. The collection medium is concentrated into the stain and allowed to air-dry. Some laboratories recommend following the first moistened swabbing with a second dry swabbing to ensure thorough sample collection. Both swabs are retained and submitted for analysis.

When the sample is air-dried, package into a paper packet and place in an envelope. For transportation purposes and to prevent cross contamination, the threads may be placed in a plastic container for no more than 2 hours. Once in a secure location, the threads must be removed from the plastic and allowed to air-dry. They may then be repackaged into a paper packet and placed in an envelope. Threads must also be taken from a negative control area, if available.

13.8.2.3 Liquid Samples

When blood is in abundance it may be collected with a syringe or other item (spoon, pipette, etc.) and stored in a sealed glass jar without additives. **Keep it cool**.

Wet bloodstains should be collected with sterile gauze or absorbent cloth soaked in saline. Rub the material collected on the stain and let it dry, then scrape it.

All samples should be labeled securely, to avoid loss of information due to falling labels. Associated information that should be labeled includes case number, sample number, source (species), and place of extraction (head neck, thorax, abdomen, etc.).

It is also important to collect a control sample that contains no blood. Employing the exact same techniques should collect this sample.

Two techniques are utilized for presumptive blood detection in veterinary forensics: the Adler test (benzidine), which is highly toxic, and the use of luminol.

13.8.3 Veterinary Trichology

Hair is evidence that is nearly always present on a site where a crime occurred that involved an animal. Animal hair goes through the same three stages of growth as humans: an intermediate period where growth slows (anagen phase), a later state where growth stops (catagen phase), and hair loss (telogen phase). Hair collected might fall as part of the normal cycle or as a result of some pathology (e.g., hypothyroidism) or direct physiological state (e.g., pregnancy).

Birds lose their feathers in certain moments of life as well, whether by natural or artificial means, or as a result of food and production management during the production of eggs.

The hair is a filamentary epidermal portion that exists in almost all animals. It has a root attached to the hair follicle (containing DNA) and a stem (which is the visible part) that contains very little DNA. In a cross section of a hair we can show that externally it has a structure called the cuticle, with its own characteristics, depending on the species. More internally, the cortex contains pigment granules that can determine the color, size, density, and distribution of hair (Diagram 13.1). This is obviously of great forensic utility.

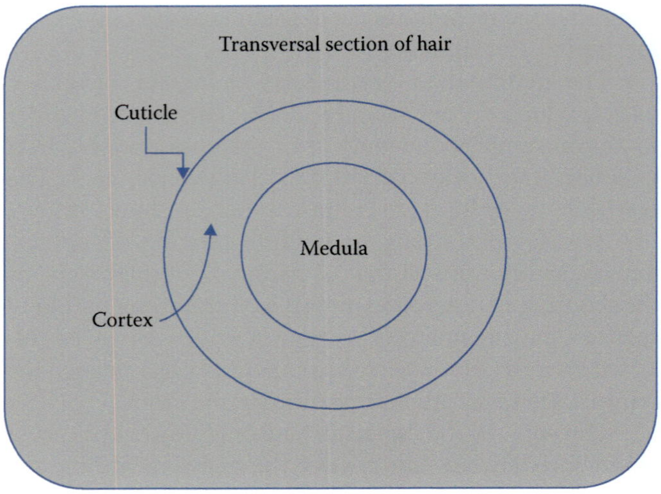

DIAGRAM 13.1 Transversal section of hair. (Víctor Toledo González Property.)

13.8.4 Tissues

In some cases, pieces of tissue from animals may be found. This tissue may be the result of rustling (animals stolen for slaughter and other uses), or in cases where the species needs to be determined from a piece of meat. In either case the identification of the species can be accomplished by immunological studies.

Internationally, there are immunochemical methods (enzyme immunoassays kits, ELISA) that allow the qualitative detection of meat species. There are commercial kits for bovine, swine, sheep, and poultry species available as well. The kits use protein antibodies against muscle heat.

13.8.5 Comparative Anatomy

The first objective of medical research is identification. Comparative anatomical knowledge is an important tool when recognizing the species by analyzing skeletal remains present at a CS. The identification of the species through anatomy could provide new evidence that may be related to the crime. This can then be incorporated into the research if necessary. Furthermore, the study of the chemical composition of the bones could tell the time of death, or the possible origin of the animal.

The greatest complication a forensic veterinarian faces is the large number of species that exist. This is why the development of a professional is required who works in the area of comparative anatomy and, moreover, may have a database with which to compare the bones found at potential crime scenes (especially when wildlife is involved). This area is also concerned with the identification of hairs, feathers, viscera, fingernails, helmets, leathers, and so on.

13.8.6 Marks (Impressions of the External Structure of Objects)

The goal of marks studies is to identify and clarify the circumstances and mechanisms surrounding their formation. Residual marks and traces can be investigated by various areas according to their origin and nature, such as traces caused by animals that use mainly their claws and fangs (the latter is treated in forensic dentistry).

13.8.7 Footprints

Footprints found on a scene may identify the species of the animal victim or perpetrator. Depending on the nature of the substrate (and how hard the animal has tread), footprints may be found with difficulty or may be clearly indicated. Through analysis, the environment in which the animal lives can be found. For example, the presence of webbing between toes in a footprint could indicate that the animal spends much time in the water, whereas the presence of the front claws in a footprint indicates the animal digs in the earth.

Other information obtained from footprint analyses could include the approximate height and weight of the animal. The distance between the anterior and posterior long members indicate whether the animal was, for example, running, walking, jogging, or dragging something.

Some animals, such as horses, use metal constructs on their feet—also known as horseshoes—which can be of different shapes and materials. These can present evidence of defects, wear, and so on, which can help identify a specimen.

Pathologies affecting nails in some animal strains include asymmetries, cracks, fractures, and other defects that could also appear as trace evidence (individual characteristics), another important anatomical element for identification.

13.8.8 Taphonomy

Taphonomy of vertebrates is the study of all the processes occurring in the bones from the time of the death of an organism, until the bones are recovered from archaeological sites or elsewhere. Taphonomy includes both natural processes, including environmental factors and the action of scavengers and small mammals, as well as cultural processes. When the bone material is preserved, it becomes a valuable source of information. In this sense, the bones provide data concerning human behavior, the faunal composition of the site and surrounding area, and may also provide data on vegetation and even the climate of the room in which the bones were recovered.

A taphonomic agent is the physical cause of modification made to a bone and the bone assemblage, and taphonomical effect is the change resulting from the alteration suffered. Rodents are a taphonomic agent that can modify deployment scenarios and can be the cause of spatial associations of materials that would not otherwise have been related. Some of the taphonomic effects of rodents commonly found in archaeological sites are the marks of their teeth found in caves or galleries. In general, their biting is located in specific areas, such as edges and salient regions of skeletal parts. These gnawed marks consist of short grooves, which usually occur in pairs, parallel or overlapping, and the bottom has either a flat or rounded groove. The burrowing behavior of rodents can also alter the spatial distribution of finds from the site. There is a removal of sediment from the interior to the surface of the ground, as the rodents are digging their burrows, causing vertical and horizontal displacement. Small materials are those that are more likely to be displaced by the burrowing activity, as many rodents simply avoided large objects (>5 cm) by digging beneath them.

Many animals view both human and animal bodies as a food source, which may cause taphonomic changes. Among the most common of these animals are dogs, rats, pigs, crows, eagles, gulls, and some fish. On the other hand, other vertebrates that are typically herbivores, such as squirrels, sheep, and cows, can gnaw bones, especially if they are in a nutritionally poor environment.

It is therefore important to be able to identify and interpret the bite marks; however, bite marks from mice, cats, small dogs, or wild animals may be difficult to distinguish between, especially if the individual is decaying. Therefore, the evaluation of the CS and the circumstances in which the body was found are important factors in the interpretation of patterns of injury, particularly if the body has been found outdoors or in the presence of animals or insects.

13.8.9 Toxicology

Many animals are victims of air pollution or poisoning from water runoff containing waste of industrial, mining, and domestic activity (Figures 13.10 through 13.12). There are many elements which may come to mind, such as smog, heavy metals, aerosols, and so on, and all of them can cause behavioral issues, physiological disorders, and even death. This death can occur in one animal or in a large number of them, depending on the sources of toxicological agent and the possibility of contact.

In the domestic environment, dog and cat poisoning can occur through consumption of harmful food (e.g., chocolate or onions), whereas in the wild, a large number of animals can access waters with heavy metals from mining waste. Therefore the investigation of the CS, along with a detailed account of its history, should be necessary in order to better establish the circumstances that could have caused injury or death.

Toxicity related to environmental contamination may be caused by natural phenomena or one linked to the ingestion of discarded human-made objects such as shotgun pellets, fishing weights, or lead vehicle batteries.

FIGURE 13.10 Dead birds from eating a dog killed by poisoning. (Photo: Carlos Muñoz Quezada and Víctor Toledo González Property.)

FIGURE 13.11 Skeletal remains of a dead dog. Normally, in these cases there is not cadaverous fauna (arthropods and flies) when animals die intoxicated. (Photo: Carlos Muñoz Quezada and Víctor Toledo González Property.)

FIGURE 13.12 Vomiting bird with suspicious content. (Carlos Muñoz Quezada and Víctor Toledo González Property.)

Other poisonings result from careless actions such as dogs given access to slug baits or cats lapping up spilled ethylene glycol. On farms, insecticides spilled or the over-enthusiastic application of agricultural chemicals pose a threat to wildlife as well.

Malicious poisoning of wildlife and domestic animals such as raptors, foxes, dogs, and cats is depressingly common as well, and often involves the use of agrochemicals or rodenticides. These poisons affect the target species individually, or en masse. Examples are rabbits contaminated with carbofuran (eggs laced with strychnine or organophosphorus insecticide). These baits are indiscriminate, though, and it may be a family dog out for a walk with the children that finds and consumes the poison.

13.8.9.1 Sampling

Overall, for toxicology studies, tissue blocks of about 200 g should be saved, with special regard to liver, kidney, stomach (rumen in cattle), and esophageal contents in the main carnivores and birds. Additionally, blood with anticoagulant and fluids may be saved, as well as samples of bait substances and suspicious (fodder or food) items.

1. Samples must be free of dust pollution, preservatives, and so on, and must be frozen after extraction.
   Blood should be sent **refrigerated** (1°–4°C in a cooler with ice pack) while the serum should be **frozen**.
2. Freeze rumen content, blood, and serum extraction posthaste to determine cyanide and ammonium.
3. Use separate containers for each sample to avoid cross contamination, change gloves, and properly label items (indicate location and nature of item).
4. Always include histopathology specimens fixed in order to confirm the diagnosis in doubt.
5. Include a toxicology form containing some observations indicated at the site of the event and general and specific characteristics.

Some modes of sample collection and preservation include the following.

Cadaver: Collect using disposable gloves (double) and conserve in a resistant bag (body bag), and store at refrigerated temperatures.

Skeletons: Collect using disposable gloves (double) and store in a resistant bag (body bag). Collect soil samples up to 15 cm deep below the bones and place in airtight container.

Bait (items containing intoxicants or poisons): Collect using disposable gloves (double) and conserve in wrap in foil (separate samples) and store in plastic or airtight containers. Store all containers in a single bag or Styrofoam container. Use of ice packs is suggested in cases involving perishable material.

Tissues (fresh or decomposed): Collect up to 2 cm in depth at site of occurrence and preserve in envelopes or sealed containers. Transport refrigerated (less than 3 hours) or frozen.

Hairs, feathers, and nails: Store sample in entirety (with root and follicle) or quills in cases involving feathers and preserve in in paper bags and maintain at an ambient temperature, refrigerate, or freeze.

Excrement: Samples must be no older than 2 or 3 days and may be collected whole or in pieces and preserved in sealed containers or envelopes. Transport to laboratory within a few hours using ice packs, or freeze.

The expert should have suspicions of intoxication when the animal had good health and had a sudden onset of symptoms (salivation, tremors, muscle spasms, dyspnea, hemorrhage, cyanosis, vomiting, diarrhea, seizures, etc.), when the sudden death of an animal occurs, when clinical symptoms are similar in different subjects (different species) at once or in successive time periods when there have been previous cases of proven or suspected poisoning in the same area, when there is presence of vomiting or bleeding from orifices, or when the bodies were found in abnormal postures.

Also, certain intoxicants that cause changes in the central nervous system might leave odors that emanate from the animal's mouth or vomit.

13.8.10 Veterinary Pathology

In general, the involvement of a veterinarian in legal cases may be useful in a variety of ways. In particular, veterinary expertise may be sought for one or more of the following: a clinical examination, a postmortem examination, laboratory investigations, a site visit, viewing radiographs or other images, examining histological sections or electron micrographs, giving advice/opinion based on reading reports, or viewing photos or video recordings.

The study of histopathological anatomy is the study of causes of death by working on the body via necropsy or in a laboratory setting by way of sample tissues. The forensic pathologist should be able to determine the etiology or pathophysiology: whether the death was accidental, intentional, natural, or of undetermined origins.

Often, it will be necessary to perform a postmortem examination at the scene of the incident. This requires that the specialist determine three things: (1) date of death; (2) cause of death; and (3) circumstances of death (e.g., how the animal died, why the animal died, how long it took to die, when he died, where he died, who was involved, and was it a sudden or unexpected death).

Before necropsy is performed, an external examination of the specimen showing and describing injuries, determining body condition, determining evidence of immersion or burial, and the taking of samples (hair, feathers, non-animal elements attached to the body), is required. Also, any insects present may be gathered for forensic entomological study (more on this below).

Once the body has been opened, internal examination is required to differentiate natural disease lesions from those which may be unnatural (e.g., abuse). The next step is to differentiate antemortem from postmortem lesions and finally take samples for histopathological, microbiological or immunological examinations. Types of samples may include toxins, infectious agents, biological material for determination of DNA, blood, body fluids, and so on.

Finally, after the examination a report must be written. This report must be in present tense, complete, and clear, using technical terminology as well as contain an explanation in layman's terms, and present conclusions.

13.8.10.1 Sampling

Many tests with cadavers must be performed no more than 24–48 hours after death, depending on ambient temperature. In cold locations (at 0°C [32°F] or less) you can perform almost all tests even beyond 48 hours. However, this still severely affects the integrity of tissue being used for histopathological analysis. Cases of common occurrence mentioned in the postmortem may have different decomposition dynamics due to climate conditions as well.

For example, dead mammals or seabirds found on beaches have a thick layer of subcutaneous fat that keeps their temperature from cooling. This facilitates decomposition and attracts scavengers such as gulls or dogs. In this case, the samples are most likely to have relevant results in toxicology, entomology and eventually PCR (polymerase chain reaction) for infectious agents, depending on the strength of the latter, over time.

Ruminants (cows, sheep, goats, etc.) are similar to the previous case in that these animals usually have a thick layer of hair or wool (sheep) and additionally, their pre-stomachs contain and maintain live fermenting bacteria. Therefore, the temperature for several hours after the death of the animal will remain stable and invite the same problems. These bacteria may also be passed onto other tissues, causing contamination. If the temperature exceeds 10°C or 15°C (50°F or 59°F), the animal carcass will be decayed at around 24–48 hours.

Additionally, animals that have agonized for some time before dying often lose all energy reserves, which can undermine tissue health even before death. In such cases, more rapid decomposition may occur. Also, animals that have suffered severe bacterial or infectious processes that result in sepsis may have bacteria in the blood that not only weakens the animal but also indicates antemortem infection.

There are diseases that are normal zoonoses that can cause major disruptions in public health. This is why it

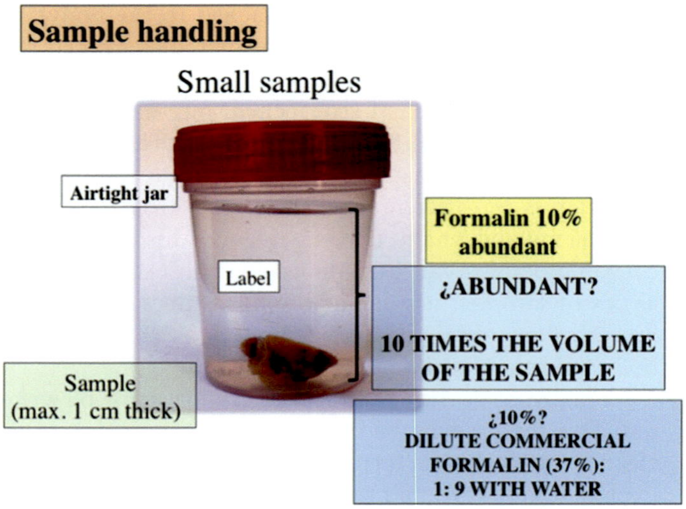

DIAGRAM 13.2 Sample handling.

is important to take adequate time to collect samples or perform an autopsy.

Some basic general considerations and procedures for samples follows:

1. *Histopathology and Histochemistry Testing*
   - Use an airtight plastic bottle with dilution of formalin (1 part water, 9 parts of 37% formalin)
   - Formalin volume should be 10 times the sample volume
   - The sample should not be more than 1 cm thick (Diagram 13.2)
   - Alcohol is not a good tissue fixative because of low tissue penetration capability

   Freezing is not a desirable preservation technique for histopathology specimens, as crystals that damage the tissue structure are formed. Refrigeration is acceptable for a period of up to 48 hours.
2. *Immunohistochemistry*
   These samples are treated the same as those used for histopathology. Samples should not spend more than 48 hours in storage.
3. *PCR*
   These samples should be frozen with utmost care taken to not contaminate the samples with foreign DNA. Wear gloves and always clean sterilized material used to extract each sample. Store samples in sterile jars or airtight bags.
4. *Virology*
   Samples must be buffered in a solution of 50% glycerol and frozen in sterile vials or bags. Lung, liver, spleen, kidney, and brain fragments may be collected at a maximum thickness of 1 cm.
5. *Bacteriology*
   Following are precautions to take during collection of samples in a corpse. These samples should be collected first if infection is suspected.

   In general, you should use an aseptic technique, clean material, and be careful not to contaminate other parts of the animal or neighboring property.

   If intestinal infection is suspected, this sample should be taken first, before proceeding to the opening of the intestine. Samples can be attached to both ends of a thread segment of between 5 and 10 cm and the entire segment may be preserved. **Do not freeze these samples.**
6. *Mushrooms*
   The sampling of these microorganisms is performed in a manner similar to the collecting of samples in microbiology.
7. *Cytology and Fluids*
   Conjunctive and trachea swabs are collected with cotton swabs to isolate epithelial cells. Then, the swab is placed on glass slides, air-dried, and fixed for 5–10 minutes at 80%–100% methanol.

   Prints obtained from tissue are gently pressed against the slide and the organ to be sampled. This should be done on absorbent paper prior to the cleaning of excess blood from the surface. Like the preceding example, this sample must be fixed with air or methanol.

   The fluids can be sent in tubes containing anticoagulant that have been centrifuged at 1500 rpm for 5 minutes. A drop of the resulting sediment is deposited on a microscope slide in a similar manner as performing a blood smear. The sample may be fixed the same way.
8. *Parasitology*
   Tissue impressions are obtained by gently pressing the slide against the organ to be sampled. The simple should be pre-cleaned with absorbent paper to remove excess blood from the surface. Like the preceding, the sample may then be fixed in air or methanol.

   The fluids can be sent in tubes with anticoagulant and then centrifuged at 1500 rpm for 5 minutes. A drop of sediment is deposited on a microscope slide and smear, similar to performing a blood smear, and fixed the same way.
   - Ticks, fleas, lice, and mites can be preserved in 70% alcohol. To perform skin scraping, the material obtained from the lesion is mixed with mineral oil on a microscope slide and covered with a coverslip.
   - Living nematodes can be immersed in 70% alcohol and dead parasites can be set in 5%–10% formalin. Heartworms, lungworms, trematodes, and cestodes may be

fixed in a formalin solution of 5%, diluted with saline.

- For determination of endoparasites, sending 10–20 g of fresh fecal material is recommended. If processing is not immediate, it is recommended to set the stool in a solution of 10% formalin for fixation of tibia eggs.
- For analysis of protozoa, a drop of fresh fecal material is mixed with a drop of Lugol's solution (or saline) on a slide. The preparation should be covered with a coverslip and examined immediately.

Also, in some cases it is necessary to **collect the full animal** or group of animals.

13.8.11 Forensic Entomology

Insects and arthropods are also used in forensic investigations. The presence of differing species can either narrow or broaden the investigation.

The insects are attracted to a corpse in order to feed and/or lay eggs. Sometimes this occurs while the animal is dying, during advanced putrefaction, or in other periods when only dried matter remains. Given this sequence, differentiated with the corpse arrival and phenological characteristics of these insects, we can determine with some accuracy the postmortem interval (PMI: time elapsed since death to sample collection period). The presence of toxic substances in the body as a possible cause of death (entomotoxicology) may also be found in this manner. This may also determine whether the animal in question had died at the crime scene or been transported from another location. Legal and forensic entomological procedures should be used both methodically and rigorously when collecting samples, and the provision of additional vital information (such as conditions and characteristics of the CS where the samples were taken) should be included.

13.8.11.1 Procedure

Before entering a crime scene where a corpse is present, it is vital to take measurements of environmental conditions. Temperature and humidity are basic examples of these conditions, but wind speed and direction should also be included (Diagram 13.3) (Figures 13.13 through 13.17).

Final Considerations: Each piece of evidence (bite marks, hair, blood patterns, etc.) should be photographed

FIGURE 13.13 Sampling of flies in photos. Take a general picture of the crime scene. (Photo: Víctor Toledo González.)

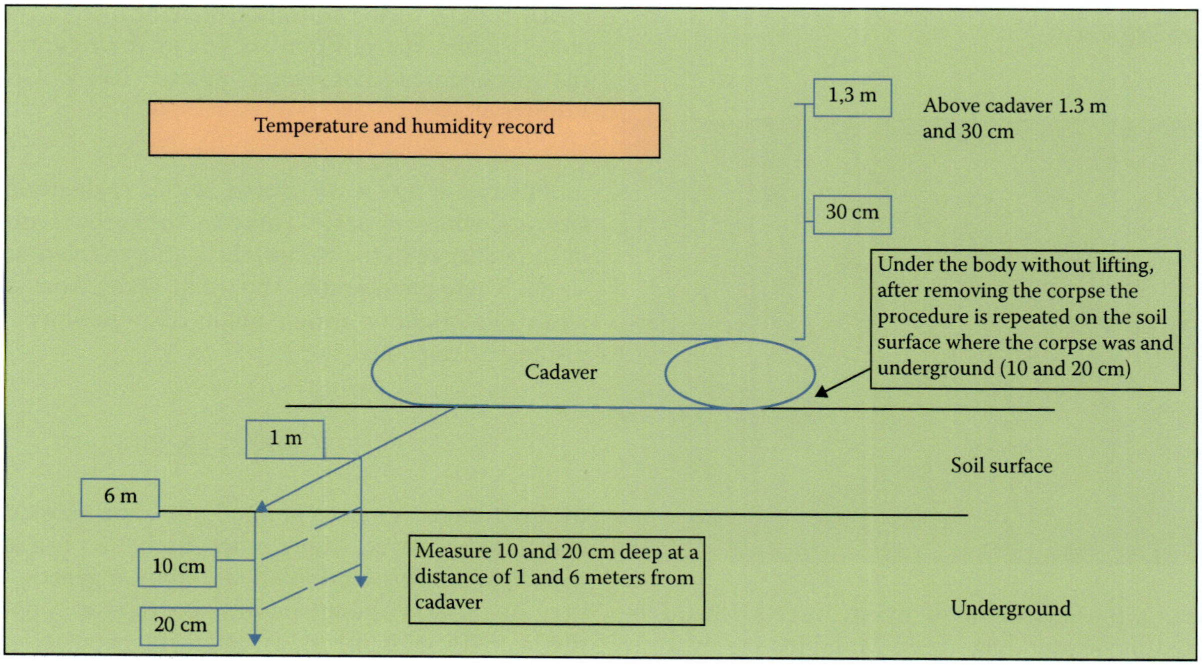

DIAGRAM 13.3 Measuring points of temperature and humidity at a crime scene.

FIGURE 13.14 Displacing the sweep net horizontally side by side. The process is repeated many times to collect the largest number of flying insects. (Víctor Toledo González Property.)

FIGURE 13.15 Collection of flying insects should be conducted in surrounding areas. Many insects fly away from the body at the time the expert approaches them. (Víctor Toledo González Property.)

FIGURE 13.16 Alternative collection of flying insects. (Víctor Toledo González Property.)

FIGURE 13.17 After collection of flying insects, the mesh should adopt the position shown in the figure so that the specimens do not escape. (Víctor Toledo González Property.)

to illustrate where it was found, with a scale (to indicate size) and without a scale. This establishes the relationship of the evidence to the victim, the victim to the room, and so on. These photographs should be taken from straight above or straight on at right angles, eliminating potential distance distortions.

13.12 CONCLUSION

In this chapter we have pointed out some views on animal forensics work. Many other disciplines can actively participate in this work (ballistic studies, genetic, chemistry, and others). However, it is necessary to supplement this activity with others of equal importance, such as work at the scene of crime, security crime scene, forensic tactics, legislations, and others.

Don't forget: Working with animals can be as varied as the number of species you can find—so forensic science is a multidisciplinary job.

ACKNOWLEDGMENTS

Dr. Carlos Muñoz Quezada (Veterinarian), expert worker in Crime Scene Investigation (Chile); Dr. Noemi Friedrich MV, MSc., Veterinary Forensic Expert (ISCET) with a Diploma in Criminology and Penology (Argentina); Dr. Ricardo Olivares P-M (Veterinary Anatomist, Favet); Dr. Ana María Ramirez (Veterinary Hematologist, Favet); and Dr. Gustavo Farias Roldán (Veterinary Toxicologist, Favet) for their huge and generous collaboration in elaboration of this chapter, for their support in the development of Forensic Veterinary Medicine in Chile and their great human qualities.

Also, Mr. Rodrigo Marcos Quezada (Criminalist Investigator), Hector Casanova Oyarzún (Ballistic Engineer), and Mr. José Manuel Duarte (Proficient in Documentology)—members of COLCRIM who have this huge challenge and contributed to its development.

Thanks to Mr. and Mrs. Cooper, who advance this discipline and write their experiences in cited books, and finally to Dr. Flavio Correa, a veterinarian from Cuba who spent most of his professional life developing veterinary forensics in his country.

BIBLIOGRAPHY

Arkow, P. and H. Munro. 2006. The veterinary profession's roles in recognizing and preventing family violence: The experiences of the human medicine field and the development of diagnostic indicators of non-accidental (injury). In: *International Handbook on Cruelty to Animals*, ed. F. R. Ascione. West Lafayette, IN: Purdue University Press, pp. 31–58.

Brown, K., G. Townsend, and T. Winning. 2005. Forensic applications of dental and oral anatomy. In: *Oral and Maxillofacial Anatomy, Histology and Embriology*, ed. S. R. Prabhu. Oxford: Oxford University Press.

Byrd, J. and J. Castner. 2000. *Forensic Entomology: The Utility of Arthropods in Legal Investigations*. Boca Raton, FL: CRC Press.

Ciocca, L (Eds.). 2010. *Odontologia Médico-Legal*. Chile: Jurídicas de Santiago.

Cooper, J. and M. Cooper. 2007. *Introduction to Veterinary and Comparative Forensic Medicine*. Oxford, UK: Wiley-Blackwell.

Cooper, J. and M. Cooper. 2013. *Wildlife Forensic Investigation*. CRC Press.

Correa, F. 2007. *Medicina forense veterinaria*. Monografía. Universidad de Granma, unidad docente de Medicina Veterinaria de Santiago de Cuba. http://www.ilustrados.com/documentos/eb-medicinaforense.doc (Accessed December 10, 2014).

David, T. J. 1986. Adjunctive use of scanning electron microscopy in bitemark analysis: A 3-D study. *J Forensic Sci* 31:1126–34.

Dorion, R. 2011. Animal bites. In: *Bitemark Evidence*, ed. R. Dorion. New York, NY: CRC Press, pp. 217–40.

Drinnan, A. J. and M. J. Melton. 1985. Court presentation of bitemark evidence. *Int Dent J* 35:316–21.

Friedrich, N. 2014. *Bienestar animal: El abuso en los animales*. Revista Información Veterinaria. Órgano oficial del Colegio Medico Veterinario de la Provincia de Córdoba. p. 177.

Gov UK. 2013. *Zoonosis diseases (zoonoses): Guidance, data and analysis*. https://www.gov.uk/government/collections/zoonotic-diseases-zoonoses-guidance-data-and-analysis (Accessed July 14, 2015).

Gutiérrez, M. 2004. *Análisis tafonómicos en el área interserrana*. Facultad de Ciencias Naturales y Museo. PhD Thesis. Universidad de la Plata, Argentina.

Haglund, W.D. and Sorg, M.H. (eds.). 1997. Rodents and humans remains. In: *Forensic Taphonomy*. Boca Raton, FL: CRC Press, pp. 422–32.

Heath, S. E. 1999. *Animal Management in Disasters*. St. Louis, MO: Mosby.

Hellman, D. S. and N. Blackman. 1966. Enuresis, fire setting and cruelty to animals: A triad predictive of adult crime. *Am J Psychiatry* 122:1431–5.

Kaiser, L., C. R. Heleski, J. Siegford, and K. A. Smith. 2006. Stress-related behaviors among horses used in a therapeutic riding program. *J Am Vet Med Assoc* 228:39–45.

Lagoni, L., C. Butler, and S. Hetts. 1994. *The Human–Animal Bond and Grief*. Philadelphia, PA: W.B. Saunders.

Morgan, M. and J. Palmer. 2007. Clinical review: Dog bites. *BMJ* 24:413–7.

Morse, D. R., J. V. Esposito, H. P. Kessler, and R. Gorin. 1994. Age estimation using dental periapical radiographic parameters: A review and comparative study of clinically based and regression models with the Operation Desert Storm victims. *Am J Forensic Med Pathol* 15:303–18.

Munro, H. M. C. and M. V. Thrusfield. 2001a. Non-accidental physical injuries found in dogs and cats. *J Small Anim Pract* 42:279–90.

Munro, H. M. C. and M. V. Thrusfield. 2001b. Battered pets: Sexual abuse. *J Small Anim Pract* 42:333–7.

Munro, R. 2008. *Animal Abuse and Unlawful Killing: Forensic Veterinary Pathology*, First edition. Philadelphia, PA: W.B. Saunders.

NFSTC Science Serving Justice. 2007. *Collection techniques*. http://projects.nfstc.org/pdi/Subject01/pdi_s01_m01_05.htm (Accessed December 25, 2014).

O'Connor, T. 2000. *The Archaeology of Animals Bones*. United States: Sutton Publishing Limited, Phoenix Mill.

Palacio, J., M. Leon, and S. García-Belenquer. 2005. *Aspectos epidemiológicos de las mordeduras caninas*. Gac Sanit, no. 1 (January–February), pp. 50–8. http://scielo.isciii.es/scielo.php?pid=s0213-91112005000100011&script=sci_arttext (Accessed June 25, 2015).

Pretty, I. A. and L. D. Addy. 2002. Associated postmortem dental findings as an aid to personal identification. *Sci Justice* 42:65–74.

Pretty, I. A. and L. D. Sweet. 2001. Forensic dentistry. *Br Dent J* 190:359–66.

Rawson, R. D., A. Bell, B. S. Kinard, and J. G. Kinard. 1979. Radiographic interpretation of contrast-media-enhanced bite marks. *J Forensic Sci* 24:898–901.

Rigdon, J. D. and F. Tapia. 1977. Children who are cruel to animals: A follow-up study. *J Oper Psychiatry* 8:27–36.

Rothwell, B. R. 1995. Bite marks in forensic dentistry: A review of legal, scientific issues. *J Am Dent Assoc* 126:223–32.

Rutty, G. N. 2001. *Essentials of Autopsy Practice*, Vol. 1. London: Springer-Verlag.

Simpson, V. R. 2006. Patterns and significance of bite wounds in Eurasian otters (*Lutra lutra*) in southern and south-west England. *Vet Rec* 158:113–9.

Souviron, R. 2011. Animal bites. In: *Bitemark Evidence*, ed. R. Dorion. New York, NY: CRC Press, pp. 209–16.

Sprayson, T. 2006. Taking the lead: Veterinary intervention in disaster relief. *In Practice* 28:48–51.

Sweet, D. and C. M. Bowers. 1998. Accuracy of bitemark overlays: A comparison of five common methods to produce exemplars from a suspect's dentition. *J Forensic Sci* 43:362–7.

Sweet, D., J. A. Lorente, M. Lorente, A. Valenzuela, and E. Villanueva. 1997. An improved method to recover saliva from human skin: The double swab technique. *J Forensic Sci* 42:320–2.

Toledo, V., L. Ibarra, V. Rojas, L. Ciocca, N. Rocha, and G. Jara. 2012. Estudio preliminar de patrones de mordedura según forma del cráneo, mediante el análisis morfológico y morfométrico de semiarcadas dentarias de perro doméstico (Canis familiaris) con fines de identificación. *Int J Morphol* 30:222–9.

Universidad de Murcia. 2005. *Guía para el envío de muestras al servicio de toxicología y veterinaria forense de la universidad de Murcia*. https://www.um.es/grupos/grupo-toxicologia/guia-muestras.pdf (Accessed July 3, 2015).

World Health Organization (WHO). 2005. Landmark Study on Domestic Violence. News Release WHO/62, 24 November 2005. World Health Organization, Geneva, Switzerland.

Yarrow, R. 2005. The tsunami and its aftermath. *Vet Rec* 156: 687.

CHAPTER 14

Ethics in Forensics

Ghada Hasabo

CONTENTS

14.1 INTRODUCTION

Forensic science is a professional occupation concerned with the scientific analysis and examination of physical evidence, its interpretation, and its presentation in court. It involves the applying of many principles, techniques, and strategies of the physical sciences, and has as its primary objective the determination of physical facts which can be important in legal cases (Figure 14.1).

It is the duty of all individuals active in the profession of forensic science to serve the interests of justice to their greatest and most effective ability at all times. For this duty, they use all the scientific tools at their command to determine all the many physical facts relative to the matters under investigation. Having created factual determinations, forensic scientists then interpret and appraise their findings. To do this, they are guided by expertise and data that will lead them to opinions and conclusions concerning the matters under study. These findings, conclusions, and opinions are then reported to criminal investigators, with all the accuracy and talent of which these experts are capable, such that everyone involved in the criminal proceeding might readily be able to place the findings in their correct relationship to the matter at hand.

In doing so, these forensic specialists are guided by those practices and procedures that are typically recognized among the profession to be in line with a high level of skilled ethics. For the best forensic practice, it is obviously necessary not only to have sufficient scientific knowledge and experience, but also to do this under the umbrella of ethics (Figure 14.2).

14.2 CODES OF ETHICS IN FORENSIC SCIENCE

The majority of forensic science practitioners work in traditional crime laboratories or identification units (Melson, 2012). Others may belong to a forensic science professional organization. It is through their employment or membership in specialized organizations, either membership societies or certification organizations, that they will become exposed to codes of ethics or rules of skilled responsibility.

Except for physicians, few laboratories or forensic units had their own codes to guide practitioners' behavior, until the American Society of Crime Laboratory Directors/Laboratory (ASCLD/LAB) Accreditation Board adopted a consistent code for their forensic laboratories. Even fewer forensic science practitioners privately follow their own specific code of ethics.

Most professionals who belong to a forensic science society work in organizations that don't have a clear code—or if they do, there's no effective social control mechanism. Consequently, for years, or maybe decades, forensic scientists were not subject to enforceable codes or alternative parameters on their behavior, except maybe through excoriation by the courts rejecting proof or reversing judgments of conviction due to professional nonfeasance or malfeasance by the forensic scientists.

The 2009 report of the National Research Council of the National Academy of Sciences recognized the inequality within the existing codes of ethics and their lack of widespread coverage (National Academies of Sciences and National Research Council 2009). One of the recommendations of the report encourages the formation of a national code of ethics with a means of

FIGURE 14.1 The three essential contributors for good forensic practices.

FIGURE 14.2 The forensic scientist must work under an umbrella of ethics.

enforcement. Such a code may be implemented through certification organizations, once a demand for individual certification becomes obligatory, as the report additionally suggested.

14.2.1 Codes of Ethics in Professional Organizations

Persons in the criminal justice community who depend on forensic science to clear a defendant could argue over the scope of codes of ethics; however, there's one thought that everyone ought to agree upon, enunciated in 1971 by Professor James Starrs: "The forensic scientist can wait no longer to tighten the outlines of the ethical guides that should *be drawn to govern his conduct in the criminal justice system.*"

Until now, forensic science societies and certification organizations were the first sources of ethics in forensic science. These societies vary in nature, from national and international societies such as the American Academy of Forensic Sciences (AAFS) and the International Association of Identification (IAI), representing a variety of forensic science disciplines; to regional societies such as the California Association of Criminalists (CAC) and the Mid-Atlantic Association of Forensic Scientists (MAAFS); to discipline-specific organizations such as the National Association of Medical Examiners (NAME) and the Society of Forensic Toxicologists (SOFT). Practitioners may belong to more than one organization. Thus, a specialist could belong to organizations that each have their own codes, differing in nature and scope from one another, some enforceable and a few not, or have no code in any respect. Once adopted by such organizations, the codes become very necessary and relevant. Regardless of their nature, however, the regular influence of these codes over the practitioner is often low.

If no social monitor mechanism is obtained for an association's code, problems related to the applied forensic science should be referred to the practitioner's senior. Until the ASCLD/LAB guidelines were adopted, very few, if any, using agencies had a code of ethics pertaining specifically to forensic specialists (again with the exception of physicians and different medical practitioners, who have had to adjust to various state medical board moral codes). Instead, employers had to fit ethical misconduct into the agency's government code of ethics—for instance, for those who primarily were government workers.* In different circumstances, the misconduct had to be handled through the performance work setup and also the employee's annual performance analysis. If the misconduct was serious enough, the entity's internal affairs division or workplace of skilled responsibility might need to investigate the alleged misconduct.

The investigative entities may fail to have any guidance on ethical issues applicable to forensic science practitioners. The disciplines among forensic science could differ from one another, and therefore the role and ethical issues of police and lawyers could also be "different from the scientist, [but] the moral responsibilities of the individual do not differ."

That concept is important in considering the different codes of ethics. Despite their variations, exceptions to the codes rely on the individual's own sense of morality. In fact, the very foundation of professional organizations' codes of ethics depends on personal morality (Schroeder, 1984). The construct of a morality-based code is recognized by some organizations, and in this there's a differentiation between codes of ethics and codes of conduct or rules of professional responsibility. Recognizing that codes of ethics place confidence in personal morality, such as not to lie, cheat, or steal, and contain broad ethical concepts, some organizations have solely a code of conduct or code of professional responsibility that is

* See the Paul Coverdell National Forensic Science Improvement Act (P.L. 106–561) grant program, 42 U.S.C. § 3797k(4), which requires as part of the application for a grant that the applicant certify that "a government entity exists and an appropriate process is in place to conduct independent external investigations into allegations of serious negligence or misconduct substantially affecting the integrity of the forensic results committed by employees or contractors of any forensic laboratory system, medical examiner's office, coroner's office, law enforcement storage facility, or medical facility in the State that will receive a portion of the grant amount."

specifically designed for the specialty represented by the organization and for its members' skilled development.

Different societies and organizations each have a code of ethics and a code of professional responsibility. Despite each code's application to a specific career, many organizations describe their code as being more aspirational than concrete ethical rules. For example, the Forensic Toxicologist Certification Board's Code of Ethics is captioned "Aims and Ideals" (FTCB, n.d.). The National Association of Doctors, however, combines aims and ideals in its "Code of Ethics and Conduct." The latter title suggests that ethics and conduct align and are, in fact, indivisible.

The misnomer in calling the document a code of ethics is readily apparent in the provisions that make it unethical to fail to abide by the organization's bylaws or constitution. The Association of Forensic DNA Analysts and Administrators (AFDAA), for example, makes it unethical not to "comply with the bylaws of the Association."

The Mid-Atlantic Association of Forensic Scientists (MAAFS), on the other hand, makes it unethical to form unauthorized public statements representing the organization (MAAFS, n.d.). The ASCLD Code of Ethics contains a similar provision.

If morality is admittedly the bedrock of ethics, it's exhausting to investigate how an organization can legislate non-compliance with bylaws and the creating of unauthorized statements as unethical conduct. In different organizations, an equivalent provision may be found within the governing documents; however, those organizations are careful to call their documents codes of *ethics* and conduct. A code of conduct that is vis-à-vis a code of ethics is more accepted to prohibit personal conduct thought to be adverse to the better interests and aims of the association.

Many of the codes are complete separate documents of the organization; others are incorporated into the governing documents of the organization, and used to be the bylaws. The incorporation model has the advantage of requiring the membership to vote for a change within the code as a modification of bylaws; the disadvantage is that the code is commonly difficult to update. For example, the Code of Ethics for the Northwest Association of Forensic Scientists is not part of its bylaws and needs solely a majority vote of the membership at any business meeting to amend it, whereas a modification to its bylaws needs a three-quarters affirmative vote of the members attending the Association Business Meeting.

Regardless of whether or not the code could be a part of the bylaw documents or a complete document, a good implementation of a code of ethics depends in great part on the membership's awareness of and commitment to it. Some codes idealistically proclaim their members' commitment. As an example, the Forensic Toxicologist Certification Board states that every member "shall pledge himself to conform to the code of ethics." The Southwestern Association of Forensic Scientists (SWAFS) goes one step further and adds that "every member can receive a copy of the Code" and imposes on the member the responsibility to "read the Code and be aware of its implications."

The sole organizations that seem to want annual avowal of the code by its members are the AAFS and NAME. Every year as a part of the annual renewal of membership, AAFS and NAME members should acknowledge their acceptance of the provisions of the code (AAFS, n.d.). NAME needs members to browse, perceive, and endorse the Code of Ethics and Conduct (NAME, n.d.). The two codes need the commitment to different codes of ethics and conduct. The NAME and also the American Academy of Psychiatry and the Law need agreement with the rules and moral principles of the American Medical Association and also the American Psychiatric Association, respectively (NAME, n.d.). The Illinois State Police (ISP) Rules of Conduct/Code of Ethics needs all "Forensic Science Command employees" to even be conversant in the state personnel rules, the State Police Directives Manual, and also the Facility Operational Manuals.

14.2.2 The Development of an Association's Code of Ethics and Conduct

The American Academy of Forensic Sciences (AAFS or the Academy) was started in 1948 as an associate interdisciplinary organization representing the different disciplines among the forensic science community. Dr. R.B.H. Gradwohl noted, because the plan of an associate academy was being developed, that

> There is no fixed border for any forensic science; each has more than necessity to rely on the others. It would thus seem fitting that a central organization be of extreme value in collating and disseminating the fundamentals of all forensic sciences.

It is no surprise that the commencement members of the Academy recognized that personal, ethical values are essential to the moral conduct of forensic scientists. On January 21, 1948, the Committee on a Permanent Organization issued its final report. The report declared that

> There can be no Justice without Truth, whether that Truth be attested by lay or expert witnesses. That Truth of which we speak is something more than the mere willingness of witnesses to relate what they saw, heard or know. Individual fidelity to this moral standard which we term honesty is only one aspect of Truth and is not always sufficient to serve the ends of ultimate Justice between two litigants or members of society.... It is commonly known that all knowledge is either consciously or unconsciously encumbered not only with the imperfections of the observer,

> but mostly by preconceived notions, prejudices and inadequate mechanisms for differentiating between appearances and reality.... Science, as an empirical method of discovering eternal truths in nature, is the one important handmaiden by which Truth and then Justice may be unfolded. And in so far as science has advanced to unroll a cloud of ignorance from the minds of men, to that extent have the legal controversies of men been more equitably adjusted.

At the 1950 scientific meeting of the Academy in Chicago, the AAFS Constitution and bylaws were adopted. Chapter 1, Section 3 provided for adverse action against "a member who will violate any of the provisions of this Constitution and bylaws." The provisions of these documents pertained primarily to membership, administration, and structure and failed to specify whether any moral standards against that action should be taken, but "a member who has been found guilty of a crime or is guilty of gross misconduct despite the fact that no criminal charge has been made." Sanctions that would be obligatory if the "charges" were sustained included censure, suspension, or expulsion.

An interesting provision in the bylaws, significantly in light of today's litigious society, explicitly states that "kindly efforts in interest of peace, conciliation or reformation, so far as possible and expedient, shall proceed the filing of formal charges affecting the character or standing of a member."

The same initiation documents provided for an Ethics Committee consisting of the three immediate past-presidents of the Academy. Such a committee was started in 1950. The committee's task, however, wasn't to make a code of ethics but to handle things wherever "incidents of conduct deemed 'detrimental to the simplest interests of any skilled society'" were reported. AAFS records don't reveal any such activity by the Ethics Committee throughout the 1950s (Field, 1998f, 33). Not till 1960, was a committee formed to make a code of ethics. That committee planned a comprehensive set of "rules" of ethics (Field, 1998g, 47, 247). A part of the preamble for the planned Rules of Ethics reads as follows:

> The purity and efficiency of judicial administration depends as much upon the character, conduct and demeanor of lawyers, physicians and forensic scientists in this great trust as upon the fidelity and ability of the courts or the honesty and intelligence of jurors.

What followed were 15 non-exclusive, general rules for guidance of its members. These rules included candor and fairness, how far a professional can move into supporting a client's case, conflict of opinion among colleagues, participation in fraud and trickery, duty on discovery of fraud or imposition, conflicting interests, confidences of a client, right to withdraw, punctuality, actions toward jury, expenses, feat interest in litigation,

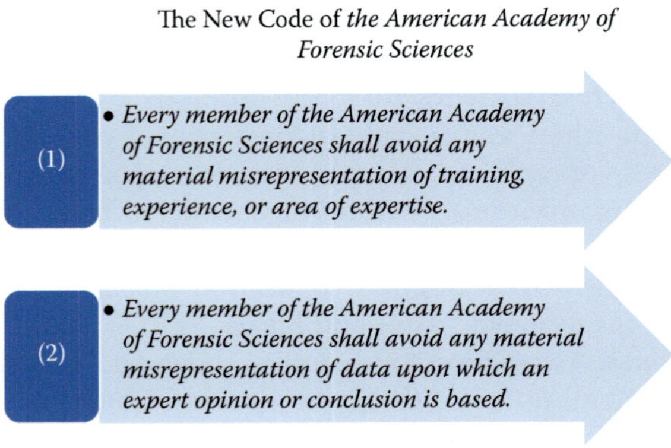

FIGURE 14.3 The new code of the American Academy of Forensic Science (AAFS).

fixing the fee, contingent fees, and membership within the academy.

The Rules of Ethics were not presented to the Academy membership for adoption. The AAFS Executive Committee met within the spring of 1963 and tabled the foundations. The explicit reason was as a result of that "it was felt that the Academy's Constitution was accepted, which it absolutely was not possible to legislate morality and integrity."

An ad hoc Committee on the Code of Ethics was formed within the mid-1970s. The Committee members recognized that the multidisciplinary nature of the Academy created a challenge. Every one of the disciplines within the Academy had completely different, discipline-specific issues. Thus, it absolutely was determined that the code of ethics had to be generic and applicable to all or any members. Four criteria drove their drafting of the planned code: it should be desirable, it should be feasible, it should be enforceable, and it should be enforced. This time, the managerial Committee, meeting within the summer of 1976, voted to the present code to the general membership, and in 1977 it absolutely was adopted at the annual meeting of the Academy.*

The new code was developed to "promote the highest quality of professional and personal conduct of its members." The two provisions the code provided are shown in Figure 14.3.

> Every member of the American Academy of Forensic Sciences shall avoid any material misrepresentation of training, experience, or area of expertise.
>
> Every member of the American Academy of Forensic Sciences shall avoid any material misrepresentation of data upon which an expert opinion or conclusion is based.

Those two provisions of the code were thought to be necessary for all members; though the adopted code

* Report to the AAFS Board of Directors from the Ethics and Long Term Planning Committee.

was far less specific than the rules that got proposed in 1963, the total modification to the Academy bylaws conjointly enclosed three voluntary "guiding principles" that were deemed "essential to the attainment of the best quality of professionalism." They were as follows:

1. The Forensic specialist should to maintain his skilled ability through existing programs of continuous education.
2. The Forensic specialist should render technically correct statements altogether written or oral reports, testimony, public addresses, or publications, and may avoid any deceptive or inaccurate claims.
3. The Forensic specialist should act in an exceedingly impartial manner and do nothing which might imply partiality or any interest in a case except the proof of the facts and their correct interpretation.

However:

> Any member whose professional or personal conduct becomes adverse to the best interests and purposes of the academy shall be liable to censure, suspension or expulsion.

The permissive investigatory action by the committee was directed to alleged violations that are related to false statement of criteria for membership, unauthorized public statements, and violations of the Code of Ethics. Curiously, the "Guiding Principles," which were solely voluntary, were not captured under the investigatory authority of the committee.

The exclusion of the guiding principles from social control was intentional, and also the next revision of the Code of Ethics eliminated those principles, separating that iteration of the code even away from the precise nature of the 1963 proposal. The 1986 revision of the code, however, specifically incorporated three new provisions that were tangentially documented through the liability and inquiring parts of the previous code's social control section (Figure 14.4).

The three new provisions were as follows:

1. Each member of the American Academy of Forensic Sciences shall refrain from practicing professional or personal conduct adverse to the best interest and aims of the Academy.
2. Misrepresentation of one or more criteria for membership within the AAFS shall represent a violation of this section of the code.
3. Each member of the AAFS shall refrain from issuing public statements that seem to represent the position of the Academy without specific authority that first gets obtained from the Board of Administrators.

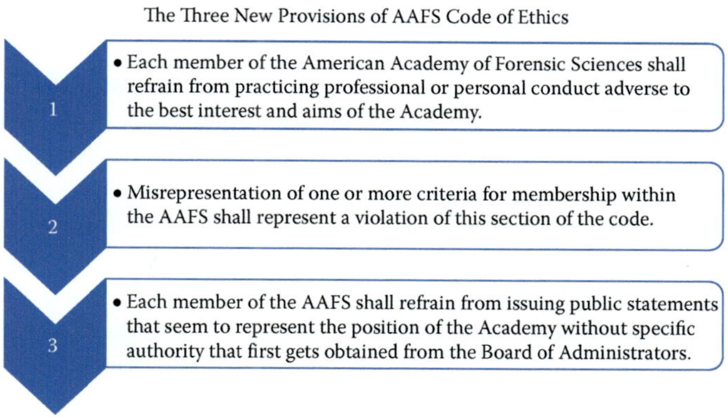

FIGURE 14.4 The three new provisions of the AAFS Code of Ethics.

In 1989, AAFS revealed within the *Journal of Forensic Sciences* a special conference on ethics in the forensic sciences, supported by the Ethics and Values board of the National Science Foundation (Peterson, 1989). The five papers constituting the conference set a vital benchmark within the development of moral concerns, and were instructive to the complete forensic science community. The introductory paragraph of the conference is instructive for its read of the relative breadth of moral standards:

> Forensic scientists are expected to be honest with respect to their qualifications, examinations, and conclusions; they should be technically competent and only use methods of proven reliability; they should remain totally objective and nonpartisan with respect to their review of evidence and delivery of expert testimony; and they are expected to present understandable and balanced reports/testimony to legal decision makers.

In the late 1990s, the Academy established an ad hoc Good Forensic Practices Committee to organize an aspirational set of guidelines to supplement the negligible, baseline provisions of the AAFS Code of Ethics. Violations of the great Forensic Practices Guidelines would not, however, be enforceable unless a violation was additionally a breach of the Code of Ethics (Barnett, 2001). These guidelines were given to the Academy's Executive Committee in 1999; however, they were never adopted by the Academy, and also the committee was disbanded.*

As of this writing, the last revision of the AAFS Code of Ethics occurred in 2008, and it remains

* Report by Dr. Robert Weinstock, Chair, Good Forensic Practice Committee to the Executive Committee, American Academy of Forensic Sciences, January 14 (1999).

general in nature with very little guidance on the actual moral and ethical obligations of forensic scientists or their professional conduct. There are two substantive changes, however, that were created within the last revision. First, "conduct adverse to the ... purposes of the Academy" was modified to "conduct adverse to the ... objectives of the Academy," as they're significantly articulated within the preamble to the bylaws. Those objectives were incorporated into the Code. Second, the prohibition on misrepresenting information was expanded to misrepresenting "scientific principles" in addition.

One contributor to the 1989 ethics conference used the AAFS Code of Ethics as an example that "many professional codes of ethics do very little more than remind us of our parent's admonitions" to not lie, cheat, steal, or kill. Another commentator has urged that "the drawback to the brevity and lack of specificity of the code of ethics of the AAFS is that it has little value as a guide to proper action in a particular circumstance."

Despite its brevity and lack of specificity, however, the AAFS Code of Ethics and Conduct might be enforced by the Academy, in contrast to some societies that had no social control provisions. The Academy was one among the few organizations that might, and did, interact in social control actions leading to sanctions against its members.

Not all codes are as general as the AAFS code. An example of a additional detailed code of ethics is that belonging to the California Association of Criminalists (CAC). Peter Barnett, a frequent author of forensic science ethics, recited the history of the CAC Code of Ethics:

> The development of the CAC Code ... was an effort by a group of early criminalists in California to help define a profession for the first time. The California criminalists who founded the CAC and adopted its code of ethics were really inventing something that had never before existed: a code of ethics that tried to bridge the gap between one profession with a strong ethical tradition—the law—and another nascent profession that was trying to develop professional recognition and a means of self-governance.

The CAC Code of Ethics, first adopted in 1957, is detailed and multi-situational. However, as Barnett points out, the in-depth code is hard to revise; as a result the opponents to any revision can argue either that the proposal is already covered in existing provision, or would conflict with different provisions already effective. Additionally, such code could be difficult to apply to uncommon circumstances. The categorization of a selected code is somewhat subjective, divided into three classes (1–10 provisions, 11–20 provisions, and 21 or a lot of provisions); however, there's a major distinction between the general code and the detailed code. The CAC Code of Ethics has 41 provisions, as an example, compared to the four provisions of the AAFS or the Association of Forensic DNA Analysts and Directors. Within the latter organization, the provisions are broad concepts:

1. Comply the bylaws of the Association.
2. Treat all data from any agency, client, or fellow member with the confidentiality needed.
3. Carry out the duties of the profession with integrity, attention to accuracy and in an unbiased manner.
4. Don't misrepresent qualifications, evidence, opinions, conclusions, or testimony.

Even broader ideas are reflected within the ABFT Code of Ethics, that exhorts its members to conduct themselves and to perform activities "with honesty and integrity" (ABFT, n.d.). The Code of Conduct of the Forensic Science Society of the UK provides less clarity, by mandating that members conduct themselves "honorably within the application of their profession" (FSSoc, n.d.). The breadth of these ethical imperatives, however, are minimal in comparison to the last provision of the ABFT Code of Ethics.* That provision instructs ABFT members to:

> Act in accordance with the long-standing precepts for ethical practice of the profession...

Compare those general provisions to the specificity provided in Section III. K. of the CAC Code of Ethics:

> K. Where the expert must prepare photographs or offer oral "background information" to the jury in respect to a specific type of analytic method, this information shall be reliable and valid, typifying the usual or normal basis for the method. The instructional material shall be of a level that will provide the jury with a proper basis for evaluating the subsequent evidence presentations, and not such as would provide them with a lower standard than the science demands.

The majority of the codes are in the intermediate category that departs from the broad principles but stays within the general classes most frequently encountered by forensic scientists. The CAC Code was adopted for criminalists, and the AAFS Code for a multidisciplinary society. The other codes target a specific category of forensic

* The American Board of Forensic Document Examiners has a document entitled "Code of Ethics and Standard Practices," the opening paragraph of which calls the same document the "Code of Ethics and Competency."

scientists, like the ASCLD/LAB Guiding Principles of Professional Responsibility for Crime Laboratories and Rhetorical Scientists. Those guidelines pertain to laboratory management and "all laboratory personnel, together with technical support personnel and those who assist Forensic scientists in their work."*

The Illinois State Police Forensic Sciences Command Rules of Conduct/Code of Ethics applies to directors, administrators, forensic scientists, toxicologists, and support personnel within the command (The Code of Ethics of the California Association of Criminalists [CAC], n.d.). The Association of Forensic DNA Analysts and Administrators code applies to those who are dealing with forensic aspects of DNA analysis, as well as to their supervisors and laboratory administrators. Unlike the AAFS Code, some additional detailed codes of ethics are divided into broad classes of moral considerations.

BIBLIOGRAPHY

American Academy of Forensic Sciences (AAFS) Board of Directors' Policy and Procedure Manual, Section 4.4.4.6, http://www.aafs.org; National Association of Medical Examiners (NAME) Code of Ethics and Conduct Section 1.g., http://thename.org/ (Accessed March 2015).

American Academy of Forensic Sciences (AAFS) Code of Ethics and Conduct, Section 1.c. http://www.aafs.org (Accessed March 2016).

American Board of Forensic Toxicology (ABFT) Code of Ethics, http://www.abft.org/.

Illinois State Police Forensic Sciences Command Rules of Conduct/Code of Ethics, http://www.isp.state.il.us/forensics/ (Accessed January 2016).

American Society of Crime Laboratory Directors (ASCLD) Code of Ethics, http://www.ascld.org/ (Accessed December 2015).

ASCLD/LAB Guiding Principles of Professional Responsibility for Crime Laboratories and Forensic Scientists, fn i. http://www.ascld-lab.org/(Accessed on Jan 2016).

Association of Forensic DNA Analysts and Administrators (AFDAA), Bylaws, Article III, E.1. http://www.afdaa.org/Welcome.html (Accessed February 2016).

P.D. Barnett, *Ethics in Forensic Science: Professional Standards for the Practice of Criminalistics*. Boca Raton, FL: CRC Press (2001), pp. 27, 28, 30.

* ASCLD/LAB Guiding Principles of Professional Responsibility for Crime Laboratories and Forensic Scientists, http://www.ascld-lab.org/. As of May 6, (2011), 385 crime laboratories were accredited by ASCLD/LAB, including 192 state laboratories, 128 local agency laboratories, 23 federal laboratories, 17 international (outside the United States) laboratories, and 25 private laboratories.

The Code of Ethics of the California Association of Criminalists (CAC), http://www.cacnews.org/ (Accessed January 2016).

K.S. Field, *History of the American Academy of Forensic Sciences, 1948–1998*. West Conshohocken, PA: American Society for Testing and Materials. (1998a), pp. 15, 33, 47, 58, 59, 189, 205, 206, 208, 247–253, 289–290.

The Forensic Science Society, UK (FSSoc) Code of Conduct, Section 2. http://www.forensicscience-society.org.uk (Accessed November 2015).

Forensic Toxicologist Certification Board (FTCB) Code of Ethics, http://home.usit.net.

D.M. Lucas, The ethical responsibilities of the forensic scientist: Exploring the limits, *Journal of Forensic Sciences* 34 (1989) 719–729, 727.

K.E. Melson, Embracing the path forward: The journey to justice continues, *New England Journal on Criminal and Civil Confinement* **36** (Summer 2010) 197.

K.E. Melson, Codes of ethics in forensic science societies: The organizational parameters of morality and conduct. In *Ethics in Forensic Science*. J.C. Upshaw Downs, A.R. Swienton, Chap. 4. New York, NY: Elsevier. (2012), pp. 81–135.

Mid-Atlantic Association of Forensic Scientists (MAAFS), Code of Ethics, 1.2.4, http://www.maafs.org (Accessed January 2016).

National Academies of Sciences, National Research Council, *Strengthening Forensic Science in the United States: A Path Forward*. Washington, DC: National Academies Press. (2009), pp. 36–37, 63–64.

National Association of Medical Examiners (NAME), http://thename.org/.

See National Association of Medical Examiners (NAME) Code of Ethics and Conduct, http://thename.org/, and American Academy of Forensic Sciences (AAFS) Code of Ethics and Conduct, http://www.aafs.org.

National Association of Medical Examiners (NAME) Code of Ethics and Conduct Section 1.a, http://thename.org/ and American Academy of Psychiatry and the Law Ethical Guidelines for the Practice of Forensic Psychiatry, Section I, http://www.aapl.org/.

National Association of Medical Examiners (NAME) Code of Ethics and Conduct Section 1.g, http://thename.org/ (Accessed December 2015).

Northwest Association of Forensic Scientists (NWAFS) Bylaws, Chapter III, Section 3.E.(1); Constitution Article VI, Section 2, http://www.nwafs.org/ (Accessed January 2016).

J.L. Peterson, Symposium: Ethical conflicts in the forensic sciences, *Journal of Forensic Sciences* 34 (1989) 717.

J.L. Peterson, J.E. Murdock, Forensic science: Developing an integrated system of support and enforcement, *Journal of Forensic Sciences* **34** (1989) 749–762, 759. "A survey of 50 criminalistics laboratories in the summer of

1987 yielded returns of only 6 such codes, many of which were of the parent police agency and not particularly relevant to forensic science matters." But see the Illinois State Police Forensic Sciences Command Rules of Conduct/Code of Ethics, http://www.isp.state. il.us/forensics/. Peterson and Murdock (1989).

O.C. Schroeder, Ethical and moral dilemmas confronting forensic scientists, *Journal of Forensic Sciences* **29** (1984) 966–986, 969.

Southwestern Association of Forensic Scientists (SWAFS), Code of Professional Conduct Section VI, http://www.swafs.us/ and Illinois State Police, Forensic Sciences Command, Rules of Conduct/Code of Ethics, Section VIII.C, http://www.isp.state.il.us/forensics/.

J.E. Starrs, The ethical obligations of the forensic scientist in the criminal justice system, *Journal of the AOAC* **54** (1971) 906–914, 914.

CHAPTER 15

Forensic Digital Imaging

Michael Dixon, Mark Wood, and Stephen Cole

CONTENTS

This chapter covers the basic principles of forensic digital imaging theory. It is not intended to cover much in the way of photographic instruction, as this is available from many other publications and websites. It is also not intended to cover acceptable court practices, since this differs too much from country to country and is highly changeable over time.

15.1 IMAGE SIZE AND RESOLUTION

Bitmap images require sufficient resolution for the end purpose. If a photograph of a football crowd is required, where every person's face needs to be clearly identifiable, it would be no good taking such a shot using a mobile phone. With photography it is the choice of camera and lens that determines the clarity of the image. The bitmap resolution of a digital camera is counted in megapixels.

Three choices affect resolution when taking a photograph:

- The maximum resolution of the camera
- The resolution set in the camera
- How the shot is framed

The maximum resolution of the camera: A 6-megapixel camera will have half the resolution of a 12-megapixel camera. The greater the megapixel count, the greater the resolution. But the quality of the lenses used also affects the level of detail in a photograph.

The resolution is set in the camera, so it is possible to set the resolution of a 12-megapixel camera to 6 megapixels—doing so, however, is a bad idea. Best practice should involve capturing as much data as possible. If later, a low-resolution file is required, then a copy of the original photograph can be resampled.

FIGURE 15.1 Photograph of a knife from a distance, effectively limiting the resolution of the photo.

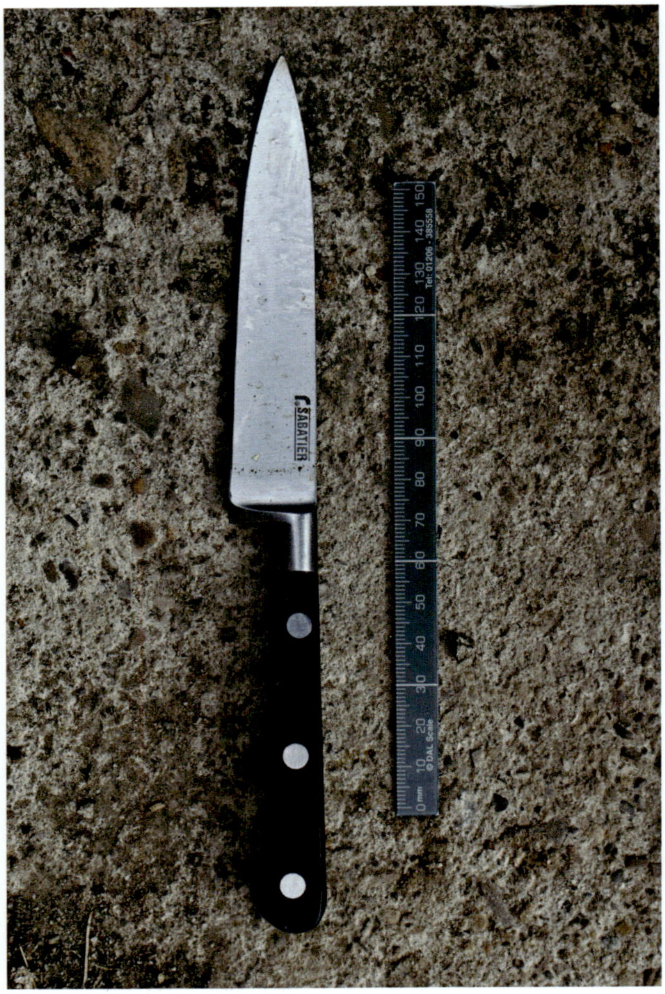

FIGURE 15.2 Close-up photograph of the same knife.

A 12-megapixel camera can comfortably produce an A3-sized print. If a high-quality lens is used the A3 image could be resampled to A2 with little or no loss of image quality. The physical size of the sensor also affects image sharpness.

Here's how the shot is framed: Take a look at the photographs above, both were taken on a 12-megapixel camera. In the photograph on the right, the knife fills the frame, top to bottom, so effectively it's a 12-megapixel image. The photograph on the left fills less than half the frame, so it's effectively smaller than 6 megapixels (Figures 15.1 and 15.2).

There are two components that form the resolution of a bitmap. The amount of pixels in an image is one part of resolution; the second is the bit depth.

From this basic overview of pixel resolution, we will now take a look at some specifics. In the examples in Figures 15.3 through 15.5, a photograph has been resampled into three sizes; each image has been sized to 14 × 14 cm, but the pixels per inch (ppi) has been changed for each. Notice how at 10 ppi, the pixel structure in the image is plainly seen, but at 30 ppi the image is decidedly acceptable. At 72 ppi, the image looks clear and sharp.

When deciding on the pixel resolution of an image, thought has to be given to the purpose of the file. It is common, and correct practice, for photographers to shoot at the maximum resolution of their camera. When scanning a document, sufficient pixel resolution for 1:1 reproduction is often desired; for example an A4 document would be scanned at a resolution that would allow it to be printed at A4.

Thus far we have briefly looked at *input resolution*, the megapixel count of the camera. Getting this part right means that high-quality image data is captured. Once captured and enhanced, this pixel data can be either printed, displayed on-screen, or stored for future use. These three options relate to output resolution.

Print and on-screen display resolutions vary. Typically, print resolution is 300 ppi, and for on-screen display the standard resolution is 72 ppi. When storing or archiving images, the output resolution should be

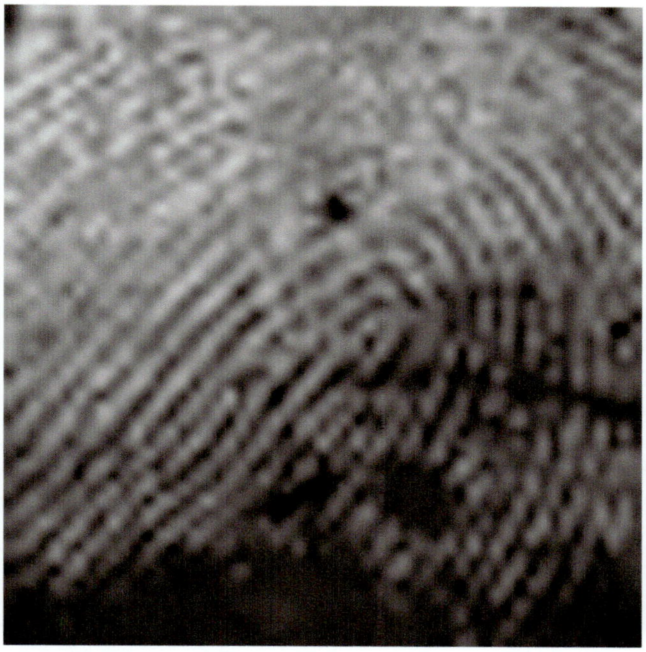

FIGURE 15.3 Fingerprint image resampled to 14 cm/10 ppi.

FIGURE 15.4 The same fingerprint image resampled to 14 cm/30 ppi.

the same as the input resolution: a 12-megapixel image should be stored as a 12-megapixel image.

Figure 15.6 is from Adobe Photoshop. It shows Photoshop's Image Size dialogue box, displaying the pixel dimensions for a 12-megapixel photograph; any other image editing software may look slightly different.

FIGURE 15.5 The same fingerprint image resampled to 14 cm/72 ppi.

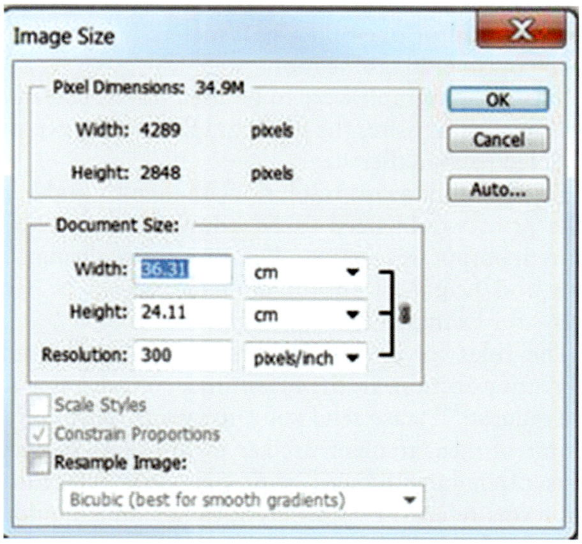

FIGURE 15.6 The Image Size dialogue box from Adobe Photoshops®. It contains information for a 12-megapixel photograph. The width and height of the photograph in pixels is 4288 and 2848, respectively. Multiplying the width and height together gives 12,212,224 pixels. A megapixel is 1 million pixels; hence, 12 megapixels.

The screen grab has a boxed area called Document Size. The 12-megapixel image will make a 36.21 × 24.11 cm print, if the required output resolution is 300 ppi. Resampling the photograph could make larger or smaller prints. Resampling is to either add or take away pixels.

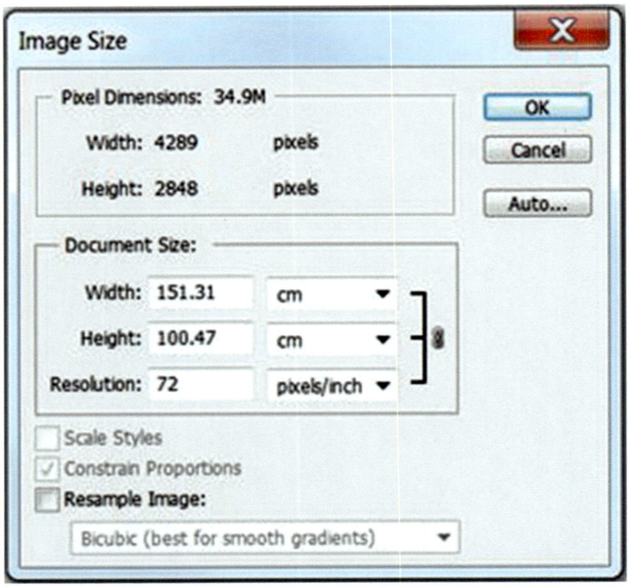

FIGURE 15.7 The Adobe Photoshop dialogue box for the image where the document size is set at 72 ppi.

Figure 15.7 shows the specifications for the same photograph, where the document size is set for on-screen display, nominally 72 ppi. The resulting image would require a monitor one-and-a-half meters high to display it at the optimal magnification.

If this photograph were to be used for on-screen display, say on a website, the photograph would have to be resampled to a smaller size.

To determine print resolution, the width and height of the print would need to be known, along with the required output resolution. For on-screen display, the width and height of the final image would be set in pixels—for example, 800 × 600 pixels.

The rules for calculating resolution are covered in the Printing section. In the meantime, consider this nonsense request: "Please send your images at 72 dpi." First, the unit of measurement used is in dpi (dots per inch); this is often interchanged with ppi. Strictly speaking, these terms refer to two different things and should not be mixed about. But for what do we have the 72 dpi or ppi image request? Because the required width and height have not been stated, there is no way to know what is being asked for. When output resolution is being specified, values for width, height, and pixel per inch have to be stated.

Pixels per inch (ppi) should be used to refer to camera or scanning resolution, being a measure of bitmap resolution, while dots per inch (dpi) should be used to describe the resolution of a printing device.

That concludes this introduction to bitmap image resolution, as measured in pixels. But there is a second component that needs to be addressed when referring to bitmap images, and that is bit depth.

15.2 BIT DEPTH

Thus far we have looked at bitmap resolution as being a grid of pixels. Now we will look at the tone and color values of those pixels. To simplify the explanation, we will consider *monochrome* images, as the same rules apply to color images.

Computers work in a binary number system, and digital images are no different. A digitized photograph is just a series of 1s and 0s. Let us consider one pixel in an image. In the most basic bitmap image, a pixel can be on or off, being set to a value of 1 or 0. In computer-speak, this would be a 1-bit image. Computer processing power goes up in binary values: 1-bit, 2-bit, 4-bit, 8-bit, 16-bit, 32-bit, and 64-bit. Modern operating systems such as Apple and Windows ship in both 32-bit and 64-bit versions.

The greater the bits, the faster instructions can be processed. When considering digital images, a bit depth of 64 bits would generate over 18 quintillion levels of tonal information. Humans perceive less than 256 levels of tone. Therefore, the bit depth of monochrome images is usually set between 8 bits and 16 bits; similar rules apply to color images.

The example in Figure 15.8 shows four grayscale bitmap images. The desired effect is to produce an image that looks like a black sphere with a specular highlight. Imagine it is a black snooker ball under bright television lights.

The 1-bit image (2^1) can only switch pixels on or off; it's black and white, so it looks cartoon-like. The 2-bit image (2^2) can have four values: black, white, and two intermediate grays—not very convincing. The 4-bit image (2^4) has 16 tones, including 2 black-and-white and 14 intermediate gray tones; steps can still be seen in the image. When such steps are visible in a photograph, it is called posterization. The 8-bit image (2^8) has 256 levels of tone, including black and white. An 8-bit image

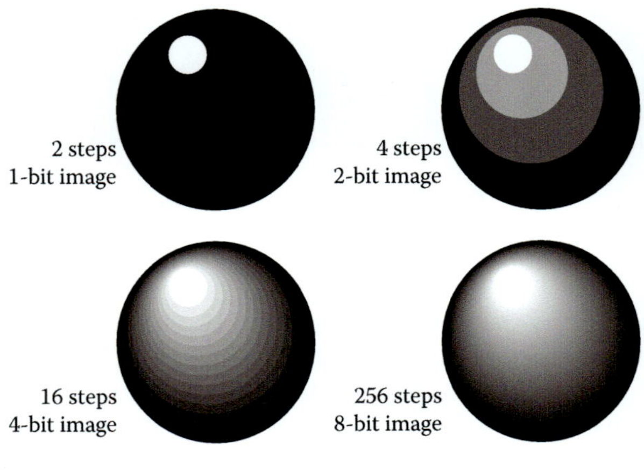

FIGURE 15.8 Four grayscale images, illustrating 1-bit, 2-bit, 4-bit, and 8-bit levels of tone, respectively.

FIGURE 15.9 Six levels of tone becomes posterized.

FIGURE 15.10 Sixteen levels of tone looks somewhat less posterized.

can correctly render a monochrome photograph without posterizing.

In the examples in Figures 15.9 through 15.11, the final photograph in each sequence only has 60 levels of tone, but still looks photographic. The other images have posterized; the six-level example clearly shows why the phenomenon is known as posterization.

FIGURE 15.11 Sixty levels of tone still looks photographic.

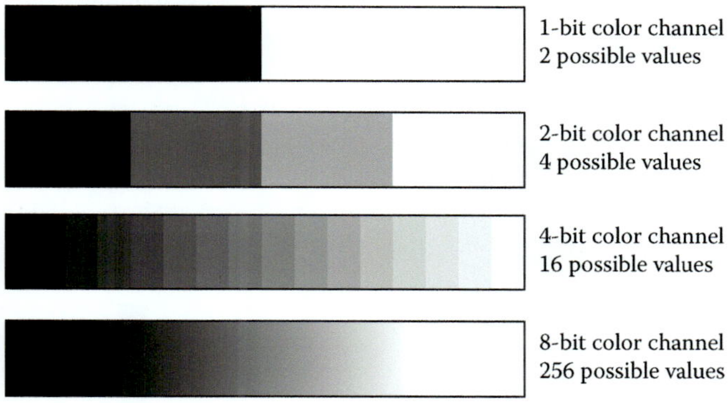

FIGURE 15.12 1-bit through 8-bit color channels.

Although an 8-bit grayscale image is sufficient to correctly render a monochrome image, scanning software can be set to scan monochrome in 16 bits, or more than 32,000 levels of tone (see Figure 15.12).

Understanding bit depth and color requires knowledge of *color channels*. Most image-capture devices, DSLRs (digital single-lens reflex cameras), compact cameras, and scanners use the additive primaries of red, green, and blue to render color. Together abbreviated RGB, each of these primary colors is assigned to a channel. So, an RGB image has three color channels of at least 8 bits per channel. When a color image is set to 8 bits, each channel contains 256 possible tones for red, green and blue. Three 8-bit channels create a 24-bit image; 2^{24} makes 16.7 million colors. (Three channels of 16 bits create a 48-bit image.)

15.3 HISTOGRAMS

Essential to understanding digital imaging is the ability to read and make sense of histograms. A histogram can be likened to a bar chart that maps out the amount of tone in an image. For example, if a grayscale image were to have 16 levels of tone, its histogram could be displayed as shown in Figure 15.13.

Reading the histogram along the horizontal axis (Figure 15.14), we can see that tones 0, 1, 2, and 3 represent the darkest tones in the image. Black is 0, and the mid-tones of the image are values 4 to 10. As this is a nighttime scene, there are far more darker tones than mids. In the highlights, values 11 to 15, there are very few pixels. White is represented by 15, and only a few of the highlights on the statue are that bright. It should be noted that 0 is a value in computing: it's not anything.

The histogram for this image looks different from the RTC scene. This histogram indicates the photograph has lots of mid-tones and highlight tones. Figure 15.15 illustrates the histogram for the same image, as it appears in Adobe Photoshop.

The histogram appears in the Input Levels area of the Levels dialogue box. Each tone is a thin black line; the lines are spread across the 256 steps of the histogram, hence the white spaces—and its histogram is full of tone (Figure 15.16).

This second Photoshop histogram shows that tones are distributed across the full tonal range of the image; the spikes, tone values that hit the top of the histogram, seen as thin black lines, are a telltale sign that this image has been enhanced.

Referring back to the previous section on Bit Depth, we explained that typically photographs are 8 bits per channel, so a monochrome photograph would have 256 tones available to render the image. Having

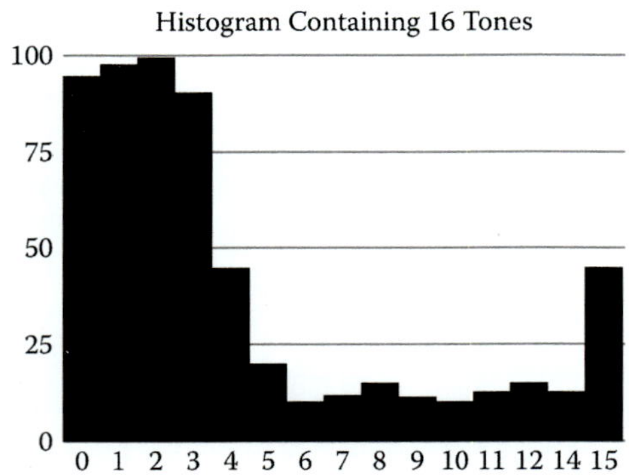

FIGURE 15.13 Histogram of a grayscale image with 16 levels of tone.

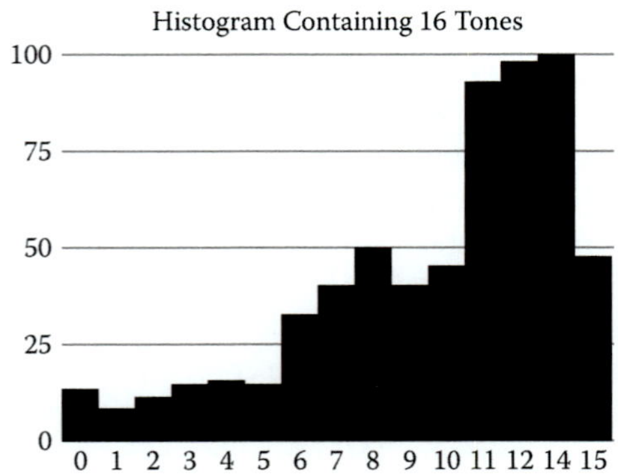

FIGURE 15.14 Reading the histogram along the horizontal axis.

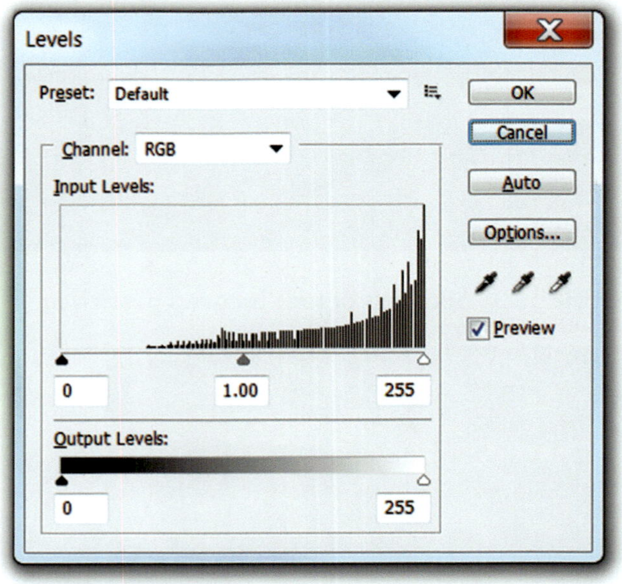

FIGURE 15.15 The histogram as it appears in Adobe Photoshop.

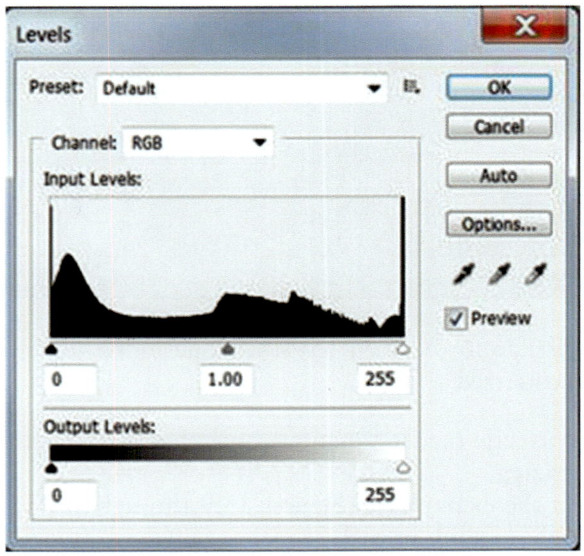

FIGURE 15.16 The histogram in the Input Levels of the Levels dialogue box.

256 tones in photography ensures that it looked photographic.

For every photographed scene (Figure 15.17a), there will be a unique histogram (Figure 15.17b). In digital photography, the histogram as displayed on a digital camera provides an excellent guide to whether the correct exposure has been achieved.

Histograms are discussed in more detail later. But to close this section, we will take a further look at Photoshop's Level Dialogue box, where you cannot only view, but also edit the histogram.

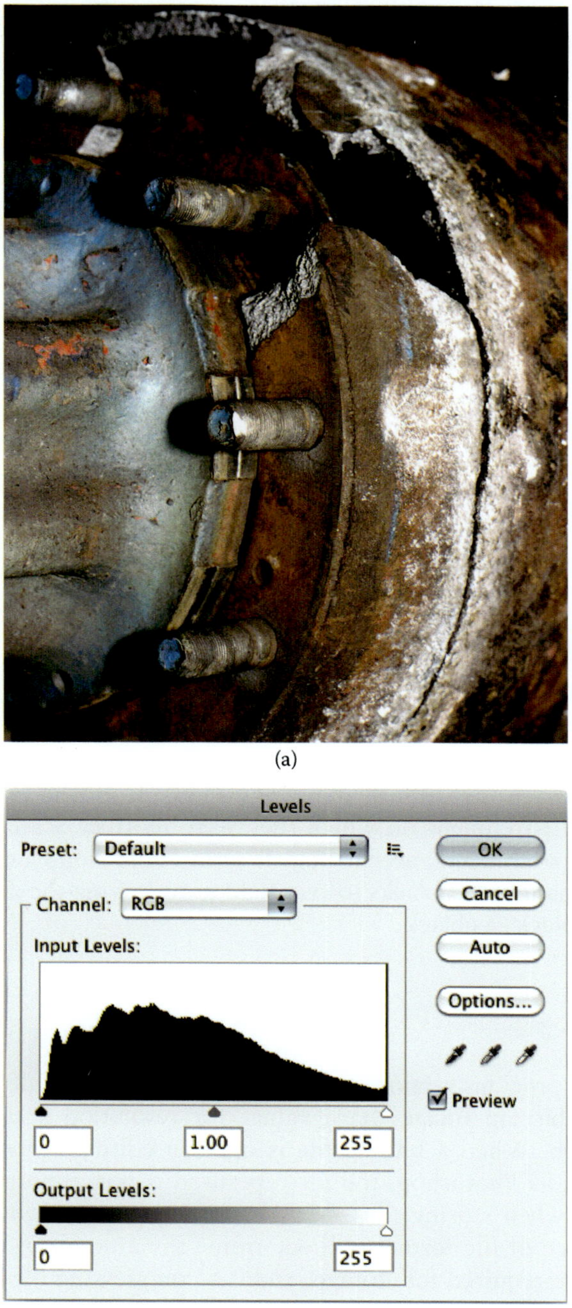

(a)

(b)

FIGURE 15.17 (a) A photograph and (b) its histogram.

In Photoshop's Levels dialogue box, the Input Levels area, which contains the histogram, are isolated. Red circles indicate the three primary editing controls for Photoshop's Levels; many software applications, such as Aperture, Photoshop Elements, and scanning software have similar controls in their respective Levels dialogue boxes.

On the far left, the red circle covers the Black Point Slider; on the far right of the histogram, the red circle covers the White Point Slider, and in the middle is the Gamma Slider. Moving these three sliders can change the tone of a bitmap image. This is done first by setting the Black and White Points and then, if necessary, adjusting the mid-tones/gamma.

In the example shown in Figures 15.18 and 15.19, a low-contrast image has been enhanced using Photoshop's Levels.

The photograph of the footprint looks too gray, as there is no strong contrast. The histogram in Figure 15.19

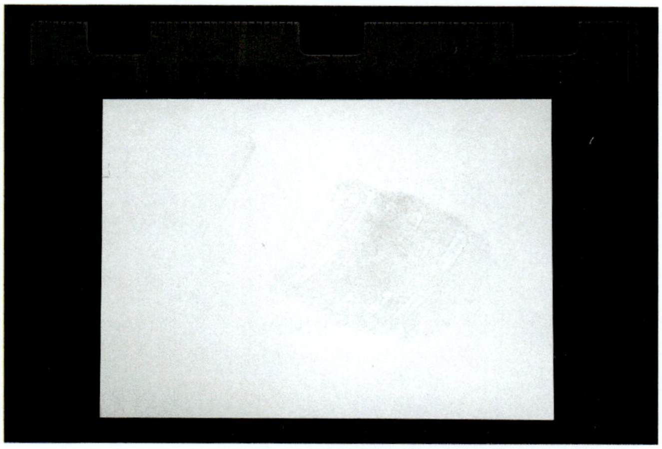

FIGURE 15.18 A low-contrast photograph enhanced.

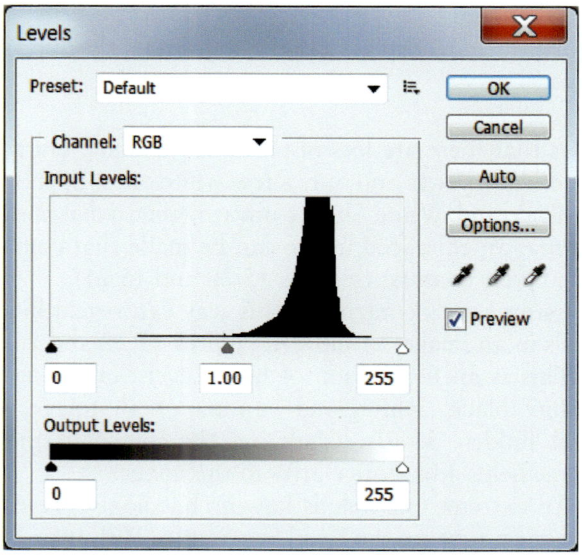

FIGURE 15.19 Display of the histogram for the image.

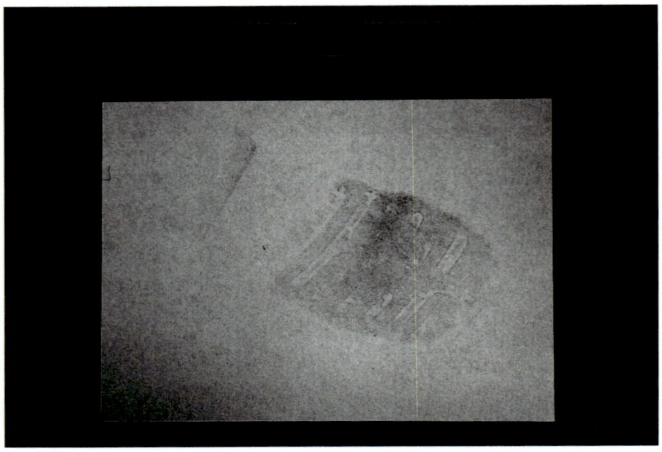

FIGURE 15.20 The photograph enhanced for improved contrast.

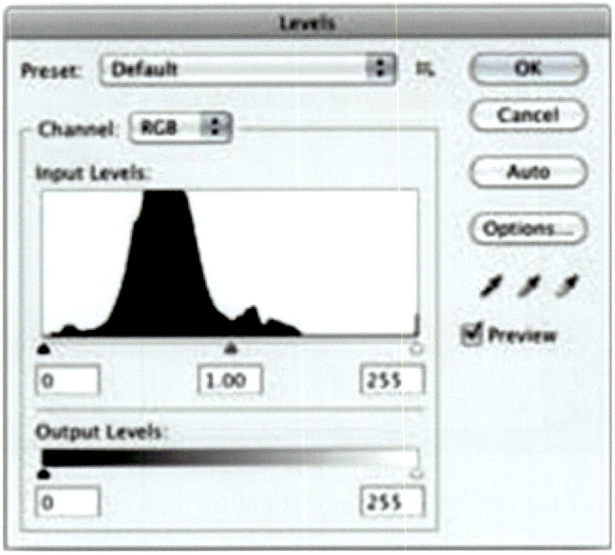

FIGURE 15.21 Display of the histogram for the improved image.

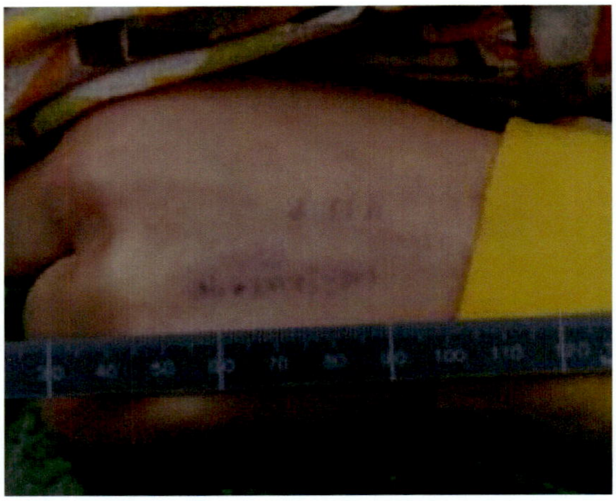

FIGURE 15.22 A color photograph.

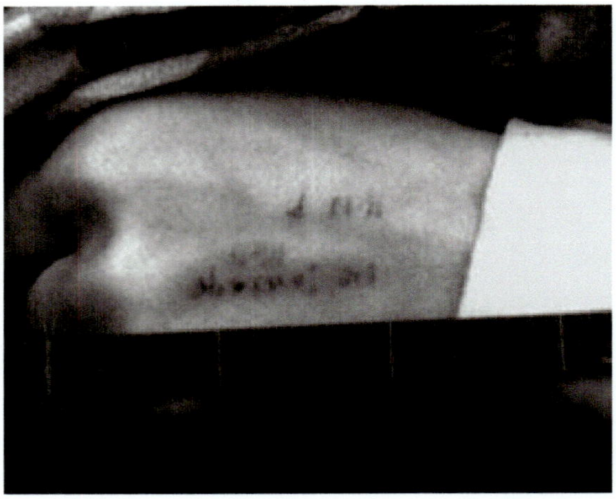

FIGURE 15.23 The same color photo converted to black and white and illustrating improved contrast.

shows that there are lots of tones in the mids, but there are no black pixels and only a few white ones. By moving the Black and White Sliders inward, then adjusting the Gamma, an enhanced image can be made that contains much better contrast (Figures 15.20 and 15.21).

Using Levels controls in this way can reveal hidden details in an image, as show in Figures 15.22 and 15.23.

This is an illustration of how Levels, changing the absolute black, white, and gamma of an image, can reveal hidden details. Changing the image to monochrome helps add more clarity to the image.

An extreme example is how archaeologists revealed the text on some of the Dead Sea Scrolls. Well over 2000 years old, some of these documents were hard to read, the black text almost indistinguishable from the blackened parchment on which they were written. Scanning the parchments, archaeologists used Photoshop's Levels to change near blacks to very light gray, leaving the darkest blacks as black.

15.4 FILE FORMATS

The previous sections outlined resolution and bit depth. All bitmap images have values for resolution and bit depth. When a bitmap file is open in editing software such as Photoshop, the file type used is not important, but when storing files—that is, saving them—then the choice of file format will determine the amount of disc space required for storage, and if a compressing file format is chosen, consideration has to be given to how much data will be lost in compression.

TABLE 15.1 File Formats

File Format	Extension	Description
Joint Photographic Expert Group	JPEG, and JPEG 2000	JPEG files are perhaps the most common image format used. JPEG format allows images to be compressed so more data can fit on storage devices such as compact flash cards and hard drives. For example, a 2-gigabit memory card in a 12-megapixel camera can store 120 raw files, or 224 high-quality JPEGs (or 867 images on BASIC JPEG). The JPEG format achieves this by resampling an image into clusters of pixels; the greater the compression, the higher the resampling. JPEG is a lossy file format: by using it, data is thrown away.
Graphic Interchange Format	GIF	Pronounced originally as "jif," then latterly with a hard *g*, "gif," this file format was introduced by CompuServe in 1987. A GIF has a maximum of 256 colors or tones, and, along with JPEGs, is a common graphic format found on websites. Because GIFs have a maximum of only 256 colors, they are not suitable for color photographs.
Portable Network Graphic	PNG (PNG-8 and PNG-24)	PNG is not a commonly used format but offers better quality to compression and transparency parameters than do GIF or JPEG, for web-based work. There are two forms of PNG: PNG-8, which can substitute for GIF, and PNG-24, which substitutes for JPEG. Sadly, Microsoft Internet Explorer, in various iterations, had problems rendering PNG files properly, so the PNG standard remains underutilized.
Portable Document Format	PDF	Adobe's creation of the PostScript computer language made the desktop publishing revolution of the 1980s possible. By the early 1990s, there were several software applications, such as Aldus PageMaker and QuarkXPress, that could generate PostScript files. However, if a design company used PageMaker and wanted to send their work to a print company that used QuarkXPress, there was no easy way to achieve this. PDFs were devised to bridge this problem. A PDF file can be generated by many software applications and viewed on any computer that can run the free Adobe Acrobat Reader software. Although often used for text-based documents, a photograph can be saved as a PDF, so that it can be viewed in Acrobat Reader.
Encapsulated PostScript	EPS	Before PDFs became the universal format to send documents to press, there was Encapsulated PostScript. Often used by graphic designers, the EPS format suits vector graphics such as logos. For example, Design Company A might have designed a logo for a sports club. Later, Design Company B is asked to design the sports club's brochure. The best file format for sending the logo would be either EPS or PDF.

File format means the method by which files are stored, whether on a camera's compact *flash card* or on a computer's hard drive. The choice of file format is important, because some methods of saving and storing damage pixel information. Table 15.1 illustrates the most common raster/bitmap file formats.

The three most significant file formats in photography are: RAW (in its many forms), TIFF, and JPEG. Later, we will discuss the merits of photographing for raw capture, versus JPEG or TIFF. But for now, here is a little bit more information on JPEG lossy compression. Once a file has been damaged through lossy compression, image data will be lost, and there is no way to recover it—despite what you might have seen in Hollywood spy movies.

The images in Figure 15.24a and b show two versions of the same photograph with increasing levels of JPEG compression applied; note the appearance of *JPEG artifacts*, a block of pixels that have been averaged to the detriment of the image.

15.5 LIGHT SOURCES

The literal meaning of "photography" is "drawing with light." Therefore, it is important to consider the four basic lighting conditions photographers use. The first is ambient light: the light of the sun, or artificial light such as incandescent bulbs, strip lights, and so on. The second and third types of light both use flash, but flash is used in two distinct ways—hence the two categories, *speed lights* and *monolights* (*flash heads*). The fourth type of light is in fact a mix of lights: for example, a sunlit room with flash used to illuminate shadow areas.

15.5.1 Ambient Light

When using ambient light, a photographer measures the available light and sets the ISO, aperture, and shutter speed of the camera to capture the optimal exposure.

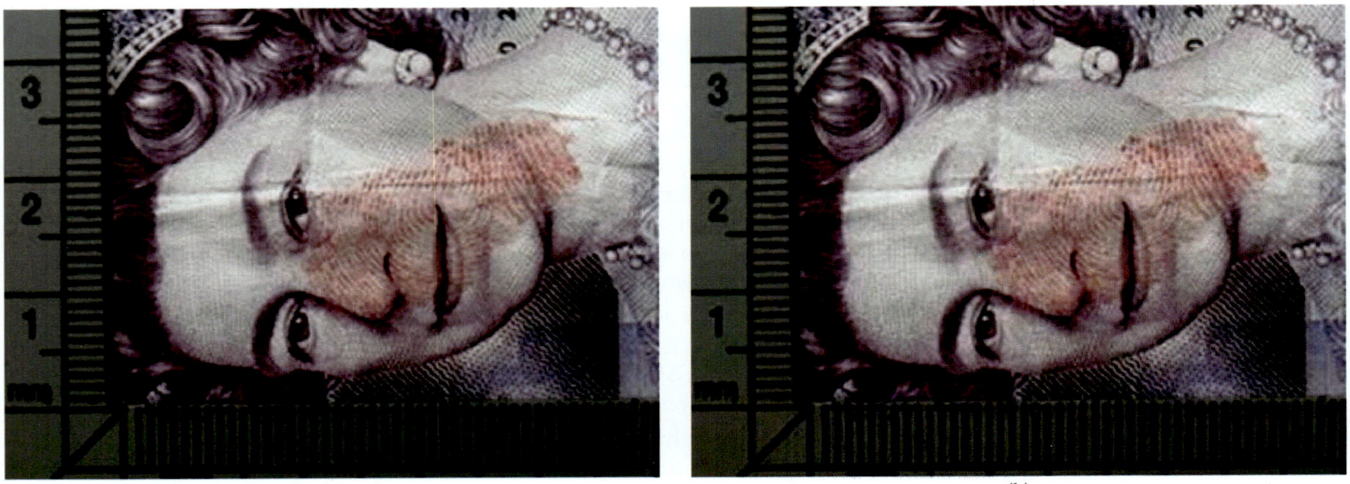

(a) (b)

FIGURE 15.24 (a) A photograph with JPEG Quality High, Best Quality. (b) The same photograph with JPEG Quality Low; artifacts have appeared in several areas of the images.

(ISO stands for International Standards Organization, which is a standardized industry scale for measuring sensitivity to light.) If the scene to be photographed is very dark, the photographer may find it impossible to get a good exposure without using a tripod.

When using a tripod, the shutter speed can be changed to several seconds, or even minutes. This could be a problem if moving objects needed to be photographed, and the action frozen.

The accuracy of modern *through-the-lens* (TTL) light meters found in DSLRs allows photographers to set their exposures purely on the values obtained from the camera. Handheld light meters are now less common, but are necessary when using monolights.

15.5.2 Speed Lights

All but the top-end DSLRs have built-in flashguns. However, all DSLRs have a *hot shoe bracket* where a speed light can be fitted. The built-in flashgun is also called a speed light, though it will have significantly less light power than an external one.

Speed lights are usually used in conjunction with the camera's TTL system, where the camera sets the flash power for the speed light. Speed lights are used by photojournalists and wedding photographers to create fill-flash. Fill-flash lightens shadow areas, revealing hidden details. In the case of portraits shot in bright midday sun, it removes the shadows from the eyes. Speed lights can augment ambient light, or fully illuminate a subject at close range. They lack the power to illuminate anything but the smallest of rooms, but are extremely versatile and easy to use.

15.5.3 Monolights (Flash Heads)

If large internal spaces need careful lighting, monolights can be used. Monolights, or flash heads, are extremely powerful devices with enough power in their *capacitors* to kill—only specialist monolights should be used outdoors.

Apart from the extra light power of monolights, their key difference from speed lights is the manner of setting exposures. With speed lights the camera's TTL system will set the correct values for exposure and flash, while with monoblocks, a handheld light meter is required to take an incident light reading.

It is standard practice for the lowest ISO on the camera to be set, and then the desired aperture. The camera's shutter speed is set to synchronize with the monolight(s), and this is usually 1/125th second. These values are set into the handheld meter, and then test flashes are made until the correct flash power for the monolights is reached. Photographers who understand this process can then illuminate complex scenes and objects in a flat, neutral way, or in a highly creative, mood-enhancing one.

15.5.4 Mixed Light

Fill-flash has already been mentioned, and is a form of mixed-light photography. "Mixed-light photography" simply means having more than one type of light source in a scene. For example, in a photograph taken in a room with large windows, on a bright sunny day, the daylight will be much brighter than the artificial light. Balancing the exposure so that the interior is properly exposed and the exterior is not burnt out can be challenging.

The relative light levels of mixed lights can be a problem, but the most regularly encountered problem when working with mixed lights are differences in the color temperature of the lights.

Human perception is such that when taking a photograph in mixed light, the untrained photographer is unlikely to notice the problem. But once the photograph is downloaded and opened on a computer monitor, the problems of mismatched white balance will be evident. If color is not critical, this is not a significant problem.

15.6 CAMERA DYNAMIC RANGE

The best digital cameras can capture up to 12 stops of light. This equates to a contrast ratio of approximately 80,000 to 1, whereas the contrast ratio on a bright sunny day is likely to be 100,000 to 1. A scene lit by bright sunlight has a dynamic range impossible to capture in camera; so, unless it's a cloudy day, or the scene to be captured has low contrast, the photographer has to decide which tonal range is essential and which tones can be lost.

The captured digital photograph's dynamic range extends beyond the gamut of computer monitors, and the contrast ratio of monitors exceeds that of print. So, digital photography is a reductive process. The skilled photographer mediates the terms of the reduction. Figures 15.25 and 15.26 illustrate low and high dynamic range, respectively.

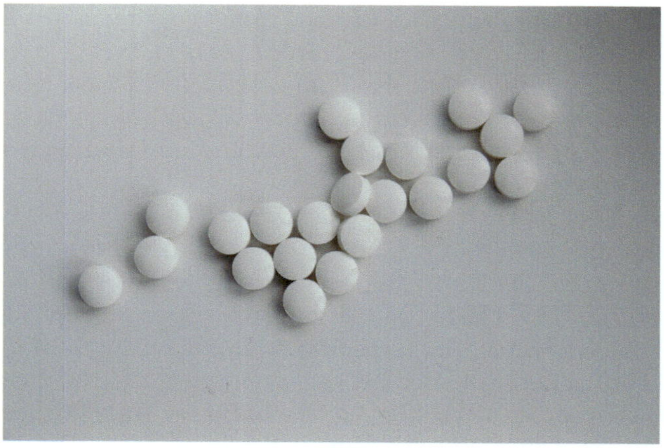

FIGURE 15.25. A photograph with low dynamic range.

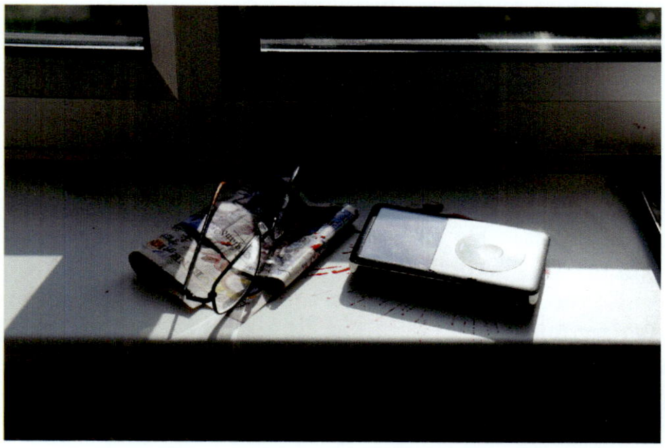

FIGURE 15.26 A photograph with high dynamic range.

15.6.1 Capture versus JPEG (and TIFF)

Professional photographers almost exclusively shoot for RAW. This has not always been the case. For the first decade of the 21st century, digital photography was dominated by JPEG (or TIFF) shooting. The shift to RAW is a good one but, thumbing through the advice of professional photo gurus, one might find advocates for JPEG.

If this is the case, check the date of the article. If the article or publication was written after 1998, the author was lagging behind the times. Please note that there is nothing wrong with shooting for JPEG; the point here is that RAW files have more tones and color to work with. Like many issues in photography, the RAW versus JPEG debate is often argued based on a fundamental misunderstanding of the digital process. RAW means unprocessed, as in raw food being not yet cooked.

RAW should be written as "raw," because it is not an acronym, nor a specific file format. However, to identify raw as a specific adjective, it is written here as RAW. All cameras capture RAW data. This data is produced by the analog-to-digital conversion of light information. Its sensor reads light passing through a camera. The sensor registers how much light is present; this is an analogue value. The camera's processing turns the analog value into a digital one. Different camera manufacturers have a variety of strategies for this process, which leads to some cameras being great for low-light photography and others more suited to sports. Professional-level cameras can be good all-around, though there are specialist camera types designed for specific types of work.

After the digital conversion takes place, the picture information has to be recorded. This is usually to a memory card, such as compact flash. Although all types of digital camera capture RAW data, not all can save RAW data to their memory cards. Consumer-level cameras are often restricted to writing JPEG files only, whereas many other types of camera can record JPEG and RAW files, and perhaps even TIFF files.

RAW files have several advantages over JPEG; this is true for camera types that can record RAW and

JPEG simultaneously. When a camera writes a JPEG (or TIFF) file to a memory card, a second level of processing is made. Both RAW and JPEGs will have analogue to digital processing, but JPEGs need an extra level of processing where specific colors and sharpening are applied.

This means photographers who record only JPEG files to a memory card have to have all their processing parameters set correctly in camera. For example, all in-camera JPEGs have some degree of sharpening applied, even if the camera's sharpening value is set to a nil value. Those shooting for RAW can defer nearly all of their RAW processing decisions to the computer stage of their workflow, including the degree of sharpening.

JPEGs are 8 bits per channel files; DSLRs are either 12 bits or 14 bits per channel. The JPEG shooter reduces bit depth in camera: 12 bits becomes 8 bits, and whatever data is lost by doing this cannot be recovered later on the computer. RAW shooters preserve the 12- or 14-bit data, giving them more scope to change tones, and helping them open up shadow areas or recover burnt-out highlights.

Extreme White Balance corrections can be made to RAW files. For instance, a camera's White Balance might be set to Daylight, but the shots made in Tungsten light. If this happens to a photographer shooting for JPEG, the chances of successfully correcting the imbalance would be slight. The RAW shooter, however, would be able to accurately reset the white point of the image post-shoot.

A RAW file is like a digital negative: it provides evidence of the original captured scene—untampered and unedited—apart from the initial analog-to-digital conversion. JPEGs are like a photographic print, and as such they sit at the end of the processing workflow. The list of RAW advantages could go on, but following are a few issues relating to RAW that need to be examined.

RAW files are much larger than JPEGs, so take up more storage space. Over time, certain RAW formats will become obsolete, and consideration has to be given to preserving ways to access older files. Until the late 1990s, processing RAW files was more complex than processing JPEGs. This is no longer true, and with the advent of software such as Apple's Aperture, it is arguably easier to process RAW than it is JPEG. However, the ease of RAW processing is dependent on the software available to you.

15.6.2 The RAW Process

This section highlights key concepts when shooting for RAW. As mentioned previously, all digital cameras process RAW data. Central to this process is the problem of taking a device that can only read luminance, black-and-white (monochrome) information, and deriving color information from it. The CMOS (complementary metal-oxide semiconductor) or CCD (charge-coupled device) sensors, used in the majority of digital cameras, cannot detect color.

They can only read how intense light is. In order for color information to be detected, a Bayer filter is placed over the sensor. The Bayer filter is a grid of RGB-colored elements. The red elements filter red to cyan light; the green elements, greens to magentas; and the blue filters, blues to yellows.

The process generates the ubiquitous RGB channel information found throughout digital imaging. Therefore, the Bayer filtering creates a patchwork of pixels. In each row of the sensor, there is an alternating pattern of green then red, or blue then green, pixels being read (see Figure 15.27).

The patchwork of RGB pixels needs to be demosaicked; the mosaic patchwork has to be resolved so that there are no gaps in the columns and rows of pixels. In areas of a detailed pattern, such as fabric, errors in demosaicking can occur. Some cameras are more prone to this problem than others, and though some RAW decoding software can mediate the problem, it is best to choose the best camera for the job.

15.6.3 The Tonal Range of RAW

In digital imaging, the histogram is a graph of the tones in an image (as discussed in the ePhotoPros article "Anatomy of the Histogram"). Photographers use the histogram, as displayed on the back of a DSLR, to evaluate the merits of the exposure settings used for a shot. It is therefore disconcerting to learn that the on-camera histogram does not accurately represent the tones of a RAW file (Figures 15.28 and 15.29).

The image displayed on the back of a DSLR is a JPEG preview of the file captured by the camera. If the captured file is a JPEG, the on-camera JPEG will generate an accurate, and therefore reliable, histogram. If the

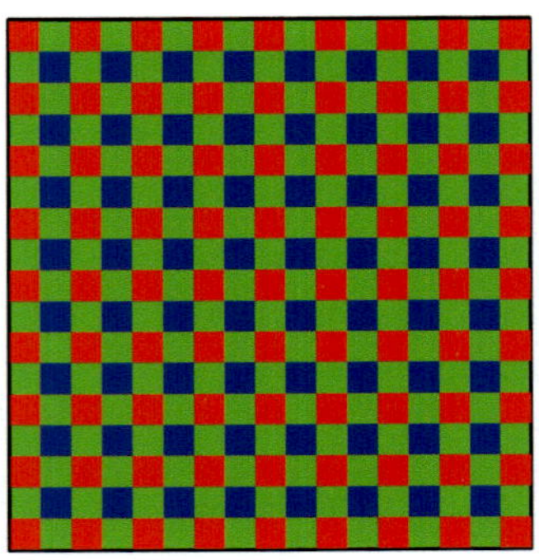

FIGURE 15.27 A photograph with low dynamic range.

captured file is RAW, the camera has no way of showing either a preview or histogram of the photograph.

So, the camera generates a JPEG preview. This is true even if the camera is set to record RAW only. Nearly all DSLRs generate a JPEG preview that is then embedded into a RAW file. It is this JPEG that is viewed on camera, and it is on this JPEG that the on-camera histogram is based. This could be problematic, but a little knowledge can be a good thing. RAW files contain more tones and a greater dynamic range than JPEG files. So, when reviewing a shot on the back of a DSLR, the RAW shooter can allow the histogram to touch the right-hand edge of the graph.

For the JPEG shooter this would mean lost data, but the seasoned RAW shooter knows that as much as 2 stops of apparently burnt-out highlight are present and recoverable.

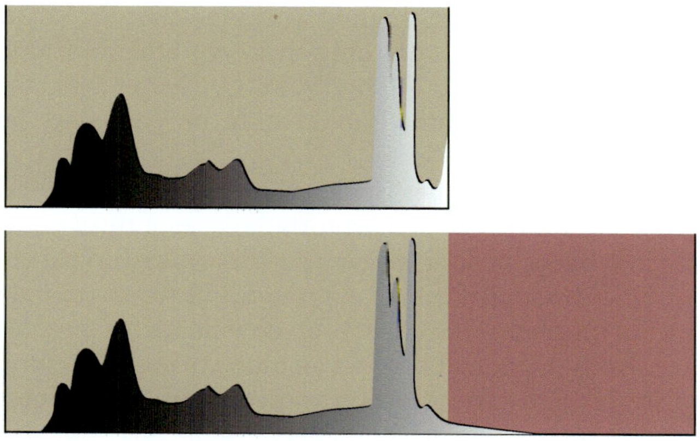

FIGURE 15.28 Histogram JPEG image. Histogram showing extended range of raw.

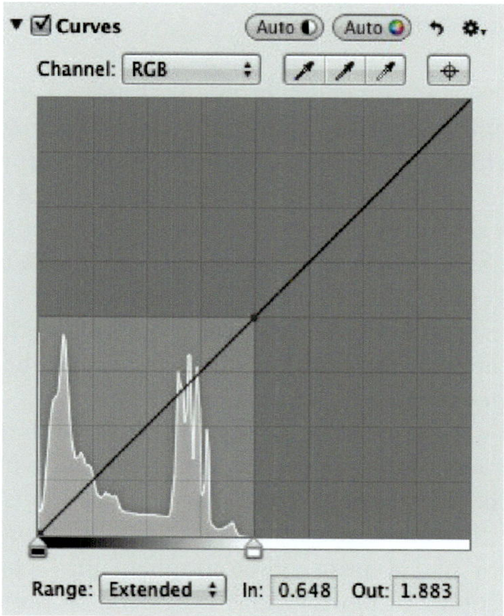

FIGURE 15.29 Curves histogram of same image.

15.6.4 Color Theory

This section outlines the broad issues of digital color and introduces the topic of color management. It is not necessary to have a comprehensive knowledge of all aspects of this section.

15.6.5 Color Models

There are four color models used by photographers: RGB, CMYK, HSL, and Lab. Most of imaging devices use the RGB color model—that is, using red, green, and blue light signals to create color (see Figure 15.30). Printing devices commonly use color based on CMYK (cyan, magenta, yellow, and black). HSL (hue, saturation, and lightness) is similar to HSB (hue, saturation, and brightness) and is used in computer graphics and digital imaging as an alternative to RGB. Lab color is a purely theoretical color model, and its significance will be described later.

In the RGB color model, the purest red may be described as Red 255, Green 0, Blue 0; this is because the scale of color levels in the RGB color model are generally described in a range of 0 to 255. Black would be described as Red 0, Green 0, Blue 0; white is defined as Red 255, Green 255, and Blue 255. Varying the RGB values creates color.

If equal values of green and blue were added to pure red (changing Red 255, Green 0, Blue 0 to Red 255, Green 200, Blue 200) a pink color would be made. Change the values to Red 255, Green 255, Blue 200, and a soft lemon yellow is made.

The RGB color model is device dependent; that is to say, the purest red (Red 255, Green 0, Blue 0) is

FIGURE 15.30 An illustration of the additive color model RGB. Red, green, and blue light combine to make white light.

FIGURE 15.31 CMYK color, also known as the subtractive color model: cyan, magenta, and yellow combine to make black. Note that the secondary colors here are red, green, and blue.

dependent on the device producing it, whether that is a camera, monitor or scanner.

The CMYK color model is also device dependent, and, perhaps confusingly, photographers using inkjet printers do not need to convert their images from RGB to CMYK, even though inkjet printers use combinations of CMYK inks.

CMYK is the color model used to print magazines, newspapers, posters, and books (see Figure 15.31). Using combinations of cyan, magenta, yellow, and black (CMYK), a variety of colors can be reproduced. When set to Cyan 0%, Magenta 0%, Yellow 0%, and Black 0%, the print would contain no ink and therefore no color, other than that of the paper or substrate.

When all the values are set to 100%, a solid black is achieved. In reality, printers do not lay down 100% of all the different inks; to do so would create pools of ink in the black areas of a print that would look heavy, and shadow detail would be lost.

Significantly, the CMYK model has a greatly reduced range of colors compared to RGB, so there are colors that can be recorded in RGB that cannot be reproduced in CMYK.

In order to help photographers print more of the colors they can see on their RGB monitors, inkjet manufacturers have introduced printers with more than just the four inks required for standard CMYK output. In addition to CMYK, these are typically light cyan and light magenta. In the case of Epson's K3 systems, two extra blacks are included; these help in the production of black-and-white prints.

The addition of light cyan and light magenta increases the gamut of a CMYK printer. To best access this extra gamut, prints are made from the RGB color model. There is an exception to this rule; for people using raster image processing (RIPs), they have to print using the CMYK color model.

Every device in the digital photography workflow has its own color space that can be defined using a color profile. So far, the RGB color space has only been referred to in a generic way; however, there are four notable RGB color spaces: Adobe RGB (1998), Color Match RGB, ProPhoto RGB, and sRGB IEC61966-1 or sRGB for short.

There is much comment on Adobe RGB being superior to sRGB; however, a digital camera does not shoot either sRGB or Adobe RGB. The camera assigns profiles to aid color management, but when shooting in RAW the pixel data downloaded from a camera has a color space larger than either sRGB or Adobe RGB.

The Adobe RGB color space is bigger than the sRGB color space; however, as a starting point, using sRGB will result in more reliable color matching. Once you are comfortable that everything is working using the sRGB working space, then, and only then, try other working spaces such as Adobe RGB (1998). Or, better still, try ProPhoto; but ProPhoto should only be embraced by advanced users.

Many devices ship with manufacturer's profiles; increasingly these are excellent. In the case of third party inks and paper, generic profiles for these inks and papers can be downloaded for your printer, but these are only generic profiles. The quality of downloadable profiles vary from manufacturer to manufacturer; therefore, it may be necessary to create your own profiles to best match your equipment and papers. To do this, you will need a spectrophotometer.

15.6.6 Assigning Profiles / Converting to a Profile

Files without an embedded profile are known as untagged images and cannot be color-managed. Assigning a profile provides color-aware applications the information needed to display or print the file accurately. Assigning a profile does not change the values of the pixels in a photographic image; rather, it allows the CMM to interpret the color appearance of an image. So assigning a grayscale profile to a photograph would make that photograph appear black and white, even though the photograph's pixels remain in full color.

Converting an image to a profile will change the physical pixel data in a photograph from the source values to the destination color space values. This would be done to achieve accurate color matching between a soft proof and a print. Photographers may choose to convert copies of photographs they send to photo-labs. Photo-labs can supply the ICC profiles for their printing machines, giving photographers the ability to soft-proof photographs and choose the best way to convert their photographs before sending them to the lab.

15.6.7 Image Audit Trail

This section outlines the importance of maintaining the integrity of a photograph; as evidence of the scene rendered by the camera. It explains why a RAW workflow is ideally suited for this purpose. For those who need to continue shooting for a JPEG workflow, alternative explanations are given.

In digital imaging, there are two terms that can mean the same thing: image manipulation and image enhancement. In the realm of digital imaging, important distinctions have to be drawn between changing the tones and colors of pixels in an image and moving pixels. It is imperative that photographic evidence is only ever enhanced. To displace or introduce new pixels into an image creates a forgery; it is image manipulation.

All digital photographs contain a text log, embedded in them, that records the original capture date and time of a photograph and subsequently tracks modifications to the file. This is true for nearly all computer data.

Furthermore, a digital camera embeds other text data in each photograph taken. All photographs from a DSLR contain date, time, camera model, lens type, ISO, aperture settings, and so on—together known as metadata. EXIF (exchangable image file format) metadata is written by devices such as cameras and is a great aid to proving the validity of an image, as well as in helping the cataloging process. Cameras with a GPS system will have the longitude and latitude of each photograph logged as EXIF metadata.

15.6.8 Camera Usage

This section briefly outlines the key concepts of camera usage, describing all the parameters that need to be considered when taking a photograph.

The parameter commonly referred to as ISO relates to light exposure; changing this parameter changes a camera's sensitivity to light. Typically, ISO 100 is the lowest setting—lowest, because on this setting, greater levels of light are required to make an exposure. The key advantage of low settings such as ISO 100 is that the best range of tones can be captured, and it has no *noise* problems (see Figure 15.32).

Noise is caused when the camera's sensitivity is increased to allow shooting in low light. Much like turning up the volume on a stereo system, background noise becomes apparent (see Figure 15.33). When high ISOs are needed, cameras such as Nikon's D3 are renowned for their low noise characteristics at very high ISO.

FIGURE 15.32 Image taken at a low ISO: there are good tones, and the image is clear.

FIGURE 15.33 Image taken at a high ISO: the image lacks contrast and detail; it looks gritty and contains colored artifacts. The grittiness is *luminance noise*, and the colored artifacts are referred to as *chroma* or *chrominance noise*.

15.6.9 Angle of View

There are two types of lens in common use: prime lenses and zoom lenses. Prime lenses have a fixed focal length, whereas the focal length can be changed on a zoom lens.

Different focal lengths result in different *angles of view*. The shorter the focal length, the wider the angle of view. The longer the focal length, the narrower the angle of view. Surveillance photographers and paparazzi use lenses with very long focal lengths to take photographs over a great distance. (See the series of photographs in Figure 15.34.)

Digital SLRs use one of two sizes of sensor; both have an aspect ratio of 3:2. The first size of sensor is "full frame." These DSLRs use a sensor roughly the same size as 35 mm film; therefore, the diagonal measure of the sensor will be 35 mm. The second type of sensor is roughly two-thirds the size of the full-frame sensor and is known as either APS-C or DX.

These two sensor sizes have a significant effect on the angle of view of lenses: for example, a Nikon 50 mm lens will fit both a Nikon FX (full-frame) camera and a Nikon DX camera.

But the angle of view for the 50 mm lens on the FX camera will be greater than the angle that would be achieved on a DX camera. The significance for surveillance work is that DX sensors yield a better telephoto value than do FX sensors—though FX (full frame) cameras, such as the Nikon D3, give exceptional image quality in low light.

FIGURE 15.34 Photographs illustrating zooms at 10 mm, 50 mm, 105 mm, and 400 mm.

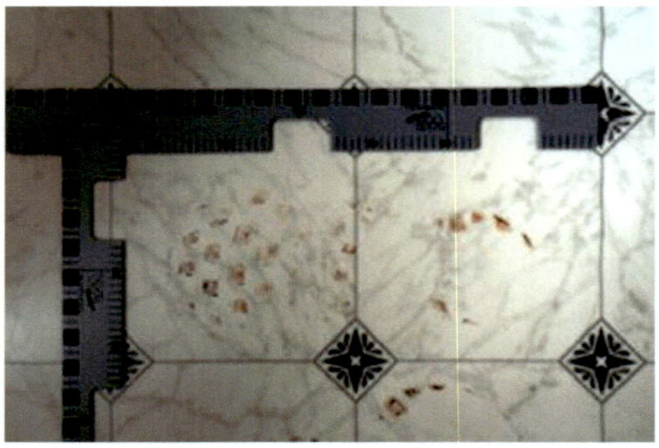

FIGURE 15.35 Image of a tile wall with minimal to no distortion.

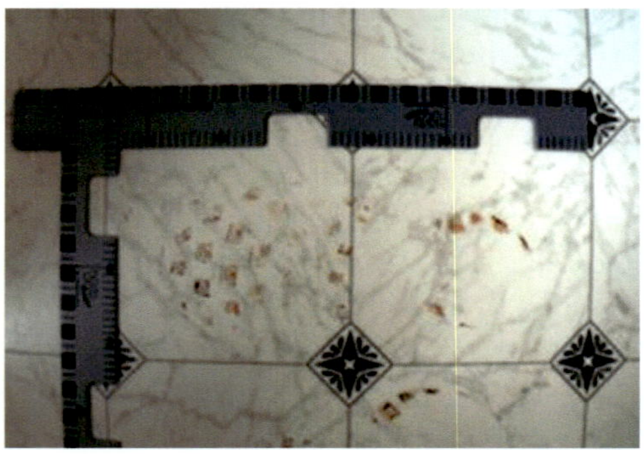

FIGURE 15.36 While most lenses will have some barrel distortion, this photograph clearly distorts the size and shape of the footprint, making a footwear match improbable.

15.6.10 Barrel Distortion

Lenses distort light; the images they produce do not faithfully map the placement of objects in a scene. Take a look at the tile wall photograph in Figures 15.35 and 15.36.

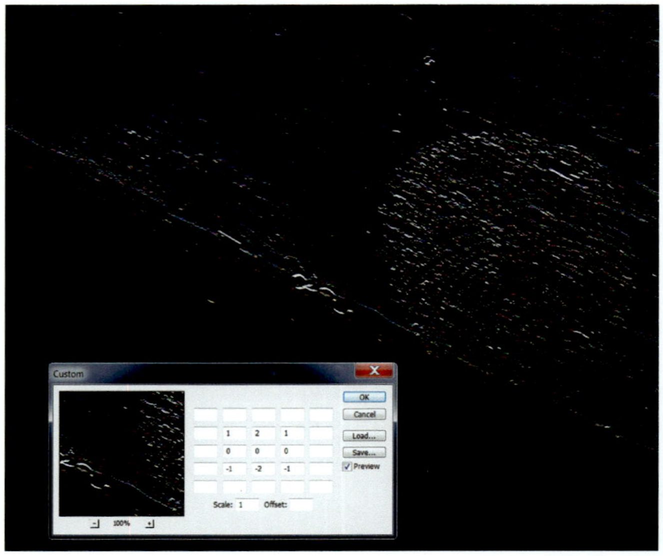

FIGURE 15.37 Illustration of the use of a *custom* filter.

This test is often used to check the distortion found in a lens. In the case of architecture shots and interiors, the lens's ability to map the placement of object can be vital, so high-quality lenses are used. These are often prime lenses.

15.6.11 Convolution Filters

Image editing packages often include what are usually called "user defined" or "custom" filters in image editing packages. A convolution matrix multiplies the central pixel value based upon the values of its neighboring pixels. This can be used to sharpen, blur, and enhance edge effects and is usually a 3 × 3 or 5 × 5 matrix (see Figure 15.37).

APPENDIX

Ethical, Legal, and Professional Aspects

The Art of Cross-Examination

Filomena Paciello and Kay Michiels

Even though forensic evidence has proven to be very reliable, and forensic scientists need only a small amount of material to, for example, come up with a DNA profile, witness testimony is still intensively presented as evidence in courtroom proceedings.

Roughly, we speak of two types of witness testimony. *Eyewitness* testimony, which, as the name suggests, is the testimony of someone who actually witnessed the alleged crime (or some other event relevant for discovering the truth). This testimony can be an alibi for the defendant or someone who says that they have seen the defendant leaving the scene of the crime or, days or weeks before the crime, having a fight with, for example, the victim.

There is also *expert* witness testimony. This testimony is not based on what someone has seen, but based on their specific knowledge of some sort. They have conducted either an investigation or analysis about some type of forensic evidence. Their knowledge is based on the fact that all forensic evidence is objective and may be in need of an subjective explanation in order to help the judge or jury to form their own independent opinion about the evidence.

The cross-examination is the forensic art of discovering the truth in the witness evidence, and it represents the principal means by which the veracity of a witness is put to the test in the courtroom (Figure A.1).

The investigative purpose is focused not on what has happened, but on what is being *said* about what has happened.

Keep in mind that the difference between the two types of witness testimony may require a different approach. For eyewitness testimony, as a lawyer you want to know if this witness is telling the truth. There has been quite a lot of research done about the reliability of eyewitness testimony. For example, we know that witnessing a crime in which a weapon is being used in general causes a distortion in remembering what has happened. This is called weapon focus. The presence of the weapon makes the witness focus more on the weapon and less on the suspect—which in the end may result in a less reliable description of the suspect.

As a game, the examination has rules drawn from a secular praxis of Anglo-American ideology. The structure consists of three fundamental stages moments: (1) direct examination, (2) cross-examination, and (3) reexamination. The subjects who ask the questions are the public prosecutor and the private party's advocates.

The direct examination is conducted by the party who asked to interrogate the witness. The direct examination's aim is to bring out facts framed in a version of history and to obtain a representation of facts as known to the witness; such facts should be useful in demonstrating the examiner's thesis. The final purpose of the direct examination is to demonstrate that the witness is reliable and credible.

The cross-examination is conducted by the party who has a competing interest: to show that the facts alleged in the direct examination are not true or are incorrect or are not complete, so to discredit the witness, who has stated on other occasions different things, and force him or her to admit certain facts.

There are basically three types of cross-examination:

1. *Apparent Cross-Examination*: This type of cross-examination does not attempt to deal with the merits or substance of the expert's testimony, but rather attacks the witness's qualifications and prejudice.
2. *Real Cross-Examination*: This cross-examination is the opposite of apparent cross-examination in that it deals with the merits and substance of the witness's testimony.
3. *Combination of Real and Apparent Cross-Examination*: This is the most common type of cross-examination employed, and, just as the description implies, deals with the merits and substance of the witness's testimony and as well as his or her prejudice and lack of qualifications.

FIGURE A.1 Film Poster—CROSS EXAMINATION (1932). (Public domain.)

FIGURE A.2 Law. (Public domain.)

> In apparent cross-examination (when you can't meet the experts head-on or on their merits), try to emphasize the witness's lack of qualifications, such as his or her lack of academic standing, with questions that relate to fields that the witness is not aware of (Figure A.2).

The basic purpose of cross-examination involves the following:

- To discredit the witness
- To elicit testimony from the witness, which discredits unfavorable testimony given by other witnesses on the same side, creating a conflict with the testimony of other witnesses on the same side
- To elicit testimony to corroborate favorable testimony
- To elicit testimony to contribute independently to the development of your case

Stated another way, the goals of cross-examination are to discredit the witness and/or witness testimony, and to discredit the other side's case and so support your case.

The commandments of cross-examination by Irving Younger, from his book *The Advocate's Deskbook*, include the following 10 tips (encapsulated and paraphrased):

1. *Be Brief*: It is important to be succinct, because the less time spent, the less the chance you will screw up, and a simple cross that restates the important part of the story in your terms is more easily absorbed and understood by the jury.
2. *Use Plain Words*: Use a language of simplicity.
3. *Use Only Leading Questions*: The law forbids questions on direct examination that suggest the answer; the lawyer is not competent to testify. On cross-examination, the law permits questions that suggest the answer and allows the attorney to put words in the witness's mouth. Cross-examination, therefore, specifically permits you to take control of the witness, taking him or her where you want to go.
4. *Be Prepared*: Advance preparation is essential to a successful cross-examination; never ask a question that you do not know the answer to. Lawyers need skills to accomplish individual tasks (tactical skills) such as selecting jurors, delivering opening statements and closing arguments, and examining witnesses, as well as those skills that integrate individual actions to achieve greater effects and drive unfolding events toward a desired outcome (strategy).
5. *Listen*: For some, cross-examination of an important witness causes stage fright; it confuses the mind and panic sets in. You have a hard time just getting the first question out, and you're generally thinking about the next question and not listening to the answer.
6. *Do Not Quarrel*: When the answer to your question is absurd, false, irrational, contradictory, or the like, stop and sit down. Resist the temptation to respond with "How can you say that?" or "How dare you make such an outrageous claim?" The answer to such a question often elicits a response that explains away the absurdity and rehabilitates the witness.
7. *Avoid Repetition*: Never allow a witness to repeat on cross-examination what he or she said on direct examination, because the more times a statement is repeated, the more likely the jury is to believe it.
8. *Disallow Witness Explanation*: Never permit the witness to explain anything on cross-examination. That is for your adversary to do.
9. *Limit Questioning*: Don't ask even one question too many. Stop when you have made your point. Leave the argument for the jury. Try to predict which witnesses will be called by the opposition and anticipate what questions your opponent will ask each witness on direct examination.

FIGURE A.3 Worldwide Justice. (Public domain.)

10. *Save for Summation*: Save the ultimate points for summation. A prepared, clear, and simple leading cross-examination does not argue the case, as any such arguments are most effective in your final summation (Figure A.3).

The reexamination seeks to again directly interrogate the witness, already submitted to your opponent's cross-examination, so to clarify, correct, and complete testimony that emerged in cross-examination and/or reestablish its credibility. The party that conducted the direct examination can propose new questions to recover the sequence of facts after the cross-examination tried to put in doubt its existence; reexamination also allows explanation of any contradictions into which the witness has fallen.

Regarding particular reexamination questions, factors or variables to keep in mind are as follows:

- The context in which a question is placed
- The elements that compose it
- The question's desired objectives and aims

A question usually is not only a question but also a covert argument: it assumes certain facts to assure relevancy, the answer's sincerity, the examiner's loyalty, and the accuracy of any objections. Questions are used not only to gain knowledge but also to influence the answers and then persuade.

The semantic composition of the question concerns the meaning of the words used and the context in which it is placed. The syntactic composition of the question concerns the relation of the words inside the phrase and other aspects, such as the tone or the frequency with which examiners have asked them.

A fundamental distinction among types of questions takes into account the objectives discussed above:

1. *Open questions*: They have the broadest response.
2. *Closed questions*: They involve a choice between clearly understood alternatives; this kind of question is preferred when communication is clear and there is a common frame of reference in which to address thorny topics.

The following sequences provide the interviewer strategic opportunities to make certain questions stand out:

- *Tunnel*: Sequence of closed questions
- *Funnel*: Sequence of questions from open to closed
- *Inverted funnel*: Sequence of questions from closed to open
- *Irregular*: Alternative sequence of open and closed questions

The issues to be considered in reexamination should be as follows:

- *The verbal*: The words that are said
- *The para verbal*: Pitch, timbre, volume, voice inflection
- *The nonverbal, also called body language*: Eye contact, body movements

Bear in mind that impediments to perceptive focus are possible in the testimony: physical interference (e.g., circumstances, light, exposure time, location), physiological interference (e.g., fatigue, sensory deficits, age), psychological interference (e.g., simplification, Gestalt perception, emotional-affective perception, distribution, cognitive attitude, expectations, gravity, personality, stereotypes).

The following questions may help you prepare for cross-examinations:

- What are the facts beyond dispute?
- What is the context for the facts beyond dispute?
- Is the fact important to the judge or jury?
- Is the fact necessary for your theory of the case?
- Which witness are able to corroborate or deny these facts?
- Is there any other evidence to corroborate or deny these facts presented by a witness?
- What is believable?

Impeachment is a subset of cross-examination: witness impeachment is a polite term for challenging the credibility of a witness.

Categories of impeachment are as follows:

- Bias, prejudice, or interest
- Inadequate perception
- Inconsistent statement
- Character (prior convictions and/or no extrinsic evidence)
- Competency
- Contradictions

FIGURE A.4 Goddess of Justice. (Public domain.)

It is important to keep in mind that during the criminal trial, the main goal is to find out the truth about what happened at the scene of a crime instead of just to convict the defendant. The judge, jury and attorney are supposed to be without prejudice against the defendant (Figure A.4).

Research has shown that judges or juries highly value witness testimony: this is because witness testimony can be used to fill in the blanks in a reconstruction of what might have happened. Looking at the exoneration forthcoming out of the Innocence Project, one can see that the majority of exonerations of those wrongly accused and imprisoned are based on eyewitness testimony.*

To conduct a good cross-examination, preparation is key. As a defense lawyer, the cross-examination may be your best opportunity to present important facts, inferences, and impressions. Some researchers are convinced that at least 70% of the effectiveness of cross-examination is determined before the cross-examination begins.†

Cross-examination is the most potent weapon in the trial lawyer's arsenal, and it determines who wins and who loses the legal battle.

* *The Innocence Project:* http://www.innocenceproject.org/causes-wrongful-conviction.

† *A Checklist of Winning Cross-Examination Concepts and Techniques:* http://publicdefender.mt.gov/training/PracticeManual-Criminal/Ch9-CrossExam.pdf.

BIBLIOGRAPHY

Clark Ronald H., Bailey William S., Dekle George R., *Cross-Examination Handbook: Persuasion Strategies & Techniques*, 2010, New York, NY: Aspen Publishers; Pap/Com edition.

Davies Leonard E., *Anatomy of Cross-Examination*, 2004, Bloomington, IN: Xlibris Corporation.

Guglielmo Gulotta, *Le 200 regole della cross-examination. Un'arte scientifica*, 2012, Italy: Giuffrè Editore.

Iannuzzi John Nicholas, *Handbook of Cross Examination: The Mosaic Art*, 2011, Bloomington, IN: Xlibris Corporation.

Loftus Elizabeth F., Loftus Geoffrey R., Messo Jane, Some Facts about Weapon Focus, *Law and Human Behavior*, vol. 11, no. 1, 55, 1987.

Maffeo Vania, *L' esame incrociato tra legge e prassi*, 2012, Italy: CEDAM Editore.

Moses E. Ray, *Cross-Examination in Criminal Defence*, 2001, Houston, TX: Center for Criminal Justice Advocacy. http://criminaldefense.homestead.com/Cross.html.

Polchinski D. Peter, *Cross-Examination Edge: A Guide to Effective Questioning*, 2010, Tucson, AZ: Lawyers & Judges Publishing.

Pozner S. Larry, Dodd Roger, *Cross-Examination: Science and Techniques*, 2004, New York, NY: LexisNexis.

Pratt A. Timothy, *The Ten Commandments of Cross-Examination*, FDCC Trial Tactics Section. http://www.thefederation.org/documents/Pratt-SP03.htm.

Randazzo Ettore, *L'esame incrociato*, 2011, Italy: Giuffrè Editore.

Read Shane D., *Winning at Trial*, 2007, Boulder, CO: LexisNexis/National Institute for Trial Advocacy.

Simpson Walter, *Pattern Cross Examination*, 2014, Costa Mesa, CA: James Publishing.

Stone Marcus, *La cross-examination. Strategie e tecniche*, 1990, Italy: Giuffrè Editore.

Torgan E. Evan, *Cross-Examination: It's Not as Hard as It Seems*, 2009, NYSBA Practical Skills–Civil Practice–The Trial.

Wellman Francis L., *The Art of Cross-Examination*, 2010, Whitefish, MT: Kessinger Publishing.

Younger Irving, The art of cross examination, The ten commandments of cross examination, in *The Advocate's Deskbook: The Essentials of Taking a Case*, pp. 292–301, 1988, New Jersey, NJ: Prentice Hall. Available at: http://www.law.uc.edu/sites/default/files/Younger10.pdf.

Index

For Product Safety Concerns and Information please contact our EU representative GPSR@taylorandfrancis.com Taylor & Francis Verlag GmbH, Kaufingerstraße 24, 80331 München, Germany

Batch number: 10722683

Printed by Printforce, the Netherlands